KAWASAKI

CONCOURS • 1986-2006

WHAT'S IN YOUR TOOLBOX?

FIRST EDITION
First Printing January, 2004

SECOND EDITION
First Printing April, 2013

Printed in U.S.A.

CLYMER and colophon are registered trademarks of Penton Business Media, Inc.

ISBN-10: 1-59969-651-7

ISBN-13: 978-1-59969-651-5

Library of Congress: 2013933863

AUTHOR: Clymer Staff.

TECHNICAL PHOTOGRAPHY: Clymer Staff, with assistance from Jordan Engineering, Oceanside CA..

TECHNICAL ILLUSTRATIONS: Errol McCarthy.

WIRING DIAGRAMS: Bob Meyer.

EDITOR: James Grooms.

PRODUCTION: Holly Messinger.

TOOLS AND EQUIPMENT: K & L Supply Co. at www.klsupply.com.

COVER: Mark Clifford at www.markclifford.com.

Associate Publisher James Grooms

EDITORIAL

Content Director
James Grooms

Editor
Steven Thomas

Associate Editor
Rick Arens

Authors
Ed Scott
Ron Wright
Michael Morlan
George Parise
Jay Bogart

Illustrators
Bob Meyer
Steve Amos
Errol McCarthy
Mitzi McCarthy

MARKETING

Marketing Manager
Steven Thomas

SALES

Sales Manager–Powersport/Marine/I&T
Matt Tusken

CUSTOMER SERVICE

Customer Service Manager
Terri Cannon

Customer Service Representatives
Becky Bigham
Dinah Bunnell
April LeBlond
Sherry Rudkin

PRODUCTION

Director of Production
Dylan Goodwin

Group Production Manager
Greg Araujo

Project Managers
Darin Watson
Adriane Wineinger

Production Editor
Ashley Bally

Associate Production Editor
Samantha Collins

P.O. Box 12901, Overland Park, KS 66282-2901 • 800-262-1954 • 913-967-1719

CONTENTS

CHAPTER THREE
LUBRICATION, MAINTENANCE AND TUNE-UP 55

CHAPTER FOUR
ENGINE TOP END 97

CHAPTER FIVE
ENGINE LOWER END 140

CHAPTER SIX
CLUTCH 181

QUICK REFERENCE DATA

MODEL:______________________________ YEAR:______________

VIN NUMBER:______________________________

ENGINE SERIAL NUMBER:______________________________

CARBURETOR SERIAL NUMBER OR I.D. MARK:______________________________

TIRE INFLATION PRESSURE[1]

	Load[2]	Pressure (cold)
1986-1999 models		
Front tire	–	250 kPa (36 psi [2.5 kg/cm^2])
Rear tire		
USA, California, Canada, Australia and South Africa models	0-200 kg (0-441 lb.)	290 kPa (41 psi [2.9 kg/cm^2])
All models except USA, California, Canada, Australia and South Africa models	0-97.5 kg (215 lb.)	250 kPa (36 psi [2.5 kg/cm^2])
	97.5-183 kg (215-404 lb.)	290 kPa (41 psi [2.9 kg/cm^2])
2000-on models		
Front tire	–	250 kPa (36 psi [2.5 kg/cm^2])
Rear tire		
USA, California, Canada and Australia models	0-200 kg (0-441 lb.)	290 kPa (41 psi [2.9 kg/cm^2])
All models except USA, California, Canada, and Australia	0-97.5 kg (215 lb.)	250 kPa (36 psi [2.5 kg/cm^2])
	97.5-183 kg (215-404 lb.)	290 kPa (41 psi [2.9 kg/cm^2])

1. Tire inflation pressures apply to original equipment tires only. Aftermarket tires may require different pressures. Refer to the tire manufacturer's specifications.
2. Load equals the total weight of the rider, passenger, accessories and all cargo.

RECOMMENDED LUBRICANTS AND FLUIDS

Fuel	Regular unleaded
Octane	87 [(R + M)/2 method] or research octane of 91 or higher
Capacity	28.5 L (7.5 U.S. gal [6.3 Imp. gal])
Air filter oil	SAE30

(continued)

RECOMMENDED LUBRICANTS AND FLUIDS (continued)

Fuel	Regular unleaded
Engine oil	
Classification	API SE, SF, SG or equivalent
Viscosity	SAE 10W-40, 10W-50, 20W-40 or 20W-50
Capacity	
Oil change only	2.7 L (2.85 U.S. qt. [2.38 Imp. qt.])
Oil and filter change	3.0 L (3.17 U.S. qt. [2.64 Imp. qt.])
Final gearcase oil	
Viscosity	
Temperature above 5° C (41° F)	SAE 90
Temperature below 5° C (41° F)	SAE 80
Grade	API GL-5 hypoid gear oil
Capacity	220 ml (7.4 U.S. oz. [7.7 Imp. oz.])
Coolant quantity (to the upper mark)	3.1 L (3.27 U.S. qt. [2.73 Imp. qt.])
Fork oil viscosity	SAE 10W-20 fork oil
Oil capacity per leg	
1986-1993 model)	
When empty	approx. 388 ml (13.1 U.S. oz. [13.7 Imp oz.])
Oil change	approx. 330 ml (11.2 U.S. oz. [11.6 Imp. oz.])
Oil level each leg (measured from top of the fully extended fork tube without spring)	355 mm (13.97 in.)
1994-on models	
When empty	approx 379 ml (12.82 U.S. oz. [13.33 Imp. oz.])
Oil change	approx. 330 ml (11.2 U.S. oz. [11.6 Imp. oz.])
Oil level each leg (measured from the top of the fully compressed fork tube without spring)	171 mm (6.73 in.)
Brake and clutch fluid	DOT 4 brake fluid

ENGINE TUNE-UP SPECIFICATIONS

Battery	
Capacity	12 V 18 AH
Idle speed	
California and 1988-on Switzerland models	1150-1250 rpm
2000-on European and French models	1250-1350 rpm
All other models	950-1050 rpm
Vacuum pressure @ idle	less than 2.7 kPa (0.787 in. Hg [2 cm Hg]) difference
Valve clearance	
Intake	0.13-0.18 mm (0.005-0.007 in.)
Exhaust	0.18-0.23 (0.007-0.009)
Spark plug gap	0.6-0.7 mm (0.024-0.028 in.)
Compression pressure	885-1350 kPa (128-196 psi) @ 300 rpm
Oil pressure @ 90° C (194° F)	265-325 kPa (38-47 psi) @ 4000 rpm
Firing order	1–2–4–3

(continued)

ENGINE TUNE-UP SPECIFICATIONS (continued)

Ignition timing (initial/advanced)*	
1986-1989 models	
1986-1989 California and 1989 Switzerland models	10° BTDC @ 1200 rpm/35° BTDC @ 3500 rpm
All other models	10° BTDC @ 1000 rpm/35° BTDC @ 3500 rpm
1990-1993 models	
California and Spain models	10° BTDC @ 1200 rpm/35° BTDC @ 3500 rpm
All other models	10° BTDC @ 1000 rpm/35° BTDC @ 3500 rpm
1994-1999 models	
California, Spain and 1996-1999 Switzerland models	10° BTDC @ 1200 rpm/35° BTDC @ 3500 rpm
All other models	10° BTDC @ 1000 rpm/35° BTDC @ 3500 rpm
2000-on models	
Europe and France models	10° BTDC @ 1300 rpm/35° BTDC @ 3500 rpm
California models	10° BTDC @ 1200 rpm/35° BTDC @ 3500 rpm
All other models	10° BTDC @ 1000 rpm/35° BTDC @ 3500 rpm

*Not adjustable.

MAINTENANCE SPECIFICATIONS

Brake pad service limit (front and rear)	1.0 mm (0.039 in.)
Brake disc runout	0.3 mm (0.012 in.)
Rear master cylinder pushrod length	43.5-45.5 mm (1.71-1.79 in.)
Throttle cable free play	2-3 mm (0.08-0.12 in.)
Choke cable free play	2-3 mm (0.08-0.12 in.)
Front fork air pressure (1986-1993 models)	50 kPa (7.1 psi)
Shock absorber air pressure	
Solo rider no load	50 kPa (7.1 psi)
Rider with load and/or passenger	200-350 kPa (28-50 psi)
Wheel runout	
Axial	0.5 mm (0.020 in.)
Radial	0.8 mm (0.031 in.)
Rear brake light switch	Activated after 10 mm (0.394 in.) of pedal travel
Radiator cap relief pressure	93-123 kPa (13.2-17.9 psi)

MAINTENANCE AND TUNE UP TORQUE SPECIFICATIONS

Item	N•m	in.-lb.	ft.-lb.
Brake caliper mounting bolts			
Front	32	–	24
Rear	34	–	25
Brake caliper bleed valve	7.8	69	–
Brake hose banjo bolt			
1986-2004	25	-	18
2005-on	34	-	25
Coolant manifold drain bolt	7.8	69	–
Cylinder drain bolts	7.8	69	–
Final gearcase drain bolt	17	–	13
Front axle nut	88	–	65
Front axle clamp bolts			
1986-1993 models	20	–	15
1994-on models	35		26

(continued)

Table 9 MAINTENANCE AND TUNE UP TORQUE SPECIFICATIONS (continued)

Item	N•m	in.-lb.	ft.-lb.
Handlebar clamp bolt	19	–	14
Handlebar mounting bolt	19	–	14
Fork bridge clamp bolts			
Lower bridge	21	–	15
Upper bridge	16	–	12
Oil filter bolt	20	–	15
Oil gallery bolt	18	–	13
Oil pipe banjo bolt	25	–	18
Pickup coil cover bolts	9.8	87	–
Rear axle nut	110	–	81
Spark plugs	14	–	10
Shock absorber bolts			
Lower	59	–	43
Upper	39	–	29
Steering head nut	39	–	29
Swing arm locknut	52	–	38
Swing arm adjuster bolt	27	–	20
Swing arm pivot mounting bolt	23	–	17
Thermostat housing bleed valve	7.8	69	–

CHAPTER ONE

GENERAL INFORMATION

This detailed and comprehensive manual covers the Kawasaki ZG1000 Concours from 1986-2006.

The text provides complete information on maintenance, tune-up, repair and overhaul. Hundreds of original photographs and illustrations created during the complete disassembly of the motorcycle guide the reader through every job. All procedures are in step-by-step form and designed for the reader who may be working on the motorcycle for the first time.

MANUAL ORGANIZATION

A shop manual is a tool and as in all Clymer manuals, the chapters are thumb tabbed for easy reference. Main headings are listed in the table of contents and the index. Frequently used specifications and capacities from the tables at the end of each individual chapter are listed in the *Quick Reference Data* section at the front of the manual. Specifications and capacities are provided in U.S. standard and metric units of measure.

During some of the procedures there will be references to headings in other chapters or sections of the manual. When a specific heading is called out in a step it will be *italicized* as it appears in the manual. If a sub-heading is indicated as being "in this section" it is located within the same main heading. For example, the sub-heading *Handling Gasoline Safely* is located within the main heading *SAFETY.*

This chapter provides general information on shop safety, tools and their usage, service fundamentals and shop supplies. **Tables 1-8** at the end of the chapter list model numbers, general motorcycle specifications and general shop technical data.

Chapter Two provides methods for quick and accurate diagnosis of problems. Troubleshooting procedures present typical symptoms and logical methods to pinpoint and repair a problem.

Chapter Three explains all routine maintenance necessary to keep the motorcycle running well. Chapter Three also includes recommended tune-up procedures, eliminating the need to constantly consult the chapters on the various assemblies.

Subsequent chapters describe specific systems such as engine, transmission, clutch, drive system, fuel and exhaust systems, suspension and brakes.

WARNINGS, CAUTIONS AND NOTES

The terms WARNING, CAUTION and NOTE have specific meanings in this manual.

A WARNING emphasizes areas where injury or even death could result from negligence. Mechanical damage may also occur. WARNINGS *should be taken seriously.*

A CAUTION emphasizes areas where equipment damage could result. Disregarding a CAUTION could cause permanent mechanical damage, though injury is unlikely.

A NOTE provides additional information to make a step or procedure easier or clearer. Disregarding a NOTE could cause inconvenience but would not cause equipment damage or personal injury.

SAFETY

Professional mechanics can work for years and never sustain a serious injury or mishap. Follow these guidelines and practice common sense to safely service the motorcycle.

1. Do not operate the motorcycle in an enclosed area. The exhaust gases contain carbon monoxide, a poisonous gas that is odorless, colorless and tasteless. Carbon monoxide levels build quickly in a small enclosed area and can cause unconsciousness and death in a short time. Make sure the work area is properly ventilated or operate the motorcycle outside.
2. *Never* use gasoline or any extremely flammable liquid to clean parts. Refer to *Cleaning Parts* and *Handling Gasoline Safely* in this chapter.
3. *Never* smoke or use a torch in the vicinity of flammable liquids, such as gasoline or cleaning solvent.
4. If welding or brazing on the motorcycle, remove the fuel tank, carburetor and shock to a safe distance at least 50 ft. (15 m) away.
5. Use the correct type and size tool to avoid damaging fasteners.
6. Keep tools clean and in good condition. Replace or repair worn or damaged equipment.
7. When loosening a tight fastener, be aware of what could happen if the tool slips.
8. When replacing fasteners, make sure the new fasteners are of the same size and strength as the original ones.
9. Keep the work area clean and organized.
10. Wear eye protection *any time* the safety of your eyes is in question. This includes procedures involving drilling, grinding, hammering, compressed air and chemicals.
11. Wear the correct clothing for the job. Tie up or cover long hair so it cannot be caught in moving equipment.
12. Do not carry sharp tools in clothing pockets.
13. Always have an approved fire extinguisher available. Make sure it is rated for gasoline (Class B) and electrical (Class C) fires.

14. Do not use compressed air to clean clothes, the motorcycle or the work area. Debris may be blown into your eyes or skin. *Never* direct compressed air at yourself or someone else. Do not allow children to use or play with any compressed air equipment.
15. When using compressed air to dry rotating parts, hold the part so it cannot rotate. Do not allow the force of the air to spin the part. The air jet is capable of rotating parts at extreme speed. The part may be damaged or disintegrate, causing serious injury.
16. Do not inhale the dust created by brake pad and clutch wear. In most cases, these particles contain asbestos. In addition, some types of insulating materials and gaskets may contain asbestos. Inhaling asbestos particles is hazardous to your health.
17. Never work on the motorcycle while someone is working under it.
18. When placing the motorcycle on a stand, make sure it is secure before walking away.

Handling Gasoline Safely

Gasoline is a volatile, flammable liquid and is one of the most dangerous items in the shop.

Because gasoline is used so often, many people forget that it is hazardous. Only use gasoline as fuel for gasoline internal combustion engines. When working on a motorcycle, remember that gasoline is always present in the fuel tank, fuel line and carburetor. To avoid a disastrous accident when working around the fuel system, observe the following precautions:

1. *Never* use gasoline to clean parts. See *Cleaning Parts* in this section.
2. When working on the fuel system, work outside or in a well-ventilated area.

2

3. Do not add fuel to the fuel tank or service the fuel system while the motorcycle is near open flames, sparks or near someone who is smoking. Gasoline vapor is heavier than air; it collects in low areas and is more easily ignited than liquid gasoline.

4. Allow the engine to cool completely before working on any fuel system component.

5. When draining the carburetor, catch the fuel in a plastic container and then pour it into an approved gasoline storage container.

6. Do not store gasoline in glass containers. If the glass breaks, a serious explosion or fire may occur.

7. Immediately wipe up spilled gasoline with rags. Store the rags in a metal container with a lid until they can be properly disposed of, or place them outside in a safe place for the fuel to evaporate.

8. Do not pour water onto a gasoline fire. Water spreads the fire and makes it more difficult to extinguish. Use a class B, BC or ABC fire extinguisher to put out a gasoline fire.

9. Always turn off the engine before refueling. Do not spill fuel onto the engine or exhaust system. Do not overfill the fuel tank. Leave an air space at the top of the tank to allow room for the fuel to expand due to temperature fluctuations.

Cleaning Parts

Cleaning parts is one of the more tedious and difficult service jobs performed in the home garage. There are many types of chemical cleaners and solvents available for shop use. Most are poisonous and extremely flammable. To prevent chemical exposure, vapor buildup, fire and serious injury, observe each product warning label and note the following:

1. Read and observe the entire product label before using any chemical. Always know what type of chemical is being used and whether it is poisonous and/or flammable.
2. Do not use more than one type of cleaning solvent at a time. If mixing chemicals is called for, measure the proper amounts according to the manufacturer's instructions.
3. Work in a well-ventilated area.
4. Wear chemical-resistant gloves.
5. Wear safety glasses.
6. Wear a vapor respirator if the instructions call for it.
7. Wash hands and arms thoroughly after cleaning parts.
8. Keep chemical products away from children and pets.
9. Thoroughly clean all oil, grease and cleaner residue from any part that must be heated.
10. Use a nylon brush when cleaning parts. Metal brushes may cause a spark.
11. When using a parts washer, only use the solvent recommended by the manufacturer. Make sure the parts washer is equipped with a metal lid that will lower in case of fire.

Warning Labels

Most manufacturers attach information and warning labels to the motorcycle. These labels contain instructions that are important to personal safety when operating, servicing, transporting and storing the motorcycle. Refer to the owner's manual for the description and location of labels. Order replacement labels from the manufacturer if they are missing or damaged.

SERIAL NUMBERS

Serial numbers are stamped onto the frame and engine. Record these numbers in the *Quick Reference Data* section at the front of the manual. Have these numbers available when ordering parts.

The vehicle identification number (VIN) (**Figure 1**) is stamped on the right side of the steering head. The engine number (**Figure 2**) is stamped on the right of the crankcase just forward of the air filter housing.

Table 1 lists VIN and engine numbers by model year.

FASTENERS

Proper fastener selection and installation is important to ensure the motorcycle operates as designed and can be serviced efficiently. Original equipment fasteners are designed for their specific applications. Make sure replacement fasteners meet all the same requirements as the originals.

Threaded Fasteners

Threaded fasteners secure most of the components on the motorcycle. Most are tightened by turning them clockwise (right-hand threads). If the normal rotation of the component would loosen the fastener, it may have left-hand threads. If a left-hand threaded fastener is used, it is noted in the text.

Two dimensions are required to match the thread size of the fastener: the number of threads in a given distance and the outside diameter of the threads.

Two systems are currently used to specify threaded fastener dimensions: the U.S. Standard system and the metric system (**Figure 3**). Pay particular attention when working with unidentified fasteners. Mismatching thread types can damage threads.

NOTE
To ensure that the fastener threads are not mismatched or cross-threaded, start all fasteners by hand. If a fastener is hard to start or turn, determine the cause before tightening it with a wrench.

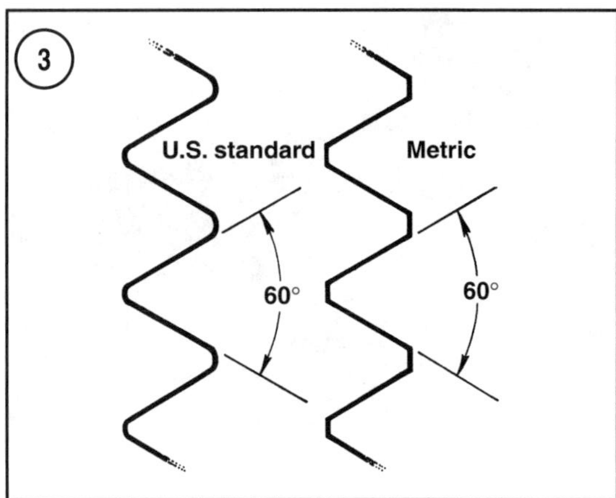

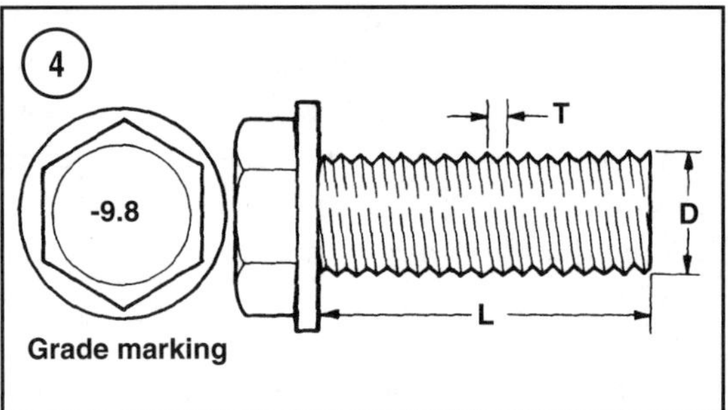

The length (L, **Figure 4**), diameter (D) and distance between thread crests (pitch) (T) classify metric screws and bolts. A typical bolt may be identified by the numbers, 8—1.25 × 130. This indicates the bolt has diameter of 8 mm, the distance between thread crests is 1.25 mm and the length is 130 mm. Always measure bolt length as shown in **Figure 4** to avoid purchasing replacements of the wrong length.

The numbers located on the top of the fastener (**Figure 4**) indicate the strength of metric screws and bolts. The higher the number, the stronger the fastener. Unnumbered fasteners are the weakest.

Many bolts and studs are combined with nuts to secure particular components. To indicate the size of a nut, manufacturers specify the internal diameter and the thread pitch.

The measurement across two parallel flats on a nut or bolt head indicates the wrench size that fits the fastener.

WARNING
Do not install fasteners with a strength classification lower than what was originally installed by the manufacturer. Doing so may cause equipment failure and/or damage.

Torque Specifications

The components of a motorcycle may be subjected to uneven stresses if the fasteners of the various subassemblies are not installed and tightened correctly. Fasteners that are improperly installed or that work loose can cause extensive damage. Use an accurate torque wrench when tightening fasteners, and tighten each fastener to its specified torque.

Torque specifications for specific components appear in the procedures and at the end of the appropriate chapters. Specifications for torque are pro-

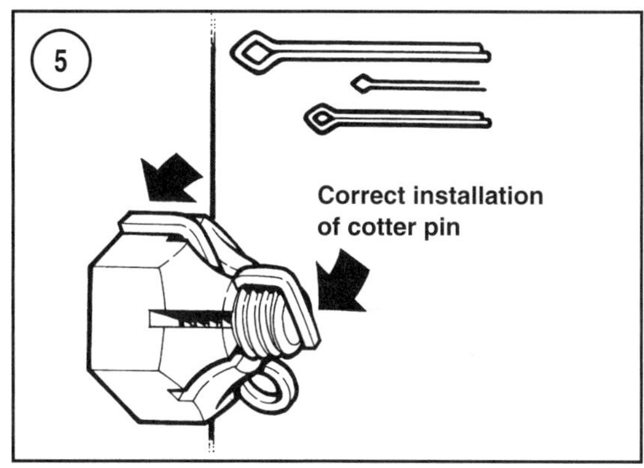

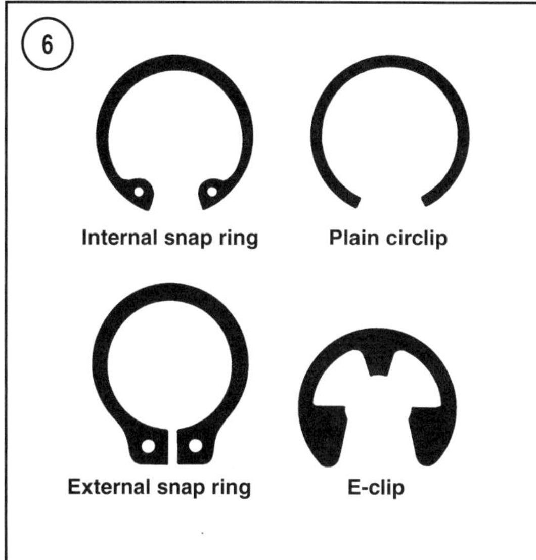

vided in Newton-meters (N•m) and in foot-pounds (ft.-lb.) or inch-pounds (in.-lb.). Refer to **Table 6** for torque conversion formulas and to **Table 4** for general torque specifications. To use the general torque specifications, determine the size of the fastener as described under *Fasteners* in this section. Locate that size fastener in **Table 4** and tighten the fastener to the indicated torque. Torque wrenches are described in *Basic Tools* in this chapter.

Self-locking Fasteners

Several types of bolts, screws and nuts use various means to create interference between the threads of two fasteners to prevent the fasteners from loosening. The most common types are the nylon-insert nut or a dry adhesive coating on the threads of a bolt.

Self-locking fasteners improve resistance to vibration and therefore provide greater holding strength than standard fasteners. Most self-locking fasteners cannot be reused. The materials used to form the lock become distorted after the initial installation and removal. Always discard and replace self-locking fasteners after their removal. Do not replace self-locking fasteners with standard fasteners.

Washers

There are two basic types of washers: flat washers and lockwashers. Flat washers are simple discs with a hole for a screw or bolt. Flat washers help distribute fastener load, they protect components from fastener damage, and they can be used as spacers and seals. Lockwashers are used to prevent a fastener from working loose.

When replacing washers, make sure the replacements are of the same design and quality as the originals.

Cotter Pins

A cotter pin is a split metal pin inserted into a hole or slot to prevent a fastener from working loose. In certain applications, such as the rear axle on an ATV or motorcycle, a cotter pin and castellated (slotted) nut is used.

To use a cotter pin, first make sure the pin's diameter is correct for the hole in the fastener. After correctly tightening the fastener and aligning the holes, insert the cotter pin through the hole and bend the ends over the fastener (**Figure 5**). Unless instructed to do so, never loosen a torqued fastener to align the holes. If the holes do not align, tighten the fastener just enough to achieve alignment.

Cotter pins are available in various diameters and lengths. Measure length from the bottom of the head to the tip of the shortest pin.

Snap Rings and E-clips

Snap rings (**Figure 6**) are circular-shaped metal retaining clips. They secure parts and gears onto shafts, pins or rods. External snap rings are used to retain items on shafts. Internal snap rings secure parts within housing bores. In some applications, in addition to securing the component(s), snap rings of varying thickness also determine end play. These are usually called selective snap rings.

Two basic types of snap rings are used: machined and stamped snap rings. Machined snap rings (**Figure 7**) can be installed in either direction since both faces have sharp edges. Stamped snap rings (**Figure 8**) are manufactured with a sharp edge and a round edge. When installing a stamped snap rings in a thrust application, install the sharp edge facing away from the part producing the thrust.

E-clips are used when it is not practical to use a snap ring. Remove E-clips with a flat blade screwdriver by prying between the shaft and E-clip. To install an E-clip, center it over the shaft groove and push or tap it into place.

Observe the following when installing snap rings:

1. Remove and install snap rings with snap ring pliers. See *Snap Ring Pliers* in this chapter.
2. In some applications, it may be necessary to replace snap rings after removing them.
3. Compress or expand snap rings only enough to install them. If overly expanded, they lose their retaining ability.
4. After installing a snap ring, make sure it seats completely.
5. Wear eye protection when removing and installing snap rings.

SHOP SUPPLIES

Lubricants and Fluids

Periodic lubrication helps ensure a long service life for any type of equipment. Using the correct type of lubricant is as important as performing the lubrication service, although in an emergency the wrong type of lubricant is better than none. The following section describes the types of lubricants most often required. Make sure to follow the manufacturer's recommendations for lubricant types.

Engine oils

Generally, all liquid lubricants are called oil. They may be mineral-based (including petroleum bases), natural-based (vegetable and animal bases), synthetic-based, or emulsions (mixtures).

Engine oil is classified by two standards: the American Petroleum Institute (API) service classification and the Society of Automotive Engineers (SAE) viscosity rating. This information is on the oil container label. Two letters indicate the API service classification (SF, SG, etc.). The number or sequence of numbers and letter (10W-40 for example) is the oil's viscosity rating. The API service classification and the SAE viscosity index are not indications of oil quality.

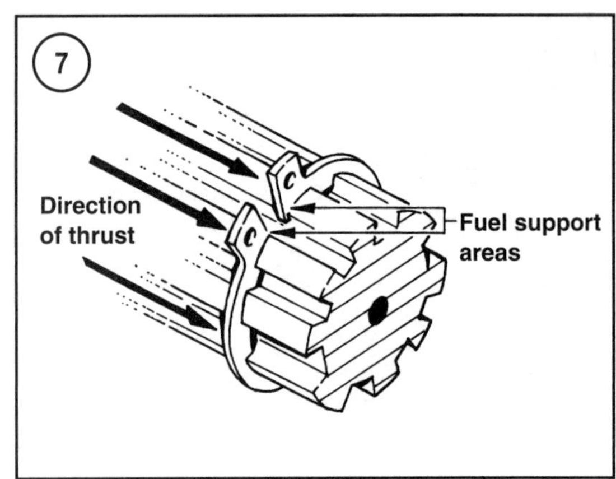

The service classification indicates the oil meets specific lubrication standards. The first letter in the classification (*S*) indicates the oil is for gasoline engines. The second letter indicates the standard the oil satisfies.

Always use oil with a classification recommended by the manufacturer. Using oil with a different classification can cause engine damage.

Viscosity is an indication of the oil's thickness. Thin oils have a lower number while thick oils have a higher number. A "W" after the number indicates that the viscosity testing was done at low temperature to simulate cold-weather operation. Engine oils fall into the 5- to 50-weight range for single-grade oils.

Most manufacturers recommend multigrade oil. Multigrade oils (for example 10W-40) are less viscous (thinner) at low temperatures and more viscous (thicker) at high temperatures. This allows the oil to perform efficiently across a wide range of engine operating conditions. The lower the number, the better the engine will start in cold climates. Higher numbers are usually recommended when operating an engine in hot weather.

Greases

Grease is oil with a thickening base added so the end product is semi-solid. Grease is often classified

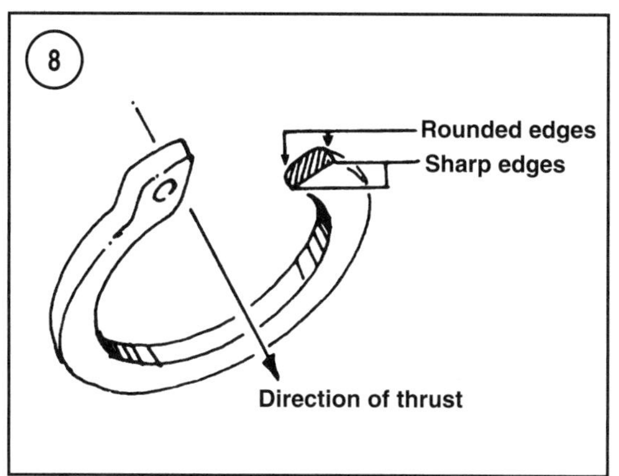

by the type of thickener added, such as lithium soap. The National Lubricating Grease Institute (NLGI) grades grease. Grades range from No. 000 to No. 6, with No. 6 being the thickest. Typical multipurpose grease is NLGI No. 2. For specific applications, manufacturers may recommend water-resistant type grease or one with an additive such as molybdenum disulfide (MoS_2).

Unless otherwise specified, use a multipurpose waterproof NLGI No. 2 grease when grease is called for in this manual.

Brake fluid

Brake fluid is the hydraulic fluid used to transmit hydraulic pressure (force) to the wheel brakes. Brake fluid is classified by the Department of Transportation (DOT). Current designations for brake fluid are DOT 3, DOT 4 and DOT 5. This classification appears on the fluid container.

Each type of brake fluid has its own definite characteristics. Do not intermix different types of brake fluid. DOT 5 fluid is silicone-based. DOT 5 is not compatible with other fluids or in systems for which it was not designed. Mixing DOT 5 fluid with other fluids may cause brake system failure. When adding brake fluid, *only* use the fluid recommended by the motorcycle manufacturer.

Brake fluid will damage plastic, painted or plated surfaces. Use extreme care when working with brake fluid. Immediately wash any spills with soap and water. Rinse the area with plenty of clean water.

Hydraulic brake systems require clean and moisture-free brake fluid. Never reuse brake fluid.

Brake fluid absorbs moisture, which greatly reduces its ability to perform correctly. Keep brake fluid containers and reservoirs properly sealed. Purchase brake fluid in small containers, and discard any small leftover quantities properly. Do not store a container of brake fluid with less than ¼ of the fluid remaining. This small amount absorbs moisture very rapidly.

WARNING

Never put a mineral-based (petroleum) oil into the brake system. Mineral oil will cause rubber parts in the system to swell and break apart, resulting in complete brake failure.

Recycling

Do it yourself maintenance and repair comes with a responsibility to properly dispose of motorcycle and shop waste products. These include: engine and transmission oils, oil filters, coolant (a petroleum product), hydraulic fluids, batteries and any cleaning chemicals. Many local organizations provide collection centers for these waste products.

Cleaners, Degreasers and Solvents

Many chemicals are available to remove oil, grease and other residue from the motorcycle. Before using cleaning solvents, consider how they will be used and disposed of, particularly if they are not water-soluble. Local ordinances may require special procedures for the disposal of various cleaning chemicals. Refer to *Safety* and *Cleaning Parts* in this chapter for more information on their use.

Generally, degreasers are strong cleaners used to remove heavy accumulations of grease from engine and frame components.

Use brake parts cleaner to clean brake system components when contact with petroleum-based products will damage seals. Brake parts cleaner leaves no residue.

Use electrical contact cleaner to clean electrical connections and components without leaving any residue.

Carburetor cleaner is a powerful solvent used to remove fuel deposits and varnish from fuel system components. Use this cleaner carefully, as it may damage finishes.

Most solvents are designed to be used in a parts washing cabinet for individual component cleaning. For safety, use only nonflammable or high flash point solvents.

Gasket Sealant

Sealants are used in combination with a gasket or seal and are occasionally used alone. Follow the manufacturer's recommendation when using sealants. Use extreme care when choosing a sealant other than the type originally recommended. Choose sealants based on their resistance to heat, various fluids and their sealing capabilities.

One of the most common sealants is RTV, or room temperature vulcanizing sealant. This sealant cures at room temperature over a specific time period. It allows the repositioning of components without damaging gaskets.

Moisture in the air causes the RTV sealant to cure. Always install the tube cap as soon as possible after applying RTV sealant. RTV sealant has a limited shelf life and will not cure properly if the shelf life has expired. Keep partial tubes sealed, and discard them if they have surpassed the expiration date.

Applying RTV sealant

Clean all old gasket residue from the mating surfaces. Remove all gasket material from blind threaded holes; it can cause inaccurate bolt torque. Spray the mating surfaces with aerosol parts cleaner, then wipe them with a lint-free cloth. The area must be clean for the sealant to adhere.

Apply RTV sealant in a continuous bead, 2-3 mm (0.08-0.12 in.) thick. Circle all the fastener holes unless otherwise specified. Do not allow any sealant to enter these holes. Assemble and tighten the fasteners to the specified torque within the time frame recommended by the RTV sealant manufacturer.

Gasket Remover

Aerosol gasket remover can help remove stubborn gaskets. This product can speed up the removal process and prevent damage to the mating surface that may be caused by a scraping tool. Most of these products are very caustic. Follow the gasket remover manufacturer's instructions for use.

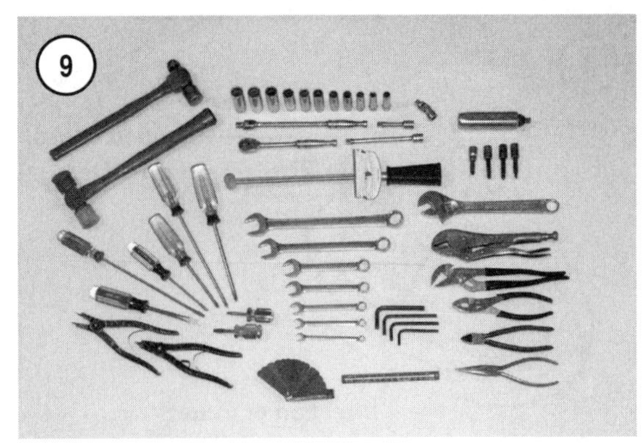

Threadlocking Compound

A threadlocking compound is a fluid applied to the threads of fasteners. After tightening the fastener, the fluid dries and becomes a solid filler between the threads. This makes it difficult for the fastener to work loose from vibration or heat expansion/contraction. Some threadlocking compounds also provide a seal against fluid leakage.

Before applying threadlocking compound, remove any old compound from both thread areas and clean them with aerosol parts cleaner. Use the compound sparingly. Excess fluid can run into adjoining parts.

Threadlocking compounds are available in different strengths. Follow the manufacturer's recommendations regarding compound selection. Two manufacturers of threadlocking compound are ThreeBond and Loctite. They both offer a wide range of compounds for various strength, temperature and repair applications.

When applying threadlock to any fastener, avoid getting it on plastic components.

BASIC TOOLS

Most of the procedures in this manual can be carried out with common hand tools and test equipment familiar to the home mechanic. Always use the correct tools for the job at hand. Keep tools organized and clean. Store them in a tool chest with related tools organized together.

Quality tools are essential. The best are constructed of high-strength alloy steel. These tools are light, easy to use and resistant to wear. Their working surface is smooth, and the tool is carefully polished. They have an easy-to-clean finish and are

10

11

comfortable to use. Quality tools are a good investment.

When building a new tool kit, consider purchasing a basic set (**Figure 9**) from a large tool supplier. These sets contain a variety of commonly used tools and they provide substantial savings when compared to individually purchased tools. As one becomes more experienced and tasks become more complicated, specialized tools can be added.

Some of the procedures in this manual require special tools. These are described in the appropriate chapter and are available froth either the motorcycle manufacturer or an aftermarket tool supplier.

In many cases, an acceptable substitute may be found in an existing tool kit. Another alternative is to make the tool or have one made. Many schools with a machine shop curriculum welcome outside work.

Screwdrivers

Screwdrivers of various lengths and types are mandatory for the simplest tool kit. The two basic types are the slotted tip (flat blade) and the Phillips tip. These are available in sets that often include an assortment of tip sizes and shaft lengths.

As with all tools, use a screwdriver designed for the job. Make sure the size of the tip conforms to the size and shape of the fastener. Use them only for driving screws. Never use a screwdriver for prying or chiseling metal. Repair or replace worn or damaged screwdrivers. A worn tip may damage the fastener, making it difficult to remove.

Wrenches

Box-end, open-end and combination wrenches (**Figure 10**) are available in a variety of types and sizes.

The number stamped on the wrench refers to the distance between the work areas. This must match the distance across two parallel flats on the bolt head or nut.

The box-end wrench is an excellent tool because it grips the fastener on all sides. This reduces the chance of the tool slipping. The box-end wrench is designed with either a 6- or 12-point opening. For stubborn or damaged fasteners, the 6-point provides superior holding ability by contacting the fastener across a wider area at all six edges. For general use, the 12-point works well. It allows the wrench to be removed and reinstalled without moving the handle over such a wide arc.

An open-end wrench is fast and works best in areas with limited overhead access. Because it contacts the fastener at only two points, an open-end wrench is subject to slipping under heavy force or if the tool or fastener is worn. A box-end wrench is preferred in most instances, especially when applying considerable force to a fastener.

The combination wrench has a box-end on one end and an open-end on the other. This combination makes it a very convenient tool.

Adjustable Wrenches

An adjustable wrench or Crescent wrench (**Figure 11**) fits nearly any nut or bolt head that has clear access around its entire perimeter. An adjustable wrench is best used as a backup wrench to hold a large nut or bolt while the other end is being loosened or tightened with a box-end or socket wrench.

Adjustable wrenches contact the fastener at only two points, which makes them more subject to slipping off the fastener. The fact that one jaw is adjustable and may loosen only aggravates this shortcoming. Make certain the solid jaw is the one transmitting the force.

Socket Wrenches, Ratchets and Handles

Sockets that attach to a ratchet handle (**Figure 12**) are available with 6-point (A, **Figure 13**) or 12-point (B) openings and different drive sizes. The drive size indicates the size of the square hole that accepts the ratchet handle. The number stamped on the socket is the size of the work area and must match the fastener head.

As with wrenches, a 6-point socket provides superior-holding ability, while a 12-point socket needs to be moved only half as far to reposition it on the fastener.

Sockets are designated for use with either hand. Impact sockets are made of thicker material for more durability. Compare the size and wall thickness of a 19-mm hand socket (A, **Figure 14**) and the 19-mm impact socket (B). Use impact sockets when using an impact driver or air tools. Use hand sockets with hand-driven attachments.

WARNING
Do not use hand sockets with air or impact tools as they may shatter and cause injury. Always wear eye protection when using impact or air tools.

Various handles are available for sockets. The speed handle is used for fast operation. Flexible ratchet heads in varying lengths allow the socket to be turned with varying force and at odd angles. Extension bars allow the socket setup to reach difficult areas. The ratchet is the most versatile wrench. It allows the user to install or remove the nut without removing the socket.

Sockets combined with any number of drivers make them undoubtedly the fastest, safest and most convenient tool for fastener removal and installation.

Impact Driver

An impact driver provides extra force for removing fasteners by converting the impact of a hammer into a turning motion. This makes it possible to remove stubborn fasteners without damaging them. Impact drivers and interchangeable bits (**Figure 15**) are available from most tool suppliers. When using a socket with an impact driver, make sure the socket is designed for impact use. Refer to *Socket Wrenches, Ratchets and Handles* in this section.

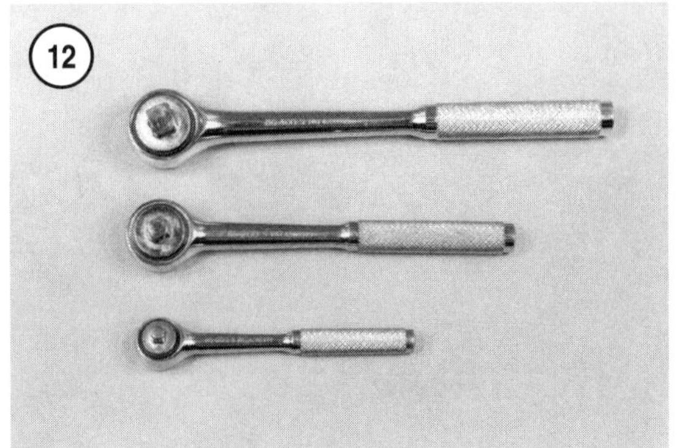

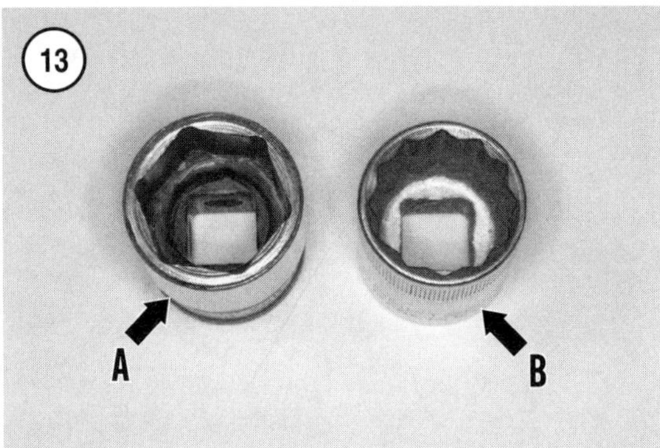

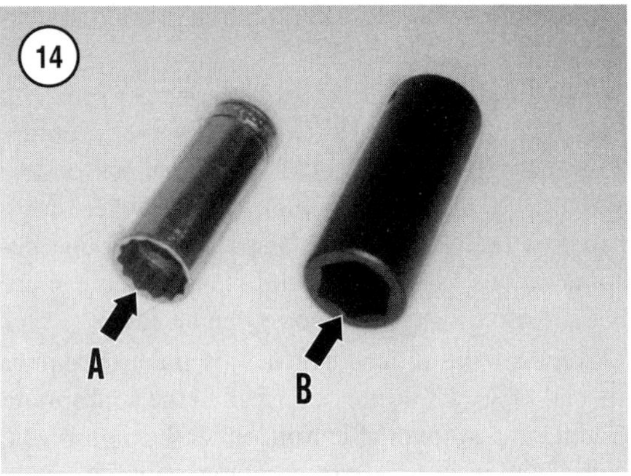

WARNING
Do not use hand sockets with air or impact tools, They may shatter and

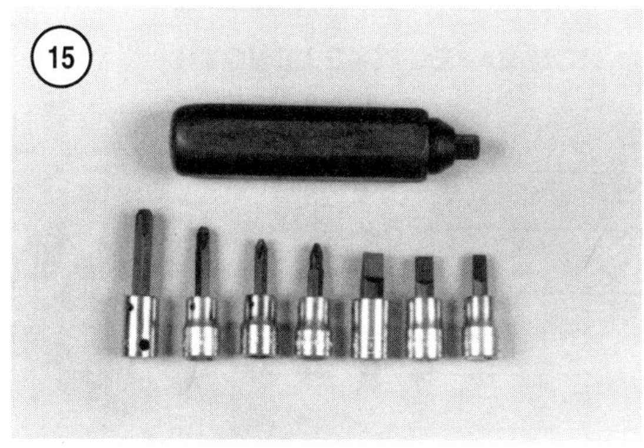
15

cause injury. Always wear eye protection when using impact or air tools.

Allen Wrenches

Allen or setscrew wrenches (**Figure 16**) are used on fasteners with hexagonal recesses in the fastener head. These wrenches are available in L-shaped bars, sockets and T-handles. A metric set is required when working on most motorcycles made by Japanese and European manufacturers. Allen bolts are sometimes called socket bolts.

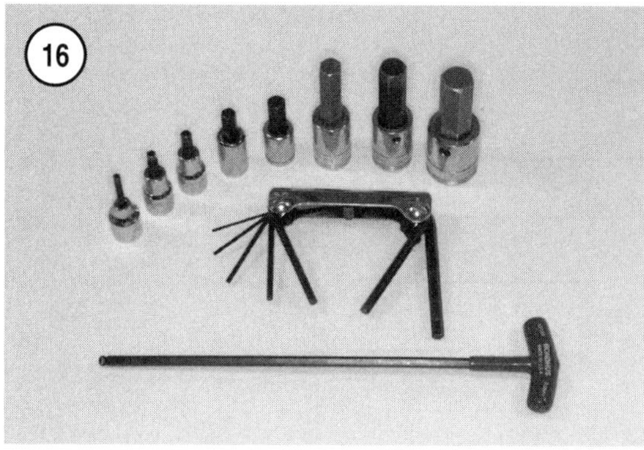
16

Torque Wrenches

A torque wrench is used with a socket, torque adapter or similar extension to tighten a fastener to a measured torque. Torque wrenches come in several drive sizes (1/4, 3/8, 1/2 and 3/4) and use various methods of reading the torque value. The drive size indicates the size of the square drive that accepts the socket, adapter or extension. Common methods of reading the torque value are the deflecting beam (A, **Figure 17**), the dial indicator (B) and the audible click (C).

When choosing a torque wrench, consider the torque range, drive size and accuracy. The torque specifications in this manual provide an indication of the range required.

A torque wrench is a precision tool that must be properly cared for to remain accurate. Store torque wrenches in cases or separate padded drawers within a toolbox. Follow the manufacturer's instructions for their care and calibration.

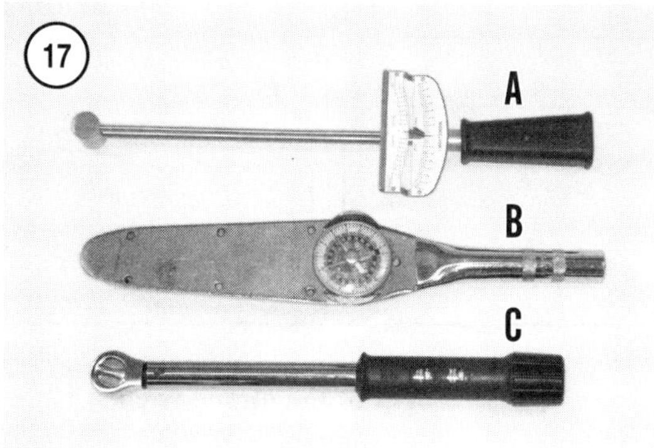

17

Torque Adapters

Torque adapters extend or reduce the reach of a torque wrench. The torque adapter shown in **Figure 18** is used to tighten a fastener that cannot be reached due to the size of the torque wrench head, drive, and socket. Since a torque adapter changes the effective lever length (**Figure 19**) of a torque wrench, the torque reading on the wrench does not equal the actual torque applied to the fastener. It is necessary to calculate the adjusted torque reading on the wrench to compensate for the change of lever length. When a torque adapter is used at a right angle to the drive head, calibration is not required, since the effective length has not changed.

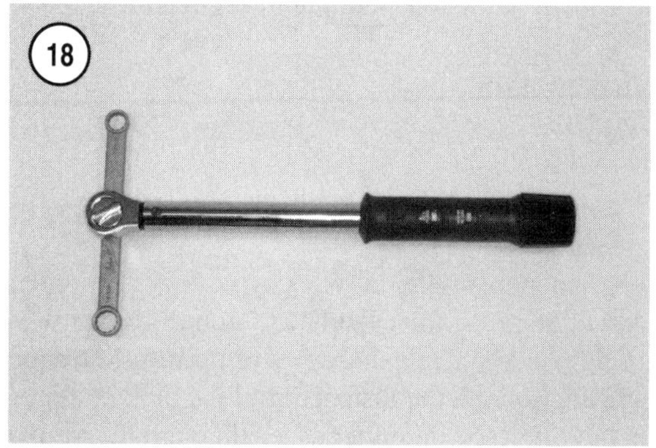
18

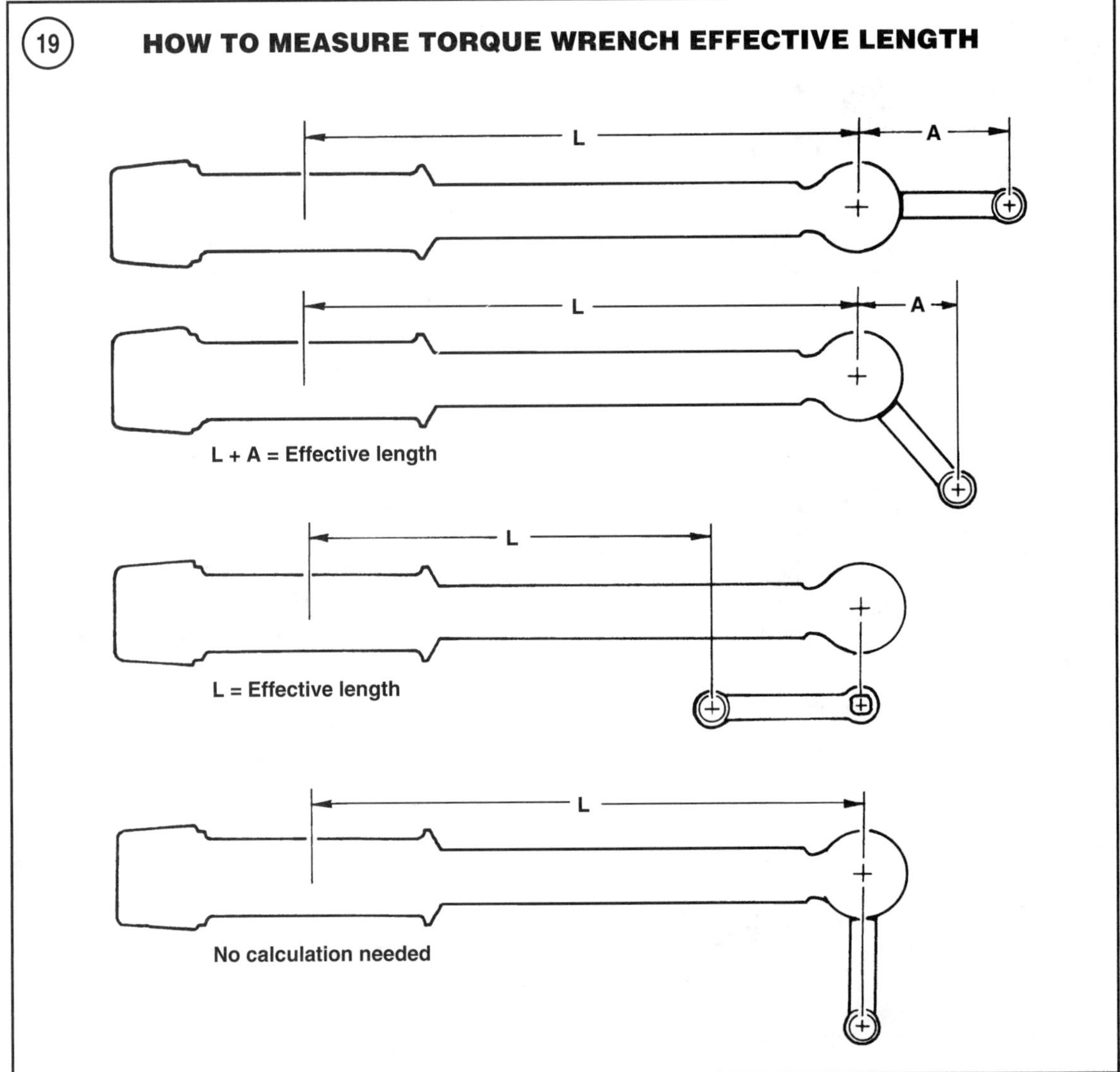

To calculate the adjusted torque reading when using a torque adapter, use the following formula.

$$TW = \frac{TA \times L}{L + A = E}$$

TW is the torque setting or dial reading on the wrench.

TA is the torque specification and the actual amount of torque applied to the fastener.

A is the amount the adapter increases (or in some cases reduces) the effective lever length as measured along the centerline of the torque wrench from the center of the drive to the center of adapter box end (**Figure 19**).

L is the lever length of the wrench as measured from the center of the drive to the center of the grip.

The effective length of the torque wrench is the sum of L and A. For example:

To apply 20 ft.-lb. to a fastener using an adapter as shown in the top example in **Figure 19**:

TA = 20 ft.-lb.
A = 3 in.
L = 14 in.

$$TW = \frac{20 \times 14}{14 + 3} = \frac{280}{17} = 16.5 \text{ ft.-lb.}$$

In this example, a click-type torque wrench would be set to the calculated torque value (TW = 16.5 ft.-lb.). When using a dial or beam-type torque wrench, tighten the fastener until the pointer aligns with 16.5 ft.-lb. In either case, although the torque

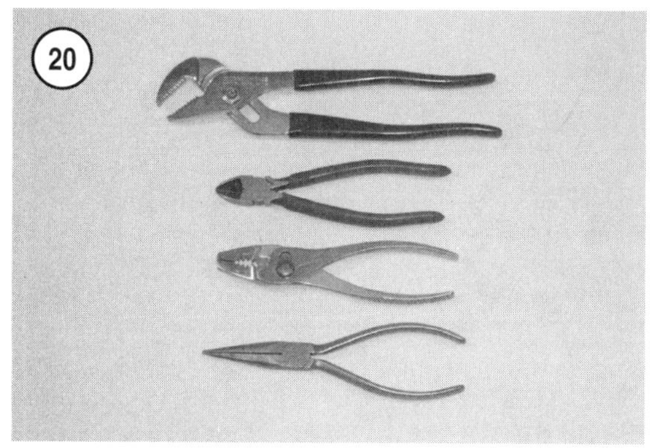
20

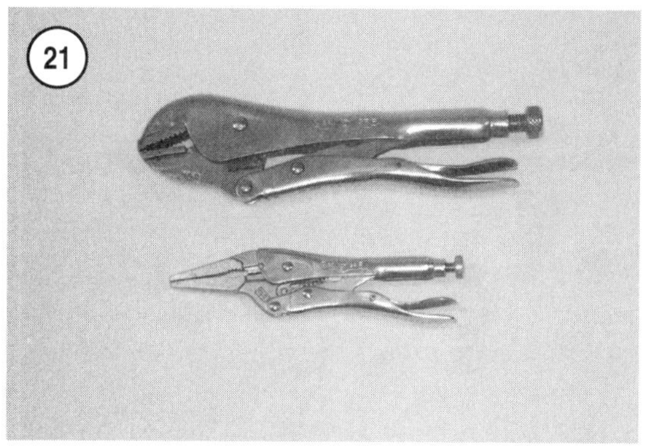
21

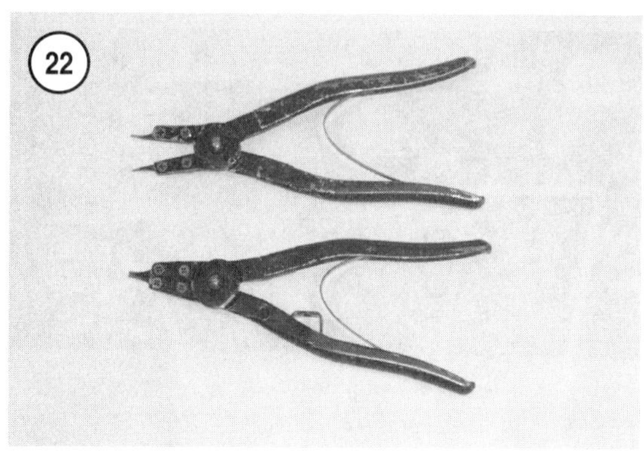
22

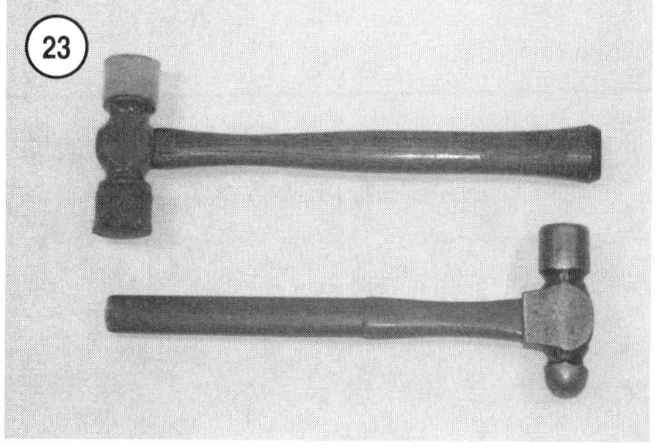
23

wrench reads 16.5 ft.-lb., the actual torque applied to the fastener is 20 ft.-lb.

1

Pliers

Pliers come in a wide range of types and sizes. Pliers are useful for holding, cutting, bending, and crimping. Do not use them to turn fasteners. **Figure 20** show several types of useful pliers. Each design has a specialized function. Slip-joint pliers are general-purpose pliers used for gripping and bending. Diagonal cutting pliers cut wire and can be used to remove cotter pins. Adjustable pliers can be adjusted to hold different size objects. The jaws remain parallel so they grip around objects such as pipe or tubing. Needlenose pliers are used to hold or bend small objects. Locking pliers (**Figure 21**), sometimes called Vise-grips, are used to hold objects very tightly. They have many uses ranging from holding two parts together to gripping the end of a broken stud. Use caution when using locking pliers. The sharp jaws will damage the objects they hold.

Snap Ring Pliers

Snap ring pliers (**Figure 22**) are specialized pliers with tips that fit into the ends of snap rings to remove and install them.

Snap ring pliers are available with a fixed action (either internal or external) or convertible (one tool works on both internal and external snap rings). They may have fixed tips or interchangeable ones of various sizes and angles. For general use, select convertible type pliers with interchangeable tips.

WARNING

Snap rings can slip and fly off during removal and installation. In addition, the tips may break. Always wear eye protection when using circlip pliers.

Hammers

Various types of hammers (**Figure 23**) are available to fit a number of applications. A ball-peen hammer is used to strike another tool, such as a punch or chisel. Soft-faced hammers are required when a metal object must be struck without damaging it. *Never* use a metal-faced hammer on engine or suspension components. Damage will occur in most cases.

Always wear eye protection when using hammers. Make sure the hammer face is in good condition and the handle is not cracked. Select the correct hammer for the job and make sure to strike the object squarely. Do not use the handle or the side of the hammer to strike an object.

PRECISION MEASURING TOOLS

Each type of measuring instrument is designed to measure a dimension with a particular degree of accuracy and within a certain range. When selecting a measuring tool, make sure it is applicable to the task.

As with all tools, measuring tools provide the best results if cared for properly. Improper use can damage the tool and result in inaccurate results. If any measurement is questionable, verify the measurement using another tool. A standard gauge is usually provided with measuring tools to check accuracy and calibrate the tool.

Precision measurements can vary according to the experience of the person taking the measurement. Accurate results are only possible if the mechanic possesses a feel for using the tool. Heavy-handed use of measuring tools produces less accurate results than if the tool is handled gently. Grasp precision measuring tools with your fingertips so the point at which the tool contacts the object is easily felt. This feel for the equipment produces consistently accurate measurements and reduces the risk of damaging the tool or component. Refer to the following sections for a description of various measuring tools.

Feeler Gauge

The feeler or thickness gauge (**Figure 24**) is used for measuring the distance between two surfaces. A common use for a feeler gauge is to measure valve clearance. Wire (round) type gauges are used to measure spark plug gap.

A feeler gauge set consists of an assortment of steel strips of graduated thicknesses. Each blade is marked with its thickness. Blades can be of various lengths and angles for different procedures.

24

25

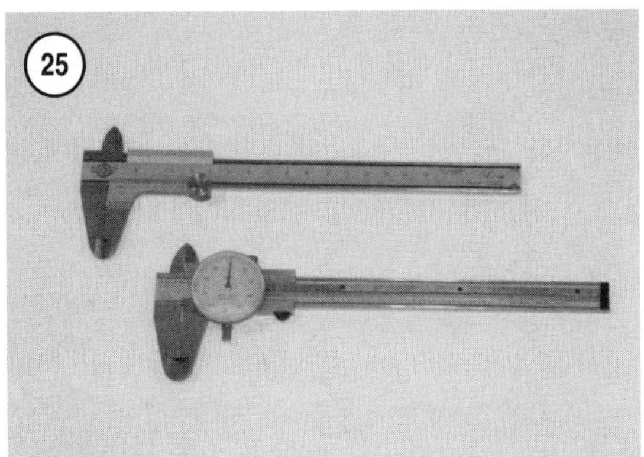

26

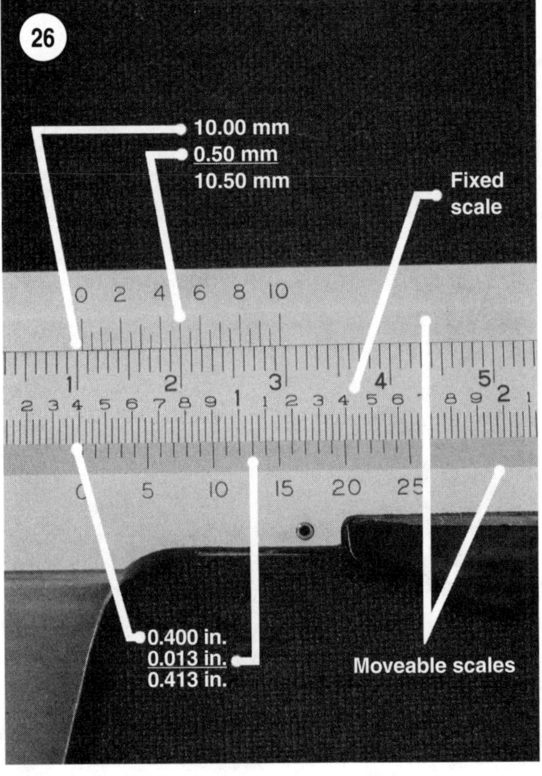

1

DECIMAL PLACE VALUES*

0.1	Indicates 1/10 (one tenth of an inch or millimeter)
0.010	Indicates 1/100 (one one-hundredth of an inch or millimeter)
0.001	Indicates 1/1,000 (one one-thousandth of an inch or millimeter)

*This chart represents the values of figures placed to the right of the decimal point. Use it when reading decimals from one-tenth to one one-thousandth of an inch or millimeter. It is not a conversion chart (for example: 0.001 in. is not equal to 0.001 mm).

Calipers

Calipers (**Figure 25**) are excellent tools for obtaining inside, outside and depth measurements. Although not as precise as a micrometer, they allow reasonable precision, typically to within 0.05 mm (0.001 in.). Most calipers have a range up to 150 mm (6 in.).

Calipers are available in dial, vernier or digital versions. Dial calipers have a dial which is easy to read. Vernier calipers have marked scales that must be compared to determine the measurement. The digital caliper uses an LCD display to show the measurement.

Properly maintain the measuring surfaces of the caliper. There must not be any dirt or burrs between the tool and the object being measured. Never force the caliper closed around an object. Close the caliper around the highest point so it can be removed with a slight drag. Some calipers require calibration. Always refer to the manufacturer's instructions when using a new or unfamiliar caliper.

To read a vernier caliper, refer to **Figure 26**. The fixed scale is marked in both inch and millimeter increments. In this example, refer to the metric scale. The ten individual lines on the fixed scale equal one centimeter. The moveable scale is marked in 0.05 mm (hundredth) increments. To obtain a reading, establish the first number by the location of the 0 line on the movable scale in relation to the first line to the left on the fixed scale. In this example, the number is 10 mm. To determine the next number, note which of the lines on the moveable scale align with a mark on the fixed scale. A number of lines will seem close, but only one will align exactly. In this case, 0.50 mm is the reading to add to the first number. The result of adding 10 mm and 0.50 mm is a measurement of 10.50 mm.

Micrometers

A micrometer is an instrument designed for linear measurement using the decimal divisions of the inch or meter (**Figure 27**). While there are many types and styles of micrometers, most of the procedures in this manual call for an outside micrometer. The outside micrometer is used to measure the outside diameter of cylindrical forms and the thickness of materials.

A micrometer's size indicates the minimum and maximum size of a part it can measure. The usual sizes (**Figure 28**) are 0-1 in. (0-25 mm), 1-2 in. (25-50 mm), 2-3 in. (50-75 mm) and 3-4 in. (75-100 mm).

Micrometers that cover a wider range of measurement are available. These use a large frame with interchangeable anvils of various lengths. This type

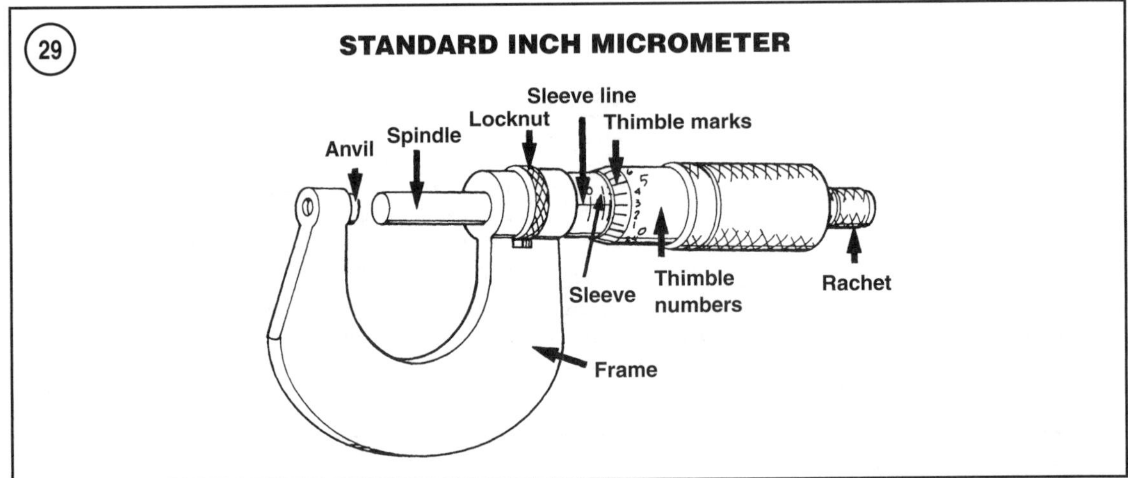

of micrometer offers a cost savings; however, its overall size may make it less convenient.

Reading a Micrometer

When reading a micrometer, read numbers from different scales and add them together. The following sections describe how to read the measurements of various types of outside micrometers.

For accurate results, properly maintain the measuring surfaces of the micrometer. There must not be any dirt or burrs between the tool and the measured object. Never force the micrometer closed around an object. Close the micrometer around the highest point so it can be removed with a slight drag. **Figure 29** shows the markings and parts of a standard inch micrometer. Be familiar with these terms before using a micrometer in the follow sections.

Standard inch micrometer

The standard inch micrometer is accurate to one-thousandth of an inch or 0.001. The sleeve is marked in 0.025 in. increments. Every fourth sleeve mark is numbered 1, 2, 3, 4, 5, 6, 7, 8, 9. These numbers indicate 0.100, 0.200, 0.300, and so on.

The tapered end of the thimble has 25 lines marked around it. Each mark equals 0.001 in. One complete turn of the thimble aligns its zero mark with the first mark on the sleeve or 0.025 in.

When reading a standard inch micrometer, perform the following steps while referring to **Figure 30**.

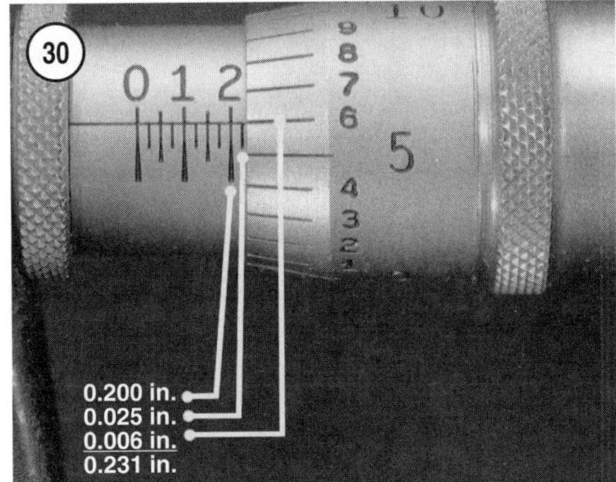

1. Read the sleeve and find the largest number visible. Each sleeve number equals 0.100 in.

2. Count the number of lines between the numbered sleeve mark and the edge of the thimble. Each sleeve mark equals 0.025 in.

3. Read the thimble mark that aligns with the sleeve line. Each thimble mark equals 0.001 in.

NOTE

If a thimble mark does not align exactly with the sleeve line, estimate the amount between the lines. For accurate readings in ten-thousandths of an inch (0.0001 in.), use a vernier inch micrometer.

4. Add the readings from Steps 1-3.

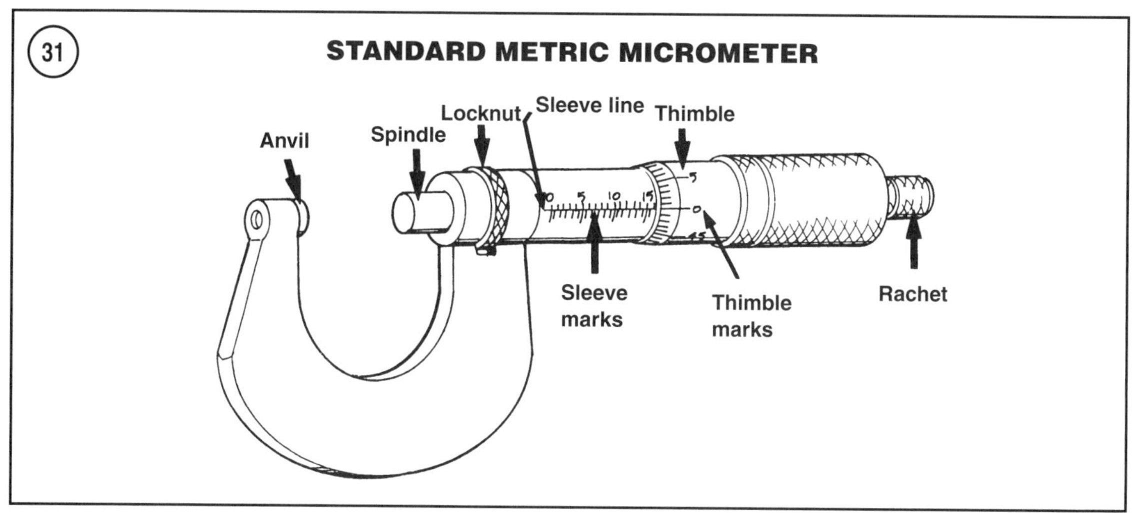

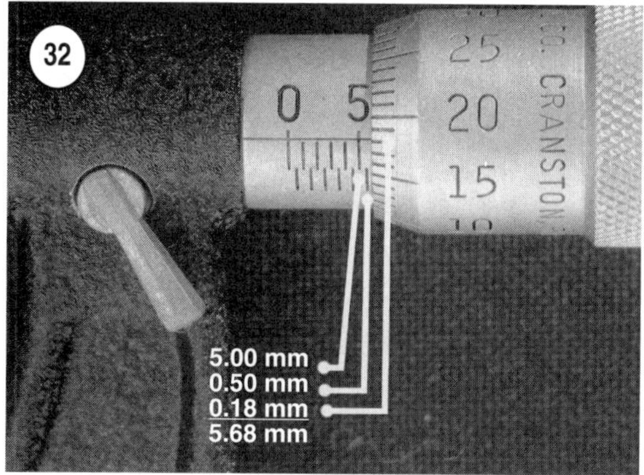

Metric micrometer

The standard metric micrometer (**Figure 31**) is accurate to one one-hundredth of a millimeter (0.01 mm). The sleeve line is graduated in millimeter and half millimeter increments. The marks on the upper half of the sleeve line equal 1.00 mm. Every fifth mark above the sleeve line is identified with a number. The number sequence depends on the size of the micrometer. A 0-25 mm micrometer, for example, has sleeve marks numbered 0 through 25, in 5 mm increments. This numbering sequence continues with larger micrometers. On all metric micrometers, each mark on the lower half of the sleeve equals 0.50 mm.

The tapered end of the thimble has 50 lines marked around it. Each mark equals 0.01 mm.

One complete turn of the thimble aligns its 0 mark with the first line on the lower half of the sleeve line or 0.50 mm.

When reading a metric micrometer, add the number of millimeters and half-millimeters on the sleeve line to the hundredths of a millimeter shown on the thimble. Perform the following steps while referring to **Figure 32**.

1. Read the upper half of the sleeve line and count the number of lines visible. Each upper line equals 1 mm.
2. See if the half-millimeter line is visible on the lower sleeve line. If so, add 0.50 to the reading in Step 1.
3. Read the thimble mark that aligns with the sleeve line. Each thimble mark equals 0.01 mm.

NOTE

If a thimble mark does not align exactly with the sleeve line, estimate the amount between the lines. For accurate readings to two-thousandths of a millimeter (0.002 mm), use a metric vernier micrometer.

4. Add the readings from Steps 1-3.

Micrometer adjustment

Before using a micrometer, check its adjustment as follows:

1. Clean the anvil and spindle faces.

2A. To check a 0-1 in. or 0-25 mm micrometer:

a. Turn the thimble until the spindle contacts the anvil. If the micrometer has a ratchet stop, use it to ensure that the proper amount of pressure is applied.

b. The adjustment is correct if the 0 mark on the thimble aligns exactly with the 0 mark on the sleeve line. If the marks do not align, the micrometer is out of adjustment.

c. Follow the manufacturer's instructions to adjust the micrometer.

2B. To check a micrometer larger than 1 in. or 25 mm, use the standard gauge supplied by the manufacturer. A standard gauge is a steel block, disc or rod that is machined to an exact size.

a. Place the standard gauge between the spindle and anvil, and measure its outside diameter or length. If the micrometer has a ratchet stop, use it to ensure the proper amount of pressure is applied.

b. The adjustment is correct if the 0 mark on the thimble aligns exactly with the 0 mark on the sleeve line. If the marks do not align, the micrometer is out of adjustment.

c. Follow the manufacturer's instructions to adjust the micrometer.

Micrometer Care

Micrometers are precision instruments. They must be used and maintained with great care. Note the following:

1. Store micrometers in protective cases or separate padded drawers in a toolbox.
2. When in storage, make sure the spindle and anvil faces do not contact each other or any other objects. If they do, temperature changes and corrosion may damage the contact faces.
3. Do not clean a micrometer with compressed air. Dirt forced into the tool will cause wear.
4. Lubricate micrometers with WD-40 to prevent corrosion.

Telescoping and Small Bore Gauges

Use telescoping gauges (**Figure 33**) and small bore gauges (**Figure 34**) to measure bores. Neither gauge has a scale for direct readings. An outside micrometer must be used to determine the reading.

To use a telescoping gauge, select the correct size gauge for the bore. Compress the movable post and carefully insert the gauge into the bore. Carefully move the gauge in the bore to make sure it is centered. Tighten the knurled end of the gauge to hold the movable post in position. Remove the gauge and measure the length of the posts with a micrometer. Telescoping gauges are typically used to measure cylinder bores.

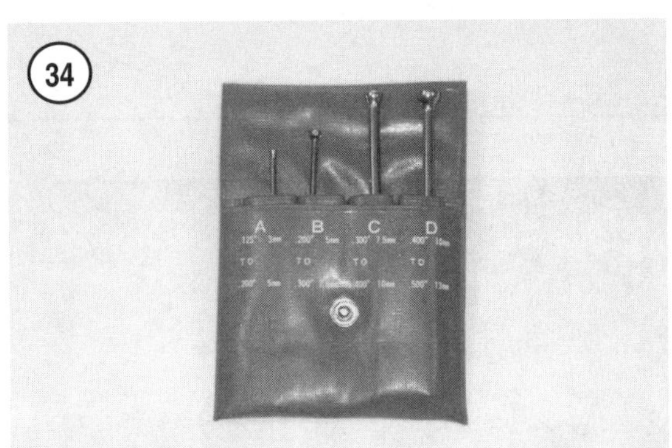

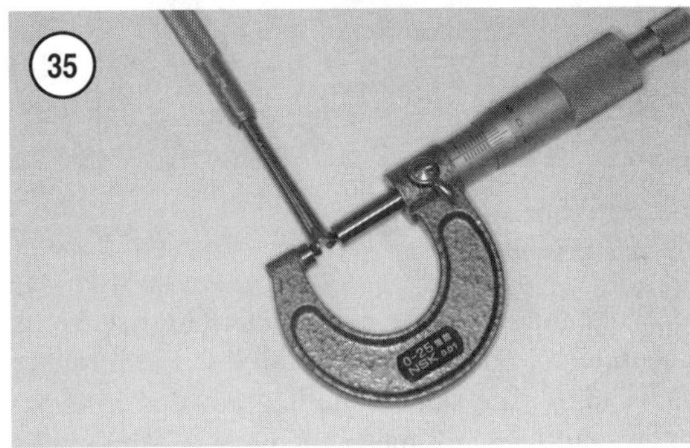

To use a small-bore gauge, select the correct size gauge for the bore. Carefully insert the gauge into the bore. Tighten the knurled end of the gauge to carefully expand the gauge fingers to the limit within the bore. Do not over tighten the gauge, as there is no built-in release. Excessive tightening can damage the bore surface and damage the tool. Remove the gauge and measure the outside dimension (**Figure 35**). Small bore gauges are typically used to measure valve guides.

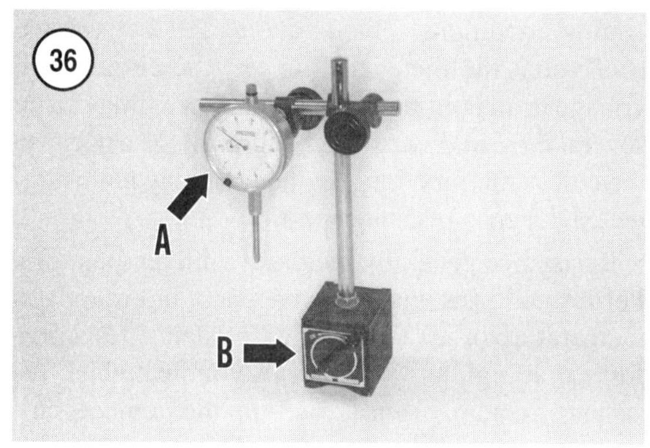

Dial Indicator

A dial indicator (A, **Figure 36**) is a gauge with a dial face and needle used to measure variations in dimensions and movements. Measuring brake rotor runout is a typical use for a dial indicator.

Dial indicators are available in various ranges and graduations. They use three basic types of mounting bases: magnetic, clamp, or screw-in stud. When purchasing a dial indicator, select the magnetic stand type (B, **Figure 36**) with a continuous dial.

Cylinder Bore Gauge

A cylinder bore gauge is similar to a dial indicator. The gauge set shown in **Figure 37** consists of a dial indicator, handle, and different length adapters (anvils) to fit the gauge to various bore sizes. The bore gauge is used to measure bore size, taper and out-of-round. When using a bore gauge, follow the manufacturer's instructions.

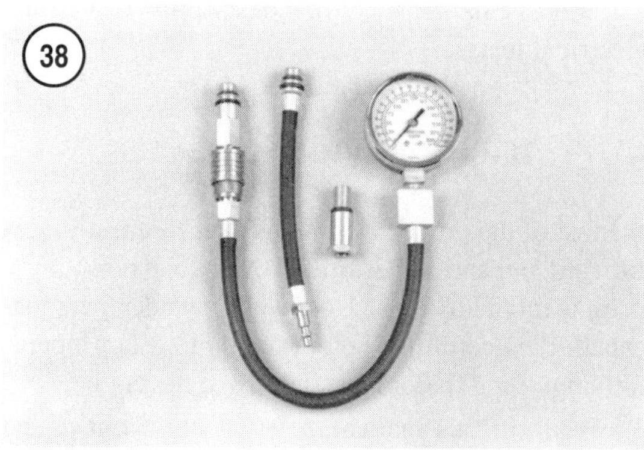

Compression Gauge

A compression gauge (**Figure 38**) measures combustion chamber (cylinder) pressure, usually in psi or kg/cm. The gauge adapter is either inserted or screwed into the spark plug hole to obtain the reading. Disable the engine so it will not start and hold the throttle in the wide-open position when performing a compression test. An engine that does not have adequate compression cannot be properly tuned. See Chapter Three.

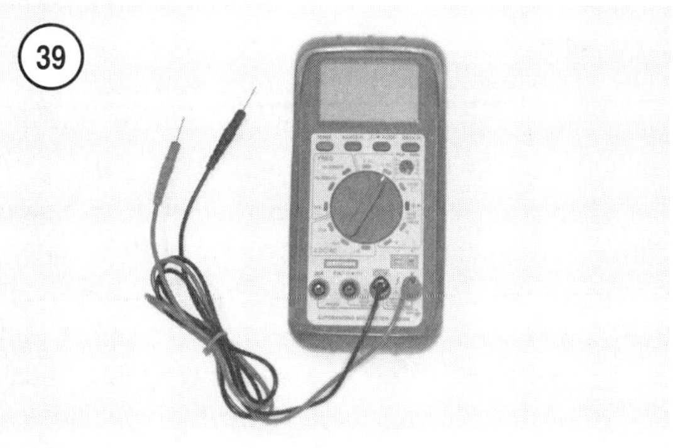

Multimeter

A multimeter (**Figure 39**) is an essential tool for electrical system diagnosis. The voltage function indicates the voltage applied or available to various electrical components. The ohmmeter function tests circuits for continuity and measures the resistance of a circuit.

Some test specifications for electrical components are based on results using a specific test meter. Results may vary if using a meter not recommend by the manufacturer. Such requirements are noted when applicable.

Ohmmeter (analog) calibration

Each time an analog ohmmeter is used or if the scale is changed, the ohmmeter must be calibrated. Digital ohmmeters do not require calibration.

1. Make sure the meter battery is in good condition.
2. Make sure the meter probes are in good condition.
3. Touch the two probes together and watch the needle. It must align with the 0 mark on the scale.
4. If necessary, rotate the set-adjust knob until the needle points directly to the 0 mark.

ELECTRICAL SYSTEM FUNDAMENTALS

A thorough study of the many types of electrical systems used in today's motorcycles is beyond the scope of this manual. However, an understanding of electrical basics is necessary to perform simple diagnostic tests.

Voltage

Voltage is the electrical potential or pressure in an electrical circuit and is expressed in volts. The more pressure (voltage) in a circuit, the more work can be performed.

Direct current (DC) voltage means the electricity flows in one direction. All circuits powered by a battery are DC circuits.

Alternating current (AC) means the electricity flows in one direction momentarily then switches to the opposite direction. Alternator output is an example of AC voltage. This voltage must be changed or rectified to direct current to operate in a battery powered system.

Resistance

Resistance is the opposition to the flow of electricity within a circuit or component and is measured in ohms. Resistance causes a reduction in available current and voltage.

Resistance is measured in an inactive circuit with an ohmmeter. The ohmmeter sends a small amount of current into the circuit and measures how difficult it is to push the current through the circuit.

An ohmmeter, although useful, is not always a good indicator of a circuit's actual ability under operating conditions. This is due to the low voltage (6-9 volts) the meter uses to test the circuit. The voltage in an ignition coil secondary winding can be several thousand volts. Such high voltage can cause the coil to malfunction, yet the fault may not be detected during a resistance test.

Resistance generally increases with temperature. Perform all tests with the component or circuit at a temperature of 20°C (68° F). Resistance tests performed at high temperatures may indicate high resistance readings and result in the unnecessary replacement of a component.

Amperage

Amperage is the unit of measure for current within a circuit. Current is the actual flow of electricity. The higher the current, the more work can be performed. However, if the current flow exceeds the circuit or component capacity, the system will be damaged.

Electrical Tests

Refer to Chapter Two for a description of various electrical tests.

BASIC SERVICE METHODS

Most of the procedures in this manual are straightforward and can be performed by anyone reasonably competent with tools. However, consider personal capabilities carefully before attempting any operation involving major disassembly of the engine.

1. *Front*, in this manual, refers to the front of the motorcycle. The front of any component is the end closest to the front of the motorcycle. The left and right sides refer to the position of the parts as viewed by the rider sitting on the seat facing forward. For example, the throttle control is on the right side of the handlebar.
2. Whenever servicing an engine or suspension component, secure the motorcycle in a safe manner.
3. Tag all similar parts for location and mark all mated parts for position. Record the number and thickness of any shims as they are removed. Identify parts by placing them in sealed and labeled plastic bags.

4. Tag disconnected wires and connectors with masking tape and a marking pen. Do not rely on memory alone.
5. Protect finished surfaces from physical damage or corrosion. Keep gasoline and other chemicals off painted surfaces.
6. Use penetrating oil on frozen or tight bolts. Avoid using heat where possible. Heat can warp, melt or affect the temper of parts. Heat also damages the finish of paint and plastics.
7. When a part is a press fit or requires a special tool for removal, the information or type of tool is identified in the text. Otherwise, if a part is difficult to remove or install, determine the cause before proceeding.
8. To prevent objects or debris from falling into the engine, cover all openings.
9. Read each procedure thoroughly and compare the illustrations to the actual components before starting the procedure. Perform each procedure in sequence.
10. Recommendations are occasionally made to refer service to a dealership or specialist. In these cases, the work can be performed more economically by the specialist than by the home mechanic.
11. The term *replace* means to discard a defective part and install a new part in its place. *Overhaul* means to remove, disassemble, inspect, measure, repair and/or replace parts as required to recondition an assembly.
12. Some operations require the use of a hydraulic press. If a press is not available, have these operations performed by a shop equipped with the necessary equipment. Do not use makeshift equipment that may damage the motorcycle.
13. Repairs are much faster and easier if the motorcycle is clean before starting work. Degrease the motorcycle with a commercial degreaser; follow the directions on the container for the best results. Clean all parts with cleaning solvent as they are removed.

CAUTION
Do not apply a chemical degreaser to an O-ring drive chain. These chemicals will damage the O-rings. Use kerosene to clean O-ring type chains.

CAUTION
Do not direct high-pressure water at steering bearings, carburetor hoses, wheel bearings, suspension and electrical components, or O-ring drive chains. The water will force the grease out of the bearings and possibly damage the seals.

14. If special tools are required, have them available before starting a procedure. When special tools are required, they will be described at the beginning of the procedure.

15. Make diagrams of similar-appearing parts. For instance, crankcase bolts are often not the same lengths. Do not rely on memory alone. It is possible that carefully laid out parts will become disturbed, making it difficult to reassemble the components correctly without a diagram.

16. Make sure all shims and washers are reinstalled in the same location and position.

17. Whenever a rotating part contacts a stationary part, look for a shim or washer.

18. Use new gaskets if there is any doubt about the condition of old ones.

19. If self-locking fasteners are used, replace them with new ones. Do not reuse a self-locking fastener. Also, do not install standard fasteners in place of self-locking ones.

20. Use grease to hold small parts in place if they tend to fall out during assembly. However, do not apply grease to electrical or brake components.

Removing Frozen Fasteners

If a fastener cannot be removed, several methods may be used to loosen it. First, apply penetrating oil such as Liquid Wrench or WD-40. Apply it liberally, and let it penetrate for 10-15 minutes. Rap the fastener several times with a small hammer. Do not hit it hard enough to cause damage. Reapply the penetrating oil if necessary.

For frozen screws, apply penetrating oil as described. Insert a screwdriver in the slot, and rap the top of the screwdriver with a hammer. This loosens the rust so the screw can be removed in the normal way. If the screw head is too damaged to use this method, grip the head with locking pliers and twist the screw out.

Avoid applying heat unless specifically instructed, as it may melt, warp or remove the temper from parts.

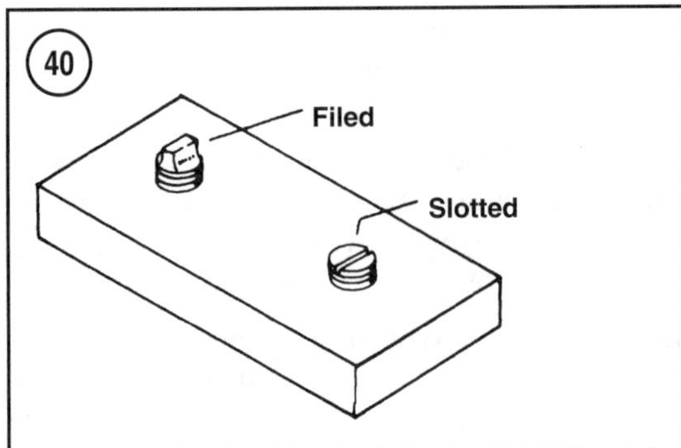

Removing Broken Fasteners

If the head breaks off a screw or bolt, several methods are available for removing the remaining portion. If a large portion of the remainder projects out, try gripping it with locking pliers. If the projecting portion is too small, file it to fit a wrench or cut a slot in it to fit a screwdriver (**Figure 40**).

If the head breaks off flush, use a screw extractor. To do this, center punch the remaining portion of the screw or bolt. Drill a small hole in the screw and tap the extractor into the hole. Back the screw out with a wrench on the extractor (**Figure 41**).

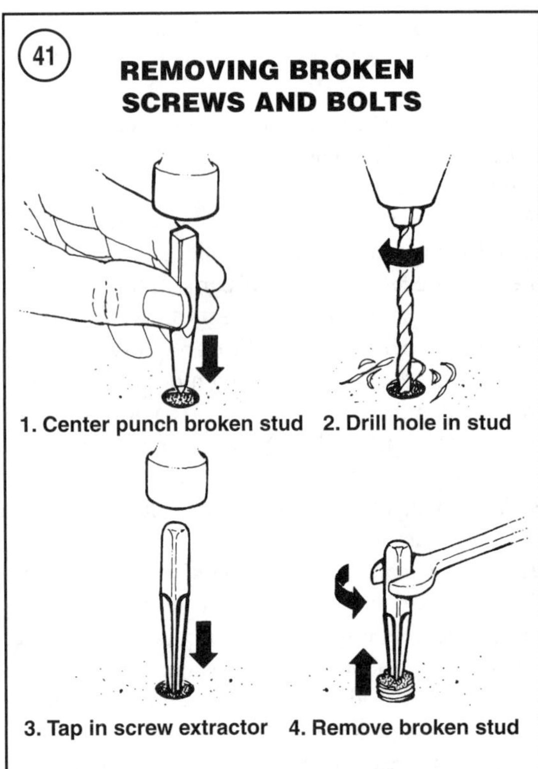

Repairing Damaged Threads

Occasionally, threads are stripped through carelessness or impact damage. Often the threads can be repaired by running a tap (for internal threads on nuts) or die (for external threads on bolts) through the threads (**Figure 42**). To clean or repair spark plug threads, use a spark plug tap.

If an internal thread is damaged, it may be necessary to install a Helicoil or some other type of thread insert. Follow the manufacturer's instructions when installing their insert.

If it is necessary to drill and tap a hole, refer to **Table 8** for metric tap and drill sizes.

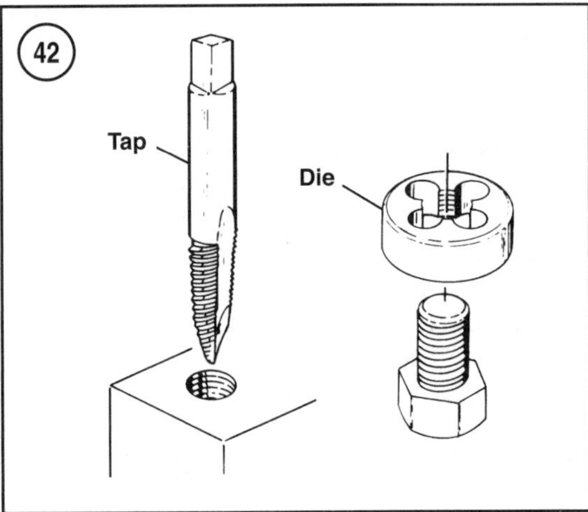

Stud Removal/Installation

A stud removal tool is available from most tool suppliers. This tool makes the removal and installation of studs easier. If one is not available, thread two nuts onto the stud and tighten them against each other. Remove the stud by turning the lower nut (**Figure 43**).

1. Measure the height of the stud above the surface.
2. Thread the stud removal tool onto the stud and tighten it, or thread two nuts onto the stud.
3. Remove the stud by turning the stud remover or the lower nut.
4. Remove any threadlocking compound from the threaded hole. Clean the threads with an aerosol parts cleaner.
5. Install the stud removal tool onto the new stud or thread two nuts onto the stud.

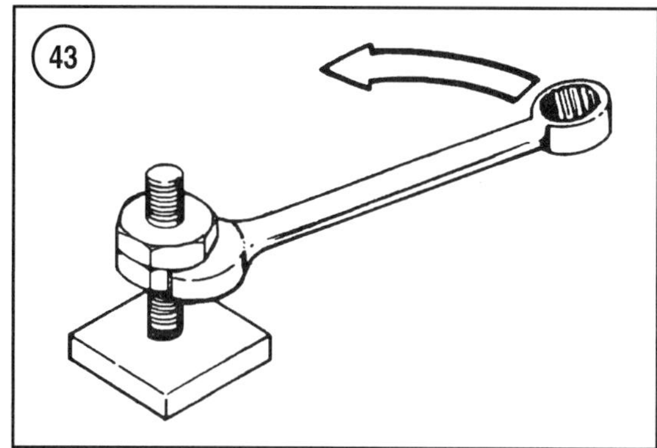

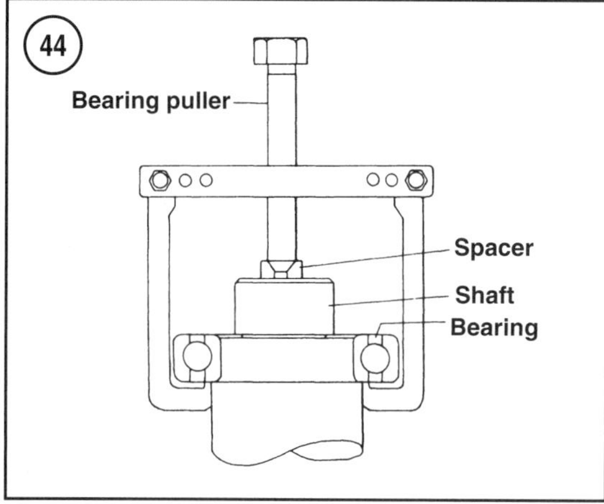

6. Apply threadlocking compound to the threads of the stud.
7. Install the stud and tighten with the stud removal tool or the top nut.
8. Install the stud to the height noted in Step 1 or torque it to specification.
9. Remove the stud removal tool or the two nuts.

Removing Hoses

When removing stubborn hoses, do not exert excessive force on the hose or fitting. Remove the hose clamp and carefully insert a small screwdriver or pick tool between the fitting and hose. Apply a spray lubricant under the hose and carefully twist the hose off the fitting. Use a wire brush to clean any corrosion or rubber hose material from the fitting. Clean the inside of the hose thoroughly. Do not use any lubricant when installing the hose (new or old). The lubricant may allow the hose to come off the fitting even with the clamp secure.

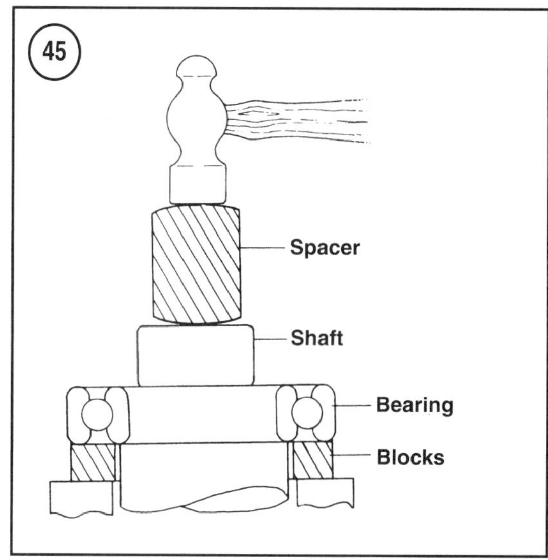

Bearings

Bearings are used in the engine and transmission assembly to reduce power loss, heat and noise resulting from friction. Because bearings are precision parts, they must be properly lubricated and maintained. If a bearing is damaged, replace it immediately. When installing a new bearing, take care to prevent damaging it. Bearing replacement procedures are included in the individual chapters where applicable; however, use the following sections as a guideline.

NOTE
Unless otherwise specified, install bearings with the manufacturer's mark or number facing outward.

Removal

While bearings are normally removed only when damaged, there may be times when a good bearing must be removed. Improper bearing removal will damage the bearing and maybe the shaft or case half. Note the following when removing bearings:

1. When using a puller to remove a bearing from a shaft, take care that shaft is not damaged. Always place a piece of metal between the end of the shaft and the puller screw. In addition, place the puller arms next to the inner bearing race. See **Figure 44**.
2. When using a hammer to remove a bearing from a shaft, do not strike the hammer directly against the shaft. Instead, use a brass or aluminum spacer between the hammer and shaft (**Figure 45**) and make

sure to support both bearing races with wooden blocks as shown.

3. A hydraulic press is the ideal tool for bearing removal. Note the following when using a press:

   a. Always support the inner and outer bearing races with a suitable size wooden or aluminum ring (**Figure 46**). If only the outer race is supported, pressure applied against the balls and/or the inner race will damage them.

   b. Always make sure the press arm (**Figure 46**) aligns with the center of the shaft. If the ram is not centered, it may damage the bearing and/or shaft.

   c. The moment the shaft is free of the bearing, it will drop to the floor. Secure or hold the shaft to prevent it from falling.

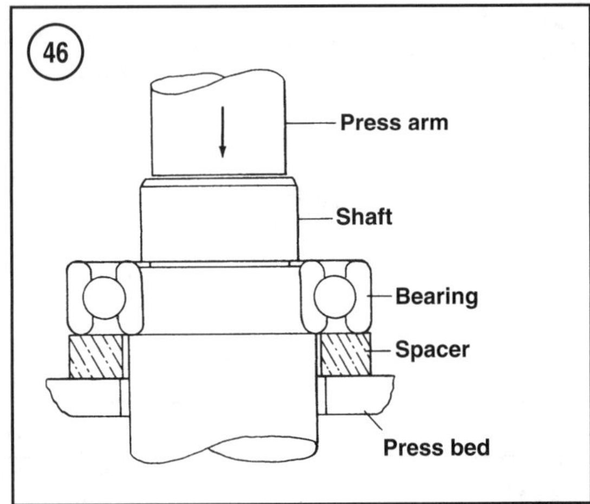

Installation

1. When installing a bearing into a housing, apply pressure to the *outer* bearing race (**Figure 47**). When installing a bearing onto a shaft, apply pressure to the *inner* bearing race (**Figure 48**).

2. When installing a bearing as described in Step 1, some type of driver is required. Never strike the bearing directly with a hammer or the bearing will be damaged. When installing a bearing, use a piece of pipe or a driver with a diameter that matches the bearing race. **Figure 49** shows the correct way to use a driver and hammer to install a bearing onto a shaft.

3. Step 1 describes how to install a bearing in a case half or over a shaft. However, when installing a bearing over a shaft and into a housing at the same time, a tight fit is required for both outer and inner bearing races. In this situation, install a spacer underneath the driver tool so that pressure is applied evenly across both races. See **Figure 50**. If the outer race is not supported as shown in **Figure 50**, the balls will push against the outer bearing race and damage it.

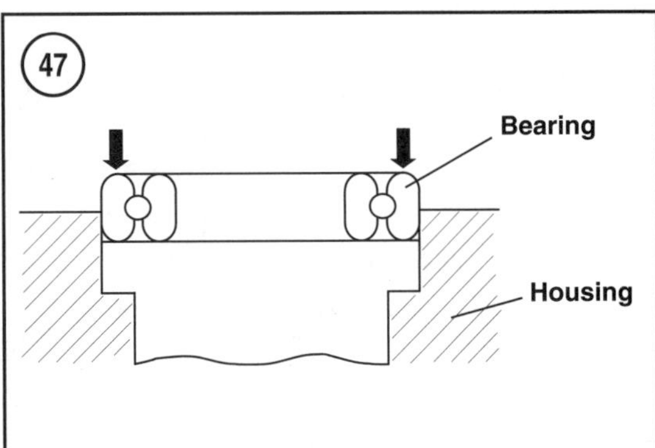

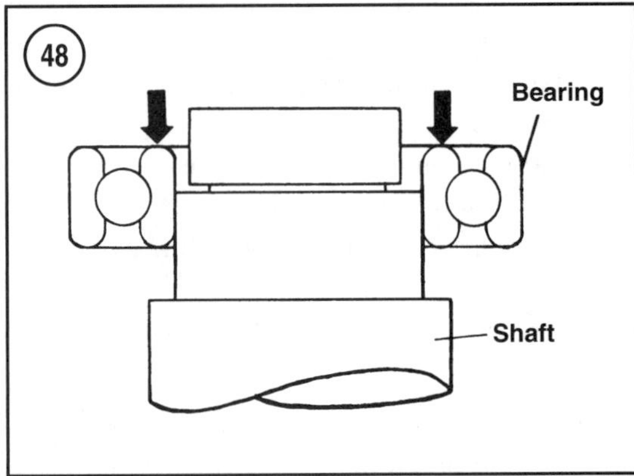

Interference fit

1. Follow this procedure when installing a bearing over a shaft. When a tight fit is required, the bearing inside diameter will be smaller than the shaft. In this case, driving the bearing onto the shaft using normal methods may cause bearing damage. Instead, heat the bearing before installation. Note the following:

   a. Secure the shaft so it is ready for bearing installation.

   b. Clean all residues from the bearing surface of the shaft. Remove burrs with a file or sandpaper.

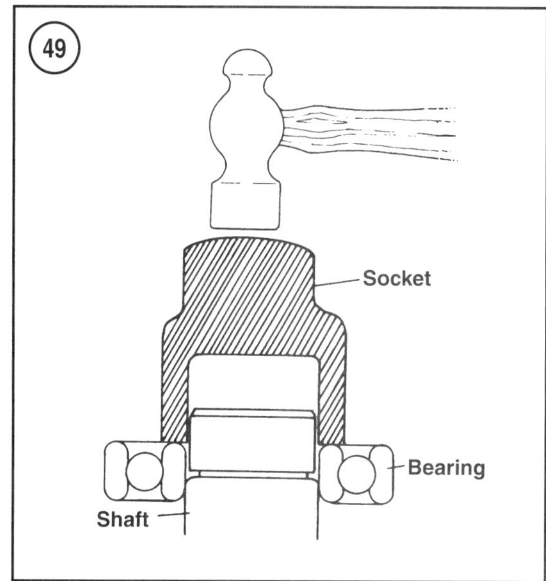

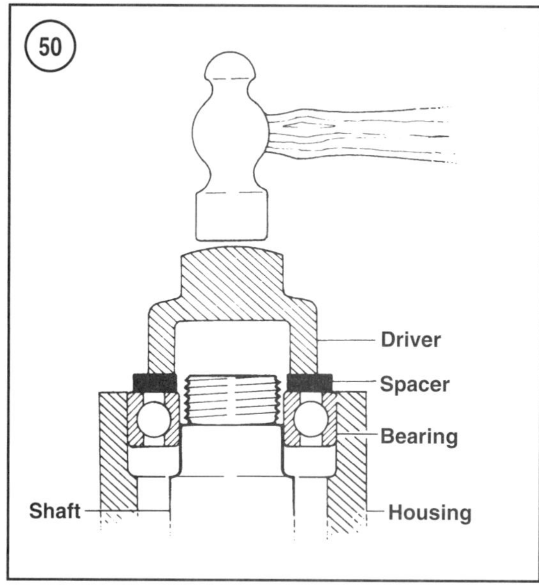

c. Fill a suitable pot or beaker with clean mineral oil. Place a thermometer rated above 120° C (248° F) in the oil. Support the thermometer so that it does not rest on the bottom or side of the pot.

d. Remove the bearing from its wrapper and secure it with a piece of heavy wire bent to hold it in the pot. Hang the bearing in the pot so it does not touch the bottom or sides of the pot.

e. Turn the heat on and monitor the thermometer. When the oil temperature rises to approximately 120° C (248° F), remove the bearing from the pot and quickly install it. If necessary, place a socket on the inner bearing race and tap the bearing into place (**Figure 49**). As the bearing chills, it will tighten on the shaft so installation must be done quickly. Make sure the bearing is installed completely.

2. Follow this step when installing a bearing in a housing. Bearings are generally installed in a housing with a slight interference fit. Driving the bearing into the housing using normal methods may damage the housing or cause bearing damage. Instead, heat the housing before the bearing is installed. Note the following:

CAUTION
Before heating the housing, wash the housing thoroughly with detergent and water. Rinse and rewash the cases as required to remove all traces of oil and other chemical deposits.

a. Heat the housing to approximately 100° C (212° F) in an oven or on a hot plate. To check the housing temperature, fling tiny drops of water onto the housing. If they sizzle and evaporate immediately, the temperature is correct. Heat only one housing at a time.

CAUTION
Do not heat the housing with a propane or acetylene torch. Never bring a flame into contact with the bearing or housing. The direct heat will destroy the case hardening of the bearing and will likely warp the housing.

b. Remove the housing from the oven or hot plate, and hold onto the housing with a kitchen potholder, heavy gloves or heavy shop cloth. It is hot!

NOTE
Remove and install the bearings with a suitable size socket and extension.

c. Hold the housing with the bearing side down and tap the bearing out. Repeat for all bearings in the housing.

d. Before heating the bearing housing, place the new bearing in a freezer. Chilling a bearing slightly reduces its outside diameter while the heated bearing housing assembly is slightly larger due to heat expansion. This will make bearing installation easier.

NOTE
Always install bearings with the manufacturer's mark or number facing outward.

e. While the housing is still hot, install the new bearing(s) into the housing. Install the bearings by hand, if possible. If necessary, lightly tap the bearing(s) into the housing with a socket placed on the outer bearing race (**Figure 47**). Do not install new bearings by driving on the inner-bearing race. Install the bearing(s) until it seats completely.

Seal Replacement

Seals (**Figure 51**) are used to contain oil, water, grease or combustion gasses in a housing or shaft. Improper removal of a seal can damage the housing or shaft. Improper installation of the seal can damage the seal. Note the following:

1. Prying is generally the easiest and most effective method for removing a seal from a housing. However, always place a rag underneath the pry tool (**Figure 52**) to prevent damage to the housing.

2. Pack waterproof grease in the seal lips before the seal is installed.

3. Install seals with the manufacturer's numbers or marks facing out.

4. Install seals with a socket placed on the outer circumference of the seal as shown in **Figure 53**. Drive the seal squarely into the housing. Never install a seal by striking the top of the seal with a hammer.

STORAGE

Several months of non-use can cause a general deterioration of the motorcycle. This is especially true in areas of extreme temperature variations. This deterioration can be minimized with careful preparation for storage. A properly stored motorcycle will be much easier to return to service.

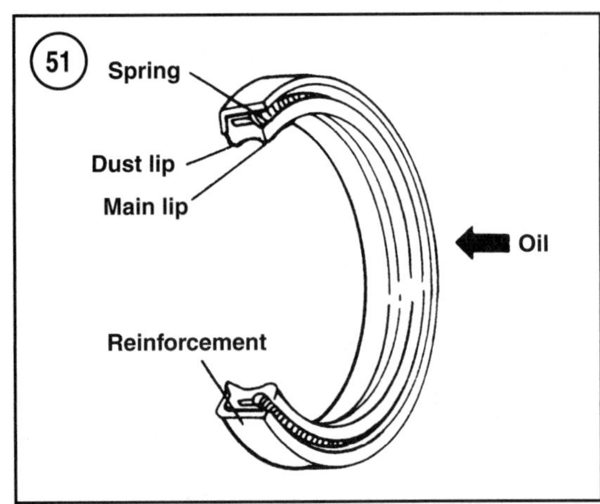

Storage Area Selection

When selecting a storage area, consider the following:

1. The storage area must be dry. A heated area is best, but not necessary. It should be insulated to minimize extreme temperature variations.

2. If the building has large window areas, mask them to keep sunlight off the motorcycle.

3. Avoid buildings in industrial areas where corrosive emissions may be present. Avoid areas close to saltwater.

4. Consider the area's risk of fire, theft or vandalism. Check with an insurer regarding motorcycle coverage while in storage.

Preparing the Motorcycle for Storage

The amount of preparation a motorcycle should undergo before storage depends on the expected length of non-use, storage area conditions and personal preference. Consider the following list the minimum requirement:

1. Wash the motorcycle thoroughly. Make sure all dirt, mud and road debris are removed.

2. Start the engine and allow it to reach operating temperature. Drain the engine oil regardless of the riding time since the last service. Fill the engine with the recommended type of oil.

3. Drain all fuel from the fuel tank, run the engine until all the fuel is consumed from the lines and carburetor.

4. Remove the spark plugs and pour a teaspoon of engine oil into the cylinders. Place a rag over the

openings and slowly turn the engine over to distribute the oil. Reinstall the spark plugs.

5. Remove the battery. Store the battery in a cool and dry location.

6. Cover the exhaust and intake openings.

7. Reduce the normal tire pressure by 20%.

8. Apply a protective substance to the plastic and rubber components. Make sure to follow the manufacturer's instructions for each type of product being used.

9. Place the motorcycle on the center stand and support the front of the engine with a jack or wooden blocks so the front wheel is off the ground. This is especially important on a motorcycle as large as the Concours. The tires can easily develop flat spots if the motorcycle is stored while resting on them.

10. Cover the motorcycle with old bed sheets or something similar. Do not cover it with plastic material that will trap moisture.

Returning the Motorcycle to Service

The amount of service required when returning a motorcycle to service after storage depends on the length of non-use and storage conditions. In addition to performing the reverse of the above procedure, make sure the brakes, clutch, throttle and engine stop switch work properly before operating the motorcycle. Refer to Chapter Three and evaluate the service intervals to determine which areas require service.

Table 1 SERIAL NUMBERS

Year/model	VIN number (U.S. manufacture)	VIN number (Japan manufacture)	Engine number
1986/ZG1000-A1	JKAZGCA1*GB500001-053400	JKAZGCA1*GA000001-005500	2GT00AE000001-on
1987/ZG1000-A2	JKAZGCA1*HB503401-504900	JKAZGCA1*HA005501-006700	2GT00AE000001-012200
1988/ZG1000-A3	JKAZGCA1*JB504901-on	JKAZGCA1*JA006701-on	2GT00AE012201-on
1989/ZG1000-A4	None	JKAZGCA1*KA008001-0090000	2GT00AE012201-on
1990/ZG1000-A5	JKAZGCA1*LB505601-506300	JKAZGCA1*LA009001-011400	2GT00AE012201-on
1991/ZG1000-A6	JKAZGCA1*MB506301-on	JKAZGCA1*MA0011401-on	2GT00AE012201-on
1992/ZG1000-A7	JKAZGCA1*NB506701-507300	JKAZGCA1*NA014001-025000	2GT00AE012201-on
1993/ZG1000-A8	JKAZGCA1*PB507301-508000	JKAZGCA1*PA025001-035000	2GT00AE012201-on

(continued)

Table 1 SERIAL NUMBERS (continued)

Year/model	VIN number (U.S. manufacture)	VIN number (Japan manufacture)	Engine number
1994/ZG1000-A9	JKAZGCA1*RB508001-on	JKAZGCA1*RA035001-on	2GT00AE012201-on
1995/ZG1000-A10	JKAZGCA1*SB508651-on	JKAZGCA1*SA038001-042000	2GT00AE012201-on
1996/ZG1000-A11	None	JKAZGCA1*TA042001-046000	2GT00AE012201-on
1997/ZG1000-A12	JKAZGCA1*VB509801-510500	JKAZGCA1*VA046001-048000	2GT00AE012201-on
1998/ZG1000-A13	JKAZGCA1*WB510501-511600	JKAZGCA1*WA048001-052000	2GT00AE012201-on
1999/ZG1000-A14	JKAZGCA1*XB511601-on	JKAZGCA1*XA052001-on	2GT00AE012201-on
2000/ZG1000-A15	JKAZGCA1*YB513301-on	JKAZGCA1*YA057001-on	2GT00AE012201-on
2001/ZG1000-A16	JKAZGCA1*1B514901-on	JKAZGCA1*1A059001-on	2GT00AE012201-on
2002/ZG1000-A17	JKAZGCA1*2B516901-on	JKAZGCA1*2A063001-on	2GT00AE012201-on
2003/ZG1000-A18	JKAZGCA1*3B518601-on	JKAZGCA1*3A068001-on	2GT00AE012201-on
2004/ZG1000-A19	JKAZGCA1*4B519901	NA	NA
2005/ZG1000-A20	JKAZGCA1*5B521300	NA	NA
2006/ZG1000A6F	JKAZGCA1*6B523201	NA	NA

NA - Not Available

Table 2 VEHICLE DIMENSIONS

Dimension	New mm (in.)
Overall length	2290 (90.1)
Overall width	
1986 models	
U.S., Canada, Australia and South Africa models	760 (29.1)
All other 1986 models	930 (36.6)
1987-1999 models	
Finland and Norway models	760 (29.9)
All other models	930 (36.6)
2000-on models	930 (36.6)
Overall height	1415 (55.7)
Wheelbase	1555 (61.2)
Minimum ground clearance	
1986-1993 models	140 (5.5)
1994-on models	130 (5.1)
Seat height	
1986-1993 models	815 (32.1)
1994-on models	790 (31.1)
Minimum turning radius	3.3 m (10.8 ft.)

Table 3 VEHICLE WEIGHT

Dry weight	
1986 models	
U.S., Canada, Australia and South Africa models	258 kg (568.8 lb.)
California models	265.5 kg (585.3 lb.)
1987-1993 models	
California models	265.5 kg (585.3 lb.)
Finland and Norway models	258 kg (568.7 lb.)
All other models	265 kg (584.2 lb.)

(continued)

Table 3 VEHICLE WEIGHT (continued)

Dry weight (continued)	
1994-1999 models	
California models	270.5 kg (596.3 lb.)
All other models	270 kg (595.2 lb.)
2000-on models	
California models	270.5 kg (596.3 lb.)
Europe and France models	273 kg (601.8 lb.)
All other models	270 kg (595.2 lb.)
Curb weight (with oil and full tank)	
Front	
1986-1993 models	142 kg (313.1 lb.)
1994-2000 models	144 kg (317.5 lb.)
2001-on models	
Europe and France models	145 kg (319.7 lb.)
All other models	144 kg (317.5 lb.)
Rear	
1986 models	
U.S., Canada, Australia and South Africa models	160 kg (352.7 lb.)
California models	160.5 kg (353.8 lb.)
All other models	152 kg (335.1 lb.)
1987-1989 models	
California models	160.5 kg (353.8 lb.)
All other models	160 kg (352.7 lb.)
1990-1993 models	
California models	160.5 kg (353.8 lb.)
Finland and Norway models	152 kg (335.1 lb.)
All other models	160 kg (352.7 lb.)
1994-1999 models	
California models	163.5 kg (360.4 lb.)
All other models	163 kg (359.3 lb.)
2000-on models	
California models	163.5 kg (360.4 lb.)
Europe and France models	165 kg (363.8 lb.)
All other models	163 kg (359.3 lb.)
Maximum load	
Total weight rider, passenger, cargo and accessories	200 kg (440.9 lb.)

Table 4 GENERAL TORQUE SPECIFICATIONS

Fastener thread diameter	N•m	in.-lb.	ft.-lb.
5	3.4-4.9	30-43	–
6	5.9-7.8	52-69	–
8	14-19	–	10-13.5
10	25-34	–	19-25
12	44-61	–	33-45
14	73-98	–	54-72
16	115-155	–	83-115
18	165-225	–	125-165
20	225-325	–	165-240

Table 5 METRIC, INCH AND FRACTIONAL EQUIVALENTS

Fractions	Decimal in.	Metric mm	Fractions	Decimal in.	Metric mm
1/64	0.015625	0.39688	33/64	0.515625	13.09687
1/32	0.03125	0.79375	17/32	0.53125	13.49375
3/64	0.046875	1.19062	35/64	0.546875	13.89062
1/16	0.0625	1.58750	9/16	0.5625	14.28750
5/64	0.078125	1.98437	37/64	0.578125	14.68437
3/32	0.09375	2.38125	19/32	0.59375	15.08125
7/64	0.109375	2.77812	39/64	0.609375	15.47812
1/8	0.125	3.1750	5/8	0.625	15.87500
9/64	0.140625	3.57187	41/64	0.640625	16.27187
5/32	0.15625	3.96875	21/32	0.65625	16.66875
11/64	0.171875	4.36562	43/64	0.671875	17.06562
3/16	0.1875	4.76250	11/16	0.6875	17.46250
13/64	0.203125	5.15937	45/64	0.703125	17.85937
7/32	0.21875	5.55625	23/32	0.71875	18.25625
15/64	0.234375	5.95312	47/64	0.734375	18.65312
¼	0.250	6.35000	¾	0.750	19.05000
17/64	0.265625	6.74687	49/64	0.765625	19.44687
9/32	0.28125	7.14375	25/32	0.78125	19.84375
19/64	0.296875	7.54062	51/64	0.796875	20.24062
5/16	0.3125	7.93750	13/16	0.8125	20.63750
21/64	0.328125	8.33437	53/64	0.828125	21.03437
11/32	0.34375	8.73125	27/32	0.84375	21.43125
23/64	0.359375	9.12812	55/64	0.859375	22.82812
3/8	0.375	9.52500	7/8	0.875	22.22500
25/64	0.390625	9.92187	57/64	0.890625	22.62187
13/32	0.40625	10.31875	29/32	0.90625	23.01875
27/64	0.421875	10.71562	59/64	0.921875	23.41562
7/16	0.4375	11.11250	15/16	0.9375	23.81250
29/64	0.453125	11.50937	61/64	0.953125	24.20937
15/32	0.46875	11.90625	31/32	0.96875	24.60625
31/64	0.484375	12.30312	63/64	0.984375	25.00312
½	0.500	12.70000	1	1.00	25.40000

Table 6 CONVERSION FORMULAS

Multiply:	By:	To get the equivalent of:
Length		
Inches	25.4	Millimeter
Inches	2.54	Centimeter
Miles	1.609	Kilometer
Feet	0.3048	Meter
Millimeter	0.03937	Inches
Centimeter	0.3937	Inches
Kilometer	0.6214	Mile
Meter	3.281	Feet
Fluid volume		
U.S. quarts	0.9463	Liters
U.S. gallons	3.785	Liters
U.S. ounces	29.573529	Milliliters
Imperial gallons	4.54609	Liters
Imperial quarts	1.1365	Liters

(continued)

Table 6 **CONVERSION FORMULAS (continued)**

Multiply:	By:	To get the equivalent of:
Fluid volume (continued)		
Liters	0.2641721	U.S. gallons
Liters	1.0566882	U.S. quarts
Liters	33.814023	U.S. ounces
Liters	0.22	Imperial gallons
Liters	0.8799	Imperial quarts
Milliliters	0.033814	U.S. ounces
Milliliters	1.0	Cubic centimeters
Milliliters	0.001	Liters
Torque		
Foot-pounds	1.3558	Newton-meters
Foot-pounds	0.138255	Meters-kilograms
Inch-pounds	0.11299	Newton-meters
Newton-meters	0.7375622	Foot-pounds
Newton-meters	8.8507	Inch-pounds
Meters-kilograms	7.2330139	Foot-pounds
Volume		
Cubic inches	16.387064	Cubic centimeters
Cubic centimeters	0.0610237	Cubic inches
Temperature		
Fahrenheit	(F – 32°) × 0.556	Centigrade
Centigrade	(C × 1.8) + 32	Fahrenheit
Weight		
Ounces	28.3495	Grams
Pounds	0.4535924	Kilograms
Grams	0.035274	Ounces
Kilograms	2.2046224	Pounds
Pressure		
Pounds per square inch	0.070307	Kilograms per square centimeter
Kilograms per square centimeter	14.223343	Pounds per square inch
Kilopascals	0.1450	Pounds per square inch
Pounds per square inch	6.895	Kilopascals
Speed		
Miles per hour	1.609344	Kilometers per hour
Kilometers per hour	0.6213712	Miles per hour

Table 7 **TECHNICAL ABBREVIATIONS**

ABDC	After bottom dead center
ATDC	After top dead center
BBDC	Before bottom dead center
BDC	Bottom dead center
BTDC	Before top dead center
C	Celsius (Centigrade)
cc	Cubic centimeters
cid	Cubic inch displacement
CDI	Capacitor discharge ignition
cu. in.	Cubic inches
DOHC	Dual overhead cam
F	Fahrenheit
ft.	Feet
ft.-lb.	Foot-pounds
gal.	Gallons
H/A	High altitude

(continued)

Table 7 TECHNICAL ABBREVIATIONS (continued)

hp	Horsepower
in.	Inches
in.-lb.	Inch-pounds
I.D.	Inside diameter
kg	Kilograms
kgm	Kilogram meters
km	Kilometer
kPa	Kilopascals
L	Liter
m	Meter
MAG	Magneto
ml	Milliliter
mm	Millimeter
N•m	Newton-meters
O.D.	Outside diameter
OEM	Original Equipment Manufacturer
oz.	Ounces
psi	Pounds per square inch
PTO	Power take off
pt.	Pint
qt.	Quart
rpm	Revolutions per minute

Table 8 METRIC TAP AND DRILL SIZE

Metric size	Drill equivalent	Decimal fraction	Nearest fraction
3 × 0.50	No. 39	0.0995	3/32
3 × 0.60	3/32	0.0937	3/32
4 × 0.70	No. 30	0.1285	1/8
4 × 0.75	1/8	0.125	1/8
5 × 0.80	No. 19	0.166	11/64
5 × 0.90	No. 20	0.161	5/32
6 × 1.00	No. 9	0.196	13/64
7 × 1.00	16/64	0.234	15/64
8 × 1.00	J	0.277	9/32
8 × 1.25	17/64	0.265	17/64
9 × 1.00	5/16	0.3125	5/16
9 × 1.25	5/16	0.3125	5/16
10 × 1.25	11/32	0.3437	11/32
10 × 1.50	R	0.339	11/32
11 × 1.50	3/8	0.375	3/8
12 × 1.50	13/32	0.406	13/32
12 × 1.75	13/32	0.406	13/32

CHAPTER TWO

TROUBLESHOOTING

The troubleshooting procedures described in this chapter provide typical symptoms and logical methods for isolating problems and their cause(s). There may be several ways to resolve a problem, but only a systematic approach will do so while avoiding wasted time and unnecessary parts replacement.

Gather as much information as possible to aid in diagnosis. Never assume anything and do not overlook the obvious. Make sure there is fuel in the tank. On carbureted models, make sure the fuel valve is in the on position. If the motorcycle has been sitting for any length of time, fuel deposits may have gummed up the carburetor jets. Gasoline loses its volatility after standing for long periods and water condensation may have diluted it. Drain the old gas and start with a fresh tank full. Make sure the engine stop switch is in the run position. Make sure the spark plug wires are attached to the spark plugs.

If a quick check does not reveal the problem, proceed with one of the troubleshooting procedures described in this chapter. After defining the symptoms, follow the procedure that most closely relates to the condition(s) encountered.

In most cases, expensive and complicated test equipment is not needed to determine whether repairs can be performed at home. A few simple checks could prevent an unnecessary repair charge and lost time while the motorcycle is at a dealership's service department. On the other hand, be realistic and do not attempt repairs beyond your personal capabilities. Many service departments will not take work that involves the reassembly of damaged or abused equipment. If they do, expect the cost to be high.

If the motorcycle does require the attention of a professional, describe the symptoms, conditions and previous repair attempts accurately and fully. The more information a technician has available, the easier it will be to diagnose.

By following the lubrication and maintenance schedule described in Chapter Three, the need for troubleshooting can be reduced by eliminating potential problems before they occur. However, even with the best of care the motorcycle may require troubleshooting.

OPERATING REQUIREMENTS

An engine needs three basic elements to run properly: correct air/fuel mixture, compression and a spark at the proper time. If any element is missing, the engine will not run. Four-stroke engine operating principles are shown in **Figure 1**.

If the machine has been sitting for any length of time and refuses to start, check and clean the spark plugs and then look to the fuel delivery system. This includes the fuel tank, fuel valve, and fuel lines to the carburetor. Gasoline deposits may have gummed up the carburetor jets and air passages. Gasoline tends to lose its potency after standing for long periods. Condensation may contaminate the fuel with water. Drain the old fuel (fuel tank, fuel

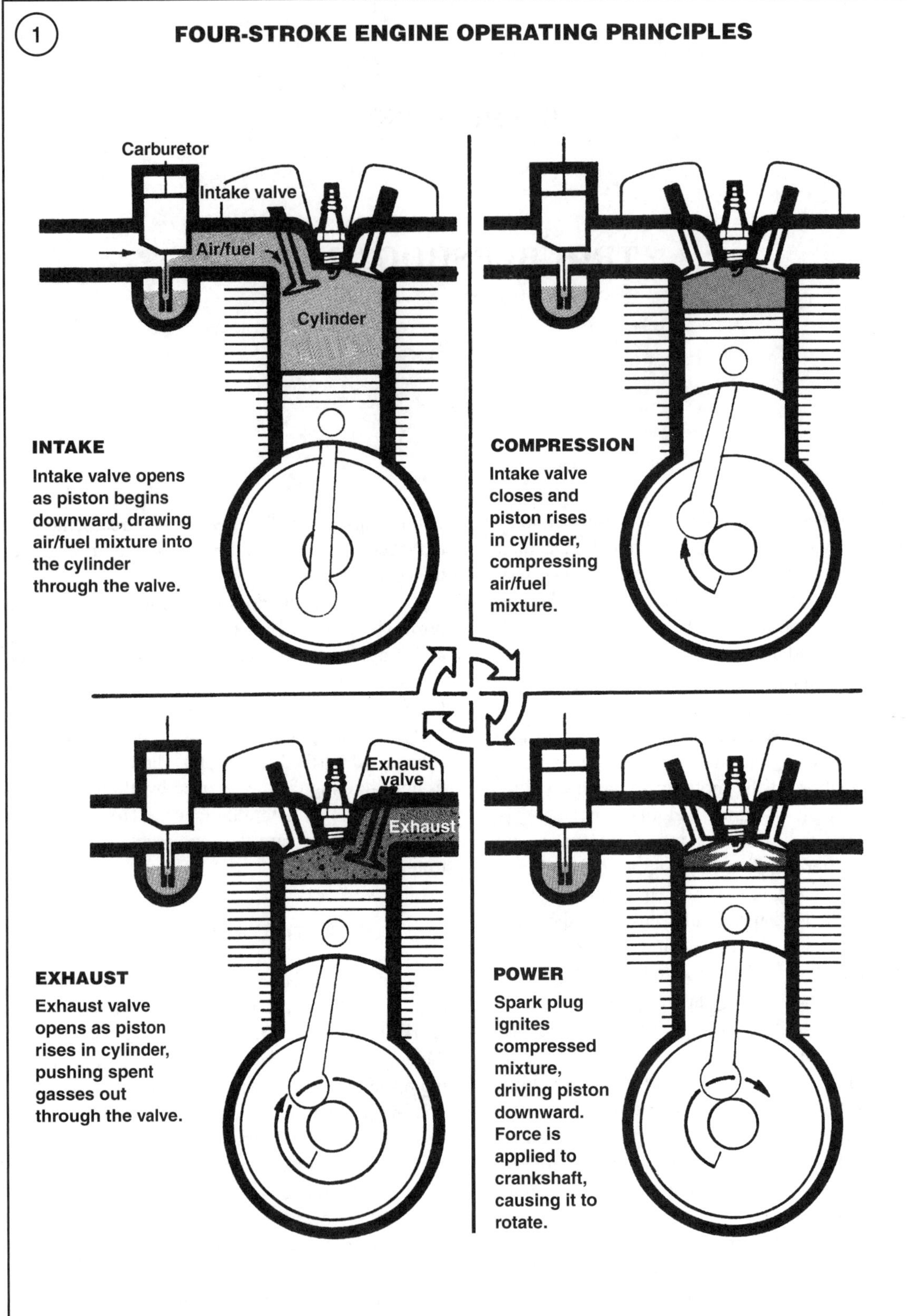
1
FOUR-STROKE ENGINE OPERATING PRINCIPLES
Carburetor
Intake valve
Air/fuel
Cylinder
INTAKE
Intake valve opens as piston begins downward, drawing air/fuel mixture into the cylinder through the valve.
COMPRESSION
Intake valve closes and piston rises in cylinder, compressing air/fuel mixture.
Exhaust valve
Exhaust
EXHAUST
Exhaust valve opens as piston rises in cylinder, pushing spent gasses out through the valve.
POWER
Spark plug ignites compressed mixture, driving piston downward. Force is applied to crankshaft, causing it to rotate.

lines and carburetor) and try starting with a tank of fresh gasoline.

STARTING THE ENGINE

Starting Notes

1. All models covered in this manual use an ignition cut-off system. The position of the sidestand can affect engine starting. Note the following:
   a. The engine cannot start when the sidestand is down and the transmission is in gear.
   b. The engine can be started when the sidestand is down and the transmission is in neutral. The engine will stop if the transmission is put in gear with the sidestand down.
   c. The engine can be started when the clutch lever is pulled in and the transmission is in gear.
2. Before starting the engine, shift the transmission into neutral and confirm that the engine stop switch is in the run position.
3. Turn the ignition switch to on and confirm the following:
   a. The neutral indicator light is on (when transmission is in neutral).
   b. The engine oil-pressure warning light is on.
4. The engine is now ready to start. Refer to the starting procedure in this section that best meets the present air temperature and engine condition.
5. The exhaust pipes may discolor under the following conditions:
   a. If the engine idles at a fast idle speed for more than five minutes.
   b. If the throttle is snapped on and off repeatedly at normal air temperature.
6. Excessive choke use can cause an excessively rich fuel mixture. This condition can wash oil off of the piston and cylinder walls, causing piston and cylinder scuffing.

CAUTION

Do not operate the starter for more than 5 seconds at a time. Wait approximately 10 seconds between starting attempts.

Starting Procedure

When experiencing engine starting troubles, it is easy to work out of sequence and forget basic starting procedures. The sections below list the recommended starting procedures for a motorcycle with the indicated ambient temperatures and engine conditions.

Cold engine with normal air temperature

Normal air temperature is considered to be between 10-35° C (50-95° F).

1. Perform the procedures in *Starting Notes*.
2. Install the ignition key and turn the ignition switch on.
3. Pull the choke lever (**Figure 2**) to the fully on position.
4. Make sure the engine stop switch (A, **Figure 3**) is in the run position.
5. Depress the starter button (B, **Figure 3**) and start the engine. Do not open the throttle when pressing the starter button.
6. With the engine running, operate the choke lever as required to keep the engine idling below 2500 rpm.
7. After approximately 30 seconds, push the choke lever (**Figure 2**) forward to the off position. If the

engine idle is rough, open the throttle slightly until the engine warms up.

Cold engine with low air temperature

Low air temperature is considered to be 10° C (50° F) or lower.

1. Perform the procedures in *Starting Notes*.
2. Install the ignition key and turn the ignition switch on.
3. Pull the choke lever (**Figure 2**) fully on.
4. Make sure the engine stop switch (A, **Figure 3**) is in the run position.

NOTE
Starting a cold engine with the choke on and the throttle open results in a lean mixture and causes hard starting.

5. Depress the starter button (B, **Figure 3**) and start the engine. Do not open the throttle when pressing the starter button.
6. With the engine running, operate the choke lever as required to keep the engine idling below 2500 rpm.
7. Continue warming the engine until the choke lever can be moved to the off position and the engine responds to the throttle cleanly.

Warm engine and/or high air temperature

High air temperature is considered to be 35° C (95° F) or higher.

1. Perform the procedures in *Starting Notes*.
2. Make sure the engine stop switch (A, **Figure 3**) is in the run position.
3. Install the ignition key and turn the ignition switch on.
4. Open the throttle slightly and depress the starter button (B, **Figure 3**). Do not use the choke.

Flooded engine

If the engine will not start after a few attempts it may be flooded. If you smell gasoline after trying to start the engine, the engine is probably flooded. To start a flooded engine:

1. Turn the engine stop switch to the run position (A, **Figure 3**).

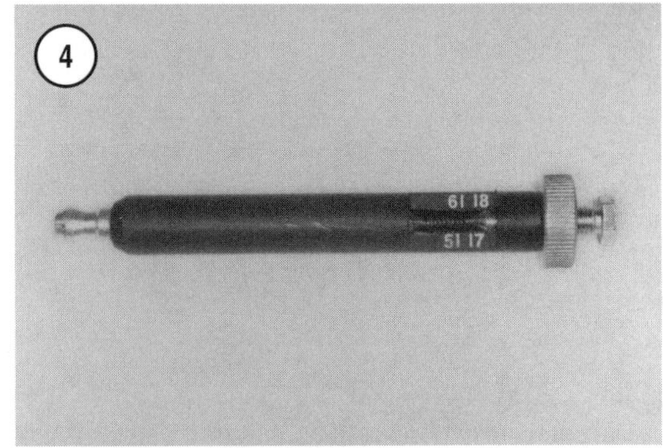

2. Push the choke lever (**Figure 2**) forward to the off position.
3. Turn the ignition switch to on.
4. Open the throttle completely and depress the starter button (B, **Figure 3**). If the engine starts, close the throttle quickly. If necessary, operate the throttle to keep the engine running until it smooths out. If the engine does not start, wait 10 seconds and then try to restart the engine by following normal starting procedures. If the engine will not start, refer to *Starting Difficulties* in this chapter.

STARTING DIFFICULTIES

When the engine turns over but is difficult to start or if it will not start at all, it does not help to drain the battery. Check for obvious problems first. Go down the following list step-by-step. Perform each step while remembering the engine operating requirements described in this chapter. If the engine still will not start, refer to the appropriate troubleshooting procedures in this chapter.

1. Make sure the choke lever (**Figure 2**) in the correct position. Open the choke for a cold engine, and close it for a warm or hot engine.

WARNING
Do not use an open flame to check fuel in the tank. A serious explosion is certain to result.

2. Make sure the engine stop switch (A, **Figure 3**) is not stuck or working improperly and that the wire is not broken or shorting out. If necessary, test the switch as described in Chapter Nine.

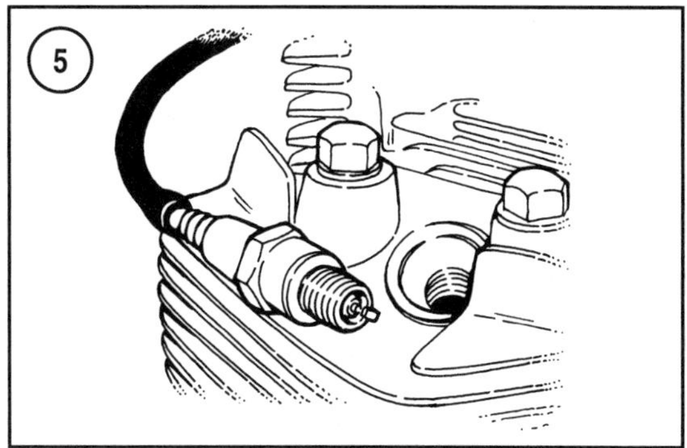

3. Make sure that the sidestand is up and that the sidestand switch operates properly. If necessary, test the switch as described in Chapter Nine.
4. Make sure all four spark plug wires are secure. Push each spark plug cap and slightly rotate it to clean the electrical connection between the plug and the connector.

NOTE
If the engine will still not start, continue with the following.

5. Perform a spark test as described in this chapter. If there is a strong spark, perform Step 6. If there is no spark or if the spark is very weak, test the ignition system as described in this chapter.

NOTE
If the fuel and ignition systems are working properly, check the mechanical system. Isolate a mechanical problem to one of these areas: top end, bottom end, clutch or transmission. Step 6 covers the top end as it relates to engine compression. Clutch and transmission problems are covered elsewhere in this chapter.

6. Check cylinder compression as described in Chapter Three.

Spark Test

Perform the following spark test to determine if the ignition system operates properly:

CAUTION
Before removing the spark plugs in Step 1, clean the area around the each plug base with compressed air. Dirt that falls into the cylinder will cause rapid piston, piston ring and cylinder wear.

1. Remove each spark plug from the cylinder head as described in Chapter Three.

NOTE
A spark tester is a useful tool for testing the ignition system's spark output. ***Figure 4*** *shows the Motion Pro Ignition System Tester (part No. 08-122). This tool is inserted in the spark plug cap and its base is grounded against the cylinder head. The tool's air gap is adjustable, and it allows you to see and hear the spark while testing the intensity of the spark. This tool is available through most motorcycle dealerships.*

NOTE
Always use a new spark plug for this test procedure if a spark tester is not available.

2. Connect each spark plug wire and connector to a spark plug (or tester) and touch each spark plug base (**Figure 5**) or tester to a good engine ground. Position the spark plug so the electrodes are visible. Position the spark tester so the terminals are visible.

WARNING
Mount the spark plug, or spark tester, away from the spark plug holes in the cylinder head so the spark plug or tester cannot ignite the gasoline vapors in the cylinder. If the engine is flooded, do not perform this test. The firing of the spark plugs or spark tester can ignite fuel ejected through the spark plug holes.

3. With the transmission in neutral, turn the ignition system to the on position and the engine stop switch to run.

WARNING
Do not hold the spark plugs, tester, wire or connector or a serious electrical shock may result.

4. Push the starter button to turn the engine over. A fat blue spark must be evident across the spark plug

electrodes or between the tester terminals. Repeat for each cylinder.

5. If the spark is good at each spark plug, the ignition system is functioning properly. Check for one or more of the following possible malfunctions:
   a. Obstructed fuel line or fuel filter.
   b. Low compression or engine damage.
   c. Flooded engine.
6. If the spark was weak or if there was no spark at one or more plugs, note the following:
   a. If there is no spark at any plug, there may be a problem in the input side of the ignition system or IC igniter, pickup coil, sidestand switch, neutral switch or starter lockout switch. Refer to *Ignition System* in this chapter.
   b. If there is no spark at one spark plug only, the spark plug is probably faulty or there is a problem with the spark plug wire or plug cap. Retest with a spark tester or use a new spark plug. If there is still no spark at that one plug, make sure the spark plug cap is installed correctly.
   c. If there is no spark with one ignition group (same ignition coil), switch the ignition coils and retest. If there is now spark (both spark plugs), the original ignition coil is faulty.
   d. Troubleshoot the ignition system as described in *Ignition System* in this chapter.

Engine is Difficult to Start

1. Check for fuel flow to the carburetors. If fuel is reaching the carburetors, go to Step 2. If not, check for one or more of the following possible malfunctions:
   a. Clogged fuel hose and/or fuel filter.
   b. Clogged fuel tank breather hose.
   c. Loose or disconnected fuel pump relay connector.
   d. Pinched, damaged or disconnected fuel valve vacuum hose.
2. Perform the spark test as described in this chapter. Note the following:
   a. If the spark plugs are wet, go to Step 3.
   b. If the spark is weak or if there is no spark, go to Step 4.
   c. If the spark is good, go to Step 5.
3. If the plugs are wet, the engine may be flooded. Check the following:
   a. Flooded carburetors.
   b. Dirty air filter.
   c. Throttle valve(s) binding or stuck open.
   d. Incorrect choke operation.
   e. Needle valve in carburetor stuck open.
   f. Fuel level too high in the float bowl(s).
4. If the spark is weak or if there is no spark, check the following:
   a. Fouled spark plug(s).
   b. Damaged spark plug(s).
   c. Loose or damaged spark plug wire(s).
   d. Loose or damaged spark plug cap(s).
   e. Damaged IC igniter.
   f. Damaged pickup coil.
   g. Damaged ignition coil.
   h. Damaged engine stop switch.
   i. Damaged ignition switch.
   j. Damaged starter lockout switch.
   k. Damaged neutral switch.
   l. Damaged sidestand switch.
   m Dirty or loose terminals.
   n. Low battery voltage.
   o. Damaged wiring.
5. If the spark is good, check the following:
   a. Try starting the engine by following normal starting procedures. If the engine does not fire, go to Step 6.
   b. If the engine starts but then stops, check for an inoperative choke, incorrect carburetor adjustment, leaking intake manifolds, improper ignition timing (faulty IC igniter) or contaminated fuel.
6. If the engine turns over and the fuel and ignition systems are working correctly, check for the following possible malfunctions:
   a. Leaking cylinder head gasket.
   b. Valve clearance too tight.
   c. Bent or stuck valve.
   d. Broken valve spring.
   e. Incorrect valve timing.
   f. Improper valve-to-seat contact.
   g. Worn cylinder or piston rings.

Engine Does Not Crank

If the engine will not turn over, check for one or more of the following:

1. Blown fuse.
2. Discharged battery.

3. Defective starter, starter solenoid or starter switch.
4. Faulty starter clutch.
5. Seized camshaft, valve or rocker arm.
6. Seized pistons or connecting rod.
7. Seized crankshaft or balancer.
8. Locked-up transmission or clutch assembly.

ENGINE PERFORMANCE

In the following checklists, it is assumed that the engine runs but is not operating at peak performance. This section serves as a starting point from which to isolate a driveability problem. Where ignition timing is mentioned as a problem, remember that the ignition timing cannot be adjusted. If the ignition timing is incorrect, a part within the ignition system is faulty. Check the individual ignition system components, and replace any faulty part(s).

Engine Will Not Idle

1. Incorrect carburetor adjustment.
2. Fouled or improperly gapped spark plug(s).
3. Faulty spark plug cap or wire.
4. Leaking head gasket(s) or vacuum leak.
5. Ignition timing incorrect (caused by damaged IC igniter, pickup coil or ignition coil).
6. Incorrect valve timing.
7. Obstructed fuel line or fuel valve.
8. Low engine compression.
9. Starter valve (choke) stuck in the open position.
10. Incorrect pilot screw adjustment.
11. Clogged pilot jet or air bleed pipe in the carburetor(s).
12. Clogged air filter element.
13. Partially plugged fuel valve vacuum hose.

Low or Poor Engine Power

1. Support the bike with the rear wheel off the ground, and spin the rear wheel by hand. If the wheel spins freely, perform Step 2. If the wheel does not spin freely, check for the following conditions:
   a. Dragging rear brake.
   b. Excessive rear axle tightening torque.
   c. Worn or damaged rear wheel bearings.
   d. Worn or damaged final gear bearings.
2. Check the tire pressure. If pressure is normal, perform Step 3. If pressure is low, check for a leak.
3. Ride the bike, and accelerate rapidly from first to second gear. If the engine speed reduces when the clutch is released, perform Step 4. If the engine speed does not change when the clutch is released, check for the following:
   a. Slipping clutch.
   b. Worn or warped clutch plates or friction discs.
   c. Weak clutch spring.
   d. Sticking clutch hydraulic system.
   e. Check the engine oil for additives.
4. Ride the bike, and accelerate lightly. If the engine speed increases relative to throttle operation, perform Step 5. If engine speed does not increase, check for the following:
   a. Choke valve opened.
   b. Clogged air filter.
   c. Fuel flow restricted.
   d. Clogged muffler.
   e. Incorrect fuel level in float bowl(s).
5. Check for one of the following:
   a. Incorrect ignition timing due to a malfunctioning ignition component.
   b. Improperly adjusted valves or worn valve seats.
   c. Low engine compression.
   d. Clogged carburetor jet(s).
   e. Fouled spark plugs.
   f. Incorrect spark plug heat range.
   g. Oil level too low or too high.
   h. Contaminated oil.
   i. Worn or damaged valve train assembly.
   j. Engine overheating. See *Engine Overheating* in this chapter.
6. If the engine knocks when accelerating or when running at high speed, check for the following:
   a. Incorrect type of fuel.
   b. Lean carburetor jetting.
   c. Advanced ignition timing.
   d. IC igniter malfunction.
   e. Excessive carbon buildup in the combustion chamber.
   f. Worn pistons and/or cylinder bores.

Poor Idle Speed or Low Speed Performance

1. Check the valve clearance. Adjust the valves as necessary.
2. Check the carburetor pilot screw adjustment as described in Chapter Eight.
3. Check for damaged intake manifolds or loose carburetor and air filter housing clamps.
4. Perform the spark test described in this chapter. Note the following:
   a. If the spark is good, go to Step 5.
   b. If the spark is weak, test the ignition system as described in this chapter.
5. Check the ignition timing as described in Chapter Three. Note the following:
   a. If the ignition timing is incorrect, the IC igniter or the pickup coil is probably faulty.
   b. If the ignition timing is correct, recheck the carburetor and fuel system.

Poor High Speed Performance

1. Check ignition timing as described in Chapter Three. If ignition timing is correct, perform Step 2. If the timing is incorrect, test the following ignition system components as described in Chapter Eight:
   a. IC igniter.
   b. Pickup coils.
   c. Ignition coils.
2. Check the valve clearance as described in Chapter Three. Note the following:
   a. If the valve clearance is correct, perform Step 3.
   b. If the clearance is incorrect, readjust the valves and test ride the bike once again.

WARNING
Some fuel may spill from the fuel tank, fuel valve or fuel hose when performing Step 3. Because gasoline is extremely flammable, perform this procedure away from all open flames (including appliance pilot lights) and sparks. Do not smoke or allow anyone to smoke in the work area. An explosion and fire may occur. Always work in a well-ventilated area. Wipe up spills immediately.

WARNING
Gasoline presents an extreme fire hazard. Do not drain or store gasoline into an open container. Drain and store the gasoline in a commercially available gas can, away from heat, sparks or flames.

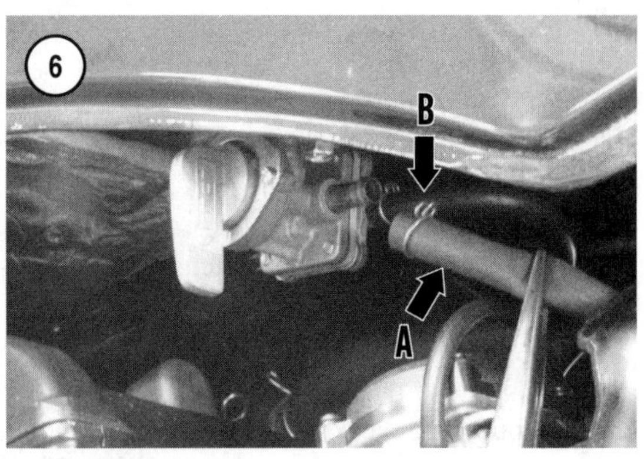

3. Check the fuel flow to the carburetors by performing the following:
   a. Disconnect the fuel hose (A, **Figure 6**) from the fuel fitting on the fuel valve. Connect a long hose to the fuel fitting, and insert the open end into a suitable container.
   b. Disconnect the vacuum hose (B, **Figure 6**) from the fuel valve, and connect a hand-operated vacuum pump to the vacuum fitting on the fuel valve.
   c. Operate the vacuum pump and apply vacuum to the fuel valve.
4. Fuel should flow freely into the container. If the fuel flows freely, perform Step 5. If fuel flow is restricted, check for the following:
   a. Empty fuel tank.
   b. Faulty fuel valve.
   c. A clogged fuel line.
   d. Clogged or dirty fuel valve.
   e. Clogged fuel tank breather.
5. Remove the carburetors as described in Chapter Eight. Then remove the float bowls and check for contamination and plugged jets. If any contamination is found, disassemble and clean each carburetor. Pour out and discard the remaining fuel in the fuel tank and flush the tank thoroughly. If no contamination was found and the jets were not plugged, perform Step 6.
6. Incorrect valve timing and worn or damaged valve springs can cause poor high speed performance. If the valve timing was set just prior to the bike experiencing this type of problem, the valve timing may be incorrect. If the valve timing was not

set or changed, and all of the other inspection procedures in this section failed to locate the problem area, remove the cylinder head and inspect the valve train assembly.

Engine Overheating

1. Cooling system malfunction. Check the following:
   a. Low coolant level.
   b. Air in cooling system.
   c. Clogged radiator, hose or engine coolant passages.
   d. Thermostat stuck closed.
   e. Worn or damaged radiator cap.
   f. Damaged water pump.
   g. Damaged electrical component. Refer to *Cooling System* in this chapter.
2. Incorrect carburetor adjustment or jet selection.
3. Improper spark plug heat range.
4. Low oil level.
5. Oil not circulating properly.
6. Valves leaking.
7. Heavy engine carbon deposits in combustion chamber.
8. Dragging brake(s).
9. Clutch slipping.
10. Dirty air filter.
11. Leaking air filter housing or air duct.

Engine Temperature Too Low

1. Thermostat stuck open.
2. Damaged cooling fan switch.
3. Damaged temperature gauge.
4. Damaged coolant temperature sensor.
5. Damaged temperature gauge.

Coolant Leaks

1. Loose hose connection/clamp.
2. Worn or damaged coolant hose.
3. Faulty pump mechanical seal.
4. Deteriorated O-rings.
5. Damaged radiator cap.
6. Worn or damaged head gasket.

Engine Backfires

1. Incorrect ignition timing (due to loose or damaged ignition system component).
2. Incorrect carburetor adjustment.

2

Engine Misfires During Acceleration

1. Incorrect ignition timing (due to loose or damaged ignition system component).
2. Incorrect carburetor adjustment.

ENGINE NOISES

Often the first evidence of an internal engine problem is a strange noise. While engine noises can indicate problems, they are difficult to interpret correctly. Inexperienced mechanics can be seriously misled by them.

Consider the following when troubleshooting engine noises:

1. A knocking or pinging during acceleration caused by using a lower octane fuel than recommended. May also be caused by poor fuel. Pinging can also be caused by a spark plug of the wrong heat range or carbon buildup in the combustion chamber. Refer to *Spark Plugs* and *Engine Compression Test* in Chapter Three.
2. Slapping or rattling noises at low speed or during acceleration (piston slap). Check the following:
   a. Excessive piston-to-cylinder wall clearance.
   b. Worn cylinder or piston.
   c. Bent connecting rod.
   d. Worn piston pin.
   e. Worn piston pin hole.

NOTE

Piston slap is easier to detect when the engine is cold and before the pistons have expanded. Once the engine has warmed up, piston expansion reduces piston-to-cylinder clearance.

3. A knocking or rapping while decelerating is usually caused by excessive rod bearing clearance.
4. A persistent knocking and vibration occurring every crankshaft rotation is usually caused by worn rod or main bearing(s). This can also be caused by broken piston rings or damaged piston pins.
5. A rapid on-off squeal may indicate a compression leak around cylinder head gasket or spark plug(s).

6. If there is excessive valve train noise, check for the following:
   a. Incorrect valve clearance.
   b. Worn or damaged camshaft bearing.
   c. Cam chain tensioner not advanced to next notch (1990-on models).
   d. Damaged cam chain tensioner.
   e. Valve sticking in guide.
   f. Broken valve spring.

ENGINE LUBRICATION

An improperly operating engine lubrication system will quickly lead to engine seizure. Check the engine oil level before each ride, and top off the oil, as described in Chapter Three. Oil pump service is described in Chapter Five.

Oil Pressure Warning Light Turns On

1. Damaged oil pump.
2. Clogged oil screen.
3. Low oil level.
4. Oil viscosity too low.
5. Worn camshaft bearings.
6. Worn crankshaft bearings.
7. Damaged oil pressure switch.
8. Stuck relief valve.
9. Damaged oil pipe O-ring.
10. Poor wiring.

Engine Leaks Oil

1. Clogged air filter breather hose.
2. Loose engine parts.
3. Damaged gasket sealing surfaces.

Black Smoke

1. Clogged air filter.
2. Carburetor fuel level too high.
3. Choke stuck open.
4. Main jet too large.

White Smoke

1. Worn valve guide.
2. Worn valve oil seal.
3. Worn piston ring oil ring.

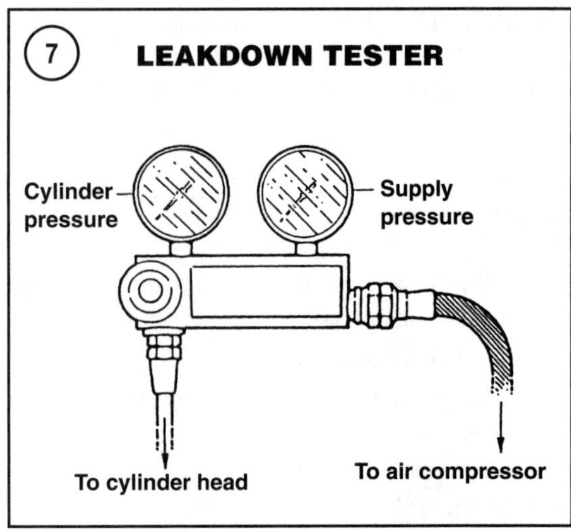

4. Excessive cylinder and/or piston wear.
5. Oil level too high.

Brown Smoke

1. Main jet too small.
2. Carburetor fuel level too low.
3. Leaking air duct.
4. Leaking air filter housing.
5. Missing air filter.

Low Oil Pressure

1. Oil level too low.
2. Oil pump damaged.
3. Oil strainer screen clogged.
4. Oil filter clogged.
5. Internal oil leakage.
6. Incorrect type engine oil.
7. Relief valve stuck open.

High Oil Pressure

1. Incorrect type engine oil being used.
2. Plugged oil filter, oil gallery or metering orifices.
3. Relief valve stuck closed.

No Oil Pressure

1. Damaged oil pump.
2. Excessively low oil level.
3. Damaged oil pump drive shaft.
4. Damaged oil pump drive sprocket.

5. Incorrect oil pump installation.

Oil Level Too Low

1. Oil level not maintained at correct level.
2. Worn piston rings.
3. Worn cylinder.
4. Worn valve guides.
5. Worn valve stem seals.
6. Piston rings incorrectly installed during engine overhaul.
7. External oil leakage.
8. Oil leaking into the cooling system.

Oil Contamination

1. Blown head gasket allowing coolant to leak into the engine.
2. Water contamination.
3. Oil and filter not changed at specified intervals or when operating conditions demand more frequent changes.

ENGINE LEAKDOWN TEST

Perform an engine leakdown test to pinpoint engine problems caused by compression leaks. While a compression test (Chapter Three) can identify a weak cylinder, a leakdown test can determine where the leak occurs. A cylinder leakdown test is made by applying compressed air through the cylinder head (with the valves closed) and then measuring the rate of leakage as a percentage. Under pressure, air leaks past worn or damaged parts. A cylinder leakdown tester and an air compressor are needed to perform this test. **Figure 7** shows a typical leakdown tester and its hose connections.

1. Start and run the engine until it is warm. Then turn the engine off.
2. Remove the fuel tank (Chapter Eight). Open and secure the throttle at its wide-open position.
3. Remove the No. 1 cylinder spark plug.
4. Set the No. 1 piston to TDC on its compression stroke as described in Chapter Three.
5. Thread the tester's 10-mm adapter into the No. 1 cylinder spark plug hole following the manufacturer's instructions. Then connect the leakdown tester onto the adapter. Connect an air compressor hose onto the tester's fitting.
6. If the engine is not too hot, remove the radiator cap.

WARNING

Because the crankshaft may spin when compressed air is applied to the cylinder, remove any tools attached to the end of the crankshaft.

NOTE

To prevent the engine from turning over as compressed air is applied to the cylinder, shift the transmission into fifth gear and have an assistant apply the rear brake.

7. Apply compressed air to the leakage tester and perform a cylinder leakdown test following the manufacturer's instructions. Read the percent of leakage on the gauge, following the manufacturer's instructions. Note the following:
   a. For a new or rebuilt engine, a leakage rate of 0 to 5 percent per cylinder is desirable. A leakage rate of 6 to 14 percent is acceptable.
   b. For a used engine, the critical rate is not the percent of leakage for each cylinder but the difference between the cylinders. On a used engine, a leakage rate of 10 percent or less between cylinders is satisfactory.
   c. A leakage rate exceeding 10 percent between cylinders points to an engine in very poor condition and requires further inspection and possible engine repair.
8. After measuring the percent of leakage, and with air pressure still applied to the combustion chamber, listen for air escaping from the following areas:

NOTE

Use a mechanic's stethoscope to help listen for air leaks in the following areas.

   a. Air leaking through the exhaust pipe indicates a leaking exhaust valve.
   b. Air leaking through the carburetor indicates a leaking intake valve.
   c. Air leaking through the crankcase breather tube suggests worn piston rings or a worn cylinder bore.
   d. Air leaking into the cooling system causes the coolant to bubble in the radiator. This condition indicates a damaged cylinder head gasket

or a warped cylinder head-to-cylinder block mating surface.
9. Remove the tester and repeat these steps for each cylinder.

CLUTCH

The basic clutch troubles and causes are listed in this section. Clutch service is found in Chapter Six.

Clutch Lever Hard to Pull In

If the clutch lever has become hard to pull in, check the following:
1. Sticking master piston.
2. Sticking slave cylinder piston.
3. Clogged hydraulic system.

Clutch Lever Soft or Spongy

1. Air in the hydraulic system.
2. Low fluid level.
3. Leaking hydraulic system.

Rough Clutch Operation

1. Excessively worn, grooved or damaged clutch hub and clutch housing slots.
2. Sticking master piston.
3. Sticking slave cylinder piston.

Clutch Slippage

If the engine speed increases without an increase in motorcycle speed, the clutch is probably slipping. Some main causes of clutch slipping are:
1. Worn clutch plates/friction discs.
2. Weak or broken clutch springs.
3. Hydraulic system clogged.
4. Worn or damaged clutch release system.
5. Unevenly worn clutch hub or housing.
6. Engine oil additive being used (clutch plates contaminated).

Clutch Drag

If the clutch will not disengage or if the bike creeps with the transmission in gear and the clutch disengaged, the clutch is dragging. Some main causes of clutch drag are:
1. Warped clutch plates.
2. Uneven clutch spring tension.
3. Loose clutch hub locknut.
4. Air in the hydraulic system.
5. Leaking or sticking hydraulic system.
6. Deteriorated brake fluid.
7. Engine oil level too high.
8. Incorrect oil viscosity.
9. Engine oil additive being used.
10. Damaged clutch housing.
11. Damaged primary or secondary cup.
12. Worn or damaged master cylinder.

FUEL SYSTEM

The following lists isolate common fuel system problems under specific complaints.

Engine Will Not Start

If the engine will not start and the electrical and mechanical systems are working correctly, check the following:
1. If there is no fuel going to the carburetors, note the following:
   a. Clogged fuel tank breather tube.
   b. Clogged fuel tank-to-fuel-valve hose or fuel-valve-to-carburetor hose.
   c. Clogged or damaged fuel valve.
   d. Incorrect float adjustment.
   e. Stuck or clogged needle valve in carburetor.
2. If the engine is flooded (too much fuel), note the following:
   a. Flooded carburetors. Needle valve in carburetor stuck open.
   b. Clogged air filter element.
3. A faulty emission control system (if equipped) can cause fuel problems. Note the following:
   a. Faulty liquid/vapor separator.
   b. Loose, disconnected or plugged emission control system hoses.
4. If you have not located the problem in Steps 1-3, check for the following:
   a. Contaminated or deteriorated fuel.
   b. Intake manifold air leak.
   c. Clogged pilot or choke circuit.

Engine Starts but Idles and Runs Poorly or Stalls Frequently

An engine that idles roughly or stalls may have one or more of the following problems:

1. Partially plugged fuel line.
2. Ignition system failure.
3. Incorrect fuel mixture.
4. Contaminated or old fuel.
5. Intake manifold air leak.
6. Incorrect fuel level adjustment.
7. Incorrect idle speed adjustment.
8. Incorrect pilot screw adjustment.
9. Plugged carburetor jets.
10. Partially plugged fuel tank breather.
11. Plugged choke circuit.
12. Fuel valve malfunction.
13. Faulty emission control system (if used).

Incorrect Fast Idle Speed

A fast idle speed can be due to one of the following problems:

1. Stuck choke valve.
2. Incorrect choke cable free play.
3. Incorrect carburetor synchronization.
4. Incorrect throttle cable adjustment.

Poor Fuel Mileage and Engine Performance

Poor fuel mileage and engine performance can be caused by infrequent engine tune-ups. Check your records to see when your bike was last tuned up and compare that interval with the recommended tune-up service intervals in Chapter Three. If the last tune-up was within the specified service intervals, check for one or more of the following problems:

1. Clogged air filter.
2. Clogged fuel system.
3. Loose, disconnected or damaged fuel and emission control vacuum hoses.
4. Faulty secondary air supply system (if used).
5. Ignition system malfunction.

Rich Fuel Mixture

One or more of the following conditions can cause a rich carburetor fuel mixture:

1. Clogged or dirty air filter.
2. Worn or damaged carburetor needle valve and seat.
3. Clogged air jets.
4. Incorrect float level (too high).
5. Choke valve damaged or stuck open.
6. Flooded carburetor(s).
7. Damaged vacuum piston(s).
8. Damaged emission control system (if used).

Lean Fuel Mixture

One or more of the following conditions can cause a lean carburetor fuel mixture:

1. Incorrect float level adjustment (too low).
2. Partially restricted fuel line.
3. Clogged carburetor jet(s).
4. Worn or damaged carburetor needle valve and seat.
5. Plugged carburetor air vent hose.
6. Damaged vacuum piston.
7. Damaged throttle valve.
8. Damaged emission control system hoses (if used).
9. Faulty fuel valve or fuel valve hose.
10. Intake air leak.

Engine Backfires or Misfires During Acceleration

Check for the following:

1. Lean fuel mixture.
2. Incorrect carburetor adjustment.
3. Ignition system malfunction.
4. Faulty vacuum hoses.
5. Vacuum leaks at the carburetor and/or intake manifold(s).
6. Fouled spark plug(s).

Engine Backfires or Misfires During Deceleration

Check for the following:

1. Lean fuel mixture.
2. Faulty air cut-off valve.
3. Secondary air system malfunction.
4. Damaged emission control system hoses (if used).

GEARSHIFT LINKAGE

The gearshift linkage assembly connects the gearshift pedal (external shift mechanism) to the shift drum (internal shift mechanism).

The external shift mechanism sits on the outside of the transmission case, and it can be serviced with the engine installed in the frame. The internal shift mechanism sits inside the transmission case, which can be removed without separating the crankcase halves. Common gearshift linkage troubles and checks to make are listed below.

Transmission Jumps Out of Gear

1. Loose gear lever mounting nut.
2. Damaged gear lever.
3. Weak or damaged lever spring.
4. Loose or damaged shift drum.
5. Bent shift fork shaft(s).
6. Bent or damaged shift fork(s).
7. Worn gear dogs or slots.
8. Damaged shift drum grooves.

Difficult Shifting

1. Incorrect clutch operation.
2. Incorrect oil viscosity.
3. Damaged or binding gear lever.
4. Damaged or binding neutral lever.
5. Bent shift fork shaft(s).
6. Bent or damaged shift fork(s).
7. Worn gear dogs or slots.
8. Damaged shift drum grooves.
9. Weak or damaged shift return springs.
10. Damaged shift pawl.

Shift Pedal Does Not Return

1. Bent shift shaft.
2. Weak or damaged shift shaft return spring.
3. Shift shaft incorrectly installed.

Incorrect Shift Lever Operation

1. Bent shift pedal or linkage.
2. Stripped shift pedal splines.
3. Damaged shift pedal linkage.

TRANSMISSION

Transmission symptoms are sometimes hard to distinguish from clutch symptoms. Common transmission troubles and checks to make are listed below. Refer to Chapter Seven for transmission service procedures. Prior to working on the transmission, make sure the clutch and gearshift linkage assemblies are not causing the trouble.

Difficult Shifting

1. Incorrect clutch operation.
2. Bent shift fork(s).
3. Damaged shift fork guide pin(s).
4. Bent shift fork shaft(s).
5. Damaged shift drum grooves.

Jumps Out of Gear

1. Loose or damaged gear lever or neutral lever.
2. Bent or damaged shift fork(s).
3. Bent shift fork shaft(s).
4. Damaged shift drum grooves.
5. Worn gear dogs or slots.
6. Worn gear grooves.
7. Worn or damaged splines on the transmission shaft(s).

Excessive Gear Noise

1. Worn or damaged transmission bearings.
2. Worn or damaged gears.
3. Excessive gear backlash.
4. Metal flakes in gear teeth.
5. Insufficient oil.

FINAL DRIVE

Excessive Final Gearcase Noise

1. Low oil level.
2. Worn or damaged pinion and ring gears.
3. Excessive pinion-to-ring gear backlash.
4. Worn or damaged pinion gear and splines.
5. Scored driven flange and wheel hub.
6. Scored or worn ring gear and driven flange.

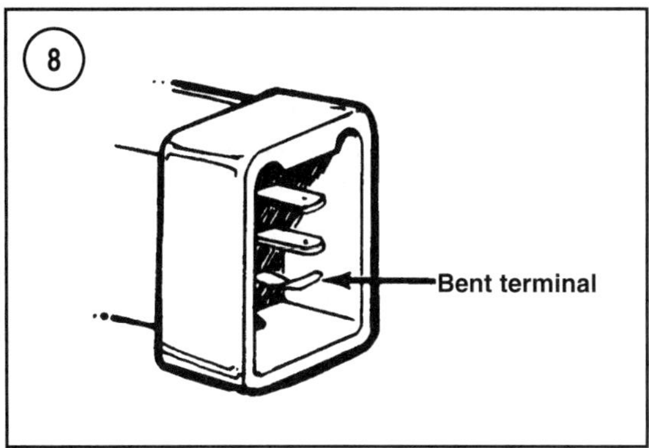

Excessive Rear Wheel Backlash

1. Worn driveshaft or coupling splines.
2. Loose gearcase bearing(s).
3. Excessive ring gear-to-pinion gear backlash.

Final Gearcase Oil Leak

1. Loose or missing cover bolts.
2. Damaged final gearcase seals.
3. Clogged breather.
4. Oil level too high.

ELECTRICAL TESTING

NOTE
Scan the QR code or search for "Clymer Manuals YouTube Tech Tips" to see an overview on electrical troubleshooting with a wiring diagram.

This section describes the basics of electrical troubleshooting and the use of test equipment.

Electrical troubleshooting can be very time-consuming and frustrating without proper knowledge and a suitable plan. Refer to the wiring diagrams at the end of the manual for component and connector identification. Use the wiring diagrams to determine how the circuit should work by tracing the current paths from the power source through the circuit components to ground. Also check any circuits that share the same fuse, ground or switch. If the other circuits work properly and the shared wiring is good, the cause must be in the wiring used only by the suspect circuit. If all related circuits are faulty at the same time, the probable cause is a poor ground connection or a blown fuse(s).

As with all troubleshooting procedures, analyze typical symptoms in a systematic manner. Never assume anything and do not overlook the obvious like a blown fuse or an electrical connector that has separated. Test the simplest and most obvious items first and try to make tests at easily accessible points on the motorcycle.

Electrical Component Replacement

Most motorcycle dealerships and parts suppliers will not accept the return of any electrical part. If you cannot determine the *exact* cause of any electrical system malfunction, have a Kawasaki dealership retest that specific system to verify your test results. If you purchase a new electrical component(s), install it, and then find that the system still does not work properly, you will probably be unable to return the unit for a refund.

Consider any test results carefully before replacing a component that tests only *slightly* out of specification, especially resistance. A number of variables can affect test results dramatically. These include: the testing meter's internal circuitry, ambient temperature and conditions under which the machine has been operated. All instructions and specifications have been checked for accuracy; however, successful test results depend to a great degree upon individual accuracy.

Preliminary Checks and Precautions

Prior to starting any electrical troubleshooting perform the following:

1. Check the main fuse (Chapter Nine). If the fuse is blown, replace it.
2. Check the individual fuses mounted in the junction box (Chapter Nine). Inspect the suspected fuse, and replace it if blown.
3. Inspect the battery. Make sure it is fully charged, and that the battery leads are clean and securely attached to the battery terminals. Refer to *Battery* in Chapter Three.

4. Electrical connectors are often the weak link. Check them carefully as follows:
   a. Disconnect an electrical connector by pulling only on the connector housing.
   b. Disconnect each connector in the suspect circuit and check the male and female terminals (**Figure 8**).
   c. Make sure the terminals (**Figure 9**) are pushed all the way into the connector.
   d. Check each wire where it enters the connector for damage.
   e. Make sure all terminals are clean and free of corrosion. Clean them, if necessary, and pack the connectors with dielectric grease.
   f. Push the connector halves together. Make sure the connectors are fully engaged and locked together (**Figure 10**).
5. Never use a self-powered test light on circuits that contain solid-state devices. The solid-state devices may be damaged.

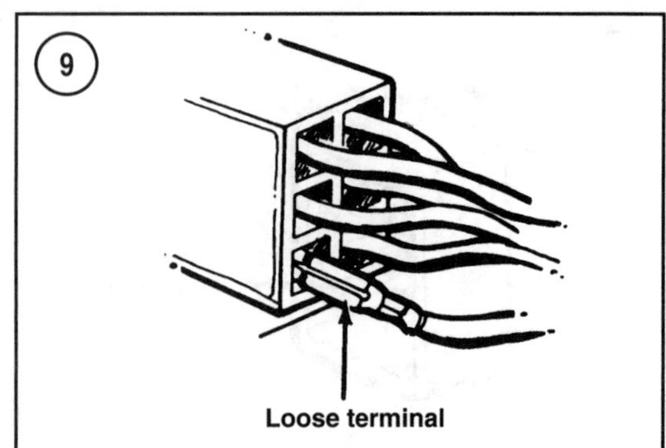

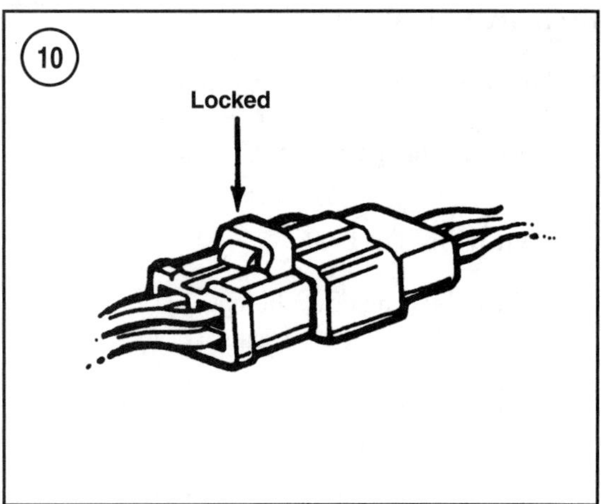

Test Light or Voltmeter

A test light can be constructed from a 12-volt light bulb with a pair of test leads carefully soldered to the bulb. To check for battery voltage in a circuit, attach one lead to ground and the other lead to various points along the circuit. The bulb lights up when battery voltage is present.

A voltmeter is used in the same manner as the test light to determine if battery voltage is present in any given circuit. The voltmeter, unlike the test light, also indicates how much voltage is present at each test point. When using a voltmeter, attach the positive lead to the component or wire to be checked and the negative lead to a good ground (**Figure 11**).

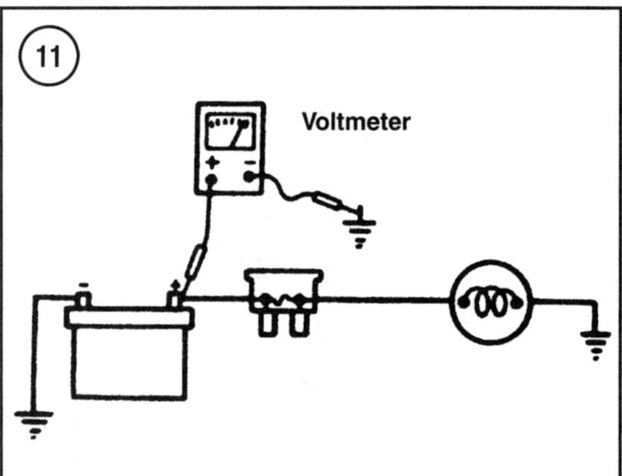

Ammeter

An ammeter measures the flow of current (amps) in a circuit (**Figure 12**). When connected in series in a circuit, the ammeter determines if current is flowing through the circuit and if that current flow is excessive because of a short in the circuit. Current flow is often referred to as current draw. Comparing actual current draw in the circuit or component to the manufacturer's specified current draw provides useful diagnostic information.

Self-powered Test Light

A self-powered test light can be constructed from a 12-volt light bulb, a pair of test leads and a 12-volt battery. When the test leads are touched together the light bulb should go on.

Use a self-powered test light as follows:

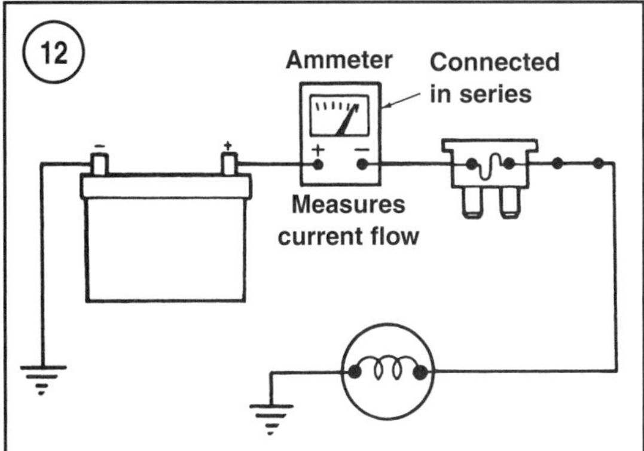

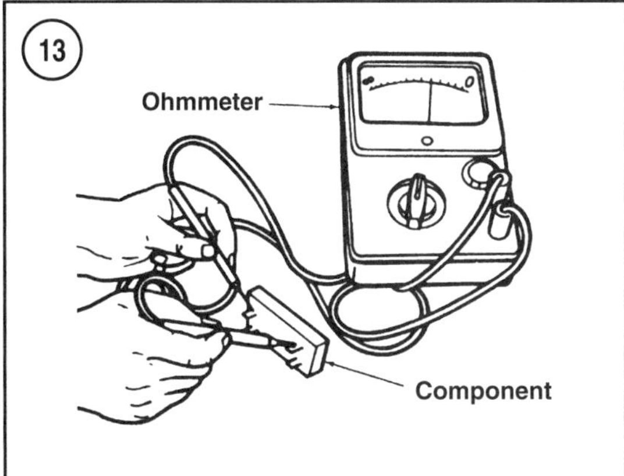

1. Touch the test leads together to make sure the light bulb goes on. If not, correct the problem prior to using it in a test.
2. Disconnect the motorcycle's battery or remove the fuse(s) that protects the circuit to be tested.
3. Select two points within the circuit where there should be continuity.
4. Attach one lead of the self-powered test light to each point.
5. If there is continuity, the self-powered test light bulb will come on.
6. If there is no continuity, the self-powered test light bulb will not come on, indicating an open circuit.

Ohmmeter

An ohmmeter measures the resistance (in ohms) to current flow in a circuit or component. Like the self-powered test light, an ohmmeter contains its own power source and should not be connected to a live circuit.

Ohmmeters may be analog type (needle scale) or digital type (LCD or LED readout). Both types of ohmmeters have a switch that allows the user to select different ranges of resistance for accurate readings. The analog ohmmeter also has a set-adjust control which is used to zero or calibrate the meter (digital ohmmeters do not require calibration).

To use an ohmmeter, connect its test leads to the terminals or leads of the circuit or component to be tested (**Figure 13**). If an analog meter is used, it must be calibrated by touching the test leads together and turning the set-adjust knob until the meter needle reads zero. When the leads are uncrossed, the needle should move to the other end of the scale indicating infinite resistance.

During a continuity test, a reading of infinity indicates there is an open in the circuit or component. A reading of zero indicates continuity; that is, there is no measurable resistance in the circuit or component being tested.

If the meter needle falls between these two ends of the scale, this indicates the actual resistance to current flow that is present. To determine the resistance, multiply the meter reading by the ohmmeter scale. For example, a meter reading of 5 multiplied by the R × 1000 scale is 5000 ohms of resistance.

CAUTION

Never connect an ohmmeter to a circuit which has power applied to it. Always disconnect the battery negative lead before using an ohmmeter.

Jumper Wire

A jumper wire is a simple way to bypass a potential problem and isolate it to a particular point in a circuit. If a faulty circuit works properly with a jumper wire installed, an open exists between the two jumper points in the circuit.

To troubleshoot with a jumper wire, first use the wire to determine if the problem is on the ground side or the load side of a device. Test the ground by connecting a jumper between the lamp and a good ground (**Figure 14**). If the lamp comes on, the problem is the connection between the lamp and ground. If the lamp does not come on with the jumper installed, the lamp's connection to ground is good so the problem is between the lamp and the power source.

To isolate the problem, connect the jumper between the battery and the lamp (**Figure 14**). If it comes on, the problem is between these two points. Next, connect the jumper between the battery and the fuse side of the switch. If the lamp comes on, the switch is good. By successively moving the jumper from one point to another, the problem can be isolated to a particular place in the circuit.

Pay attention to the following when using a jumper wire:

1. Make sure the jumper wire gauge (thickness) is the same as that used in the circuit being tested. Smaller gauge wire will rapidly overheat and could melt.
2. Install insulated boots over alligator clips. This prevents accidental grounding, sparks or possible shock when working in cramped quarters.
3. Jumper wires are temporary test measures only. Do not leave a jumper wire installed as a permanent solution. This creates a severe fire hazard that could easily lead to complete loss of the motorcycle.

When using a jumper wire always install an inline fuse/fuse holder (available at most auto supply stores or electronic supply stores) to the jumper wire. Never use a jumper wire across any load (a component that is connected and turned on). This would result in a direct short and will blow the fuse(s).

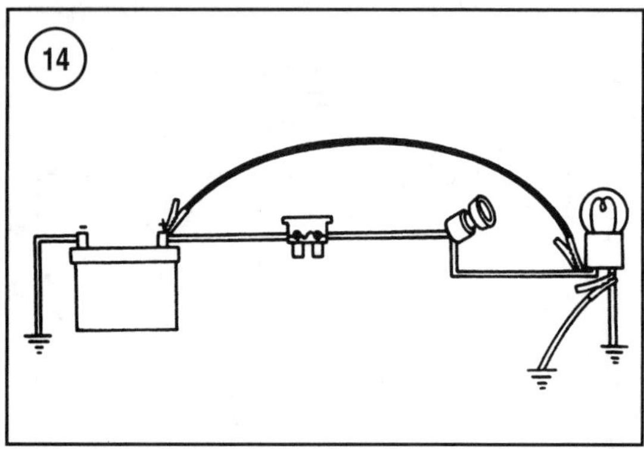

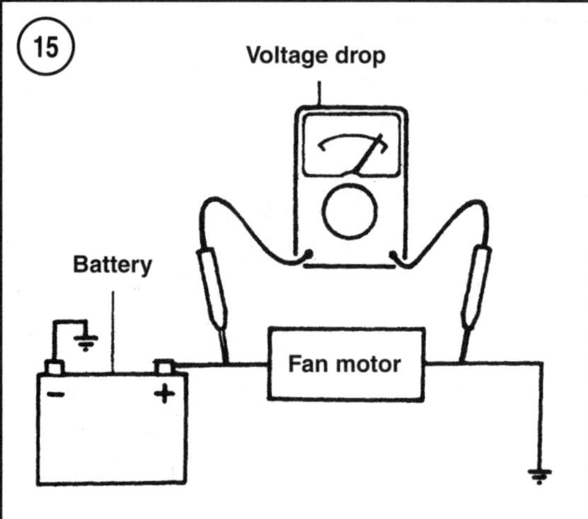

Voltage Testing

Unless otherwise specified, make sure all voltage tests are with the electrical connectors still connected. Insert the test leads into the back of the connector housing. Make sure the test lead touches the electrical wire or metal terminal within the housing. If the test lead only touches the wire insulation, you will get a false reading.

Always check both sides of the connector as one side may be loose or corroded thus preventing electrical flow through the connector. This type of test can be performed with a test light or a voltmeter. A voltmeter gives the best results.

NOTE
If using a test light, it does not make any difference which test lead is attached to ground.

1. Attach the voltmeter negative test lead to a good ground (bare metal). Make sure the part used for ground is not insulated with a rubber gasket or rubber grommet.
2. Attach the voltmeter positive test lead to the point (electrical connector, etc.) to be tested (**Figure 11**).
3. Turn the ignition switch on. If using a test light, the test light will come on if voltage is present. If using a voltmeter, note the voltage reading. The reading should be within 1 volt of battery voltage. If the voltage is less, there is a problem in the circuit.

Voltage Drop Testing

Since resistance causes voltage to drop, a voltmeter can be used to determine resistance in an active circuit. A voltage drop test measures the difference between the voltage at the beginning of the circuit and the available voltage at the end of the circuit while the circuit is operating. If the circuit has no resistance, there is no voltage drop so the voltmeter indicates 0 volts. The greater the resistance in a circuit, the greater the voltage drop reading. A voltage drop of 1 or more volts indicates that a circuit has excessive resistance.

It is important to remember that a 0 reading on a voltage drop test is good. Battery voltage, on the other hand, indicates an open circuit. A voltage drop test is an excellent way to check the condition of solenoids, relays, battery cables and other high-current electrical components.

1. Connect the voltmeter positive test lead to the end of the wire or device closest to the battery.

2. Connect the voltmeter negative test lead to the ground side of the wire or device (**Figure 15**).

3. Turn the components on in the circuit.

4. The voltmeter should indicate 0 volts. If there is a drop of 1 volt or more, there is a problem within the circuit. A voltage drop reading of 12 volts indicates an open in the circuit.

Peak Voltage Testing

Peak voltage tests check the voltage output of the ignition coil, ignition pulse generator, and the exciter coil at normal cranking speed. These tests make it possible to identify ignition system problems quickly and accurately.

Peak voltage tests require a specific peak voltage adapter from the motorcycle manufacturer and a commercially available digital multimeter (minimum impedance: 10 M ohms/DCV). If these tools are not available, refer the tests to a dealership or other qualified service shop.

WARNING
High voltage is present during ignition system operation. Do not touch ignition components, wires or test leads while cranking or running the engine.

NOTE
All peak voltage specifications are minimum values. If the measured voltage meets or exceeds the specification, the test results are satisfactory. On some components, the voltage may greatly exceed the minimum specification.

Continuity Testing

A continuity test is used to determine the integrity of a circuit, wire or component. A circuit has continuity if it forms a complete circuit; that is if there are no opens in either the electrical wires or components within the circuit. A circuit with an open, on the other hand, has no continuity.

This type of test can be performed with a self-powered test light or an ohmmeter. An ohmmeter gives the best results. If using an analog ohmmeter, calibrate the meter by touching the leads together and turning the calibration knob until the meter reads zero.

1. Disconnect the negative battery cable.

2. Attach one test lead (test light or ohmmeter) to one end of the part of the circuit to be tested.

3. Attach the other test lead to the other end of the part or the circuit to be tested.

4. The self-powered test light comes on if there is continuity. An ohmmeter reads 0 or very low resistance if there is continuity. A reading of infinite resistance indicates no continuity; the circuit has an open.

Testing for a Short with a Self-powered Test Light or Ohmmeter

1. Disconnect the negative battery cable.

2. Remove the blown fuse from the junction box.

3. Connect one test lead of the test light or ohmmeter to the load side (battery side) of the fuse terminal in the junction box.

4. Connect the other test lead to a good ground (bare metal). Make sure the part used for a ground is not insulated with a rubber gasket or rubber grommet.

5. Starting next to the junction box, wiggle the wiring harness relating to the suspect circuit. If the test light blinks or the needle on the ohmmeter moves, there is a short-to-ground at that point in the harness.

6. Move 15.2 cm (6 in.) away from the junction box, and wiggle the wire. Continue down the harness, wiggling the wire at 15.2 cm (6 in.) intervals watching for a short-to-ground.

Testing For a Short with a Test Light or Voltmeter

1. Remove the blown fuse from the junction box.
2. Connect the test light or voltmeter across the fuse terminals in the junction box. Turn the ignition switch on and check for battery voltage.
3. Starting at the junction box, locate the wiring harness relating to the suspect circuit. Wiggle the wiring harness. If the test light blinks or the needle on the voltmeter moves, there is a short-to-ground at that point in the harness.
4. Move 15.2 cm (6 in.) away from the junction box, and wiggle the wire. Continue down the harness, wiggling the wire at 15.2 cm (6 in.) intervals watching for a short-to-ground.

CHARGING SYSTEM

The charging system consists of the battery, alternator voltage and a voltage regulator/rectifier, which is part of the alternator. A 30 amp main fuse protects the circuit.

Alternating current generated by the alternator is rectified to direct current. The voltage regulator maintains the voltage to the battery and additional electrical loads at a constant voltage regardless of variations in engine speed and load.

The basic charging system problems are:
1. Battery overcharging.
2. Battery undercharging.

Battery Undercharging

1. Check the main fuse.
2. Check the battery as described in Chapter Three.
3. Perform the current draw test (Chapter Nine). Locate and repair any short in the circuit.
4. Perform the charging voltage test (Chapter Nine).
   a. If the charging voltage exceeds 13.5 volts, perform the regulator operational test.
   b. If the charging voltage is less than 13.5 voltage, proceed to Step 5.
5. Measure the length of the carbon brushes.
6. Measure the diameter of the rotor slip rings.
7. Perform the rectifier resistance test.
8. Perform the stator resistance and continuity tests.
9. Perform the rotor resistance and continuity tests.

Battery Overcharging

1. Perform the regulator operational test (Chapter Nine).
2. Perform the rotor resistance and continuity tests.

IGNITION SYSTEM

1. Inspect the main fuse and the ignition fuse as described in this chapter.
2. Check the battery as described in Chapter Three.
3. Check the condition of each spark plug as described in Chapter Three.
4. Perform the spark test described in this chapter.
5. Check the resistance of each ignition coil (Chapter Nine).
6. Check the resistance of each pickup coil (Chapter Nine).
7. Check the continuity of the ignition switch (Chapter Nine).
8. Check the continuity of the engine stop switch (Chapter Nine).
9. Check the continuity of the neutral switch (Chapter Nine).
10. Check the continuity of the sidestand switch (Chapter Nine).
11. Check the continuity of the starter lockout switch (Chapter Nine).
12. Perform the junction box diode test (Chapter Nine).
13. Check the connections in the entire ignition system.
14. Have a Kawasaki dealership or other qualified service shop check the IC igniter.

STARTING SYSTEM

CAUTION
Do not operate the starter for more than 5 seconds at a time. Let it cool approximately 10 seconds, then use it again.

1. Check the main fuse.
2. Check the battery as described in Chapter Three.
3. Perform the starter operational test described in Chapter Nine.
4. Test the starter relay (Chapter Nine).
5. Check the continuity of the ignition switch (Chapter Nine).

6. Check the continuity of the engine stop switch (Chapter Nine).
7. Check the continuity of the neutral switch (Chapter Nine).
8. Check the continuity of the sidestand switch (Chapter Nine).
9. Check the continuity of the starter lockout switch (Chapter Nine).
10. Check the continuity of the starter switch (Chapter Nine).
11. Check the wiring and each connector in the starting circuit.

COOLING SYSTEM

1. Inspect the main fuse and horn fuse as described in Chapter Nine.
2. Inspect the battery as described in Chapter Three.
3. Check the ignition switch (Chapter Nine).
4. Check the temperature gauge.
5. Perform the fan motor operational test (Chapter Nine).
6. Perform the fan switch test (Chapter Nine).
7. Perform the coolant temperature sensor test (Chapter Nine).
8. Check the wiring and connectors in the cooling system circuit.

FRONT SUSPENSION AND STEERING

Poor handling may be caused by improper tire pressure, a damaged/bent frame or front steering components, a worn front fork assembly, worn wheel bearings or dragging brakes.

Steering is Sluggish

1. Incorrect steering stem adjustment (too tight).
2. Damaged steering head bearings.
3. Bent steering head.
4. Tire pressure too low.
5. Worn or damaged tire.

Steers to One Side

1. Bent front or rear axle.
2. Bent frame, swing arm or fork(s).
3. Worn or damaged wheel bearings.
4. Worn or damaged swing arm pivot bearings.
5. Damaged steering head bearings.
6. Bent swing arm.
7. Incorrectly installed wheels.
8. Front and rear wheels are not aligned.
9. Front fork legs positioned unevenly in steering stem.
10. Fork legs unbalanced (oil level, air pressure, damping not the same).

Front Suspension Noise

1. Loose mounting fasteners.
2. Damaged fork(s) or rear shock absorber.
3. Low fork oil capacity.
4. Fork oil too thin.
5. Weak or damaged fork springs.
6. Loose or damaged fairing mounts.

Front Wheel Wobble/Vibration

1. Worn tire.
2. Worn swing arm pivot bearing.
3. Loose or damaged wheel rim.
4. Loose handlebar clamp bolt.
5. Loose steering head.
6. Loose front wheel axle.
7. Loose or damaged wheel bearing(s).

Rear Wheel Wobble/Vibration

1. Damaged wheel rim(s).
2. Loose or damaged wheel bearing(s).
3. Damaged wheel rims.
4. Loose rear wheel axle.
5. Loose swing arm pivot bolts.
6. Unbalanced tire and wheel assembly.
7. Damaged tire.

Hard Suspension (Front Fork)

1. Insufficient tire pressure.
2. Damaged steering head bearings.
3. Incorrect steering head bearing adjustment.
4. Bent fork tubes.
5. Binding slider.
6. Incorrect weight fork oil.
7. Fork oil too low.

8. Weak fork spring.
9. Incorrect fork air pressure (1986-1993 models).
10. Plugged fork oil passage.

Hard Suspension (Rear Shock Absorber)

1. Excessive rear tire pressure.
2. Incorrect air pressure.
3. Incorrect shock adjustment.
4. Damaged shock absorber bushing(s).
5. Damaged swing arm pivot bearings.
6. Poorly lubricated suspension components.

Soft Front Suspension

1. Insufficient tire pressure.
2. Insufficient fork oil level or fluid capacity.
3. Incorrect oil viscosity.
4. Weak or damaged fork springs.

Soft Rear Suspension

1. Insufficient rear tire pressure.
2. Damaged shock absorber.
3. Incorrect shock absorber adjustment.
4. Leaking damper unit.

BRAKES

The front and rear brake units are critical to riding performance and safety. Inspect the front and rear brakes frequently, and repair any problem immediately. When adding or changing the brake fluid, use only DOT 4 brake fluid from a closed container. See Chapter Fourteen for additional information on brake fluid selection and disc brake service.

When checking brake pad wear, verify that the brake pads in each caliper contact the disc squarely. If one of the brake pads is wearing unevenly, suspect a warped or bent brake disc or damaged caliper.

Brake Drag

1. Clogged brake hydraulic system.
2. Sticking caliper pistons.
3. Sticking master cylinder piston.
4. Master cylinder relief port is plugged.
5. Incorrectly installed brake caliper.
6. Warped brake discs.
7. Incorrect wheel alignment.
8. Contaminated brake pad and discs.
9. Excessively worn brake disc or pad.
10. Caliper not sliding correctly.

Brakes Grab

1. Contaminated brake pads and disc.
2. Incorrect wheel alignment.
3. Warped brake discs.
4. Caliper not sliding correctly.

Brake Squeal or Chatter

1. Contaminated brake pads and disc.
2. Incorrectly installed brake caliper.
3. Warped brake discs.
4. Incorrect wheel alignment.

Soft or Spongy Brake Lever or Pedal

1. Low brake fluid level.
2. Air in brake hydraulic system.
3. Leaking brake hydraulic system.
4. Clogged brake hydraulic system.
5. Worn brake caliper seals.
6. Worn master cylinder seals.
7. Caliper not sliding correctly.
8. Sticking caliper piston.
9. Sticking master cylinder piston.
10. Damaged front brake lever.
11. Damaged rear brake pedal.
12. Contaminated brake pads and disc.
13. Excessively worn brake disc or pad.
14. Warped brake discs.

Hard Brake Lever or Pedal Operation

1. Clogged brake hydraulic system.
2. Sticking caliper piston.
3. Sticking master cylinder piston.
4. Worn caliper piston seal.
5. Glazed or worn brake pads.
6. Damaged front brake lever.
7. Damaged rear brake pedal.
8. Caliper not sliding correctly.

CHAPTER THREE

LUBRICATION, MAINTENANCE AND TUNE-UP

This chapter describes lubrication, maintenance and tune-up procedures. Minor problems found during these inspections are generally simple and inexpensive to correct. However, they could lead to major problems if not corrected promptly.

When inspecting components in this chapter, compare any measurements to the tune-up and maintenance specifications in **Table 7** and **Table 8** at the end of this chapter. Replace any part that is damaged, worn to the service limit or out of specification. Refer to *Shop Supplies* in Chapter One for general lubricant information.

FUEL REQUIREMENTS

The ZG1000 engine is designed to use unleaded gasoline with a pump octane rating [(R+M)/2 method)] of 87 or higher. The pump octane rating is normally displayed at the service station fuel pump. Using gasoline with a lower octane rating can cause pinging or spark knock. Either condition can lead to engine damage.

When adding fuel, note the following:

1. Do not overfill the fuel tank. There should be no fuel in the filler neck located between the fuel cap and the tank.
2. Oxygenated fuels are used to help meet clean air regulations in some areas of the United States and Canada. When using an oxygenated fuel, make sure it meets the 87 minimum octane rating.
3. Oxygenated fuels can damage plastic and painted parts. Take care not to spill these fuels on the motorcycle when refueling.
4. An ethanol (ethyl or grain alcohol) gasoline that contains more than 10% ethanol (by volume) may cause engine starting and performance problems.
5. A methanol (methyl or wood alcohol) gasoline that contains more than 5% methanol (by volume) may cause engine starting and performance problems. Gasoline that contains methanol must have corrosion inhibitors to protect metal, plastic and rubber parts in the fuel system.

MAINTENANCE INTERVALS

Table 1 shows the recommended maintenance schedule. Strict adherence to these recommendations will help ensure a long service life from the motorcycle. If the motorcycle is operated in an area of high humidity, the lubrication services must be performed more frequently to prevent rust and corrosion.

For convenience, most of the procedures listed in **Table 1** are described in this chapter. Those procedures that require more than minor disassembly or adjustment are covered in the appropriate chapter in the manual. Refer to the *Table of Contents* or *Index* to locate a particular procedure.

CYLINDER NUMBERING AND FIRING ORDER

The cylinders are numbered 1 through 4, starting with the cylinder on the left side, as shown in **Figure 1**. Left and right refer to the rider's point of view while sitting on the seat facing forward.

The cylinder firing order is 1-2-4-3.

ENGINE ROTATION

During operation, engine rotation is counterclockwise when viewed from the left side. When required to manually rotate the engine during service, always turn the crankshaft *counterclockwise*.

TUNE-UP

Perform the engine tune-up procedures at the intervals specified in **Table 1**. More frequent tune-ups may be required if the motorcycle is primarily operated in stop-and-go traffic.

The Vehicle Emission Control Information label provides tune-up specifications and is located on the rear fender. Always refer to the specifications on this label when servicing the motorcycle. If the specifications on the Vehicle Emission Control Information label differ from those in **Table 7** or **Table 8**, use the specifications from the label.

When performing a tune-up, service the following items as described in this chapter:

1. Air filter.
2. Spark plugs.
3. Engine compression.
4. Ignition timing.
5. Valve clearance.
6. Engine oil and filter.
7. Carburetor adjustment.
8. Brake system.
9. Suspension components.
10. Tires and wheels.
11. Fasteners.

SPARK PLUGS

Removal

A spark plug reading can be used to help determine the operating condition of its cylinder. As each spark plug is removed, label it with its cylinder number. If anything turns up during an inspection, knowing which cylinder a plug came from is critical.

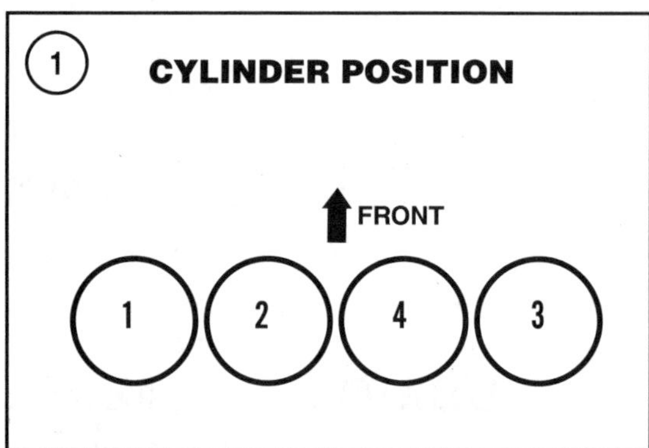

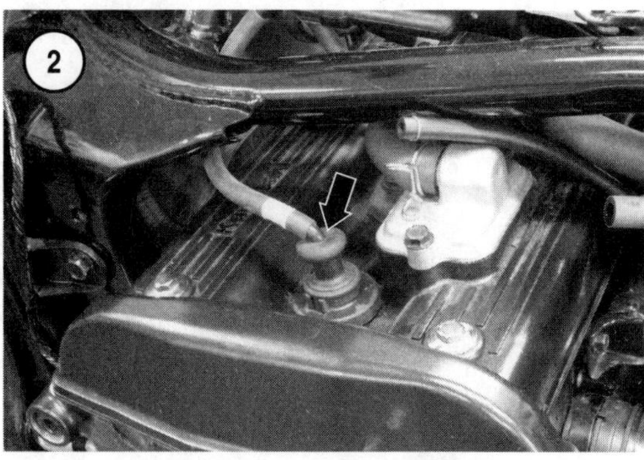

1. Remove the lower, middle and front fairings as described in Chapter Fifteen.
2. Remove the fuel tank (Chapter Eight).

CAUTION
Whenever a spark plug is removed, dirt around it can fall into the plug hole. This can cause serious engine damage.

3. Blow away all loose dirt, then wipe off the top surface of the cylinder head cover. Remove all loose debris that could fall into the cylinder head spark plug tunnels.
4. Carefully disconnect the spark plug cap (**Figure 2**) from each spark plug. The plug caps form a tight seal on the cylinder head cover as well as the spark plugs. Twist the cap to break the seal. Carefully pull the plug cap up and off the spark plug. If it is stuck to the plug, twist it slightly to break it loose.

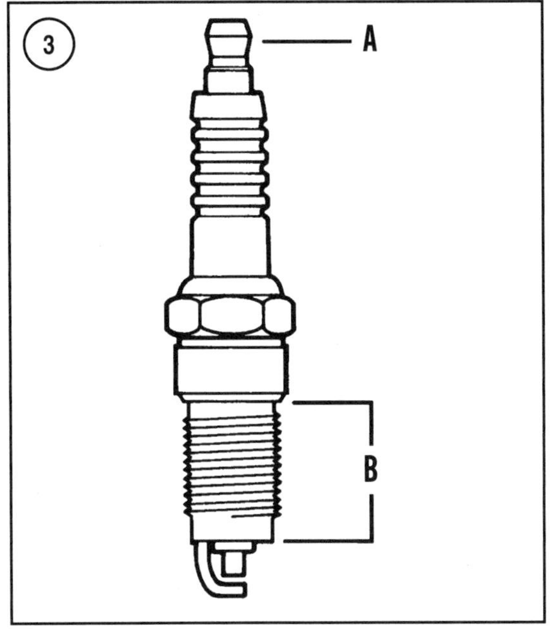

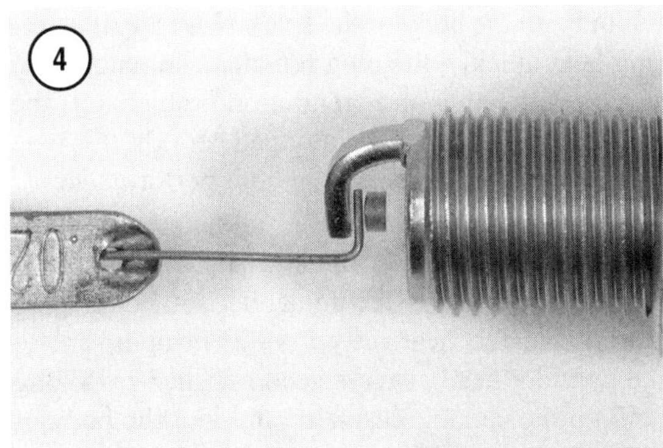

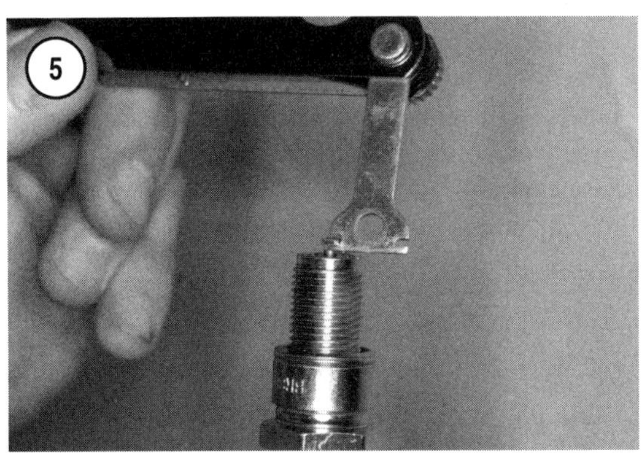

NOTE
If a plug is difficult to remove, apply penetrating oil around base of plug and let it soak in about 10-20 minutes.

5. Remove the spark plugs with a 5/8-in. spark plug wrench with a rubber insert to hold the plug. Label each spark plug by its cylinder number.
6. Repeat for the remaining three spark plugs.

CAUTION
Do not clean the spark plugs with a sand-blasting device. While this type of cleaning is thorough, it can leave abrasive cleaning material on the plug. A spark plug must be absolutely clean. Any material left on the plug will fall into the cylinder during operation and cause damage.

7. Inspect the spark plug carefully. Look for a plug with broken center porcelain, excessively eroded electrodes, and excessive carbon or oil fouling. Replace such a plug. If deposits are light, the plug may be cleaned in solvent with a wire brush. Regap the plug as described in this section.
8. Inspect the spark plug caps and wires for cracks, hardness or other damage.

Gap and Installation

Carefully gap the spark plugs to ensure a reliable, consistent spark.

1. Remove the new spark plugs from the boxes. If installed, unscrew the terminal nut (A, **Figure 3**) from the end of the plug.
2. Insert a wire feeler gauge between the center and side electrodes of the plug (**Figure 4**). The specified gap is listed in **Table 7**. If the gap is correct, you will feel a slight drag as you pull the wire through. If there is no drag or if the gauge will not pass through, bend the side electrode with a gaping tool (**Figure 5**) and set the gap to specification.
3. Apply a light coat of antiseize compound to the threads of the spark plug before installing it. Do not use engine oil on the plug threads.

CAUTION
The cylinder head is aluminum. Cross threading the spark plug can easily damage the threads in plug hole.

4. Turn the spark plug into the cylinder by hand until it seats. Very little effort is required. If force is necessary, the plug is cross-threaded. Unscrew it and try again.

5. Use the same tool set-up used during removal, and hand tighten the plug until it seats. Torque the plug to 14 N•m (10 ft-lb.).

CAUTION
Do not use a plastic hammer or any type of tool to tap the plug cap onto the spark plug. The assembly will be damaged. Use only your fingers.

NOTE
Be sure to push the plug cap all the way down to make full contact with the spark plug post. If the cap does not completely contact the plug, the engine may start to falter and cut out at high engine speeds.

6. Install each plug cap onto the correct spark plug. Carefully press the cap onto the spark plug by hand while rotating the assembly slightly in both directions. Make sure it is attached to the spark plug and to the sealing surface of the cylinder head cover.
7. Install the fuel tank (Chapter Eight) and the fairings (Chapter Fifteen).

Selection

Refer to **Table 5** for spark plug recommendations.

NOTE
The following sections provide general information and operation fundamentals that apply to all spark plugs. However, before changing to plugs other than what is recommended by the Kawasaki, check with the spark plug manufacturer for specific part numbers and equivalents that apply to this machine. Poor performance or engine damage can occur by installing spark plugs that are not compatible with this engine.

Heat range

Spark plugs are available in several heat ranges to accommodate the load and performance demands put on the engine. The standard spark plug recommended by the manufacturer is usually a medium heat-range plug that operates well over a wide range of engine speeds. As long as engine speeds vary, these plugs will stay relatively clean and perform well.

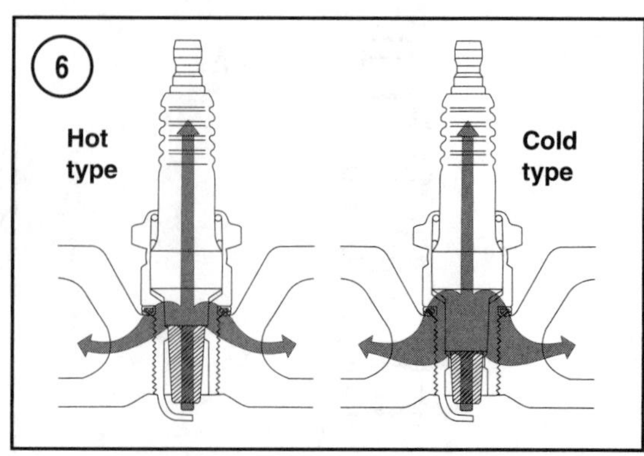

If the engine is run in hot climates, at high speed or under heavy loads for prolonged periods, a spark plug with a colder heat range is recommended. A colder plug quickly transfers heat away from its firing tip and to the cylinder head (**Figure 6**). This is accomplished by a short path up the ceramic insulator and into the body of the spark plug. By transferring heat quickly, the plug remains cool enough to avoid overheating and preignition problems. If the engine is run slowly for prolonged periods, this type of plug will foul and result in poor performance.

If the engine is run in cold climates or at slow speed for prolonged periods, a spark plug with a hotter heat range is recommended. A hotter plug slowly transfers heat away from its firing tip and to the cylinder head. This is accomplished by a long path up the ceramic insulator and into the body of the spark plug (**Figure 6**). By transferring heat slowly, the plug remains hot enough to avoid fouling and buildup. If the engine is run in hot climates or fast for prolonged periods, this type of plug will overheat, cause preignition problems and possibly melt the electrode. Damage to the piston and cylinder assembly is possible.

If you choose to change a spark plug to a different heat range, go one step hotter or colder from the recommended plug. Do not try to correct poor carburetor or ignition problems by using different spark plugs. This will only compound the existing problems and possibly lead to engine damage.

Reach

Reach is the length of the threaded portion of the plug (**B, Figure 3**). Always use a spark plug that is

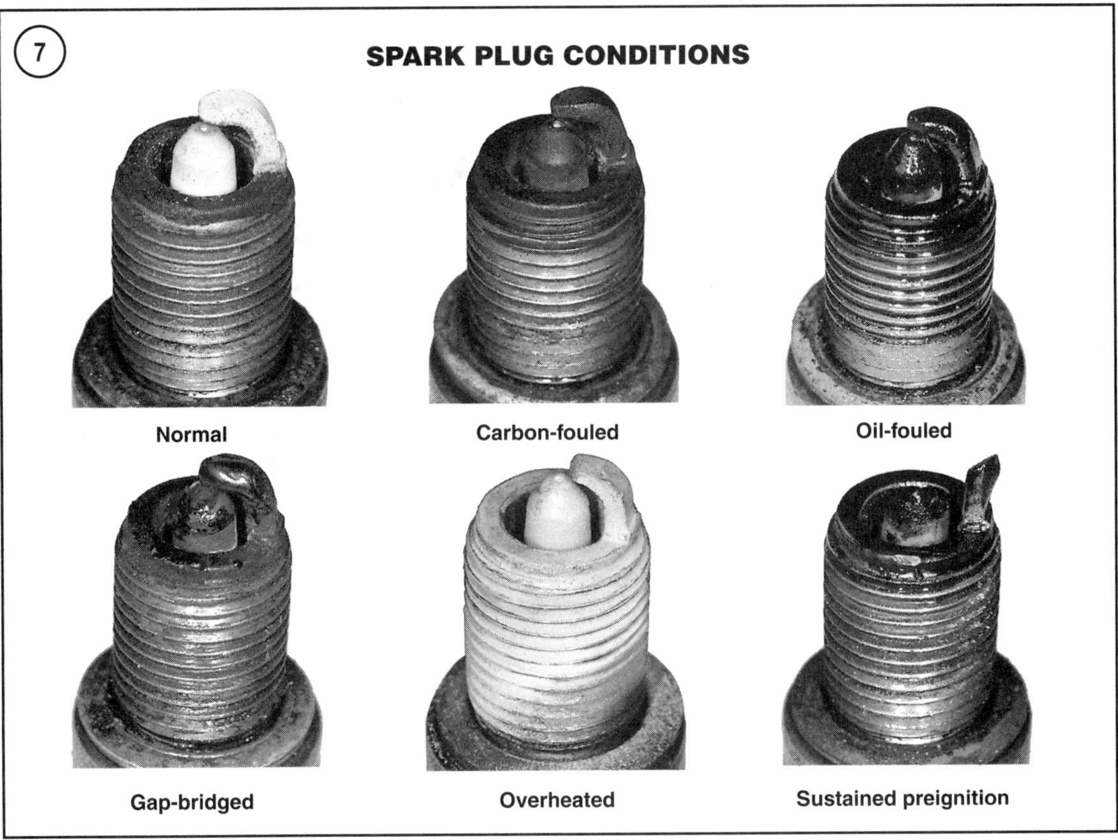

the correct reach. Too short of a reach can lead to deposit buildup or burning of the exposed threads in the cylinder head. Misfiring can also occur since the tip of the plug is shrouded and not exposed to the fuel mixture. If the reach is too long, the exposed plug threads can burn, causing preignition. It is possible the piston may contact the plug on the upstroke, causing severe engine damage.

Inspection

Inspecting or reading the spark plugs can provide a significant amount of information regarding engine performance/condition. Reading plugs that have been in use will give an indication of spark plug operation (correct heat range), air/fuel mixture composition and engine conditions (oil consumption). Before checking new spark plugs, operate the motorcycle under a medium load for approximately 6 miles (10 km). Avoid prolonged idling before shutting off the engine. Remove the spark plugs as described in this section and compare them to those in **Figure 7**.

Normal condition

A light tan or gray-colored deposit on the firing tip and no abnormal gap wear or erosion indicate good engine, ignition and air/fuel mixture conditions. A plug with the proper heat range is being used. It may be serviced and returned to use.

Carbon-fouled

Soft, dry, sooty deposits covering the entire firing end of the plug are evidence of incomplete combustion. Even though the firing end of the plug is dry, the deposits decrease the plug's insulation. The carbon forms an electrical path that bypasses the electrodes resulting in a misfire condition. One or more of the following conditions can cause carbon fouling:

1. Air/fuel mixture too rich.
2. Spark plug heat range too cold.
3. Clogged air filter.
4. Improperly operating ignition component.
5. Ignition component failure.
6. Low engine compression.

7. Prolonged idling.

Oil-fouled

An oil fouled plug has a black insulator tip, a damp oily film over the firing end and a carbon layer over the entire nose. The electrodes are not worn. Common causes for this condition are:

1. Incorrect air/fuel mixture.
2. Low idle speed or prolonged idling.
3. Ignition component failure.
4. Spark plug heat range too cold.
5. Engine still being broken in.
6. Valve guides worn.
7. Piston rings worn or broken.

Oil fouled spark plugs may be cleaned in an emergency, but it is better to replace them. It is important to correct the cause of fouling before the engine is returned to service.

Gap bridging

Plugs with this condition have deposit buildup between the electrodes. The deposits reduce the gap and eventually close it entirely. If this condition is encountered, check for excessive carbon or oil in the combustion chamber. Be sure to locate and correct the cause of this condition.

Overheating

Badly worn electrodes and premature gap wear are signs of overheating, along with a gray or white blistered porcelain insulator surface. This condition is commonly caused by a spark plug with a heat range that is too hot. If you have not changed to a hotter spark plug and the plug is overheated, consider the following causes:

1. Lean air/fuel mixture.
2. Improperly operating ignition component.
3. Engine lubrication system malfunction.
4. Cooling system malfunction.
5. Engine air leak.
6. Improper spark plug installation (overtightening).
7. No spark plug gasket.

Worn out

Corrosive gases formed by combustion and high voltage sparks have eroded the electrodes. A spark plug in this condition requires more voltage to fire under hard acceleration. Install a new spark plug.

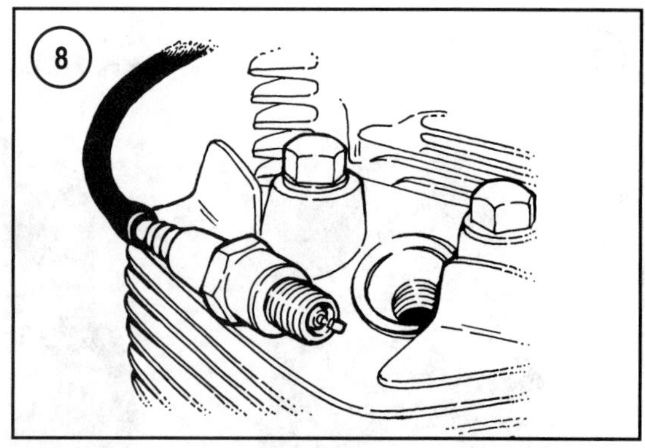

Preignition

If the electrodes are melted, preignition is almost certainly the cause. Check for carburetor mounting or intake manifold leaks and advanced ignition timing. The plug heat range may also be too hot. Find the cause of the preignition before returning the engine into service. For additional information on preignition, refer to Chapter Two.

ENGINE COMPRESSION TEST

An engine compression test is one of the quickest ways to check the condition of the rings, head gasket, piston and cylinder. Record the compression readings during each tune-up, and compare the current readings with those taken during earlier tune-ups. This will help you spot any developing problems.

Use a screw-in type compression gauge with a flexible adapter when performing this test. Check the rubber gasket on the end of the adapter before each use. This gasket seals the cylinder to ensure accurate compression readings.

1. Remove the lower, middle and front fairings as described in Chapter Fifteen.
2. Warm the engine to normal operating temperature.
3. Remove the spark plug. Insert the plug into the plug cap, and ground the plug against the cylinder head (**Figure 8**).
4. Install a compression gauge into the cylinder-head spark plug hole (**Figure 9**). Make sure the gauge is seated properly against the hole.

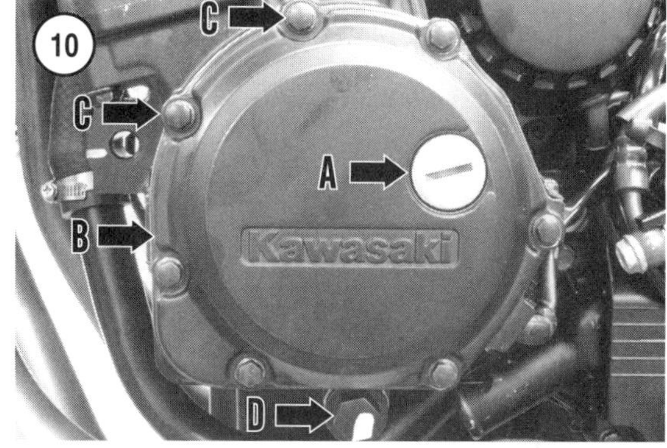

5. Turn the engine stop switch off.

NOTE
The battery must be fully charged or a false compression reading may be obtained. The engine must be turning at least 300 rpm.

6. Hold the throttle wide open and crank the engine with the starter for several revolutions until the gauge stabilizes at its highest reading. Record the pressure reading, and compare it to the compression specification (**Table 7**).
7. Remove the compression gauge and install it in the next cylinder. Repeat the test for each cylinder.
8. If the reading is higher than normal in one of the cylinders, there may be carbon buildup in the combustion chamber or on the piston crown. This condition can cause detonation and overheating. Service the piston as described in Chapter Five.
9. If a reading in a cylinder is low, allow the engine to cool, and then adjust the valves as described in this chapter.
   a. Warm up the engine to normal operating temperature, and perform another compression test. The problem has been corrected if the compression reading is within specification.
   b. If the reading is still low, this indicates a leaking cylinder head gasket, a leaking valve, or worn, stuck or broken piston rings. To determine which, pour about a teaspoon of engine oil through the spark plug hole onto the piston crown. Rotate the engine once to distribute the oil, then make another compression test and record the reading. If the compression increases significantly, the valves are good but the rings are worn or damaged. If compression does not increase, the valves or the cylinder head gasket is leaking. A valve could be hanging open or a piece of carbon could be on the valve seat.
10. Reinstall the spark plugs and the fairings.

3

IGNITION TIMING

The fully transistorized ignition system is not adjustable. However, periodically check the ignition timing to confirm that all ignition system components function correctly. If the ignition timing is incorrect, troubleshoot the ignition system as described in Chapter Two. Incorrect ignition timing can cause a drastic loss of engine performance and efficiency. It may also cause overheating.

Before starting this procedure, check all electrical connections and grounds in the ignition system circuit. They must be tight and free from corrosion.

WARNING
Do not start and run the motorcycle in an enclosed area. Exhaust gasses contain carbon monoxide; an odorless, colorless and tasteless poisonous gas. Carbon monoxide levels build quickly in a small, enclosed area. It can cause unconsciousness and death in a short time.

1. Remove the lower, middle and front fairings as described in Chapter Fifteen.
2. Start the engine and let it warm up for approximately 2-3 minutes.
3. Shut off the engine, and securely support the motorcycle on a level surface.
4. Remove the cap (A, **Figure 10**) from the timing inspection window in the pickup coil cover.

5. Connect a portable tachometer, following the manufacturer's instructions (the motorcycle's tachometer is not accurate enough in the low rpm range). Set the tachometer to the 0-2000 rpm range.
6. Connect a timing light to the No. 1 spark plug following the manufacturer's instructions.
7. Start the engine and let it idle at the engine speed listed in **Table 7**.
8. Aim the timing light at the inspection window, and pull the trigger. The F-mark on the timing rotor should align with the index mark on the crankcase (**Figure 11**).

NOTE
This engine uses two ignition coils. One coil fires the No. 1 and No. 4 cylinders; the other fires the No. 2 and No. 3 cylinders. Operation of the No. 2 and No. 3 cylinder coils can be checked by connecting a timing light to the No. 2 spark plug wire.

9. If the ignition timing is incorrect, troubleshoot the ignition system as described in Chapter Two. The ignition timing cannot be adjusted.
10. Turn the ignition switch off. Disconnect the timing light and tachometer.
11. Install the timing inspection cap. Lubricate a new O-ring with oil and tighten the cap securely.

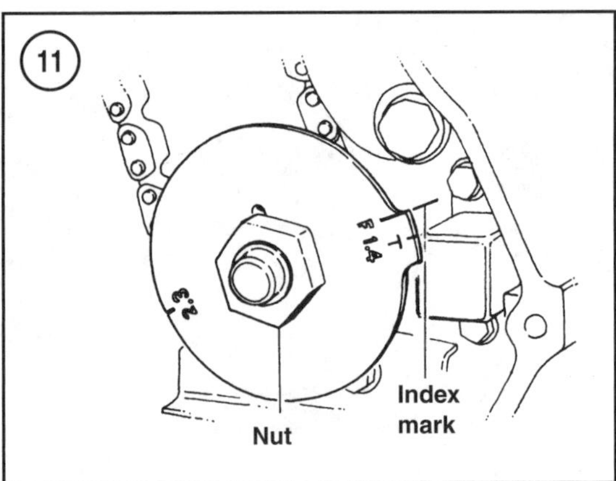

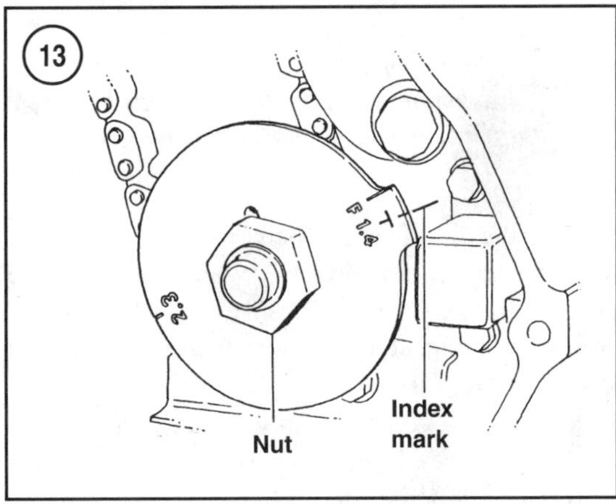

VALVE CLEARANCE

Measurement and Adjustment

Check and adjust the valve clearance while the engine is cold (below 35° C or 95° F).
1. Remove the lower, middle and front fairings as described in Chapter Fifteen.
2. Securely support the motorcycle on level ground.
3. Remove the cylinder head cover (Chapter Four).
4. Remove the spark plugs so the engine will turn easily.
5. Set an oil pan beneath the pickup coil cover, and remove the cover (B, **Figure 10**) from the left side.

NOTE
*The valves must be adjusted with the camshafts properly positioned. Examine the timing marks on the left side of the camshaft sprockets (**Figure 12**).*

6. Use the timing rotor nut (**Figure 13**) to rotate the engine counterclockwise until the No. 1.4 T-mark on the rotor aligns with the index mark on the crankcase.
7. Check the timing marks on the camshaft sprockets (**Figure 12**). They should be positioned at 9 o'clock (EX) and 3 o'clock (IN) as shown in **Figure 14**. If not, rotate the crankshaft one full turn coun-

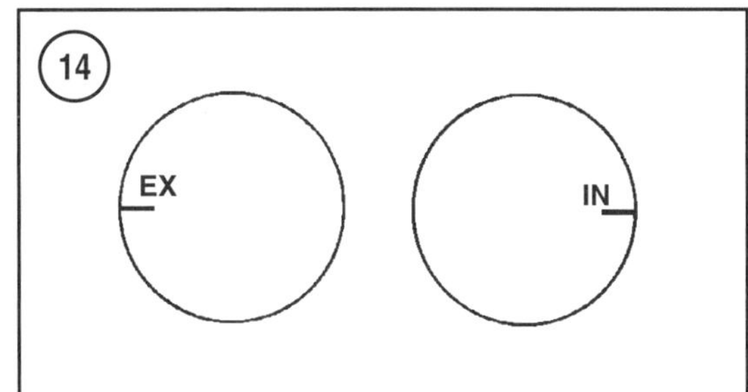

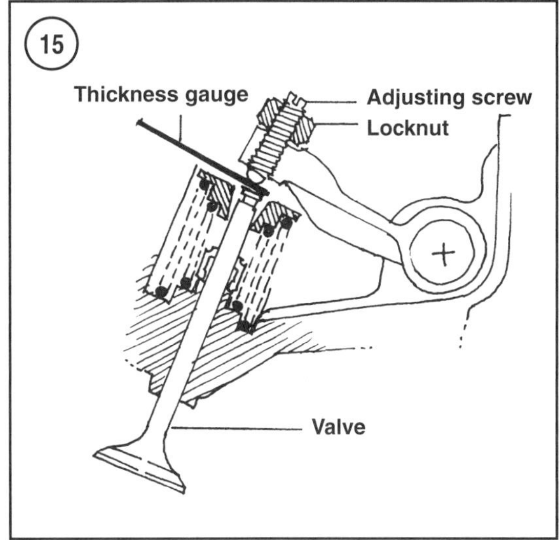

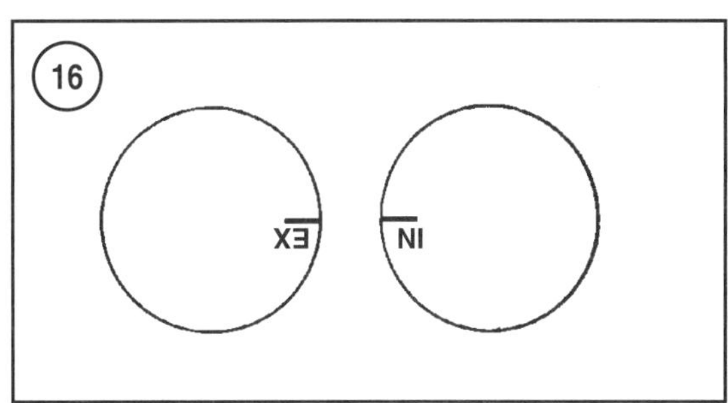

terclockwise. The No. 1.4 T-mark on the rotor should align with the index mark (**Figure 13**) and the timing marks on the camshaft sprockets should appear as shown in **Figure 14**. The No. 4 cylinder is now set to top dead center on the compression stroke.

8. Insert a thickness gauge between the adjusting screw and the valve stem (**Figure 15**), and check the clearance of the following valves:

   a. No. 2 cylinder intake valves.

   b. No. 3 cylinder exhaust valves.

   c. No. 4 cylinder intake and exhaust valves.

9. If any clearance is outside the range specified in **Table 7**, adjust the clearance by performing the following:

   a. Loosen the adjuster locknut.

   b. Turn the adjusting screw until the valve clearance is within the specified range.

   c. Hold the adjusting screw, and tighten the locknut to 25 N•m (18 ft.-lbs.).

   d. Recheck the valve clearance.

10. Rotate the crankshaft one turn counterclockwise until the No. 1.4 T-mark again aligns with the index mark on the crankcase (**Figure 13**). Check the timing marks on the camshaft sprockets. The EX mark should be at 3 o'clock and the IN mark at 9 o'clock. See **Figure 16**. The No. 1 cylinder is now set to top dead center on the compression stroke.

11. Check the valve clearance (**Figure 15**) of the following valves:

   a. No. 1 cylinder intake and exhaust valves.

   b. No. 2 cylinder exhaust valves.

   c. No. 3 cylinder intake valves.

12. If any clearance is outside the range specified in **Table 7**, adjust the clearance as described in Step 9.

13. Install the pickup coil cover (B, **Figure 10**) by performing the following:

   a. Apply silicon sealant to the pickup coil grommet (A, **Figure 17**) in the crankcase and to the crankcase where the two case halves mate (B).

   b. Fit the pickup coil cover into place on the crankcase.

   c. Apply Loctite 242 to the threads of the two indicated cover bolts (C, **Figure 10**), and torque the cover bolts to 9.8 N•m (87 in.-lb.).

3

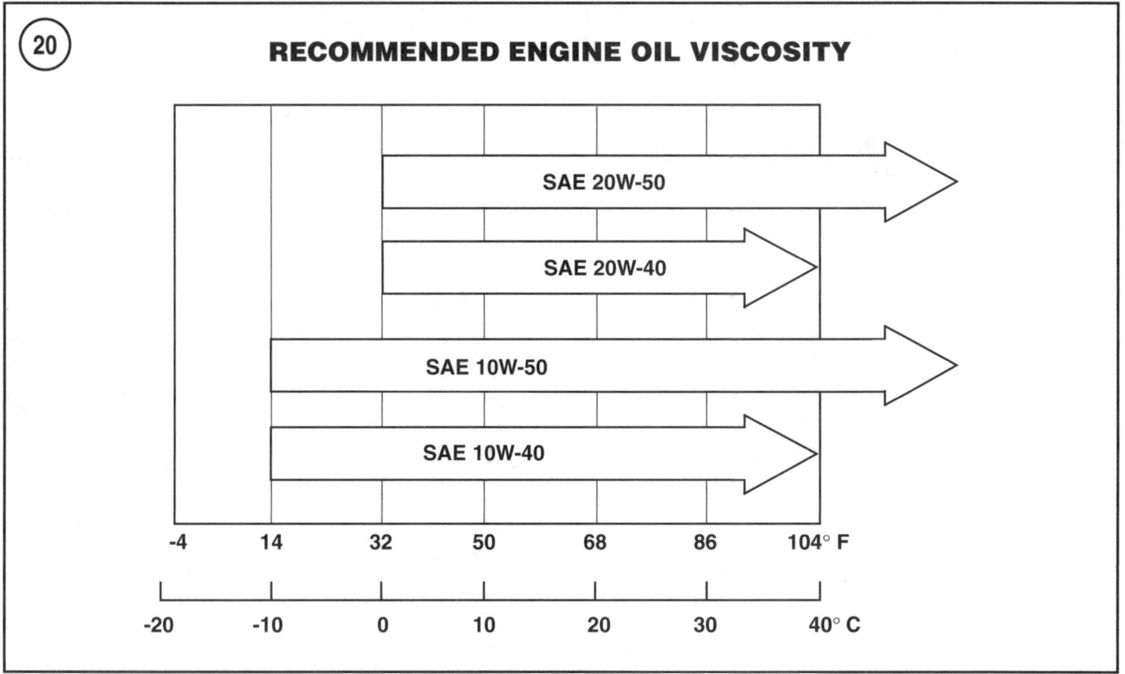

ENGINE OIL AND FILTER

Engine Oil Level Check

Check the engine oil level at the oil inspection window (**Figure 18**) on the left side of the crankcase.

1. Move the motorcycle to a level surface and support it on the centerstand.
2. Run the engine until it reaches operating temperature.
3. Turn the engine off, and let the oil settle.

CAUTION
Do not check the oil level with the motorcycle on its sidestand. This produces an inaccurate reading.

4. The oil level should be between the upper and lower level lines on the oil inspection window (**Figure 18**).
5. Remove the oil filler cap (**Figure 19**), and add the recommended oil (**Table 4**) until the oil level rises to the upper level line on the oil inspection window. Add oil slowly to avoid overfilling.
6. Inspect the O-ring on the oil filler cap. Replace the O-ring if it is torn, deteriorated or brittle.
7. Install the oil filler cap, and tighten it securely.
8. Recheck the oil level. Adjust it as necessary.

Engine Oil and Filter Change

Regular oil and filter changes contribute more to engine longevity than any other maintenance ser-

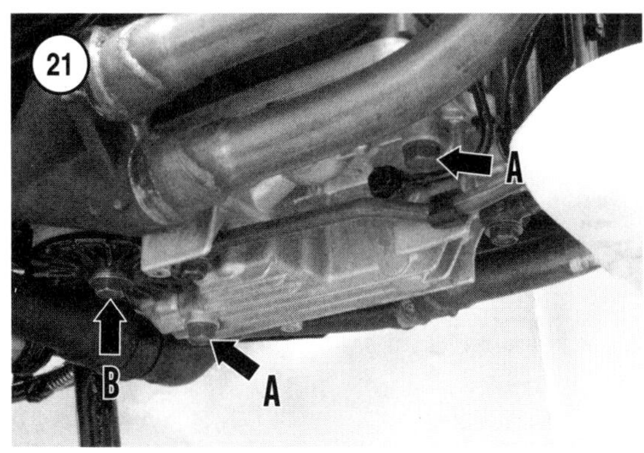

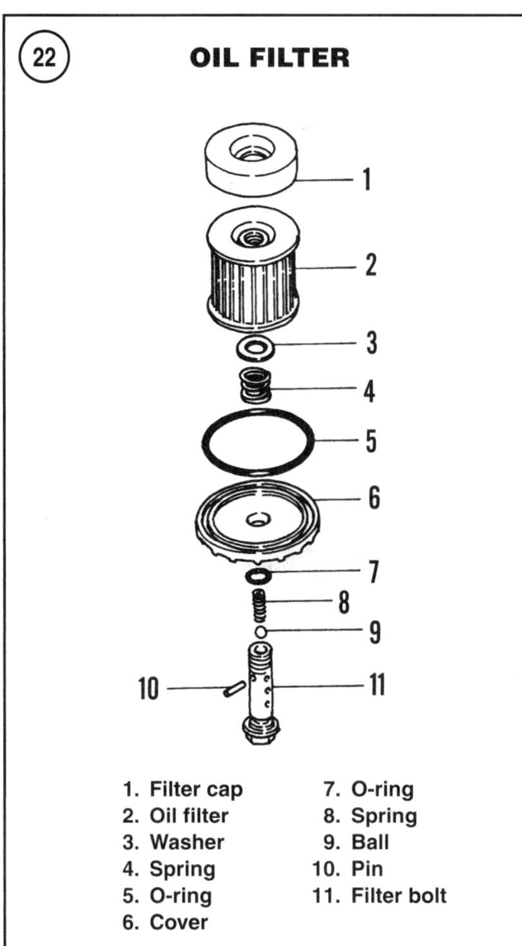

1. Filter cap
2. Oil filter
3. Washer
4. Spring
5. O-ring
6. Cover
7. O-ring
8. Spring
9. Ball
10. Pin
11. Filter bolt

vice. The recommended oil and filter change interval is listed in **Table 1**. This recommendation assumes that the motorcycle is operated in moderate climates. If the motorcycle is operated under dusty conditions, the oil becomes dirty more quickly. Consequently, it should be changed more frequently than recommended.

Use only a quality engine oil with an API classification of SE, SF or SG. Always try to use the same brand of oil. Refer to **Figure 20** when selecting an oil. Note that the temperature in the chart refers to ambient air temperature (not engine oil temperature).

CAUTION

Do not use engine oils labeled energy conserving. These oils contain friction modifiers specifically designed for automobile engines. When used in motorcycle engines, these oils may cause clutch plate slipping and deterioration, starter clutch slipping, and pitting on transmission gears.

1. Remove the lower fairing as described in Chapter Fifteen.
2. Securely support the motorcycle on a level surface.
3. Start the engine and let it warm up for approximately 2-3 minutes. Shut the engine off.
4. Loosen the oil filler cap (**Figure 19**). This speeds up the flow of oil.
5. Drain the oil by performing the following:
   a. Place a drain pan under one of the two oil drain bolts (A, **Figure 21**).
   b. Remove the oil drain bolt (A, **Figure 21**) and its gasket from the bottom of the oil pan.
   c. Allow the oil to completely drain.
   d. Inspect the drain bolt gasket for damage. Replace a gasket if necessary. Install the oil drain bolt, and tighten it securely.
   e. Move the oil pan beneath the other drain bolt, and repeat substeps a through d.
6. Inspect the condition of the drained oil for contamination.
7. Replace the oil filter (**Figure 22**), by performing the following:

CAUTION

*The oil filter bolt (B, **Figure 21**) is made of a soft material. Only use a socket or box end wrench on this bolt.*

   a. Remove the oil filter bolt (B, **Figure 21**), and lower the oil filter assembly (**Figure 23**) from the oil pan.
   b. Remove the filter cap (A, **Figure 24**) from the oil filter (B).

c. Hold the filter, and turn the mounting bolt to remove the filter.
d. Remove the washer (A, **Figure 25**) and spring (B) from the oil filter bolt. Discard the filter.
e. Pull the oil filter bolt (C, **Figure 25**) from the cover.
f. Inspect the oil filter cover O-ring (D, **Figure 25**) and the oil filter bolt O-ring (7, **Figure 22**). Replace both O-rings if either is brittle, cracked, deformed or if the oil filter leaked. To ease installation, apply grease to the new O-rings.
g. Clean all oil residue from the oil filter cover and cap.
h. Clean the oil filter bolt in solvent, and check the operation of the bypass valve in the bolt. Inspect the bolt, bypass valve and the bolt head. Replace the bolt as necessary.

NOTE
To remove the bypass valve, drive the retaining pin from the oil filter bolt. Remove the spring and bypass valve ball. Replace as necessary.

i. Assemble the oil filter by reversing the disassembly procedure. Lightly grease the rubber washer on each side of the new oil filter.

8. Thoroughly clean the oil-filter sealing surface on the crankcase. This surface must be clean to achieve a good seal with the oil filter cover.
9. Set the oil filter assembly in the oil pan, and torque the oil filter bolt (**Figure 26**) to 20 N•m (15 ft.-lb.).
10. Insert a funnel into the oil filler hole and add the quantity of oil specified in **Table 4**.
11. Remove the funnel and screw in the oil filler cap (**Figure 19**) securely.
12. Start the engine, and let it idle.
13. Check the oil filter bolt, cover and drain bolts for leaks. Tighten either if necessary.
14. Turn off the engine, and check the engine oil level as described in this section.
15. Reinstall the lower fairing (Chapter Fifteen).

NOTE
Never dispose of engine oil in the trash, on the ground or down a storm drain. Many service stations and oil retainers accept used oil for recycling. Do not combine other fluids with engine oil for recycling. To locate a recycler, contact the American Petroleum Institute (API) at www.recycleoil.org.

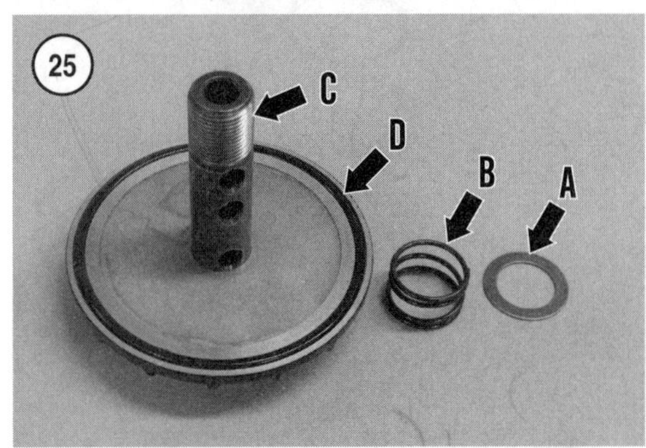

Engine Oil Screen

Refer to *Oil Pump* and *Oil Pan* in Chapter Five for information on removing and inspecting the oil sump screens.

Engine Oil Pressure Test

Check the oil pressure after installing a new oil pump, reassembling the engine or when troubleshooting the lubrication system.

The Kawasaki oil pressure gauge (part No. 57001-164) and adapter (part No. 57001-1188) or equivalents are required to test the pressure.

1. Start the engine and let it warm up to normal operating temperature [90° C (194° F)]. The engine must be at operating temperature for accurate results.
2. Shut off the engine.
3. Securely support the motorcycle on a level surface.

CAUTION
Hot oil will drain from the crankcase when the plug is removed. Take the necessary precautions so you will not be burned.

4. Remove the plug (D, **Figure 10**) from the test port beneath the pickup coil cover.
5. Install the adapter into the test port, and connect the oil pressure gauge to the adapter.
6. Start the engine. Run the engine at 4000 rpm and read the gauge.
7. If the engine oil pressure is significantly less than the value specified in **Table 8**, inspect the oil pump and relief valve. If these components are not the source of the problem, check the remainder of the lubrication system.

3

CLUTCH

The clutch is hydraulically operated and does not require routine adjustment.

Clutch Fluid Level Check

Check the hydraulic fluid in the clutch master cylinder at the interval specified in **Table 1** or whenever the fluid level drops. Refer to Chapter six for clutch bleeding and service.

CAUTION
If the clutch operates correctly in cool weather or when the engine is cold but it operates erratically (or not at all) in hot weather or after the engine warms, air has entered the system. Bleed the clutch as described in Chapter Six.

1. Securely support the motorcycle in an upright position on level ground.
2. Turn the handlebar so the clutch master cylinder is level.
3. The brake fluid in the inspection window (**Figure 27**) must be above the lower level mark on the reservoir.

NOTE
If the reservoir is empty, air has entered the system. Bleed the clutch as described in Chapter Six.

4. If the fluid level is at or below the lower level line, add brake fluid by performing the following:
   a. Wipe off the master cylinder cover.
   b. Remove the cover screws, reservoir cap, diaphragm plate (1992-on models) and diaphragm.
   c. Add fresh DOT 4 brake fluid until the fluid level rises to the upper level line in the reservoir.

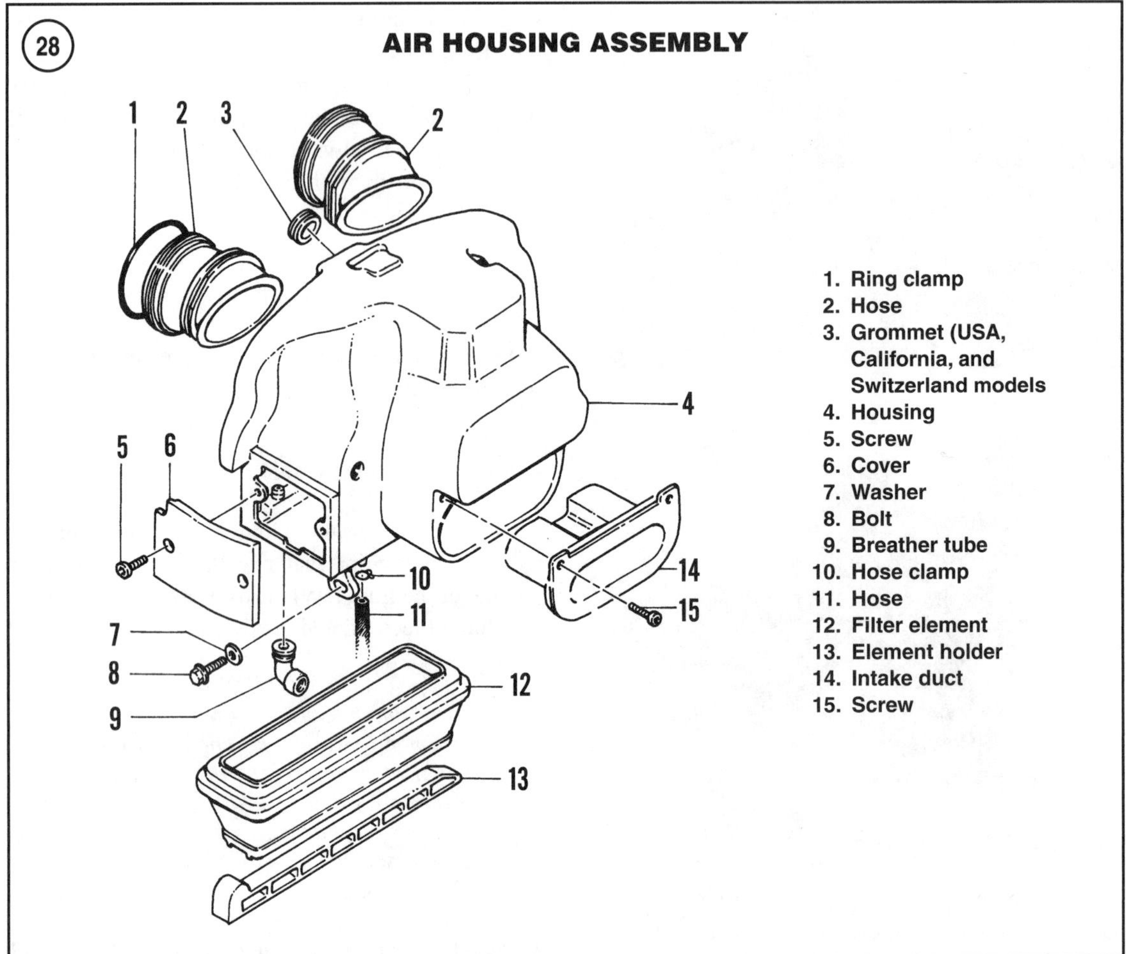

d. Install the diaphragm, diaphragm plate and reservoir cap. Tighten the cap screws securely.

Clutch Hydraulic Line Inspection

Check the clutch line between the master cylinder and the clutch slave cylinder. If any leaks are found, tighten the connections and bleed the clutch as described in Chapter Six. If this does not stop the leak or if the clutch line is obviously damaged, cracked or chafed, replace the clutch line and bleed the system.

Clutch Lever Adjustment

The distance between the clutch lever and the handlebar grip can be adjusted to suit rider preference. Position 1 sets the lever to the maximum distance from the grip; position 4 is the closest.

1. Turn the adjuster on the clutch lever and align a number with the arrow on the lever.

2. Check the operation of the clutch. Make sure the clutch disengages when the lever is pulled toward the handlebar grip.

AIR FILTER

Replacement

The air filter removes dust and abrasive particles from the air before it enters the carburetors and engine. If the filter is torn or damaged, very fine particles can enter the engine, cause rapid wear of the piston rings, cylinder and bearings and clog the small passages in the carburetor. A clogged air fil-

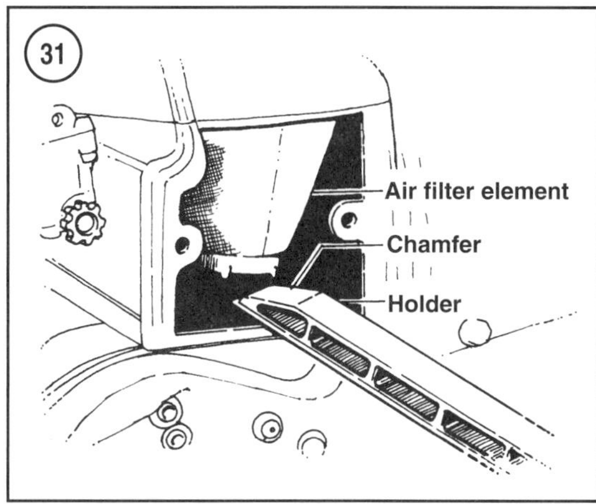

ter, on the other hand, decreases the efficiency and life of an engine.

Never run the motorcycle without the air filter element installed. Replace the air filter at the intervals specified in **Table 1**.

Refer to **Figure 28**.

1. Remove the left side cover (Chapter Fifteen).
2. Remove the cover screws (A, **Figure 29**), and remove the cover (B) from the air filter housing.
3. Pull the element holder (A, **Figure 30**) from the housing, and then slide out the air filter (B).
4. Inspect the air filter element for tears or other damage that would admit unfiltered air into the engine. Check the element's sponge gasket for tears. Replace the element as necessary.
5. Clean the element by performing the following:
   a. Lower the element into a high-flashpoint solvent bath so that only the outside of the element soaks in the solvent. Do not let the dirty solvent touch the inside of the element. This will contaminate the element.
   b. Once the outer side of the element is clean, pour clean solvent into the inside of the element and let it drain.
   c. Dry the element by directing compressed air to the inside of the element. If compressed air is not available, let the element drip dry.
   d. Saturate a clean, lint-free cloth with SAE-30 weight oil. Apply oil to the outside of the element by tapping the cloth against the element. Set the element on clean newspapers to soak up any excess oil.
6. Install the air filter element into the housing without the holder, and press the element up against the filter housing. (**Figure 31**).
7. Slide the element holder along the rim of the filter. The chamfered side of the holder must face up.
8. Install the air filter housing cover (B, **Figure 29**) and the left side cover.

CARBURETOR

Idle Speed Adjustment

Before adjusting the idle speed, clean the air filter element and check engine compression as described in this chapter. The idle speed cannot be properly set unless the filter is clean and the engine has adequate compression.

1. Make sure the throttle cable free play is adjusted correctly. Adjust free play if necessary as described in this chapter.

NOTE
The engine must be at normal operating temperature for accurate idle speed adjustment.

2. Start the engine and let it warm up to normal operating temperature. Make sure the choke lever is in the off position (all the way forward).
3. Turn the idle speed knob (C, **Figure 29**) in or out and adjust the idle speed to the specification in **Table 7**.
4. Open and close the throttle a couple of times. Check for variations in idle speed, and readjust if necessary.

WARNING
With the engine running at idle speed, move the handlebar from side to side. If idle speed increases during this movement, the throttle cable needs adjusting or may be incorrectly routed through the frame. Correct this problem immediately. Do not ride the motorcycle in this unsafe condition.

Pilot Screw Adjustment

The pilot screw (idle mixture screw) is pre-set and should not be reset. Do not adjust the pilot screws unless the carburetors have been overhauled. If so, refer to *Carburetor* in Chapter Eight.

Carburetor Synchronization

This procedure equalizes the vacuum at each intake port so the same air/fuel mixture is delivered to each cylinder. When the carburetors are not synchronized, the engine idles roughly, accelerates poorly and operates with reduced fuel economy.

Various synchronization tools are available. Some measure engine vacuum with a vacuum gauge or by the movement of mercury within a glass tube (**Figure 32**). Others perform the function electronically. The only way to accurately synchronize the carburetor is to measure the vacuum of all four carburetors at the same time.

Prior to synchronizing the carburetors, clean the air filter element and adjust the valve clearance. Also check the ignition timing to assure the ignition system is operating properly.

1. Remove the lower and middle fairings as described in Chapter Fifteen.
2. Start the engine and let it reach normal operating temperature.
3. Adjust the idle speed as described in this section, then shut off the engine.

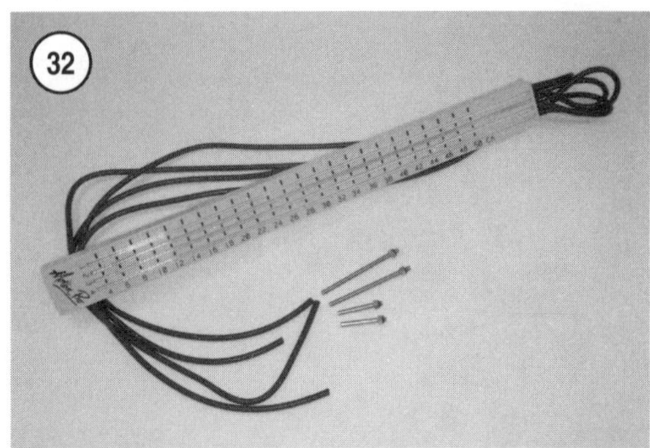
32

33

4. Balance the vacuum gauge set following the manufacturer's instructions.
5. Remove the fuel tank, and attach an auxiliary tank to the carburetors.
6. Following the gauge manufacturer's instructions, connect the vacuum gauge to the vacuum fitting on each carburetor (A, **Figure 33**).
7. Start the engine and let it idle at the specified idle speed. If necessary, turn the idle speed knob (C, **Figure 29**) to set the idle speed.
8. The carburetors are correctly balanced if the vacuum gauge readings are the same or if the difference between any two carburetors is less than 2.7 kPa (0.787 in. Hg).
9. The carb assembly has three carburetor adjuster screws (**Figure 34**). If the carburetors require adjusting perform the following:
   a. Turn the screw on the left side (B, **Figure 33**) to synchronize carburetor No. 1 to carburetor No. 2.
   b. Use the screw on the right side to synchronize carburetor No. 3 to No. 4.

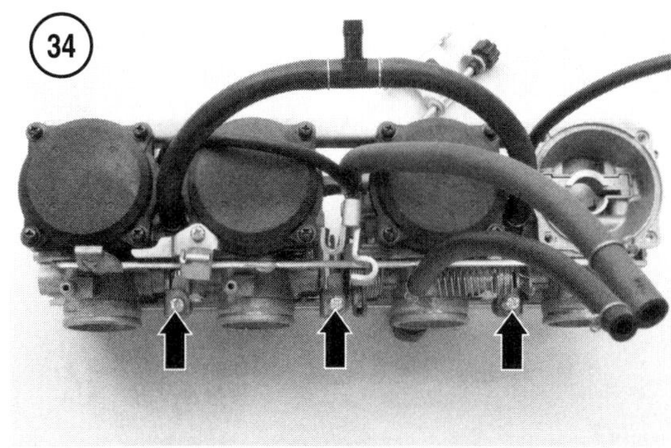

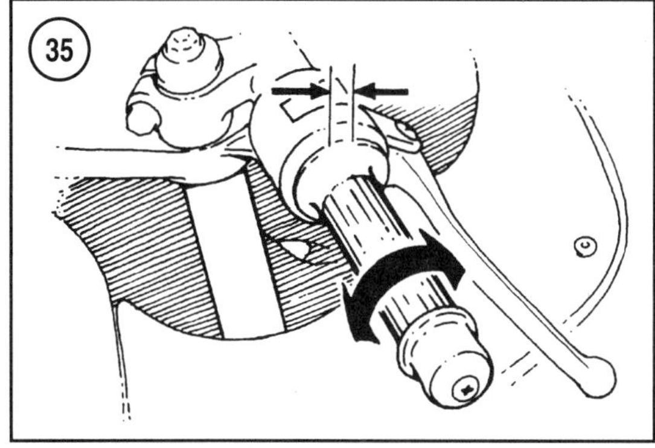

c. Turn the center screw to synchronize the left pair or carburetors (No. 1 and No. 2) to the right pair (No. 3 and No. 4).

10. Shut off the engine.

11. Remove the vacuum gauge, and reconnect the vacuum hoses to their respective fittings. Make sure they are properly seated to avoid vacuum leak.

12. Restart the engine and reset the engine idle speed to the value specified in **Table 7**, if necessary.

13. Shut off the engine.

Fuel Line Inspection

Inspect the fuel lines at the interval specified in **Table 1**. Check all fuel hoses from the fuel tank to the carburetor assembly. Replace any hose that is cracked, brittle or starting to deteriorate. Make sure the hose clamps are in place and secure.

WARNING
A damaged or deteriorated fuel line presents a dangerous fire hazard. Fuel could spill onto the hot engine or exhaust pipe.

Fuel Valve/Filter

Remove and drain the fuel tank. Remove the fuel shutoff valve and clean it of all dirt and debris. Replace worn of damaged O-rings and gaskets as described in Chapter Eight.

THROTTLE CABLE

Check the throttle operation at the interval indicated in **Table 1**. Operate the throttle grip. Check for smooth throttle operation from fully closed to fully open, then back to the fully closed position. The throttle should automatically return to the fully closed position without any hesitation.

Check the throttle cables for damage, wear or deterioration. Make sure the cables are not kinked at any place.

If the throttle does not return to the fully closed position smoothly and if the exterior of the cable sheaths appears to be in good condition, lubricate the throttle cables as described in this chapter.

If cable lubrication does not solve the problem, the throttle cables must be replaced as described in Chapter Eight.

Free Play Inspection/Adjustment

Check the throttle cables from the throttle grip to the carburetors. Make sure they are not kinked or chafed. Replace the cables if necessary.

Make sure the throttle grip rotates smoothly from fully closed to fully open. Check free play with the handlebars at the center, full-left, and full-right steering positions.

1. Shift the transmission into neutral.
2. Start the engine and let it idle.
3. While the engine idles, slowly twist the throttle to raise engine speed. Note the amount of throttle-grip rotational movement (**Figure 35**) required to raise the engine speed off idle. This amount of movement is the throttle cable free play.
4. If throttle cable free play is outside the range specified in **Table 8**, proceed to Step 5 and adjust the free play.

NOTE
Before adjusting the throttle cable free play, check and adjust engine idle speed and carburetor synchroniza-

3

tion. Both must be within specification.

5. At the throttle grip, loosen the pull cable adjuster locknut (A, **Figure 36**).

6. Turn the adjuster (B, **Figure 36**) in either direction until the throttle cable free play is within the range specified in **Table 8**.

7. If the correct amount of free play cannot be achieved at the handlebar, adjust the free play at the carburetor by performing the following:

  a. Remove the fuel tank as described in Chapter Eight.

  b. Loosen the two locknuts (A, **Figure 37**) on the pull cable (B), and loosen the two locknuts on the return cable (C).

  c. Turn the pull cable adjuster (B, **Figure 37**) and the return cable adjuster (C) completely into carburetor bracket. This increases free play to its maximum.

  d. Make sure the throttle grip is completely closed, and turn out the return cable adjuster (C, **Figure 37**) until the inner cable becomes tight. Tighten the return cable locknuts.

  e. Turn out the pull cable adjuster (B, **Figure 37**) until the free play at the throttle grip is within specification. Tighten the pull cable locknuts (A, **Figure 37**).

8. Operate the throttle grip several times, and then check the throttle linkage at the carburetor throttle wheel. It should rest against the throttle stop when the throttle grip is closed.

9. Start the engine and let it idle in neutral. Listen to the engine speed as you turn the handlebar from steering lock to steering lock. If idle speed changes as you turn the handlebar, the throttle cable is routed incorrectly or there is insufficient cable free play. Make the necessary corrections.

CHOKE CABLE

Inspect the choke cable at both ends for fraying or other damage. Operate the choke lever. It should move smoothly between its fully open and fully closed positions. If the choke lever movement is not smooth, lubricate the choke cable as described in this chapter, check the cable for kinks or damage, and check the choke lever for damage.

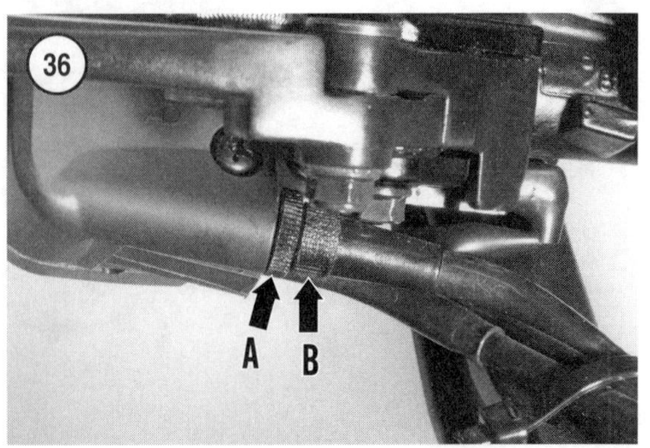

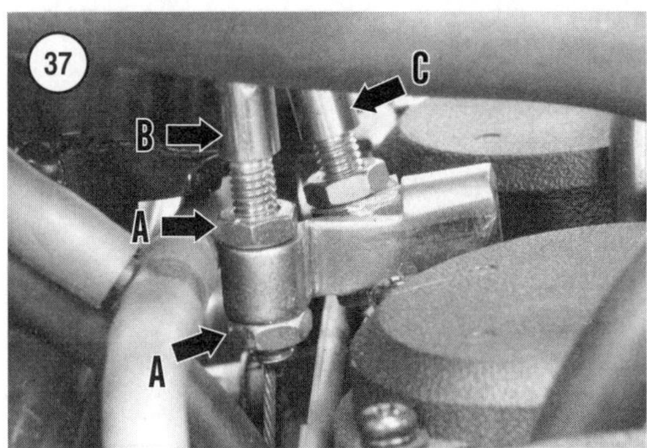

Free Play Inspection/Adjustment

1. Remove the fuel tank as described in Chapter Eight.

2. Push the choke lever (**Figure 38**) to its fully off position.

3. Operate the choke lever while watching the choke plate (**Figure 39**) on the carburetor.

4. Choke cable free play is measured at the choke lever. It equals the distance the choke lever (**Figure 38**) moves until the choke plate begins to act on the starter plunger.

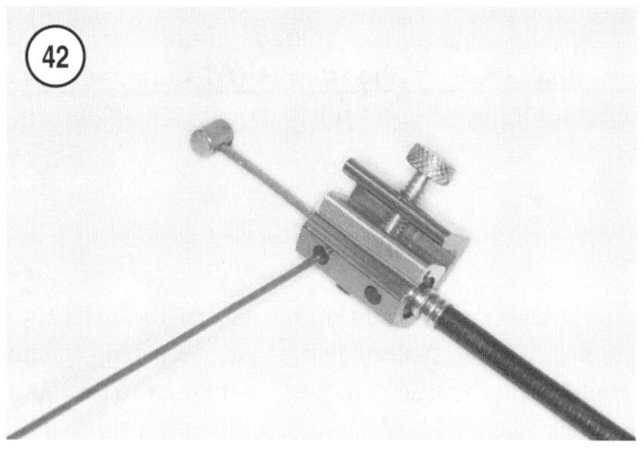

5. If this distance is outside the range specified in **Table 8**. Adjust the free play by performing the following:

   a. Loosen the choke adjuster locknut (A, **Figure 40**) on the left side of the frame.
   b. Turn the choke cable adjuster (B, **Figure 40**) until the choke cable free play is within specification, then tighten the locknut securely.

6. If the free play cannot be adjusted at the adjuster, turn to the carburetor. Loosen the locknut (**Figure 41**) on the cable holder. Reposition the choke cable in the holder and tighten the locknut. Recheck the free play.

CONTROL CABLE LUBRICATION

Clean and lubricate the throttle and choke cables at the intervals indicated in **Table 1**. In addition, check the cables for kinks and signs of wear, damage or fraying that could cause the cables to fail or stick.

The most positive means of control cable lubrication involves the use of a cable lubricator like the one shown in **Figure 42**. A can of cable lube or an aerosol general lubricant is required. Do *not* use chain lube as a cable lubricant.

CAUTION

If the original equipment cables have been replaced with nylon-lined cables, do not lubricate them as described. Nylon-lined cables are generally used dry. Oil and most cable lubricants will cause liner expansion, pinching the liner against the cable. When servicing nylon-lined and other aftermarket cables, follow the cable manufacturer's instructions.

1A. Disconnect the throttle cable at both ends as described in *Throttle Cable Replacement* in Chapter Eight.

1B. Disconnect the choke cable at both ends as described in *Choke Cable Replacement* in Chapter Eight.

2. Attach a cable lubricator to the end of the cable following the manufacturer's instructions.

NOTE

If lubricant does not flow out the opposite end, check the cable for fraying, bending or other damage.

3

Attempt to lubricate the cable from the opposite end.

3. Insert the lubricant can nozzle into the lubricator. Press and hold the button on the can until the lubricant begins to flow out of the other end of the cable. Place a shop cloth at the opposite end of the cable to catch excess lubricant that flows from the end.
4. Remove the lubricator and wipe excess lubricant from the cable.
5. Dab a bit of grease onto the cable ends before reconnecting them. Reconnect the cable(s), and adjust them as described in this chapter.

6A. After lubricating the throttle cables, operate the throttle at the handlebar. It should open and close smoothly with no binding.

6B. After lubricating the choke cable, operate the choke lever at the handlebar. It should open and close smoothly with no binding.

7. Adjust the throttle or choke cable as described in this chapter.

GENERAL LUBRICATION

Lubricate these items at the service interval indicated in **Table 1** or whenever the motorcycle has been operated in wet or rainy conditions or after cleaning the motorcycle with a high pressure spray. Remove any old grease and clean off dirt, rust or other contaminants before applying the indicated lubricant.

1. Use engine oil to lubricate the following:
   a. Centerstand.
   b. Sidestand.
   c. Clutch and brake levers.
   d. Rear brake pedal.
   e. Rear brake clevis pin.
   f. Shift pedal and linkage.
2. Lubricate the following items with grease:
   a. Throttle cable ends.
   b. Choke cable end.
   c. Speedometer inner cable (lower end).

EMISSION CONTROL SYSTEM

Inspection

The emission control system includes a crankcase breather system, an evaporative emission control system and a secondary air system. The evaporative emission control system captures fuel vapors and stores them in the charcoal canister so they will not be released into the atmosphere. The secondary air system introduces fresh air into the exhaust ports to reduce exhaust emission levels.

All models sold in California are equipped with an evaporative emission control system. A secondary air system is used on all California models, 1988-on U.S. and Switzerland models, and on 1997-on German models. Inspect these systems at the interval specified in **Table 1**. Check all hoses for cracks, deterioration or loose connections and check the charcoal canister for damage. The vacuum hose routing diagram and emission control information appear on labels on the rear fender. Refer to these labels and to the appropriate section of Chapter Eight for additional information.

Crankcase Breather Inspection

The crankcase breather cover (**Figure 43**) routes blow by gasses from the crankcase to the air filter housing. From here, the gasses are drawn into the combustion chamber and burned with the incoming air/fuel mixture.

Visually inspect the crankcase breather. Make sure the elbow on the air box (A, **Figure 44**) securely connects to the fitting (B) on the crankcase breather cover.

BATTERY

The battery is an important part of the motorcycle's electrical system, yet most electrical system troubles can be traced to battery neglect. Clean and inspect the battery at periodic intervals. The

Concours is equipped with a lead-acid battery. The electrolyte level in the battery must be checked regularly. During hot weather periods, check the electrolyte level more frequently.

Normal motorcycle vibration can seriously shorten the life of the battery. The tool box also serves as the battery hold down. Make sure the tool box is securely fastened as described in Chapter Fifteen.

On all models covered in this manual, the negative side is grounded. When removing the battery, disconnect the negative (–) cable first, then disconnect the positive (+) cable. This minimizes the chance of a tool shorting to ground when the battery positive cable is disconnected.

NOTE
The battery's lead plates and the plastic case can be recycled. Most motorcycle dealers will accept your old battery in trade when you purchase a new one. Never place an old battery in your household trash. In most states, it is illegal to place any acid or lead (heavy metal) contents in landfills.

Safety Precautions

Note the following precautions:

1. When working with batteries, use extreme care to avoid spilling or splashing the electrolyte. This solution contains sulfuric acid, which can ruin clothing and cause serious chemical burns. If any electrolyte is spilled or splashed on your clothing or skin, immediately neutralize it with a solution of baking soda and water, then flush with an abundance of clean water.

WARNING
Electrolyte splashed into the eyes is extremely harmful. Always wear safety glasses while working with batteries. If you get electrolyte in your eyes, force your eyes open and flood them with cool, clean water for approximately 15 minutes and seek medical attention.

CAUTION
Always remove the battery from the motorcycle before connecting charging equipment. If a battery is left connected to the motorcycle, the charger may damage the diodes within the rectifier.

2. While batteries are being charged, highly explosive hydrogen gas forms in each cell. Some of this gas escapes through filler cap openings and may form an explosive atmosphere in and around the battery. This condition can persist for several hours. Sparks, an open flame or a lit cigarette can ignite the gas, causing an explosion and possible serious personal injury. Note the following precautions to prevent an explosion:
   a. Do not smoke or permit any open flame (including gas-appliance pilot lights) near a battery being charged or one that has been recently charged.
   b. Do not disconnect live circuits at battery terminals since a spark usually occurs when a live circuit is broken.
   c. Use caution when connecting or disconnecting any battery charger. Be sure its power switch is off before making or breaking connections. Poor connections are a common cause of electrical arcs, which can cause explosions. Keep children and pets away from charging equipment and batteries.

Removal/Installation

1. Remove the seat and tool box as described in Chapter Fifteen.
2. Disconnect the electrical cable from the negative battery terminal (A, **Figure 45**).
3. Move the negative cable out of the way so it will not accidentally contact the battery negative terminal.

4. Pull back the boot and disconnect the electrical cable from the positive battery terminal (B, **Figure 45**).
5. Installation is the reverse of removal. Pay attention to the following:
   a. Apply dielectric grease to each battery terminal.
   b. Connect the positive cable first, then connect the negative cable.
   c. Tighten each terminal mounting screw securely.
   d. Route the breather hose along the same path noted during removal.

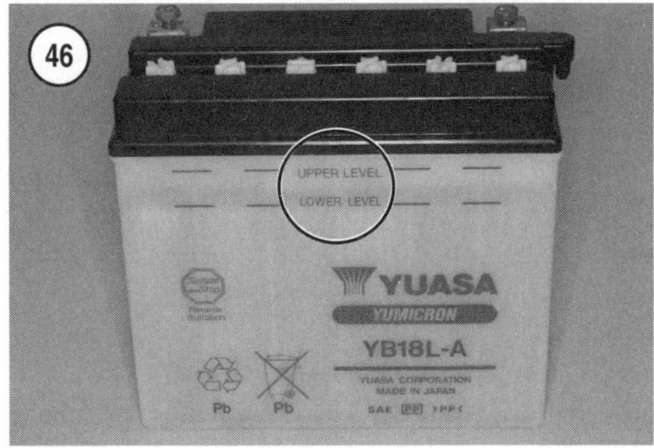

Inspection

1. Inspect the battery box for contamination or damage. Clean the box with a solution of baking soda and water.
2. Check the entire battery case for cracks or other damage. If the battery case is warped, discolored or has a raised top, the battery has overcharged or overheated.
3. Check the back of the tool box for acid damage, cracks or other wear. Replace if damaged.
4. Check the battery terminal bolts, spacers and nuts for corrosion or damage. Clean parts thoroughly with a solution of baking soda and water. Replace severely corroded or damaged parts.

CAUTION
Keep cleaning solution out of the battery cells or the electrolyte level will be seriously weakened.

5. Clean the top of the battery with a stiff bristle brush, using a baking soda and water solution.
6. Check the battery cable terminals for corrosion and damage. If corrosion is minor, clean the battery cables with a stiff wire brush. Replace severely worn or damaged cables.

CAUTION
Do not overfill the battery cells in Step 7. The electrolyte expands due to heat from charging and will overflow if the level is above the upper level line.

7. Visually inspect the electrolyte level in each cell. The fluid level should be between the upper- and lower-level lines on the battery case (**Figure 46**). If necessary, remove the caps and add distilled water to bring the level within the upper- and lower-level lines.

Testing

Hydrometer testing is the best way to check the condition of a lead-acid battery. Use a hydrometer with numbered graduations from 1.100 to 1.300 rather than one with just color-coded bands. To use the hydrometer, squeeze the rubber ball, insert the tip into the cell and release the ball (**Figure 47**).

NOTE
Do not attempt to test a battery with a hydrometer immediately after adding water to the cells. Charge the battery for 15-20 minutes at a rate high enough to cause vigorous gassing and allow the water and electrolyte to mix thoroughly.

Draw enough electrolyte to float the weighted float inside the hydrometer. When using a tempera-

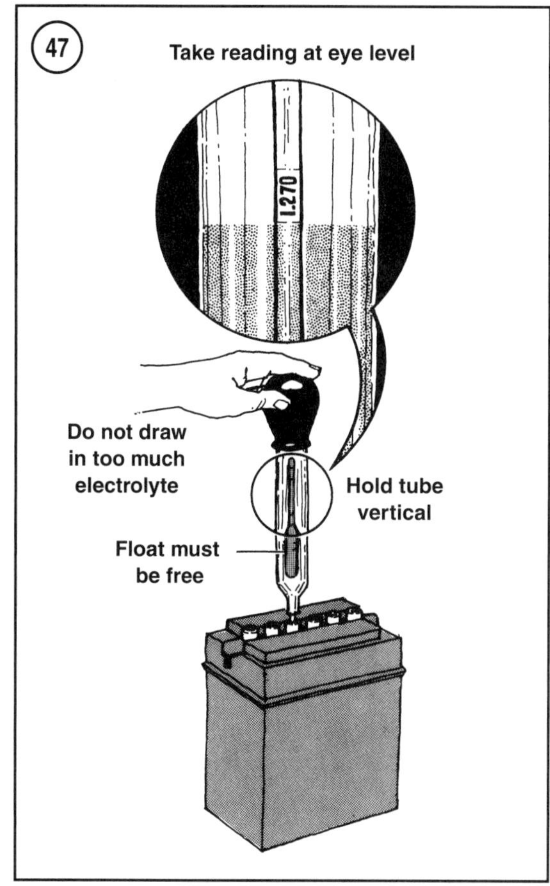

ture-compensated hydrometer, release the electrolyte and repeat this process several times to make sure the thermometer has adjusted to the electrolyte temperature before taking the reading.

Hold the hydrometer vertically and note the number aligned with the surface of the electrolyte (**Figure 47**). This is the specific gravity for this cell. Return the electrolyte to the cell it came from. The specific gravity of the electrolyte in each battery cell is an excellent indication of that cell's condition (**Table 6**). A fully charged cell will read 1.260-1.280. A specific gravity below 1.230 indicated that the battery should be charged. Charging is also necessary if any two cells vary by more than 0.050.

NOTE

If a temperature-compensated hydrometer is not used, add 0.001 to the specific gravity reading for every 3° above 77° F or subtract 0.001 points of specific gravity for every 3° below 77° F.

Charging

During charging, the cells will show signs of gas bubbling. If one cell has no gas bubbles or if its specific gravity is low, the cell is probably shorted.

If a battery not in use loses its charge within a week after charging or if the specific gravity drops quickly, the battery is defective. A good battery should only self-discharge approximately 1% each day.

NOTE

Some maintenance chargers can be used while the battery is connected to the motorcycle. These types of chargers are specifically designed for motorcycle batteries and will not damage the diodes in the regulator/rectifier.

1. Remove the battery from the motorcycle as described in this chapter.
2. Measure the battery voltage with a digital voltmeter.
3. Connect the positive charger lead to the positive battery terminal and the negative charger lead to the negative battery terminal.
4. Remove all vent caps from the battery, set the charger to 12 volts, and switch it on. The battery should be charged at 1.8 amps.

CAUTION

The electrolyte level must be maintained at the upper level during the charging cycle; check and refill with distilled water as necessary.

5. The charging time depends on the discharged condition of the battery. The chart in **Figure 48** can be used to determine approximate charging times at different specific gravity readings.
6. After the battery has been charged for the pre-determined time, turn the charger off, disconnect the leads and check the specific gravity. It should be within 1.260-1.280. If it is, and if the battery remains stable for one hour, the battery is charged.

Replacement

Make sure a new battery is charged completely before installing it in the motorcycle. Failure to do so will reduce the life of the battery. Using a new

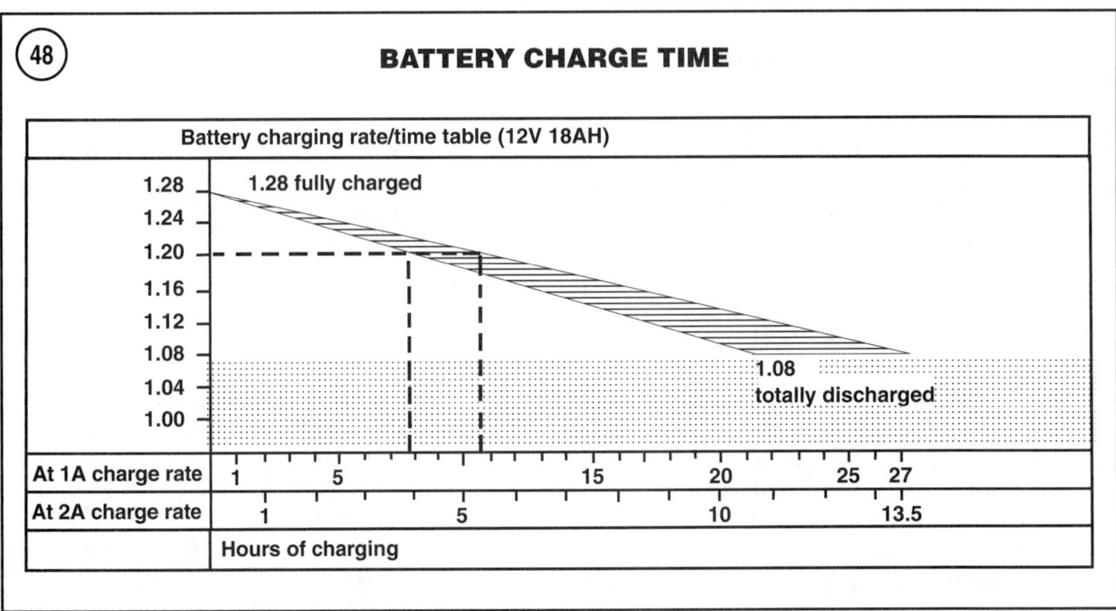

battery without an initial charge causes permanent battery damage. That is, the battery will never be able to hold more than an 80% charge. Charging a new battery after it has been used will not bring its charge to 100%. When purchasing a new battery from a dealership or parts store, verify its charge status. If necessary, have the store perform the initial or booster charge to bring the battery up to 100% charge prior to picking up the battery.

NOTE

***Recycle your old battery**. The lead plates and the plastic case can be recycled. Most motorcycle dealerships will accept your old battery in trade when you purchase a new one. Never place an old battery in your household trash. Placing any acid or lead (heavy metal) contents in landfills is illegal in most states.*

COOLING SYSTEM

Check the coolant and inspect the cooling system at the intervals specified in **Table 1**.

WARNING

Never remove the radiator cap, loosen a coolant drain bolt or disconnect a coolant hose while the engine and radiator are hot. Hot fluid and steam may be blown out under pressure and cause serious injury.

Coolant Type

Use only a high quality, ethylene glycol based coolant specifically designed for aluminum engines. Mix the coolant with distilled water in a 50:50 ratio. Cooling system capacity is listed in **Table 4**. *Never* use tap water or saltwater when mixing coolant with water. The minerals in them will damage engine parts. Distilled (or purified) water can be purchased at supermarkets or drug stores in gallon containers.

CAUTION

Many anti-freeze solutions contain silicate inhibitors to protect aluminum parts from corrosion damage. However, silicate inhibitors cause premature wear to water pump seals. Do not use anti-freeze solutions that contain silicate inhibitors.

Coolant Level

1. Securely support the motorcycle in an upright position on level ground.

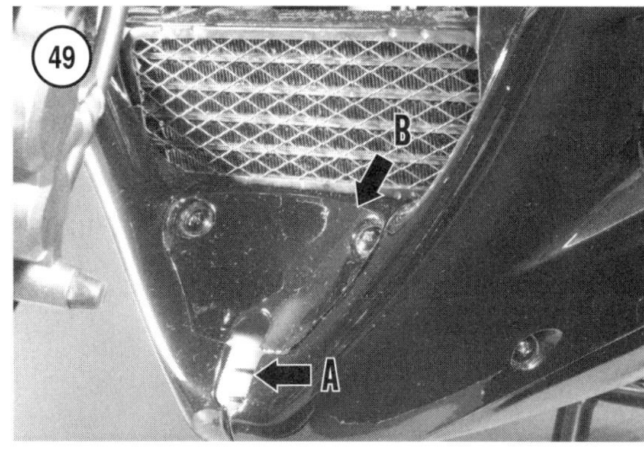

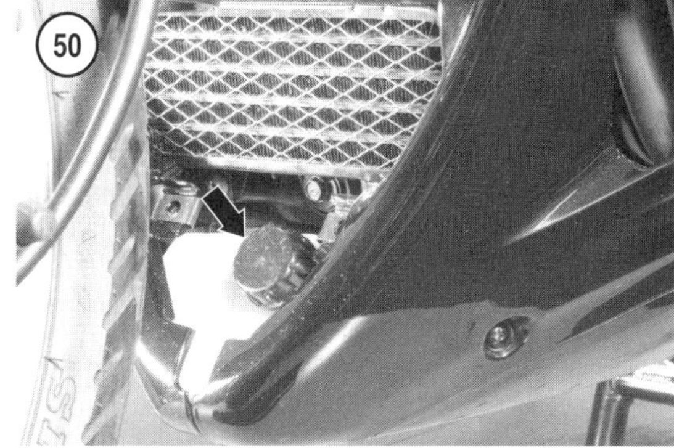

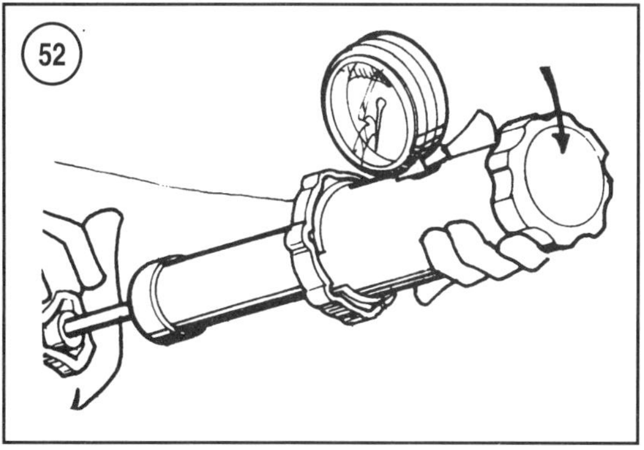

NOTE
Coolant level must be checked while the engine is cold.

2. Check the level of the coolant in the reservoir. Coolant level should be between the upper (A, **Figure 49**) and lower level lines on the reservoir.
3. If necessary, add coolant by performing the following:
   a. Remove the mounting screws, and lift the reservoir cover (B, **Figure 49**) from the middle fairing.
   b. Remove the cap (**Figure 50**) from the coolant reservoir.
   c. Add coolant to bring the level to the upper level line.
   d. Reinstall the reservoir cap and the reservoir cover (B, **Figure 49**).

3

Cooling System Inspection

A cooling system pressure tester is required to test the cooling system.

1. Remove the lower, middle and front fairings as described in Chapter Fifteen.
2. Remove the fuel tank (Chapter Eight).
3. Check all cooling system hoses for damage or deterioration. Replace any hose that is questionable. Make sure all hose clamps are tight.
4. Carefully clean any debris from the radiator core. Use a whisk broom, compressed air or low-pressure water. If the radiator has bent fins, carefully straighten them with a screwdriver.
5. Pressure test the radiator cap by performing the following:
   a. Remove the radiator cap (**Figure 51**).
   b. Use a cooling system tester to pressure test the radiator cap (**Figure 52**, typical) following the tester manufacturer's instructions. The cap must hold pressure up to the specified radiator cap relief pressure (**Table 8**). Replace the radiator cap if it does not hold pressure or if relief pressure is outside the specified range.

CAUTION
Do not exceed the indicated test pressure. If test pressure exceeds the specifications, the radiator may be damaged.

6. Pressure test the cooling system by performing the following:
   a. Leave the radiator cap off, and install the cooling system pressure tester to the cap fitting on the radiator filler neck (**Figure 53**, typical).
   b. Pressure test the entire cooling system. The cooling system should be pressurized up to, but not exceeding, the maximum radiator cap relief pressure specified in **Table 8**. The system must be able to hold this pressure. If the pressure does not hold steady, check the system for leaks. Replace or repair any component that fails this test.
7. Reinstall the radiator cap and fairings.

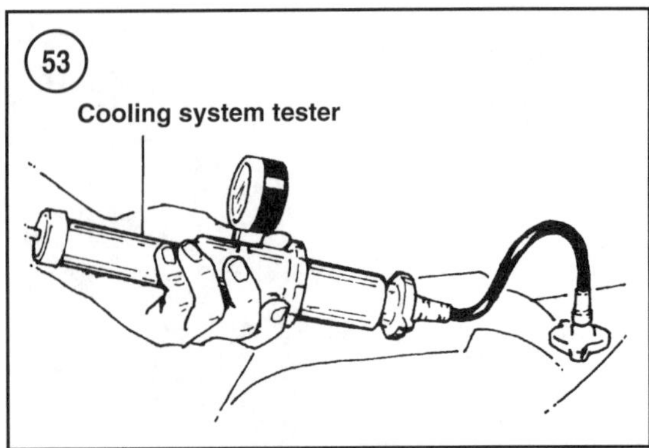

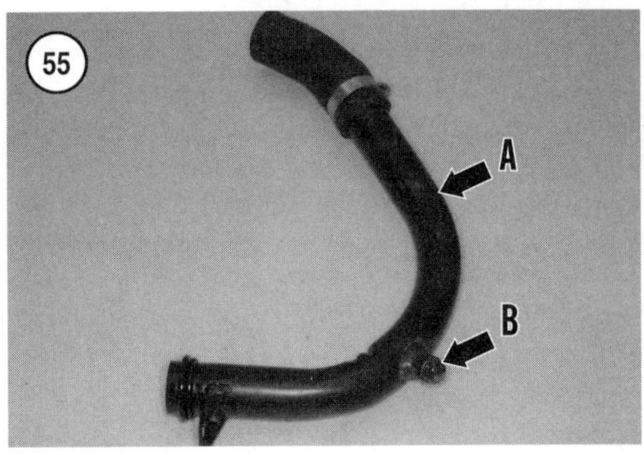

Coolant Change

Change the coolant at the interval indicated in **Table 1**.

It is sometimes necessary to remove the radiator or drain the coolant from the system in order to perform a service procedure on some part of the motorcycle. If the coolant is still in good condition, it can be reused if it is kept clean. Drain the coolant into a clean drain pan and pour it into a clean, sealable container like a plastic milk or bleach bottle. This coolant can then be reused if it is still clean.

WARNING
Waste antifreeze is toxic and may never be discharged into storm sewers, septic systems, waterways, or onto the ground. Place used antifreeze in the original container and dispose of it according to local regulations. Do not store coolant where it is accessible to children or pets.

WARNING
*Do **not** remove the radiator cap when the engine is HOT. The coolant is under pressure. Severe scalding could result if the escaping coolant comes in contact with your skin. Allow the system to cool down before loosening the cap, and then turn the cap slowly to the first detent to allow any built-up pressure to escape safely.*

WARNING
Be careful not to spill antifreeze on painted surfaces. Antifreeze will damage painted surfaces. Wash a spill immediately with soapy water, and rinse the area thoroughly with clean water. Coolant is also slippery. Be sure to clean up any spilled coolant that may get on the ground or on the tire treads.

Perform the following procedure when the engine is cold.

1. Securely support the motorcycle on a level surface.

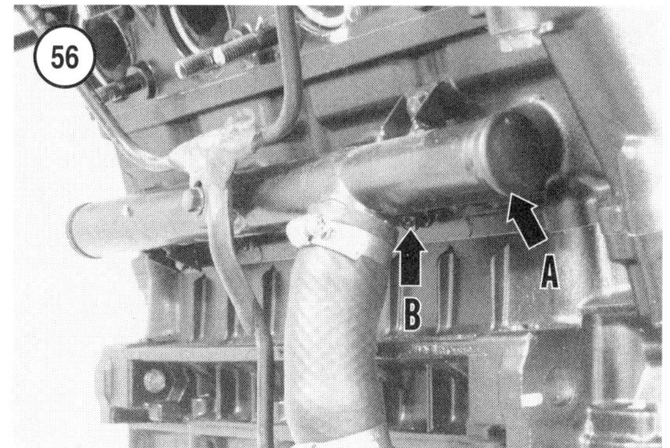

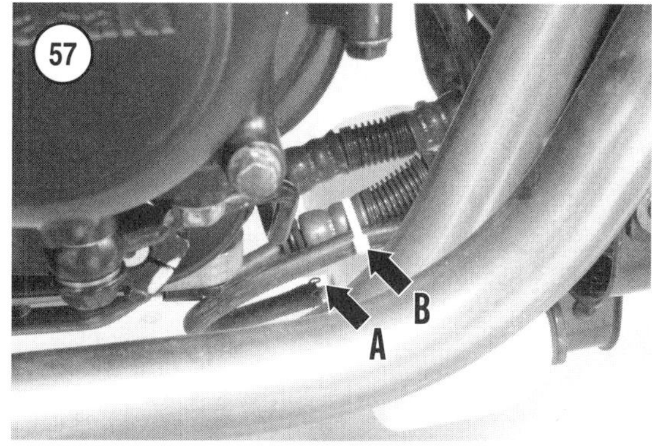

2. Remove the lower, middle and front fairings as described in chapter Fifteen.

3. Remove the fuel tank (Chapter Eight).

4. Remove the radiator cap (**Figure 51**) from the filler neck.

5. Drain the coolant from the radiator and engine by performing the following:

NOTE
*The coolant manifold pipe (**Figure 54**) connects the water pump output port to the coolant manifold on the front of the cylinder block.*

a. Locate the coolant manifold pipe (A, **Figure 55**) on the left side.
b. Place a drain pan under the drain bolt (B, **Figure 55**) on the pipe.
c. Remove the drain bolt, and drain the coolant from the radiator and engine.
d. Install a new sealing washer onto the drain bolt, reinstall the bolt and torque it to 7.8 N•m (69 in.-lb.).

NOTE
Further coolant draining is not necessary for most repair procedures. If the cylinder block or engine is being removed or if the coolant is being replaced, continue with Step 6.

6. Drain the coolant from the cylinder block by performing the following:

a. Remove the radiator (Chapter Ten) and the exhaust pipes (Chapter Eight).
b. Remove the coolant manifold (A, **Figure 56**) as described in Chapter Ten.
c. Place a drain pan under one cylinder drain bolt (B, **Figure 56**).
d. Remove the bolt and drain the coolant from the cylinders.
e. Repeat substeps c and d for the other cylinder drain bolt.
f. Reinstall the cylinder drain bolts. Install a new sealing washer on each drain bolt, and torque each bolt to 7.8 N•m (69 in.-lb.).

7. Drain the coolant from the reservoir by performing the following:

NOTE
Be prepared to catch residual coolant as each hose is removed from the coolant reservoir.

a. Disconnect the reservoir hose from the rear fitting on the reservoir (A, **Figure 57**). Note the zip tie (B, **Figure 57**) that secures this hose to the oil cooler pipe. This tie keeps the hose away from the exhaust pipe. If this zip tie is removed, install a new one during assembly.
b. Note how the overflow hose (A, **Figure 58**) is routed up behind the oil cooler, over the clutch cover (**Figure 59**), then secured to the

3

swing arm. This hose must be rerouted along the same path during assembly.

c. Remove the reservoir bracket bolts (B, **Figure 58**), and lower the reservoir and it bracket from the radiator bracket.

d. Disconnect the overflow hose from the fitting on the top of the coolant reservoir. Remove the reservoir. Pour out any coolant from the reservoir.

8. Reinstall the parts removed in Step 6 and Step 7.

9. Add coolant and bleed the system by performing the following:

a. Loosen the bleed bolt (**Figure 60**) on the water pump.

b. Place a funnel in the radiator filler neck. Slowly refill the radiator and engine with a 50:50 mixture of antifreeze and distilled water. Add the mixture slowly so air will be expelled from the system. Refer to **Table 4** for cooling system capacity.

c. A combination of air and coolant should flow from the water pump bleed bolt. Continue adding coolant until only coolant flows from the air bleeder.

d. Tighten the water-pump bleed bolt (**Figure 60**) securely, and open the bleed valve (**Figure 61**) on the thermostat housing.

e. Continue adding coolant to the filler neck until the coolant emerges from the thermostat housing bleed valve (**Figure 61**). Torque the bleed valve to 7.8 N•m (69 in.-lb.).

10. Once the system has been bled, add coolant to the filler neck until the neck is full.

11. Install the radiator cap (**Figure 51**) onto the filler neck. Turn the radiator cap clockwise to the first stop. Press the cap down, and turn it clockwise to the second stop.

12. Remove the cap (**Figure 50**) from the coolant reservoir, and add coolant until the level reaches the upper mark (A, **Figure 49**) on the reservoir.

13. Start the engine, and let it idle until the engine reaches normal operating temperature. Make sure there are no bubbles in the coolant.

14. Let the engine cool and check the fluid level in the coolant reservoir. It should be at the upper level mark.

15. Test ride the motorcycle. Adjust the coolant level in the reservoir as necessary.

TIRES AND WHEELS

Tire Pressure

Check and adjust the tire pressure to maintain good traction and handling and to prevent rim damage. A simple, accurate gauge can be purchased for a few dollars and should be carried in your tool kit. The recommended tire pressures for OEM tires are shown in **Table 3**. Make sure to install the valve stem cap.

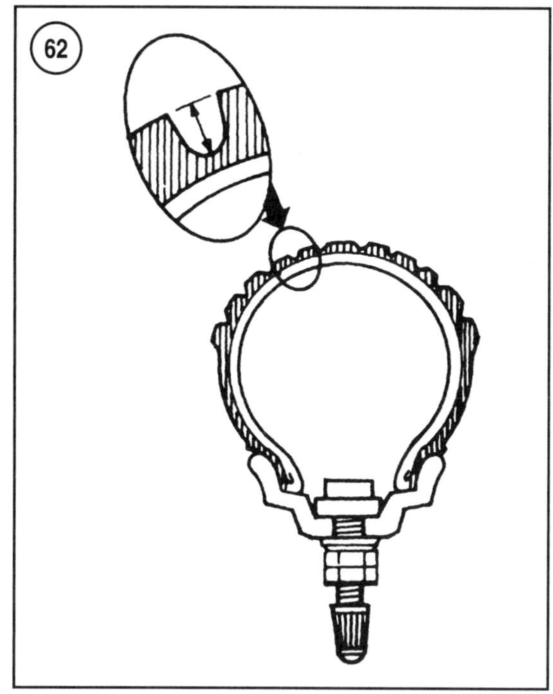

62

63

Tire Inspection

The tires take a lot of punishment due to the variety of terrain they roll over. Inspect them weekly for wear, cuts, abrasions, etc. If you find a nail or other object in the tire, mark its location with a light crayon prior to removing it. This will help locate the hole for repairs. Refer to the tire changing procedure in Chapter Eleven.

Measure the tread depth at the center of the tire tread (**Figure 62**) using a tread depth gauge or small ruler. Kawasaki recommends that the original equipment tires be replaced when the tread has worn to the dimensions specified in **Table 2**.

Rim Inspection and Runout

Frequently inspect wheel rims for cracks, warp or dents. A damaged rim may cause an air leak or knock the wheel out of alignment. If the rim portion of an alloy wheel is damaged, the wheel must be replaced. It cannot be serviced or repaired.

Wheel rim runout is the amount of wobble a wheel shows as it rotates. Check runout with the wheels on the motorcycle by simply supporting the motorcycle with the wheel off the ground. Slowly turn the wheel while holding a pointer solidly against a fork leg or the swing arm with the other end against the wheel rim. If a large amount of runout is noticed, measure the runout with a dial indicator as described in Chapter Eleven.

Wheel Bearings

Inspect the wheel bearings at the intervals specified in **Table 1**. Check the bearings whenever the wheels are removed or whenever there is the likelihood of water or other contamination. Non-sealed wheel bearings should be cleaned and repacked as needed. Sealed bearings should be inspected at the same intervals for leaking or damaged seals. Inspect the seals for severe wear, hardness, cracks or other damage. Pack the lips of each seal with a waterproof bearing grease. Service procedures are described in Chapter Eleven.

STEERING HEAD BEARINGS

Inspection

Inspect the steering head bearings (**Figure 63**) at the intervals specified in **Table 1**.

1. Securely support the motorcycle with the front wheel off the ground.

NOTE
When performing Step 2, make sure the control cables do not interfere with handlebar movement.

2. Hold onto the handlebars. Rotate them from side to side and check for bearing preload. The steering head should rotate smoothly with absolutely no

preload. If any binding or roughness is noted, adjust the steering head bearings as described in *Steering Head* in Chapter Twelve.

NOTE
Learning to recognize bearing free play can take time. Be patient when checking free play and try to feel the bearings rocking within their races.

3. Grasp the fork legs (**Figure 64**). Check for bearing free play by gently rocking the fork legs back and forth. There should be little or no free play, that is, little or no rocking in the steering head.

4. Support the motorcycle so both wheels are on the ground. Sit on the motorcycle and hold onto the handlebars. Apply the front brake lever and try to push the front fork forward. If any movement is detected in the steering head area, adjust the steering head bearings as described in *Steering Head* in Chapter Twelve.

FRONT SUSPENSION

Front Suspension Inspection

Periodically inspect the front suspension.

1. Wipe the each front fork leg with a soft wet cloth. Remove any dirt, road tar or bugs from the fork legs. This debris will eventually work its way into the seals and cause an oil leak.

2. Check the fork tubes for signs of leaks or damage.

3. Apply the front brake and pump the front fork up and down as vigorously as possible. Check for smooth operation and for any oil leaks.

4. Make sure the upper (**Figure 65**) and lower fork bridge clamp bolts (**Figure 66**) are tight.

5. Check the front axle clamp bolt (A, **Figure 67**) on each fork leg, and check the front axle nut (B). They must be tight.

CAUTION
If any previously mentioned fastener is loose, refer to Chapter Eleven or Twelve for correct tightening procedures and torque specifications.

64

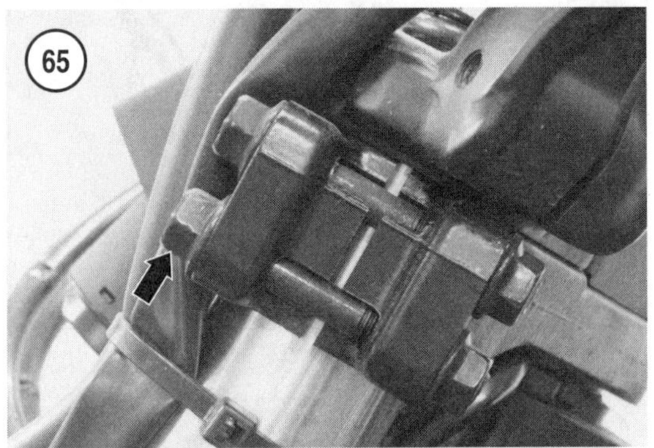
65

66

67

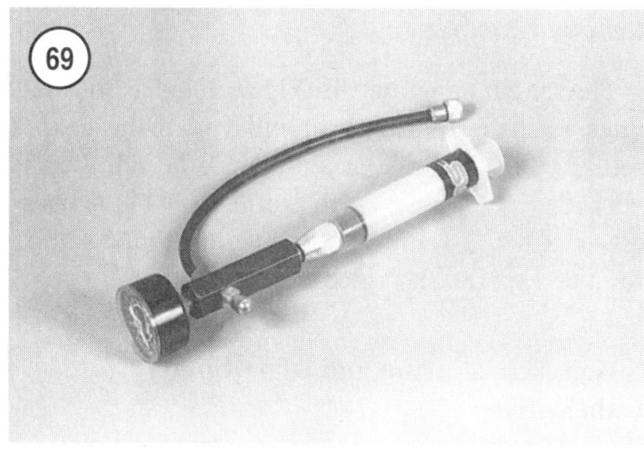

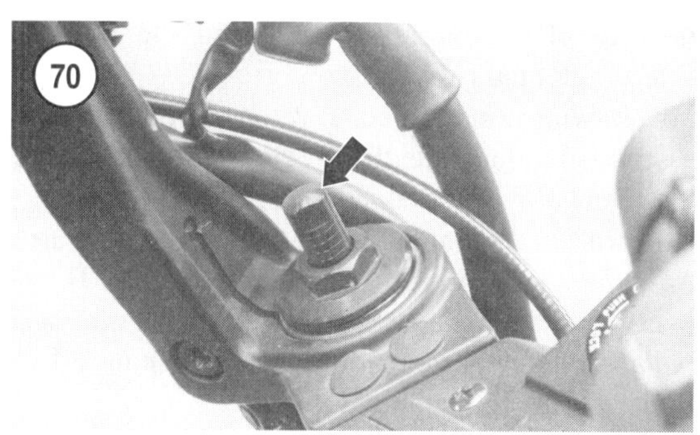

Fork Oil Change

The fork legs on 1986-1993 models are equipped with drain screws. Changing the fork oil on all models requires partial disassembly of the fork legs. Refer to Chapter Twelve for fork oil service procedures.

Fork Air Pressure Adjustment (1986-1993 models)

The fork springs and air pressure supports the motorcycle on these models. Measure air pressure when the fork legs are at normal room temperature.

The air pressure can be varied to suit the load and rider preference. In general, increase air pressure for heavy loads. Do not use a high-pressure air source to adjust the fork air pressure. It can quickly add excessive pressure and damage the fork seals. Use a manual pump so air can be added slowly. Consider the following when adjusting fork air pressure:

1. Securely support the motorcycle with the front wheel off the ground.

NOTE
A single air valve supplies air to both fork legs.

2. Remove the air valve cap (**Figure 68**).

CAUTION
Do not exceed 250 kPa (36 psi). The fork seals could be damaged by excessive air pressure.

3. Connect a manual pump (**Figure 69**) to the valve, and pump the fork to about 20 psi.

NOTE
Do not use a tire gauge to measure fork air pressure. A typical gauge cannot adequately seal on the air valve resulting in inaccurate measurement.

4. Slowly bleed off the air until the pressure reaches the desired value. The standard pressure is listed in **Table 8**.
5. Add the valve cap.

Fork Preload Adjustment (1994-on models)

Turn the preload adjuster (**Figure 70**) clockwise to increase the spring preload. Turn it counterclockwise to decrease preload. Make sure both adjusters are turned to the same setting.

The adjusters have seven grooves. For a 68 kg (150 lb.) rider without a passenger, the standard setting is the fifth groove from the top.

REAR SUSPENSION

Rear Suspension Inspection

1. With both wheels on the ground, check the shock absorber by bouncing the seat several times.

2. Securely support the motorcycle on a stand with the rear wheel off the ground.
3. Have an assistant steady the motorcycle.
4. Push hard on the rear wheel (sideways) to check for side play in the swing arm bearings.
5. Check the shock absorber for oil leaks, loose mounting fasteners or other damage.
6. Check the rear suspension for loose or missing fasteners.
7. Make sure the rear axle nut is tight.

CAUTION
If any previously mentioned fastener is loose, refer to Chapter Thirteen for correct tightening procedures and torque specifications.

Rear Shock Absorber Adjustment

The shock absorber can be adjusted to suit various riding conditions by adjusting air pressure and/or rebound damping. Both adjusters are located behind the side cover on the right side of the motorcycle (**Figure 71**).

Air pressure

Do not use a high-pressure hose to adjust the fork air pressure. It can quickly add excessive pressure and damage the fork seals. Use a manual pump so air can be added slowly. Consider the following when adjusting the shock absorber air pressure:

1. Securely support the motorcycle on the centerstand with the rear wheel off the ground.
2. Remove the right side cover as described in Chapter Fifteen.

NOTE
Do not use a tire gauge to measure fork air pressure. A typical tire gauge cannot adequately seal around the shock valve and thus yields inaccurate readings.

3. Remove the cover from the air valve (A, **Figure 71**). Measure the air pressure when the shock absorber is cold. Kawasaki recommends a pressure of 50 kPa (7.1 psi) for a 68 kg (150 lb.) rider with no load.
4. Slowly add or release air to adjust the pressure (**Table 8**). In general, more air pressure stiffens the ride.

Rebound damper

The rebound damper (B, **Figure 71**) has four settings. Push the adjuster in or pull it out to the desired setting. The No. 1 setting (when the adjuster is pushed all the way in) is the softest; No. 4 the hardest. The No. 2 setting is the recommended setting for a 68 kg (150 lb.) rider with no load.

Swing Arm Bearing and Drive Shaft Lubrication

Lubricate the swing arm bearing assemblies and the drive shaft coupling at the intervals in **Table 1**. Use a high quality, waterproof grease.

The swing arm must be removed and partially disassembled to lubricate the needle bearings. Remove the swing arm as described in Chapter Thirteen.

Kawasaki recommends removing the swing arm to lubricate the driveshaft-sliding coupling. However, general practice is to remove the final gearcase (Chapter Thirteen) to expose the shaft splines. Lubricate with high temperature grease.

FINAL GEARCASE

Oil Level Check

1. Place the motorcycle on its centerstand on a level surface.
2. Clean the area around the oil filler cap (A, **Figure 72**), and remove the cap from the final gearcase. If the oil level is low, inspect the final drive gearcase for leaks.
3. A small amount of oil should flow from the oil filler hole. If the oil level is low, add the recommended gear oil (**Table 4**) through the oil filler hole to correct the oil level.

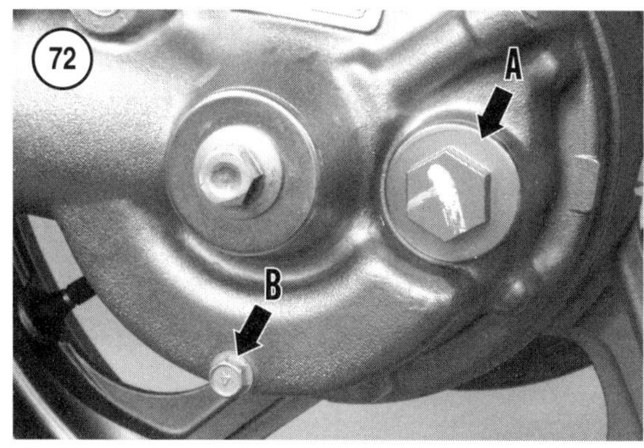

4. Inspect the O-ring on the oil filler cap. Replace the O-ring if it is brittle or deteriorated.
5. Apply gear oil to the O-ring, install the oil filler cap, and tighten the cap securely.

Oil Change

The recommended oil change interval is listed in **Table 1**. Discard old oil in the same manner described in *Engine Oil Change* in this chapter.

1. Ride the motorcycle until it reaches normal operating temperature.
2. Park the motorcycle on a level surface, and support it on the centerstand. Turn the engine off.
3. Place a drain pan underneath the final gearcase.
4. Remove the drain bolt (B, **Figure 72**) and the oil filler cap (A). Drain the oil.
5. Replace the drain bolt's sealing washer if it is damaged or was leaking.
6. Install the drain bolt and sealing washer. Torque the bolt to the 17 N•m (13 ft.-lb.).
7. Inspect the O-ring on the oil filler cap. Replace the O-ring if it is brittle or deteriorated.
8. Insert a funnel into the oil filler hole and add the recommended type and quantity of gear oil (**Table 4**).
9. Remove the funnel. Some oil should flow from the oil filler hole. Add additional oil if necessary.
10. Apply gear oil to the O-ring, install the oil filler cap and tighten the cap securely.
11. Test ride the motorcycle and check for leaks. After the test ride, recheck the oil level. Adjust the oil level if necessary.

BRAKES

Check the brake fluid in each master cylinder at the interval listed in **Table 1**. At the same time, inspect the brake pads for wear. Brake bleeding, brake component service and brake pad replacement are covered in Chapter Fourteen.

Disc Brake Hoses

Check the brake hoses between each master cylinder and each brake caliper assembly.

If there is any leakage, tighten the connections and bleed the brakes as described in Chapter Fourteen. If tightening the connection does not stop the leak or if the brake hose(s) is obviously damaged, cracked or chafed, replace the brake hose(s) and bleed the system as described in Chapter Fourteen.

Brake Fluid Selection

Use DOT 4 brake fluid in the front and rear master cylinder reservoirs. Always use the same brand of brake fluid. One manufacturer's brake fluid may not be compatible with another's. Do not mix different brands of brake fluids.

Remember that brake fluid will damage painted, plated and plastic surfaces. Protect the motorcycle so brake fluid cannot spill onto these parts. If spills occur, wash the area immediately with soap and water. Rinse the area thoroughly with clean water.

WARNING
Use brake fluid clearly marked DOT 4 from a sealed container. Other types may vaporize and cause brake failure. Do not use silicone based (DOT 5) brake fluid. It can cause brake component damage leading to brake system.

Front Brake Fluid Level Check

1. Park the motorcycle on level ground. Support it so it is upright.
2. Turn the handlebar so the front master cylinder is level.
3. The brake fluid in the inspection window must be above the lower level line (**Figure 73**) on the reservoir.

WARNING
If the reservoir is empty, air has entered the brake system. Bleed the front brakes as described in Chapter Fourteen.

4. If the fluid level is at or below the lower level line, add brake fluid by performing the following:
   a. Wipe off master cylinder cover.
   b. Remove the cover screws, reservoir cap, diaphragm plate (1992-on models) and diaphragm.
   c. Add fresh DOT 4 brake fluid until the fluid level rises to the upper level line in the reservoir.
   d. Install the diaphragm, diaphragm plate (1992-on models) and reservoir cap. Tighten the cap screws securely.

NOTE

Low brake fluid usually indicates brake pad wear. As the pads wear, the brake caliper pistons automatically extend farther out of their bores, which lowers the fluid level in the master cylinder. However, if the brake fluid level is low, and the brake pads are not excessively worn, check all brake lines and connections for leaks.

5. If the fluid level was low, check the brake pads for excessive wear as described in this section.

Rear Brake Fluid Level Check

1. Park the motorcycle on level ground. Support it so it is upright.
2. Remove the right side cover as described in Chapter Fifteen.
3. The brake fluid level must be between the upper and lower level lines on the rear master cylinder reservoir (**Figure 74**).

WARNING

If the reservoir is empty, air has entered the brake system. Bleed the rear brakes as described in Chapter Fourteen.

4. If the fluid level is at or below the lower level line, add brake fluid by performing the following:
   a. Wipe off the master cylinder reservoir cap.
   b. Unscrew the cap from the reservoir.
   c. Add fresh DOT 4 brake fluid until the fluid level rises to the upper level line on the master cylinder reservoir (**Figure 74**).
   d. Install the reservoir cap, and tighten it securely.

NOTE

Low brake fluid usually indicates brake pad wear. As the pads wear, the brake caliper pistons automatically extend farther out of their bores, which lowers the fluid level in the master cylinder. However, if the brake fluid level is low, and the brake pads are not excessively worn, check all brake lines and connections for leaks.

5. If the fluid level was low, check the brake pads for excessive wear as described later in this chapter.

Brake Fluid Change

Every time the reservoir top cover and diaphragm are removed, a small amount of dirt and moisture enter the brake fluid system. The same thing happens if a leak occurs or if any part of the hydraulic brake system is loosened or disconnected. Dirt can clog the system and cause unnecessary wear. Water in the brake fluid vaporizes at high temperature, im-

pairing the hydraulic action and reducing the brake's stopping ability.

To maintain peak braking efficiency, change the brake fluid at the interval listed in **Table 1**. To change brake fluid, drain the fluid and bleed the brakes as described in Chapter Fourteen.

Brake Pad Wear

Inspect the brake pads at the intervals specified in **Table 1**. Refer to the brake pad replacement procedure in Chapter Fourteen.

Front Brake Lever Adjustment

The distance between the front brake lever and the throttle grip can be adjusted to suit rider preference. Position 1 sets the lever to the maximum distance from the throttle grip, position 4 is the closest.

1. Turn the adjuster on the brake lever and align a number with the arrow on the brake lever.
2. Support the motorcycle with the front wheel off the ground. Spin the front wheel by hand, and apply the front brake several times. Make sure the brakes operate properly and that front wheel turns without any brake drag.

Brake Pedal Height

The brake pedal height is adjusted by changing the rear master cylinder pushrod length. Refer to *Pushrod Adjustment* in Chapter Fourteen. When adjusting the brake pedal height, make sure the pushrod length is within the range specified in **Table 8**.

3

Rear Brake Light Switch Adjustment

1. Turn the ignition switch on.
2. Depress the brake pedal. The brake light should turn on just before the brakes begin to apply.
3. If the brake light comes on too late, perform the following:

NOTE

The brake pedal/footpeg assembly has been removed for photographic clarity. The rear brake light switch can be adjusted while the assembly is installed on the motorcycle.

   a. Hold the brake light switch body, and turn the adjuster (**Figure 75**) as needed to make the light turn on earlier.
   b. Recheck the rear brake light operation.
4. Turn the ignition switch off.

FASTENERS

Constant vibration can loosen many of the fasteners on a motorcycle. Check the tightness of all nuts, bolts and other fasteners.

1. Check the tightness of all exposed fasteners. Refer to the appropriate chapter for torque specifications.
2. Check that all hose clamps, cable stays and safety clips are properly installed. Replace missing or damaged items.

Tables 1-9 are on the following pages.

Table 1 MAINTENANCE SCHEDULE[1]

Odometer reading	Procedure
Initial 500 miles (800 km)	Check and adjust the valve clearance Clean the air filter element. Replace the element after every fifth cleaning Check and adjust the throttle free play Check and adjust the engine idle speed Check carburetor synchronization; adjust as necessary Inspect the emission control system on models so equipped Change engine oil and filter Change the final gearcase oil Check the fluid level in the clutch reservoir; adjust as necessary Check the fluid level in the front and rear brake reservoirs; adjust as necessary Check the operation of each brake light switch Check the steering head bearings for looseness or binding Check the battery electrolyte level Check all fasteners. Tighten them as necessary
3000 miles (5000 km)	Check the condition of the spark plugs; clean and adjust the gap as necessary Check the secondary air valve on models so equipped Check and adjust the engine idle speed Check carburetor synchronization; adjust as necessary Check the condition of the fuel hoses; replace them as necessary Inspect the emission control system on models so eqiupped Check the fluid level in the clutch reservoir; adjust as necessary Check the condition of the brake hoses and connections Check the brake pads Check the fluid level in the front and rear brake reservoirs; adjust as necessary Check the operation of each brake light switch Check the steering head bearings for looseness or binding Check the battery electrolyte level Check the tires for wear Perform the general lubrication procedures described in Chapter Three
6000 miles (10,000 km)	Perform the 3000 mile (5000 km) checks Check and adjust the valve clearance Clean the air filter element. Replace the element after every fifth cleaning Check and adjust the throttle free play Check the condition of the fuel system Change engine oil and filter at this interval or every year Inspect the condition of the coolant and hoses at this interval or every year, whichever comes first Check the oil level in the final gearcase Lubricate the driveshaft Lubricate the swing arm pivot and the uni-trak pivots Check all fasteners. Tighten them as necessary
	(continued)

Table 1 MAINTENANCE SCHEDULE[1] (continued)

Odometer reading	Procedure
9000 miles (15,000 km)	Perform the 3000 mile (5000 km) checks
12,000 miles (20,000 km)	Perform the 3000 mile (5000 km) checks
	Check and adjust the valve clearance
	Replace the air filter element at this interval or after every fifth cleaning
	Check and adjust the throttle free play
	Check the condition of the fuel system
	Change engine oil and filter at this interval or every year, whichever comes first
	Inspect the condition of the coolant hoses at this interval or every year, whichever comes first
	Check the oil level in the final gearcase
	Change the fluid in the clutch system
	Change the fluid in the front and rear brake systems
	Lubricate the steering head bearings
	Lubricate the swing arm pivot and the uni-trak pivots
	Check all fasteners. Tighten them as necessary
15,000 miles (25,000 km)	Perform the 3000 mile (5000 km) checks
18,000 miles (30,000 km)	Perform the 6000 mile (10,000 km) checks
	Change the coolant at this interval or every 2 years, whichever comes first
	Change the final gearcase oil
	Change the fork oil
Every 2 years	Replace coolant
	Replace brake and clutch fluid
	Replace the cups and seals in the clutch master cylinder[2]
	Replace the seals in the clutch slave cylinder[2]
	Replace the cups and seals in the brake master cylinders[2]
	Replace the seals in the front and rear brake calipers[2]
Every 4 years	Replace the fuel hoses[2]
	Replace the brake hoses[2]

1. Use this maintenance schedule as a guide to general maintenance and lubrication. Service items more frequently if the motorcycle is exposed to mud, water, sand, high humidity or run harder than normal.
2. Recommended by manufacturer.

Table 2 TIRE SPECIFICATIONS

Front tire	Tubeless
Size, Manufacturer	
1986-1993 models	110/80 VR18, Dunlop K105F or 110/80 V18, Metzeler ME33 Laser
1994-1999 Germany models	110/80 V18, Pirelli MT09 or 120/70 ZR18, Bridgestone Battrax BT54F
All 1994-1999 models except Germany models	120/70 R18 59V, Dunlop K 701F
2000-on models	120/70 R18 59V, Dunlop K 701F
Rear tire	Tubeless
Size, Manufacturer	
1986-1993 models	150/80 VR16, Dunlop K700G or 150/80 VB16, Metzeler ME99 A2
1994-1999 Germany models	150/80 VB16, Pirelli MT08 or 150/80 VR16 V250, Bridgestone Battrax BT53V R

(continued)

3

Table 2 TIRE SPECIFICATIONS (continued)

Rear tire (continued)	
Size, manufacturer (continued)	
All 1994-1999 models except	
Germany models	150/80 R16 71V, Dunlop K 700J
2000-on models	150/80 R16 71V, Dunlop K 700J
Minimum tread depth	
Front	1.0 mm (0.04 in.)
Rear	
Under 130 km/h	2.0 mm (0.08 in.)
Over 130 km/h	3.0 mm (0.12 in.)

Table 3 TIRE INFLATION PRESSURE[1]

	Load[2]	Pressure (cold)
1986-1999 models		
Front tire	–	250 kPa (36 psi [2.5 kg/cm^2])
Rear tire		
USA, California, Canada, Australia, and South Africa models	0-200 kg (0-441 lb.) load	290 kPa (41 psi [2.9 kg/cm^2])
All models except USA, California, Canada, Australia, and South Africa models	0-97.5 kg (215 lb.) load	250 kPa (36 psi [2.5 kg/cm^2])
	97.5-183 kg (215-404 lb.)	290 kPa (41 psi [2.9 kg/cm^2])
2000-on models		
Front tire	–	250 kPa (36 psi [2.5 kg/cm^2])
Rear tire		
USA, California, Canada, and Australia models	0-200 kg (0-441 lb.)	290 kPa (41 psi [2.9 kg/cm^2])
All models except USA, California, Canada, and Australia	0-97.5 kg (215 lb.)	250 kPa (36 psi [2.5 kg/cm^2])
	97.5-183 kg (215-404 lb.)	290 kPa (41 psi [2.9 kg/cm^2])

1. Tire inflation pressures apply to original equipment tires only. Aftermarket tires may require different pressures. Refer to the tire manufacturer's specifications.
2. Load equals the total weight of the rider, passenger, accessories and all cargo.

Table 4 RECOMMENDED LUBRICANTS AND FLUIDS

Fuel	Regular unleaded
Octane	87 [(R + M)/2 method] or research octane of 91 or higher
Capacity	28.5 L (7.5 U.S. gal [6.3 Imp. gal])
Air filter oil	SAE30
Engine oil	
Classification	API SE, SF, SG or equivalent
Viscosity	SAE 10W-40, 10W-50, 20W-40 or 20W-50

(continued)

3

Table 4 RECOMMENDED LUBRICANTS AND FLUIDS (continued)

Fuel	Regular unleaded
Engine oil (continued)	
Capacity	
Oil change only	2.7 L (2.85 U.S. qt. [2.38 Imp. qt.])
Oil and filter change	3.0 L (3.17 U.S. qt. [2.64 Imp. qt.])
Final gearcase oil	
Viscosity	
Temperature above 5° C (41° F)	SAE 90
Temperature below 5° C (41° F)	SAE 80
Grade	API GL-5 hypoid gear oil
Capacity	220 ml (7.4 U.S. oz. [7.7 Imp. oz.])
Coolant capacity (to the upper mark)	3.1 L (3.27 U.S. qt. [2.73 Imp. qt.])
Fork oil viscosity	SAE 10W-20 fork oil
Oil capacity per leg	
1986-1993 model)	
When empty	approx. 388 ml (13.1 U.S. oz. [13.7 Imp oz.])
Oil change	approx. 330 ml (11.2 U.S. oz. [11.6 Imp. oz.])
Oil level each leg (measured from top of the fully extended fork tube without spring)	355 mm (13.97 in.)
1994-on models	
When empty	approx 379 ml (12.82 U.S. oz. [13.33 Imp. oz.])
Oil change	approx. 330 ml (11.2 U.S. oz. [11.6 Imp. oz.])
Oil level each leg (measured from the top of the fully compressed fork tube without spring)	171 mm (6.73 in.)
Brake and clutch fluid	DOT 4 brake fluid

Table 5 RECOMMENDED SPARK PLUGS

Spark plug gap	0.6-0.7 mm (0.024-0.028 in.)
Recommended spark plug	
1986-1989 models	
USA and California models	
Standard	NGK D8EA, ND X24ES-U
High-speed riding	NGK D9EA, ND X27ES-U
Low-speed riding	NGK D7EA, ND X22ES-U
Canada models	
Standard	NGK DR8ES-L, ND X24ESR-U
High-speed riding	NGK DR8ES, ND X27ESR-U
Low-speed riding	NGK DR7ES, ND X22ESR-U
Australia, Italy, South Africa models	NGK D9EA, ND X27ES-U
All other models	NGK DR8ES, ND X27ESR-U
1990-1993 models	
USA and California models	
Standard	NGK D8EA, ND X24ES-U
High-speed riding	NGK D9EA, ND X27ES-U
Low-speed riding	NGK D7EA, ND X22ES-U

(continued)

Table 5 RECOMMENDED SPARK PLUGS (continued)

1990-1993 models (continued)	
Canada models	
Standard	NGK DR8ES-L, ND X24ESR-U
High-speed riding	NGK DR7ES, ND X22ESR-U
Low-speed riding	NGK DR8ES, ND X27ESR-U
Australia models	NGK D9EA, ND X27ES-U
All other models	NGK DR8ES, ND X27ESR-U
1994-1996 USA and California models	NGK D8EA, ND X24ES-U
1997-1999 USA and California models	NGK DR8EA, ND X24ESR-U
1994-1999 Canada models	NGK DR8EA, ND X24ESR-U
All other 1994-1999 models	NGK DR9EA, ND X27ESR-U
2000-on models	
USA, California, and Canada models	
Standard	NGK DR8EA, ND X24ESR-U
High-speed riding	NGK DR9EA, ND X27ESR-U
Low-speed riding	NGK DR7EA, ND X22ESR-U
All other models	NGK DR9EA, ND X27ESR-U

Table 6 BATTERY STATE OF CHARGE

Specific gravity reading	Percentage of charge remaining
1.120–1.140	0
1.135–1.155	10
1.150–1.170	20
1.160–1.180	30
1.175–1.195	40
1.190–1.210	50
1.205–1.225	60
1.215–1.235	70
1.230–1.250	80
1.245–1.265	90
1.260–1.280	100

Table 7 ENGINE TUNE-UP SPECIFICATIONS

Battery	
Capacity	12 V 18 AH
Idle speed	
California and 1988-on Switzerland models	1150-1250 rpm
2000-on European and French models	1250-1350 rpm
All other models	950-1050 rpm
Vacuum pressure @ idle	less than 2.7 kPa (0.787 in. Hg [2 cm Hg]) difference
Valve clearance	
Intake	0.13-0.18 mm (0.005-0.007 in.)
Exhaust	0.18-0.23 (0.007-0.009)
Spark plug gap	0.6-0.7 mm (0.024-0.028 in.)
Compression pressure	885-1350 kPa (128-196 psi) @ 300 rpm
Oil pressure @ 90° C (194° F)	265-325 kPa (38-47 psi) @ 4000 rpm

(continued)

Table 7 ENGINE TUNE–UP SPECIFICATIONS (continued)

Firing order	1–2–4–3
Ignition timing (initial/advanced)*	
1986-1989	
California and 1989 Switzerland models	10° BTDC @ 1200 rpm/35° BTDC @ 3500 rpm
All other models	10° BTDC @ 1000 rpm/35° BTDC @ 3500 rpm
1990-1993 models	
California and Spain models	10° BTDC @ 1200 rpm/35° BTDC @ 3500 rpm
All other models	10° BTDC @ 1000 rpm/35° BTDC @ 3500 rpm
1994-1999 models	
California, Spain and 1996-1999 Switzerland models	10° BTDC @ 1200 rpm/35° BTDC @ 3500 rpm
All other models	10° BTDC @ 1000 rpm/35° BTDC @ 3500 rpm
2000-on models	
Europe and France models	10° BTDC @ 1300 rpm/35° BTDC @ 3500 rpm
California models	10° BTDC @ 1200 rpm/35° BTDC @ 3500 rpm
All other models	10° BTDC @ 1000 rpm/35° BTDC @ 3500 rpm

*Not adjustable

Table 8 MAINTENANCE SPECIFICATIONS

Brake pad service limit (front and rear)	1.0 mm (0.039 in.)
Brake disc runout	0.3 mm (0.012 in.)
Rear master cylinder pushrod length	43.5-45.5 mm (1.71-1.79 in.)
Throttle cable free play	2-3 mm (0.08-0.12 in.)
Choke cable free play	2-3 mm (0.08-0.12 in.)
Front fork air pressure (1986-1993 models)	50 kPa (7.1 psi)
Shock absorber air pressure	
Solo rider no load	50 kPa (7.1 psi)
Rider with load and/or passenger	200-350 kPa (28-50 psi)
Wheel runout	
Axial	0.5 mm (0.020 in.)
Radial	0.8 mm (0.031 in.)
Rear brake light switch	Activated after 10 mm (0.394 in.) of pedal travel
Radiator cap relief pressure	93-123 kPa (13.2-17.9 psi)

Table 9 MAINTENANCE AND TUNE UP TORQUE SPECIFICATIONS

Item	N•m	in.-lb.	ft.-lb.
Brake caliper mounting bolts			
Front	32	–	24
Rear	34	–	25
Brake caliper bleed valve	7.8	69	–
Brake hose banjo bolt	25	–	18
Coolant manifold drain bolt	7.8	69	–
Cylinder drain bolts	7.8	69	–
Final gearcase drain bolt	17	–	13
Front axle nut	88	–	65

(continued)

Table 9 MAINTENANCE AND TUNE UP TORQUE SPECIFICATIONS (continued)

Item	N•m	in.-lb.	ft.-lb.
Front axle clamp bolts			
1986-1993 models	20	–	15
1994-on models	35		26
Handlebar clamp bolt	19	–	14
Handlebar mounting bolt	19	–	14
Fork bridge clamp bolts			
Lower bridge	21	–	15.5
Upper bridge	16	–	12
Oil filter bolt	20	–	15
Oil gallery bolt	18	–	13
Oil pipe banjo bolt	25	–	18
Pickup coil cover bolts	9.8	87	–
Rear axle nut	110	–	81
Spark plugs	14	–	10
Shock absorber bolts			
Lower	59	–	43
Upper	39	–	29
Steering head nut	39	–	29
Swing arm locknut	52	–	38
Swing arm adjuster bolt	27	–	20
Swing arm pivot mounting bolt	23	–	17
Thermostat housing bleed valve	7.8	69	–
Valve adjuster locknut	25	–	18

CHAPTER FOUR

ENGINE TOP END

4

This chapter provides complete service and overhaul procedures for the engine top end components. This includes the cylinder head cover, camshafts, cam chain tensioner, valves, cylinder head, piston and rings. Refer to Chapter Three for valve adjustment procedures. When inspecting components described in this chapter, compare measurements to the service specifications in the tables at the end of this chapter. Replace any part that is worn, out of specification or damaged. During assembly, tighten fasteners to the specified torque.

All Concours models feature a four-stroke, liquid-cooled, dual overhead camshaft (DOHC) in-line four-cylinder engine with a balancer shaft. The camshafts are chain-driven off the crankshaft. Chain tension is controlled by a spring–loaded, automatic tensioner that bears against the rear run of the cam chain.

SERVICING ENGINE IN THE FRAME

The following components can be serviced while the engine is in the frame:

1. External gearshift mechanism.
2. Clutch.
3. Carburetors.
4. Starter.
5. Cylinder head.
6. Cylinder block.
7. Alternator.

CYLINDER HEAD COVER

Removal

Refer to **Figure 1**.

1. Securely support the motorcycle on level ground.
2. Remove the lower, middle and front fairings as described in Chapter Fifteen.
3. Remove the fuel tank (Chapter Eight).
4. On models with secondary air systems:
   a. Remove the vacuum switch as described in Chapter Eight.
   b. Remove the reed valve cover bolts (**Figure 2**), and lift each reed valve cover from the cylinder head cover.

NOTE
*The engine shown in **Figure 3** has been removed for photographic clar-*

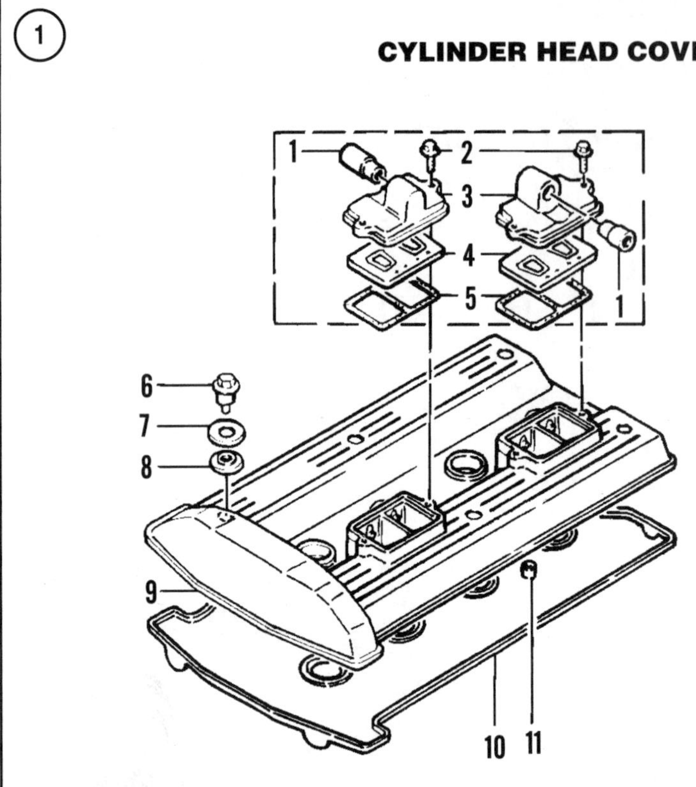

ity. The cylinder head cover can be removed while the engine is in the frame.

5. Remove the cylinder head cover bolts (**Figure 3**).

CAUTION

Four dowels are used to align the cylinder head cover on the cylinder head. One or more dowels may drop into the engine when the cover is removed. If this occurs, do not turn the engine until the dowels are accounted for.

6. Remove the cylinder head cover (**Figure 4**) and gasket. Watch for the dowels installed beneath the cover.

Installation

1. Inspect the gasket for nicks, tears or other damage. Replace the gasket (**Figure 5**) as necessary.
2. Remove all gasket residue from the cylinder head cover and from the mating surfaces on the cylinder head.

3. Apply Kawasaki Bond: No. 54019-120 or an equivalent silicon sealant to the cutouts (**Figure 6**) in the cylinder head.
4. Apply a small amount of gasket seal to the dowels, and set them into place in the cylinder head cover.
5. Set the cylinder cover onto the head. Make sure the half-rounds in the gasket mate with the cutouts in the cylinder head.
6. Install each cylinder head cover bolt with a washer and seal. Evenly tighten the bolts, and torque them to 9.8 N•m (87 in.-lb.).

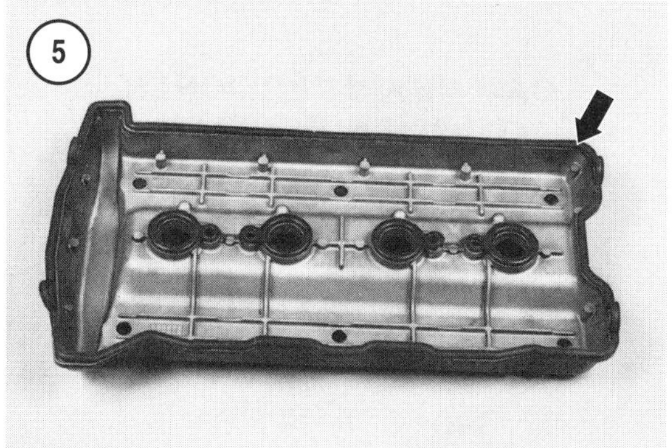

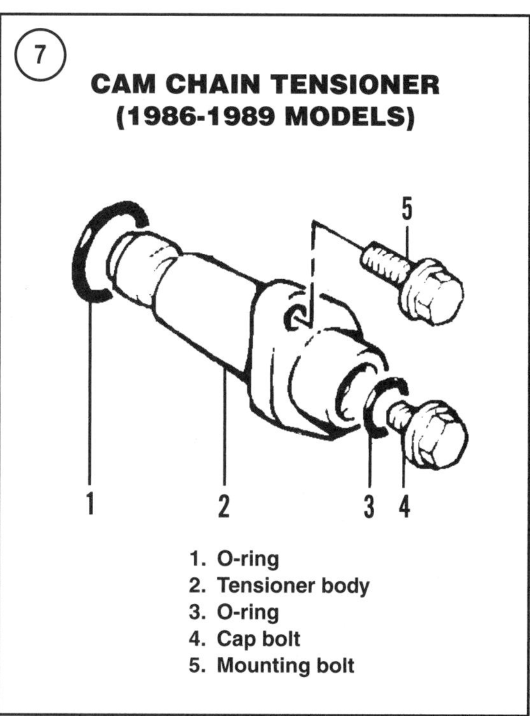

CAM CHAIN TENSIONER (1986-1989 MODELS)

1. O-ring
2. Tensioner body
3. O-ring
4. Cap bolt
5. Mounting bolt

CAM CHAIN TENSIONER

A non-ratcheting cam-chain tensioner is used on 1986-1989 models. A ratcheting-type tensioner is used in 1990-on models. Refer to the appropriate procedure.

Both style tensioners are non-return type tensioners. The tensioner pushrod freely moves inward, but it cannot move out. Whenever the cam chain tensioner mounting bolts are loosened, the tensioner assembly must be completely removed and reset as described in each respective procedure.

Removal/Installation (1986-1989 Models)

Refer to **Figure 7**.

1. Loosen the tensioner cap bolt (A, **Figure 8**).
2. Remove the tensioner mounting bolts (B, **Figure 8**), and pull the tensioner from the cylinder block. Watch for the O-ring behind the tensioner body.
3. Check the tensioner body (**Figure 9**) for cracks or other damage. Replace the tensioner assembly if necessary.
4. Install the cam chain tensioner by performing the following:
   a. Remove the cap bolt and O-ring.
   b. Install a new O-ring onto the tensioner body.

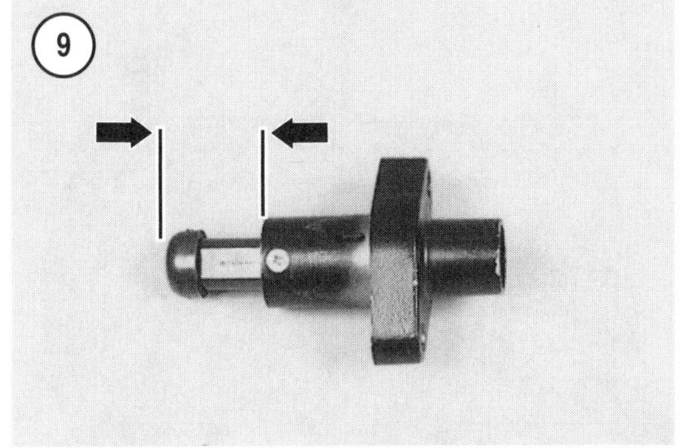

c. Insert a screwdriver into the tensioner (**Figure 10**).

CAUTION
Do not turn the screwdriver counterclockwise. The pushrod could detach from the assembly so the tensioner cannot be reinstalled.

d. Press the pushrod into the body while turning the screwdriver clockwise until the pushrod extends approximately 10 mm from the tensioner body as shown in **Figure 9**. Do not remove the screwdriver at this time.
e. Insert the tensioner into the cylinder block while holding the screwdriver. Do not release the screwdriver until the tensioner is seated in the cylinder block.
f. Press the tensioner against the cylinder block, remove the screwdriver and install the mounting bolts. Evenly finger-tighten the bolts to hold the tensioner in place.
g. Torque the cam chain tensioner mounting bolts to 9.8 N•m (87 in.-lb.).
h. Install the cap bolt and a new O-ring.

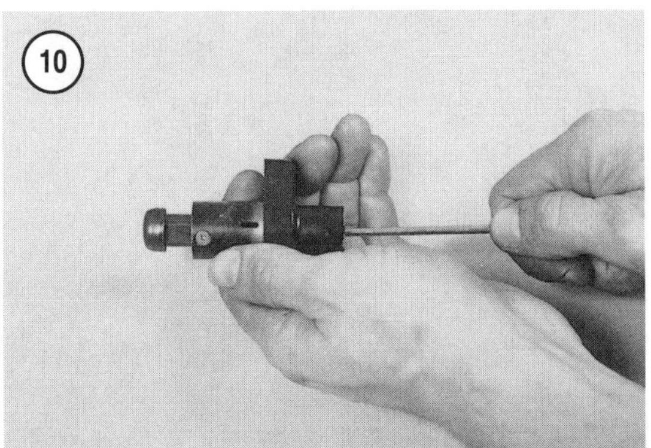

Removal/Installation (1990-on Models)

Refer to **Figure 11**.

1. Remove the cap bolt (A, **Figure 12**) and the copper washer from the cam chain tensioner body, then remove the rod and spring (A, **Figure 13**).
2. Remove the mounting bolts (B, **Figure 13**), and pull the cam chain tensioner from the rear side of the cylinder block. Watch for the tensioner gasket.
3. Inspect the cam chain tensioner by performing the following:

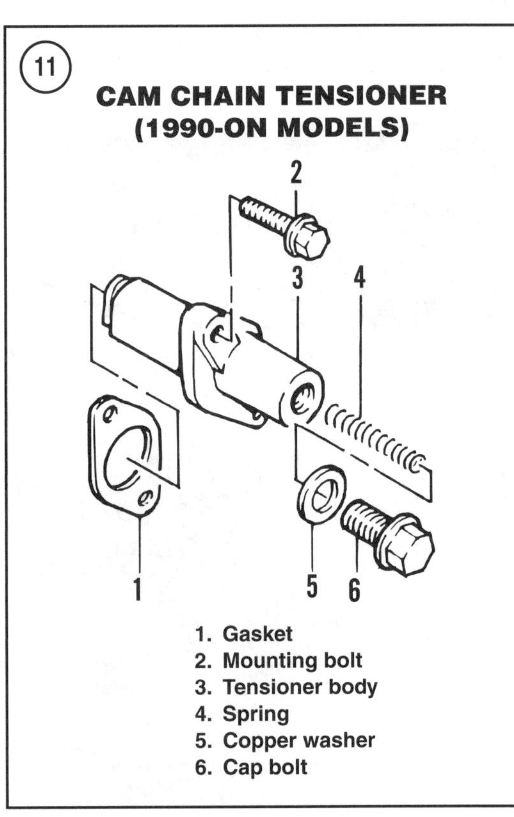

12

13

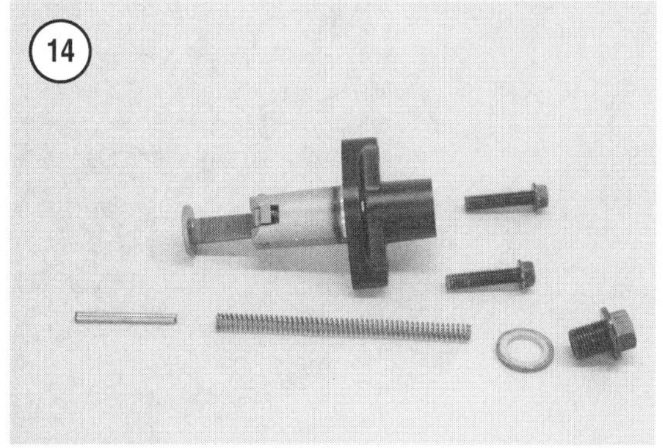
14

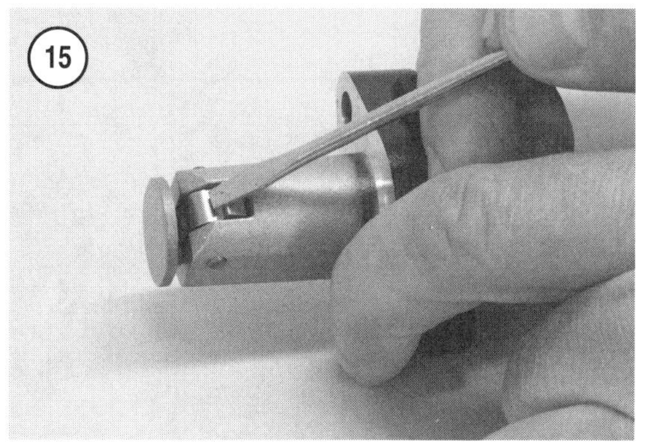
15

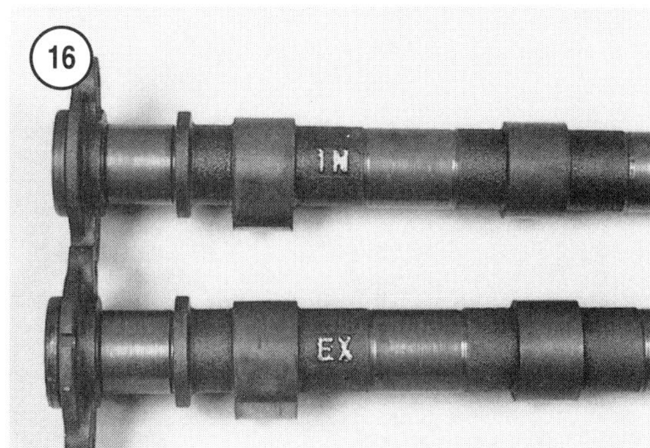

16

a. Visually inspect the cam chain tensioner assembly for wear or damage. If any part is damaged, replace the chain tensioner assembly. See **Figure 14**.

b. Check the operation of the tensioner by pressing the one-way cam (**Figure 15**) and pushing the tensioner pushrod into the body. The pushrod should move smoothly. If it does not, replace the chain tensioner assembly.

4. Install the cam chain tensioner as follows:

a. If necessary, release the one-way cam, and press the pushrod all the way into the tensioner body (**Figure 15**).

b. Seat the tensioner body and a new gasket into place in the rear of the cylinder block.

c. Install the cam chain tensioner mounting bolts (B, **Figure 13**), and torque them to 9.8 N•m (87 in.-lb.)

d. Install the spring and rod (**Figure 13**) into the tensioner body.

e. Make sure a new copper washer is in place on the cap bolt (A, **Figure 12**), and install the tensioner cap bolt. Tighten the cap bolt securely.

CAMSHAFT

The camshafts mount in the top of the cylinder head. Each camshaft is identified by the EX (exhaust) or IN (intake) cast into the shaft (**Figure 16**). The camshafts are chain driven by the timing sprocket on the left end of the crankshaft.

Since cam lobe wear, journal wear and camshaft runout affect valve timing, inspect the camshafts whenever they are removed or when experiencing valve timing problems.

Refer to **Figure 17**.

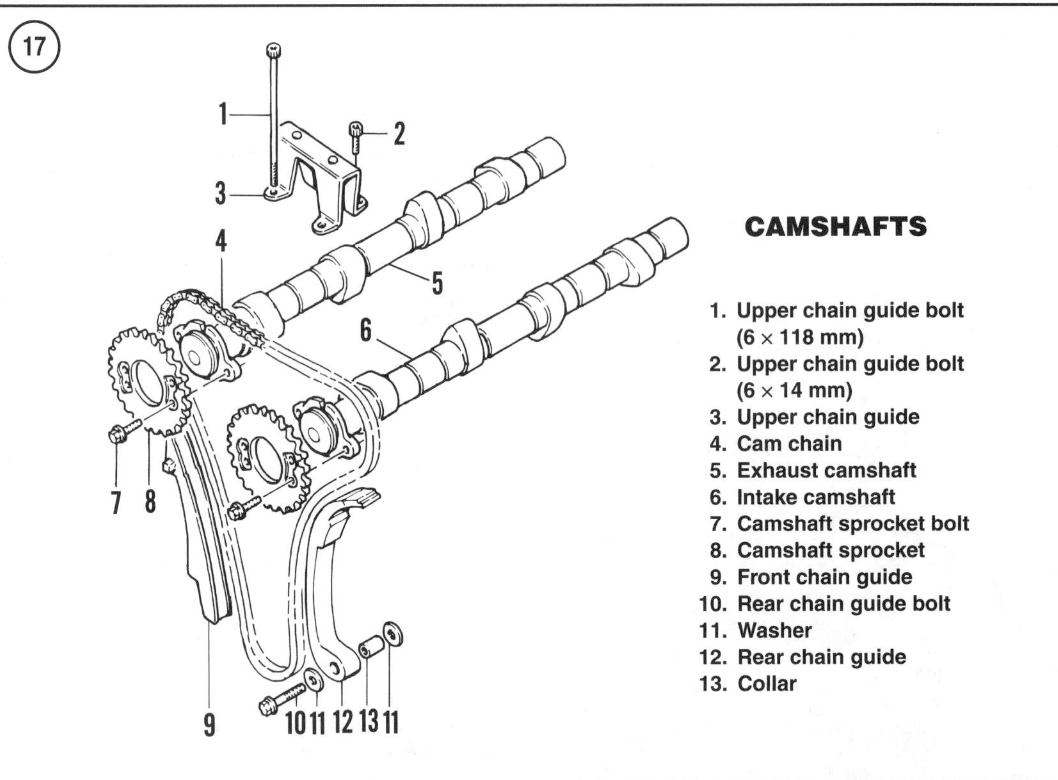

Camshaft Removal

NOTE
The camshafts can be removed with the engine mounted in the frame. The procedure is shown with the engine removed for photographic clarity.

1. Disconnect the negative battery cable (**Figure 18**).
2. Remove the cylinder head cover as described in this chapter.

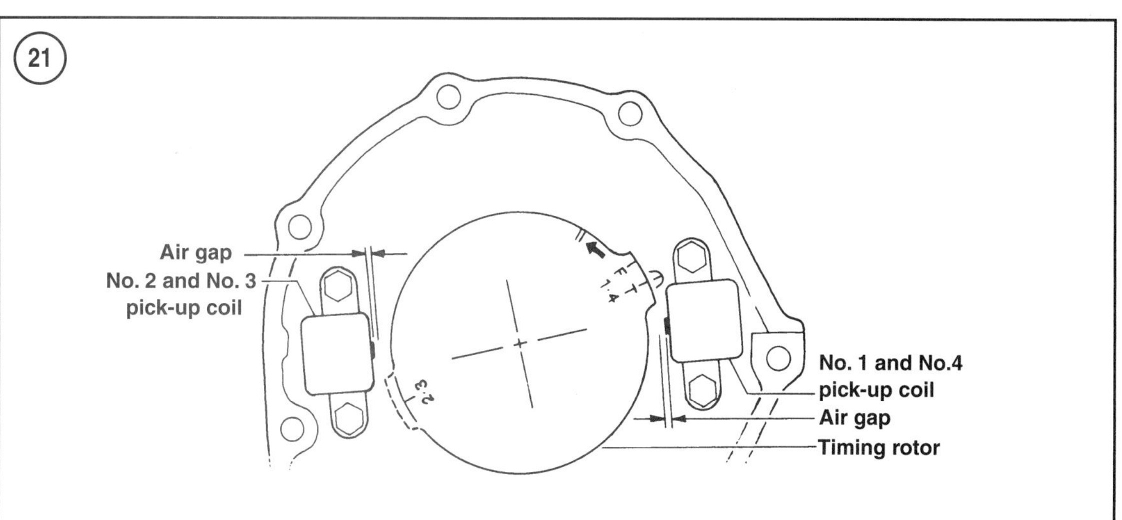

3. Remove the spark plugs so the engine will turn easily.

4. Set an oil pan beneath the pickup coil cover and remove the cover (A, **Figure 19**) from the left side.

5. Use the timing rotor nut (**Figure 20**) to rotate the engine counterclockwise until the No. 1.4 T-mark on the rotor aligns with the index mark on the crankcase (**Figure 21**). This sets the No. 1 and No. 4 cylinders to top dead center.

6. Remove the upper chain guide (**Figure 22**) from the cylinder head.

7. Loosen the valve adjuster locknuts and loosen the adjusters (**Figure 23**).

NOTE

*Each cam cap is stamped with an arrow (pointing forward) and a location number (**Figure 24**). If these marks are illegible, label the cam caps so each cap can be reinstalled in its proper location and with the proper orientation.*

8. Evenly loosen the cam cap bolts (**Figure 25**) for one camshaft. Loosen the bolts in the reverse of the tightening sequence shown in **Figure 26**, and remove the bolts.

9. Remove the cam caps. Watch for the two dowels (**Figure 27**) beneath each cam cap.

10. Slowly remove the camshaft and its sprocket so neither the cam lobes nor the bearing surfaces are damaged.

11. Tie a safety wire to the cam chain, and secure the other end to the engine so the cam chain will not fall into the engine.

12. Repeat Steps 7-9 and remove the other camshaft.

CAUTION

If the crankshaft must be turned while the camshafts are removed, pull the cam chain taut against the timing

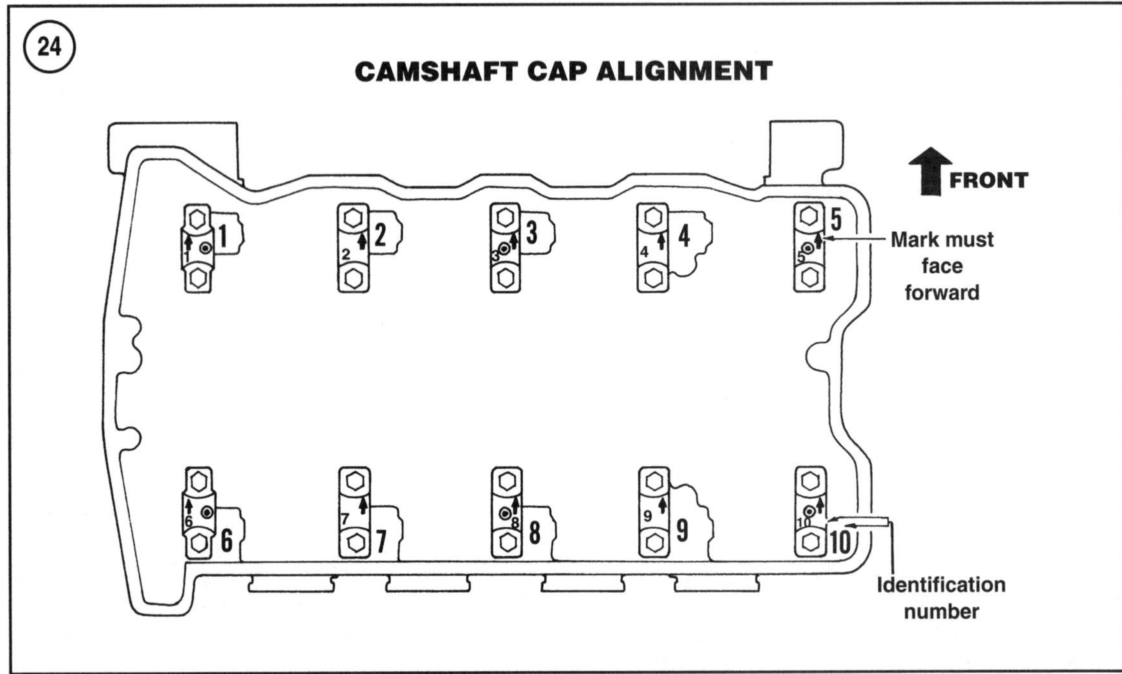

sprocket so the chain will not be damaged while the engine is turned.

13. Inspect the camshafts as described in this chapter.

Camshaft Installation

1. Make sure that the No. 1.4 T-mark on the timing rotor still aligns with the index mark on the crankcase (**Figure 21**). If necessary, use the rotor nut to rotate the crankshaft counterclockwise and align the marks. Hold the cam chain taut against the timing sprocket as you rotate the crankshaft.
2. Coat the cam lobes, camshaft journals, cam caps and bearing surfaces in the cylinder head with clean engine oil. If installing new camshafts or a new cylinder head, apply a thin coat of molybdenum disulfide grease to these parts.
3. Remove the safety wire from the cam chain.
4. Lift the cam chain, insert the exhaust camshaft through the chain and lower the camshaft into the front side of the cylinder head. Repeat this procedure and install the intake camshaft into the rear side of the head.
5. Without turning the crankshaft, lift the cam chain off each sprocket and reposition the camshaft so the sprocket's IN- or EX-index mark on each respective sprocket aligns with the top edge of the cylinder head. See **Figure 28** and **Figure 29**.

6. Locate the first cam chain pin that aligns with the exhaust sprocket's EX mark. Starting with this mark, count 35 cam chain pins toward the intake sprocket. The 35th pin must align with the IN mark on the intake sprocket.If it does not, recount and reposition the intake or exhaust camshaft as required.
7. Check that the cam chain is properly seated against the front and rear chain guides.

CAUTION
The cam caps are align-bored with the cylinder head during manufactur-

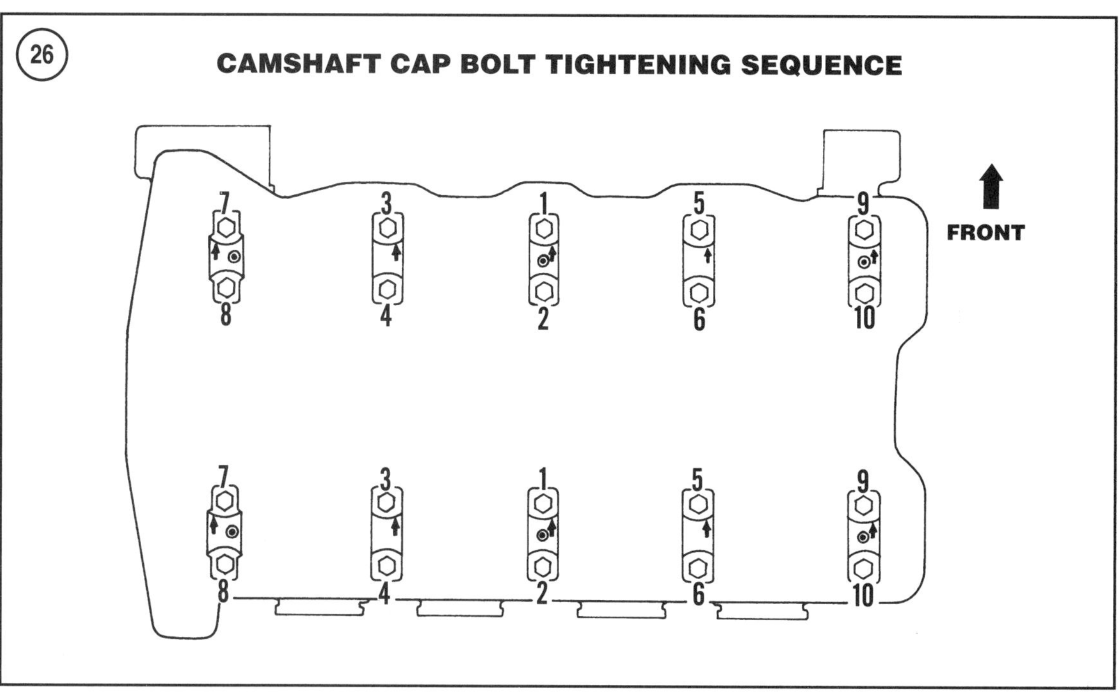

ing. The camshaft may seize if the caps are not installed in their original locations.

8. Install the cam cap dowels into the cylinder head and set each cam cap into its proper location. The arrow on each cam cap must point forward and the location number on each cap must match the number cast into the cylinder head. See **Figure 24**.

9. Seat the camshafts by tightening cam cap bolts No. 1 and 2 on each shaft (**Figure 26**).

10. Evenly tighten the bolts in a crisscross pattern. Following the tightening sequence shown in **Figure 26**, torque the cam cap bolts to 12 N•m (106 in.-lb.).

CAUTION

If any binding is felt while turning the crankshaft ***stop*** *and recheck the timing marks. Improper timing will cause valve and piston damage.*

11. Use the rotor nut to slowly turn the crankshaft two full turns counterclockwise and align the No. 1.4 T-mark with the index mark on the crankcase (**Figure 21**).

   a. Check the timing marks on the cam sprockets. They should align with the top edge of the cylinder head as shown in **Figure 28**.

4

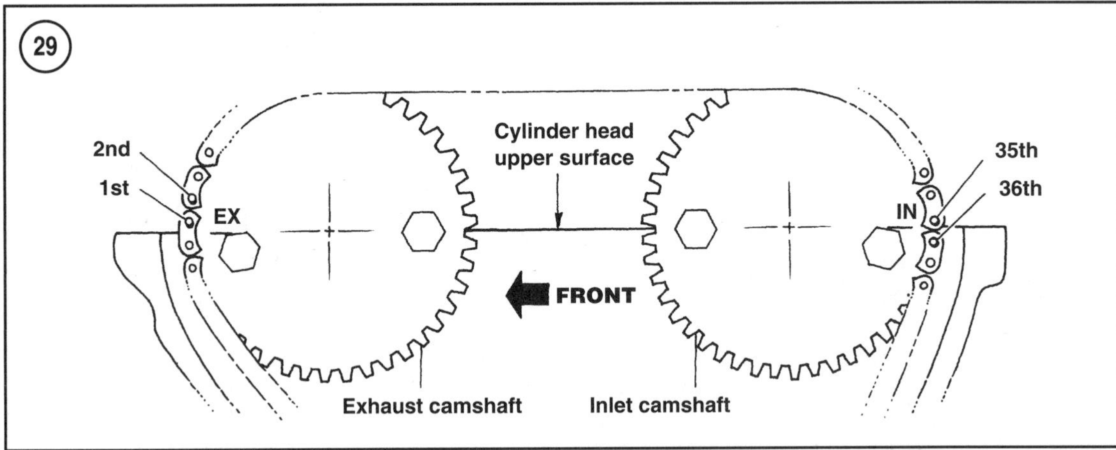

b. If the timing marks do not properly align, remove the cam caps and reposition the camshafts as described in Steps 5-10.

12. Install the pickup coil cover (A, **Figure 19**) by performing the following:

a. Apply silicon sealant to the pickup coil grommet (A, **Figure 30**) in the crankcase and to the crankcase where the two case halves mate (B).

b. Fit the pickup coil cover and gasket into place on the crankcase.

c. Apply Loctite 242 to the threads of the two indicated cover bolts (B, **Figure 19**), and torque the cover bolts to 9.8 N•m (87 in.-lb.).

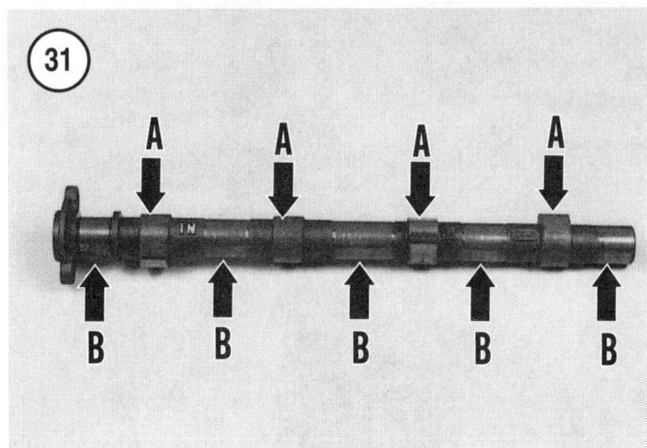

Camshaft Inspection

1. Clean all parts in solvent and blow them dry with compressed air.

2. Visually inspect each camshaft lobe (A, **Figure 31**) for wear. The lobes should not be scored and the edges should be square. Slight damage can be removed with silicon carbide oil stone. Use No. 100-120 grit initially and then polish the lobe with No. 280-320 grit.

3. Measure the height (**Figure 32**) of each cam lobe with a micrometer. Replace the camshaft if a lobe is worn beyond the service limit specified in **Table 2**.

4. Visually inspect each camshaft journal (B, **Figure 31**) for wear and scoring. Replace the camshaft if necessary.

5. Measure the diameter of the camshaft journals with a micrometer (**Figure 33**). Replace the camshaft if a journal is worn beyond the service limit in **Table 2**.

6. Measure the camshaft runout with a dial indicator and V-blocks. Replace the camshaft if the runout exceeds the service limit in **Table 2**.

NOTE

If a camshaft sprocket is worn, also inspect the cam chain, chain guides

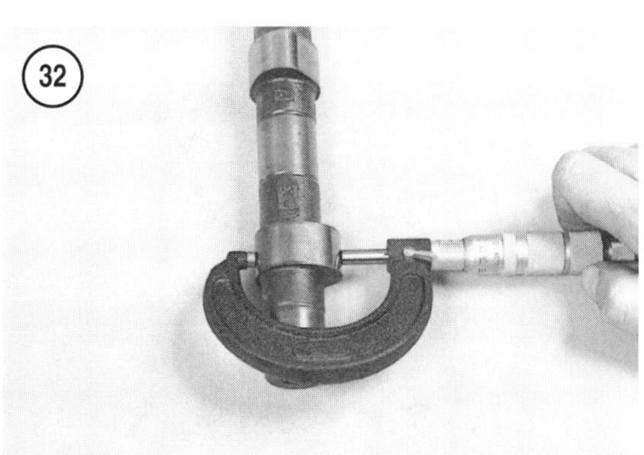
32

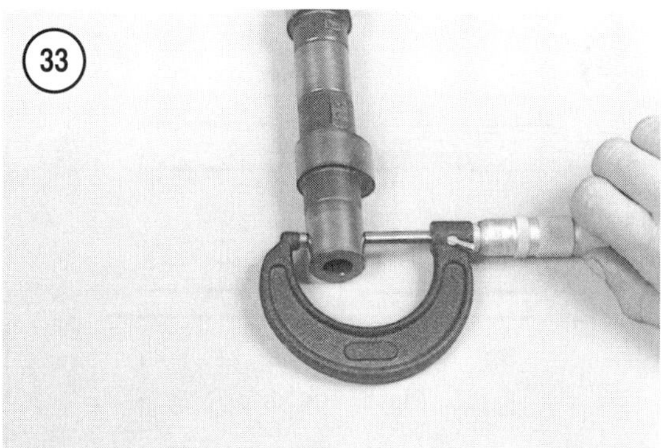
33

34

35

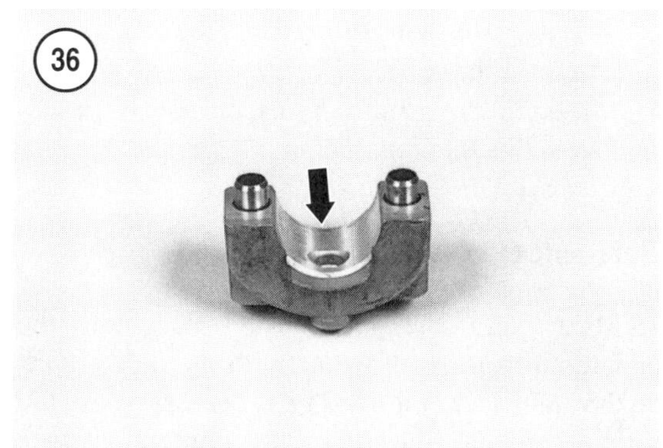
36

and the timing sprocket on the crankshaft. Refer to Chapter Five.

7. Inspect the camshaft sprocket for worn or missing teeth (**Figure 34**). Replace the sprocket if necessary.

NOTE
The cylinder head must be removed during rear cam chain guide replacement. Refer to the cylinder head removal procedure in this chapter.

8. Check the sliding surfaces of the front, rear and upper cam chain guides for wear or damage.
9. Inspect the bearing surfaces in the cylinder head (**Figure 35**) and camshaft caps (**Figure 36**). They should not be scored or excessively worn. If necessary, replace the cylinder head and all camshaft caps as a set.
10. If the cam caps are reusable, measure the camshaft bearing inside diameter by performing the following:
   a. Install the cam-cap dowels into the cylinder head.
   b. Loosely install each cam cap in its proper location in the cylinder head. The arrow on the cap must point forward, and the cam-cap location number must match the number in the cylinder head. See **Figure 24**. Do not install the camshafts.
   c. Install the cam cap bolts and torque them to 12 N•m (106 in.-lb.).
   d. Measure the inside diameter of each camshaft bearing with a bore gauge or telescoping gauge. Record the measurement for each bearing.
   e. If any camshaft bearing inside diameter exceeds the service limit specified in **Table 2**,

4

replace the cylinder head and the cam caps as a set (**Figure 37**).

11. Measure the camshaft oil clearance as described in this section.

Camshaft Oil Clearance

1. Make sure the No. 1.4 T-mark on the pickup-coil rotor still aligns with the index mark on the crankcase (**Figure 21**). If necessary, use the rotor nut to rotate the crankshaft counterclockwise and align the marks. Hold the cam chain taut against the timing sprocket as you rotate the crankshaft.
2. Wipe all oil from the camshafts and install each camshaft into its location in the cylinder head.
3. Place a piece of Plastigage lengthwise on each camshaft journal (**Figure 38**). The Plastigage must run parallel to the crankshaft.
4. Install the cam cap dowels into the cylinder head (**Figure 27**) and set each cam cap into its proper location. The arrow on each cam cap must point forward and the location number on each cap must match the number cast into the cylinder head. See **Figure 24**.
5. Seat the camshafts by tightening cam cap bolts No. 1 and No. 2 on each shaft (**Figure 26**).
6. Evenly tighten the cam cap bolts in a crisscross pattern.
7. Following the tightening sequence shown in **Figure 26**, torque the cam cap bolts to 12 N•m (106 in.-lb.).

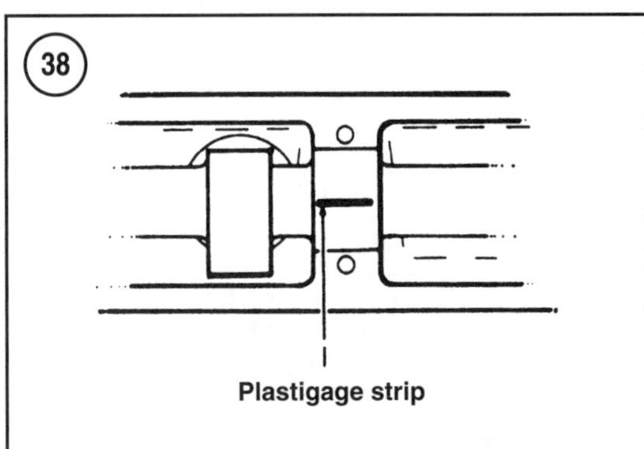

CAUTION

Do not rotate the camshaft while Plastigage is in place.

8. Reverse the order of the tightening sequence (**Figure 26**) and evenly loosen the cam cap bolts. Remove the bolts and carefully remove the cam caps.
9. Measure the width of each piece of Plastigage at its widest part (**Figure 39**).

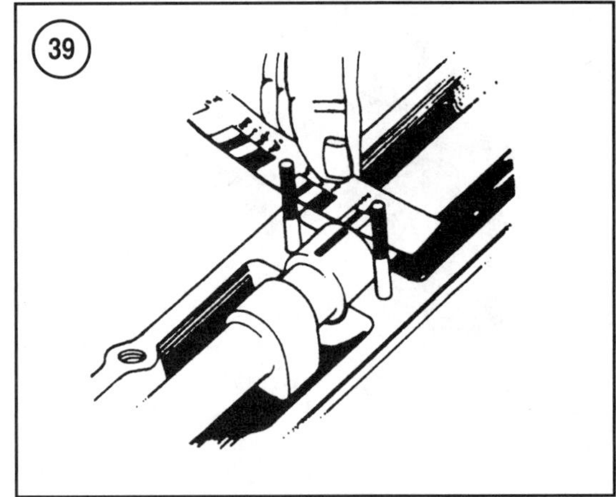

10. If the clearance exceeds the service limit specified in **Table 2**, measure the camshaft journal diameter with a micrometer (**Figure 33**). If the journal diameter is less than the specification in **Table 2**, replace the camshaft. If journal diameter is within specification, replace the cylinder head and cam caps (**Figure 37**) as a set.

CAUTION

Plastigage must not be left in the engine. It can plug an oil control orifice, which will cause severe engine damage.

11. Remove all Plastigage from the camshaft bearing journals, cam caps and the bearing surface in the cylinder head. Clean the camshaft bearing groove.

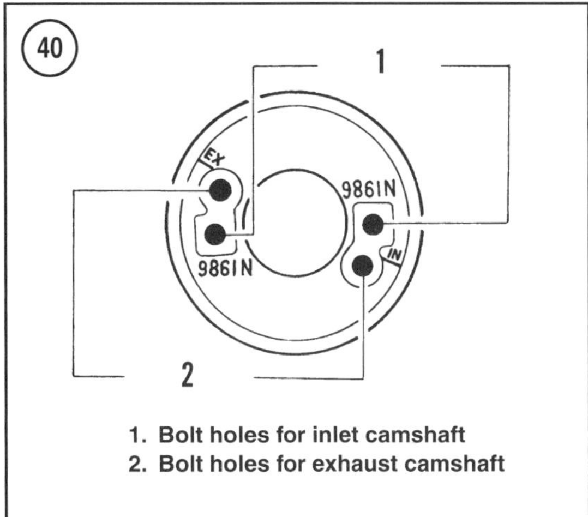

1. Bolt holes for inlet camshaft
2. Bolt holes for exhaust camshaft

Camshaft Sprocket Replacement

The intake and exhaust sprockets are identical. Four holes are drilled through each sprocket: two marked IN and two marked EX. Use the appropriate holes on the sprocket when replacing a sprocket. See **Figure 40**.

1. Install a sprocket onto the camshaft so the side marked IN and EX faces out toward the left side of the engine.
2. Align the bolt holes marked IN with the bolt holes on the intake camshaft. Align the EX sprocket holes with the bolt holes on the exhaust camshaft.
3. Apply Loctite 242 to the sprocket bolts. Torque the bolts to 15 N•m (11 ft.-lb.).

CAM CHAIN AND CHAIN GUIDES

Refer to **Figure 17** when servicing the cam chain or chain guides.

Removal

1. Remove the timing rotor as described in Chapter Nine.
2. Remove the cylinder head as described in this chapter.
3. If necessary, remove the cam chain plate bolts and remove the plate (**Figure 41**).
4. Remove the rear chain guide as follows:
   a. Remove the rear chain-guide bolt (**Figure 42**) and washer.
   b. Remove the collar (**Figure 43**) from the chain guide.
   c. Pull the rear chain guide from the cam chain tunnel (**Figure 44**). Watch for the washer behind the chain guide. Remove the washer.
5. Remove the cam chain from the timing sprocket and pull the chain from the cam chain tunnel.

6. Lift the front chain guide from its seat in the cylinder block and remove the guide from the cam chain tunnel (**Figure 45**).
7. Inspect the cam chain and the chain guides as described in this section.

Installation

1. Insert the front chain guide through the cam chain tunnel (**Figure 45**) and seat the guide in the boss in the cylinder block.
2. Lower the cam chain through the cam chain tunnel and fit the chain on the timing sprocket (**Figure 46**). Secure the chain with a safety wire so it will not fall into the tunnel.
3. Install the rear chain guide by performing the following:
   a. Insert the collar into the rear chain guide and lower the guide through the cam chain tunnel.
   b. Apply Loctite 242 to the threads of the rear chain guide bolt.
   c. Install a washer on each side of the rear chain guide.
   d. Secure the guide and washers in place with the rear chain guide bolt (**Figure 42**). Torque the bolt to 20 N•m (15 ft.-lb.).
4. Install the cylinder head as described in this chapter.

Inspection

1. Inspect the sliding surface of the front, rear and upper chain guides. Replace a guide as necessary.
2. Visually inspect the cam chain for signs of excessive wear or damage. If damage is noted, also inspect the cam chain and timing sprockets for damage.
3. Stretch the cam chain taut on the bench and measure a 20-link length (21 pins) as shown in **Figure 47**. Replace the cam chain if the measurement exceeds the service limit specified in **Table 2**.

ROCKER ARM ASSEMBLY

Two rocker arm shafts are used in this engine. Each shaft secures four rocker arms and their springs in place. The rocker arms are made of a spe-

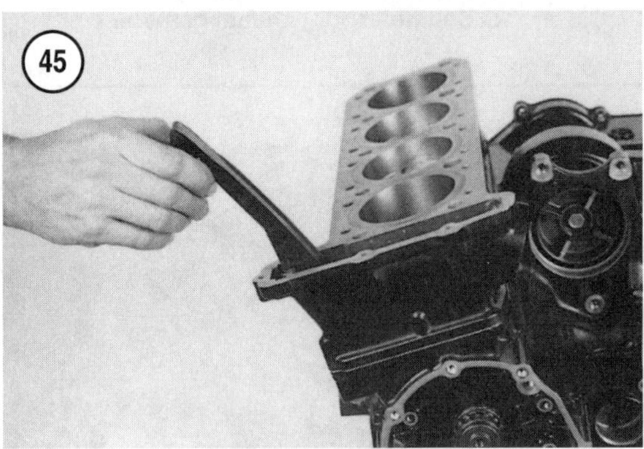

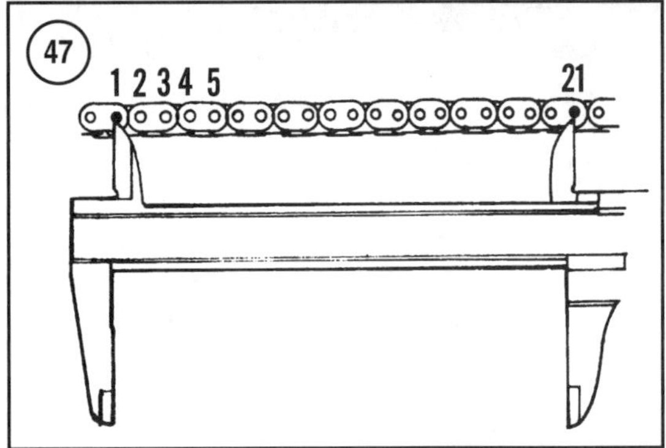

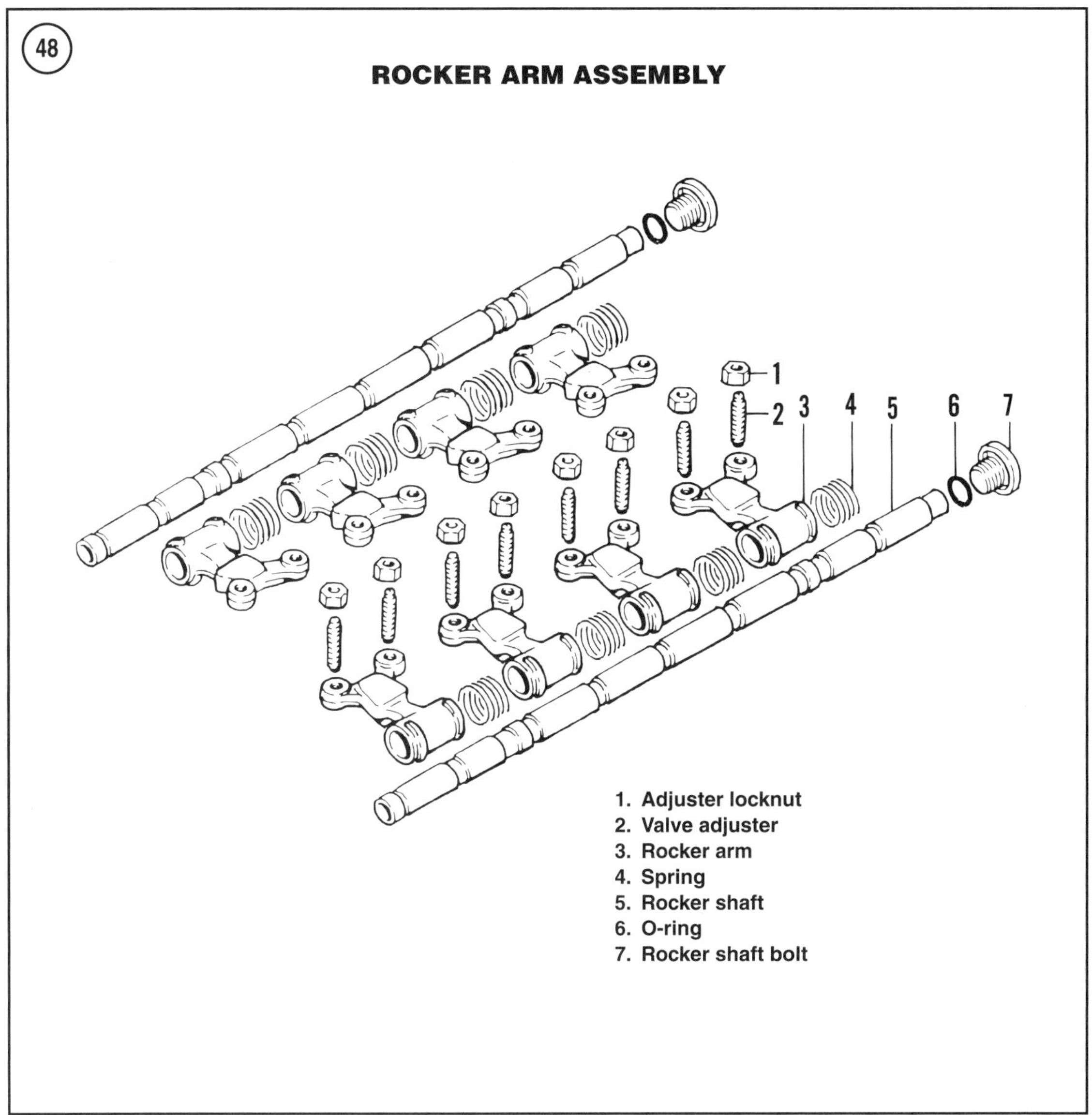

cial steel alloy for durability. The surfaces that contact the cams and the valve adjusters have been heat-treated for surface hardness.

The intake and exhaust rockers arms are identical. However, since they develop wear patterns during use, all parts should be labeled during removal so they can be reinstalled in their original positions.

Excessive rocker arm-to-shaft clearance results in excessive noise. Check this clearance whenever the rocker arms are removed. The rocker arms and shafts can be serviced while the engine is in the frame.

Removal

Refer to **Figure 48** when servicing the rocker arms.

1. Remove the camshafts as described in this chapter.

2. Remove the four oil pipe bolts and the two cylinder head oil pipes (**Figure 49**). Note the oil pipe bolts are color coded. The bolt on the intake side of each oil pipe is black, on the exhaust side the bolt is white. These bolts must be installed on the correct side of the cylinder head during assembly.

3. Remove the rocker shafts by performing the following:
   a. Use an Allen wrench to turn out the two shaft plugs (**Figure 50**).
   b. Turn a M8 × 1.25 bolts (approximately 30-mm long) into the end of the intake rocker shaft and pull the shaft out of the cylinder head (**Figure 51**).
4. Lift the rocker arms and springs (**Figure 52**) from the cylinder head. Note that the spring sits on the right side of each rocker arm. See **Figure 53**. Keep the rocker arms in order so they can be reinstalled in their original positions.
5. Repeat Steps 3 and 4 for the exhaust side.
6. Inspect the rocker arm assemblies as described in this section.

Installation

1. Coat the rocker shaft and rocker arm bores with engine oil.
2. Fit the spring onto the right side of each rocker arm (**Figure 53**) as the rocker arm faces the center of the engine. See **Figure 54** for reference.
3. Set each rocker arm and spring assembly into its original location in the cylinder head. The springs should face the right side and the valve adjusters should rest on the valves when the rocker arms are installed correctly. See **Figure 52**.
4. Turn the bolt used during removal into the end of one rocker shaft. Insert the rocker shaft (**Figure 51**) through the cylinder head, rocker arms and springs. Make sure the exhaust rocker shaft is installed on the exhaust side of the cylinder head and the intake shaft is installed on the intake side.
5. Once the shaft is seated in the opposite side of the cylinder head, remove the bolt from the rocker shaft.
6. Repeat Steps 4 and 5 for the remaining rocker shaft.
7. Apply oil to the rocker shaft plug O-ring, and install each rocker shaft plug (**Figure 50**). Torque the plugs to 9.8 N•m (87 in.-lb.).
8. Set the two cylinder head oil pipes into place in the head and secure them with the four oil pipe bolts (**Figure 49**). The bolts are color coded. A black bolt must be installed on the intake side, and a white bolt on the exhaust side, of each oil pipe.

53

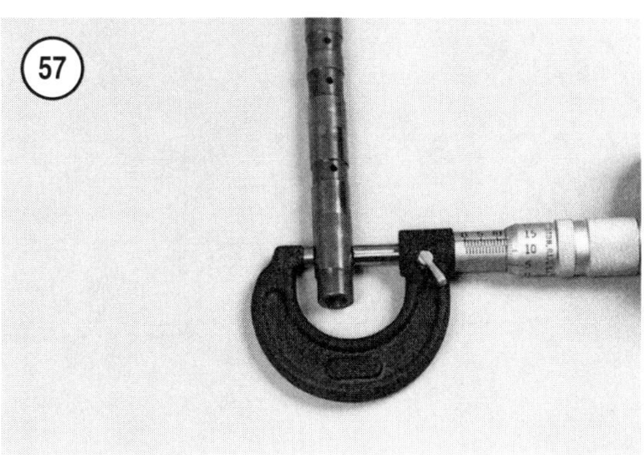
57

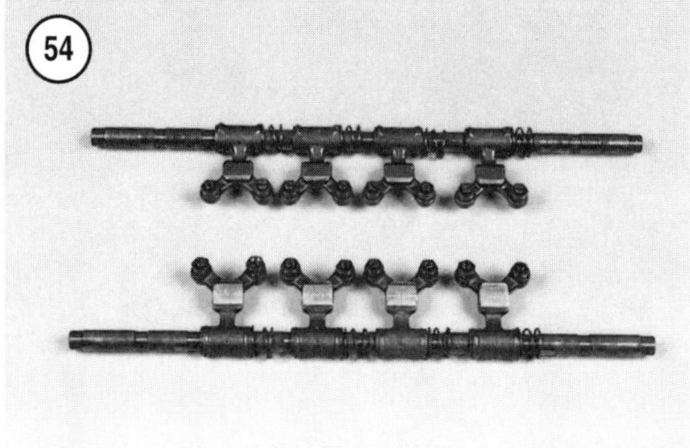
54

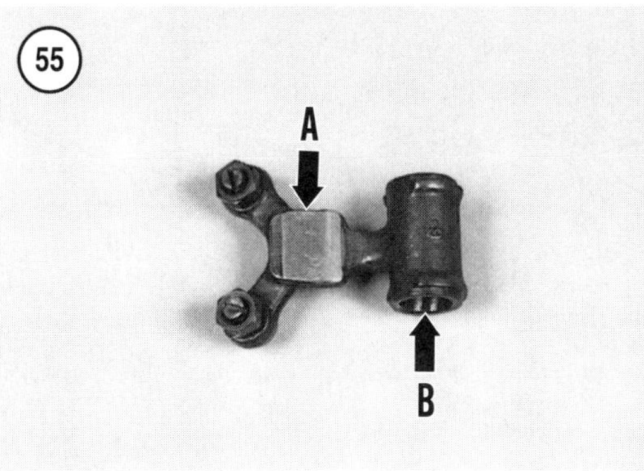

55

56

Torque the cylinder-head oil pipe bolts to 9.8 N•m (87 in.-lb.).

9. Install the camshafts as described in this chapter.

Inspection

1. Wash all parts (**Figure 54**) in clean solvent. Dry them thoroughly.

2. Check each rocker arm spring for fatigue, cracks or other damage. Replace as necessary.

3. Inspect the rocker arm pad (A, **Figure 55**) where it rides on the cam lobe. If a pad is scratched or unevenly worn, inspect its mated cam lobe for damage. Replace the rocker arm as necessary.

4. Inspect the valve adjusters (**Figure 56**) where they contact the valve stems. Replace as necessary.

5. Measure the inside diameter of the rocker arm bore (B, **Figure 55**) with a small bore gauge. Replace any rocker arm if its bore exceeds the service limit specified in **Table 2**.

6. Inspect the rocker shaft for wear or scoring. Measure its outside diameter with a micrometer (**Figure 57**). Replace a rocker shaft if it is worn to the specified service limit.

7. Examine the cylinder head oil pipes (**Figure 58**) for cracks or other abnormal condition. Pay particular attention to the brazed joints (**Figure 59**).

8. Flush the oil pipes and their bolts with solvent. Blow them clear with compressed air.

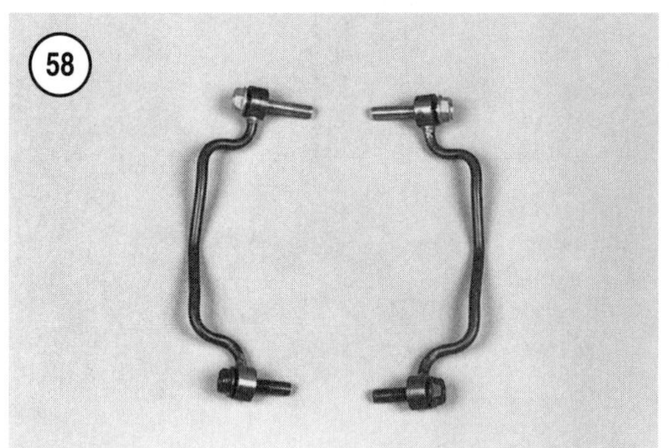
58

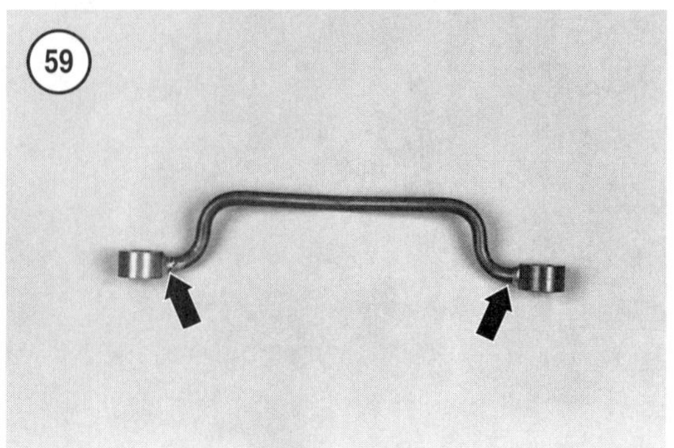
59

60

CYLINDER HEAD

1. Mounting bolt
2. Clamp
3. Banjo bolt
4. Copper washer
5. Main oil pipe
6. Cam cap bolt
7. Cam cap
8. Exhaust header stud
9. Dowel
10. Cylinder head
11. Cylinder head bolt (11 mm)
12. Washer
13. Cylinder head oil pipe bolt (white)
14. Cylinder head oil pipe bolt (black)
15. Cylinder head oil pipe
16. Cylinder head bolt (10 mm)
17. Washer
18. Clamp
19. Intake manifold
20. Valve guide
21. O-ring (1986-1987 models)
22. Cylinder head gasket

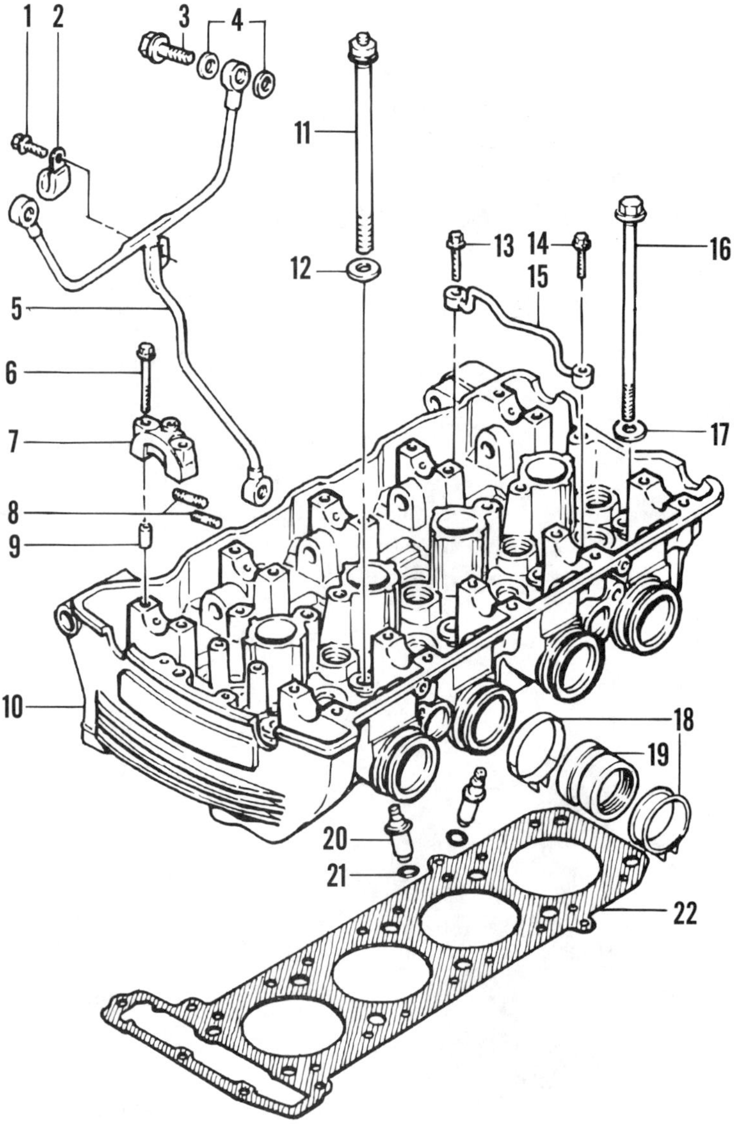

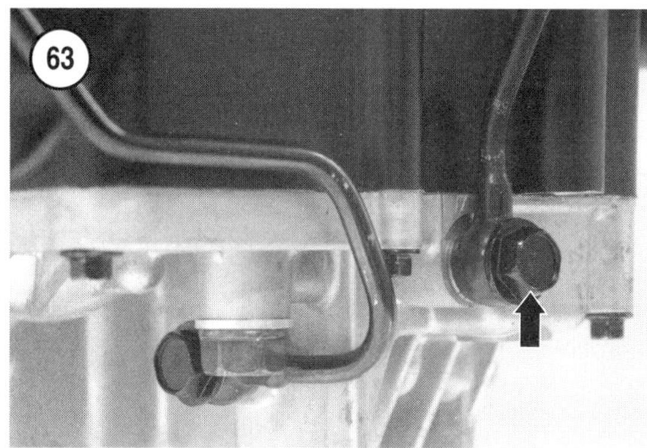

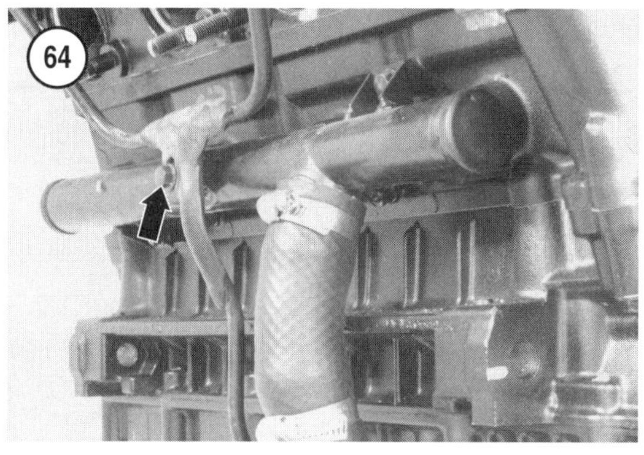

CYLINDER HEAD

Removal

The cylinder head (**Figure 60**) can be removed with the engine in the frame. The photographs show the engine removed for photographic clarity.

1. Drain the engine oil and the coolant as described in Chapter Three.
2. Remove the thermostat assembly, radiator and the radiator bracket (Chapter Ten).
3. Remove the exhaust pipes and carburetors (Chapter Eight).
4. Remove the cylinder head cover and camshafts as described in this chapter. If the valves or the cylinder head requires service, remove the rocker arm assemblies (this chapter).
5. Remove the main oil pipe (**Figure 61**) by performing the following:
    a. Remove the banjo bolts (**Figure 62**) that secure the main oil pipe to the cylinder head. Watch for the two sealing washers installed with each banjo bolt.
    b. Remove the banjo bolt (**Figure 63**) that secures the main oil pipe to the oil pan.
    c. Remove the mounting bolt (**Figure 64**) that secures the main oil pipe to the coolant manifold and pull the oil pipe from the engine.
6. Support the engine with a hydraulic jack or wooden block so the engine will not move once the front engine mounting hardware is removed in the next step.
7. Remove the front engine mounting nut and bolt from each side (**Figure 65**). Watch for any alignment shim(s) installed on the left side.

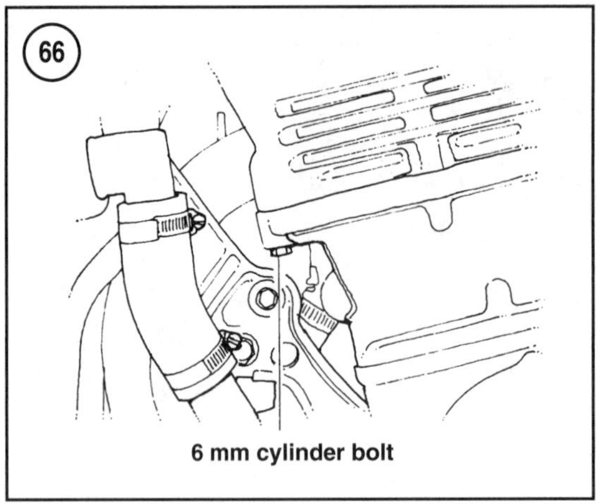

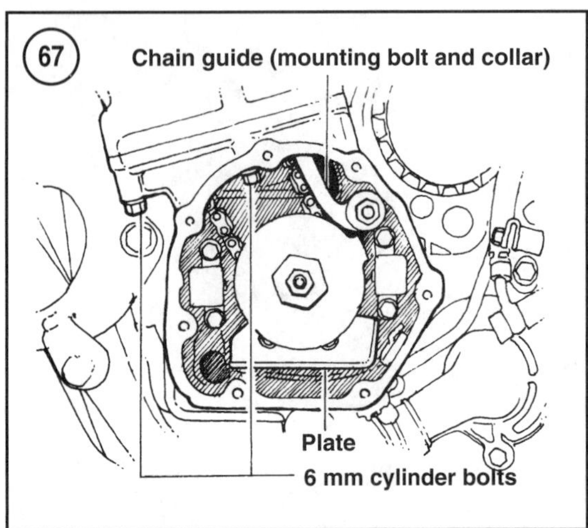

8. Remove the 6-mm cylinder head bolt (**Figure 66**).

CAUTION
The cylinder head bolts secure both the cylinder head and cylinder block in place. The 6-mm cylinder bolts must be removed during cylinder head removal so they will not be unduly stressed once the cylinder head bolts are removed.

9. Remove the 6-mm cylinder bolts (**Figure 67**).

10. Evenly loosen and remove the cylinder head bolts. Follow the reverse of the tightening sequence shown in **Figure 68**.

NOTE
Some cylinder head bolts cannot be removed from the head while the engine is in the frame. Lift these bolts enough to provide sufficient clearance to remove the head.

11. Use a soft-faced mallet to tap around the perimeter of the cylinder head.

12. Remove the cylinder head (**Figure 69**) by lifting it straight up and off the cylinder. Watch for the two dowels beneath the head.

13. Stuff a clean shop rag into cam-chain tunnel in the cylinder block so parts will not fall into the crankcase.

14. Remove the two dowels (A, **Figure 70**) and cylinder head gasket (B).

15. Inspect the cylinder head as described in this section.

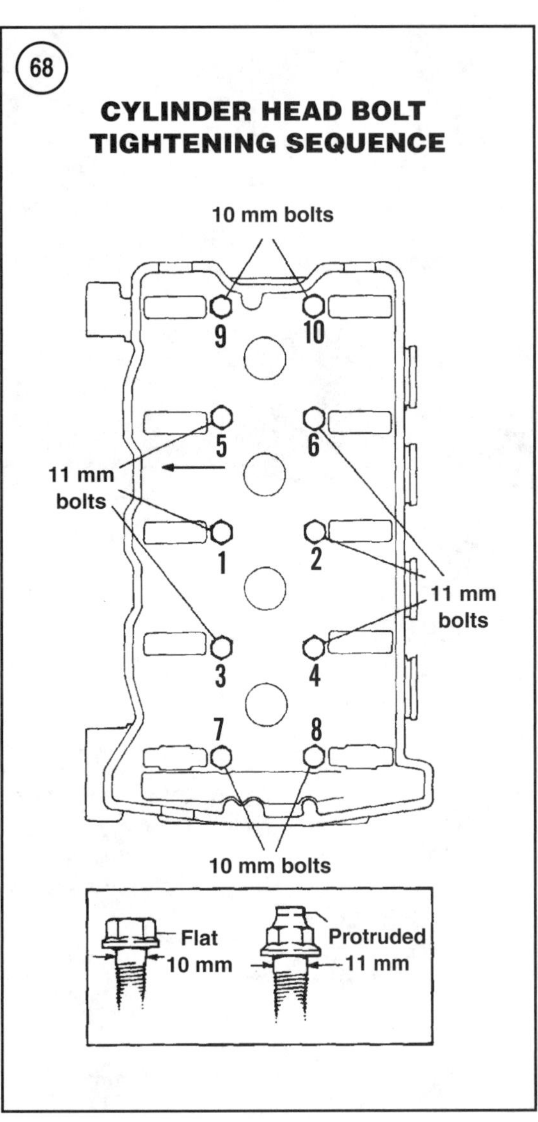

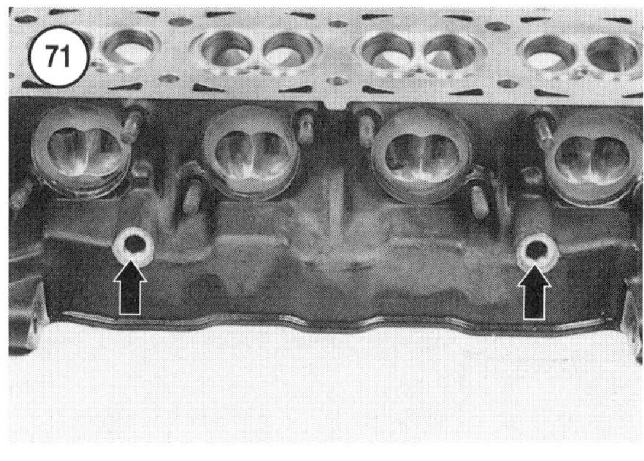

Installation

1. Clean all gasket residue from the cylinder head and cylinder mating surfaces.
2. Blow out the cylinder head oil passages (**Figure 71**) with compressed air.
3. Install a new cylinder head gasket (B, **Figure 70**) and the two dowels (A).
4. Feed the cam chain up through the cam chain tunnel in the cylinder head and lower the cylinder head (**Figure 69**) onto the cylinder. Secure the cam chain with a safety wire so it will not fall into the crankcase.

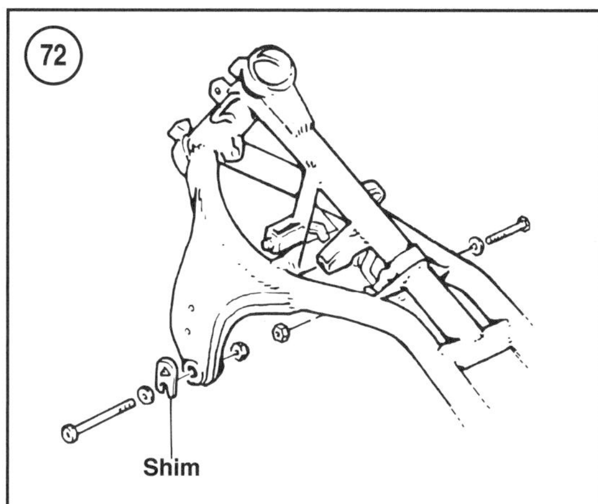

5. Apply molybdenum disulfide grease to both sides of each cylinder head bolt washer.
6. Install the cylinder head bolts with their washers. Evenly tighten the cylinder head bolts in the sequence shown in **Figure 68**.

NOTE
Kawasaki provides two sets of torque specifications for the cylinder head bolts: new and used. When installing a new cylinder head with new bolts and new washers, tighten the cylinder head bolts to the new specifications. If reusing either the cylinder head, bolts or washers; tighten the bolts to the used specifications.

7. Torque the 10 and 11 mm cylinder head bolts in the sequence shown in **Figure 68** to the specification in **Table 3**.
8. Install the 6 mm cylinder bolts (**Figure 67**), and torque them to 15 N•m (11 ft.-lb.).
9. Install the 6 mm cylinder head bolt (**Figure 66**), and torque it to 9.8 N•m (89 in.-lb.).
10. Loosely install the front engine mounting bolt, washer and nut on each side (**Figure 65**). If a shim was found during removal, install it between the front engine mounting bolt and the left side of the frame (**Figure 72**).
11. Check the adjustment shim by performing the following:
    a. Insert a 2.0 mm shim between the cylinder head and the frame.
    b. If the 2.0 mm shim does not fit, try a 1.2 mm shim.

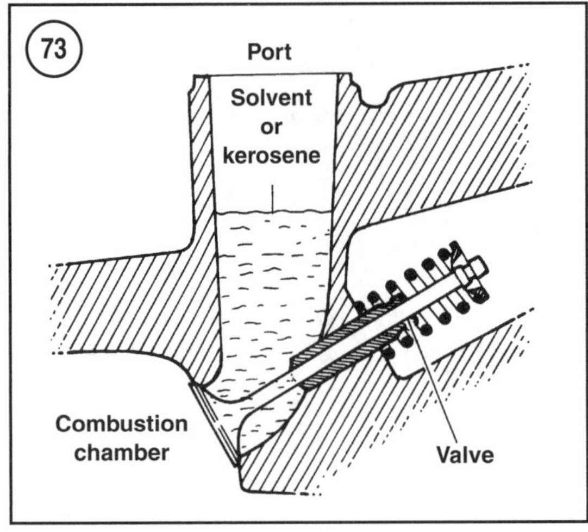

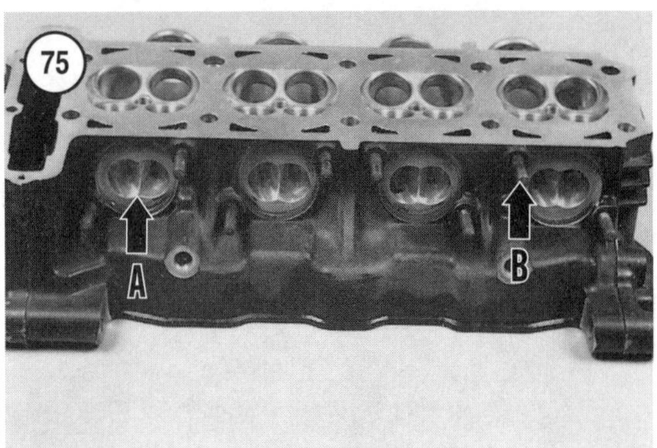

c. If the 1.2 mm shim does not fit, no shim is required.

12. Evenly tighten the front engine mounting nut and bolt on each side of the motorcycle. Torque each nut to 54 N•m (40 ft.-lb.).

13. Install the main oil pipe (**Figure 61**) onto the front of the engine. Use a new sealing washer on each side of the oil pipe fittings, and torque the banjo bolts (**Figure 62** and **Figure 63**) to 25 N•m (18 ft.-lb.) Tighten the oil pipe mounting bolt (**Figure 64**) securely.

14. Install the camshafts and cylinder head cover as described in this chapter.

15. Install the exhaust pipes and carburetors (Chapter Eight).

16. Install the radiator bracket, radiator and thermostat assembly (Chapter Ten).

17. Fill the engine with fresh engine oil and coolant (Chapter Three).

Inspection

1. Before removing the valves or cleaning the cylinder head, perform the following leakage test:
   a. Position the cylinder head so the exhaust ports face up. Pour solvent or kerosene into each port opening (**Figure 73**).
   b. Turn the head over slightly and check each exhaust valve area on the combustion chamber side. If the valve and seats are in good condition, no leakage past the valve seats will be found. If any area is wet, the valve seat is not sealing correctly. This can be caused by a damaged valve seat and/or valve face or by a bent or damaged valve. Remove the valve and inspect the valve and seat for wear or damage.
   c. Pour solvent into the intake ports and check the intake valves.

2. Remove all traces of gasket material from the mating surfaces on the cylinder head and the cylinder block.

CAUTION

Cleaning the combustion chamber with the valves removed can damage the valve seat surfaces. A damaged or

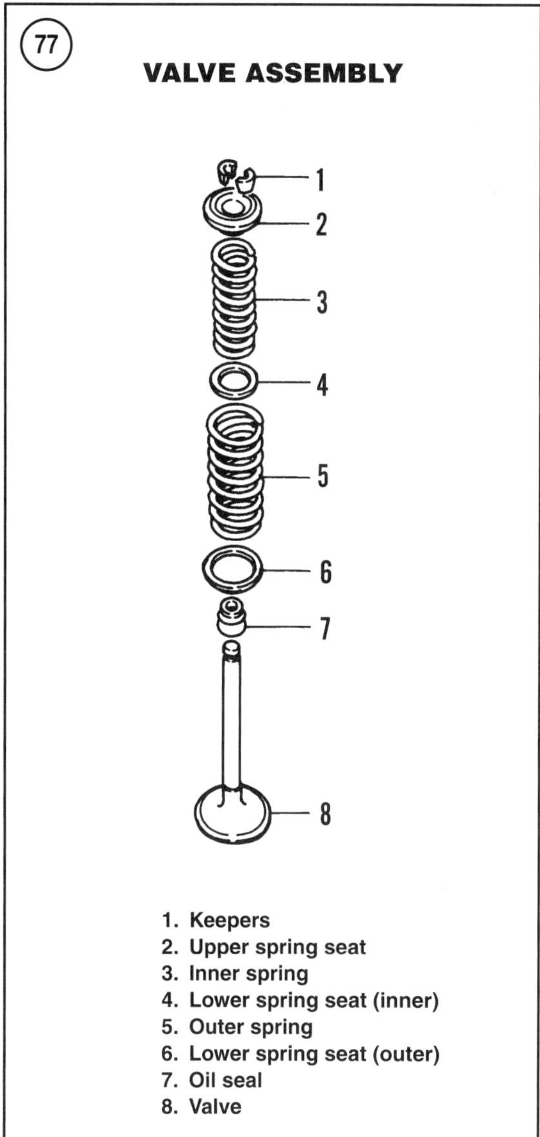

even slightly scratched valve seal will cause poor valve seating.

3. Without removing the valves, remove all carbon deposits from each combustion chamber. Use a fine wire brush dipped in solvent or make a scraper from hardwood. Take care not to damage the head, valves or spark plug threads.

4. Examine the spark plug threads for damage. If damage is minor or if the threads are dirty or clogged with carbon, use a spark plug thread tap to clean the threads (**Figure 74**). If the damage is severe, restore the threads by installing a steel thread insert. Thread insert kits can be purchased at automotive supply stores or installed at a Kawasaki dealership.

5. After all carbon is removed from the combustion chambers and valve ports, clean the entire head in solvent.

6. Check for cracks in the combustion chambers, intake ports and exhaust ports (A, **Figure 75**). A cracked head must be replaced.

7. Inspect the threads on the exhaust pipe mounting studs (B, **Figure 75**). Clean the threads with an appropriate size metric die. Replace a stud if damage is severe.

8. After the head has been thoroughly cleaned, place a straightedge across the gasket surface at several points. Measure the warp by inserting a feeler gauge between the straightedge and the cylinder head at each location (**Figure 76**). Maximum allowable cylinder head warp is listed in **Table 2**. If warp exceeds specification, the cylinder head must be replaced or resurfaced. Consult a Kawasaki dealership or machine shop experienced in this type of work.

9. Check the intake manifolds for cracks or damage that would admit unfiltered air into the engine. Also inspect the hose clamps for cracks or signs of fatigue. Replace the parts as necessary.

10. Visually inspect the cylinder head cover mating surface. Pay particular attention to the crescent-shaped cutouts on the each side of the head.

11. Inspect the valves and valves guides as described below in this chapter.

VALVES AND VALVE COMPONENTS

Complete valve service requires a number of special tools. The following procedures describe how to check for valve component wear and to determine what type of service is required. A valve spring compressor is needed to remove and install the valves.

Valve Removal

Refer to **Figure 77**.

CAUTION

Keep all components of a particular valve assembly together. Do not mix components from different valve assemblies. Excessive wear may result.

4

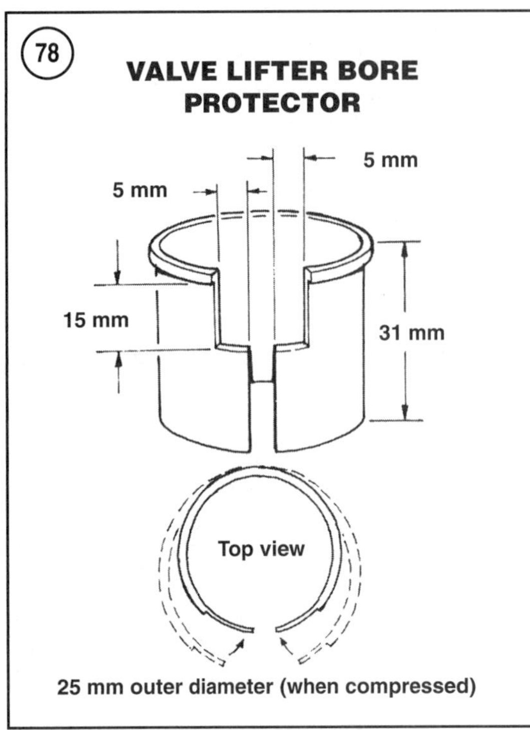

1. Remove the cylinder head and the rocker arm assemblies as described in this chapter.

NOTE
*A bore protector (**Figure 78**) can be made from a plastic 35 mm film canister. Cut out the bottom of the canister and part of its side. Cutaway enough of the canister so it slides between the valve assembly and the side of the bore. The plastic canister will prevent the valve spring compressor from marring the bore.*

2. Fit a bore protector between the valve assembly and the bore.

3. Install a valve spring compressor squarely over the upper spring seat (**Figure 79**). Make sure the opposite end of the compressor rests against the valve head.

CAUTION
To avoid loss of spring tension, do not compress the springs any more than necessary to remove the valve keepers.

4. Tighten the compressor until the valve keepers (**Figure 80**) separate from the valve stem. Remove

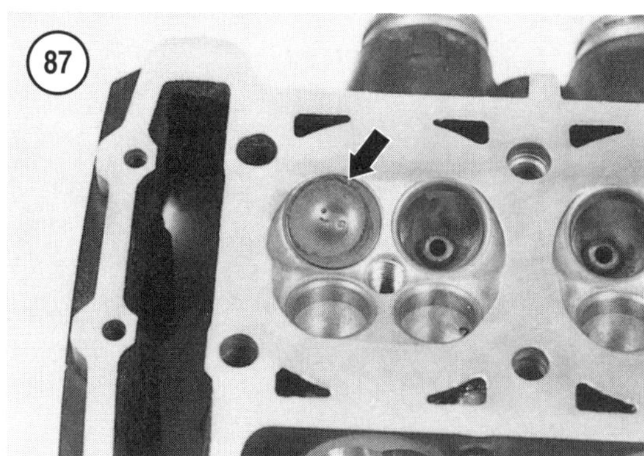

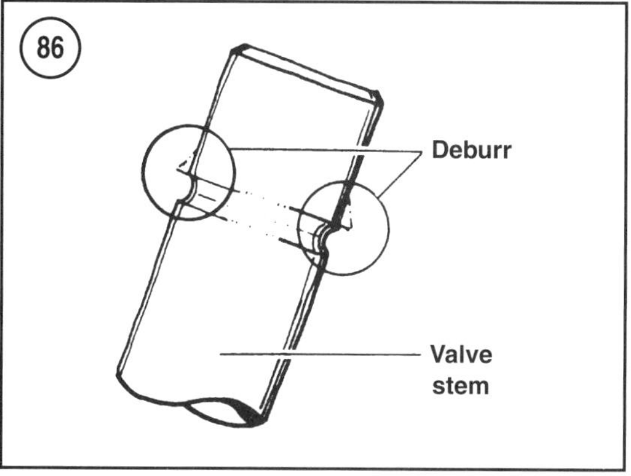

both valve keepers with a magnet, tweezers or needlenose pliers.

5. Remove the valve spring compressor and the bore protector.

6. Remove the upper spring seat (**Figure 81**).

7. Remove the inner valve spring (**Figure 82**) and the outer spring (**Figure 83**).

8. Remove the inner valve-spring seat (**Figure 84**) and the outer spring seat (**Figure 85**).

CAUTION

Remove any burrs from the valve stem grooves before removing the valve. Burrs on the valve stem will damage the valve guide when the stem passes through it.

9. Remove any burrs (**Figure 86**) from the valve stem grooves.

10. Rotate the valve slightly, and remove it from the combustion chamber side of the head (**Figure 87**).

11. Pull the oil seal (**Figure 88**) from the valve guide. Discard the oil seal.

CAUTION

*All the components of each valve assembly must be kept together (**Figure 89**).*

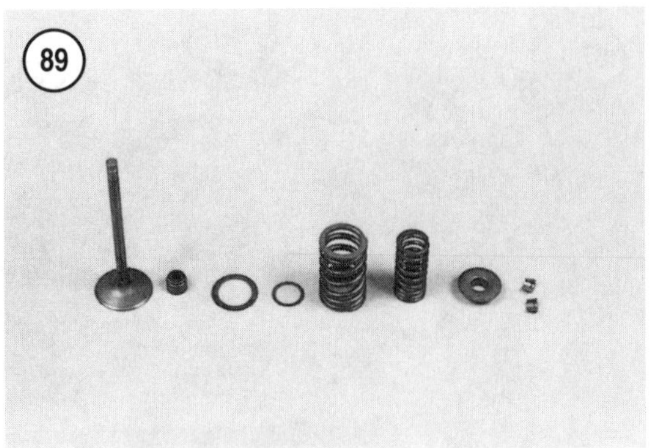

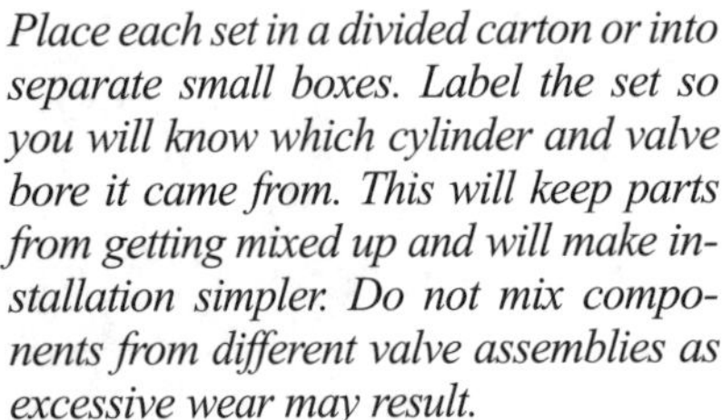
Place each set in a divided carton or into separate small boxes. Label the set so you will know which cylinder and valve bore it came from. This will keep parts from getting mixed up and will make installation simpler. Do not mix components from different valve assemblies as excessive wear may result.

12. Repeat Steps 2-11 for the remaining valve assemblies. Keep the parts from each valve assembly separate.

Valve Installation

Refer to **Figure 77** when installing the valves.

1. Clean the end of the valve guide.
2. Apply engine oil to a new oil seal and seat the seal on the end of the valve guide (**Figure 90**).
3. Apply molybdenum disulfide grease to the valve stem. Install the valve partway into the guide. Slowly turn the valve as it enters the oil seal, and continue turning the valve until it is completely installed (**Figure 87**).
4. Install the outer valve-spring seat (**Figure 85**) and then install the inner spring seat (**Figure 84**).
5. Install the outer valve spring (**Figure 83**) and then the inner spring (**Figure 82**). Install each spring so the end with the closer wound coils (**Figure 91**) faces in toward the cylinder head.
6. Seat the upper spring seat (**Figure 81**) on top of the springs.
7. Fit a bore protector between the valve assembly and the bore.
8. Install a valve spring compressor squarely over the spring retainer. Be sure the opposite end of the compressor sits against the valve head. See **Figure 79**.

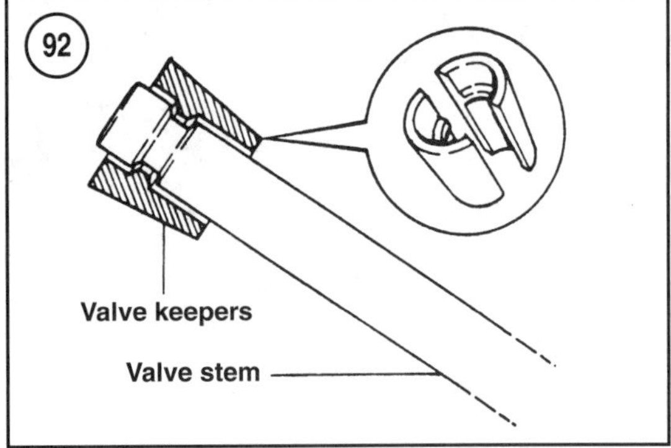

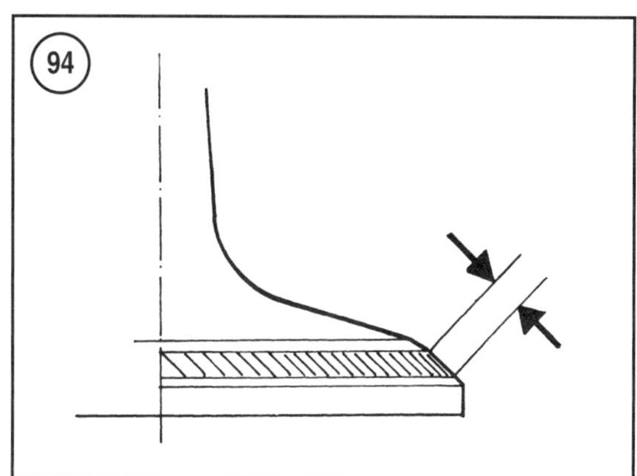

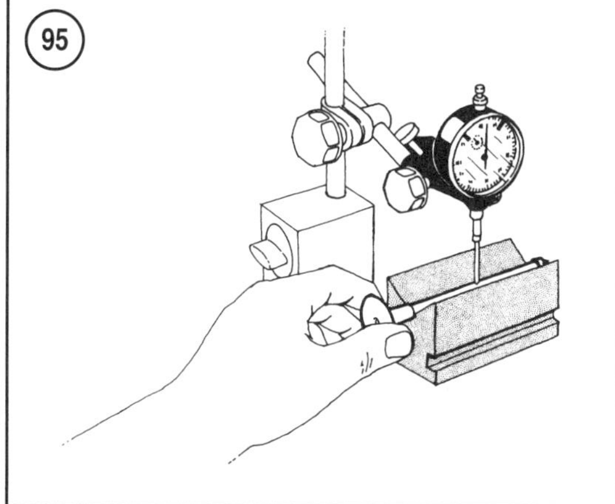

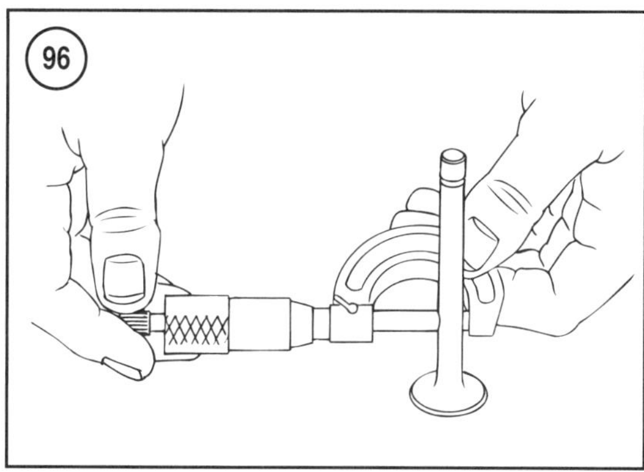

CAUTION
To avoid loss of spring tension, do not compress the springs any more than necessary to install the valve keepers.

9. Compress the valve springs with a valve spring compressor, and install the valve keepers (**Figure 92**).

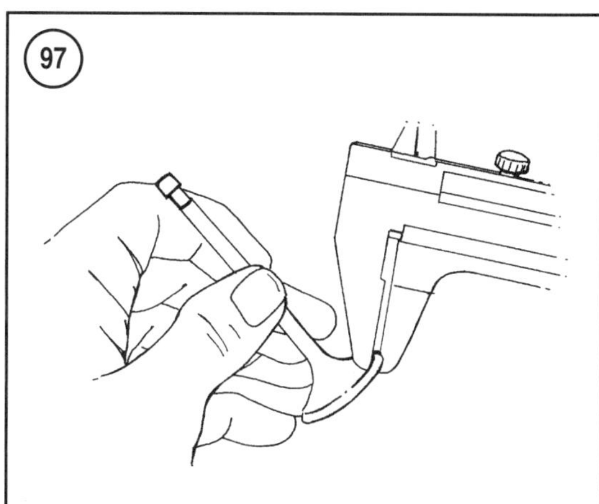

10. When both valve keepers are seated around the valve stem, slowly release the compressor. Remove the compressor and inspect the keepers (**Figure 93**). Place a drift on the end of the valve stem and tap the drift to assure the keepers are properly seated.
11. Repeat Steps 1-10 for the remaining valves.
12. Install the cylinder head as described in this chapter.
13. Adjust the valve clearance as described in Chapter Three.

Valve Inspection

During inspection, compare all measurements to the specifications in **Table 2**. Replace any part that is damaged, out of specification or worn to the service limit.

1. Clean the valve in solvent. Do not gouge or damage the valve-seat surface.
2. Inspect the surface of each valve face (**Figure 94**) for burning. Minor roughness or pitting can be removed by lapping the valve as described in this section. Excessive unevenness indicates the valve is not serviceable and should be replaced.
3. Inspect the valve stem for wear and roughness. Measure the valve stem runout with a dial indicator (**Figure 95**).
4. Measure the outside diameter of the valve stem with a micrometer (**Figure 96**).
5. Measure the valve seat width (**Figure 97**).
6. Remove all carbon and varnish from the valve guides with a stiff spiral wire brush.
7. Measure the inside diameter of the valve guide with a small bore gauge and micrometer (**Figure

98). Take a measurement at the top, middle and bottom of the guide.

8. Insert the valve into its guide, and attach a dial indicator so the plunger contacts the valve stem as shown in **Figure 99**. Hold the valve slightly off its seat and rock it sideways in two directions. Watch the dial indicator while rocking the valve. Compare the valve stem-to-guide clearance (wobble method) to the specification in **Table 2**.

9. Check the valve springs as follows:

   a. Visually inspect each valve spring for bends or other signs of distortion.

   b. Measure each valve spring free length with a vernier caliper (**Figure 100**).

   c. Use a square to measure the tilt of each spring (**Figure 101**). Tilt should be marginal.

   d. If any spring is worn or defective, replace the inner and outer springs as a set.

10. Check the spring seats and valve keepers for cracks or other damage.

11. Inspect each valve seat (**Figure 102**) as described in this section.

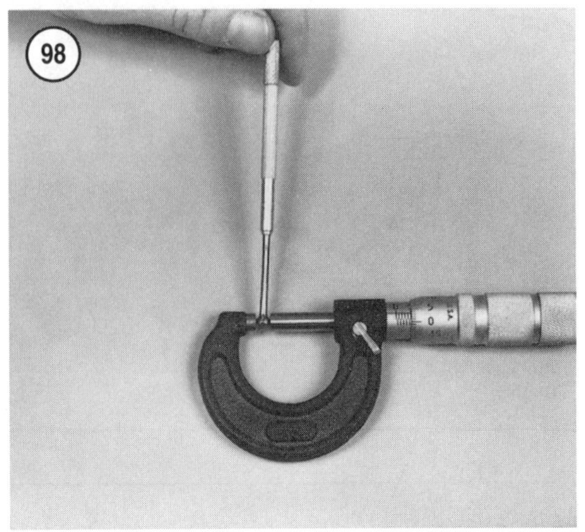

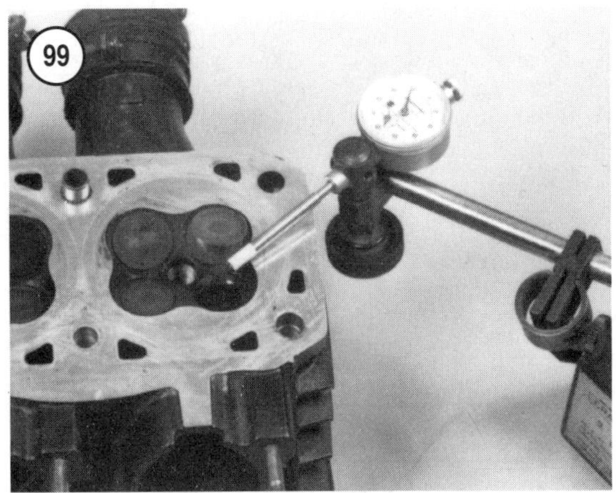

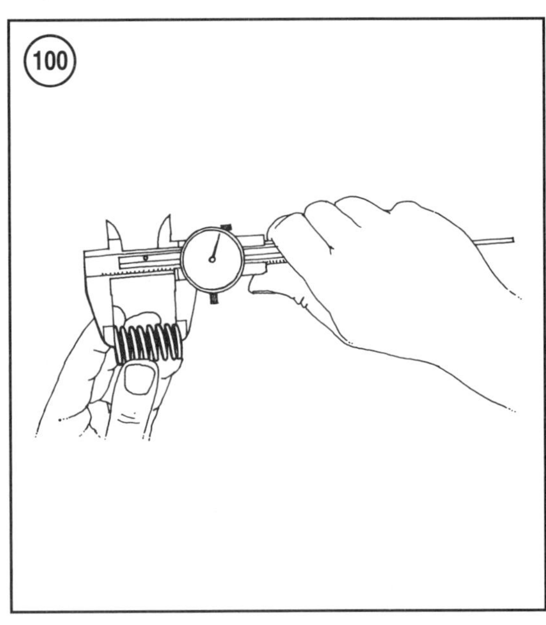

Valve Guide Replacement

When valve stem-to-guide clearance is excessive, the valve guides must be replaced. If a valve guide is replaced, also replace its respective valve.

The Kawasaki valve guide arbor (part No. 57001-1021) and valve guide reamer (part No. 57001-1079) are required to replace the valve guides.

General practice is to entrust cylinder head service to a machine shop.

NOTE

Chilling the valve guides causes them to contract, which reduces the overall diameter of the guides. On the other hand, heating the cylinder head slightly increase the diameter of the guide bore due to expansion. Since the valve guides have a slight interference fit, chilling the guides and heating the head makes installation easier.

1. Place the valve guides in a freezer overnight.

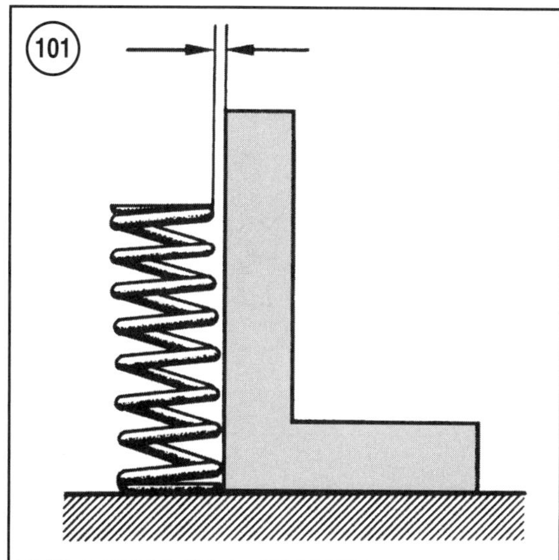

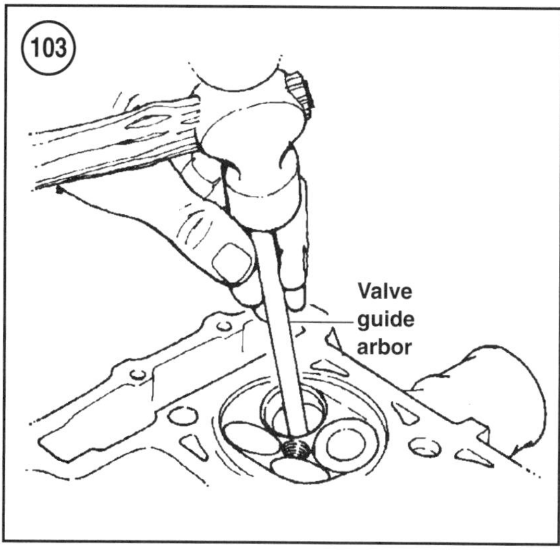

CAUTION

The cylinder head must be evenly heated. Never bring a flame into contact with the cylinder head. Direct flame can warp the head.

2. Place the cylinder head in a shop oven and warm it to 100° C (212° F). Use tiny drops of water to check the temperature. The cylinder head is heated to the proper temperature if the drops sizzle and evaporate immediately.
3. Using heavy gloves or kitchen pot holders, remove the cylinder head from the oven and place it onto wooden blocks with the combustion chamber facing up.
4. From the combustion-chamber side of the head, drive the old valve guide out of the cylinder head with the valve guide arbor and a hammer (**Figure 103**).
5. Remove and discard the valve guide. On 1986-1987 models, also remove the O-ring. *Never* reinstall a used valve guide. They are no longer true nor within tolerance.
6. After the cylinder head cools, check the guide bore for carbon or other contamination. Clean the bore thoroughly.
7. Reheat the cylinder head as described in Step 2.
8. Using heavy gloves or kitchen pot holders, remove the cylinder head from the oven and place it onto wooden blocks with the combustion chamber facing down.
9. Remove one valve guide from the freezer.

CAUTION

Failure to lubricate the new valve guide and guide bore will result in damage to the cylinder head and/or valve guide.

10. Apply clean engine oil to the new valve guide and to the valve guide bore in the cylinder head. On 1986-1988 models, install a new ring (if available) onto the valve guide.
11. From the top side of the cylinder head (camshaft side), drive the new valve guide into the cylinder head with a hammer and the valve guide arbor. Drive the valve guide until it is completed seated against the cylinder head.
12. After the cylinder head has cooled, ream the new valve guides by performing the following:

4

a. Apply cutting oil to both the new valve guide and to the valve guide reamer.

CAUTION

Always rotate the valve guide reamer clockwise. The valve guide will be damaged if the reamer is rotated counterclockwise.

b. Insert the valve guide reamer from the combustion chamber side of the cylinder head (**Figure 104**) and rotate the reamer *clockwise*. Continue to rotate the reamer and work it down through the entire length of the new valve guide. Continue to apply additional cutting oil during this procedure.

c. Rotate the reamer clockwise until it has traveled all the way through the new valve guide.

d. Rotate the reamer *clockwise*, and completely withdraw the reamer from the valve guide.

e. Measure the inside diameter of the valve guide with a small hole gauge. Measure the gauge with a micrometer. Replace the valve guide if it is not within specification (**Table 2**).

13. If necessary, repeat Steps 1-12 for any other valve guide.

14. Thoroughly clean the cylinder head and valve guides with solvent to wash out all metal particles. Dry the head with compressed air.

15. Lightly oil the valve guides to prevent rust.

16. Recondition the valve seats as described in this chapter.

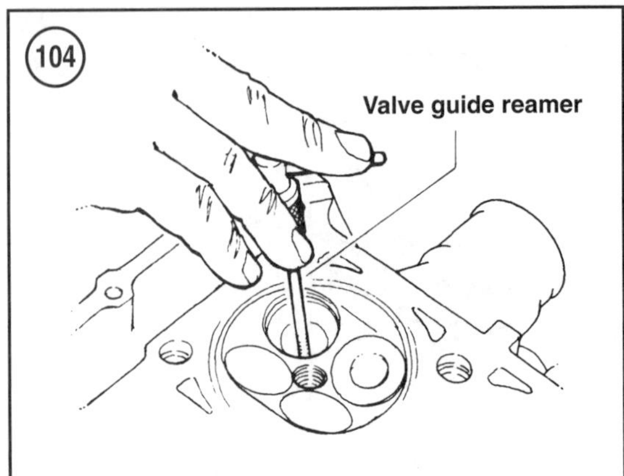

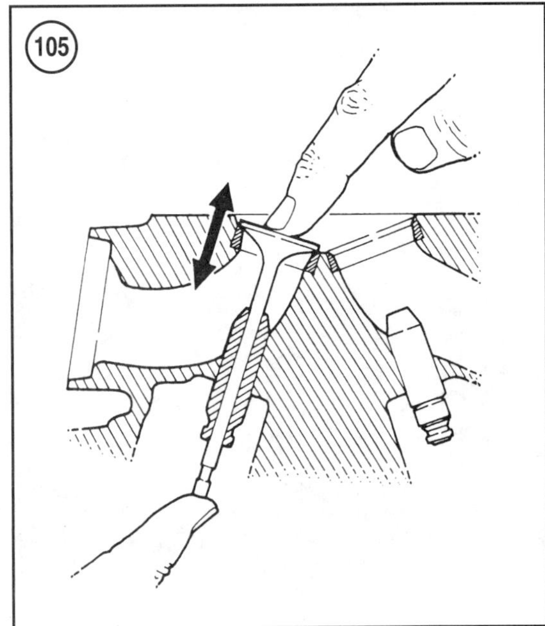

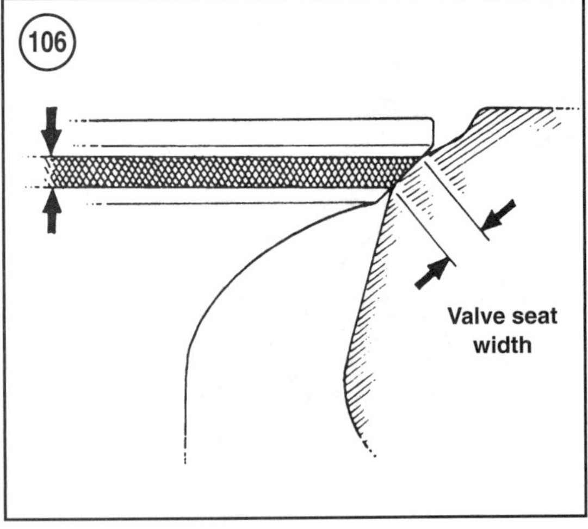

Valve Seat Inspection

1. Remove the valves as described in this section.

2. The most accurate means for checking the valve seal is to use marking compound, available from auto parts stores or machine shops. To check the valve seal with marking compound, perform the following:

a. Thoroughly clean all carbon deposits from the valve face with solvent or detergent. Completely dry the valve face.

b. Spread a thin layer of marking compound evenly on the valve face.

c. Insert the valve into its guide.

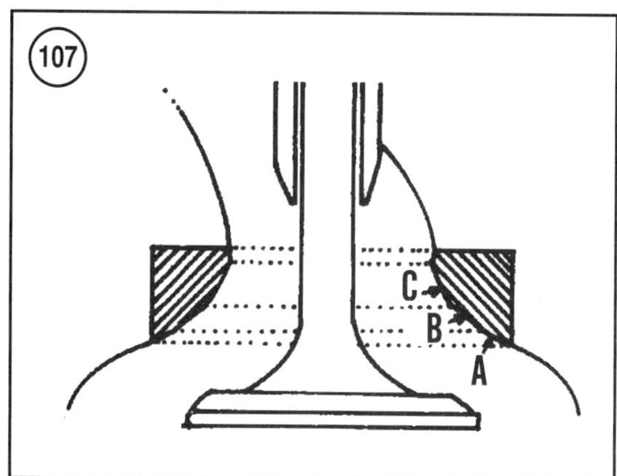

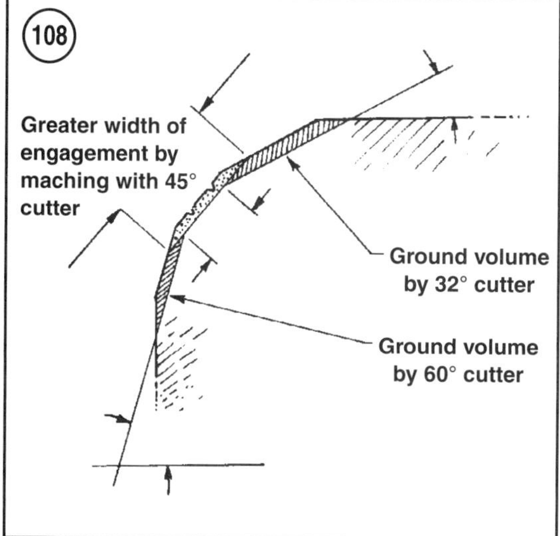

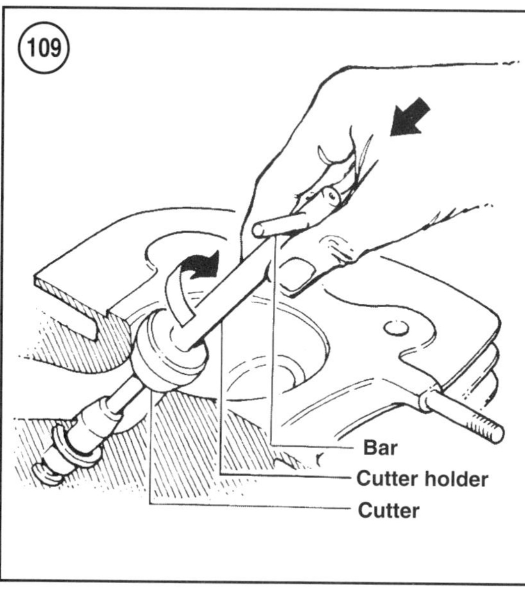

d. Support the valve by hand (**Figure 105**), and tap the valve up and down in the cylinder head. Do not rotate the valve; a false impression will result.

e. Remove the valve and examine the impression left by the marking compound. If the impression left in the dye (on the valve or in the cylinder head) is not even and continuous and if the valve seat width (**Figure 106**) is not within the tolerance specified in **Table 2**, the valve seat must be reconditioned.

3. Closely examine the valve seat in the cylinder head (**Figure 102**). It should be smooth and even, with a polished seating surface.

4. Measure the valve seat width (**Figure 106**) with a vernier caliper.

5. If the valve seat is within specification, install the valves as described in this section.

6. If the valve seat is not correct, recondition the valve seat in the cylinder head as described in this chapter.

Valve Seat Reconditioning

A valve seat cutter set consisting of 32°, 45° and 60° cutters is required to service the valve seats.

Due to the cost of the equipment and experience needed, general practice is to entrust cylinder head service to a machine shop.

The valve seats for both the intake valves and exhaust valves are machined to the same angles as follows:

1. The area below the contact surface (closest to the combustion chamber) is cut to a 32° angle (A, **Figure 107**).

2. The valve contact surface is cut to a 45° angle (B, **Figure 107**).

3. The area above the contact surface (closest to the camshafts) is cut to a 60° angle (C, **Figure 107**).

4. Using the 45° cutter, descale and clean the valve seat (**Figure 108**) with one or two turns (**Figure 109**).

CAUTION

Measure the valve seat contact area in the cylinder head after each cut to make sure the contact area is correct and to prevent removing too much material. If too much material is re-

moved, the cylinder head must be replaced.

5. If the seat is still pitted or burned, turn the 45° cutter additional turns until the surface is clean.
6. Remove the valve cutter from the cylinder head.
7. Use marking compound to inspect the valve seat and measure the valve seat width as described in *Valve Seat Inspection* in this section.

NOTE
The 32° and 60° cutters are used to make the 45° seat consistently wide around its entire surface. Differences in seat width create uneven cooling of the valve and can lead to valve warping. The 32° and 60° cutters also shift the seat up or down, depending upon the readings taken with marking compound.

8. Install the 32° cutter onto the valve tool and lightly cut the valve seat to remove 1/4 of the existing seat.

CAUTION
The 60° cutter removes material quickly. Work carefully and check your progress often.

9. Install the 60° cutter onto the valve tool and lightly cut the valve seat to remove the lower 1/4 of the existing valve seat.
10. Measure the valve seat with a vernier caliper. If necessary, fit the 45° cutter onto the valve tool and cut the valve seat to the specified width. See **Figure 108**.
11. Once the valve seat width is correct, use marking compound to inspect the valve seat and measure the valve seat width as described in *Valve Seat Inspection* in this section.
   a. The valve contact area should be approximately centered in the valve seat area.
   b. If the contact area is too high on the valve, lower the seat with the 32° cutter.
   c. If the contact area is too low on the valve, raise the seat with the 60° cutter.
   d. After the desired valve seat position and width is obtained, use the 45° cutter and very lightly clean away any burrs that may have been caused by the previous cuts—remove only enough material as necessary to clean burrs.

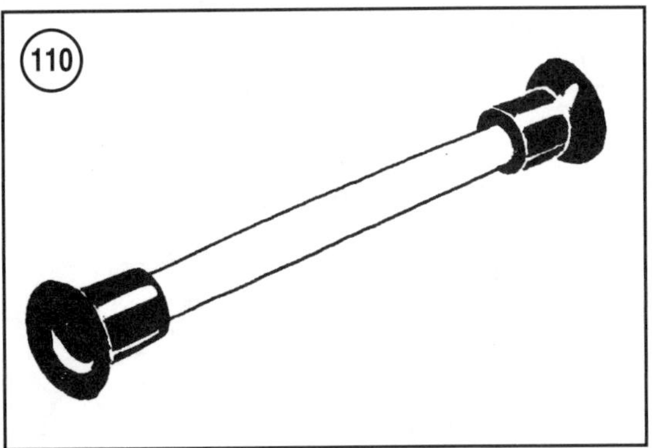

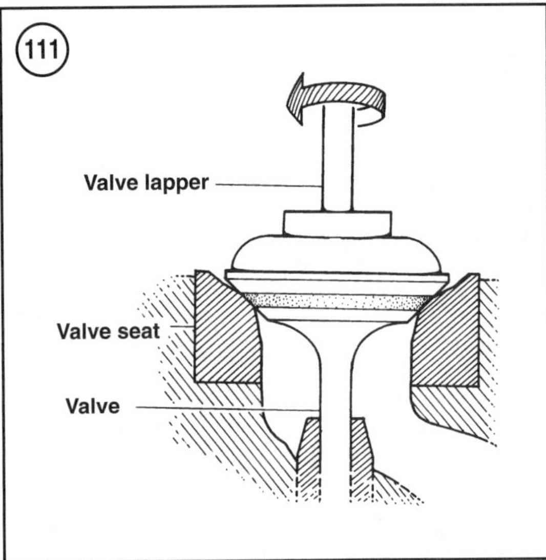

12. Check that the finish has a smooth and velvety surface, it should not be shiny or highly polished. The final seating will take place when the engine is first run.
13. Repeat Steps 1-12 for all remaining valve seats.
14. After the valve seat has been reconditioned, lap the seat and valve as described in this section.

Valve Seat Lapping

Valve lapping is a simple operation that can restore the valve seal without machining if the amount of wear or distortion is not too great. Lapping is also recommended after the valve seat has been serviced.

1. Smear a light coating of fine grade valve lapping compound onto the seating surface of the valve.
2. Insert the valve into the cylinder head.

3. Wet the suction cup of the lapping tool (**Figure 110**), and stick it onto the valve head (**Figure 111**).

4. Lap the valve to the valve seat by performing the following:

   a. Lap the valve by rotating the lapping tool between your hands in both directions.

   b. Every 5 to 10 seconds, stop and rotate the valve 180° in the cylinder head.

   c. Continue lapping until the contact surfaces of the valve and the valve seat in the cylinder head are a uniform gray. Stop as soon as they turn this color to avoid removing too much material.

5. Thoroughly clean the cylinder head and all valve components in solvent, followed by a wash with detergent and hot water.

6. After the lapping has been completed and the valve assemblies reinstalled into the cylinder head, test the valve seal as described under *Cylinder Head Inspection* in this chapter.

7. After the cylinder head and valve components are cleaned in detergent and hot water, apply a light coat of engine oil to all bare metal surfaces to prevent rust.

CYLINDER BLOCK

The cylinder block has pressed-in sleeves, which can be bored to 0.5 mm (0.020 in.) oversize.

Removal

1. Remove the cylinder head as described in this chapter.
2. Remove the cam chain and chain guides as described in this chapter.
3. If still installed, remove the cylinder head gasket and dowels (**Figure 112**).
4. Remove the timing rotor as described in Chapter Nine.
5. Remove the coolant manifold as described in Chapter Ten.
6. Loosen the cylinder block (**Figure 113**) by tapping around its perimeter of with a rubber mallet.
7. Pull the cylinder block straight up off the pistons and remove the block from the crankcase. Watch for the dowels (**Figure 114**) beneath the block.
8. Remove the dowels and base gasket from the crankcase.
9. Stuff clean rags into the crankcase openings to keep objects out of the crankcase.
10. Inspect the cylinder block as described in this section.

Installation

1. Make sure all gasket residue has been cleaned from the top and bottom mating surfaces of the cylinder block.
2. Insert the two dowels (**Figure 114**) into their fittings in the crankcase.

3. Set a new base gasket onto the crankcase. Make sure the holes in the gasket properly align with their mates in the crankcase.
4. Liberally lubricate the cylinder bores with engine oil. Lightly lubricate the piston skirts with molybdenum disulfide grease.

NOTE
Since this engine has no studs to guide the cylinder block, the pistons must be supported during cylinder installation. Work carefully so a piston ring is not damaged. Have an assistant standing by to help.

5. Use small blocks of 1/4-inch plywood to support the front and back of the No. 2 and No. 3 pistons as shown in **Figure 115**. Turn the crankshaft and lower pistons No. 2 and No. 3 so they apply a bit of pressure to the wooden blocks.
6. Carefully align the cylinder bores with their respective pistons and lower the cylinder block over pistons No. 2 and No. 3 until all the piston rings are inside the cylinder. Compress each piston ring as it enters its cylinder.
7. Once the No. 2 and No. 3 pistons are installed, turn the crankshaft to raise pistons No. 1 and No. 4. Move the wooden blocks and support these two outside pistons.
8. Turn the crankshaft so pistons No. 1 and No. 4 apply pressure to the blocks and carefully push the cylinder block down until all the pistons rings are inside their respective cylinders. Again, compress each piston ring as it enters the cylinder.
9. Remove the wooden blocks and lower the cylinder block until it seats on the gasket.
10. Install the coolant manifold as described in Chapter Ten.
11. Install the cam chain and chain guides as described in this chapter.
12. Install the timing rotor as described in Chapter Nine.
13. Install the cylinder head as described in this chapter.

Inspection

1. Wash the cylinder block in solvent to remove any oil and carbon. The cylinder bores must be thoroughly cleaned before taking any measurements. A dirty bore will yield inaccurate readings.

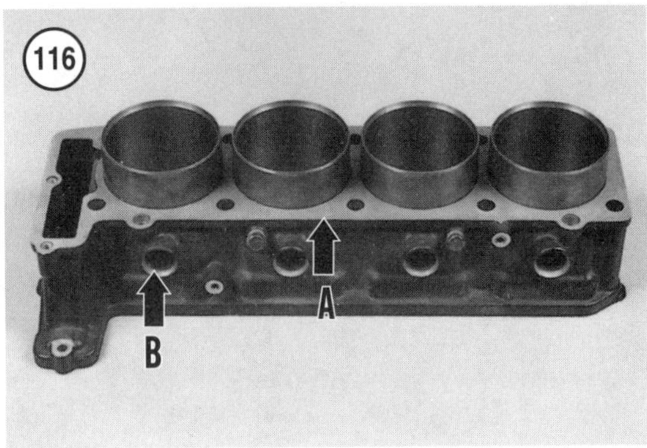

2. Remove all gasket residue from the top and bottom (A, **Figure 116**) mating surfaces of the cylinder block.
3. Clean the coolant ports (B, **Figure 116**) in the cylinder block.
4. Measure each cylinder bore inside diameter with a cylinder gauge or an inside micrometer. Measure the diameter at three locations within the cylinder: one 10 mm from the top of the cylinder, the second 60 mm from the top, and the third 20 mm from the bottom of the cylinder. Take two measurements at each height: one in-line with the piston pin and one at 90° to the pin (**Figure 117**). Take a total of six measurements in each cylinder.
5. If any of the six measurements exceeds the service limit specified in **Table 2** or if the difference between any two measurements is greater than 0.05 mm, the cylinders must be bored to the next oversize and a new piston and rings installed. Bore all cylinders even if only one is worn.

NOTE
The new pistons should be obtained before the cylinders are bored so that the pistons can be measured. Slight

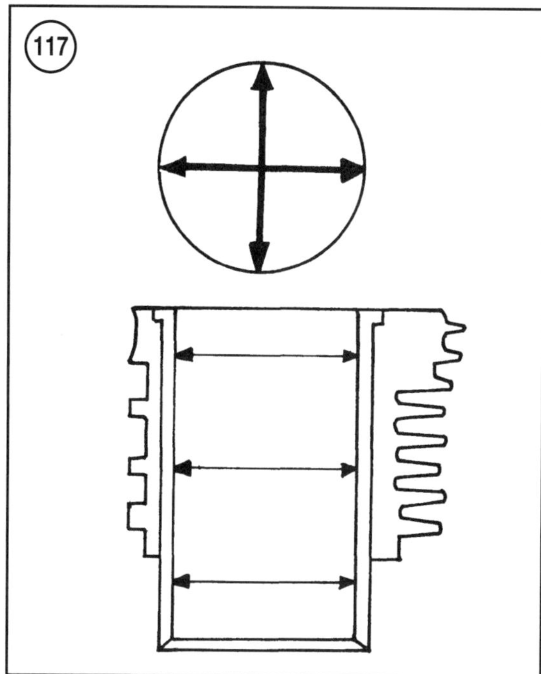

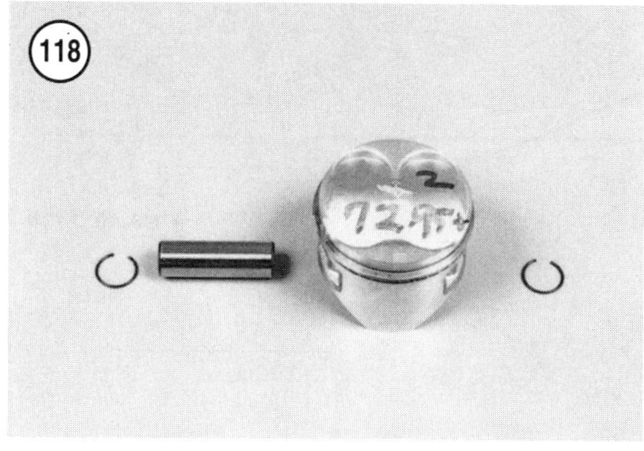

manufacturing tolerances must be taken into account to determine the actual size and working clearance.

NOTE
The service limit of a bored cylinder equals the new diameter of the cylinder bore plus 0.1 mm. The service limit of an oversized piston is the new piston's original diameter minus 0.15 mm.

6. If the cylinder is within specification, thoroughly check each bore surface for scratches or gouges. If damaged in any way, the cylinder will require boring and reconditioning.

7. If the cylinders require boring, remove all dowels from the cylinder block and take them to a dealer or machine shop for service.

8. After the cylinders have been serviced, perform the following:

CAUTION
A combination of soap and hot water is the only solution that will completely clean cylinder walls. Solvent and kerosene cannot wash fine grit out of cylinder crevices. Any grit left in the cylinders will act as a grinding compound and cause premature wear to the new rings.

a. Wash each cylinder bore with hot soapy water.
b. Also wash out any fine grit material from the cooling cores surrounding each cylinder.
c. After washing the cylinder walls, run a clean white cloth through each cylinder wall. It should not show any traces of grit or debris. If the rag is the slightest bit dirty, the wall is not thoroughly cleaned and must be rewashed.
d. After the cylinder is cleaned, lubricate the cylinder walls with clean engine oil to prevent rust.

PISTONS

Piston Removal/Installation

Figure 118 shows a typical piston assembly.

1. Remove the camshafts, cylinder head and cylinder block as described in this chapter.
2. Stuff clean shop cloths into the crankcase's cylinder openings to prevent objects from falling into the crankcase.
3. Lightly write the cylinder number on the top of the pistons. Also check the arrow that indicates the exhaust side (front) of the piston. If the arrow is illegible, draw one now.
4. Remove the piston rings as described in this section.
5. Before removing the piston, hold the rod tightly and rock the piston (**Figure 119**, typical). Any rocking motion (do not confuse with the normal sliding motion) indicates wear on the piston pin, piston pin bore or connecting rod small-end bore (more likely a combination of these). Mark the pis-

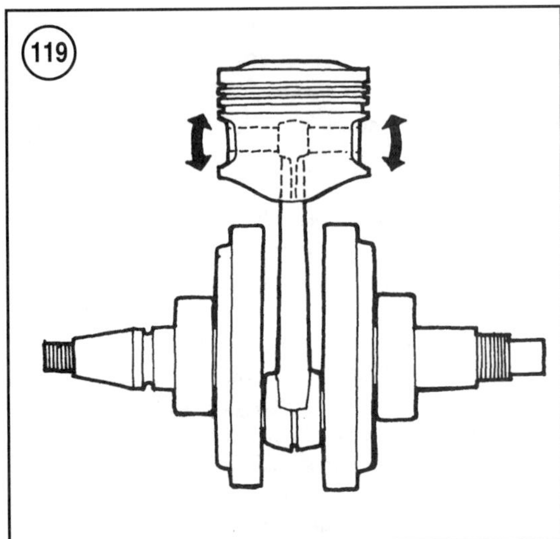

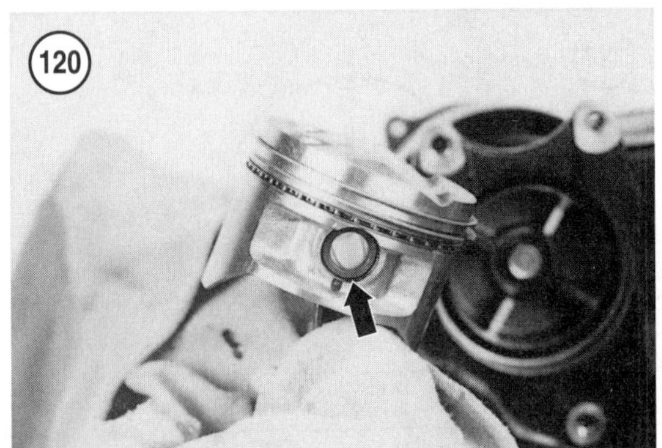

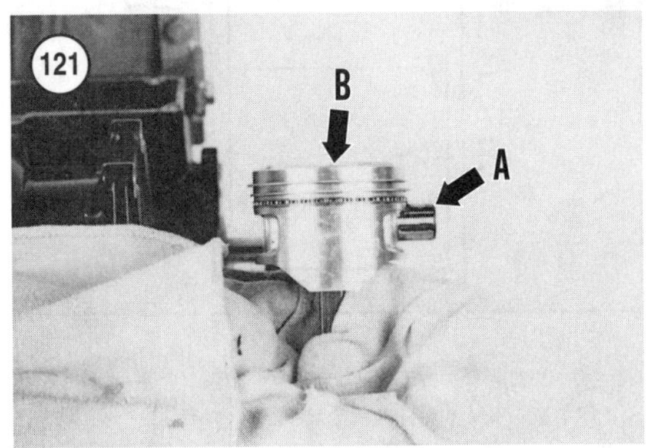

ton and pin so that they will be reassembled as a set.

NOTE
Never reuse piston pin clips. New clips must be installed during assembly.

6. Remove the piston pin clips from each side of the piston pin bore (**Figure 120**) with a small screwdriver, scribe or needlenose pliers. Hold your thumb over one edge of the clip to prevent it from springing out. Discard the clips.
7. Use a proper size wooden dowel or socket extension and push out the piston pin (A, **Figure 121**).
8. If the piston pin is difficult to remove, use a homemade tool as shown in **Figure 122**. Do not drive the piston pin out. This action may damage the piston pin or connecting rod.
9. Lift the piston (B, **Figure 121**) off the connecting rod.
10. Repeat Steps 4-9 for the remaining pistons.
11. Inspect the pistons as described in this section.

NOTE
*In the next step, install the piston pin clips so the end gap does not sit in the piston cutout (**Figure 123**).*

12. Install a new piston pin clip into the inboard side of each piston.
13. Oil the piston pin, piston and connecting rod with engine oil.

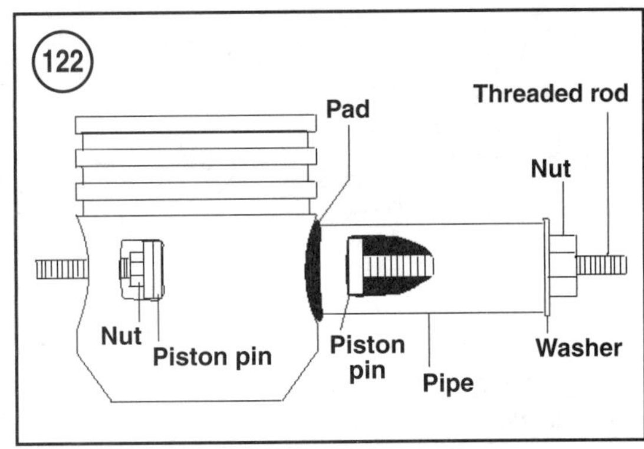

14. Insert the piston pin into the piston until its end extends slightly beyond the inside of the boss (**Figure 124**).

NOTE
Install the No 2 piston first, then install pistons No. 1, 3 and 4.

15. Set the No. 2 piston onto the No. 2 connecting rod so the arrow points to the front (exhaust side) of the engine.

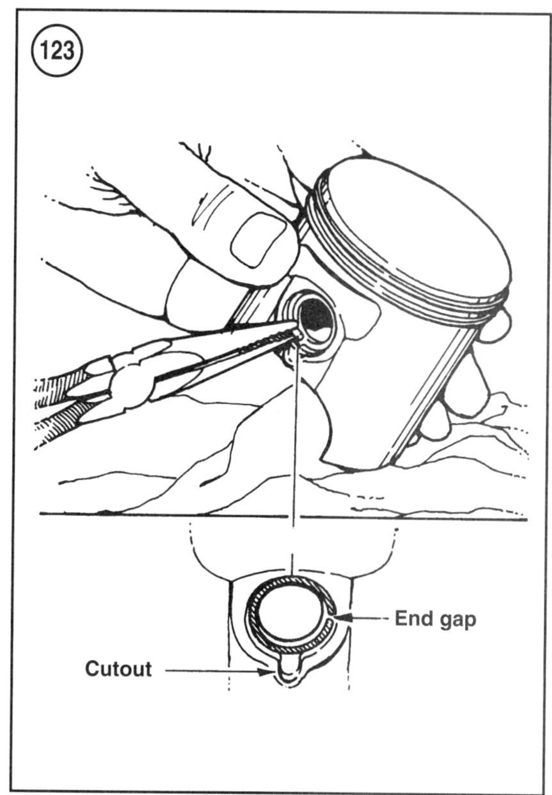

If you are installing the old pistons, make sure the piston is installed on the correct connecting rod. If the cylinders were bored, install the new pistons in the cylinder indicated by the machinist's marks (**Figure 125**).

16. Line up the piston pin with the hole in the connecting rod. Push the piston pin through the connecting rod and into the other side of the piston until the pin bottoms against the piston pin clip.

17. Install the second piston pin clip so its end gap is not opposite the cutout in the piston (**Figure 123**). Make sure each clip is completely seated in the clip groove.

18. Check the installation by rocking the piston back and forth around the pin axis and from side to side along the axis. It should rotate freely back and forth but not from side to side.

19. Install the piston rings as described in this chapter.

20. Repeat Step 15-19 for pistons No. 1, then No. 3 and finally No. 4.

Piston Inspection

NOTE

Kawasaki does not provide service dimensions for the piston-pin outside diameter or for the piston-pin-bore inside diameter.

1. Carefully clean the carbon from the piston crown (**Figure 126**) with a soft scraper. Do not remove or damage the carbon ridge around the circumference of the piston above the top ring land. If the piston, rings and cylinder are found to be dimensionally correct and can be reused, removal of the carbon ring from the top of the piston or the

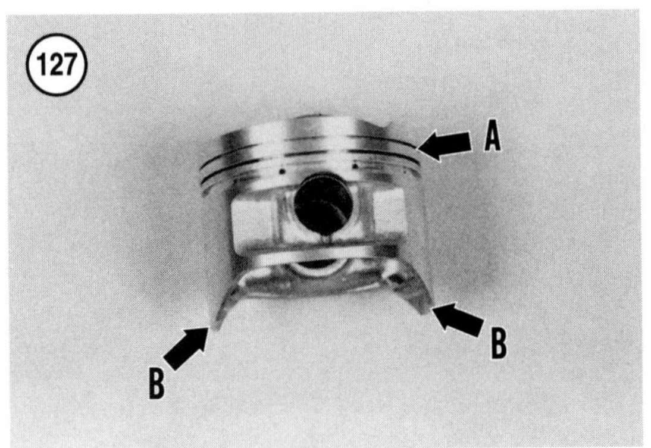

carbon ridge from the top of the cylinder will promote excessive oil consumption.

CAUTION
Do not use a wire brush on the piston skirts or ring lands. A wire brush will scratch and remove the Teflon coating from the piston skirts. A wire brush also removes aluminum. This increases piston clearance and rounds the corners of the ring lands, which results in decreased support for the piston rings.

2. Examine each ring groove (A, **Figure 127**) for burrs, dented edges and wide wear. Pay particular attention to the top compression ring groove. It usually wears more than the other grooves.
3. Check the piston skirts (B, **Figure 127**) for galling and abrasion, which may have been caused by piston seizure. If light galling is present, smooth the affected area with No. 400 emery paper and oil or a fine oilstone. However, if galling is severe or if the piston is deeply scored, replace it.
4. Check the oil control holes (**Figure 128**) for carbon or oil sludge buildup. Clean the holes with a small diameter drill bit and blow them out with compressed air.
5. Inspect the clip grooves in the piston pin bore on each side of the piston. If either groove is damaged, replace the piston.
6. If damage or wear indicates piston replacement is required, select a new piston as described in this chapter.
7. Inspect the piston pin for chrome flaking or cracks. Replace if necessary.
8. Measure the piston-to-cylinder clearance as described in this section.

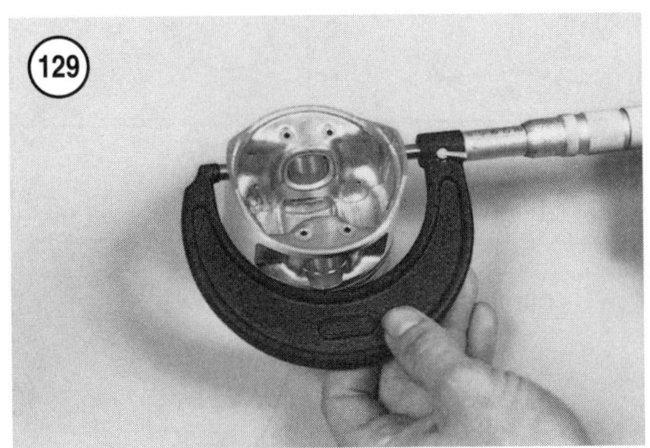

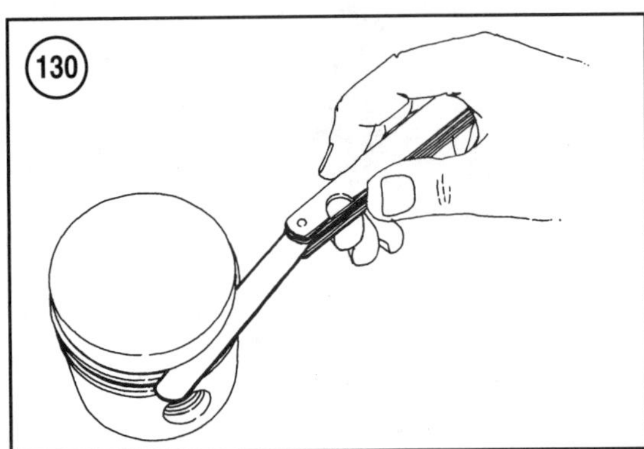

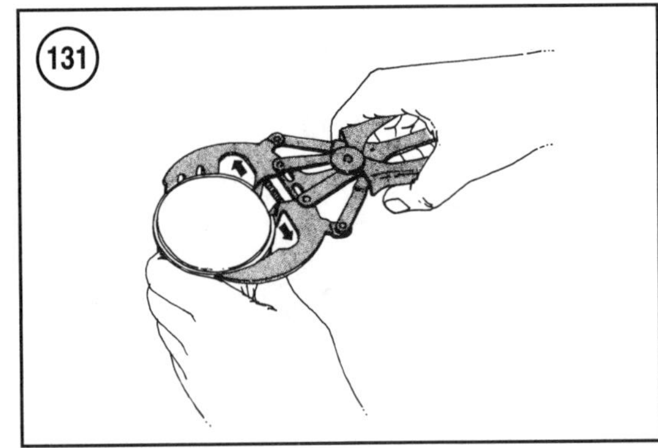

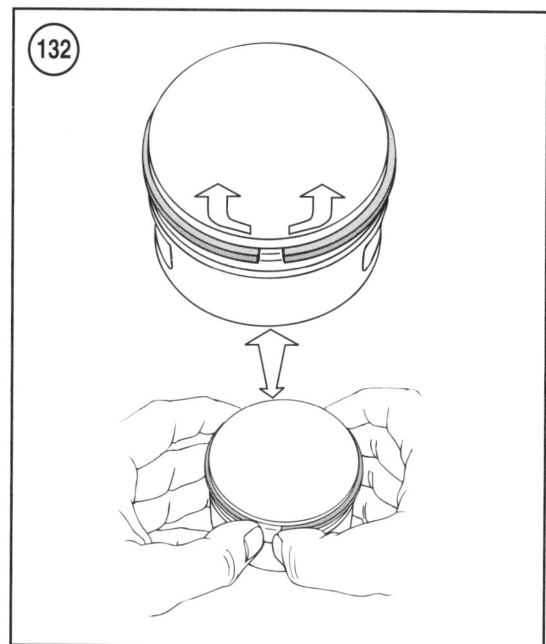

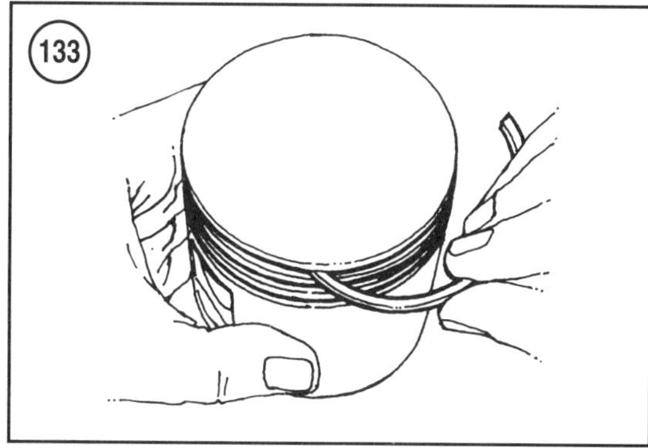

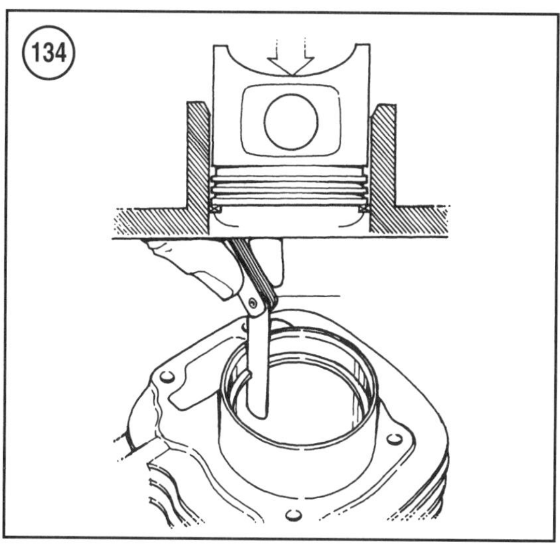

Piston-To-Cylinder Clearance

1. Make sure the piston and cylinder walls are clean and dry.
2. Measure the inside diameter of the cylinder bore as described in *Cylinder Block Inspection* in this chapter.
3. Measure the outside diameter of the piston (**Figure 129**) at right angles to the piston pin. Measure the diameter at a point 5 mm (0.20 in.) up from the bottom of the piston skirt.
4. Subtract the measured diameter of the piston from the cylinder inside diameter. Compare this difference to the piston-to-cylinder clearance listed in **Table 2**.
5. If new pistons are required, purchase them first. Measure the piston diameter and add the specified piston-to-cylinder clearance to determine the proper cylinder bore diameter.

Piston Ring Removal/Installation

WARNING
The edges of all piston rings are very sharp. Be careful when handling them to avoid cutting your fingers.

1. Measure the ring-to-groove clearance of each ring with a flat feeler gauge (**Figure 130**). If the clearance exceed the service limit specified in **Table 2**, the rings must be replaced. If the clearance is still excessive with the new rings, the piston must also be replaced.
2. Remove the old rings with a ring expander tool (**Figure 131**) or by spreading the ends with your thumbs just enough to slide the ring up over the piston (**Figure 132**). Repeat for the remaining rings.
3. Carefully remove all carbon buildup from the ring grooves with a broken piston ring (**Figure 133**).
4. Inspect the grooves carefully for burrs, nicks or broken and cracked lands. Recondition or replace the piston if necessary.
5. Check the end gap of each ring. To check the ring, insert a ring into the bottom of the cylinder bore, and push it about 20 mm (0.79 in.) into the bore. Push the ring with the crown of the piston to ensure that the ring is square in the cylinder bore. Measure the gap with a flat feeler gauge (**Figure 134**) and compare the gap to the specification in **Table 2**. If the ring end gap is greater than specified,

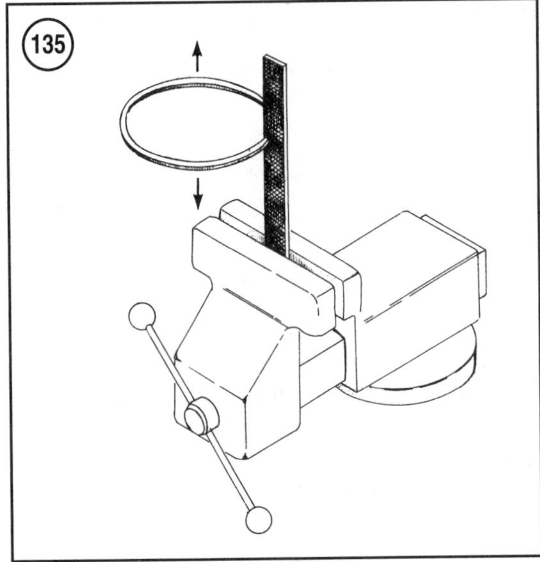

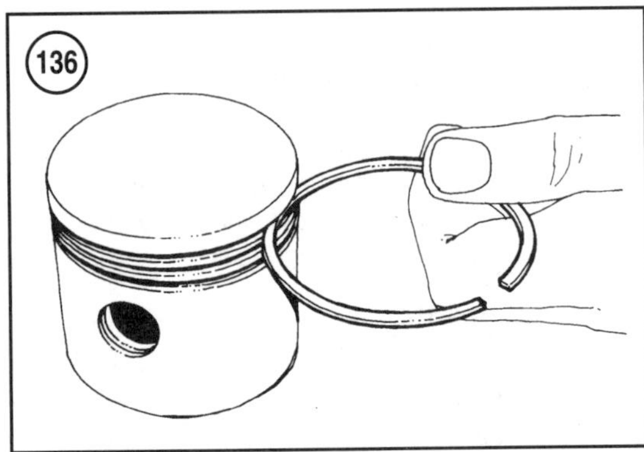

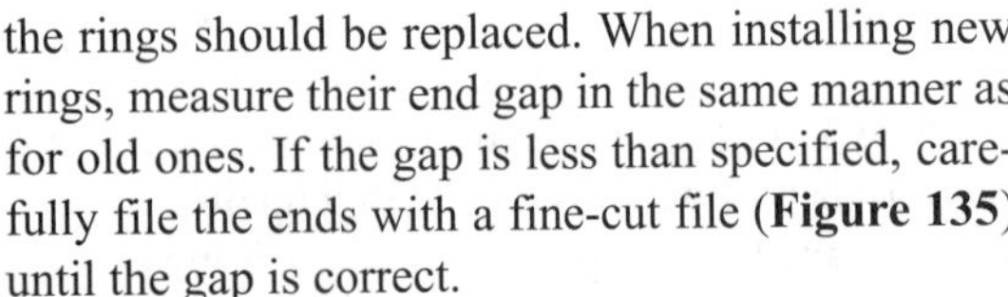

the rings should be replaced. When installing new rings, measure their end gap in the same manner as for old ones. If the gap is less than specified, carefully file the ends with a fine-cut file (**Figure 135**) until the gap is correct.

6. Roll each ring around its piston groove as shown in **Figure 136** to check for binding. If there is any binding, there may still be a carbon or oil sludge buildup that was not removed. Reclean the ring groove with solvent. After cleaning with solvent, reclean the groove with a broken piston ring (**Figure 133**).

7. Do not confuse the top and second rings. They can be identified by the manufacturer's marks shown in **Figure 137**.

8. Install the piston rings. Install the bottom oil control ring assembly first, then the second ring, then the top ring. Carefully spread the ends of each

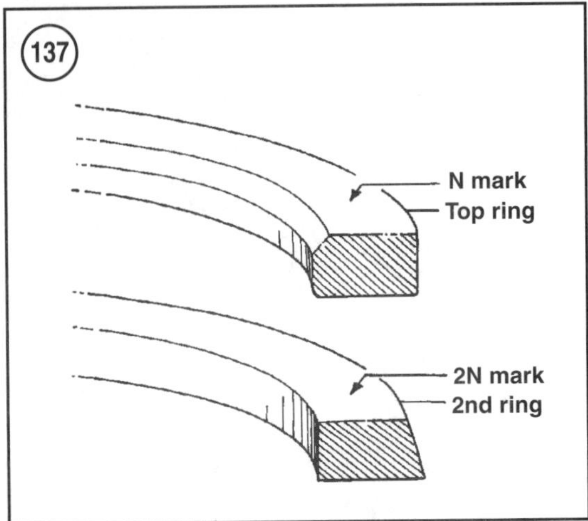

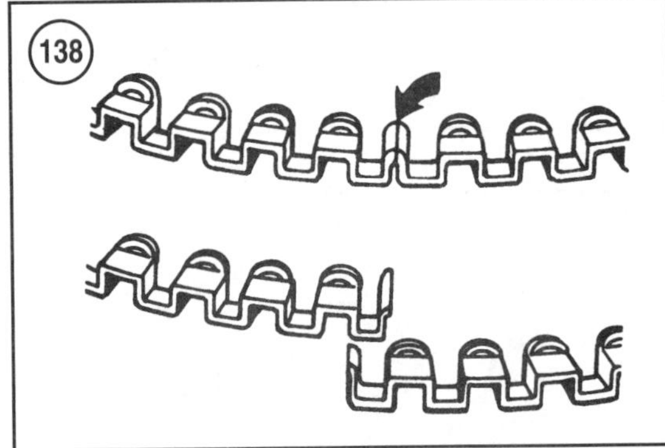

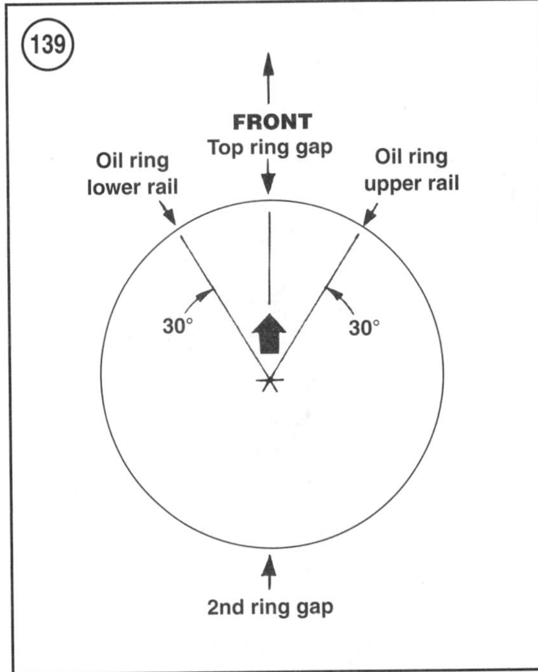

ring with your thumbs and slip the ring over the top of the piston. The piston rings must be installed with the manufacturer's mark or paint mark facing the top of the piston. Install the rings as follows:

a. Install the oil control ring assembly. First, install the oil control expander. Be sure the ends of the expander butt together as shown in **Figure 138**. They must not overlap. Next, install the lower oil ring steel rail, and finally the upper oil-ring steel rail.
b. Install the second ring and then the top ring. These rings are not symmetrical. Each must be installed as shown in **Figure 137**.

9. Make sure the rings are seated completely in their grooves all the way around the piston. Distribute the end gaps around the piston as shown in **Figure 139**. Be sure the ring gaps are not aligned with each other when installed in the cylinder.
10. After the rings are installed, apply clean engine oil to the rings. Rotate the rings several complete revolutions in their respective grooves. This will assure proper oiling when the engine is first started after piston service.
11. When installing oversized piston rings, the number on the rings must be the same as the piston oversize number.
12. When new rings are installed, the cylinder must be honed or deglazed so the rings will seat properly. Refer honing to a Kawasaki dealership. After honing, measure the ring end gap (**Figure 134**) and ring-to-groove clearance (**Figure 130**) as described above.

Table 1 GENERAL ENGINE SPECIFICATIONS

Item	Specification
Engine type	Four-stroke, liquid-cooled, DOHC
Bore × stroke	74.0 x 58.0 mm (2.91 × 2.28 in.)
Displacement	997 cc (60.84 cu. in.)
Compression ratio	10.2:1
Compression pressure	885-1350 kPa (128-196 psi) @ 300 rpm
Firing order	1-2-4-3

Table 2 ENGINE TOP END SPECIFICATIONS

Item	New mm (in.)	Service limit mm (in.)
Cylinder head warp	–	0.05 (0.002)
Camshaft		
Cam lobe height	35.243-35.385 (1.3875-1.3931)	35.14 (1.3835)
Camshaft bearing inside diameter	25.000-25.021 (0.9843-0.9851)	25.08 (0.9874)
Camshaft journal outside diameter	24.900-24.922 (0.9803-0.9812)	24.87 (0.9791)
Camshaft oil clearance	0.078-0.121 (0.0030-0.0047)	0.21 (0.0082)
Camshaft runout	–	0.01 (0.0039)
Cam chain 20-link length	158.8-159.2 (6.252-6.268)	161.5 (6.358)

(continued)

Table 2 ENGINE TOP END SPECIFICATIONS (continued)

Item	New mm (in.)	Service limit mm (in.)
Rocker arm inside diameter	12.500-12.518 (0.4921-0.4928)	12.55 (0.4941)
Rocker shaft outside diameter	12.466-12.484 (0.4908-0.4915)	12.44 (0.4988)
Valves		
Valve clearance		
Intake	0.13-0.18 (0.005-0.007)	–
Exhaust	0.18-0.23 (0.007-0.009)	–
Valve stem runout	–	0.05 (0.002)
Valve stem outside diameter		
Intake	5.475-5.490 (0.2155-0.2161)	5.46 (0.2150)
Exhaust	5.455-5.470 (0.2147-0.2154)	5.44 (0.2142)
Valve guide inside diameter	5.500-5.512 (0.2165-0.2170)	5.58 (0.2197)
Valve stem-to-guide clearance (wobble method)		
Intake	0.02-0.08 (0.0008-0.0031)	0.22 (0.0087)
Exhaust	0.07-0.14 (0.0028-0.0055)	0.27 (0.0106)
Valve head margin thickness		
Intake	0.5 (0.0197)	0.25 (0.0098)
Exhaust	1.0 (0.0394)	0.7 (0.0276)
Valve seat surface		–
Outside diameter		
Intake	28.3-28.5 (1.1141-1.1220)	–
Exhaust	24.0-24.2 (0.9448-0.9527)	–
Width (intake and exhaust)	0.5-1.0 (0.0197-0.0394)	
Valve seat cutting angle	32, 45, 60°	
Valve springs free length		
Inner spring	36.3 (1.429)	35 (1.378)
Outer spring	42 (1.654)	40 (1.575)
Cylinder inside diameter	73.994-74.006 (2.9131-2.9136)	74.11 (2.9177)
Piston outside diameter*	73.935-73.964 (2.9108-2.9119)	73.79 (2.9051)
Piston-to-cylinder clearance	0.044-0.071 (0.0017-0.0028)	–
Piston ring-to-groove clearance		
Top	0.03-0.07 (0.0012-0.0027)	0.17 (0.007)
Second	0.02-0.06 (0.0007-0.0024)	0.16 (0.006)
Piston ring groove width		
Top	1.02-1.04 (0.0402-0.0409)	1.12 (0.0441)
Second	1.01-1.03 (0.0398-0.0405)	1.11 (0.0437)
Oil	2.51-2.53 (0.0988-0.0996)	2.6 (0.1024)
Piston ring thickness (top and second)	0.97-0.99 (0.0382-0.0390)	0.9 (0.035)
Piston ring end gap		
Top and second	0.20-0.35 (0.0079-0.0138)	0.70 (0.0276)
Oil	0.2-0.7 (0.0079-0.0276)	1.0 (0.0393)
Oversize piston and rings	+ 0.5	
Secondary air system		
Vacuum switch valve pressure: open-close	54-68 kPa (410-510 mm Hg)	–

*Measured 5 mm (0.20 in.) from the bottom of the piston skirt.

Table 3 ENGINE TOP END TORQUE SPECIFICATIONS

Item	N•m	in.-lb.	ft.-lb.
Cam cap bolts	12	106	–
Cam chain tensioner mounting bolts	9.8	87	–
Camshaft sprocket bolts*	15	–	11
Cooling system drain bolt	7.8	69	–
Cylinder bolts (6 mm)	15	–	11
Cylinder head bolts			
6 mm	9.8	87	–
10 mm			
New	39	–	29
Used	36	–	27
11 mm			
New	51	–	38
Used	48	–	35
Cylinder head cover bolts	9.8	87	–
Cylinder head oil pipe bolts	9.8	87	–
Front engine mounting nuts	54	–	40
Main oil pipe banjo bolts	25	–	18
Oil filter bolt	20	–	15
Oil gallery bolt	18	–	13
Pickup coil cover bolts	9.8	87	–
Rear chain guide bolt*	20	–	15
Rocker shaft plugs	9.8	87	–
Upper chain guide bolt	9.8	87	–
Valve adjuster locknut	25	–	18

*Apply Loctite 242 (blue) or an equivalent medium strength threadlocking compound.

CHAPTER FIVE

ENGINE LOWER END

This chapter provides complete service and overhaul procedures for the following lower end components:

1. Crankcase assembly.
2. Crankshaft.
3. Balancer shaft.
4. Connecting rods.
5. Alternator chain.
6. Alternator shaft and starter clutch.
7. Oil pump.
8. Oil sump and oil cooler.

The crankshaft is supported by five main bearings in a horizontally split crankcase. The engine and transmission share a common case and the same wet-sump oil supply. The hydraulic, wet-plate clutch sits on the right side of the engine. Refer to Chapter Six for clutch service; refer to Chapter Seven for transmission service.

One of the most important aspects of a successful engine overhaul is preparation. Before removing the engine, degrease the engine and frame. Have all necessary hand and special tools available. Make sure the work area is clean and well lit. Identify and store individual parts and assemblies in appropriate storage containers. Carefully label hoses and wire harness connections with masking tape and a permanent marker.

The text makes frequent references to the left and right side of the engine. This refers to the engine as it sits in the frame, not how it may sit on the workbench.

When servicing components described in this chapter, compare measurements to the service specifications listed in the tables at the end of this chapter. Replace any part that is out of specification or damaged. During assembly, tighten fasteners to the specified torque.

SERVICING ENGINE IN THE FRAME

The following components can be serviced while the engine is in the frame:

1. External gearshift mechanism.
2. Clutch.
3. Carburetors.
4. Starter.
5. Cylinder head.
6. Cylinder block.
7. Alternator.

Figure 1

ENGINE MOUNTS

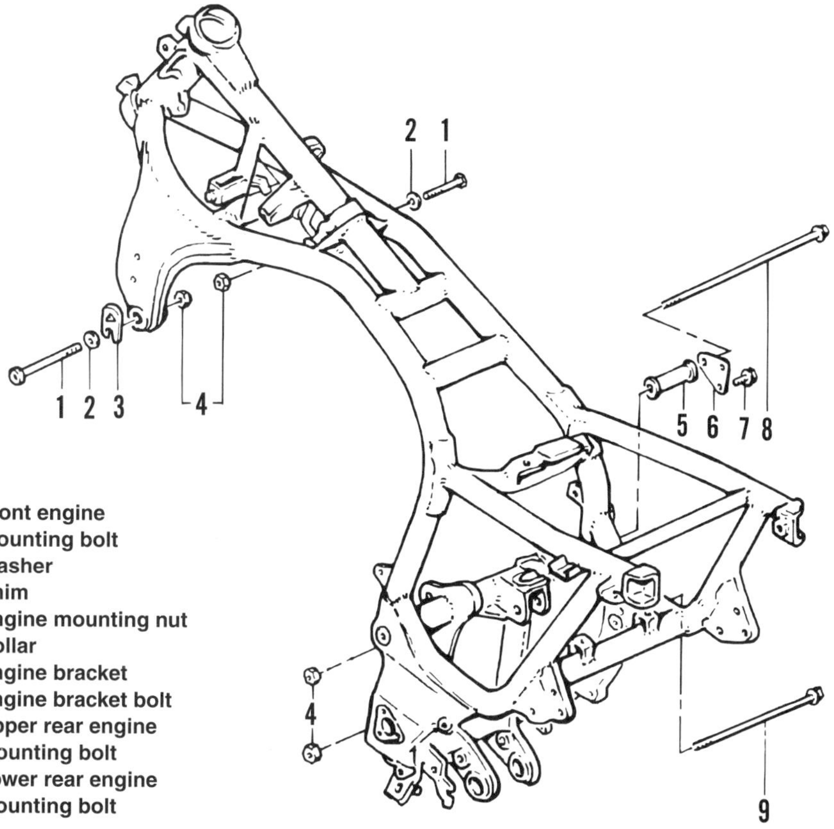

1. Front engine mounting bolt
2. Washer
3. Shim
4. Engine mounting nut
5. Collar
6. Engine bracket
7. Engine bracket bolt
8. Upper rear engine mounting bolt
9. Lower rear engine mounting bolt

Figure 2

ENGINE

Removal

Refer to **Figure 1**.

1. Remove the lower, middle and front fairings as described in Chapter Fifteen.
2. Drain the engine oil and the coolant (Chapter Three).
3. Disconnect the negative battery cable (**Figure 2**).
4. Remove the fuel tank, carburetor assembly, air filter housing and exhaust system (Chapter Eight).
5. Remove the radiator, radiator bracket, thermostat housing and water pump (Chapter Ten).
6. If not already done, remove the coolant manifold (Chapter Ten), remove the drain bolts from the front of the cylinder block and drain the coolant from the block.
7. On models with a secondary air system, remove the vacuum switch (Chapter Eight).
8. Remove the swing arm and the drive shaft (Chapter Thirteen).
9. Disconnect the following electrical connectors:
   a. Pull back the boot and disconnect the starter cable from the starter terminal (**Figure 3**).

b. Engine ground cable (**Figure 4**) from the upper crankcase bolt on the right side.
c. Disconnect the electrical connector from the neutral switch (A, **Figure 5**) on the lower crankcase.
d. Pull back the boot (B, **Figure 5**) and disconnect the connector from the oil pressure switch.
e. Twist the spark plug cap from each plug.

10. If the engine requires disassembly, removing the large sub-assemblies is easier while the engine sits in the frame. Removing these sub-assemblies also makes the engine lighter and less bulky. Remove the following:

NOTE

The crankcases on this engine can be split while the camshafts, cylinder head, cylinder block, and crankshaft are in place. If the transmission, alternator shaft or starter clutch are the only parts that requires service, ignore substep a.

a. Camshafts, cylinder head and cylinder block (Chapter Four).
b. Clutch (Chapter Six) and alternator chain (this chapter).
c. Alternator and pickup coils (Chapter Nine).
d. Starter (Chapter Nine).
e. Bevel gearcase and the external shift mechanism (Chapter Seven).

11. If the countershaft will be serviced, loosen the damper cam nut now. This nut is torqued to 225 N•m (166 ft.-lb.). Breaking it loose while the engine sits in the frame is much easier than trying to loosen the nut while on the bench. Perform the following:
  a. Remove the outer circlip (A, **Figure 6**) from the countershaft, and pull the needle bearing (B).
  b. Remove the inner snap ring (A, **Figure 7**).
  c. Hold the damper cam with the Kawasaki damper cam holder (part No. 57001-1025) or equivalent tool, and loosen the damper cam nut (B, **Figure 7**).

12. Support the engine with a hydraulic jack and wooden blocks.

13. Loosen the engine mounting nut at each mount.

14. Remove the front engine mounting nut and bolt from each left and right sides. Watch for the any alignment shim(s) installed on the left side.

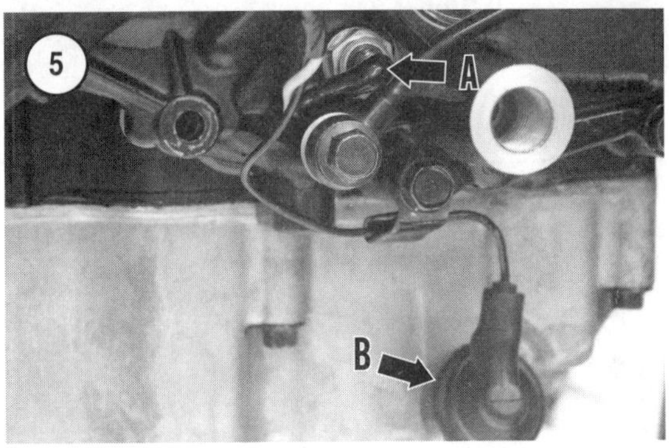

15. Remove the upper and lower rear engine mounting bolts. Watch for the collar installed on the upper rear engine mounting bolt.

16. Lower the engine and remove it from the frame.

Installation

1. Set the engine into position in the frame.
2. Install the rear engine mounting bolts and the two front engine mounting bolts. Install the collar on the upper-rear engine mounting bolt and install a washer on each front engine mounting bolt.

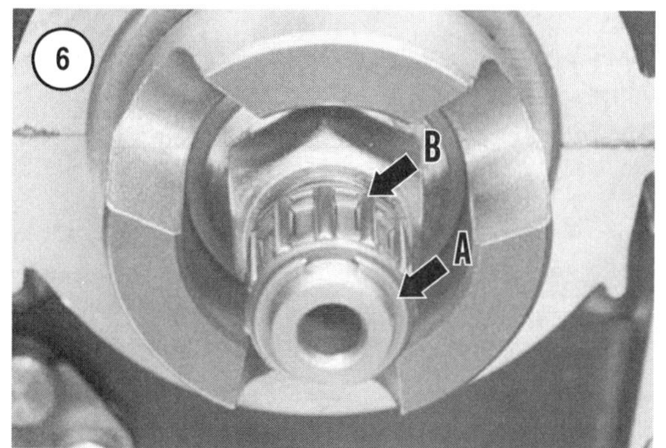

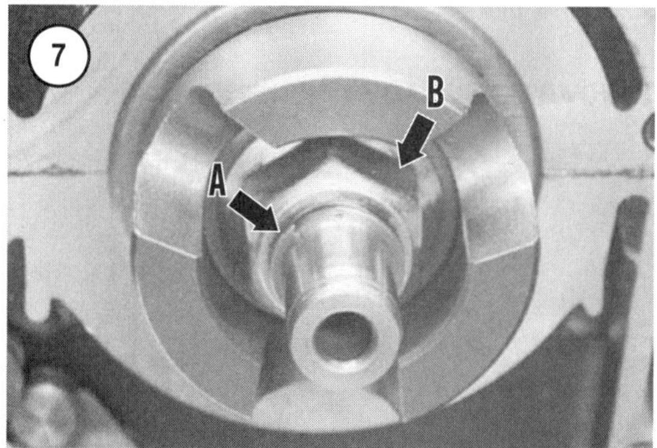

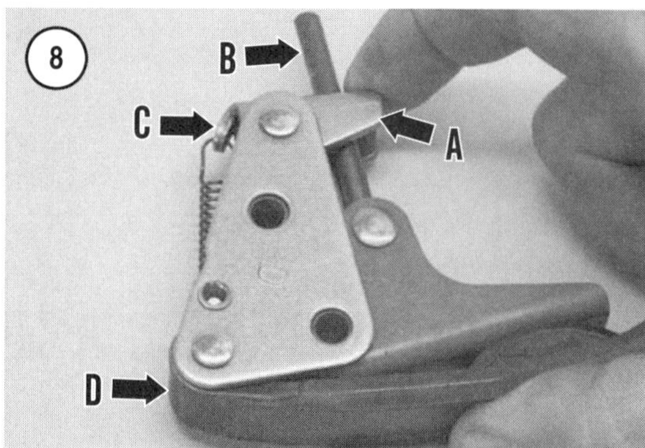

3. Loosely install a nut on each mounting bolt. If a shim was found during removal, install it between the washer and the frame on the left upper engine mount (3, **Figure 1**).

4. Check the adjustment shim by performing the following:
   a. Insert a 2.0 mm shim between the washer and the frame.
   b. If the 2.0 mm shim does not fit, try the 1.2 mm shim.
   c. If the 1.2 mm shim does not fit, no shim is required.

5. Evenly tighten the engine mounting nuts. Torque each nut to 54 N•m (40 ft.-lb.).

6. If the countershaft was serviced, complete the countershaft assembly as follows:
   a. Hold the damper cam with the damper cam holder (part No. 57001-1025) or equivalent tool. Tighten the lubricated damper cam nut (B, **Figure 7**) to 225 N•m (166 ft.-lb.).
   b. Install the inner snap ring (A, **Figure 7**) so it is completely seated in the countershaft groove.
   c. Slide the needle bearing (B, **Figure 6**) onto the countershaft, and install the outer snap ring (A).

7. Complete engine assembly by reversing Steps 1-10 of the engine removal procedure.

8. Add engine oil and coolant as described in Chapter Three.

9. Adjust the throttle cable and the choke cable (Chapter Three).

5

ALTERNATOR CHAIN ASSEMBLY

Chain Tensioner Removal/Installation

The alternator chain tensioner consists of a guide plate (A, **Figure 8**) and pin (B). The chain tensioner must be collapsed and locked before it is removed or installed. To collapse the chain tensioner, press the end of the guide plate (A, **Figure 8**) up the pin (B) until the plate locks against the pin stop.

To release the tensioner, press the spring end (C, **Figure 8**) of the guide plate.

1. Remove the clutch cover as described in Chapter Six.

2. Press the end of the guide plate (**Figure 9**) up the pin until the plate locks into position. **Figure 10** shows a locked chain tensioner.

12

STARTER CLUTCH/ALTERNATOR SHAFT

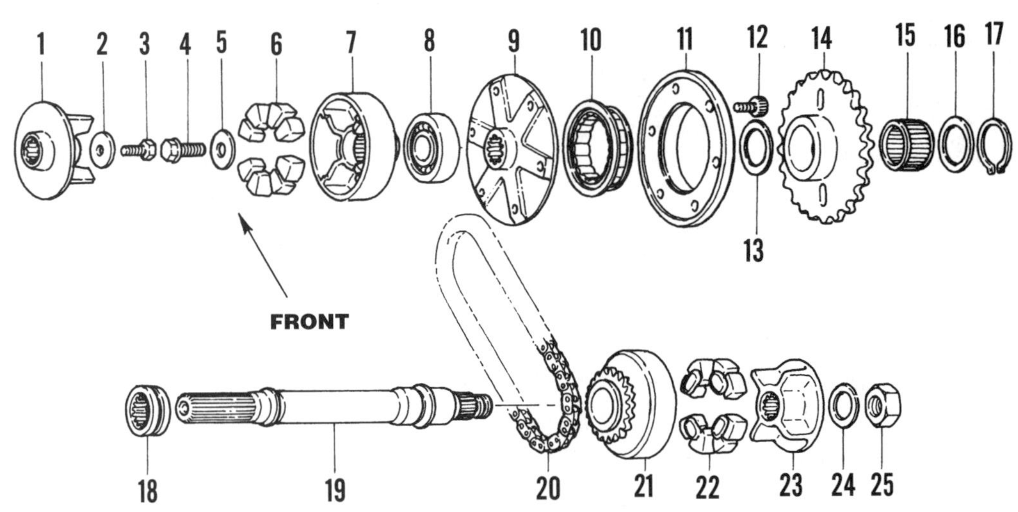

1. Right outer coupling
2. Washer
3. Bolt
4. Bolt
5. Washer
6. Right rubber dampers
7. Right inner coupling
8. Bearing
9. Coupling boss
10. One-way clutch
11. One-way clutch race
12. Allen bolt
13. Washer
14. Sprocket
15. Needle bearing
16. Washer
17. Snap ring
18. Needle bearing
19. Alternator shaft
20. Chain
21. Left inner coupling
22. Left rubber dampers
23. Left outer coupling
24. Washer
25. Nut

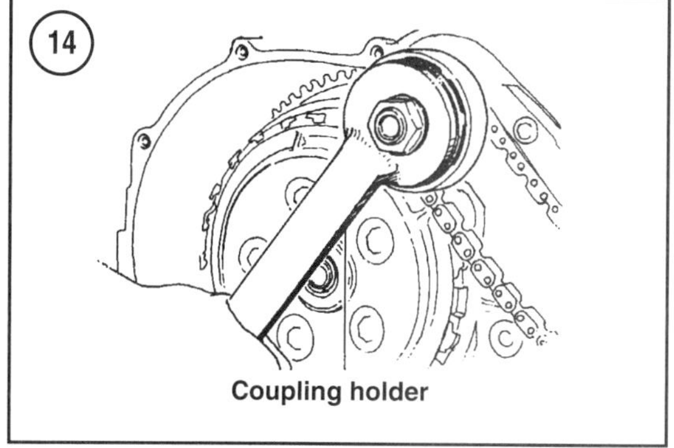

Coupling holder

3. Remove the tensioner bolts (A, **Figure 10**), and lift the chain tensioner from the crankcase.
4. Installation is the reverse of removal. Pay attention to the following:
   a. Collapse and lock the chain tensioner before installation.
   b. Apply Loctite 242 to the tensioner bolts (A, **Figure 10**), and tighten the bolts securely.
   c. Release the chain tensioner by pressing the rear of the guide plate as shown in **Figure 11**. **Figure 9** shows a released chain tensioner.

Chain and Sprocket Removal/Installation

Refer to **Figure 12**.

1. Remove the chain tensioner as described earlier in this section.
2. Remove the chain guide bolt (A, **Figure 13**), and slide the chain guide off its locator stud (B).
3. Hold the alternator shaft with the Kawasaki coupling holder (part No. 57001-1189). See **Figure 14**.
4. Remove the alternator shaft nut (A, **Figure 15**) and the drive sprocket bolt (B). Watch for the washer behind the alternator shaft nut.
5. Remove the washer and pull the right outer coupling from the alternator shaft.
6. If necessary, remove the dampers (**Figure 16**) from the right inner coupling.
7. Slide the right inner coupling, alternator chain and drive sprocket from the crankcase as an assembly. See **Figure 17**.
8. Inspect the components as described in this section.
9. Installation is the reverse of removal. Torque the alternator shaft nut (A, **Figure 15**) to 59 N•m (43 ft.-lb.). Tighten the drive sprocket bolt (B, **Figure 15**) securely.

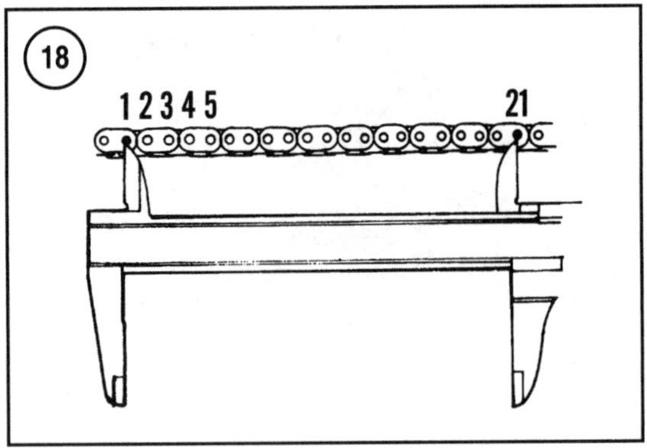

Inspection

1. Inspect the sliding surface of the chain guide and chain tensioner (D, **Figure 8**).
2. Visually inspect the alternator chain for signs of excessive wear or damage. If damage is noted, also inspect the chain and sprockets for damage.
3. Stretch the alternator chain taut on the bench and measure a 20-link length (21 pins) as shown in **Figure 18**. Replace the alternator chain if the measurement exceeds the service limit specified in **Table 1**.
4. Inspect the sprocket teeth on the right inner coupling and on the drive sprocket. See **Figure 19**. Replace as necessary.
5. Inspect the rubber dampers for wear or damage. Replace the dampers as a set if necessary.

STARTER CLUTCH AND ALTERNATOR SHAFT

Preliminary Inspection

1. Remove the starter as described in Chapter Nine.
2. While standing on the left side of the motorcycle, try to turn the starter idler gear (**Figure 20**) by hand. It should turn freely counterclockwise, but not turn clockwise.
3. If the starter clutch fails either portion of this test, remove, disassemble and inspect the starter clutch.

Removal/Installation

Refer to **Figure 12**.

1. Remove the alternator chain, sprockets and alternator chain tensioner as described in this chapter.

22

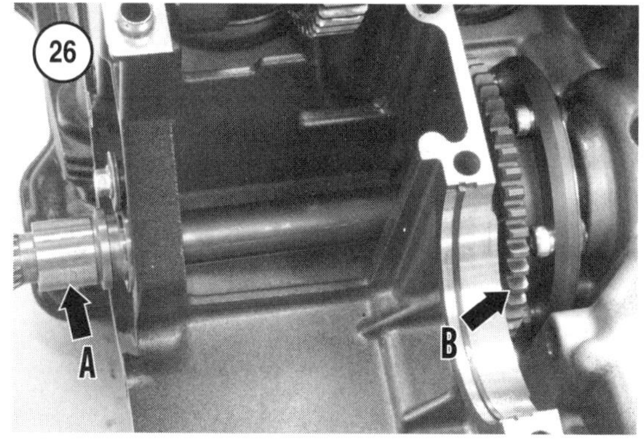

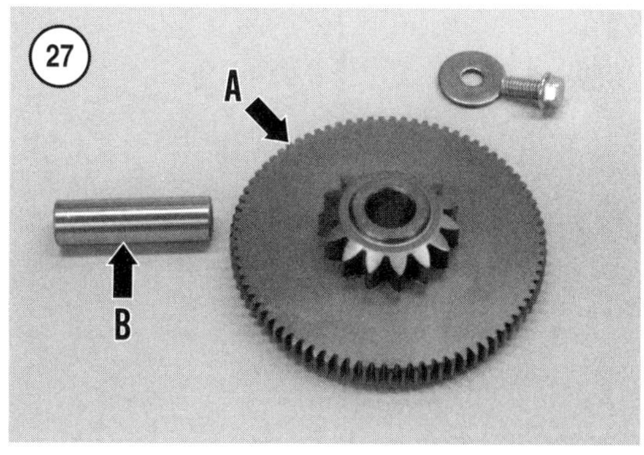

NOTE

If you are only servicing the starter clutch and alternator shaft, you can separate the crankcase halves with the cylinder head and cylinder block installed on the engine.

2. Remove the engine and separate the crankcase halves as described in this chapter.

3. Remove the dampers from the left inner coupling from the alternator shaft (**Figure 21**).

4. Remove the coupling bolt and washer (**Figure 22**).

5. Slide the left inner coupling (**Figure 23**) from the alternator shaft.

6. Remove the idler gear bolt (**Figure 24**) and washer from the right side of the crankcase.

7. Pull the idler gear shaft (A, **Figure 25**) and lift out the starter idler gear (B).

8. Pull the alternator shaft (A, **Figure 26**) from the crankcase and remove the starter clutch (B).

9. If necessary, disassemble and inspect the starter clutch as described in this section.

10. Inspect the starter idler gear (A, **Figure 27**) for tooth damage.

11. Check the idler gear shaft (B, **Figure 27**) for wear, scoring or heat discoloration.

12. Check the splines of the alternator shaft (**Figure 28**) for severe wear or cracks. Check the bearing surfaces for deep scoring, excessive wear or heat discoloration.

13. Replace worn or damaged parts as necessary. Inspect the starter clutch as described in this section.

14. Installation is the reverse of removal.

a. Apply engine oil to all bearing surfaces.

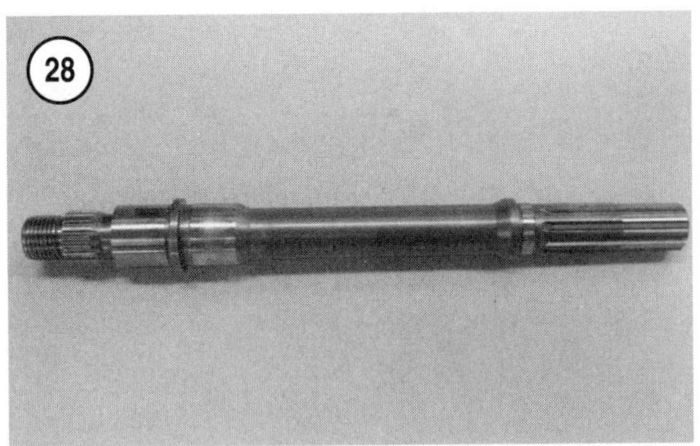

b. Set the starter clutch into the crankcase so the sprocket (B, **Figure 26**) faces the right side of the engine.
c. Insert the alternator shaft (A, **Figure 26**) through the bearing in the right side of the upper crankcase. Pass the shaft through the starter clutch and seat the shaft in the bearing on the left side. See **Figure 29.**
d. Install the idler gear (B, **Figure 25**) so it meshes with the starter clutch sprocket as shown.
e. Oil the idler gear shaft.

NOTE
The washer installed behind the idler gear bolt (A, ***Figure 24****) holds the idler gear shaft in place. If replacing the washer and bolt, use identical replacement parts from Kawasaki.*

f. Apply Loctite 242 (blue) to the idler gear bolt. Install the bolt and washer, and tighten the bolt securely.

Disassembly/Assembly

1. Remove the snap ring (**Figure 30**) and the washer (A, **Figure 31**).
2. Remove the starter clutch sprocket (B, **Figure 31**) from the hub on the coupling boss.
3. Lift out the needle bearing (**Figure 32**) and the washer (A, **Figure 33**).
4. Remove the one way clutch bolts (B, **Figure 33**), and lift the one way clutch race (C) from the coupling boss.
5. Remove the one-way clutch (A, **Figure 34**) from the coupling boss.
6. Inspect the starter clutch as described in this section.
7. Installation is the reverse of removal.

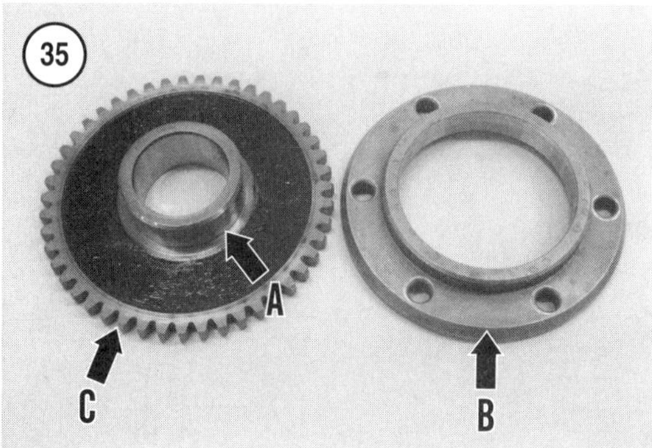

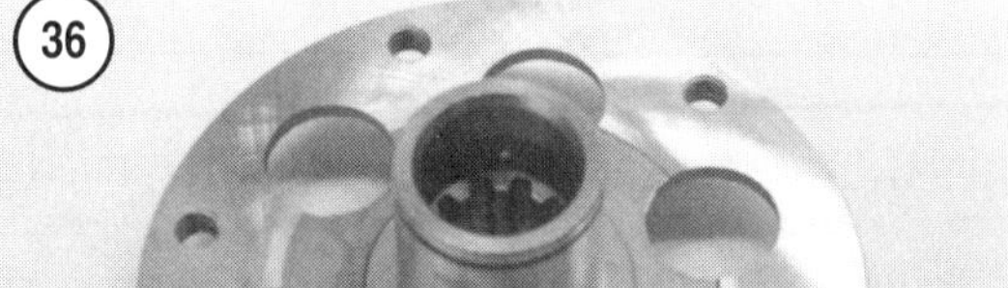

a. Set the one-way clutch (A, **Figure 34**) onto the coupling boss (B) so the larger diameter side faces down onto the boss.

b. Apply Loctite 242 (blue) to the threads of the one way clutch bolts (B, **Figure 33**) and torque the bolts to 12 N•m (106 in.-lb.).

c. Make sure the snap ring (**Figure 30**) is completely seated in its groove in the coupling boss.

d. Hold the starter clutch assembly and turn the sprocket. It should turn smoothly in one direction but not at all in the other. If it slips or makes a noise, disassemble and repair the problem.

Inspection

1. Inspect the bearing surfaces of the sprocket (A, **Figure 35**) and the one way clutch race (B).
2. Inspect the sprocket teeth (C, **Figure 35**) for excessive wear or damage.
3. Inspect the bearing surface and inner splines of the coupling boss (**Figure 36**).
4. Inspect the inside and outside surfaces of the one-way clutch (**Figure 37**) for scoring or galling.
5. Inspect the bearing needles (**Figure 38**) for uneven wear or damage.
6. Replace any part that is worn or damaged.

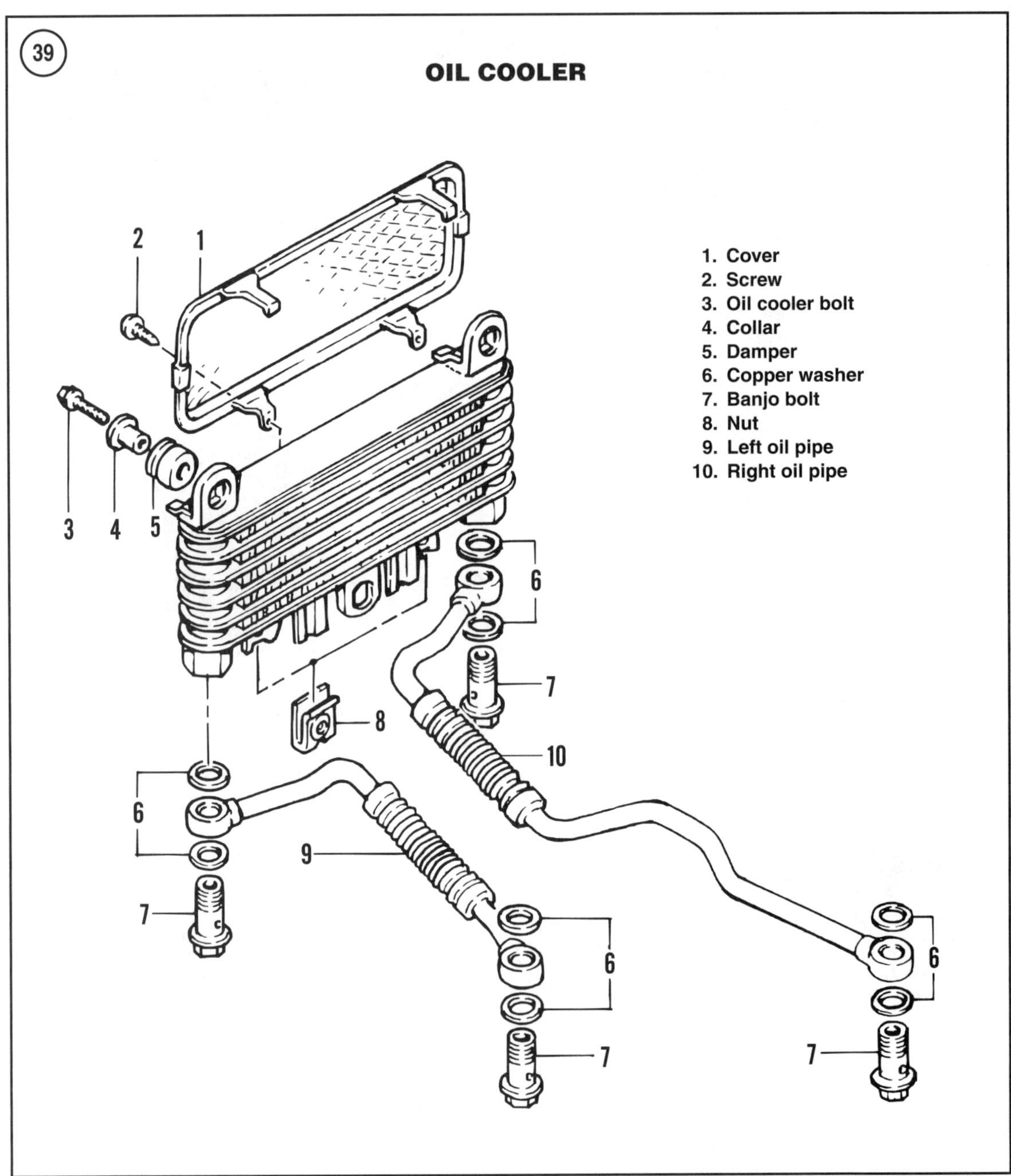

OIL COOLER

The oil cooler mounts to the bottom of the radiator bracket. The oil cooler can be removed without removing this bracket, however, it is difficult to do so without straining and possibly bending the oil lines. Oil cooler removal is easier if the radiator bracket is removed from the engine and then the oil cooler pulled from the bracket.

Removal/Installation

Refer to **Figure 39**.

1. Remove the lower, middle and front fairings as described in Chapter Fifteen.
2. Drain the engine oil and the coolant (Chapter Three).
3. Remove the radiator and then remove the radiator bracket (Chapter Ten).

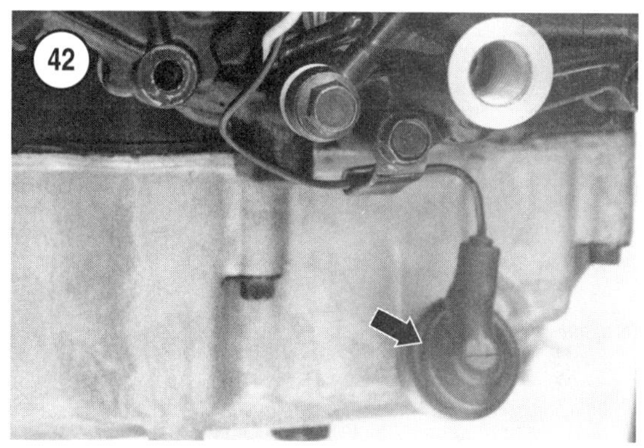

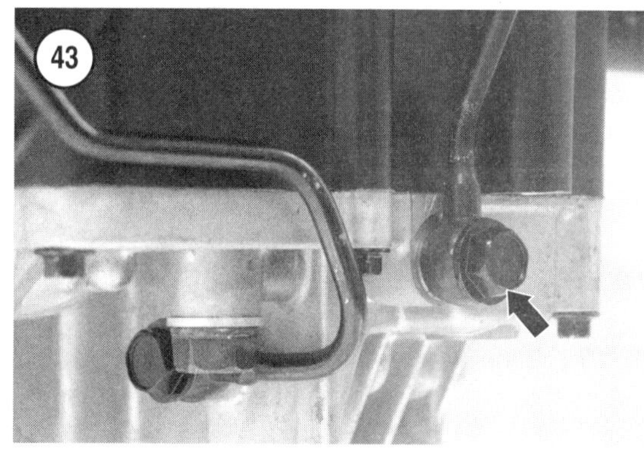

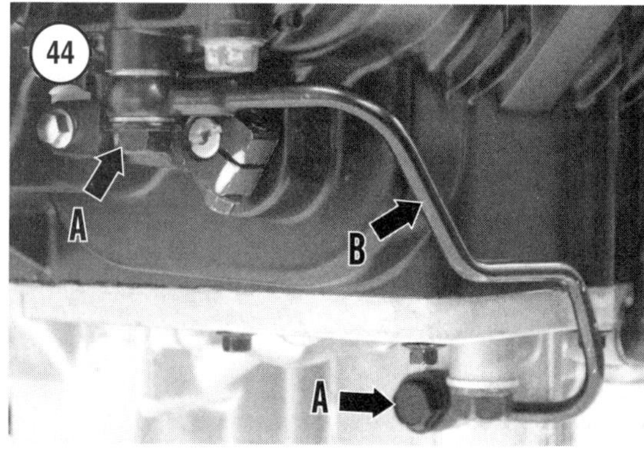

4. Remove the mounting bolts (**Figure 40**) and remove the oil cooler from the radiator bracket.
5. Installation is the reverse of removal.
   a. Make sure the oil pipes rest on the coolant reservoir as shown in **Figure 41**.
   b. Install a collar and damper with each mounting bolt.
   c. If the oil pipes were removed from the oil cooler, install new copper washers when reinstalling them. Torque each oil pipe-to-oil cooler banjo bolt to 25 N•m (18 ft.-lb.).
   d. Reinstall the radiator bracket as described in Chapter Ten.

OIL PAN

Removal/Installation

1. Drain the engine oil and remove the oil filter as described in Chapter Three.
2. Drain the engine coolant (Chapter Three).
3. Remove the radiator and the radiator bracket (Chapter Ten).
4. Remove the mufflers and exhaust pipes (Chapter Eight).
5. Disconnect the electrical connector (**Figure 42**) from the oil pressure switch.
6. Remove the banjo bolt (**Figure 43**) that secures the main oil pipe to the front of the oil pan. Discard the two copper washers.
7. Remove both banjo bolts (A, **Figure 44**) and lower the clutch cover oil pipe (B) from the engine. Discard the two copper washers installed on each end of the oil pipe.
8. Keep the drain pan under the engine. Loosen all the oil pan bolts (**Figure 45**) and let any residual oil drain from the engine.

9. Remove the oil pan bolts and lower the pan from the engine.

10. Remove the oil pan gasket.

11. Inspect the oil pan as described in this section.

12. Installation is the reverse of removal. Note the following.

   a. The O-ring (A, **Figure 46**) installed between the oil pump bracket and the oil pan must be installed so its flat side faces the bracket.
   b. Apply engine oil to all exposed O-rings.
   c. Install the large O-ring (**Figure 47**) into the oil pan.
   d. Remove all gasket residue from the oil pan and crankcase.
   e. Apply silicone sealant to the areas of the oil pan and the lower crankcase shown in **Figure 48**.
   f. Install a new gasket. Make sure the bolt holes align properly.
   g. Apply Loctite 242 (blue) to the four oil pan bolts indicated by the arrowheads (**Figure 49**) cast onto the pan and tighten the bolts securely.
   h. Install a new oil filter and refill the engine with clean oil.

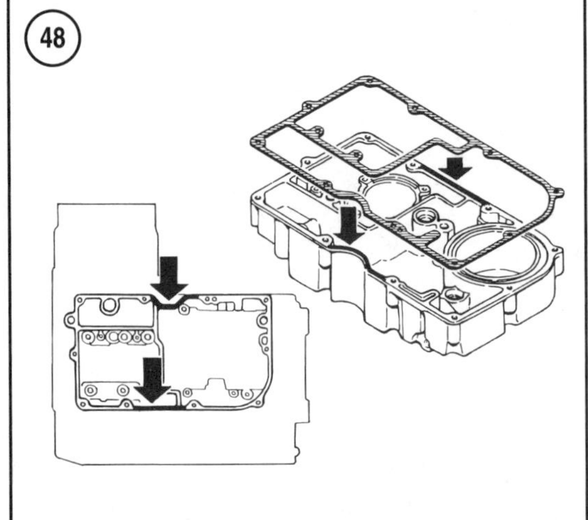

Inspection

1. Remove the large O-ring (**Figure 47**) from the oil pan.

2. Check the inside of the oil pan for metal or fiber debris that may indicate engine, clutch or transmission problems.

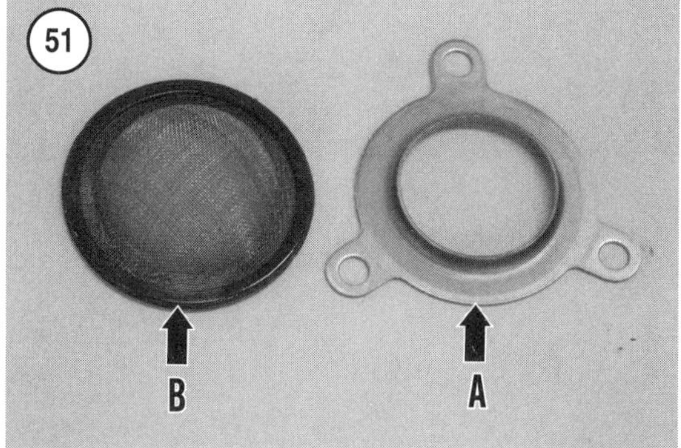

3. Service the oil screen as follows:
   a. Remove the Philips screws (**Figure 50**) from the oil screen plate.
   b. Lift the oil screen plate (A, **Figure 51**) and the oil screen (B) from the oil pan.
   c. Check the oil screen for metal or fiber debris.
   d. Clean the oil screen in solvent and dry it thoroughly.
   e. Check the oil screen for tears of other damage. Replace the screen as necessary.
   f. Installation is the reverse of removal. Apply Loctite 242 (blue) to the threads of the Philips screws (**Figure 50**). Tighten the screws securely.
4. Inspect all five exposed O-rings (A and B, **Figure 46**) in the crankcase for wear of damage. Replace any O-ring as necessary.

OIL PUMP

Removal

The oil pump can be removed with the engine installed in the frame. The engine is shown removed for photographic clarity.

1. Remove the oil pan as described in this chapter.
2. Remove the nozzle (**Figure 52**) from the crankcase.
3. Pull the oil screen assembly (**Figure 53**) from the oil pipe.
4. Lift the large oil pipe (**Figure 54**) from its ports in the crankcase and remove it.
5. Remove the small oil pipe (**Figure 55**).

NOTE
*The flats of the oil pump shaft (**Figure 56**) engage a slot in the oil pump gear.*

Oil pump removal is difficult if the slot is not vertical.

6. Remove the pickup coil cover. Rotate the crankshaft until the slot in the oil pump gear (**Figure 57**) sits vertically in the crankcase.
7. Remove the three oil pump mounting bolts (**Figure 58**) and the oil pump.
8. Watch for the dowel (A, **Figure 59**) and nozzle (B) installed behind the oil pump bracket. They may come out with the oil pump assembly or may remain in the crankcase. Remove them so they will not be misplaced.

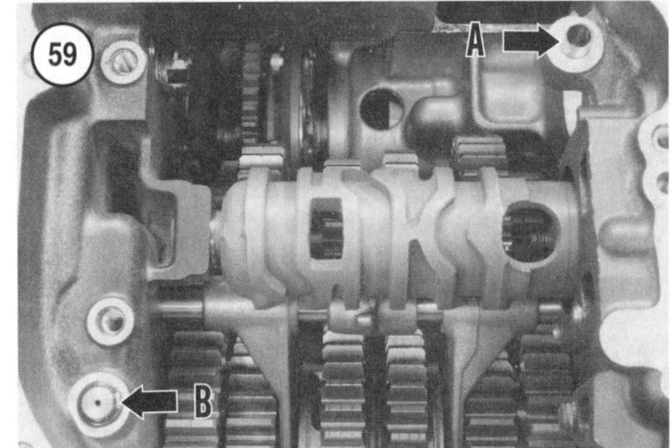

Installation

CAUTION
If the screen is contaminated with metal or clutch particles, inspect the lower end and oil lines for contamination.

1. Check the oil pump screen (**Figure 60**) for debris buildup or damage. Thoroughly clean the

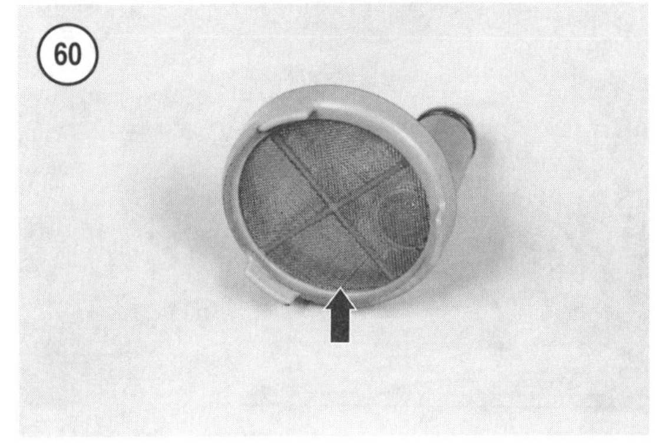

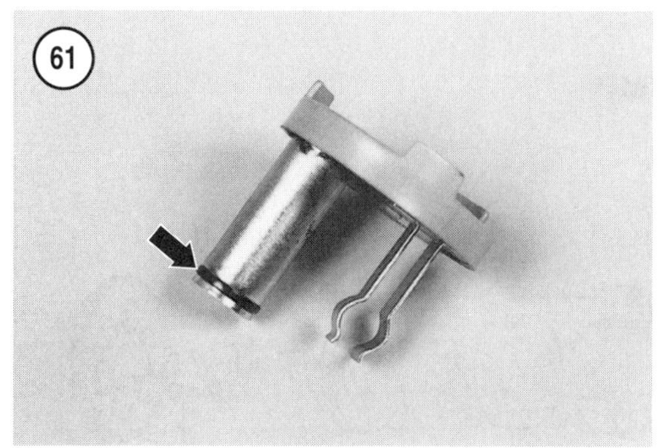

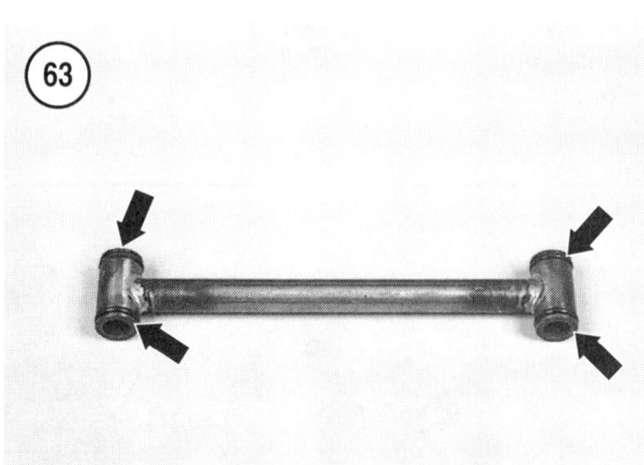

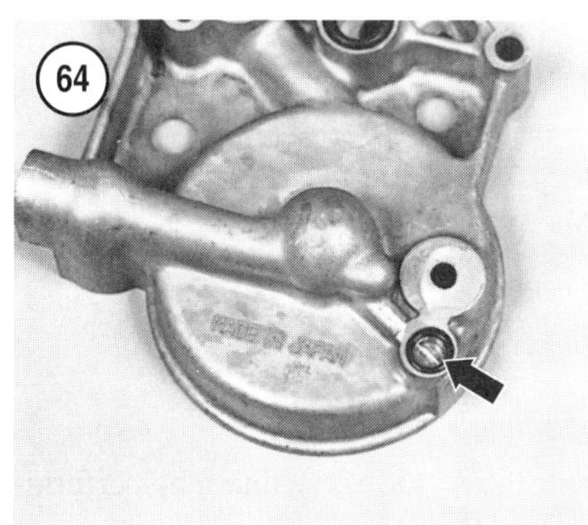

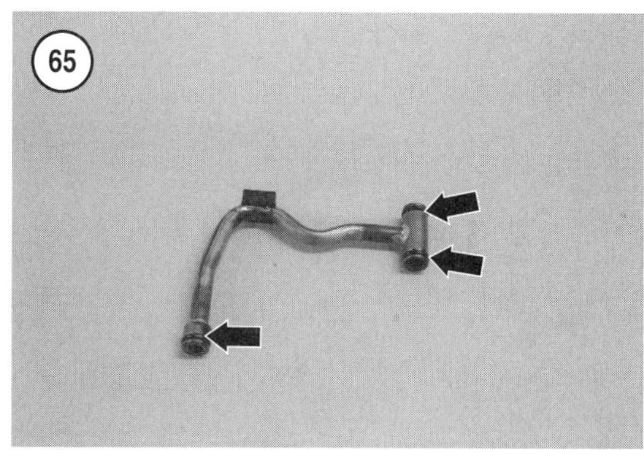

screen in solvent and let it completely dry. Replace the screen assembly if necessary.

NOTE
Lubricate the O-rings with engine oil before installing them.

2. Replace the oil pump screen O-ring (**Figure 61**).
3. Check the soldered joints (**Figure 62**) in the large oil pipe for cracks or other damage. Replace the four O-rings (**Figure 63**) on this oil pipe.
4. Replace the O-ring (**Figure 64**) in the oil pump bracket.
5. Replace the three O-ring in the small oil pipe (**Figure 65**).
6. Install the dowel (A **Figure 59**) and nozzle (B) into the crankcase. Install the nozzle into the fitting shown in B, **Figure 59**. The small hole in the nozzle must face out away from the crankcase.
7. Install the oil pump as follows:
   a. Pour clean engine oil into the oil pump.
   b. If necessary, rotate the crankshaft so the slot in the oil pump gear (**Figure 57**) sits vertically in the crankcase. If the water pump is installed, rotate the water pump shaft so its slot also sits vertically in the crankcase.
   c. Rotate the oil pump shaft so the flats on each end face up and down.
   d. Install the oil pump into the crankcase so the flats on one end of the oil pump shaft slide into the slot in the oil pump gear (**Figure 57**) and the flats on the opposite end slide into the slot in the water pump shaft. Seat the oil pump bracket on the dowel (A **Figure 59**) and nozzle (B).
   e. Apply Loctite 242 to the threads of the oil pump mounting bolts (**Figure 58**) and evenly tighten the bolts. Torque the oil pump mounting bolts to 12 N•m (106 in.-lb.).

(66)

OIL PUMP

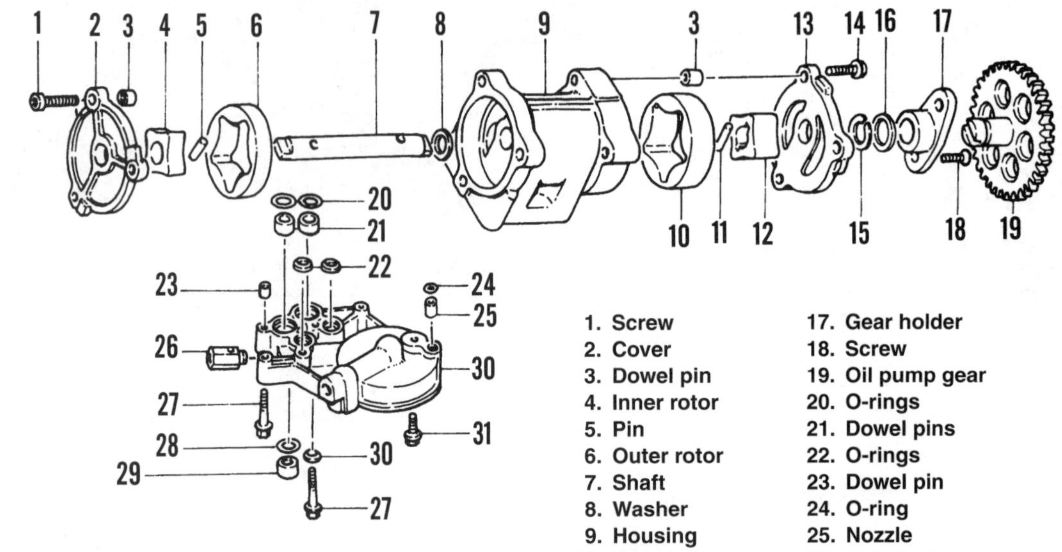

1. Screw
2. Cover
3. Dowel pin
4. Inner rotor
5. Pin
6. Outer rotor
7. Shaft
8. Washer
9. Housing
10. Outer rotor
11. Pin
12. Inner rotor
13. Cover
14. Screw
15. Snap ring
16. Washer
17. Gear holder
18. Screw
19. Oil pump gear
20. O-rings
21. Dowel pins
22. O-rings
23. Dowel pin
24. O-ring
25. Nozzle
26. Relief valve
27. Bolt
28. O-ring
29. Dowel pin
30. O-ring
31. Bolt

Disassembly/Assembly

Refer to **Figure 66**.

1. Remove the oil pump as described in this section.
2. If still installed, remove the O-ring (**Figure 64**) from the oil pump bracket.
3. Remove the oil pump bracket bolts (**Figure 67**) and separate the oil pump housing (**Figure 68**) from the oil pump bracket.
4. Remove the two dowels and their O-rings (A, **Figure 69**) from the oil pump bracket, and remove the two remaining O-rings (B).
5. If necessary, unscrew the relief valve (C, **Figure 69**) from the oil pump bracket.

NOTE
*The sides of the oil pump are identified by an A or B stamped on each respective cover. See A, **Figure 70**. The A side of the pump is disassembled first, followed by the B side.*

(67)

6. Disassemble the A side of the pump by performing the following:

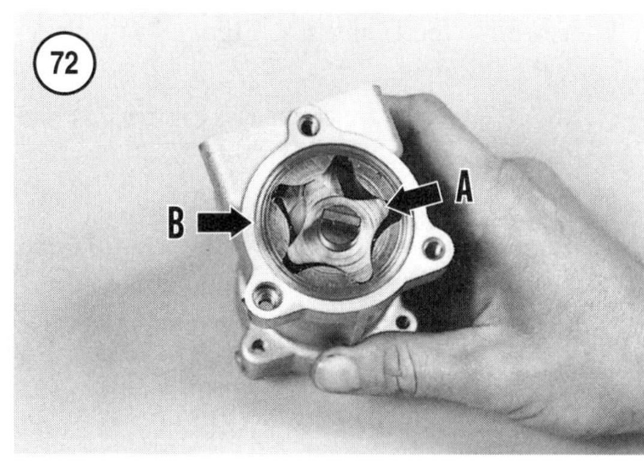

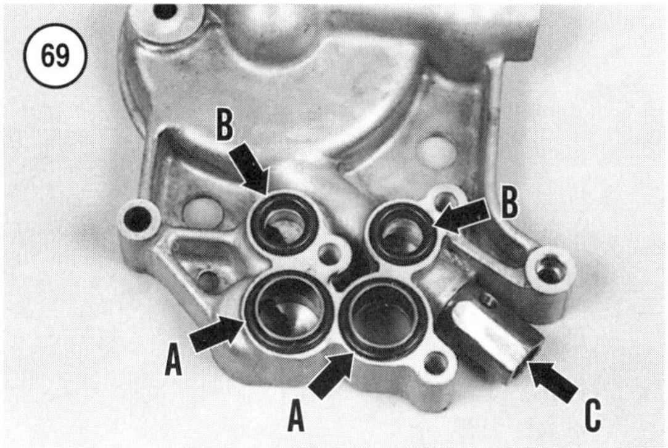

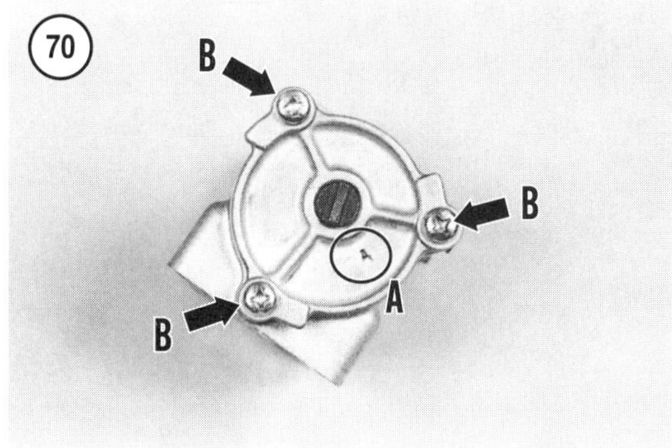

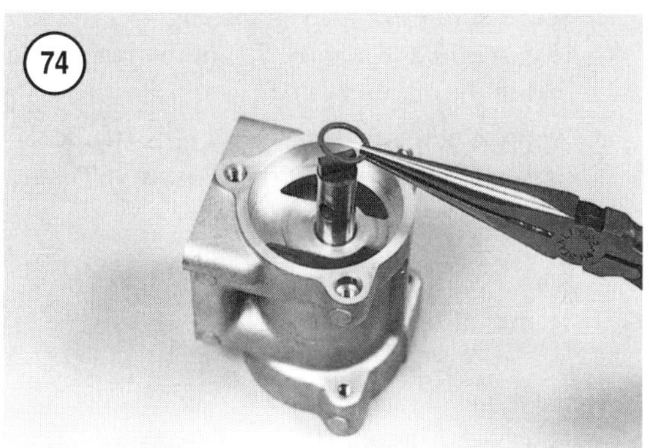

a. Remove the cover screws (B, **Figure 70**) and remove the A cover.
b. Remove the dowel (**Figure 71**) from the pump housing.
c. Remove the inner rotor (A, **Figure 72**) and the outer rotor (B).
d. Remove the pin (**Figure 73**) from the shaft and lift out the washer (**Figure 74**).
e. Store these parts in a reclosable plastic bag so they will not be mixed with the parts from the B side of the pump.

7. Disassemble the B side (A, **Figure 75**) by performing the following:

   a. Remove the cover screws (B, **Figure 75**) and lift the cover from the housing.
   b. Remove the dowel (**Figure 76**).
   c. Remove the outer rotor (A, **Figure 77**) and the inner rotor (B) from the pump housing.
   d. Remove the pin (**Figure 78**) from the pump shaft.
   e. Remove the shaft (**Figure 79**) from the housing.

8. Inspect the oil pump by performing the following.

   a. Inspect pump housing (**Figure 80**) for cracks or bore damage.
   b. Check the pump shaft for scoring, pin hole damage or signs of seizure.
   c. Check the rotor for scoring or damage.

9. Assemble the oil pump by reversing the disassembly procedure. Note the following:

   a. Lubricate all parts with clean engine oil.
   b. Assemble the A side of the pump first and then assemble the B side.
   c. Make sure each inner rotor engages the pin (**Figure 73** and **Figure 78**) in the respective end of the oil pump shaft.
   d. Apply Loctite 242 to the threads of the oil pressure relief valve (C, **Figure 69**) and tighten the valve securely.

Gear Removal/Installation

1. Remove the clutch as described in Chapter Six.
2. Rotate the oil pump gear so its two mounting screws (A, **Figure 81**) are accessible.
3. Remove the mounting screws (A, **Figure 81**), and lower the oil pump gear assembly (B) from the crankcase.
4. Installation is the reverse of removal. Note the following:

   a. Align the notch on the oil pump gear with the cutouts in the oil pump shaft.
   b. Apply Loctite 242 (blue) to the mounting screws (A, **Figure 81**) and tighten the screws securely.
   c. Install the clutch as described in Chapter Six.

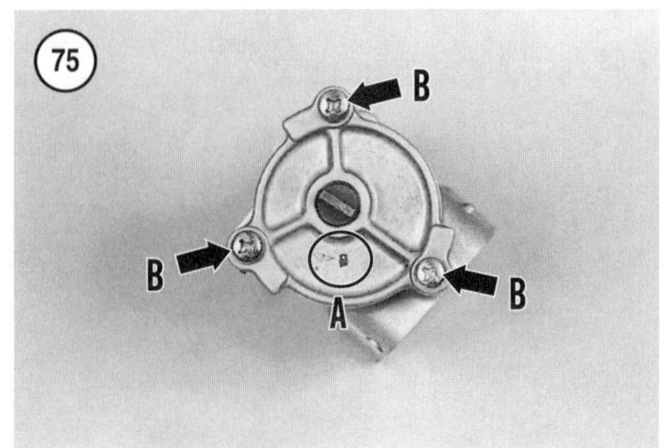

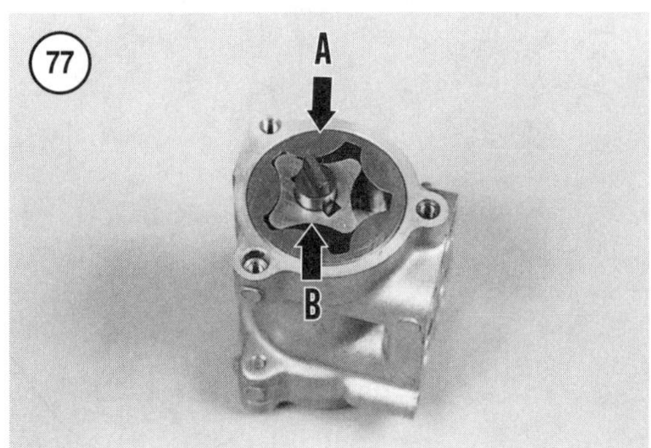

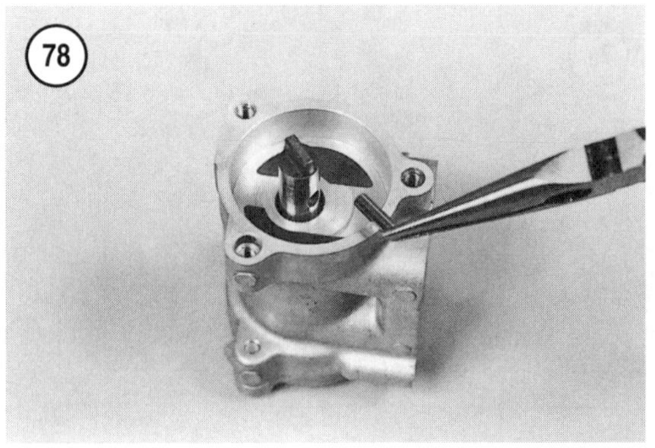

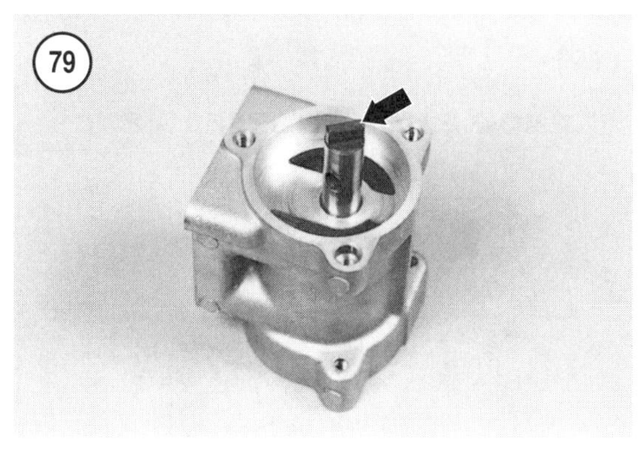

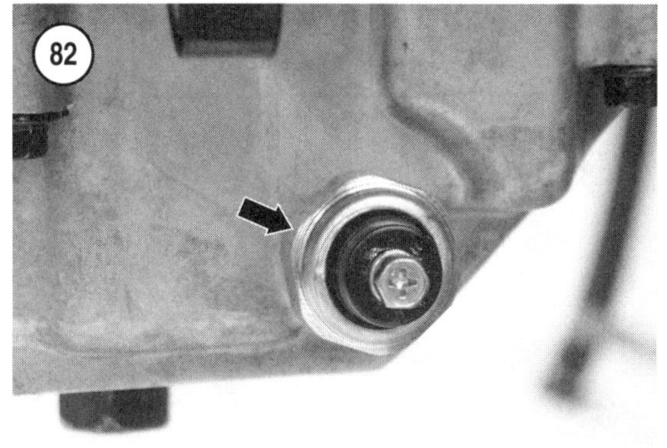

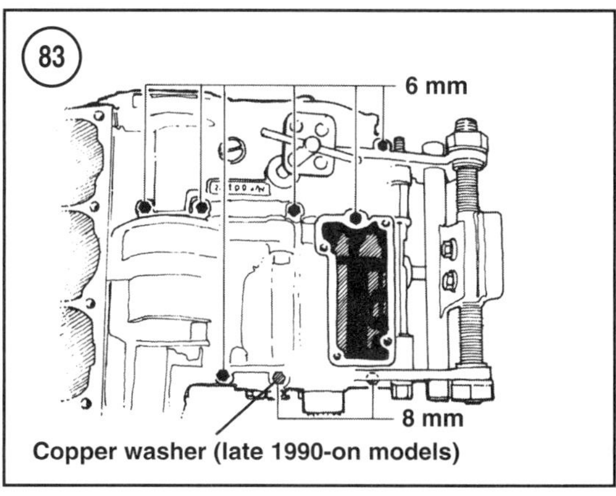

OIL PRESSURE SWITCH

Removal/Installation

1. Drain the engine oil as described in Chapter Three.
2. Disconnect the electrical connector from the oil pressure switch.
3. Unscrew the oil pressure switch (**Figure 82**) from the oil pan.
4. Installation is the reverse of removal. Note the following:
   a. Clean the threads in the oil pan and the surrounding area.
   b. Apply Loctite 242 (blue) to the threads of the oil pressure switch and torque the switch to 15 N•m (11 ft.-lb.).
   c. Refill the engine with clean oil.

CRANKCASE

Separation

NOTE
The crankcase halves can be separated while the camshafts, cylinder head, cylinder block and crankshaft are in place.

1. Remove the relevant external assemblies and the engine from the frame. See *Engine* in this chapter.
2. Set the engine on the bench so the upper crankcase half faces up.
3. Loosen the 6 mm upper crankcase bolts then loosen the 8 mm bolts. See **Figure 83**. Remove the bolts. On 1990-on models, watch for the copper

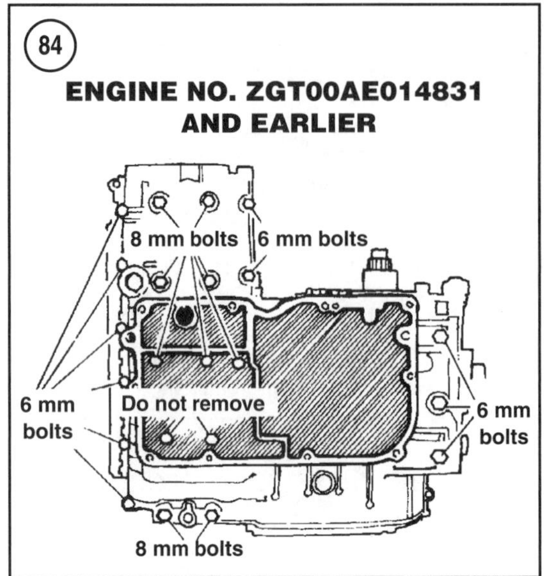

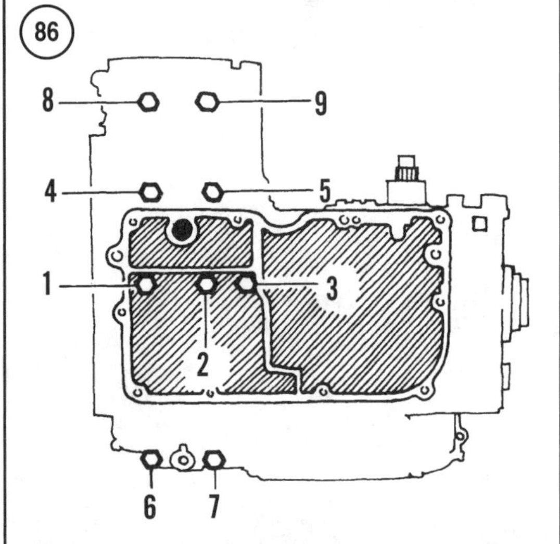

washer installed under the forward 8-mm upper crankcase bolt.

4. Turn the engine over so the lower crankcase half faces up.

5. If still installed, remove the oil pan and the oil pump as described in this chapter.

NOTE

*The sizes of some lower crankcase bolts were changed in mid-production of 1990 models. **Figure 84** shows the bolt sizes used in models with engine number ZGT00AE014831 or earlier (1986 through early-1990 models). **Figure 85** shows the bolt sizes for models with engine number ZGT00AE014832 or later (late-1990-on models). Refer to the appropriate drawing when removing and installing the lower crankcase bolts.*

6. Evenly loosen the 6 mm and 7 mm lower crankcase bolts, and then remove them. See **Figure 84** or **Figure 85**.

NOTE

Do not remove the crankshaft main bearing cap and bolts when separating the case halves. The case halves can be separated with them in place.

7. Reverse of the tightening sequence cast into the lower crankcase (**Figure 86**) and evenly loosen the

87

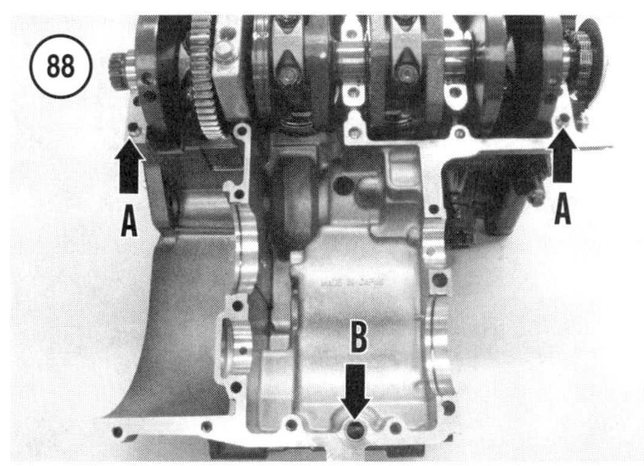

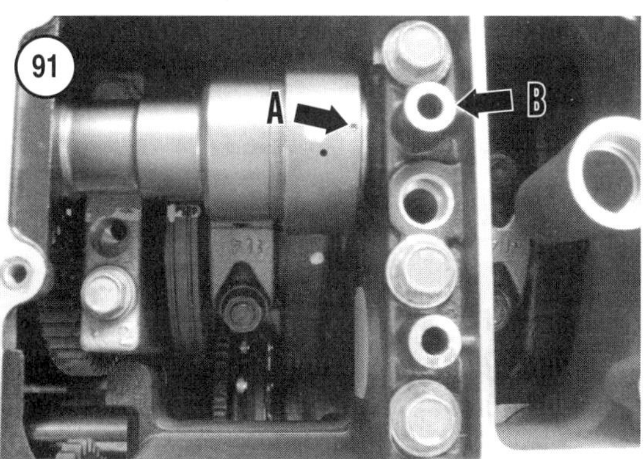

8 mm bolts (**Figure 84**) or 9 mm bearing bolts (**Figure 85**). Remove the bolts. Watch for the flat washer installed beneath the three bolts shown in **Figure 87**.

CAUTION
If necessary, pry the case halves apart at the pry points cast into the crankcase. Do not pry the crankcase between any gasket surface. The crankcase halves are machined as a set. Damage to one will require replacing both.

5

8. Tap around the perimeter of the crankcase with a plastic mallet to separate the case halves. If necessary, pry the case halves apart at the four pry points cast into the crankcase assembly.
9. Lift the lower crankcase from the upper crankcase. Watch for the locating dowels. Two dowels (A, **Figure 88**) are used on 1986-1994 models, three (A and B) on 1995-on models.
10. Disassemble and inspect the crankcase as described in this section.

Joining

1. Assemble the upper crankcase as described in *Assembly* in this section.
2. Set the shift drum to neutral. The shift drum is in neutral when the neutral lever (**Figure 89**) engages the detent on the shift cam.
3. Position the shift forks (**Figure 90**) so they can engage the slots in the sliding transmission gears.

NOTE
*Do not confuse the balancer indexing dot with its oil hole. The indexing dot (A, **Figure 91**) sits closest to the balancer's inboard edge.*

4. Rotate the balancer so its indexing dot (A, **Figure 91**) aligns with the center of the oil passage hole (B).
5. On 1986-1994 models, make sure the two dowels (A, **Figure 88**) are in place in the upper crankcase. On 1995-on models, three dowels (A and B, **Figure 88**) are used.
6. Confirm that the transmission sits in neutral.
7. Rotate the crankshaft so the connecting rods sit at top and bottom dead center. If the case halves were split with the top end installed, rotate the crankshaft so the T-mark for the No. 1 and 4 cylin-

ders align with the timing mark on the crankcase (**Figure 92**).

8. Apply a thin coat of black Kawasaki Liquid Gasket (part No. 92104-1003) or an equivalent gasket sealer to the mating surfaces of the lower crankcase. Make the coating as thin as possible, but completely cover the sealing surface. Make sure gasket sealer does not get into the bearings (**Figure 93**).

CAUTION
The crankcase halves should fit together without force. If they do not completely mate with one another, do not attempt to pull them together with the crankcase bolts. Separate the crankcase halves and determine the cause of the interference. Do not risk crankcase damage by trying to force the case halves together.

9. Position the lower crankcase over the upper case and join both halves. Set the front portion down first and lower the rear while making sure the shift forks properly engage the transmission assemblies. Make sure the balancer indexing mark (A, **Figure 91**) remains aligned with the oil passage hole (B).

10. Slowly spin the transmission shafts and shift the transmission through all six gears.

NOTE
*The size of some lower crankcase bolts were changed during production of 1990 models. See the earlier note and refer to **Figure 84** or **Figure 85** when installing the lower crankcase bolts.*

11. Apply oil to the threads of the lower crankcase bolts. Install and finger-tighten all bolts. Lightly tighten the bolts until they are snug.

12A. On models with engine number ZGT00AE-014831 or lower (1986-early 1990 models), torque the lower crankcase bolts (**Figure 84**) as follows:

a. Following the tightening sequence cast into the crankcase (**Figure 86**), first torque the 8 mm bolts to 14 N•m (10 ft.-lb.) and then torque them to 27 N•m (20 ft.-lb.).
b. Torque the 6-mm bolts to 15 N•m (11 ft.-lb.).

12B. On models with engine number ZGT00AE-014832 or higher, (late-1990-on models) tighten the lower crankcase bolts (**Figure 85**) as follows:

a. Following the tightening sequence cast into the crankcase (**Figure 86**), first torque the 9-mm bolts to 9.8 N•m (87 in.-lb.) and then torque them to 32 N•m (24 ft.-lb.).

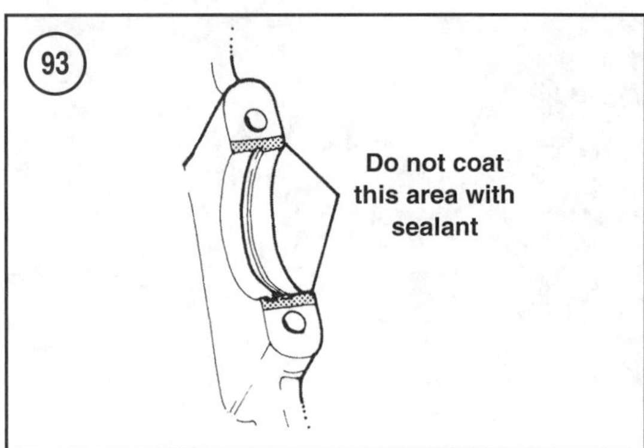

b. Torque the 7-mm bolt to 18 N•m (13 ft.-lb.).
c. Torque the 6-mm bolts to 15 N•m (11 ft.-lb.).

13. Check the transmission by rotating the countershaft and shifting through all six gears.

14. Turn the engine over so the upper crankcase faces up.

15. Apply engine oil to the threads of the upper crankcase bolts (**Figure 83**) and install the bolt. On models with engine number ZGT00AE014832 or later (late 1990-on models), install a copper washer under the indicated 8 mm bolt.

16. Lightly snug down the upper crankcase bolts. Torque the upper crankcase bolts as follows:

   a. First torque the 8 mm bolts to 14 N•m (10 ft.-lb.) and then to 27 N•m (20 ft.-lb.).
   b. Torque the 6 mm bolts to 15 N•m (11 ft.-lb.).

Disassembly

1. Remove the engine and separate the crankcase halves as described in this section.
2. Before removing the transmission, check the transmission gear lash by performing the following:
   a. Secure a dial indicator in place so its plunger rests against a tooth on one gear. See **Figure 94**.
   b. Hold the gear's mate on the other shaft, and rotate the gear slightly back and forth.
   c. Gear backlash equals the difference between the highest and lowest readings on the dial indicator.
   d. Repeat this for each set of mated gears.
3. Remove the countershaft assembly (A, **Figure 95**) and the mainshaft assembly (B) from the upper crankcase half. Insert each shaft assembly in a labeled, reclosable plastic bag until its is serviced.
4. Remove the dowel (A, **Figure 96**) and the C-ring (B) from the bearing bosses for each shaft.
5. Remove the alternator shaft and starter clutch from the upper crankcase half as described in this chapter.
6. Remove the crankshaft from the upper crankcase half as described in this chapter.
7. Remove the internal mechanism from the lower crankcase half as described in Chapter Seven.
8. Remove the balancer from the lower crankcase half as described in this chapter.
9. Inspect the crankcase halves as described in this section.

5

Assembly

1. Install the balancer into the lower crankcase half as described in this chapter.
2. Install the internal shift mechanism into the lower crankcase (Chapter Seven).
3. Install the crankshaft into the upper crankcase half (this chapter).
4. Install the alternator shaft and starter clutch into the upper crankcase half (this chapter).
5. Install the transmission assemblies into the upper crankcase by performing the following:
   a. Apply engine oil to the assembled shafts and to the bearing surfaces in the crankcase.
   b. Install the dowels (A, **Figure 96**) and C-rings (B) into the bearing bosses in the crankcase.
   c. Lower the mainshaft (B, **Figure 95**) into the upper crankcase so the C-ring engages the groove in the bearing (A, **Figure 97**). Rotate the bearing race (B, **Figure 97**) until its pin hole engages the dowel in the bearing boss.

98

99

d. Repeat substep c for the countershaft. Make sure each gear meshes with its mate on the mainshaft.

e. Check the bearing outer races (**Figure 98** and **Figure 99**). The transmission shafts are correctly seated when there is no clearance between crankcase and the bearing outer races.

6. Join the crankcase halves together as described in this section.

100

Inspection

1. Use solvent to thoroughly clean the inside and outside of both crankcase halves. Thoroughly dry the cases with compressed air. Make sure no residual solvent remains in either case half. It will contaminate the engine.
2. Blow all oil galleries clear with compressed air.
3. Check the crankcase for cracks or other damage. Inspect the mating surface of each case half. These surfaces must be free of gouges, burrs or other damage that could cause an oil leak.
4. Inspect the main bearings as described in *Crankshaft* in this chapter.
5. Check the threads of the cylinder head bolt holes in the upper crankcase (**Figure 100**). If necessary, dress the threads with an appropriate size tap. Apply kerosene to the tap before use.
6. Check the shift mechanism studs (**Figure 101**) in the lower crankcase. Each stud should be tight and its threads in good condition. Slight thread damage can be repaired with a file or die. If necessary, replace a damaged stud. Follow the procedure described in Chapter One.
7. Remove the main oil gallery plugs (**Figure 102**) and flush the gallery with solvent. Dry the gallery thoroughly with compressed air. Install a new O-ring with each plug and tighten the plugs securely.

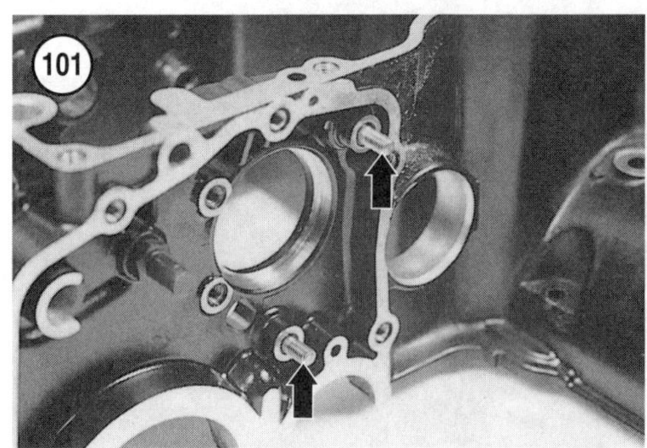
101

102

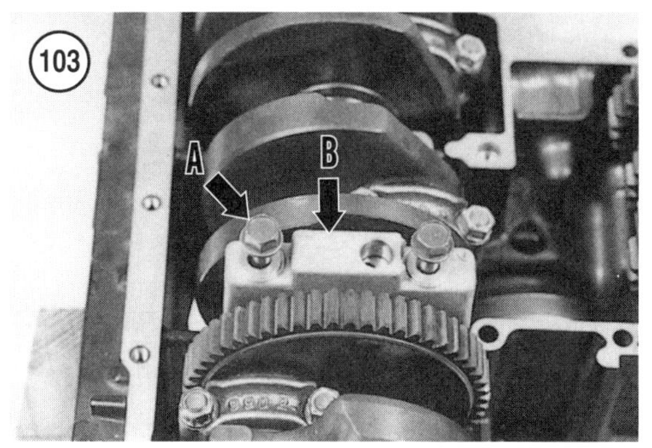

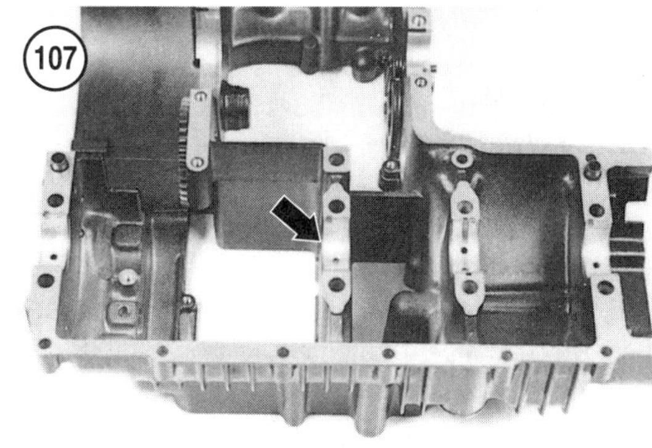

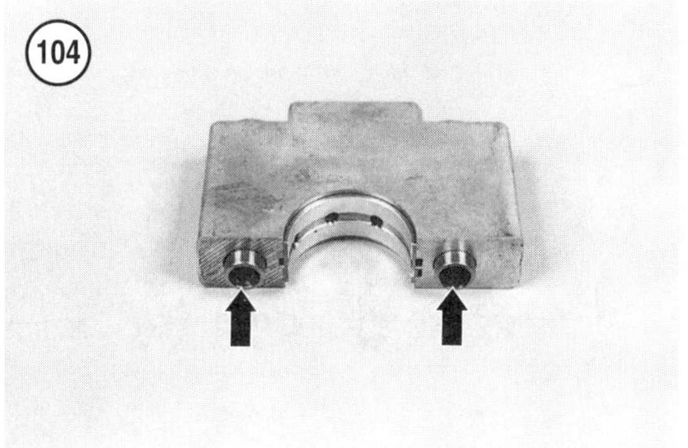

CRANKSHAFT

Removal/Installation

1. Remove the engine as described in this chapter.
2. Remove the pistons as described in Chapter Four.
3. Separate the crankcase halves as described in this chapter.
4. Remove the main bearing cap bolts (A, **Figure 103**) along with their washers and remove the bearing cap (B) from the upper crankcase.
5. Remove the two dowels (**Figure 104**) from the cap.
6. Rotate the crankshaft so the connecting rods are at top and bottom dead center and lift the crankshaft (**Figure 105**) from the crankcase.
7. Remove the crankcase main bearings from the upper (**Figure 106**) and lower (**Figure 107**) crankcase halves. Counting from the left side, mark the back of each bearing with a 1, 2, 3, 4, or 5 and U (upper) or L (lower) so each bearing can be installed in its original location. Do not forget to mark the bearing (**Figure 108**) in the main bearing cap.
7. Installation is the reverse of removal. Note the following:

a. Press each bearing into its original location.
b. Make sure the tab of the bearing locks into the notch in the bearing boss or the main bearing cap (**Figure 108**).
c. Install the dowels (**Figure 104**) into the bearing cap. Set the cap into place so the arrow cast into the cap points forward.
d. Install the main bearing cap bolts (**Figure 109**) along with their flat washers and torque the bearing cap bolts to 34 N•m (25 ft.-lb.).
e. If new main bearings were installed, measure the crankshaft oil clearance as described in this section.

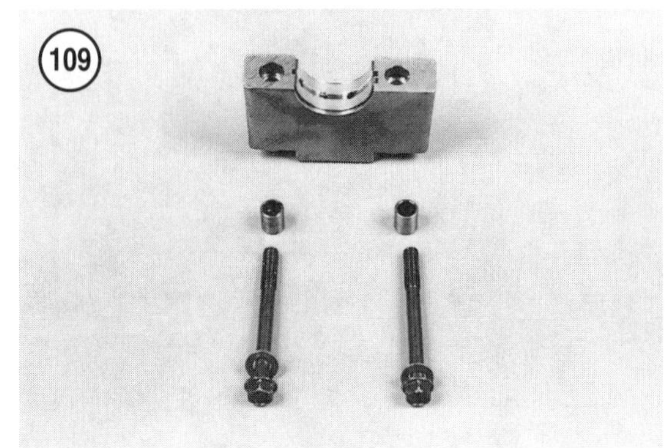

Inspection

During inspection, compare all measurements to the specifications in **Table 1**. Replace any part that is damaged, worn to the service limit or out of specification.

1. Clean the crankshaft thoroughly in solvent. Clean the oil holes with rifle cleaning brushes or pipe cleaners. Flush the crankshaft and thoroughly dry it with compressed air. Lightly oil the journals and other machined surfaces to prevent rust.
2. Inspect each journal (**Figure 110**) for scratches, ridges, scoring, nicks or other damage.
3. Measure each journal outside diameter with a micrometer (**Figure 111**).
4. Place the crankshaft of a set of V-blocks and measure the runout with a dial indicator (**Figure 112**). Replace the crankshaft if runout exceeds the service limit.
5. Check the primary drive gear (**Figure 113**) and the sprockets on each end of the crankshaft for worn, broken or cracked teeth. Replace the crankshaft as necessary.
6. Set the crankshaft into the upper crankcase. Make sure the main bearings are installed in the crankcase half. Insert a feeler gauge between the crankshaft's main bearing cap and the No. 2 machined web. If the side clearance exceeds the specified service limit (**Table 1**), replace the crankshaft.

Oil Clearance

This procedure requires the use of Plastigage, which can be purchased from auto supply stores. Make sure the Plastigage is small enough to measure the oil clearance specified in **Table 1**.

1. Remove the crankshaft as described in this section.
2. Check the inside and outside surfaces of each bearing for wear, bluish tint, flaking or scoring. If any bearing is questionable, replace all the main bearings as a set.
3. Clean the bearing surfaces of the main bearings and the crankshaft.

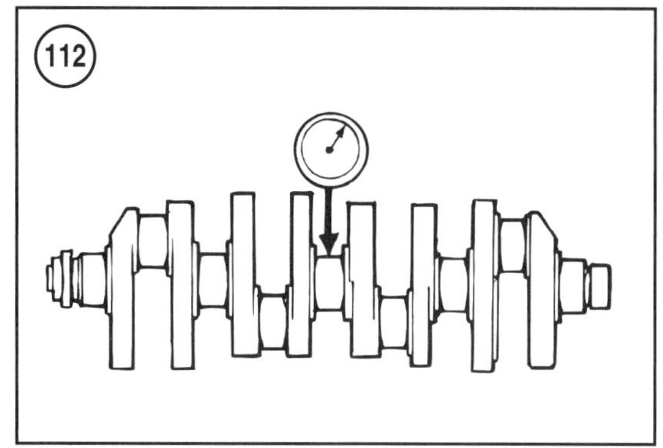
112

113

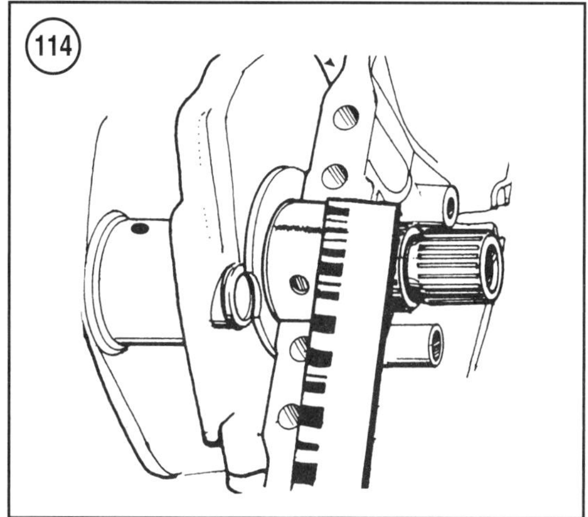
114

4. Set both case halves on the bench so their insides face up.

5. Install the existing bearings into their original locations in the upper (**Figure 106**) and lower (**Figure 107**) crankcase and the main bearing cap (**Figure 108**). Make sure the notch on each bearing locks into the slot on the bearing boss or cap.

6. Set the crankshaft into the upper crankcase half.

CAUTION

Do not rotate the crankshaft while Plastigage is in place. Also do not place Plastigage directly over an oil hole.

7. Place a piece of Plastigage over each crankshaft journal parallel to the crankshaft (**Figure 114**).

8. Install the dowels into the main bearing cap (**Figure 104**) and set the cap into the upper crankcase so its arrow points forward. Install the cap bolts with their flat washer and torque the cap bolts to 34 N•m (25 ft.-lb.).

9. On 1986-1994 models, make sure the two dowels (A, **Figure 88**) are in place in the upper crankcase. On 1995-on models, three dowels (A and B, **Figure 88**) are used.

10. Position the lower crankcase over the upper case and join both halves.

NOTE

*The size of some lower crankcase bolts were changed during production of 1990 models. Refer to **Figure 84** or **Figure 85** when installing the lower crankcase bolts.*

11. Apply oil to the threads of the 8 mm or 9 mm lower crankcase bolts. Install and finger tighten these bolts. Lightly tighten the bolts until they are snug.

12. Follow the tightening sequence cast into the crankcase (**Figure 86**) and torque the bolts in two stages.

   a. On models with engine number ZGT00AE014831 or lower (1986-early 1990 models), first torque the 8 mm bolts (**Figure 84**) to 14 N•m (10 ft.-lb.), then torque them to 27 N•m (20 ft.-lb.).
   b. On models with engine number ZGT00AE014832 or higher, (late-1990 and later models), first torque the 9 mm bolts (**Figure 85**) to 9.8 N•m (87 in.-lb.), then torque them to 32 N•m (24 ft.-lb.).

13. Reverse the tightening sequence and remove the bolts. Carefully lift the lower crankcase and measure the width of each flattened Plastigage (**Figure 114**) following the manufacturer's instructions. Measure at each end of the strip. A difference of more than 0.025 mm (0.001 in.) indicates a tapered journal.

14. Interpret the results as follows:

5

a. If the crankshaft journal oil clearance is within the new specification listed in **Table 1**, bearing replacement is not required. Remove the Plastigage from all bearing journals.

NOTE
*Main bearings are color coded. The markings are on the side of the bearings (**Figure 115**). If any bearing requires replacement, install a complete set of bearings.*

b. If the oil clearance is greater than 0.044 mm (0.00173 in.) but less than 0.08 mm (0.00315 in.), install a complete set of blue bearings and recheck the oil clearance. The clearance may exceed 0.044 mm (0.00173 in.) slightly, but it must not be less than 0.020 mm (0.00078 in.).

c. If the oil clearance exceeds the service limit (0.08 mm [0.00315 in.), measure the crankshaft journal outside diameter. If any journal outside diameter exceeds the service limit, install a new crankshaft and replace the main bearings. Refer to *Main Bearing Selection*.

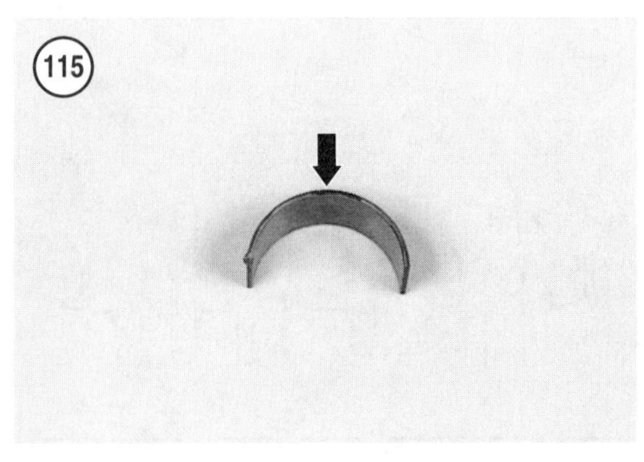

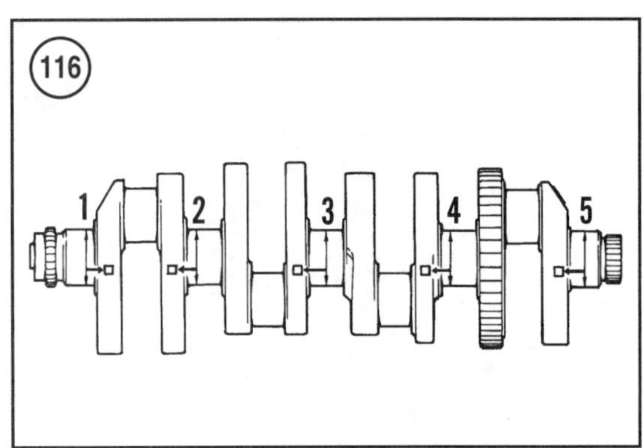

Main Bearing Selection

NOTE
*An identification mark (a **1** or no mark) stamped on an adjacent crankweb (**Figure 116**) indicates the diameter of each crankshaft journal. Another mark (an **O** or no mark) stamped on the upper crankcase (**Figure 117**) indicates the inside diameter of each bearing bore.*

1. Purchase a new crankshaft.
2. Record the crankshaft identification mark for each crankshaft journal (**Figure 116**).
3. Record the crankcase identification mark for each bearing boss (**Figure 117**).
4. Refer to **Table 2**. Cross-reference the crankshaft journal mark with its corresponding crankcase bearing bore mark and use these marks to select a new bearing for each location.
5. Install the new bearings and crankshaft. Recheck the oil clearance.
6. If the oil clearance is outside the new range specified in **Table 1**, but it does not exceed the service limit, perform the following:

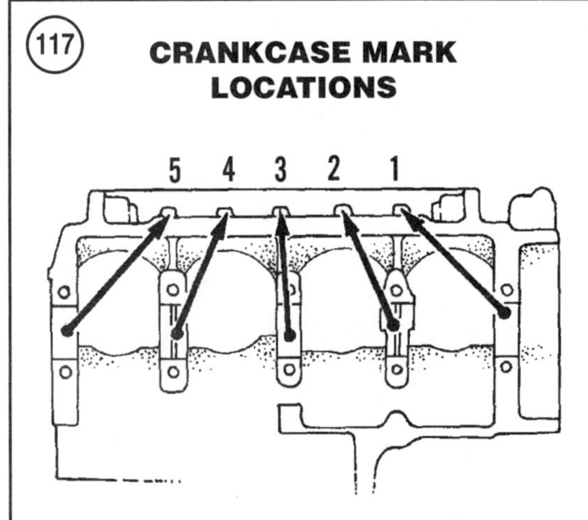

a. Assemble the crankcase without the crankshaft.

b. Use a bore gauge to measure the inside diameter of each bearing bore. Write down each measurement.

c. If the measured crankcase bearing bore inside diameter is not within the range indicated by the crankcase identification marks (see **Table 1**),

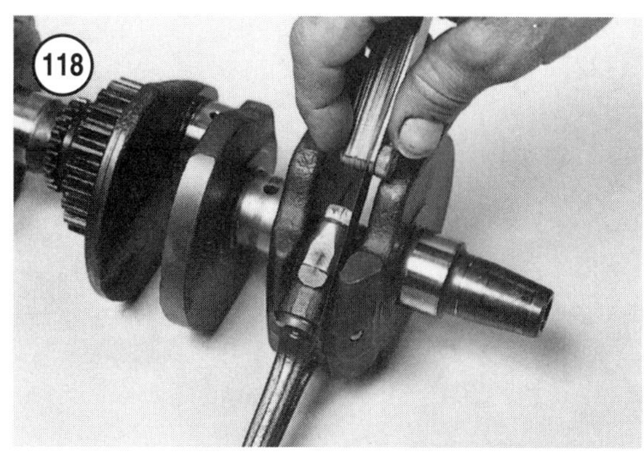

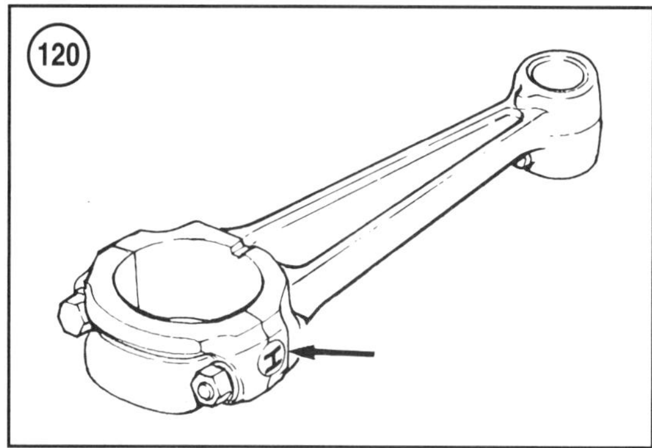

remark the crankcase (**Figure 117**) based on the measured diameter. If a measured bearing bore is 39.00-39.008 mm, use an *O* to mark that bore. If the measured diameter of a bearing bore is 39.009-39.016 mm, no mark is necessary.

d. Refer to **Table 2**. Cross-reference the crankshaft journal marks with these new crankcase marks and select new main bearings.

CONNECTING RODS

Removal

CAUTION
The connecting rod bolts are designed to stretch when tightened. These bolts must be replaced whenever the connecting rods are removed. Do not reinstalled used bolts.

1. Remove the engine as described in this chapter.
2. Remove the pistons (Chapter Four). Separate the crankcase halves and remove the crankshaft (this chapter).
3. Measure the connecting rod big end side clearance for each connecting rod. Insert a feeler gauge between the connecting rod and either machined crankweb (**Figure 118**) and record each measurement. If the clearance is excessive, replace the connecting rod(s) and recheck the clearance. If the clearance is still excessive, replace the crankshaft.

NOTE
Mark each connecting rod and cap with its cylinder number, starting on the left side.

4. Remove the connecting rod cap nuts (**Figure 119**) lift the cap from the rod bolts and separate the rod from the crankshaft. Immediately install the cap onto its rod and make sure the weight mark (a letter) on the rod aligns with the mark on the cap (**Figure 120**).

NOTE
*Some connecting rods do not have a diameter mark on the side (**Figure 121**). If there is no mark on a connecting rod, draw a line across the big end cap with an indelible pen to indicate alignment.*

NOTE
*Keep each connecting rod bearing (**Figure 122**) in its original location*

in the rod or cap. They must be installed in their original locations if reused. If a bearing comes out during connecting rod removal, immediately reinstall it in its proper location or mark the back of the bearing with its cylinder number and an R (rod) or C (cap) so its proper location can be positively identified.

Installation

1. If removed, install the bearings into their original locations. Make sure the bearing tab locks into the notch in the connecting rod or cap (**Figure 123**).

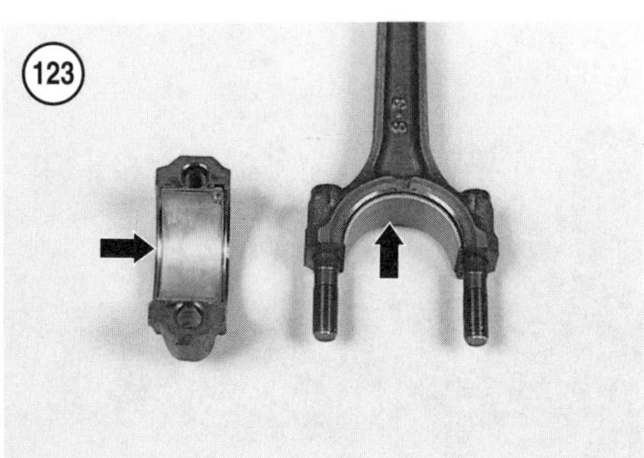

2. When installing a bearing, apply molybdenum disulfide grease to the inside of the connecting rod big end. See **Figure 124**. However, do not apply grease to a bearing or to the inside of the rod cap.
3. Check the connecting rod oil clearance after installing new bearings.
4. The two left connecting rods (No. 1 and 2) and the two right connecting rods (No. 3 and 4) are matched (same weight) to reduce vibration. If replacing the rods, make sure each rod in a pair has the same weight mark (**Figure 120**) as its mate.
5. Install each connecting rod onto its original crankpin. Make sure the weight mark on the connecting rod aligns with the mark on the rod cap (**Figure 120**).

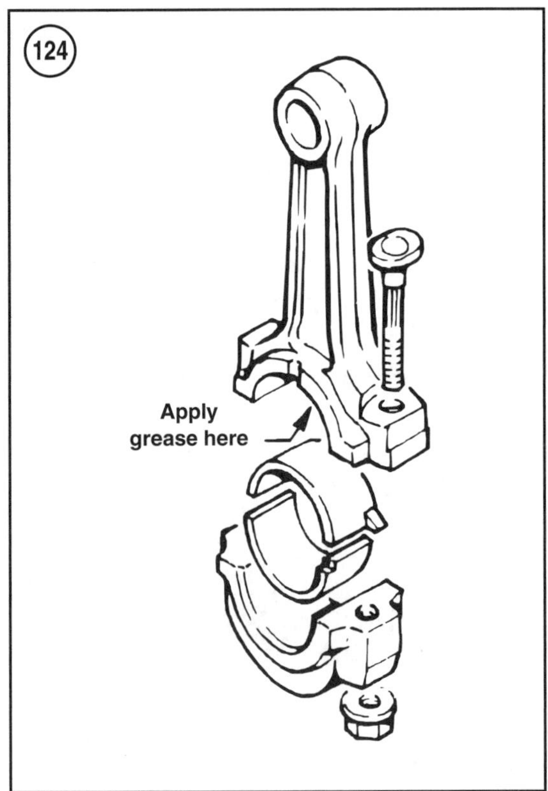

6. The new connecting rod bolts and nuts are coated with an anti-rust material. Remove this material by cleaning the bolts in solvent. Dry them thoroughly.
7. Apply clean engine oil to the threads and seating surfaces of the bolts (**Figure 125**) and nuts.
8. Torque the connecting rod nut as follows:
   a. When using a new nut, torque the nut to 29 N•m (22 ft.-lb.). If reusing a nut, torque the nut to 26 N•m (19 ft.-lb.).
   b. Place an indexing mark on each nut and its connecting rod. Tighten each rod nut and additional 120°. Do not turn a nut more than 120°. See **Figure 126**.

WARNING
An excessively stretched bolt may break during operation and cause extensive engine damage. This could result in engine lockup and loss of control of the motorcycle.

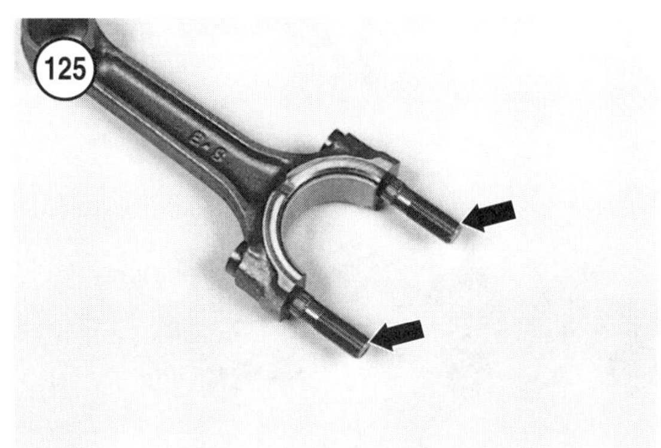

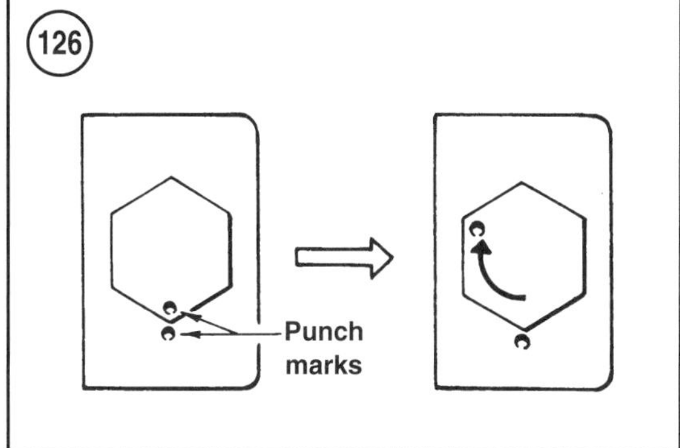

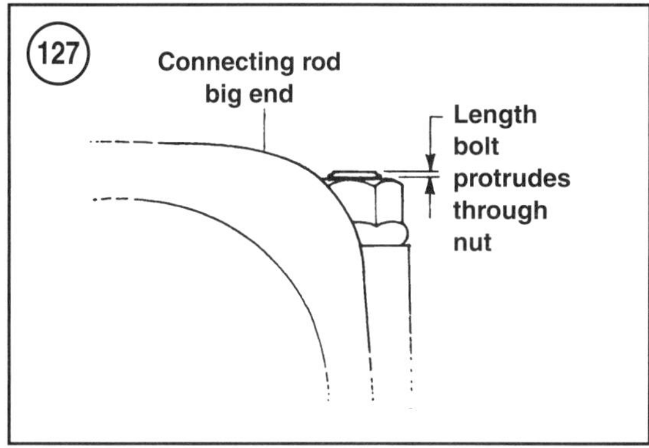

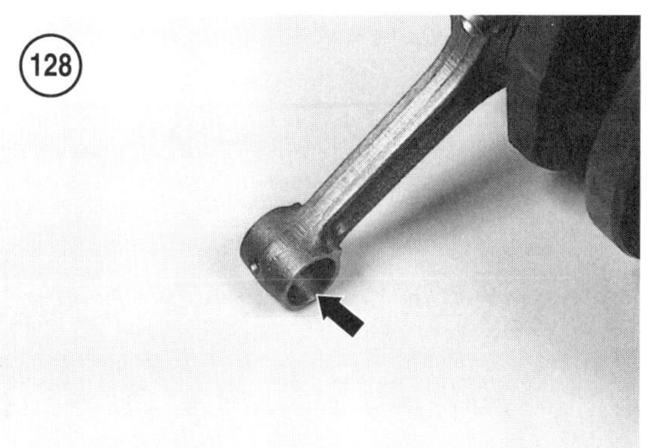

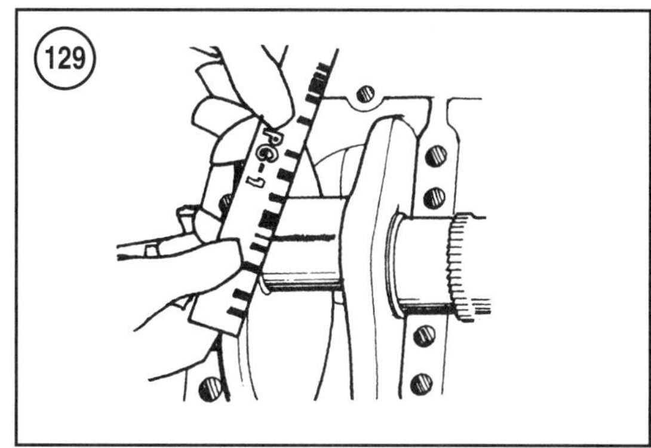

c. Measure the exposed length of each connecting rod bolt (**Figure 127**). If a bolt extends more than 0.8 mm (0.031 in.) beyond the nut, the bolt has stretched too far. Replace the bolt and nut.

Inspection

1. Check each rod for obvious damage such as cracks and burns.
2. Check the small end bore (**Figure 128**) for wear, scoring or heat discoloration.
3. Take the rods to a machine shop and have them checked for twists and bends. The service limits in **Table 1** are with a 100 mm arbor inserted through the small end.
4. Examine the bearings (**Figure 123**) for wear, scoring or burning. Good bearings can be reused.
5. Discard all connecting rod bolts. New bolts *must* be used during assembly.
6. Check the connecting rod oil clearance.

Oil Clearance

This procedure requires the use of Plastigage. Plastigauge is available in several sizes. Purchase Plastigage small enough to measure the connecting rod oil clearance specified in **Table 1**.

CAUTION
If the old connecting rod bearings are being reused, install each bearing in its original location.

1. Wipe all oil from the bearings and the crankpins.
2. Place a piece of Plastigage on one crankpin parallel to the crankshaft (**Figure 129**). Do not place Plastigage over an oil hole.

NOTE
Perform this procedure using the old connecting rod bolts.

3. Install a connecting rod with its mated cap onto its original location. Make sure the weight mark on the cap aligns with the mark on the connecting rod.
4. Apply clean engine oil to the threads and seating surfaces of the old bolts and nuts.
5. Torque the cap nuts to 26 N•m (19 ft.-lb.). Place an indexing mark on each nut and connecting rod and tighten each nut an additional 120°. See **Figure 126**. Do not overtighten the nuts.

CAUTION
Do not rotate the crankshaft while Plastigage is in place.

6. Repeat Steps 1-5 for the remaining connecting rods.
7. Remove the rod caps and measure the flattened Plastigage according to the manufacturer's instructions. Record the measurements.
8. Measure the Plastigage at both ends. A difference of .025 mm (0.001 in.) indicates a tapered crankpin. Confirm this by measuring the crankpin diameter with a micrometer (**Figure 130**). Replace the crankshaft if a crankpin is tapered.
9. Use the same strip to measure the oil clearance. Interpret the results as follows:
   a. If the connecting rod oil clearance is within the new specification listed in **Table 1**, bearing replacement is not required. Remove the Plastigage from all crankpins.

NOTE
*Connecting rod bearings are color coded. The markings are on the side of the bearings (**Figure 123**). If any bearing requires replacement, install a complete set of bearings.*

   b. If the connecting rod oil clearance is greater than 0.067 mm (0.0026 in.) but less than 0.11 mm (0.0043 in.), install a complete set of blue bearings and recheck the oil clearance. The oil clearance may exceed 0.067 mm (0026 in.) slightly, but it must not be less than the minimum 0.046 mm (0.0018 in.) clearance. The bearings will seize if clearance is less than minimum.

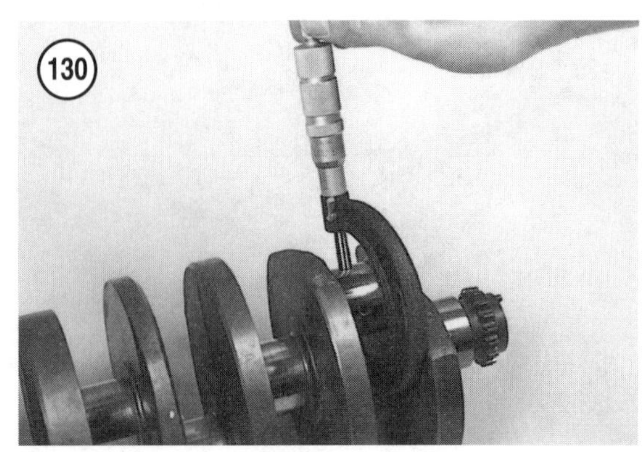
130

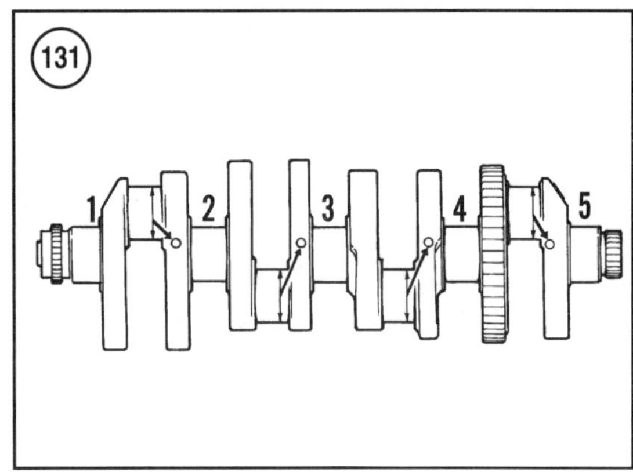

131

   c. If the connecting rod oil clearance exceeds the service limit of 0.11 mm (0.0043 in.), measure the crankpin outside diameter.

10. If any crankpin outside diameter exceeds the service limit (**Table 1**), install a new crankshaft and replace the connecting rod bearings. Refer to *Bearing Selection* in this section.
11. If the crankpin outside diameter does not exceed the service limit, and the crankpin marks on the crankshaft (**Figure 131**) do not correspond with the measured diameter, apply new marks to indicate the actual diameter of the crankpin(s). If the crankpin diameter is 34.984-34.992 mm (1.3773-1.3776 in.), no mark is needed. If the measured diameter is 34.993-35.000 mm (1.3777-1.3779 in.), add an *O* mark. Refer to **Table 3** and use these new marks to select new bearings.

Bearing Selection

NOTE
*A mark (an **O** or no mark) stamped on an adjacent crankweb **(Figure 131)***

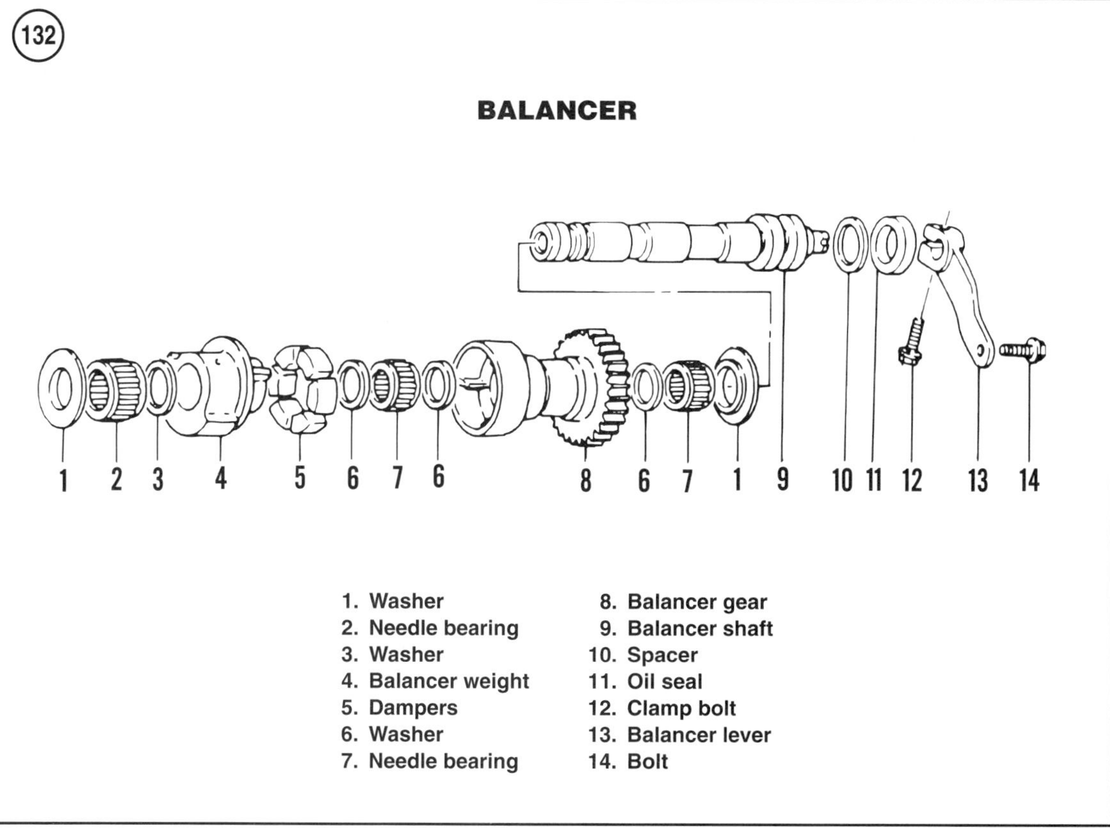

*indicates the diameter of each crankpin. A connecting rod identification rod mark (**Figure 120**) (an **O** around the weight mark or no mark) indicates the inside diameter of each connecting rod big end.*

1. Purchase a new crankshaft.
2. Record the crankpin identification mark for each crankpin (**Figure 131**).
3. Install each rod cap onto its connecting rod without the bearings. Torque the cap bolts as described in *Oil Clearance*.
4. Use a bore gauge to measure the inside diameter of each connecting rod big end. Write down each measurement.
5. The measured diameter of each connecting rod should be within the range indicated by identification mark on the side of that rod (**Figure 120**). See **Table 1**.
   a. If the measured inside diameter is not within the specified range, remark the rod based on the measured diameter.
   b. If a big end inside diameter is 38.00-38.008 mm, no mark is needed. If the measured inside diameter is 38.009-38.016 mm, add an *O* mark.
6. Refer to **Table 3**. Cross-reference the crankpin identification marks with the connecting rod identification marks and select new main bearings.
7. Install the new bearings and crankshaft. Recheck the oil clearance.

BALANCER

Removal

Refer to **Figure 132**.

1. Remove the engine and separate the case halves as described in this chapter.
2. Loosen the balancer lever clamp bolt.
3. Remove the mounting bolt and slide the lever from the shaft.
4. Remove the bolt and lift the guide plate (**Figure 133**) from the crankcase.

5. Remove the guide pin (**Figure 134**).
6. Pull the balancer shaft (**Figure 135**) and its oil seal from the right side of the crankcase.
7. Lift the weight assembly (**Figure 136**) from the crankcase. See **Figure 137**.

Installation

The weight assembly must be assembled onto the balancer shaft and then the shaft must be removed from the assembly for installation.

1. Hold onto the washer at each end of the weight assembly (A, **Figure 138**) and pull the balancer shaft (B) from the assembly.
2. Lower the weight assembly (**Figure 136**) into the crankcase.
3. Oil the bearing surfaces of the balancer shaft.
4. Insert the balancer shaft through the right side of the crankcase (**Figure 135**), through the weight assembly and seat the shaft in the boss.
5. Install the guide pin through the crankcase and into the slot in the balancer shaft. Make sure the pin end faces up (**Figure 139**).

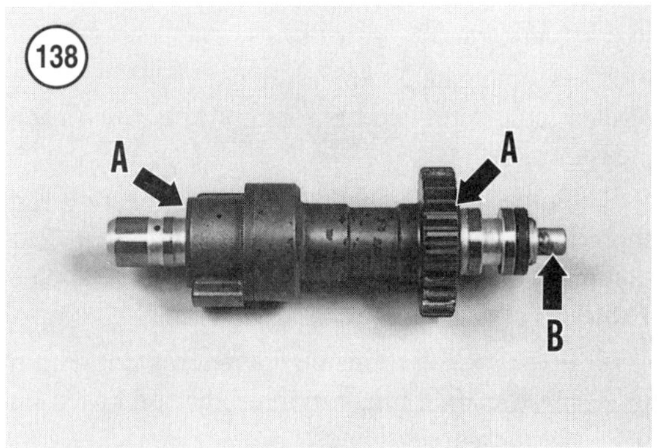

139

143

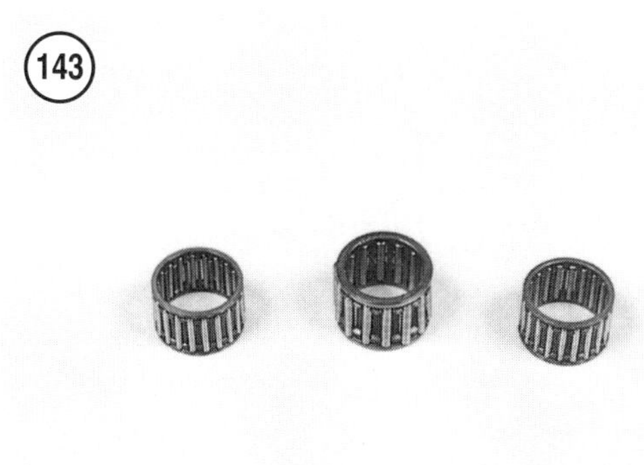

140

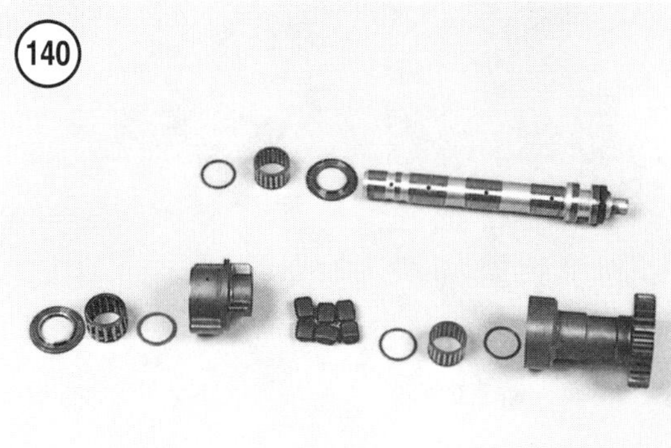

141

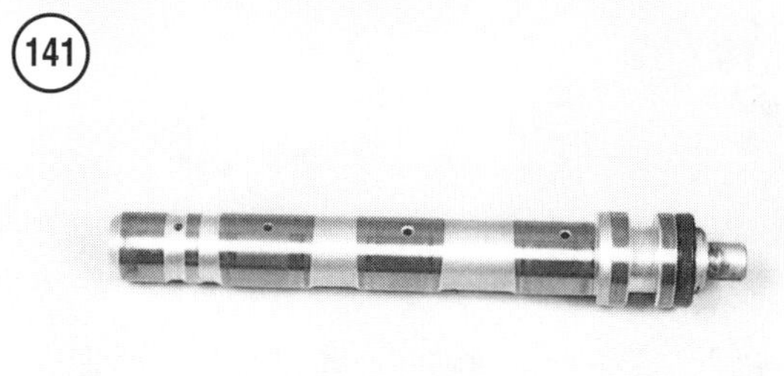

142

6. Set the guide plate into place so the hole in the plate engages the pin (**Figure 133**). Apply Loctite 242 (blue) to the plate mounting bolt and tighten the bolt securely.

7. Rotate the balancer shaft (**Figure 135**) so the slot on the end of the shaft points to the front of the crankcase.

8. Slide the balancer lever onto the shaft.

9. Apply Loctite 242 (blue) to the threads of the lever bolt and loosely install the lever bolt. Tighten the clamp bolt securely and then tighten the lever bolt.

10. Adjust the balancer as described in this section.

Disassembly/Inspection

1. Disassemble the weight assembly, and lay out the parts as shown in **Figure 140**.

2. Clean all parts in solvent and let them dry completely.

3. Check the balancer shaft (**Figure 141**) for cracks, deep scoring, excessive wear or heat discoloration. Make sure the oil holes in the shaft are clear.

4. Replace the balancer oil seal (**Figure 142**).

5. Check the needle bearings (**Figure 143**) for loose or damaged needles and check for a cracked needle cage.

6. Check the washers (**Figure 144**).

7. Check the dampers (**Figure 145**) for deterioration or cracks.

8. Check the balancer gear (**Figure 146**) for cracked or worn teeth.

9. Replace worn or damaged parts.

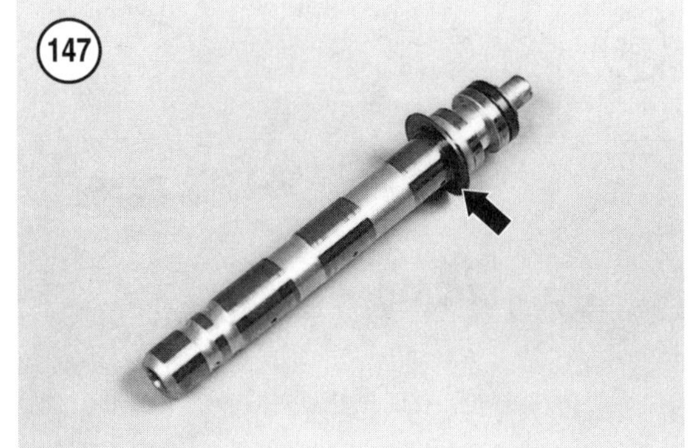

Assembly

The weight assembly must be assembled onto the balancer shaft and then the shaft must be removed from the assembly for installation.

1. Install the washer (**Figure 147**) onto the balancer shaft so the shoulder of the washer faces away from the oil seal.

> NOTE
> *Two different size needle bearings (**Figure 143**) are used in this assembly. The single large needle bearing is installed in the middle of the shaft.*

2. Slide one of the small needle bearings (**Figure 148**) onto the balancer shaft followed by another washer (**Figure 149**).
3. Install the gear assembly (**Figure 150**) onto the balancer shaft.
4. Install a washer (A, **Figure 151**) the large needle bearing (B) and another washer (C). Seat them inside the gear assembly.
5. Hold the assembly upright, and install the rubber dampers (**Figure 152**). Make sure the dampers are seated in the housing as shown in **Figure 153**.

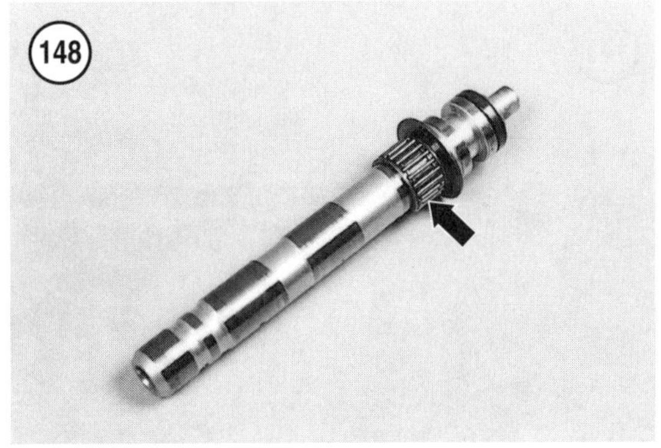

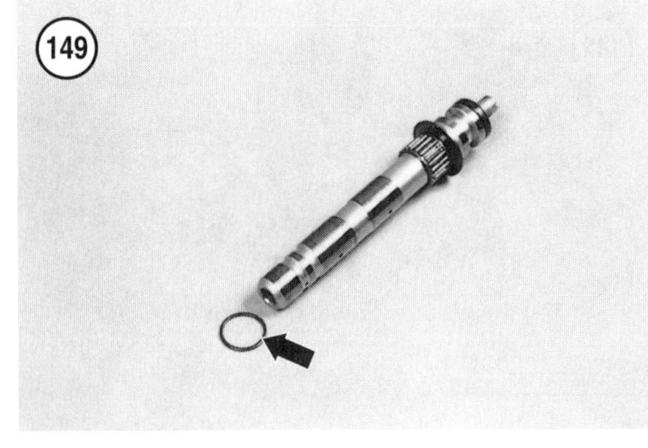

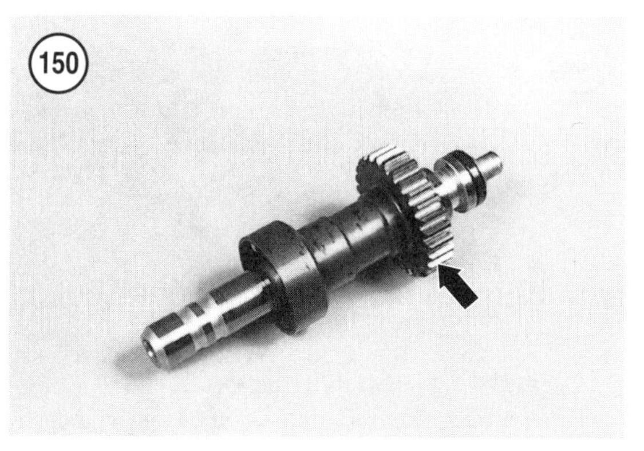

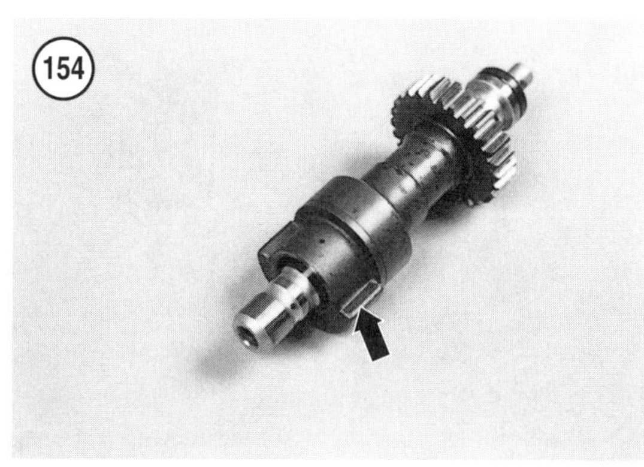

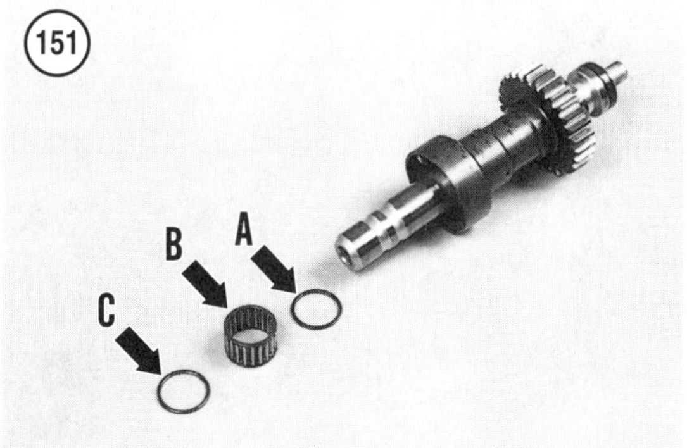

6. Install the weight (**Figure 154**) onto the gear assembly. Make sure the dot on the weight (**Figure 155**) aligns with the mark on the gear assembly.

7. Install the washer (**Figure 156**) and the other small needle bearing (**Figure 157**). Seat them inside the weight.

8. Install the washer (**Figure 158**) so the washer's shoulder faces the needle bearing. Seat the washer so it sits flush with the weight.

9. Install the balancer into the lower crankcase half as described in this section.

157

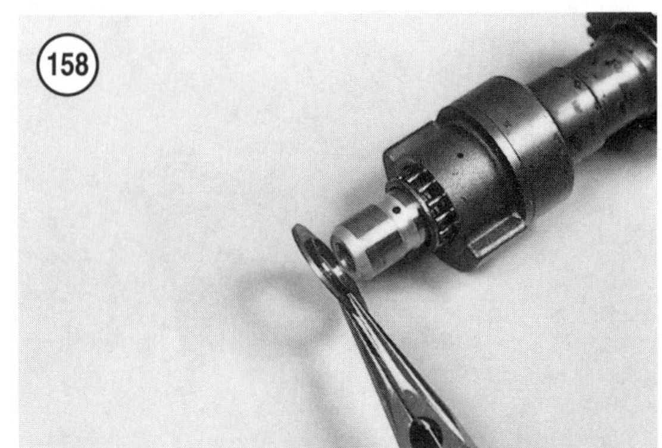
158

Adjustment

NOTE
This procedure must be performed when the engine is cold. Have the proper size screwdriver and wrench ready before starting the engine.

1. Mark the lever (A, **Figure 159**) opposite the balancer shaft slot to indicate the starting point.
2. Start the engine and let it idle.

NOTE
The balancer shaft can turn once the clamp bolt is loosened. Hold the shaft with a screwdriver before loosening the clamp bolt.

3. Hold the balancer shaft with a screwdriver and loosen the clamp bolt (B, **Figure 159**).
4. Rotate the balancer shaft counterclockwise until you hear a distinct whirring or chirping.
5. Rotate the balancer shaft clockwise until the noise disappears.
6. Tighten the clamp bolt (B, **Figure 159**) securely and shut the engine off.

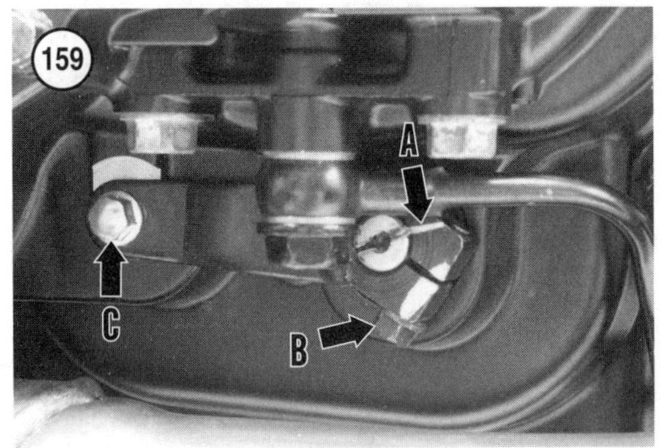

159

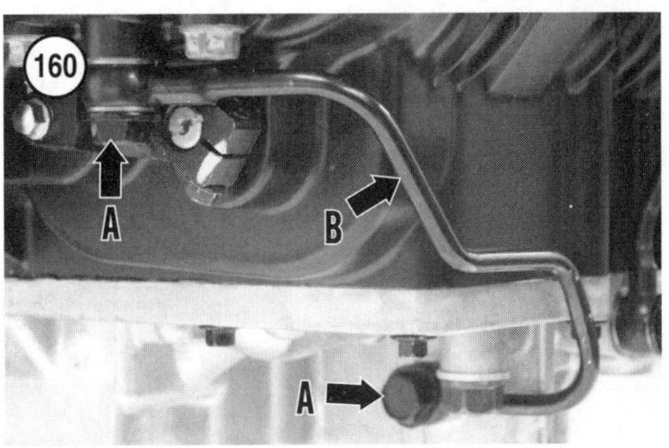

160

Oil Seal Replacement

The balancer oil seal can be replaced without removing the balancer from the engine.

1. Drain the engine oil as described in Chapter Three.
2. Remove both banjo bolts (A, **Figure 160**) and lower the clutch cover oil pipe (B) from the engine. Discard the two copper washers installed on each end of the oil pipe.
3. Mark the lever (A, **Figure 159**) opposite the balancer shaft slot.
4. Loosen the clamp bolt (B, **Figure 159**) on the balancer lever. Remove the lever mounting bolt (C, **Figure 159**) and pull the lever from the balancer shaft.
5. Pry the oil seal out of the crankcase and remove it from the balancer shaft.
6. Lubricate a new oil seal with clean engine oil. Slide the oil seal over the balancer shaft and seat it against the crankcase. Use the appropriate size socket to drive the oil seal into place.
7. Slide the balancer lever onto the shaft so the mark made earlier (A, **Figure 159**) aligns with the slot in the balancer shaft.

8. Apply Loctite 242 (blue) to the threads of the lever mounting bolt and loosely install the lever bolt. Tighten the clamp bolt securely, then tighten the lever bolt.

9. Install the clutch-cover oil pipe (B, **Figure 160**) with new copper washers. Torque each banjo bolt (A, **Figure 160**) to 25 N•m (18 ft.-lb.).

10. Refill the engine with clean oil (Chapter Three).

Table 1 ENGINE LOWER END SPECIFICATIONS

Item	New mm (in.)	Service limit mm (in.)
Connecting rod		
Rod bend	–	0.2/100 (0.0079/3.94)
Rod twist	–	0.2/100 (0.0079/3.94)
Big end side clearance	0.13-0.33 (0.0051-0.0130)	0.50 (0.0197)
Connecting rod oil clearance	0.046-0.067 (0.0018-0.0026)	0.11 (0.0043)
Crankpin outside diameter		
Identification mark		
None	34.984-34.992 (1.3773-1.3776)	34.97 (1.3767)
O	34.993-35.000 (1.3777-1.3779)	34.97 (1.3767)
Connecting rod big end inside diameter		
Identification mark		
None	38.000-38.008 (1.4961-1.4964)	–
O	38.009-38.016 (1.4964-1.4966)	–
Connecting rod bearing thickness		
Brown	1.470-1.475 (0.0579-0.0581)	–
Black	1.475-1.480 (0.0581-0.0583)	–
Blue	1.480-1.485 (0.0583-0.0585)	
Crankshaft runout	–	0.05 (0.00196)
Crankshaft journal oil clearance	0.020-0.044 (0.00078-0.00173)	0.08 (0.00315)
Crankshaft journal outside diameter		
Idenfification mark		
None	35.984-35.992 (1.4167-1.4170)	35.96 (1.4157)
1	35.993-36.000 (1.4170-1.4173)	35.96 (1.4157)
Crankcase bearing bore inside diameter		
Identification mark		
O	39.000-39.008 (1.5354-1.5357)	–
None	39.009-39.016 (1.5358-1.5361)	–
Crankshaft main bearing thickness		
Brown	1.490-1.494 (0.0587-0.0588)	–
Black	1.494-1.498 (0.0588-0.0590)	–
Blue	1.498-1.502 (0.0590-0.0591)	
Crankshaft side clearance	0.05-0.20 (0.0019-0.0079)	0.40 (0.0157)
Alternator chain 20-link length	158.8-159.2 (6.25-6.27)	161.5 (6.36)
Transmission gear lash	0.06-0.23 (0.002-0.009)	0.3 (0.012)

Table 2 CRANKSHAFT MAIN BEARING SELECTION

Crankcase bearing bore mark	Crankshaft journal mark	Bearing color	Journal number
O	1	Brown*	2, 4
O	1	Brown	1, 3, 5
None	None	Blue*	2, 4
None	None	Blue	1, 3, 5
O	None	Black*	2, 4
None	1	Black	1, 3, 5

*The bearings for journals No. 2 and 4 have oil grooves. No groove is used in the bearings for journals No. 1, 3 and 5.

5

Table 3 CONNECTING ROD BEARING SELECTION

Connecting rod mark	Crankpin mark	Bearing color
O	O	Black
None	None	Black
O	None	Blue
None	O	Brown

Table 4 ENGINE LOWER END TORQUE SPECIFICATIONS

Item	N•m	in.-lb.	ft.-lb.
Alternator coupling bolt	9.8	87	–
Alternator shaft bolt (left side)	25	–	11
Alternator shaft nut (right side)	59	–	43
Cooling system drain bolt	7.8	69	–
Connecting rod cap nuts	See text		
Crankcase bolts			
6 mm	15	–	11
7 mm (late 1990-on models)	18	–	13
8 mm (1986 to early 1990 models)			
First stage	14	–	10
Final stage	27	–	20
9 mm (late 1990-on models)			
First stage	9.8	87	–
Final stage	32	–	24
Crankshaft bearing cap bolt			
1986-1989 models	34	–	25
1990-on models	32	–	24
Damper cam nut[2]	225	–	166
Engine mounting nuts	54	–	40
Main bearing cap bolts	34	–	25
Main oil pipe banjo bolt	25	–	18
Oil cooler banjo bolts			
Oil pipe-to-oil cooler banjo bolt	25	–	18
Oil pipe-to-oil pan banjo bolt	34	–	25
Oil filter bolt	20	–	15
Oil gallery bolt	18	–	13
Oil pressure switch[1]	15	–	11
Oil pump mounting bolts[1]	12	106	–
Pickup coil rotor nut	25	–	18
Starter one-way clutch bolts[1]	12	106	–

1. Apply Loctite 242 (blue) or an equivalent medium-strength threadlock.
2. Lubricate the flange and threads with oil containing molybdenum disulfide.

CHAPTER SIX

CLUTCH

When inspecting clutch components, compare any measurements to the clutch specifications in **Table 1** at the end of this chapter. During assembly, tighten clutch fasteners to the specified torque.

The clutch is a multiplate type that operates immersed in the engine oil. It is mounted on the right side of the transmission mainshaft. The clutch can be serviced with the engine in the frame.

The operating mechanism consists of a clutch master cylinder on the left handlebar, a slave cylinder on the left side of the engine and a pushrod that runs through the mainshaft.

When the clutch lever is pulled, the piston in the master cylinder moves and pressurizes the hydraulic fluid in the clutch line. The hydraulic pressure moves the slave cylinder piston, which in turn pushes the pushrod. This action lifts the pressure plate against the clutch springs, disengaging the clutch.

The hydraulic clutch release mechanism requires no routine adjustment. As the friction plates wear, the slave cylinder piston extends beyond the elastic limit of its seal. The seal slips slightly which allows the piston to move to a new position. This compensates for the difference in plate wear and the clutch lever stroke remains unchanged.

CLUTCH SYSTEM BLEEDING

Brake fluid will damage any painted, plated or plastic surfaces on a motorcycle. Before servicing any part of the clutch system, especially portions of the hydraulic system, read *Brake Service, Preventing Brake Fluid Damage* and *Brake Bleeding Tips* in Chapter Fourteen.

Manual Bleeding

1. Check that all banjo bolts in the system are tight.
2. Remove the rubber cover from bleed valve on the clutch slave cylinder.
3. Connect a length of clear tubing to the bleed valve (**Figure 1**, typical). Place the other end of the tube into a clean container. Fill the container with enough fresh brake fluid to keep the end submerged. The tube should be long enough so that its loop can be higher than the bleed valve to prevent air from being drawn into the slave cylinder during bleeding.

4. Turn the handlebars to level the clutch master cylinder.

5. Clean all debris from the top of the master cylinder reservoir. Remove the top cover, diaphragm plate (1992-on models) and the diaphragm from the reservoir.

6. Add DOT 4 brake fluid to the reservoir until the fluid level reaches the upper limit. Loosely install the diaphragm and the cover. Leave them in place during bleeding to keep dirt out of the system and so brake fluid cannot spurt out of the reservoir.

7. Pump the clutch lever a few times and then release it.

8. Apply the clutch lever until it stops and hold it in this position.

9. Use a wrench to open the bleed valve on the slave cylinder. Let the clutch lever move to the limit of its travel and then close the bleed valve. Do not release the clutch lever while the bleed valve is open.

NOTE
As brake fluid enters the system, the level in the reservoir drops. Add brake fluid as necessary to keep the fluid level 10 mm (3/8 in.) below the reservoir top so air will not be drawn into the system.

10. Repeat Steps 7-9 until the brake fluid flowing from the hose is clear and free of air. If the system is difficult to bleed, tap the master cylinder or slave cylinder with a soft mallet to release trapped air bubbles.

11. Test the feel of the clutch lever. It should feel firm and offer the same resistance each time it is operated. If the lever feels soft, air is still trapped in the system. Continue bleeding the system.

12. When bleeding is complete, disconnect the hose from the bleed valve and torque the bleed valve to 7.8 N•m (69 in.-lb.).

13. Add brake fluid to the master cylinder to correct the fluid level.

14. Install the diaphragm, diaphragm plate (1992-on models) and top cover. Be sure the cover is secured in place.

15. Test ride the motorcycle and make sure the clutch operates properly.

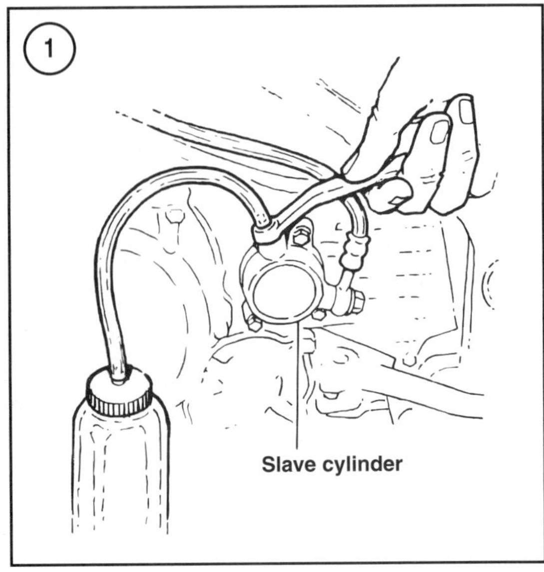

Vacuum Bleeding

1. Check that all banjo bolts in the system are tight.
2. Remove the rubber cap from the bleed valve on the clutch slave cylinder.
3. Turn the handlebars to level the clutch master cylinder.
4. Clean all debris from the top of the master cylinder reservoir. Remove the top cover diaphragm plate (1992-on models) and the diaphragm from the reservoir.
5. Add DOT 4 brake fluid to the reservoir until the fluid level reaches the upper limit. Loosely install the diaphragm and the cover. Leave them in place during bleeding to keep dirt out of the system and so brake fluid cannot spurt out of the reservoir.
6. Assemble the vacuum tool following the manufacturer's instructions.
7. Connect the pump's hose to the bleed valve on the clutch slave cylinder (**Figure 2**, typical).

NOTE
When using a vacuum pump, keep an eye on the brake fluid level in the reservoir. It will drop quite rapidly. Stop often and check the brake fluid level. Maintain the level a 10 mm (3/8 in.) from the top of the reservoir so air will not be drawn into the system.

8. Operate the vacuum pump to create vacuum in the hose.

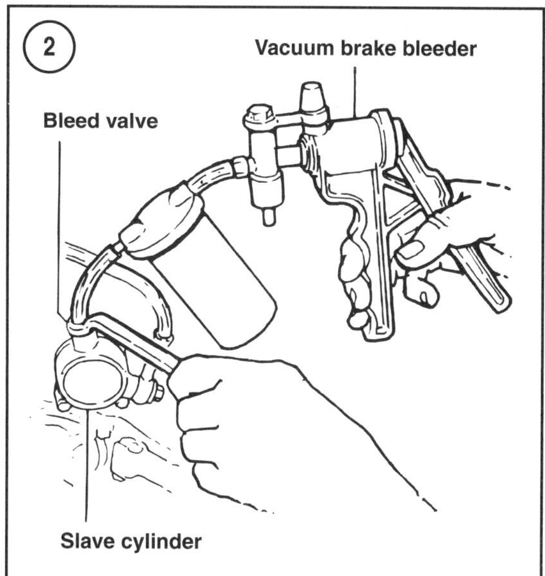

9. Use a wrench to open the bleed valve. The vacuum pump should pull fluid from the system. Close the bleed valve before the brake fluid stops flowing from the system or before the master cylinder reservoir runs empty. Add fluid to the reservoir as necessary.

10. Operate the clutch lever a few times and release it.

11. Repeat Steps 8 through 10 until the fluid leaving the bleed valve is clear and free of air bubbles. If the system is difficult to bleed, tap the master cylinder and slave cylinder with a soft mallet to release trapped air bubbles.

12. Test the feel of the clutch lever. It should feel firm and offer the same resistance each time it is operated. If the clutch lever feels soft, air is still trapped in the system. Continue bleeding.

13. When bleeding is complete, disconnect the hose from the bleed valve and torque the bleed valve to 7.8 N•m (69 in.-lb.).

14. Add DOT 4 brake fluid to the master cylinder to correct the fluid level.

15. Install the diaphragm, diaphragm plate (1992-on models) and the top cover. Be sure the cover is secured in place.

16. Test ride the motorcycle slowly at first to make sure the clutch operates properly.

BRAKE FLUID DRAINING

Before disconnecting a clutch hose, drain the brake fluid. Draining the fluid reduces the amount of fluid that can spill out when clutch system components are removed.

This section describes two methods for draining the brake system: manual and vacuum.

Manual Draining

An empty bottle, a length of clear hose and a wrench are required when performing this procedure.

1. Check that all banjo bolts in the system are tight.
2. Remove the rubber cover from the bleed valve on the clutch slave cylinder.
3. Connect a length of clear tubing to the bleed valve. Place the other end of the tube into a clean container (**Figure 1**, typical).
4. Turn the handlebars to level the clutch master cylinder.
5. Apply the clutch brake lever until it stops. Hold the lever in this position.
6. Open the bleed valve with a wrench and let the lever move to the limit of its travel. Close the bleed valve.
7. Release the lever and repeat Steps 5 and 6 until brake fluid stops flowing from the bleed valve.
8. Discard the brake fluid.

Vacuum Draining

A hand-operated vacuum pump is required when performing this procedure.

1. Check that all banjo bolts in the system are tight.
2. Remove the rubber cap from the bleed valve on the clutch slave cylinder.
3. Connect the pump's hose to the bleed valve on the clutch slave caliper (**Figure 2**, typical).
4. Operate the vacuum pump to create vacuum in the hose.
5. Use a wrench to open the bleed valve. The vacuum pump should pull fluid from the system.
6. When fluid has stopped flowing through the hose, close the bleed valve.
7. Repeat Steps 5-6 until brake fluid no longer flows from the bleed valve.
8. Discard the brake fluid.

CLUTCH COVER

Removal/Installation

1. Securely support the motorcycle on level ground.
2. Remove the lower and middle fairings as described in Chapter Three.
3. Drain the engine oil as described in Chapter Three.
4. Remove the banjo bolts (A, **Figure 3**) and remove the clutch cover oil pipe (B). Discard the two copper washers installed with each banjo bolt.

NOTE
Three different length bolts are used to secure the clutch cover in place. Note where the short, medium and long bolts are located so they can be identified during installation.

5. Remove the clutch cover bolts (**Figure 4**) and pull the clutch cover from the crankcase. If necessary, tap the cover lightly with a plastic mallet to break the gasket seal.

CAUTION
Be careful when removing gasket residue. Do not damage the mating surfaces on the cover or crankcase. A gouge or scratch could cause an oil leak.

6. Remove and discard the clutch cover gasket. Clean all gasket residue from the clutch cover and from the crankcase.
7. Check the oil pipe (A, **Figure 5**) inside the clutch cover. The banjo bolt (B, **Figure 5**) and the mounting bolt (C) must be tight. If the engine oil appears contaminated or dirty, remove the oil pipe and blow it clear with compressed air. Tighten the banjo bolt and mounting bolt securely when installing the oil pipe.
8. The damper cover (**Figure 6**) holds a noise damper in place. The cover and damper are non-wearing items. However, check the bolts that hold the cover in place. If any are loose, remove the bolts and reinstall them with a drop of Loctite 242 applied to the threads. Tighten the bolts securely.
9. Apply Kawasaki Bond (part No. 56019-120) or an equivalent silicone sealant to the gasket surfaces on the crankcase where the two case halves come together.

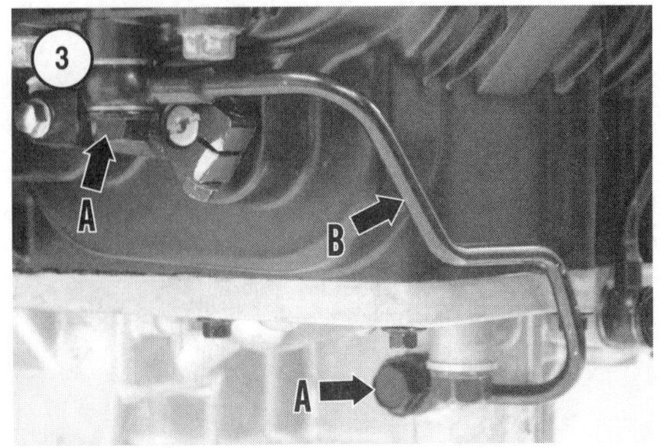

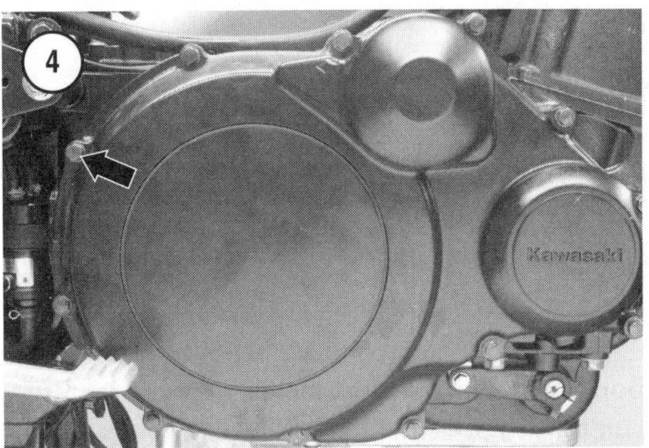

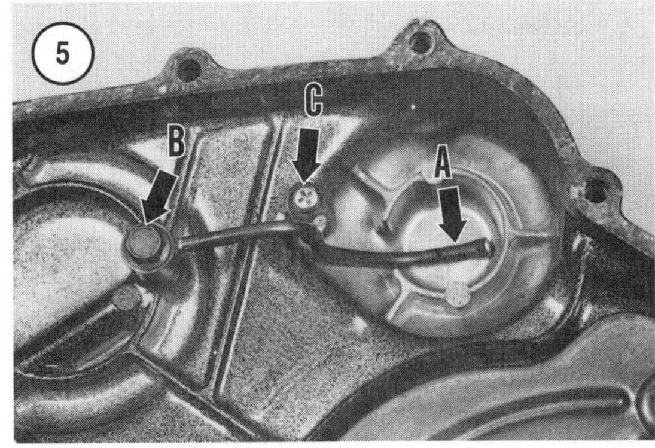

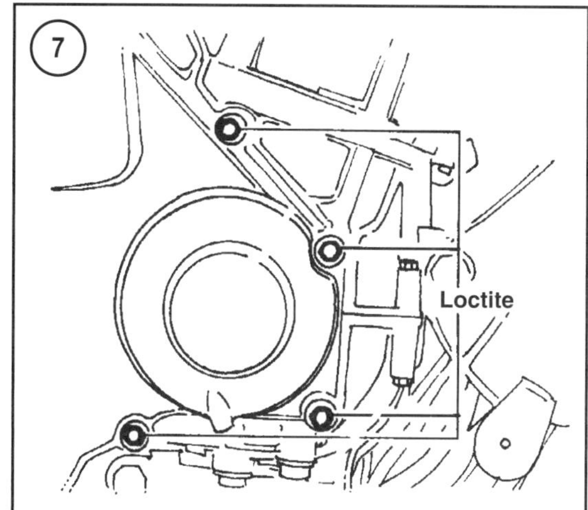

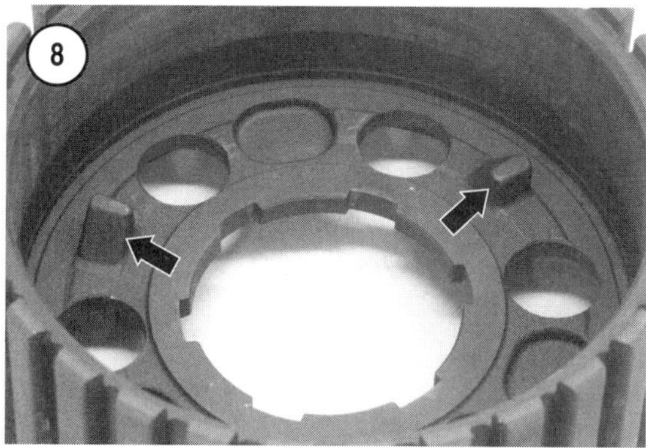

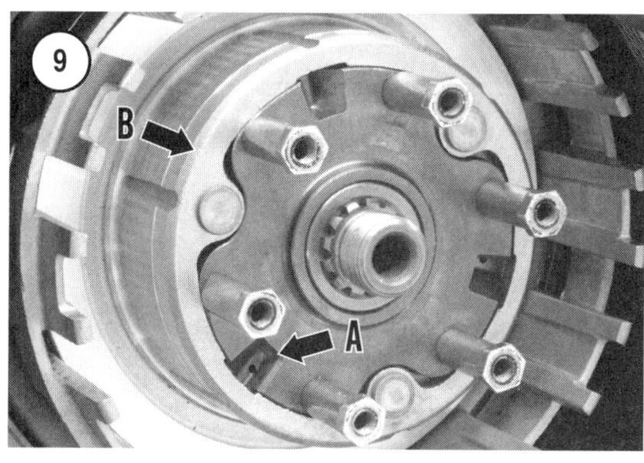

10. Since dowels are not used on the cover, insert two clutch cover bolts through the clutch cover and fit a new gasket onto the cover. The bolts will hold the gasket in place during cover installation.

NOTE
Insert the clutch cover bolts into the holes in the clutch cover. Each bolt should stick out the same amount. If not, make the necessary adjustments.

11. Set the cover into place on the crankcase. Apply Loctite 242 (blue) to the four bolts indicated in **Figure 7** and finger-tighten the bolts.
12. Install the remaining clutch cover bolts and tighten all the bolts securely.

CLUTCH

The clutch is a slipper clutch that releases slightly to prevent wheel hop during engine braking. Ramps in the sub-hub (**Figure 8**) operate against stops in the clutch hub (A, **Figure 9**) which relieves pressure on the plates so the clutch slips slightly.

The Kawasaki clutch holder (part No. 57001-1243) or its equivalent and a new clutch nut are needed when removing and installing the clutch.

Refer to **Figure 10**.

Removal/Disassembly

1. Remove the clutch cover as described in this chapter.

NOTE
The clutch discs and plates can be serviced with the alternator chain guide installed. However, any other clutch work is difficult when the chain guide is in place.

2. Remove the alternator chain tensioner and the alternator chain guide as described in Chapter Five.
3. Evenly loosen the clutch spring bolts (**Figure 11**) in a crisscross pattern.
4. Remove the clutch spring bolts (**Figure 11**), spring retainers and clutch springs.
5. Remove the pressure plate (A, **Figure 12**). The clutch lifter (B) should come out with the pressure plate.
6. Remove the friction discs (**Figure 13**) and clutch plates (**Figure 14**). Stack the discs and plates in their order or removal.

NOTE
When removing the clutch nut, hold the clutch sub-hub with the Kawasaki clutch holding tool (part No. 57001-1243), a Grabbit, or an equiv-

(10)

CLUTCH

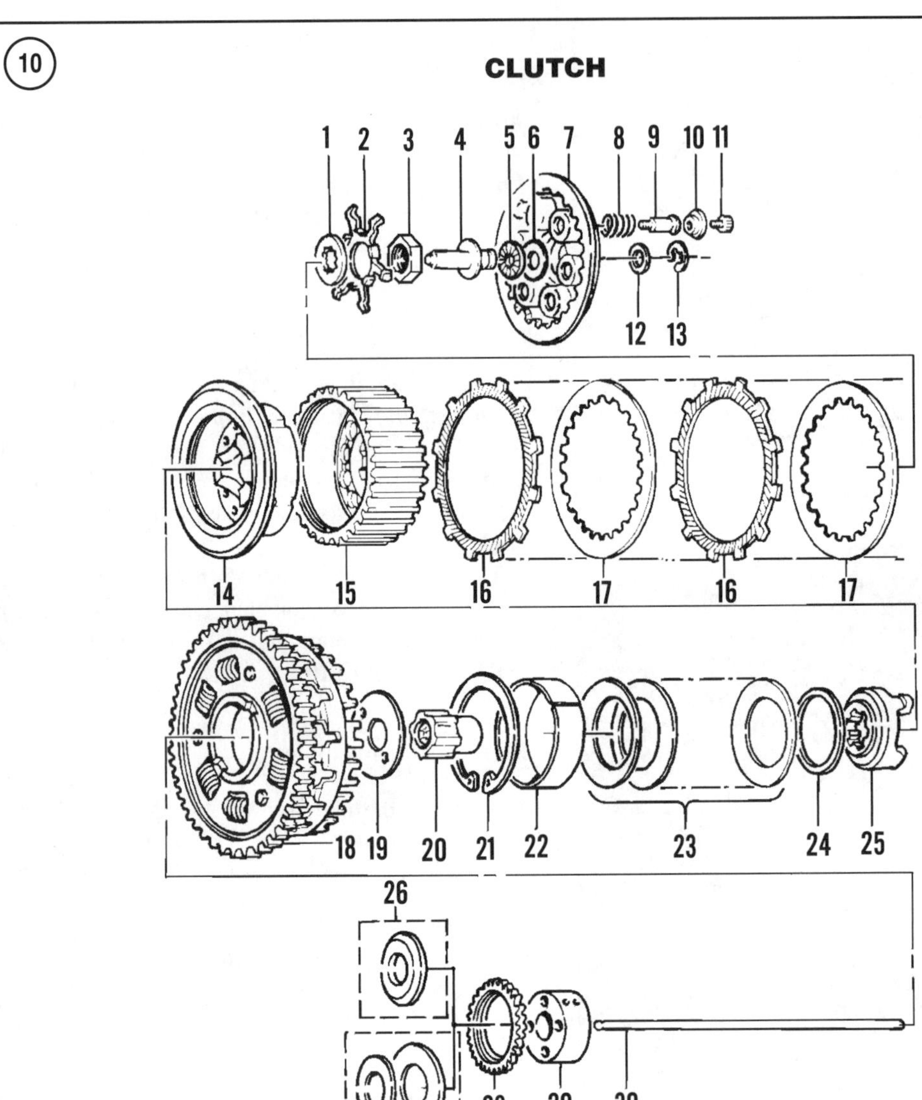

1. Washer
2. Leaf spring
3. Clutch nut
4. Clutch lifter
5. Bearing
6. Bushing
7. Pressure plate
8. Clutch spring
9. Clutch bolt
10. Spring retainer
11. Clutch spring bolt
12. Washer
13. E-clip
14. Clutch hub
15 Sub-hub
16. Friction disc (9)
17. Clutch plate (8)
18. Clutch housing
19. Thrust washer
20. Sleeve
21. Retainer
22. Bushing
23. Damper spring
24. Outer spacer
25. Cam follower
26. Inner spacer*
27. Inner spacers*
28. Oil pump spur gear
29. Clutch housing bearing collar
30. Pushrod

*On engine numbers ZGT00AG001560, ZGT00AE011635 and earlier, a single spacer is used. On engine numbers ZGT00AG001561, ZGT00AE011636 and later, two spacers are used.

alent tool, available from motorcycle dealers. Do not clamp the special tool too tightly. The tool could damage the grooves in the clutch boss.

7. Hold the clutch sub-hub (**Figure 15**) and loosen the clutch nut. Remove and discard the clutch nut (A, **Figure 16**). It is a self-locking nut, which must be replaced.

NOTE
A single leaf spring is used on 1986-1993 models. Two leaf springs are used on 1994-on models.

8. Remove the leaf spring(s) (B, **Figure 16**) and washer (**Figure 17**).
9. Remove the sub-hub (**Figure 18**) from the clutch housing and remove clutch hub assembly (B, **Figure 9**).
10. Remove the sleeve (A, **Figure 19**) and thrust washer (B) from the clutch housing.

NOTE
The clutch housing bearing collar must be removed before the clutch

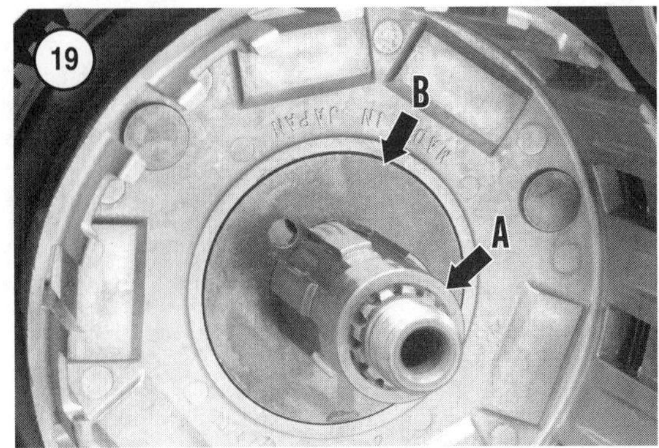

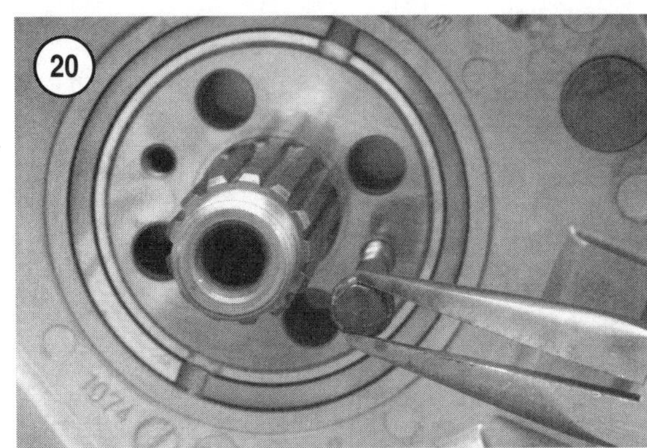

housing. The housing cannot clear the alternator chain sprocket if the collar is installed.

11. Turn two clutch cover bolts into the clutch housing bearing collar (**Figure 20**). Pull the bolts and remove the collar.
12. Remove the clutch housing (**Figure 21**) from the mainshaft.
13. Remove the oil pump spur gear from the back of the clutch housing.

NOTE
The inner spacer on the clutch was redesigned in mid-production. On engine numbers ZGT00AG001560, ZGT00AE011635 and earlier, a single spacer is used. On engine numbers ZGT00AG001561, ZGT00AE011636 and later, two spacers are used (A, ***Figure 22*** *and* ***Figure 23****).*

14. Remove the inner spacer(s).
15. If necessary, disassemble the clutch hub assembly by performing the following:
    a. Support the hub in a hydraulic press.

23

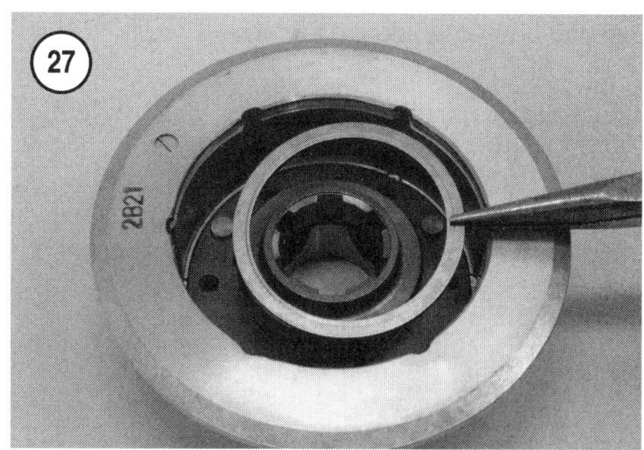
27

24

28

25

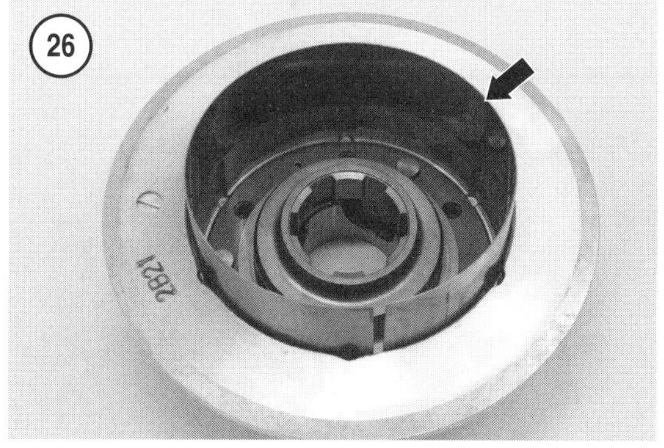
26

b. Using the appropriate size socket or bearing driver, compress the damper spring assembly and remove the retainer (**Figure 24**).

c. Release the press ram and remove the damper springs (**Figure 25**). The damper springs are directional. Note which way the concave side faces on each spring.

d. Remove the bushing (**Figure 26**), the outer spacer (**Figure 27**) and the cam follower (**Figure 28**).

14. Inspect the clutch as described in this section.

Assembly/Installation

NOTE

If the pressure plate, friction discs or clutch plates are being replaced, assemble the clutch on a spare mainshaft and measure the pressure plate free play before installing the clutch.

1A. On models with engine numbers ZGT00AG001560, ZGT00AE011635 and earlier, install the inner spacer so the chamfered side faces in toward the crankcase.

1B. On models with engine numbers ZGT00AG001561, ZGT00AE011636 and later, install the smaller diameter inner spacer (A, **Figure 22**) and then install the larger spacer (**Figure 23**).

2. Install the oil pump spur gear (**Figure 29**) onto the back of the clutch housing.
3. Install the clutch housing bearing collar onto the mainshaft.
4. Install the clutch housing onto the bearing collar. Rotate the housing (**Figure 21**) until the teeth of the oil pump gear (B, **Figure 22**) align with the oil pump spur gear on the back of the clutch housing. Gently push the clutch housing onto the mainshaft until the housing bottoms.
5. If removed, install the pushrod into the mainshaft.
6. Install the thrust washer (B, **Figure 19**) and the sleeve (A).
7. Assemble the clutch hub by performing the following:
   a. The damper spring stack consists of seven concave springs. Six springs are paired. In each paired set, the concave side of one spring faces the concave side of its mate. The seventh spring sits alone atop the stack. Its concave side faces out. Assembly the stack as shown in **Figure 30**.
   b. Install the cam follower (**Figure 28**) into the clutch hub so the cam follower engages the ramps in the hub.
   c. Install the outer spacer (**Figure 27**) over the cam follower and install the bushing (**Figure 26**) around the inner circumference of clutch hub.
   d. Install the damper spring stack (**Figure 31**) so the end with the non-paired spring faces out of the hub. See **Figure 25**.
   e. Support the hub in a hydraulic press.
   f. Using the appropriate size socket or bearing driver, compress the damper spring assembly and install the retainer (**Figure 24**).
   g. Release the press ram and inspect the clutch hub. Make sure the retainer is completely seated in its groove.
8. Install the clutch hub (B, **Figure 9**) so its inner splines engage those of the sleeve.
9. Install the sub-hub (**Figure 18**).

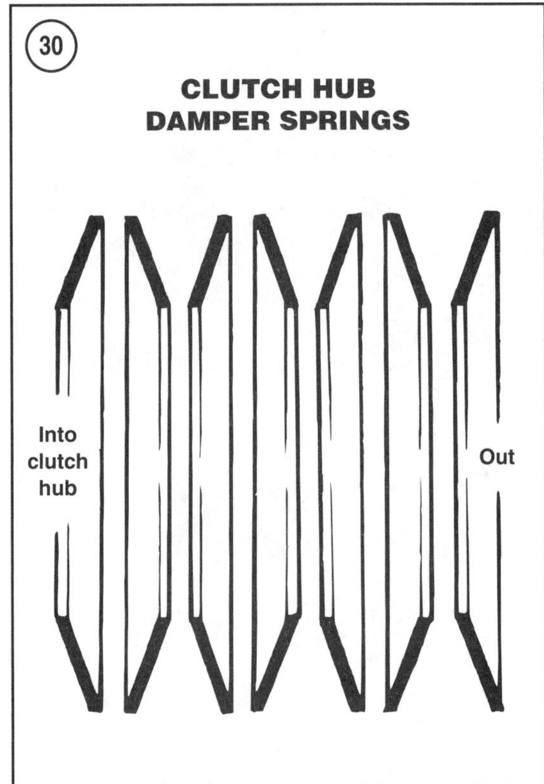

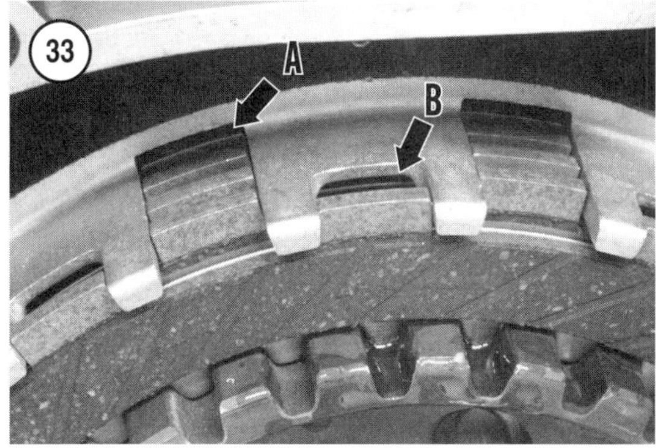

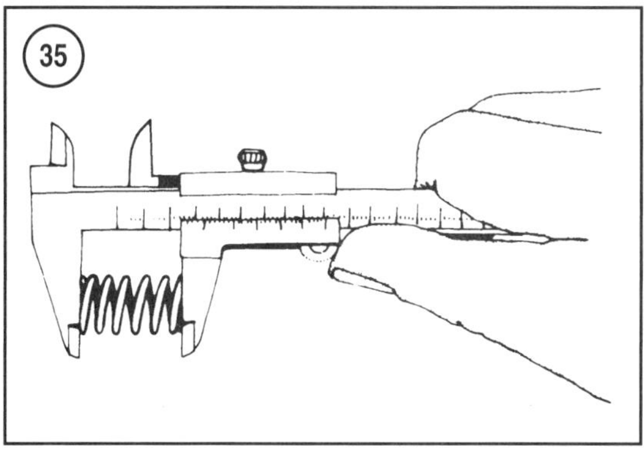

10. Install the washer (**Figure 17**) so its splines engage those of the mainshaft.

NOTE
A single leaf spring was used in 1986-1993 models. Two leaf springs are used in 1994-on models.

11. Install the leaf spring(s) (B, **Figure 16**) so the small arms engage the slots in the sub-hub.
12. Install a new clutch nut. The side with the shorter shoulder must face in. Hold the sub-hub with the special tool (**Figure 15**) and torque the nut to 130 N•m (98 ft.-lb.).

CAUTION
Apply oil to the friction material on the friction discs.

13. Install the first friction disc (**Figure 32**) onto the clutch hub. Note the following when installing the first eight friction discs:
   a. A disc's tabs must fit in the deep slots (A, **Figure 33**) in the clutch housing.
   b. The radial groove cut in the friction material must point toward the center of the clutch when the clutch rotates counterclockwise.
14. Install the first clutch plate (**Figure 14**) and then install the next friction disc.
15. Continue installing a clutch plate and then a friction disc until the last clutch plate is installed.
16. Install the last friction disc (**Figure 13**) so its tabs engage the shallow slots (B, **Figure 33**) in the clutch housing.
17. Apply molybdenum disulfide grease to the end of clutch lifter (A, **Figure 34**) and install the pressure plate (A, **Figure 12**).
18. Install the clutch springs, spring retainers and clutch bolts (**Figure 11**).
19. Evenly tighten the clutch bolts in a crisscross pattern and torque them to 11 N•m (97 in.-lb.).

Inspection

When inspecting the clutch, compare all measurements to the clutch specifications in **Table 1**. Replace any part that is damaged or out of specification.

1. Clean all clutch parts in a petroleum-based solvent such as kerosene and dry them thoroughly with compressed air.
2. Measure the free length of each spring (**Figure 35**). Replace all clutch springs as a set.

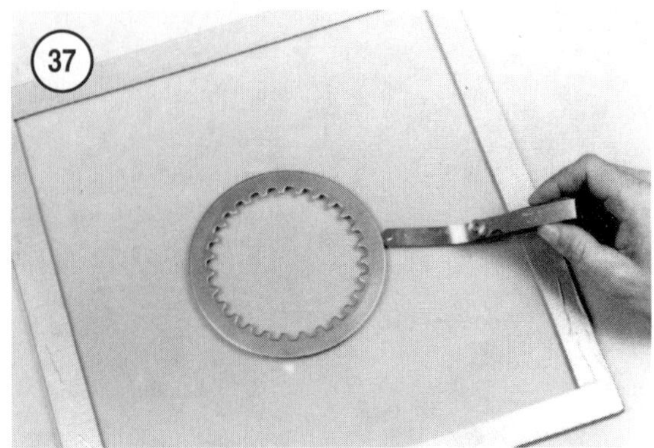

3. Inspect the clutch bolts and spring retainers for wear or thread damage.

4. The friction disc material is bonded to an aluminum disc for warp resistance and durability. Inspect the friction material for excessive wear, cracks and other damage.

5. Check the frictions disc tangs for surface damage. Pay attention to the sides of the tangs where they slide along the clutch housing fingers. If these tangs are not smooth, the clutch will not disengage and engage correctly.

6. Measure the thickness of each friction disc (**Figure 36**) at several places around each disc. If any measurement is smaller than the service limit specified in **Table 1**, replace all the friction discs as a set.

7. Check the inner splines on the clutch plates. Minor roughness can be cleaned with an oilstone or fine file. If any one plate has excessive roughness or wear, replace all the clutch plates as a set.

8. Check the warp of the clutch plates and the friction discs by performing the following:
   a. Set each clutch plate on a surface plate or piece of glass and measure the warp of each clutch plate with a feeler gauge (**Figure 37**). If the warp of any clutch plate exceeds the service limit, replace all the clutch plates as a set.
   b. Measure the warp of each friction disc. If the warp of any disc exceeds the service limit, replace all friction discs as a set.

9. Inspect the outer splines of the sub-hub (A, **Figure 38**) and inspect the slots (B) that engage the arms (**Figure 39**) of the leaf spring. If damage is noted, inspect the inner splines of the clutch plates and the arms of the leaf spring.

10. Inspect the clutch housing by performing the following:
   a. Check the clutch housing slots (A, **Figure 40**) for cracks, nicks or galling where they contact the friction disc tabs. Remove minor damage with an oilstone. If severe damage is evident, the housing must be replaced.
   b. Inspect the teeth of the clutch driven gear (B, **Figure 40**). Replace the clutch housing as

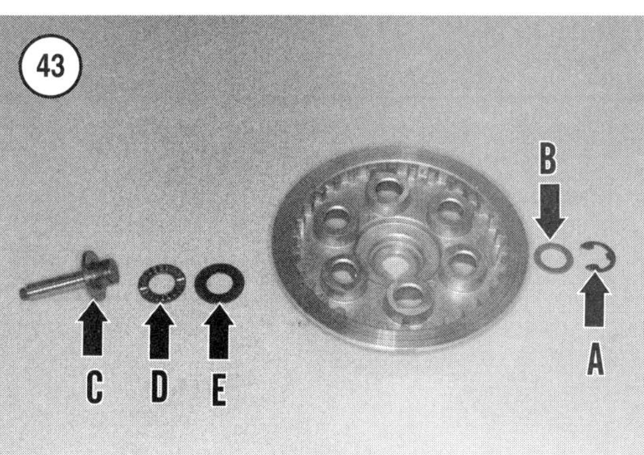

necessary. If the clutch driven gear is damaged, inspect the primary drive gear on the crankshaft.

c. Inspect the damper springs (A, **Figure 41**). If they are sagged, cracked or broken, replace the clutch housing.

d. Inspect the bushing (B, **Figure 41**) for flaking or other signs of wear.

11. Inspect the teeth of the oil pump spur gear (**Figure 42**). Replace the gear as necessary. If the oil pump spur gear is damaged, inspect the oil pump gear.

12. Inspect the clutch hub for the following:

a. Inspect the studs in the clutch hub for thread damage or cracks.

b. Inspect the inner splines in the hub in the boss for damage. Remove any small nicks with an oilstone. If damage is excessive, the clutch hub must be replaced.

13. Inspect the pressure plate splines (B, **Figure 34**) and spring towers (C) for cracks or wear.

14. Measure the pressure plate/clutch lifter clearance as described in this section.

15. Disassemble the clutch lifter by performing the following:

a. Remove the E-clip (A, **Figure 43**) from the groove in the lifter and remove the clip and washer (B) from the outside of the pressure plate.

b. Remove the clutch lifter (C, **Figure 43**), the lifter bearing (D) and the bushing (E) from the inside of the pressure plate.

c. Inspect the clutch lifter for chatter, cracks or signs of wear.

d. Turn the lifter bearing inner race by hand. The bearing should turn smoothly without roughness or damage.

e. Assemble the pressure plate by reversing the removal procedure.

16. Inspect pushrod for cracks or wear. Roll the pushrod along a surface plate or a piece of glass to check for warp.

Pressure Plate Free Play

Insufficient pressure plate free play results in excessive clutch pressure during engagement, which results in wheel hop. Excessive free play, however, causes the clutch lever to feel spongy or to pulsate during clutch engagement. Perform this test if these symptoms are evident.

Also check the pressure plate free play when the pressure plate, friction discs or clutch plates are replaced.

1. Secure a spare mainshaft in a vise with soft jaws so the clutch end of the mainshaft is up.
2. Follow the assembly procedures described in this section and assemble the following clutch parts onto the spare mainshaft:
   a. Spacer (s).
   b. Oil pump spur gear onto the clutch housing.
   c. Clutch housing bearing collar.
   d. Clutch housing.
   e. Thrust washer.
   f. Sleeve.
   g. The assembled clutch hub.
   h. Friction discs and clutch plates.
   I. Assembled pressure plate.
3. Secure a dial indicator in place so its plunger rests against the end of clutch lifter (**Figure 44**).
4. Grasp the clutch gear and rotate it clockwise and counterclockwise from stop to stop. The free play equals the difference between the highest and lowest readings on the dial indicator.

5A. If the free play exceeds the specified range listed in **Table 1**, perform the following:
   a. Install seven new standard-sized clutch plates (2.3 mm) and one new oversized clutch plate (2.6 mm).
   b. Also adjust the pressure plate/clutch lifter clearance so it is smaller than the current measurement but still within specification.

5B. If the free play is less than specification, perform the following:
   a. Install seven new standard-sized clutch plates (2.3 mm) and one new undersized clutch plate (2.0 mm).
   b. Also adjust the pressure plate/clutch lifter clearance so it is larger than the current measurement but still within the specified range.

44

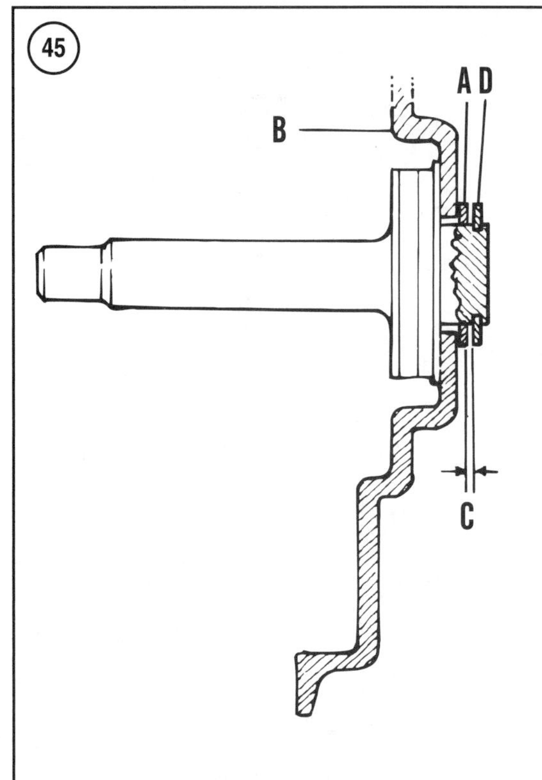

45

Pressure Plate/Clutch Lifter Clearance

1. Press the washer (A, **Figure 45**) against the pressure plate (B).
2. Use a feeler gauge (**Figure 46**) to measure the gap (C, **Figure 45**) between the washer (A) and the E-clip (D).
3. If the clearance is outside the range specified in **Table 1**, replace the washer. Washers are available in 0.2-mm increments from 0.8-1.8 mm.

46

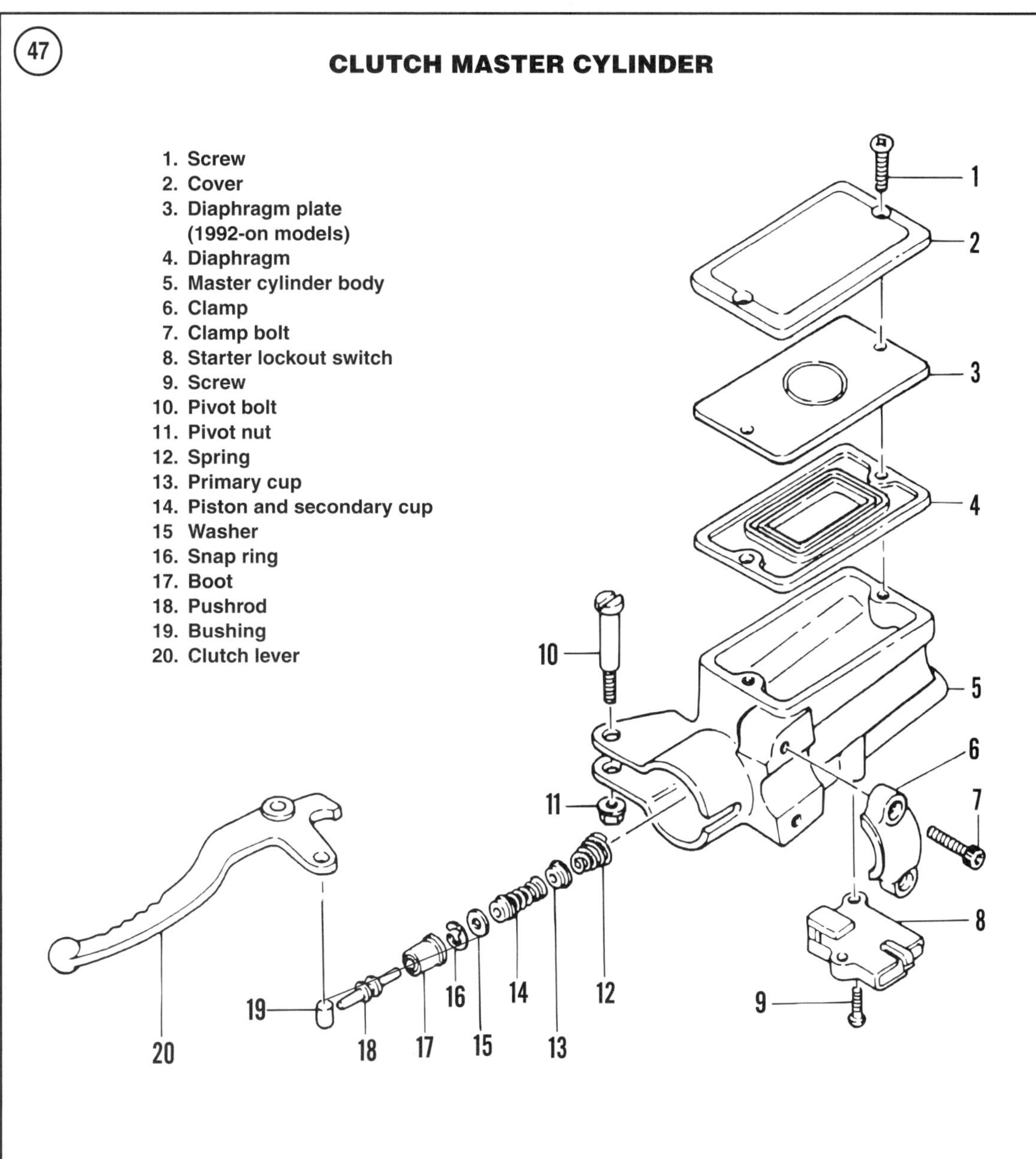

a. Remove the E-clip (A, **Figure 46**) and washer (B) from the end of the lifter.

b. Install the new washer and a new E-clip. Make sure the E-clip is seated within the lifter groove.

CLUTCH MASTER CYLINDER

Refer to **Figure 47**.

Removal/Installation

CAUTION

Cover the fuel tank and front fender with a heavy cloth or plastic tarp to protect them from brake fluid spills. Wash spilled brake fluid off any painted, plated or plastic surfaces immediately with soapy water and rinse the area completely.

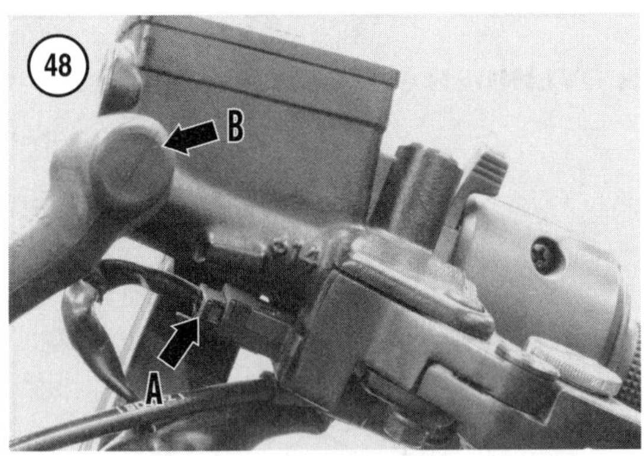

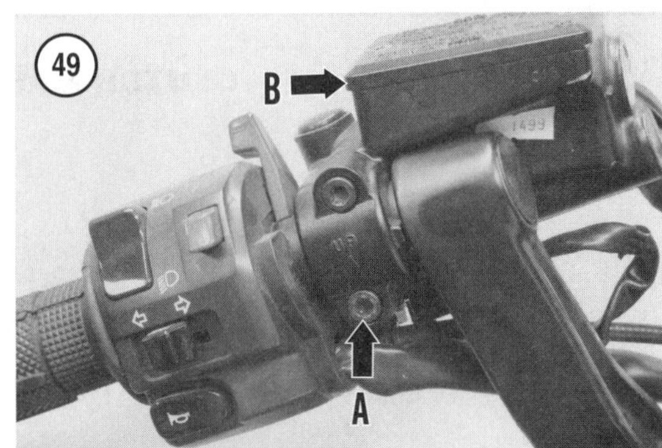

1. Securely support the motorcycle on a level surface.
2. Drain the brake fluid from the clutch master cylinder as described earlier in this chapter.
3. Disconnect the electrical lead (A, **Figure 48**) from the starter lockout switch.
4. Pull the rubber boot (B, **Figure 48**) away from the banjo bolt. Place a rag beneath the banjo bolt. Remove the bolt from the master cylinder reservoir and separate the clutch hose from the reservoir. Discard the two copper washers.
5. Place the loose end of the clutch hose into a reclosable plastic bag so brake fluid will not drip onto the motorcycle. Tie the loose end of the hose up to the handlebar.
6. Remove the clutch master cylinder clamp bolts (A, **Figure 49**) and the clamp. Remove the clutch master cylinder (B, **Figure 49**) from the handlebar.
7. Drain any residual brake fluid from the master cylinder reservoir. Dispose of the fluid properly.
8. If the master cylinder will not to be serviced, place it in a reclosable plastic bag to protect it from foreign matter.
9. Check for hydraulic fluid in the area of the clutch lever boot. If leaks are noted, the primary and secondary cups are worn and should be replaced.
10. Installation is the reverse of removal. Note the following:
   a. Position the clamp with the UP mark pointing up and install the master cylinder clamp bolts (A, **Figure 49**). Torque the clamp bolts to 8.8 N•m (78 in.-lb.). Tighten the upper clamp bolt first and then tighten the lower bolt.
   b. Install the clutch hose onto the master cylinder. Install a new copper washer onto each side of the hose fitting and torque the banjo bolt to 29 N•m (21 ft.-lb.).

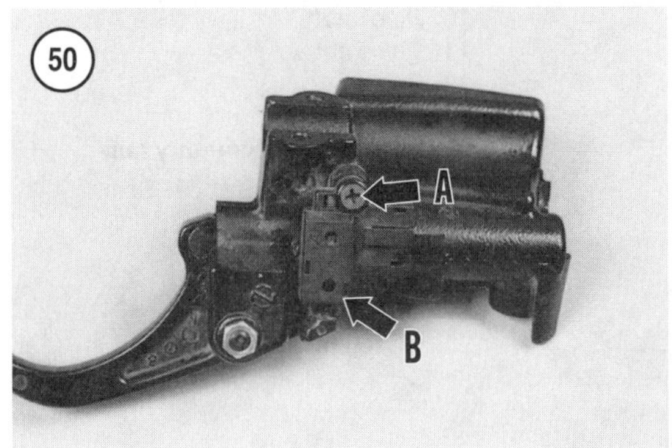

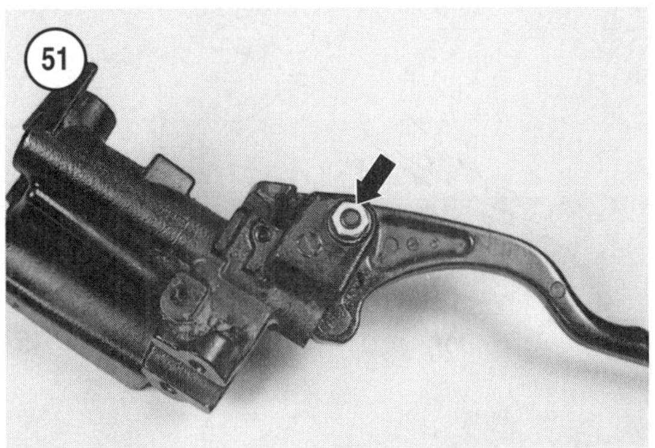

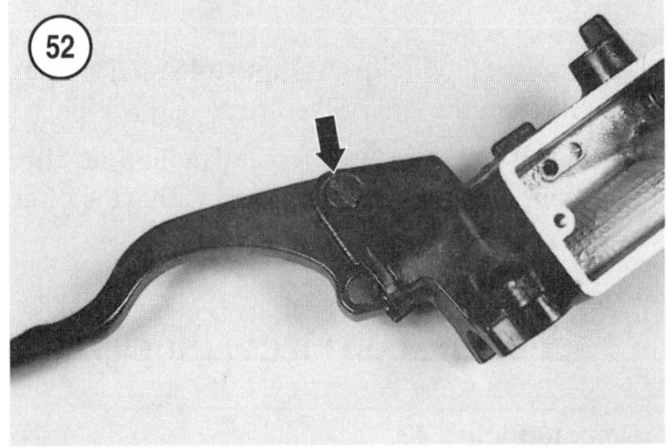

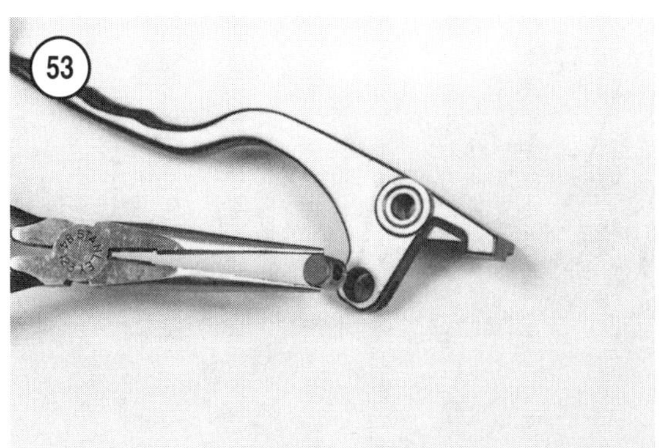
53

54

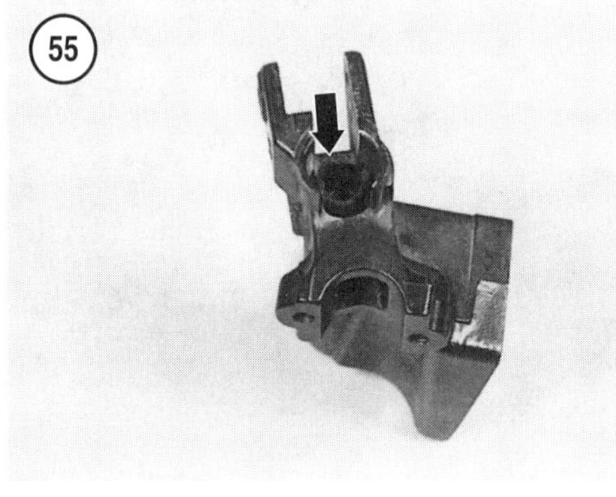
55

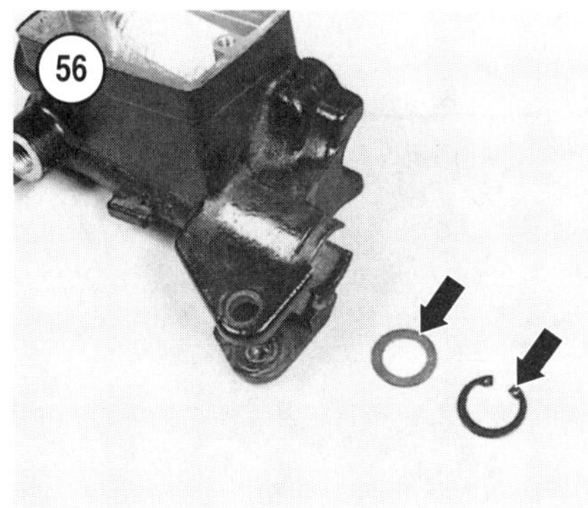
56

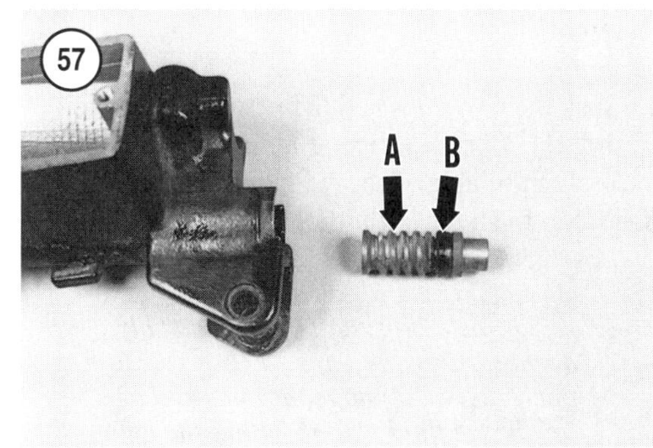

57

c. Reconnect the electrical connector to the starter lockout switch (A, **Figure 48**).

d. Refill the clutch master cylinder reservoir with fresh DOT 4 brake fluid and bleed the clutch system as described in this chapter.

Disassembly

Refer to **Figure 47**.

1. Remove the master cylinder as described in this section.

2. If still in place, remove the reservoir cover, diaphragm plate (1992-on models) and the diaphragm. Pour out and discard any the remaining brake fluid.

3. Remove the mounting screw (A, **Figure 50**) and lift the starter lockout switch (B) from the master cylinder body.

4. Remove the nut (**Figure 51**) from the pivot bolt and remove the bolt (**Figure 52**).

5. Carefully pull the clutch lever from the master cylinder and remove the bushing (**Figure 53**) from the clutch lever.

6. Pull the pushrod (**Figure 54**) from the master cylinder.

7. Roll the boot (**Figure 55**) from the master cylinder bore.

8. Remove the snap ring (**Figure 56**) and washer from cylinder bore.

9. Remove the piston (A, **Figure 57**) along with the secondary cup (B).

10. Remove the spring (A, **Figure 58**) with the primary cup (B).

Assembly

1. Soak the new cups and the new master piston in fresh DOT 4 brake fluid for at least 15 minutes to make them pliable. Coat the inside of the cylinder bore with fresh brake fluid.

CAUTION

When installing the piston assembly, do not allow the cups to turn inside out. This will damage the cups and allow brake fluid to leak within the cylinder bore.

2. Fit the spring (A, **Figure 58**) onto the primary cup (B) and install the assembly into the cylinder bore.
3. Roll the new secondary cup (B, **Figure 57**) onto the piston (A) and install the piston assembly into the cylinder bore. Make sure the large end of the piston presses against the primary cup.
4. Install the washer (**Figure 56**) into the cylinder bore. Press the washer into the bore and secure it in place with a new snap ring. The snap ring must be seated in the groove inside the cylinder bore.
5. Lubricate the boot with fresh brake fluid. Slip the boot over the pushrod until the boot seats in the pushrod groove. The round end of the pushrod must emerge from the lipped end of the boot.
6. Install the pushrod/boot assembly into the cylinder. Make sure the round end of the pushrod faces inward and that the lips of the boot are completely seated in the cylinder bore (**Figure 55**). Lubricate the pushrod end (A, **Figure 59**) with grease.
7. Lubricate the pushrod bushing with grease and install the bushing (B, **Figure 59**) into the clutch lever. Rotate the pushrod bushing within the lever so the bushing hole appears in the lever window. Slide the clutch lever into place so the pushrod (A, **Figure 59**) passes through the lever window and into the hole in the pushrod bushing.
8. Lubricate the lever pivot bolt with grease and secure the brake lever to the body with the pivot bolt (**Figure 52**) and nut (**Figure 51**). Torque the pivot nut to 5.9 N•m (52 in.-lb.).
9. Set the starter lockout switch (B, **Figure 50**) onto the master cylinder and secure the switch in place with the screw (A).
10. Install the diaphragm cover (1992-on models) and cover after the master cylinder has been installed on the handlebar.

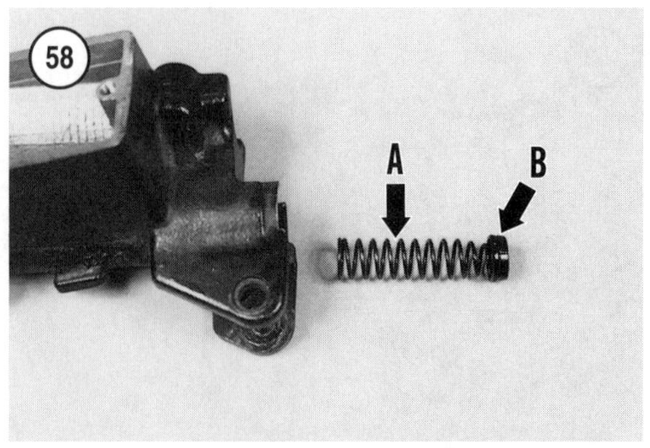

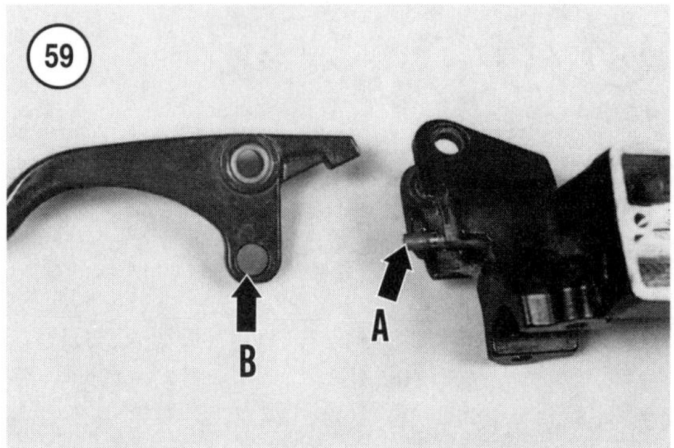

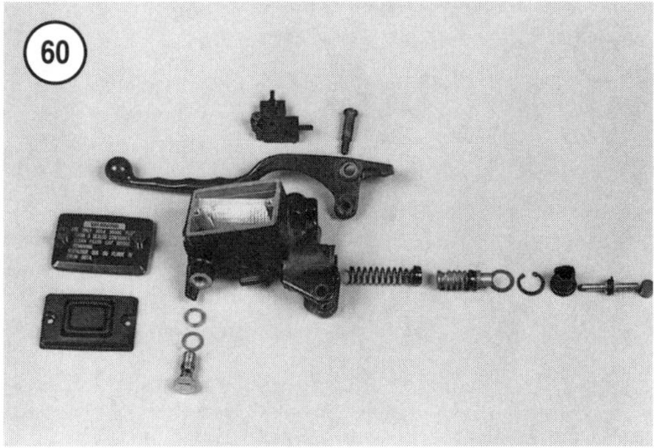

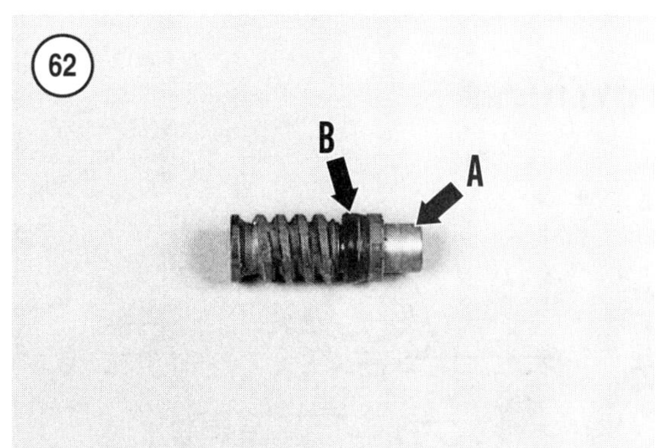

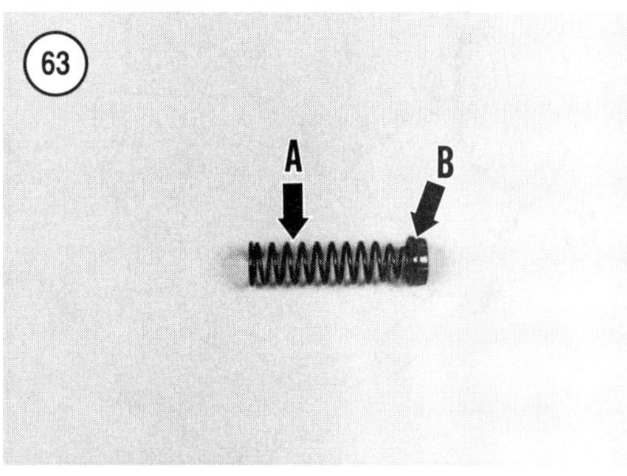

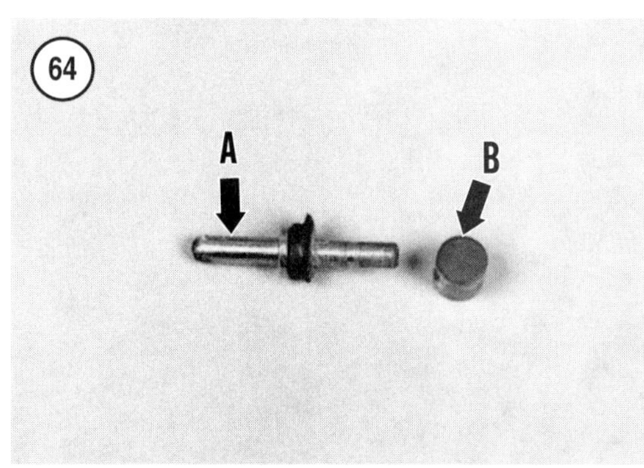

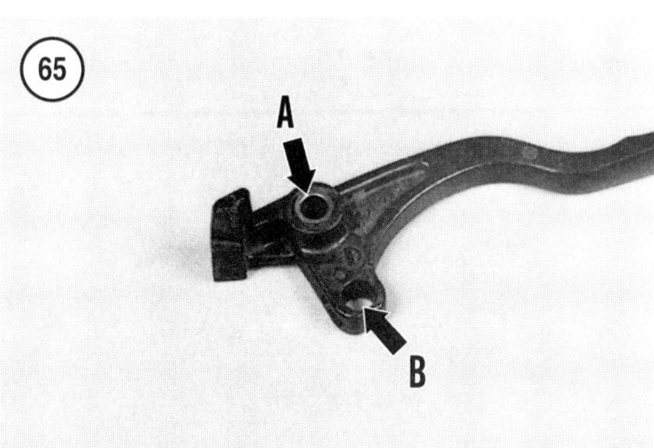

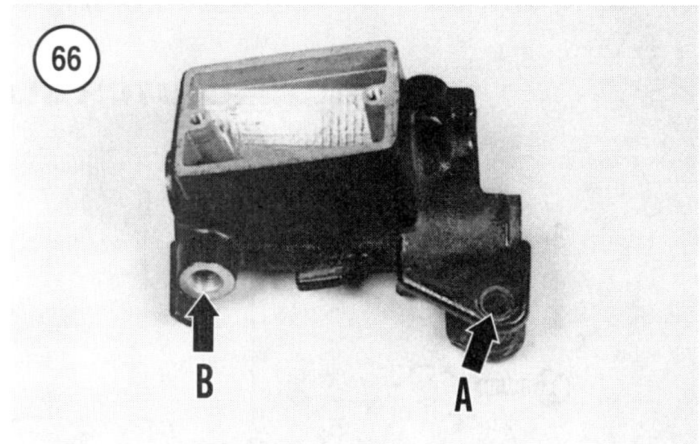

Inspection

1. Clean all parts (**Figure 60**) in fresh DOT 4 brake fluid. Place the master cylinder components on a clean lint-free cloth.
2. Inspect the cylinder bore and piston contact surfaces for scratches, wear or other signs of damage.
3. Inspect the inside of the reservoir for scratches, wear or other signs of damage. Make sure the passages in the bottom of the fluid reservoir (**Figure 61**) are clear.

NOTE
The spring, primary cup, secondary cup and master piston are sold as a piston kit. If any part is worn or damaged, they all must be replaced.

4. Check the end of the piston (A, **Figure 62**) for wear. Check the secondary cup (B, **Figure 62**) for tears, wear or swelling.
5. Check the spring (A, **Figure 63**) for cracks or fatigue. Inspect primary cup (B, **Figure 63**) for damage, softness or for swollen conditions.
6. Inspect the ends of the pushrod (A, **Figure 64**). Replace the pushrod if it is worn.
7. Remove the pushrod bushing (B, **Figure 64**) from the brake lever. Inspect the hole in the bushing. Replace the bushing if it is worn or damaged or if the hole is elongated.
8. Inspect clutch lever pivot hole (A, **Figure 65**) and bushing hole (B). Replace the clutch lever if either is worn or elongated.
9. Inspect the lever boss (A, **Figure 66**) on the reservoir for cracks or damage.
10. Inspect the threads in the master cylinder fluid port (B, **Figure 66**). If the threads are damaged or partially stripped, replace the master cylinder body.
11. Inspect the threads of the banjo bolt.
12. Replace any part that is worn or damaged.

67

CLUTCH SLAVE CYLINDER

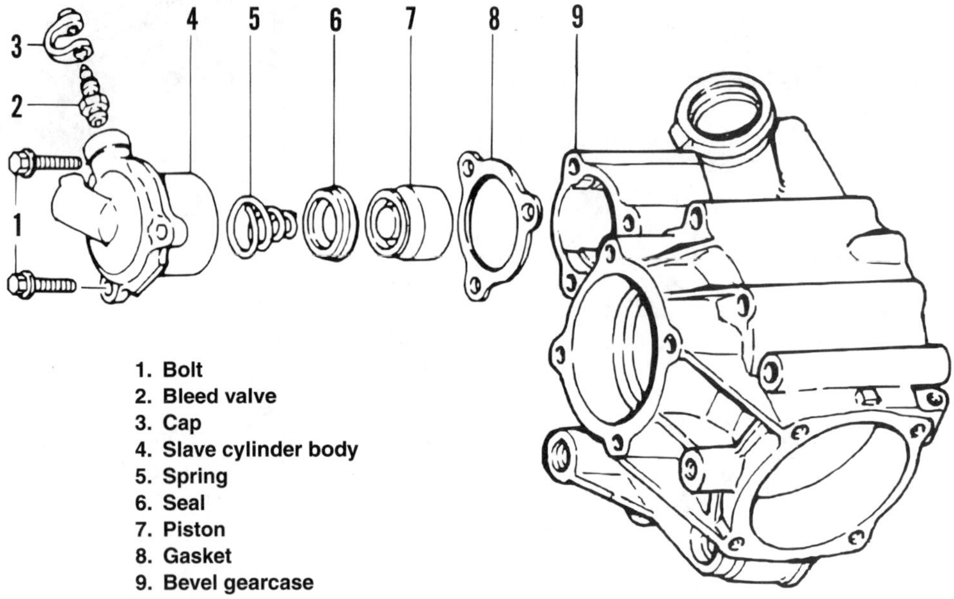

1. Bolt
2. Bleed valve
3. Cap
4. Slave cylinder body
5. Spring
6. Seal
7. Piston
8. Gasket
9. Bevel gearcase

CLUTCH SLAVE CYLINDER

Removal/Installation

Refer to **Figure 67**.

1. Remove the cap and bleed the clutch as described earlier in this chapter.
2. Place a rag under the banjo bolt (A, **Figure 68**) and remove the banjo bolt and copper washer. Insert the end of the clutch hose into a reclosable plastic bag so brake fluid will not drip onto the motorcycle.
3. Remove the slave cylinder mounting bolts (B, **Figure 68**) and pull the slave cylinder from its housing.
4. Discard the slave cylinder gasket.
5. Installation is the reverse of removal. Pay attention to the following:
   a. Install a new slave cylinder gasket.
   b. Apply Loctite 242 to the slave cylinder mounting bolts (B, **Figure 68**) and tighten the bolts securely.
   c. Secure the hose to the slave cylinder with the banjo bolt. Make sure the hose fitting sits inside the stop ©, **Figure 68**) on the slave cylinder. Install a new copper washer on each side

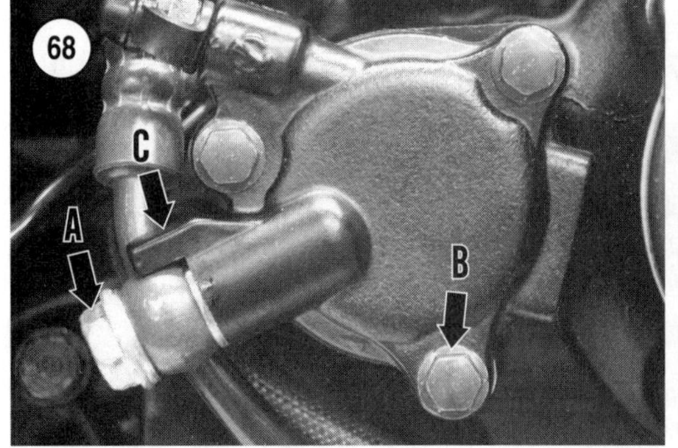

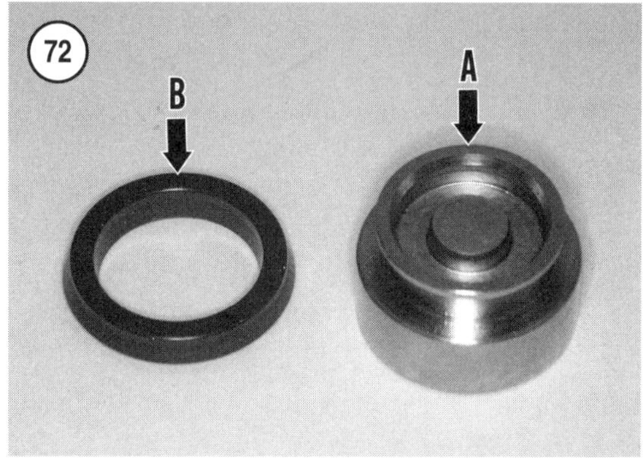

of the hose fitting and torque the banjo bolt to 29 N•m (21 ft.-lb.).

d. Refill the system with fresh DOT 4 brake fluid and bleed the system as described in this chapter.

Disassembly/Assembly

1. Securely support the slave cylinder on wooden blocks.

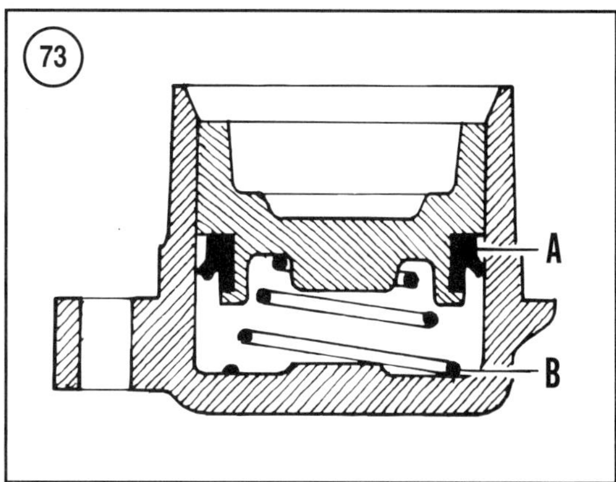

2. Apply compressed air to the hydraulic port (**Figure 69**) and blow the piston from the slave cylinder body.
3. Remove spring (A, **Figure 70**) from the piston.
4. Remove the piston seal (B, **Figure 70**) from the piston. Discard the old seal.
5. Inspect the housing (**Figure 71**) and piston (A, **Figure 72**) for scratches, wear and rust. If either part must be replaced, replace the housing and piston as a set.
6. Inspect the spring for wear, rust or fatigue. Replace the spring as necessary.
7. Lubricate the piston (A, **Figure 72**) and the new piston seal (B) with fresh DOT 4 brake fluid. Slip the seal onto the piston so the seal's lip (B, **Figure 70**) faces away from the piston. See A, **Figure 73**.
8. Fit the small end of the spring onto the piston.

CAUTION

When installing the piston assembly, make sure the lip on the piston seal does not fold over onto itself. This will damage the seal and allow brake fluid to leak past the seal.

9. Install the piston into the housing. The large end of the spring (B, **Figure 73**) should face into the housing.

CLUTCH HOSE REPLACEMENT

Check the clutch hose at the clutch system inspection intervals listed in Chapter Three. Replace the hose if it is cracked, bulging or shows signs of chafing, wear or other damage.

Refer to **Figure 74.**

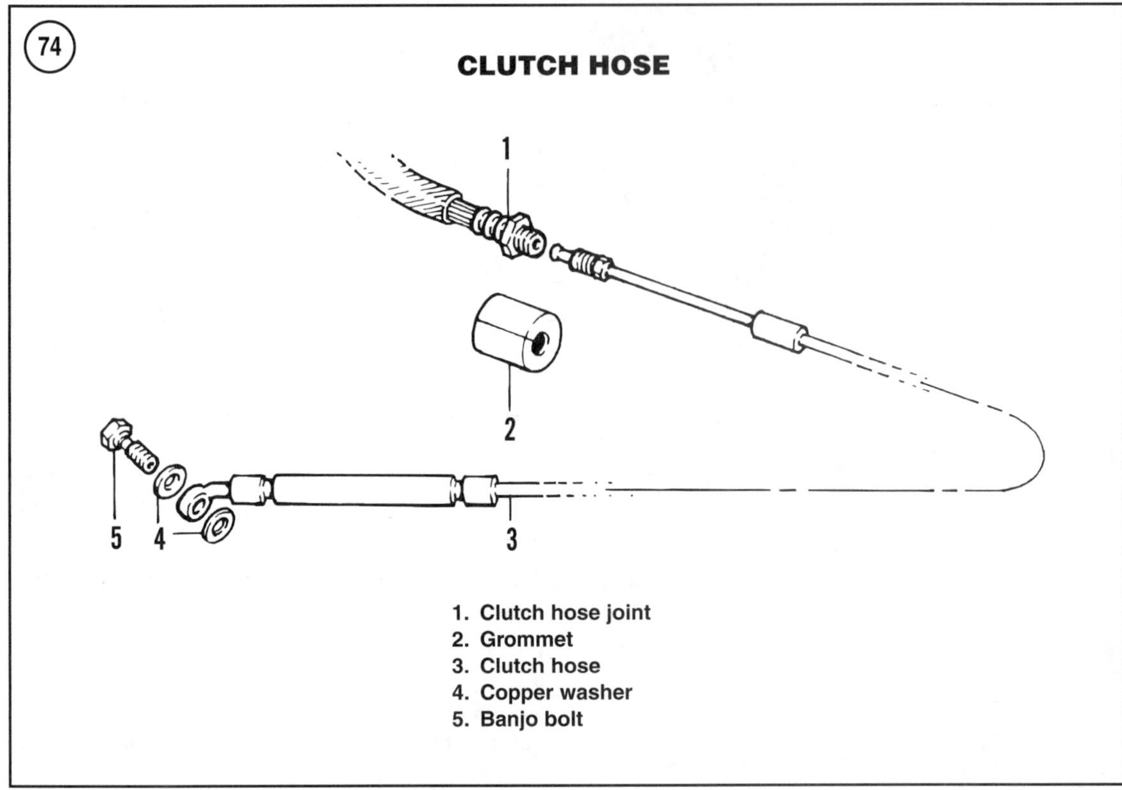

1. Clutch hose joint
2. Grommet
3. Clutch hose
4. Copper washer
5. Banjo bolt

1. Remove the lower, middle and front fairings as described in Chapter Fifteen.

2. Securely support the motorcycle on level ground.

3. Use a tarp or plastic drop cloth to cover areas of the motorcycle where hydraulic fluid could spill.

4. Follow the procedures described in this chapter and drain the brake fluid from the clutch system.

5. Note how the clutch line is routed through the motorcycle. Make a drawing so the new line can be routed along the same path as the original hose or pipe.

6. Remove any clamp or ties securing the line to the motorcycle. Also note the location of these clamps or ties.

7. Note how the hose fitting is installed on the master and slave cylinders. The new hose fitting must sit on the same side of the post.

8. Remove the banjo bolt securing the hose fitting on each end of the hose. Discard the copper washer on each side of a hose fitting.

9. Reverse these steps to install a new clutch hose. Note the following:

a. Compare the new and old hoses. Make sure they are the same.

b. Clean the banjo bolts and hose ends to remove any contamination.

c. Refer to the notes made during removal and route the new hose along the same path as the original hose. Secure the hose to the motorcycle at the same locations noted during removal.

d. Replace any banjo bolt with a damaged head or threads.

e. Install a new copper washer on each side of a clutch hose fitting.

f. Tighten thc banjo bolts to 29 N•m (21 ft.-lb.).

g. If removed, tighten the clutch hose joint to 18 N•m (13 ft.-lb.).

h. After replacing the hose, turn handlebars from side to side to make sure the hose does not rub against any part or pull away from its clutch component.

i. Refill the master cylinder and bleed the clutch as described in this chapter.

Table 1 CLUTCH SPECIFICATIONS

Item	New mm (in.)	Service limit mm (in.)
Clutch spring free length	33.2 (1.307)	32.1 (1.264)
Pressure plate free play (usable range)	0.4-1.0 (0.016-0.039)	–
Friction disc thickness	2.9-3.1 (0.114-0.122)	2.8 (0.110)
Friction disc warp	less than 0.2 (0.008)	0.3 (0.012)
Clutch plate thickness		
Standard	2.3 (0.091)	–
Oversize	2.6 (0.102)	–
Undersize	2.0 (0.079)	–
Clutch plate/friction disc warp	less than 0.2 (0.008)	0.3 (0.012)
Pressure plate/clutch lifter clearance	0.05-0.25 (0.0020-0.0098)	–
Primary gear/clutch gear backlash	0.03-0.10 (0.0012-0.0039)	0.14 (0.0055)

6

Table 2 CLUTCH TORQUE SPECIFICATIONS

Item	N•m	In.-lb.	ft.-lb.
Clutch spring bolts	11	97	–
Clutch hose banjo bolt	29	–	21
Clutch hose joint	18	–	13
Clutch hub nut	130	–	96
Clutch lever pivot nut	5.9	52	–
Master cylinder clamp bolts	8.8	78	–
Slave cylinder bleed valve	7.8	69	–

CHAPTER SEVEN

TRANSMISSION, BEVEL GEARCASE AND SHIFT MECHANISM

This chapter describes service procedures for servicing the internal and external shift mechanisms, transmission and the bevel gearcase. When servicing these components, compare any measurements to the specifications in the tables at the end of this chapter. Replace any component that is worn, damaged or out of specification. During assembly, tighten fasteners to the specified torque.

SHIFT PEDAL

Removal/Installation

Refer to **Figure 1**.

1. Remove the lower fairing as described in Chapter Fifteen.
2. Remove the boot (A, **Figure 2**) from the shift pedal pivot.
3. Remove the snap ring and washer from the shift pedal pivot bolt.
4. Loosen the clamp bolt (A **Figure 3**) on the shift lever. Note that the index mark (B, **Figure 3**) on the shift shaft aligns with the slot in the lever.
5. Simultaneously pull the shift pedal from its pivot post on the bracket and pull the shift lever from the shift shaft. Watch for the washer behind the shift pedal.
6. If the shift pedal pivot shaft must be replaced, apply Loctite 242 (blue) to the threads of the new pivot shaft and torque the shift pedal pivot shaft to 25 N•m (18 ft.-lb.).
7. Installation is the reverse of removal. Note the following:
   a. Install the washer onto the shift pedal pivot shaft.
   b. Slide the shift pedal onto the pivot shaft and slide the shift lever onto the shift shaft. Make sure the index mark (B, **Figure 3**) on the shift shaft aligns with the slot in the shift lever.
   c. Tighten the shift lever clamp bolt (A, **Figure 3**) securely.
   d. Secure the shift pedal to the pivot shaft with the washer and circlip.

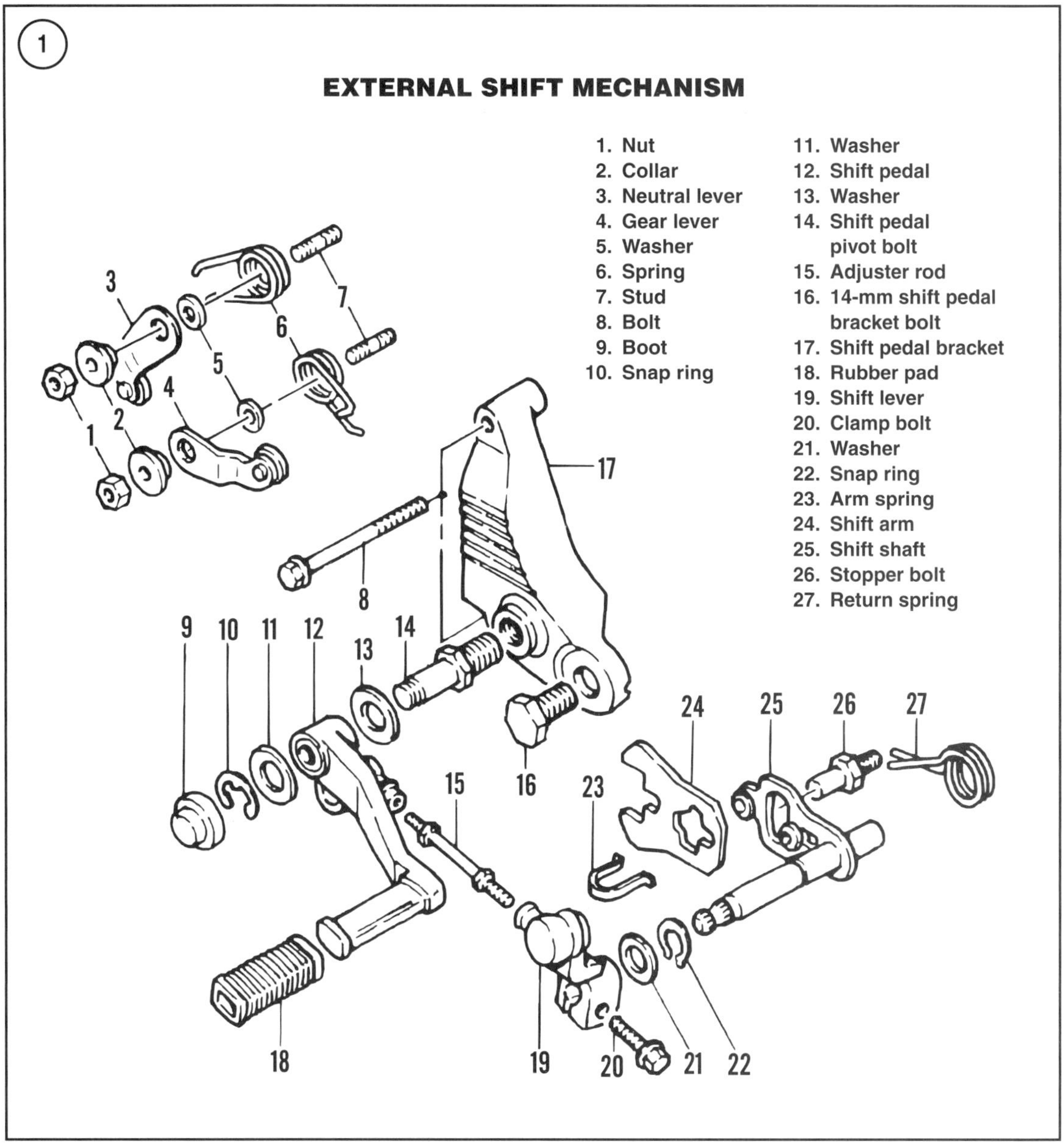

1
EXTERNAL SHIFT MECHANISM
1. Nut
2. Collar
3. Neutral lever
4. Gear lever
5. Washer
6. Spring
7. Stud
8. Bolt
9. Boot
10. Snap ring
11. Washer
12. Shift pedal
13. Washer
14. Shift pedal pivot bolt
15. Adjuster rod
16. 14-mm shift pedal bracket bolt
17. Shift pedal bracket
18. Rubber pad
19. Shift lever
20. Clamp bolt
21. Washer
22. Snap ring
23. Arm spring
24. Shift arm
25. Shift shaft
26. Stopper bolt
27. Return spring

2
C
A
B
C

3
A
B

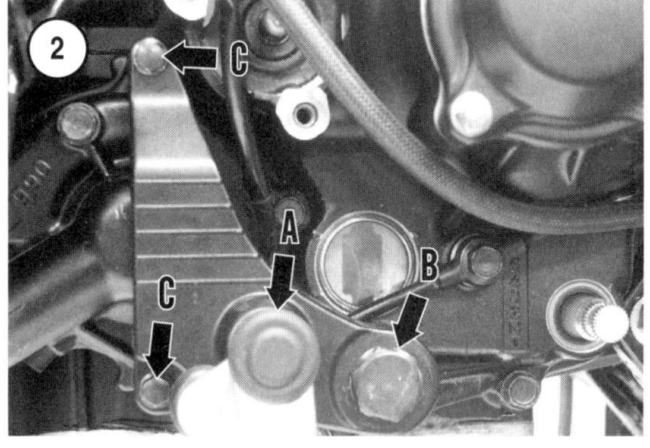

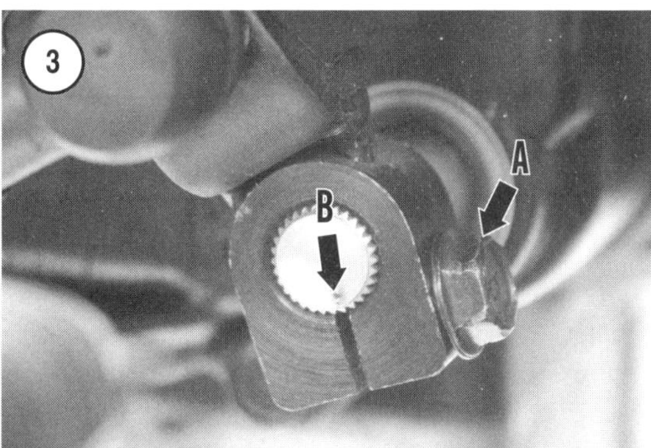

SHIFT PEDAL BRACKET

Removal/Installation

Refer to **Figure 1**.

1. Remove the lower fairing as described in Chapter Fifteen.
2. Drain the engine coolant (Chapter Three).
3. Remove the clutch slave cylinder (Chapter Six). Remove the clutch pushrod from the mainshaft so the rod will not be damaged.
4. Loosen the clamp bolt (A, **Figure 3**) on the shift lever. Note that the index mark (B, **Figure 3**) on the shift shaft aligns with the slot in the lever.
5. Slide the shift lever from the shift shaft.

NOTE

*Two of the shift pedal mounting bolts (C, **Figure 2**) also secure the water pump to the crankcase. Watch for the pump once the bracket is removed. The pump will no longer be secured to the crankcase.*

6. Remove the shift pedal bracket bolts (B and C, **Figure 2**).
7. Lower the shift pedal bracket and shift pedal from the motorcycle. Watch for the water pump behind the bracket. If necessary, loosely install the two shift pedal bracket bolts (C, **Figure 2**) to hold the water pump in place.
8. Installation is the reverse of removal.
   a. Slide the shift lever onto the shift shaft. Make sure the index mark (B, **Figure 3**) on the shift shaft aligns with the slot in the shift lever.
   b. Tighten the shift lever clamp bolt (A, **Figure 3**) securely.
   c. Install the shift pedal bracket bolts (B and C, **Figure 2**). Torque the 14-mm bolt to 78 N•m (58 ft-lb.). Tighten the other bolts securely.

EXTERNAL SHIFT MECHANISM

Removal/Disassembly

Refer to **Figure 1**.

1. Remove the bevel gearcase as described in this chapter.
2. Press the shift arm (A, **Figure 4**) rearward to disengage the shift pawls from the shift drum pins and pull the shift shaft assembly from the crankcase. Watch for the washer and snap ring on the shift shaft.

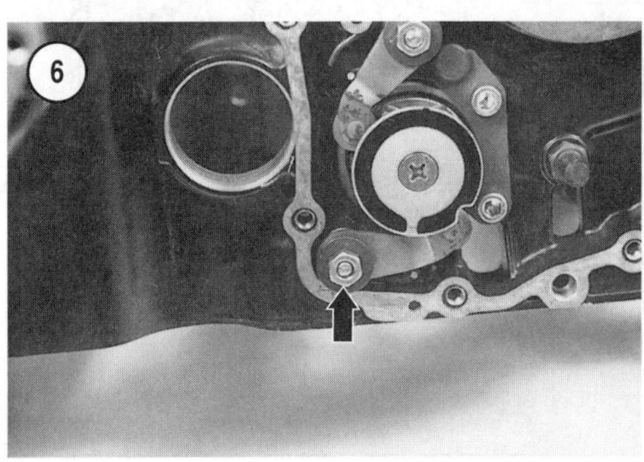

NOTE

Keep the neutral and gear lever parts separate. The neutral and gear levers are identical. However, their springs are different. The neutral lever spring is painted blue.

3. Remove the gear lever (A, **Figure 5**) by performing the following:

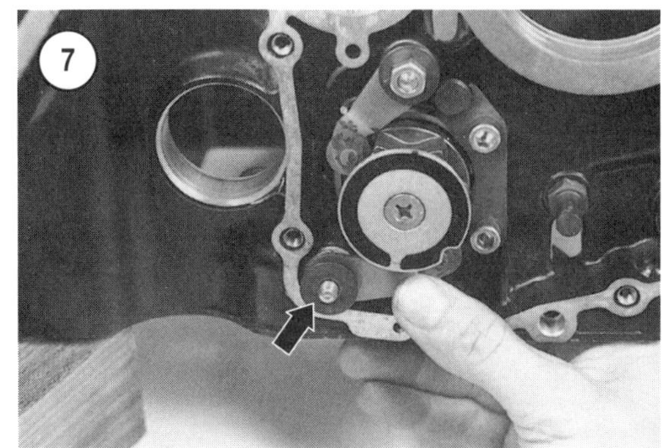

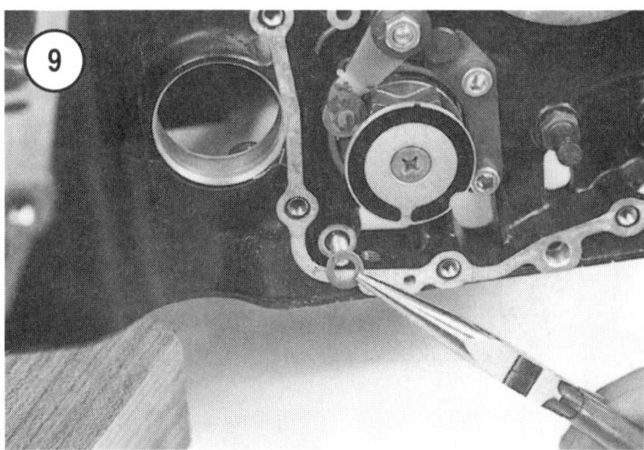

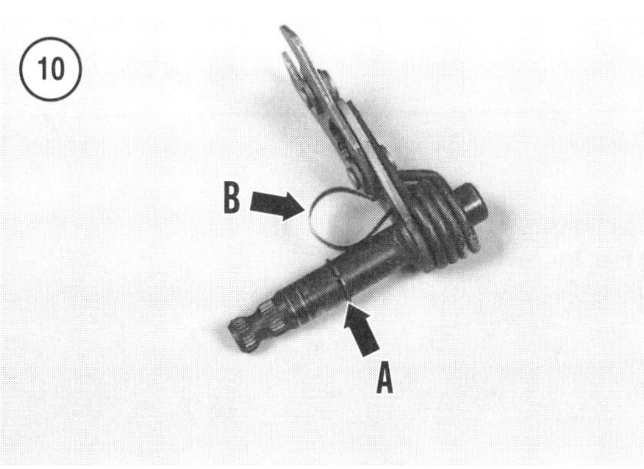

a. Remove the lever nut (**Figure 6**) and collar (**Figure 7**).
b. Pull the gear lever (**Figure 8**) and its spring from the crankcase.
c. Remove the washer (**Figure 9**) from the crankcase stud.

4. Repeat Step 3 to remove the neutral lever (B, **Figure 5**). The neutral lever spring is painted blue. Label the spring if the paint is worn off.
5. Inspect the parts as described in this chapter.

Installation

1. Install the gear lever (A, **Figure 5**) by performing the following:
   a. Install the washer (**Figure 9**) onto the gear lever stud.
   b. Install the gear lever and spring (**Figure 8**). Make sure the lever roller engages the shift cam.
   c. Install the collar (**Figure 7**).
   d. Apply Loctite 242 (blue) to the stud threads and install the nut securely.
2. Repeat Step 1 to install the neutral lever (B, **Figure 5**). The neutral lever spring is painted blue.
3. Install the shift shaft assembly by performing the following:
   a. Set the shift shaft into its boss in the crankcase.
   b. Press the shift arm (A, **Figure 4**) rearward so the shift pawls clear the shift drum. Slide the shift shaft into the crankcase until it bottoms. The arms of the return spring must straddle the stopper bolt (B, **Figure 4**).
   c. Release the shift arm. Make sure the pawls engage the pins in the shift drum.
   d. If removed, install the washer onto the shift shaft and slide it against the snap ring.
4. Install the bevel gearcase as described in this chapter.

Inspection

1. Inspect the shift shaft for bending or spline damage. Make sure the snap ring (A, **Figure 10**) is in place on the shaft.
2. Inspect the shift-arm spring (B, **Figure 10**) and the shift-shaft return spring (**Figure 11**) for cracks or other signs of fatigue. Make sure the arms of the

11

12

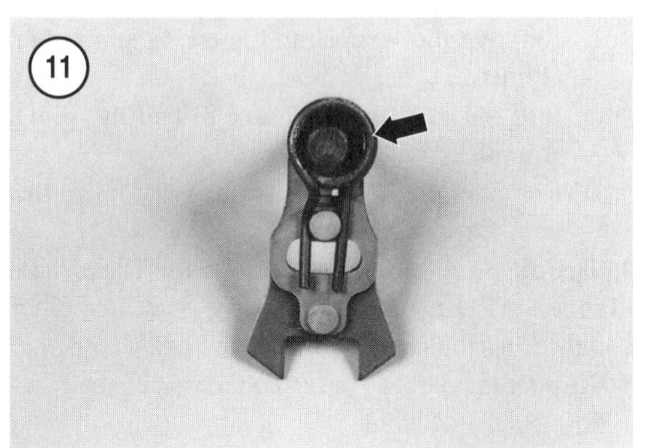

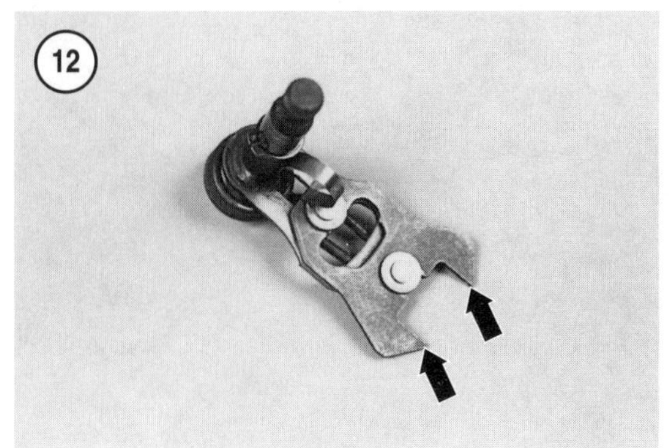

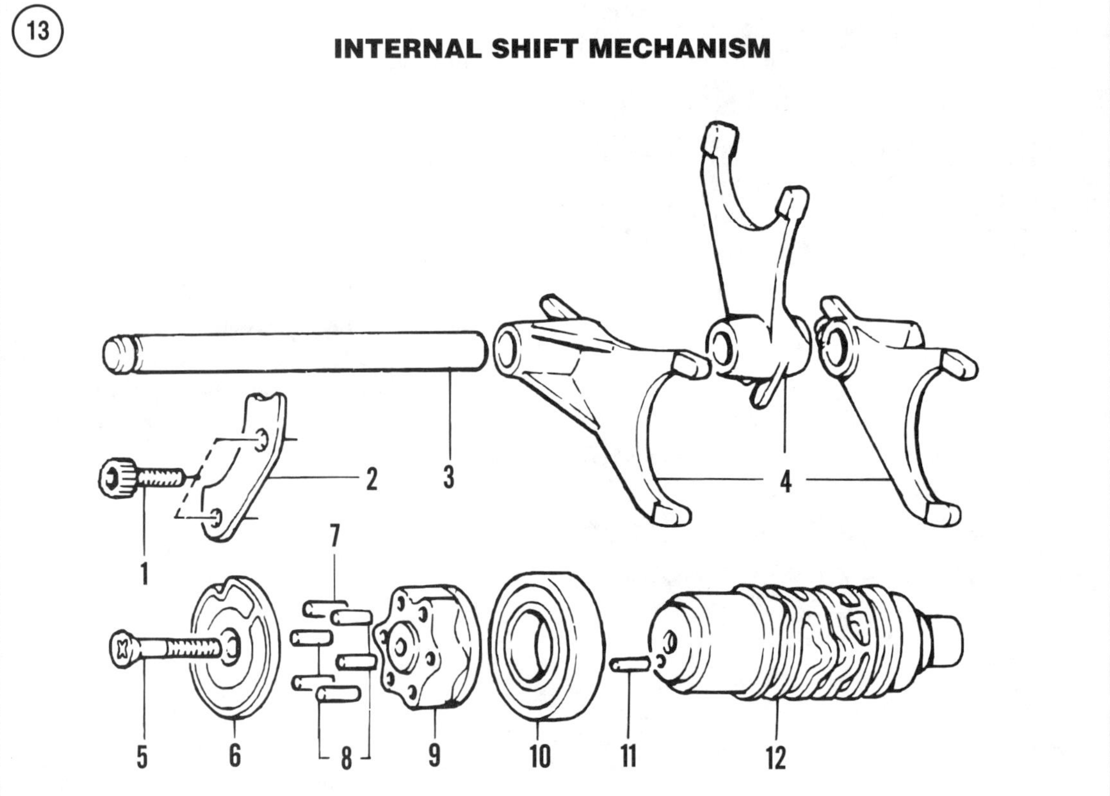

13
INTERNAL SHIFT MECHANISM
1
2
3
4
5
6
7
8
9
10
11
12

1. Allen bolt
2. Bearing retainer
3. Shift fork shaft
4. Shift fork
5. Screw
6. Pin plate
7. Pin (17.8 mm long)
8. Pin (15.8 mm long)
9. Shift cam
10. Bearing
11. Pin (8 mm long)
12. Shift drum

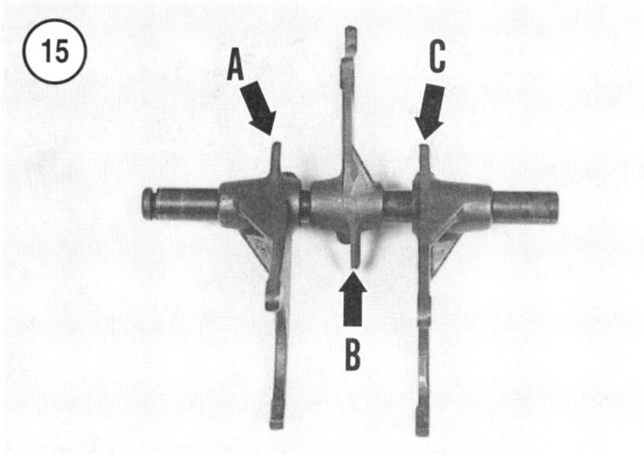

return spring straddle the pin as shown in **Figure 11**.

NOTE
If the shift drum pins are worn or damaged, replace the pins as described in this chapter.

3. Inspect the shift pawls (**Figure 12**) at the end of the shift arm for wear or other signs of damage.
4. Inspect the roller on the neutral lever and on the gear lever. Replace a lever if its roller is worn or does not turn freely.
5. Inspect the neutral lever spring and the gear lever spring.
6. Inspect the stopper bolt in the crankcase. If it is damaged or loose, perform the following:
   a. Remove stopper bolt.
   b. Apply Loctite 242 to the threads of the stopper bolt.
   c. Install the stopper bolt and tighten it securely.
7. Replace any part that is worn or damaged.

INTERNAL SHIFT MECHANISM

Removal

Refer to **Figure 13**.

1. Remove the engine and separate the case halves as described in Chapter Five.
2. Remove the external shift mechanism as described in this chapter.
3. Remove the Allen bolts (A, **Figure 14**) and remove the bearing retainer (B).

NOTE
*The shift forks are identified by shape: the left shift fork (A, **Figure 15**), the center shift fork (B) and the right shift fork (C). Label each shift fork as it is removed so the forks can be reinstalled in their original positions.*

4. Remove the shift forks by performing the following:
   a. Partially withdraw the shift fork shaft from the crankcase and remove the right shift fork (**Figure 16**).
   b. Withdraw the shaft further and remove the center shift fork (**Figure 17**).

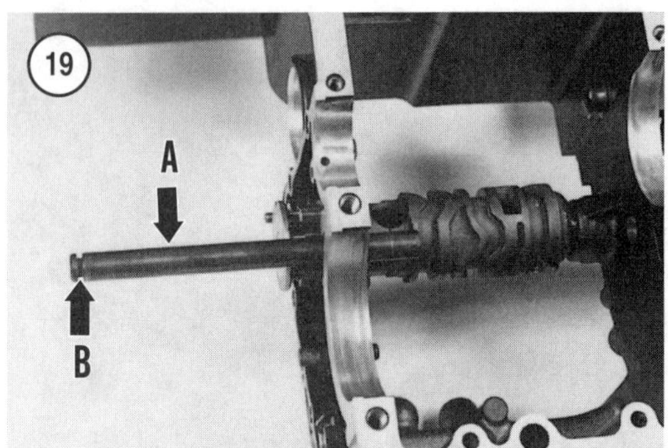

c. Remove the left shift fork (**Figure 18**) from the shaft and remove the fork shaft (A, **Figure 19**) from the crankcase.

5. Carefully pull the shift drum (**Figure 20**) out of the lower crankcase half. Remove the drum slowly to prevent damaging the crankcase bearing surface.

6. Inspect the internal shift mechanism as described in this chapter.

Installation

1. Apply clean engine oil to the bearing surfaces at each end of the shift drum and insert the drum into the lower crankcase (**Figure 20**).

2. Insert the shift shaft (A, **Figure 19**) into the crankcase so the end of the shaft with the groove (B) faces out.

3. Slide the left shift fork (**Figure 18**) onto the shaft.

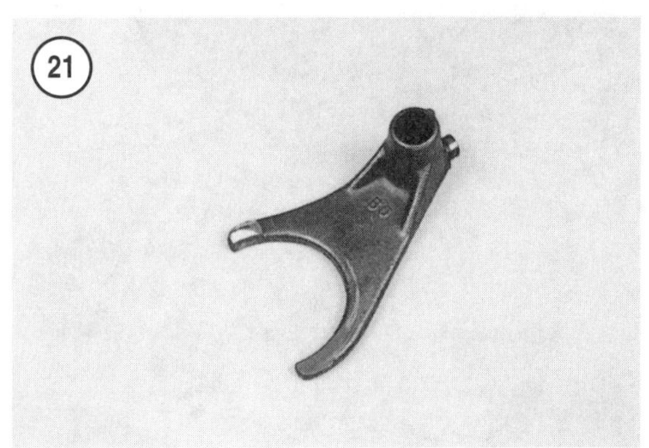

NOTE
When installing a shift fork, make sure the fork's guide pin engages its groove in the shift drum.

4. Push the shift fork shaft further into the case and install the center shift fork (**Figure 17**).

5. Push the shaft further into the case and install the right shift fork (**Figure 16**).

6. Push the shift fork into the case until it bottoms in its boss.

7. Fit the bearing retainer (B, **Figure 14**) into place on the crankcase and secure it with the Allen bolts (A). Apply Loctite 242 (blue) to the threads of the bolts and tighten them securely.

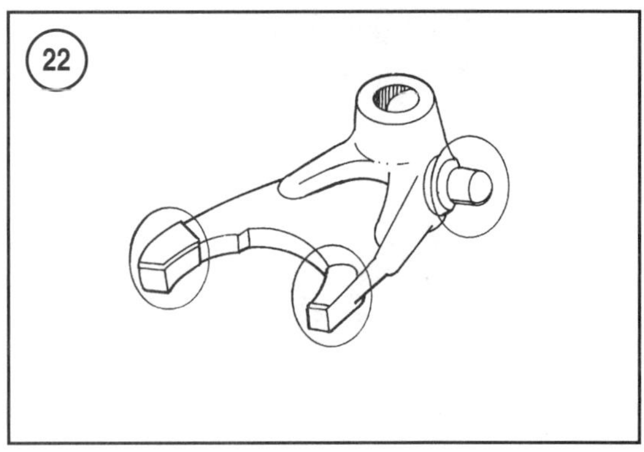

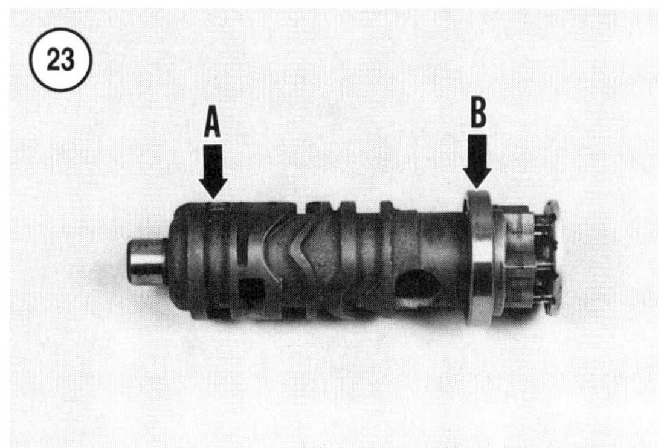

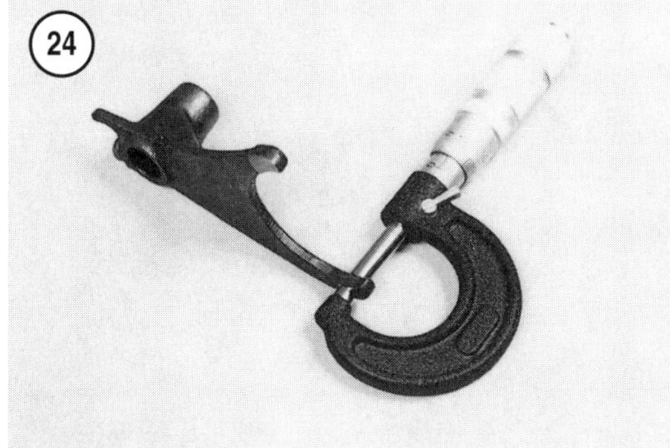

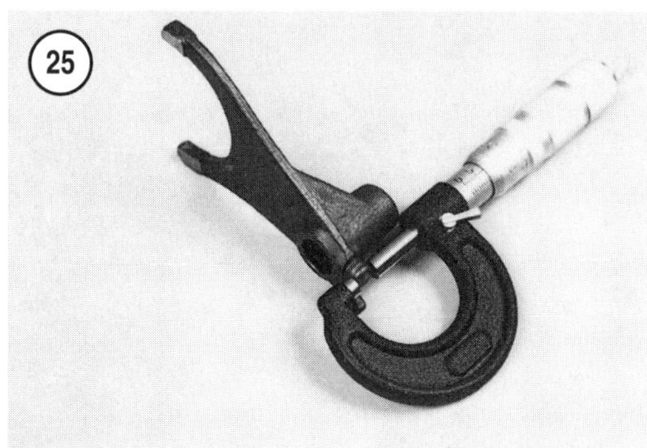

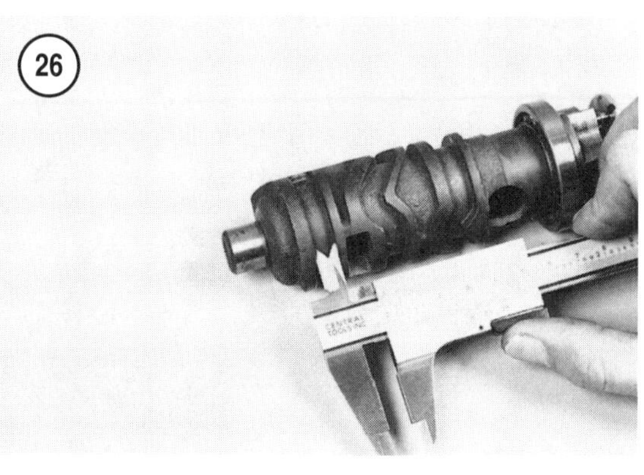

Inspection

1. Inspect each shift fork (**Figure 21**) for signs of wear or cracking. Examine each fork at the points where the fingers contact the groove in the sliding gears and where the guide pin contacts the shift drum. See **Figure 22**. These surfaces should be smooth with no signs of wear or damage.
2. Make sure each fork slides smoothly on its shaft (**Figure 15**). If any binding is noted, replace the fork shaft and the shift fork(s).
3. Visually inspect the shift forks. Replace any fork that is bent.
4. Visually inspect the grooves in the shift drum (A, **Figure 23**) and in the transmission sliding gears. Replace the shift drum or the gear if a groove is worn.
5. Measure the thickness of the shift fork fingers (**Figure 24**).
6. Measure the diameter of the shift fork guide pin (**Figure 25**).
7. Measure the width of the shift drum grooves (**Figure 26**).
8. Measure the width of the sliding gear grooves (**Figure 27**).
9. Replace any part that exceeds the service limit specification in **Table 1**.
10. Roll the fork shaft along a surface plate or piece of glass. Any clicking sounds indicate that the shaft is bent and must be replaced.
11. Visually inspect the ramps and pins in the shift cam for wear. If any require replacement, disassemble the shift drum as described in this section.
12. Spin the drum bearing (B, **Figure 23**) and check for excessive play or roughness. If any is noted, disassemble the shift drum and inspect the bearing as described in this section.

7

Shift Drum Disassembly/Inspection

The shift drum contains several pins, which can easily be lost. Use three or four small containers to store parts as they are removed.

NOTE

An impact driver with a Phillips bit or an air gun is needed to remove the shift drum screw. A screwdriver my tear the screw head.

1. Remove the shift drum screw (**Figure 28**).
2. Lift the pin plate (**Figure 29**) from the shift drum.
3. Lift the shift cam (**Figure 30**), with its pins, from the shift drum.

NOTE

Since three different length pins are used in the shift drum, the pins are identified by their length. All the pins are 4 mm in diameter.

4. Remove the long pin (17.8 mm) from the hole opposite the flat ear in the shift cam (**Figure 31**).
5. Remove the five short pins (15.8 mm) from the holes opposite the pointed ears in the shift cam (**Figure 32**).
6. Remove the ball bearing (**Figure 33**) from the shift drum.
7. Remove the neutral pin (8 mm) from the shift drum. See **Figure 34**.
8. Wash all the parts in clean solvent.
9. Inspect the shift drum bearing as follows:

WARNING

Do not spin the bearing while drying it with compressed air. The bearing is not lubricated and it can be damaged.

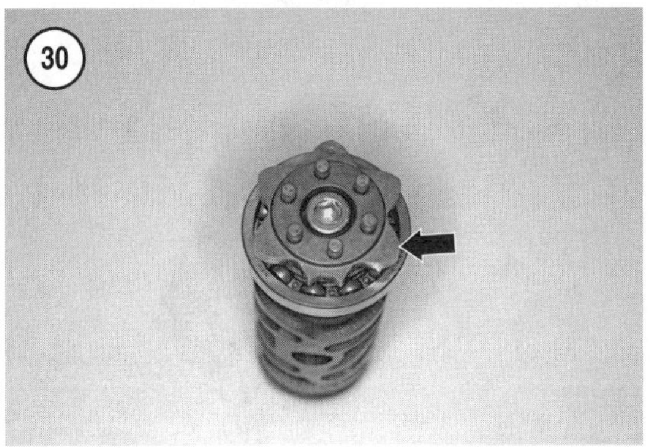

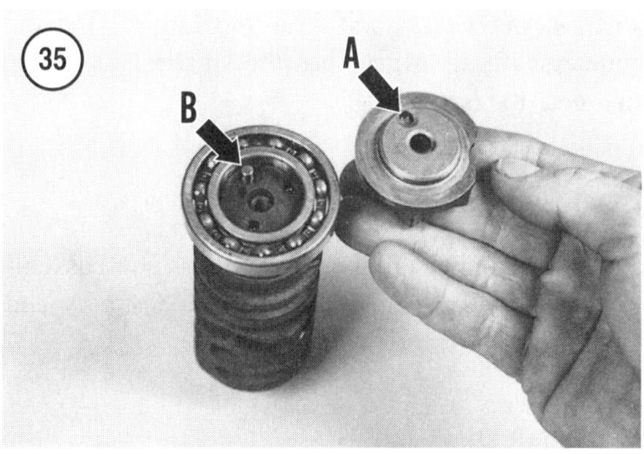

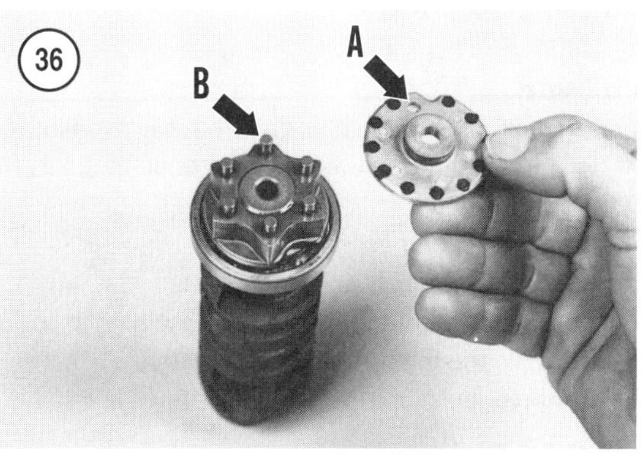

Furthermore, air can spin a bearing faster than its rating, which can cause the bearing to fly apart and cause injury.

a. Wash the shift drum bearing by slowly rotating it in clean solvent.
b. Hold the bearing with your hand so it cannot spin and dry the bearing with compressed air.
c. Once the bearing is completely dry, lubricate the bearing with clean engine oil.
d. Spin the bearing by hand. If roughness or excessive play is noted, repeat the cleaning two or three times. If the bearing still turns roughly, replace the bearing.

10. Inspect the pin holes in the shift drum and shift cam for wear or cracks.

11. Replace any worn or damaged part.

7

Shift Drum Assembly

1. Insert the 8 mm neutral pin into the shift drum (**Figure 34**).

2. Install the ball bearing onto the land in the shift drum (**Figure 33**).

3. Install the five short pins (15.8 mm) into the holes opposite the pointed ears of the shift cam. See **Figure 32**.

4. Install the long pin (17.8 mm) into the hole opposite the flat ear of the shift cam (**Figure 31**).

5. Align the hole in the back of the shift cam (A, **Figure 35**) with the neutral pin in the shift drum (B) and install the shift cam. See **Figure 30**.

NOTE
The pin plate must lie perfectly flat across the pins in the shift cam. If the plate is not flat, the long pin (17.8 mm) has been installed in the wrong hole. Refer to Steps 3 and 4 and reinstall the pins.

6. Align the hole in the back of the pin plate (A, **Figure 36**) with the pin opposite the flat ear (B) of the shift cam and install the pin plate. See **Figure 29** and **Figure 37**.

7. Install the shift drum screw (**Figure 28**). Apply Loctite 242 to the threads of the screw and tighten it securely.

TRANSMISSION

Neutral Finder Operation

Countershaft fifth gear has a neutral finder that keeps the transmission from overshooting neutral during shifts from first gear to neutral while the motorcycle is stopped. The fifth gear has three holes machined 120° apart with a 5/32 in. steel ball fitted into each hole.

However, when the motorcycle is moving, the centrifugal force created by the rotating countershaft forces the balls away from the countershaft. This allows upshifting into second gear. When the motorcycle is stopped, however, the ball on top falls into a slot in the countershaft. This prevents the gear from sliding so upshifting is locked out.

Troubleshooting

Refer to Chapter Two when troubleshooting a transmission problem.

Service Notes

1. Use a large egg flat (the type that restaurants get their eggs in) to help maintain correct alignment and positioning of the parts. As each part is removed, set it in one of the depressions in the egg flat in the same position it had when on the transmission shaft. See **Figure 38**. This is an easy way to retain the correct relationships between all parts.
2. The snap rings fit tightly on the transmission shafts. They usually become distorted during removal. All snap rings must be replaced during assembly.
3. Snap rings will turn and fold over, making removal and installation difficult. To ease replacement, open a snap ring with a pair of snap ring pliers while at the same time holding the back of the ring with a pair of pliers.
4. Install a snap ring so its flat side faces away from the direction of thrust. See **Figure 39**.
5. Position each snap ring so its end gap sits above a groove in the transmission shaft as shown in **Figure 40**.
6. Apply engine oil to the each gear during assembly.
7. The gears on a particular shaft can be identified by their diameter. On the mainshaft, first gear has the smallest diameter; sixth gear the largest. On the countershaft, sixth gear has the smallest diameter; first gear the largest.

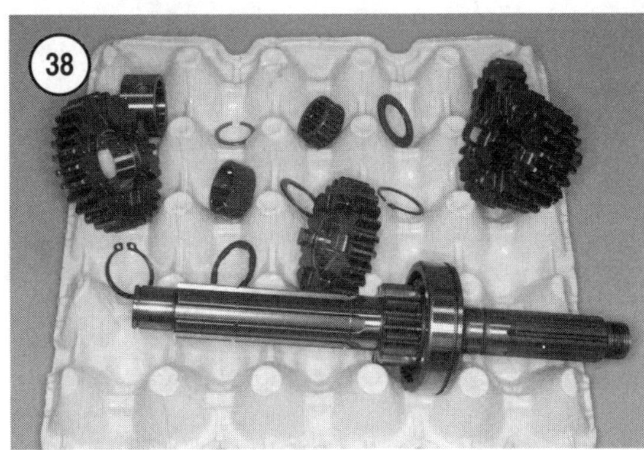

Removal/Installation

Remove and install the transmission shaft assemblies as described in *Crankcase Disassembly* and *Crankcase Assembly* in Chapter Five.

Mainshaft Disassembly

Refer to **Figure 41**.

1. Slide the bearing race from the end of the mainshaft.
2. Pry the snap ring from its groove in the mainshaft.
3. Remove the needle bearing and the thrust washer.
4. Remove second gear.
5. Remove sixth gear and its bushing.
6. Remove the splined washer and the snap ring.
7. Remove the third-fourth combination gear.
8. Remove the snap ring and the splined washer.
9. Remove fifth gear.

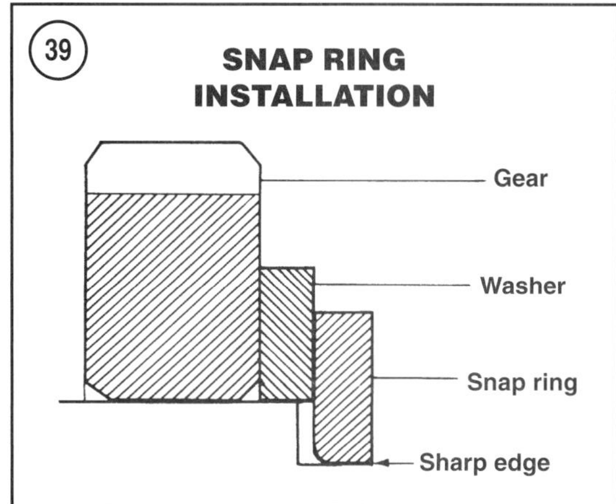

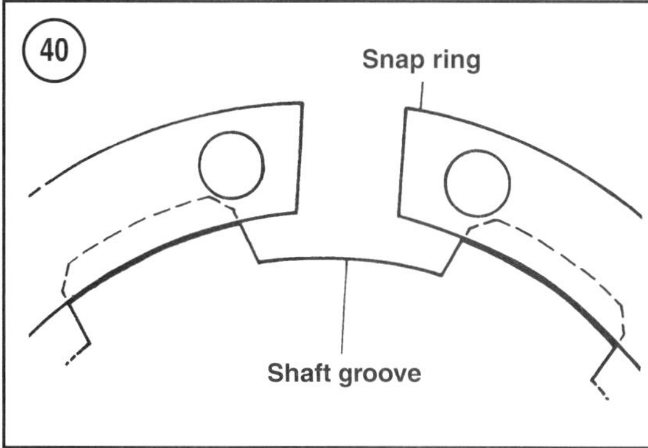

10. Inspect the mainshaft as described in this section.

Mainshaft Assembly

1. Slide fifth gear (**Figure 42**) onto the mainshaft so its dogs face out away from first gear.
2. Slide a splined washer (A, **Figure 43**) against fifth gear and install a new snap ring (B). Make sure the snap ring is completely seated in its groove and that the flat side of the snap ring faces away from fifth gear.
3. Install the third-fourth combination gear so the smaller diameter gear (third gear) faces in. Make sure the oil hole in the gear aligns with the two oil holes in the mainshaft. See **Figure 44**.
4. Install a new snap ring (**Figure 45**) so its flat side faces in toward fourth gear and seat the snap ring in its groove.
5. Install the splined washer (A, **Figure 46**) and the bushing (B). Make sure the oil hole in the bushing aligns with the hole in the mainshaft.
6. Install sixth gear (**Figure 47**) with its dogs facing in toward fourth gear.
7. The splines on one side of second gear are beveled (**Figure 48**); those on the other side are flat. Install second gear (A, **Figure 49**) so the side with the beveled splines faces in toward sixth gear.
8. Install the thrust washer (B, **Figure 49**).
9. Install the needle bearing (A, **Figure 50**) and then the snap ring (B). Make sure the snap ring is completely seated in the groove in the end of the mainshaft.
10. Install the bearing race (**Figure 51**) over the needle bearing.
11. Make sure each gear properly engages it adjoining gear where applicable. See **Figure 52**.

7

Countershaft Disassembly

A hydraulic press is needed to disassemble and assemble the countershaft. Refer to **Figure 41** when servicing the countershaft.

1. Slide the bearing race from the needle bearing on the end of the countershaft.
2. Remove the snap ring, needle bearing and washer from the countershaft.
3. Remove countershaft first gear.
4. Remove countershaft fifth gear by performing the following:
   a. Grasp third gear and hold the countershaft assembly upright so fifth gear is on top.
   b. Spin the countershaft and lift fifth gear off the shaft.
   c. Watch for the three 5/32 in. balls.
5. Remove the snap ring from the countershaft.
6. Remove countershaft third gear and its bushing.
7. Remove countershaft fourth gear.
8. Remove the washer and remove countershaft sixth gear.
9. If still installed, remove the damper cam by performing the following:
   a. Remove the outer snap ring (A, **Figure 53**) from the countershaft and pull off the needle bearing (B).
   b. Remove the inner snap ring (C, **Figure 53**) from the countershaft.
   c. Hold the damper cam with the Kawasaki damper cam holder (part No. 57001-1025) or equivalent and remove the damper cam nut (D, **Figure 53**).
   d. Remove the damper cam.

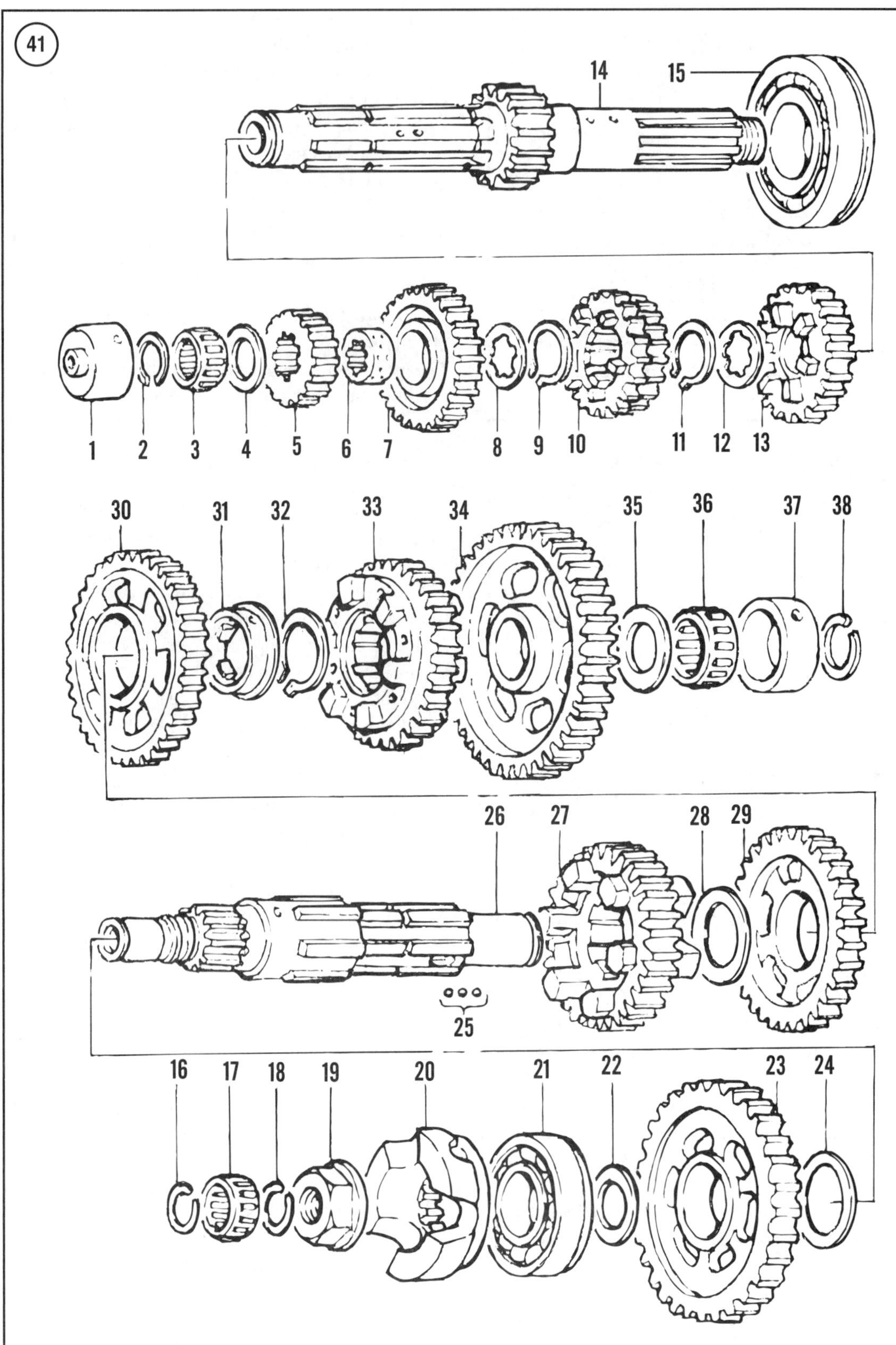
41
14
15
1
2
3
4
5
6
7
8
9
10
11
12
13
30
31
32
33
34
35
36
37
38
26
27
28
29
25
16
17
18
19
20
21
22
23
24

TRANSMISSION

1. Bearing race
2. Snap ring
3. Needle bearing
4. Thrust washer
5. Mainshaft second gear
6. Bushing
7. Mainshaft sixth gear
8. Splined washer
9. Snap ring
10. Mainshaft third-fourth combination gear
11. Snap ring
12. Splined washer
13. Mainshaft fifth gear
14. Mainshaft/first gear
15. Bearing
16. Snap ring
17. Needle bearing
18. Snap ring
19. Damper cam nut
20. Damper cam
21. Bearing
22. Spacer
23. Countershaft second gear
24. Spacer
25. Balls (3)
26. Countershaft
27. Countershaft sixth gear
28. Washer
29. Countershaft fourth gear
30. Countershaft third gear
31. Bushing
32. Snap ring
33. Countershaft fifth gear
34. Countershaft first gear
35. Washer
36. Needle bearing
37. Bearing race
38. Snap ring

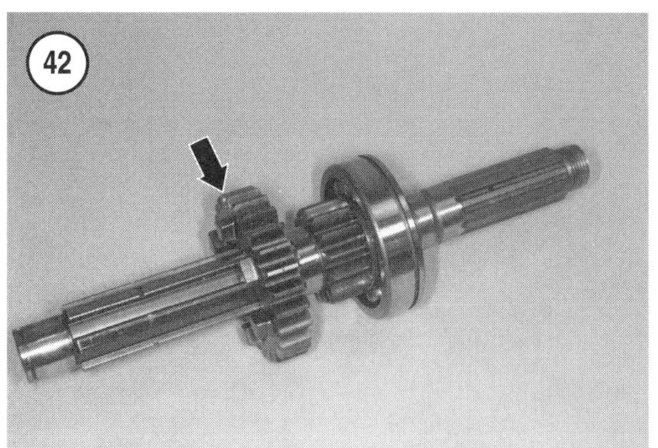

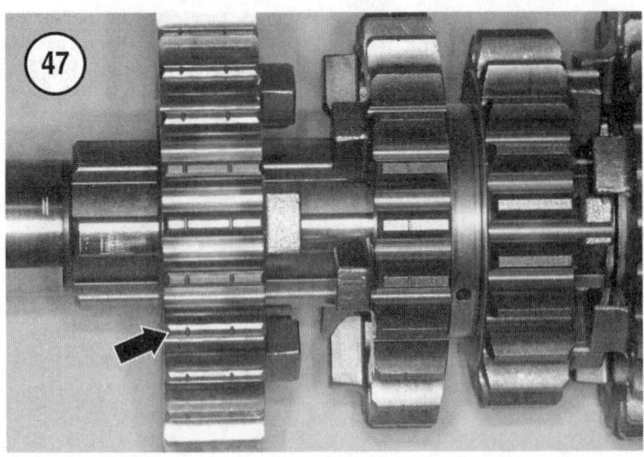

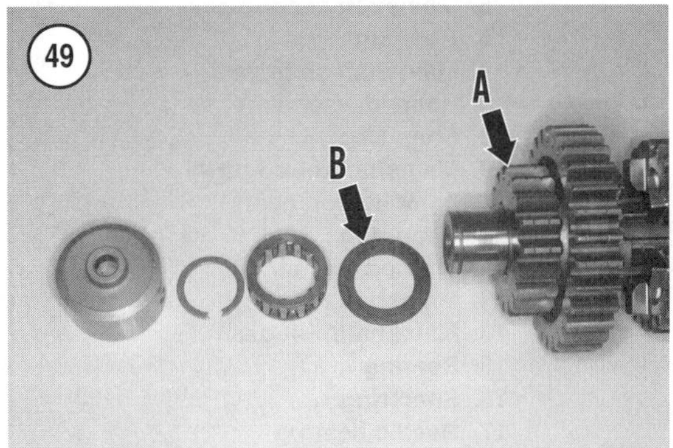

10. Support countershaft assembly in a hydraulic press and press the shaft from the damper cam, bearing and countershaft second gear (**Figure 54**). Watch for the spacer behind the bearing and the spacer behind the gear. Note which side of second gear faces in toward the stop on the countershaft. Mark this side so the gear can be reinstalled with the same orientation.

Countershaft Assembly

1. Slide the spacer (**Figure 55**) over the damper cam end of the countershaft and seat it against the stop on the shaft.
2. Install countershaft second gear (A, **Figure 56**) so the side with the large shoulder faces the stop on the countershaft.
3. Install the spacer (B, **Figure 56**).
4. Lubricate the countershaft and bearing with engine oil.
5. Set the bearing onto the countershaft so the side with the snap ring groove (**Figure 57**) faces in toward second gear. Support the assembly in the press and press the bearing into place with a bearing

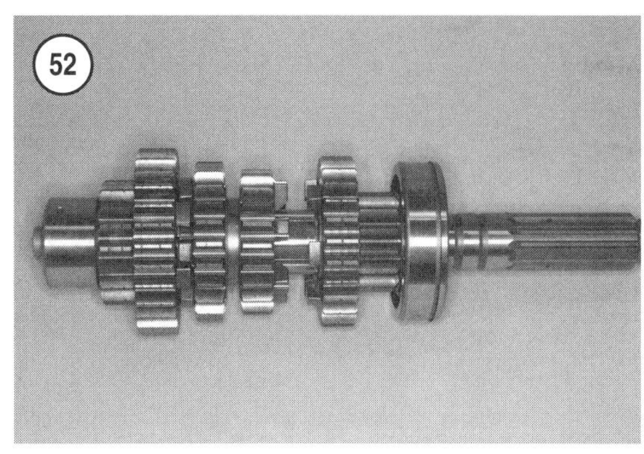

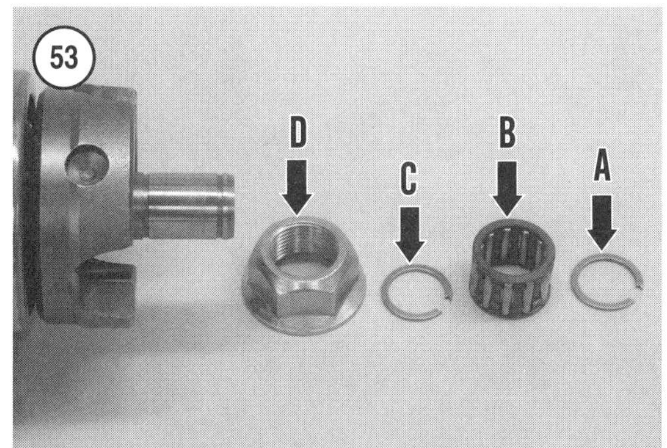

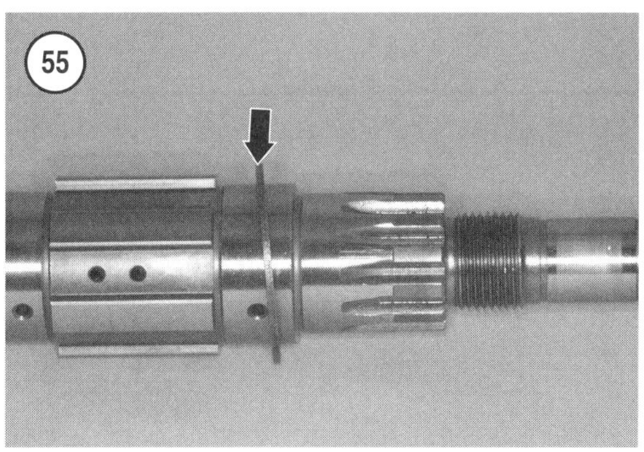

driver or pipe with a diameter that matches the diameter of the bearing inner race (**Figure 58**).

6. Oil the splines of the countershaft and damper cam with oil and set the damper cam onto the countershaft. Press the damper cam (**Figure 59**) until it is completely seated on the shaft (**Figure 60**).

7. Slide countershaft sixth gear (**Figure 61**) over the opposite end of the countershaft. Make sure the gear teeth face in toward second gear and that the oil hole in the shift fork groove aligns with the holes in the countershaft.

8. Install the washer (**Figure 62**).
9. Install countershaft fourth gear (**Figure 63**) so its recessed side faces in toward sixth gear.

NOTE
*Mark the edge of the bushing (**Figure 64**) to indicate the oil hole location. This hole will not be visible once the bushing sits on countershaft third gear.*

10. Install the bushing into the recessed side of countershaft third gear (**Figure 65**).
11. Install the third gear/bushing assembly so the flat side of the gear (**Figure 66**) faces in toward fourth gear. Make sure the oil hole mark on the bushing aligns with the hole in the countershaft.
12. Install a new snap ring so its flat side faces out away from third gear (**Figure 67**).

NOTE
Countershaft fifth gear has two sets of holes along its inside diameter. The small holes are for the indexing balls. Mark these holes so they can be easily identified. Do not use grease to hold the balls in place. They must be able

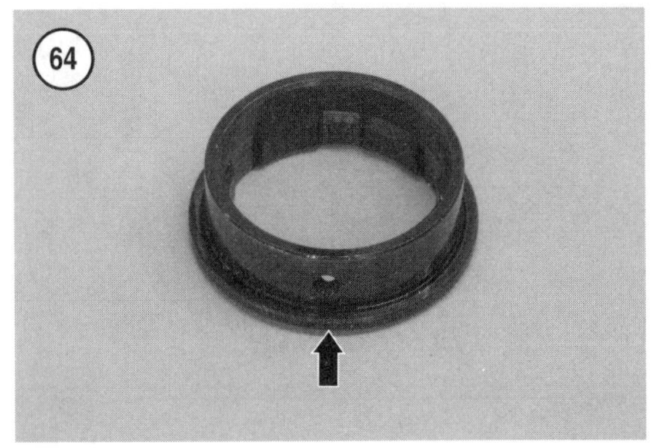

to move freely during normal transmission operation.

13. Install countershaft fifth gear by performing the following:
    a. Insert a 5/32 in. ball into each of the small holes in fifth gear (**Figure 68**).
    b. Hold the countershaft assembly upright on the bench.
    c. Position fifth gear over the countershaft so the side with the shift fork groove face in toward third gear. See **Figure 69**.
    d. Align the ball holes in fifth gear with the ball slots on the countershaft (**Figure 69**) and lower the gear onto the shaft.
14. Install countershaft first gear (**Figure 70**) so the recessed side faces in toward fifth gear.
15. Install the washer (A, **Figure 71**), needle bearing (B) and snap ring (C). Completely seat the snap ring in the groove at the end of the countershaft. See **Figure 72**.
16. Slide the bearing race (**Figure 73**) over the needle bearing.
17. Lubricate the damper cam nut (D, **Figure 53**) flange and threads with oil containing molybdenum

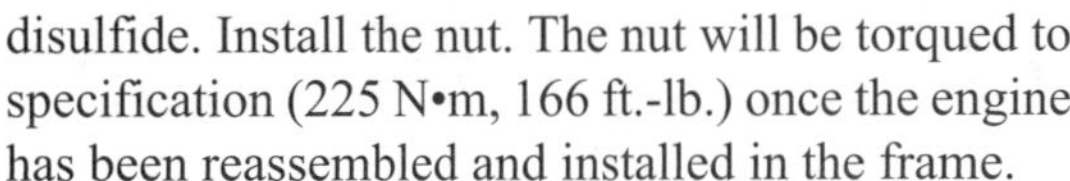

disulfide. Install the nut. The nut will be torqued to specification (225 N•m, 166 ft.-lb.) once the engine has been reassembled and installed in the frame.

Inspection

1. Clean all parts in solvent and thoroughly dry them with compressed air. Make sure any oil hole (A, **Figure 74**) in a shaft is clear.

NOTE
Replace any defective gear. It is also advisable to replace the gear's mate from the opposite shaft even though this mate may not show as much wear or damage. Worn parts usually cause accelerated wear on new parts. Replace gears in sets to ensure proper mating and wear.

2. Inspect the gears visually for cracks or chips as well as for broken or burnt teeth.
3. Check the engagement dogs (A, **Figure 75**) and engagement slots (A, **Figure 76**). Replace any gear with rounded or damaged edges on the dogs or within the slots.
4. Inspect the bearing surface (B, **Figure 76**) in each free wheeling gear for wear, discoloration and galling. Also inspect the bearing surface on the appropriate shaft. If there is any metal flaking or visual damage, replace both parts.
5. Inspect the splines (B, **Figure 74**) on each shaft for wear or discoloration. Also check the internal splines on the sliding gears (B, **Figure 75**). If no visual damage is apparent, install each gear onto its respective shaft and work the gear back and forth to make sure it moves smoothly.
6. Inspect the snap ring grooves (C, **Figure 74**) in each shaft. If uncertain about a groove's suitability,

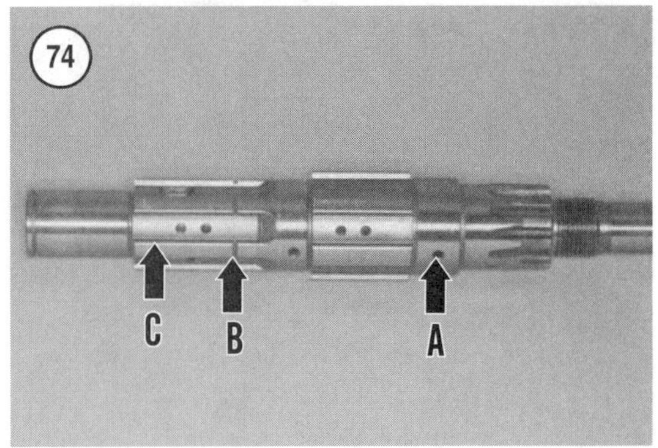

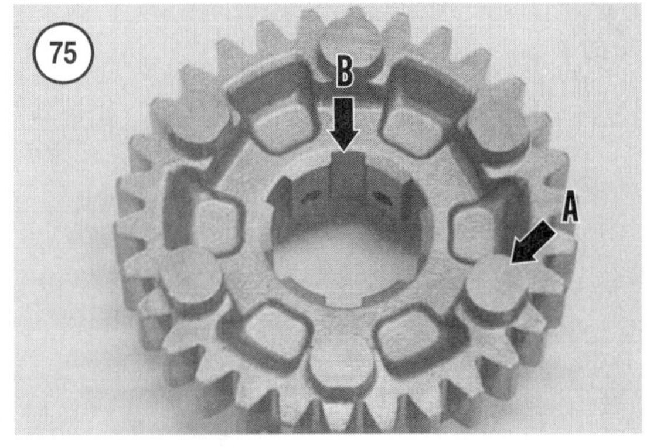

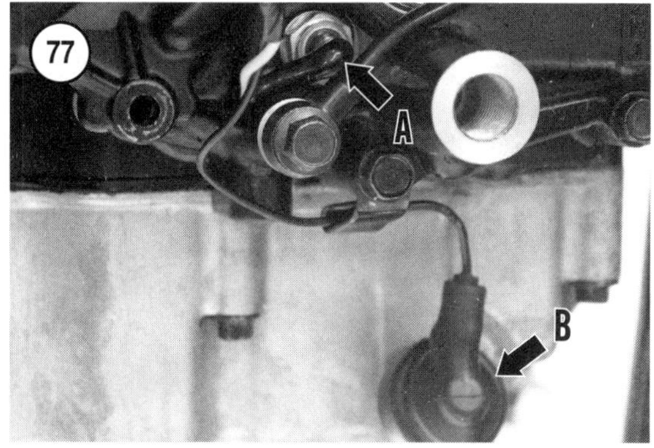

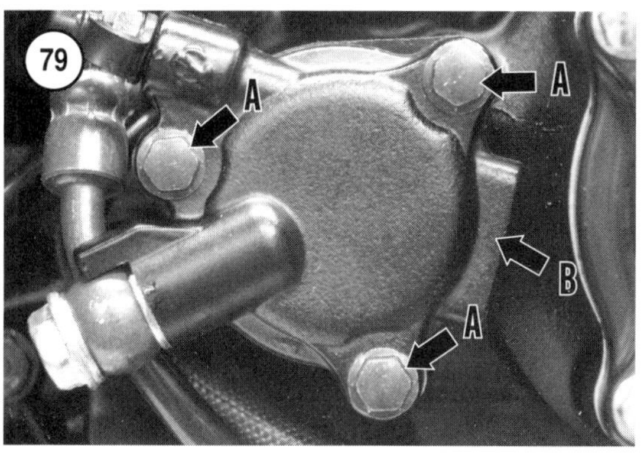

install a new snap ring in the groove. The snap ring should sit tightly within the groove with no appreciable side play. If a groove is damaged, replace the shaft.

7. Inspect the shift fork groove in the sliding gears for wear or damage. Replace the gear(s) if necessary.

8. Replace any washers that show wear.

9. Discard all snap rings and replace them during assembly.

10. Spin each ball bearing. If any noise or roughness is noted, replace the bearing.

11. Inspect the needles and cage of the needle bearings.

12. If any transmission parts are worn or damaged, disassemble and inspect the shift drum and shift forks as described in this chapter.

BEVEL GEAR ASSEMBLY

Bevel Gearcase Removal

1. Securely support the motorcycle on level ground.

2. Drain the engine oil and the coolant as described in Chapter Three.

3. Disconnect the electrical connector from the neutral switch (A, **Figure 77**) and from the oil pressure switch (B).

4. Remove the rear wheel, final gearcase and the swing arm as described in Chapter Thirteen.

5. Pull the driveshaft as described in Chapter Thirteen. Watch for the lockpin (**Figure 78**) that secures the driveshaft to the driven coupling. This small pin can fall out when the bevel gearcase is removed. If possible, use a magnet to remove it now. Store the lockpin in a reclosable plastic bag.

6. Loosen the clamp and remove the U-joint boot from the bevel gearcase.

7. Remove the muffler cover (Chapter Eight).

8. Remove the shift pedal bracket as described in this chapter.

9. Remove the water pump as described in Chapter Ten.

10. Remove the mounting bolts (A, **Figure 79**) and pull the slave cylinder (B) from the bevel gearcase. Insert the slave cylinder into a reclosable plastic bag and suspend the slave cylinder from the motorcycle with a bungee cord.

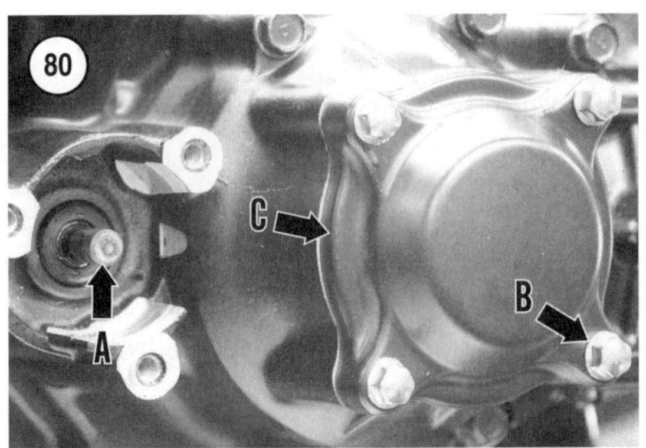

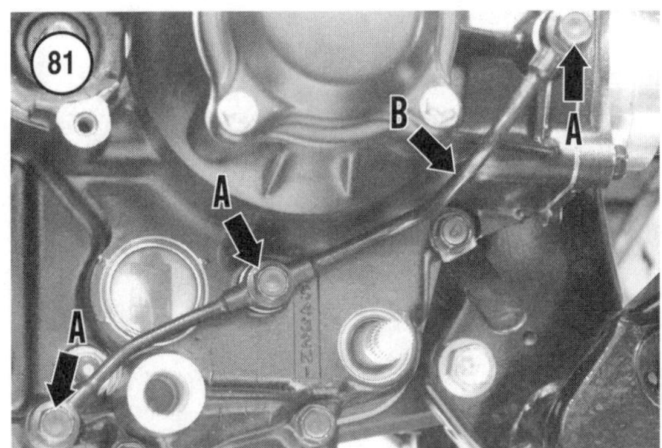

11. Remove the clutch pushrod (A, **Figure 80**) from the mainshaft so the rod will not be damaged as the final gearcase is removed.
12. Remove the banjo bolts (A, **Figure 81**) and lower the oil pipe (B) from the bevel gearcase. Discard the two copper washers installed with each banjo bolt.
13. If the bevel gearcase will be serviced, remove the mounting bolts (B, **Figure 80**) and remove the bevel gear cover (C) from the bevel gearcase. Watch for the O-ring (A, **Figure 82**) behind the cover.
14. Remove the bevel gearcase mounting bolts. Wire clamps (**Figure 83**) are installed behind three gearcase bolts. Note the location of these bolts. A wire clamp must be installed behind these three bolts during assembly.
15. Pull the bevel gearcase (A, **Figure 84**) from the crankcase. Watch for the dowels behind the gearcase. The cam follower (A, **Figure 85**) and damper spring (B) should come out with the gearcase.
16. Remove the gasket and dowels (A, **Figure 86**).

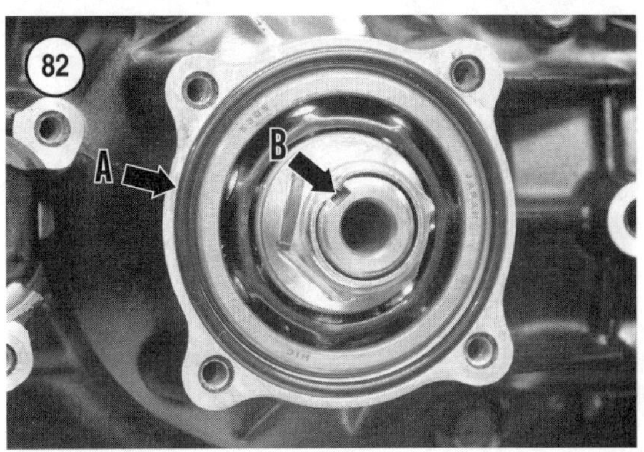

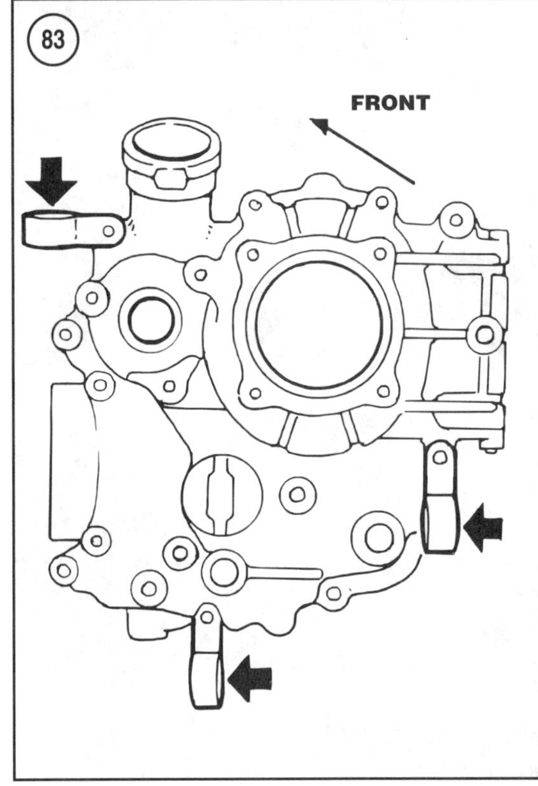

Bevel Gearcase Installation

The Kawasaki oil seal guide (part No. 57001-264) or equivalent is needed when installing the bevel gearcase.

1. Apply a high-temperature grease to the lips of the shift shaft oil seal in the bevel gearcase.
2. Protect the shift shaft oil seal with the Kawasaki oil seal guide so the seal will not be torn when the gearcase is installed. If this tool is not available, apply electrical tape to the splines (B, **Figure 86**) of the shift shaft.
3. If removed, install the damper cam (A, **Figure 85**) and spring (B) onto the bevel drive shaft.

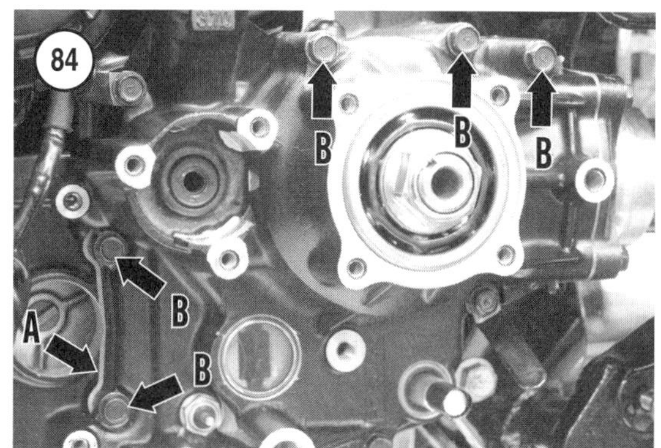

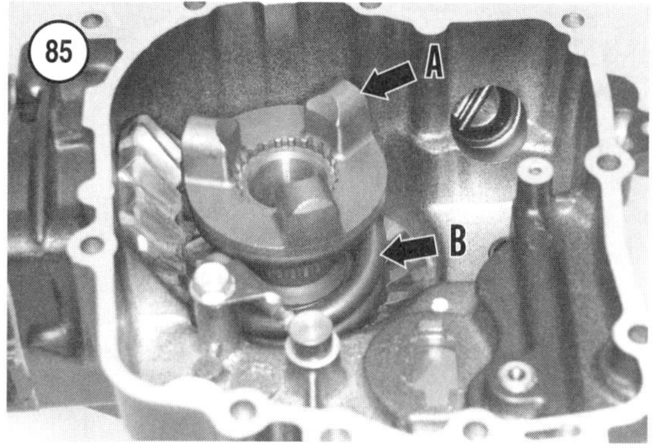

4. Apply sealant to the gearcase mating surfaces on the crankcase where to two case halves meet. See **Figure 87**.
5. Install the dowels (A, **Figure 86**) and a new gasket onto the crankcase.
6. Fit the bevel gearcase into place on the crankcase.
   a. Apply Loctite 242 to the threads of the five bevel gearcase bolts indicated by B, **Figure 84**.
   b. Install the wire clamps where shown in **Figure 83**.
   c. Tighten all the bevel gearcase bolts securely.
7. Install the oil pipe (B, **Figure 81**) onto the bevel gearcase and secure it with the banjo bolts (A). Install two new copper washers, one on either side of the oil fitting, with each banjo bolt. Torque the banjo bolts to 12 N•m (106 in.-lb.).
8. Install the clutch pushrod (A, **Figure 80**) into the mainshaft. Apply oil to the inboard end of the pushrod so the seal will not be damaged.
9. Fit the clutch slave cylinder (B, **Figure 79**) into place on the bevel gearcase. Apply Loctite 242 to the slave-cylinder mounting bolts (A, **Figure 79**) and tighten the bolts securely.
10. Complete the assembly by reversing Steps 1-9 of the removal procedure.

Bevel Gearcase Disassembly

Special tools

The following Kawasaki special tools are needed to service the bevel gearcase. Do not begin work without these tools or their equivalent. The bevel gearcase can not be properly assembled and adjusted without them.

1. Drive gear holder (part No. 57001-1026).
2. Driven gear holder (part No. 57001-1027).
3. Dial gauge holder (part No. 57001-1049).

Procedure

Refer to **Figure 88**.

1. Remove the damper cam and spring (**Figure 89**) from the bevel drive shaft.
2. Remove the mounting bolt (A, **Figure 90**) and remove the oil pipe from inside the bevel gear case. Watch for the O-ring installed on the oil pipe nozzle (B, **Figure 90**).

(88)

BEVEL GEARCASE

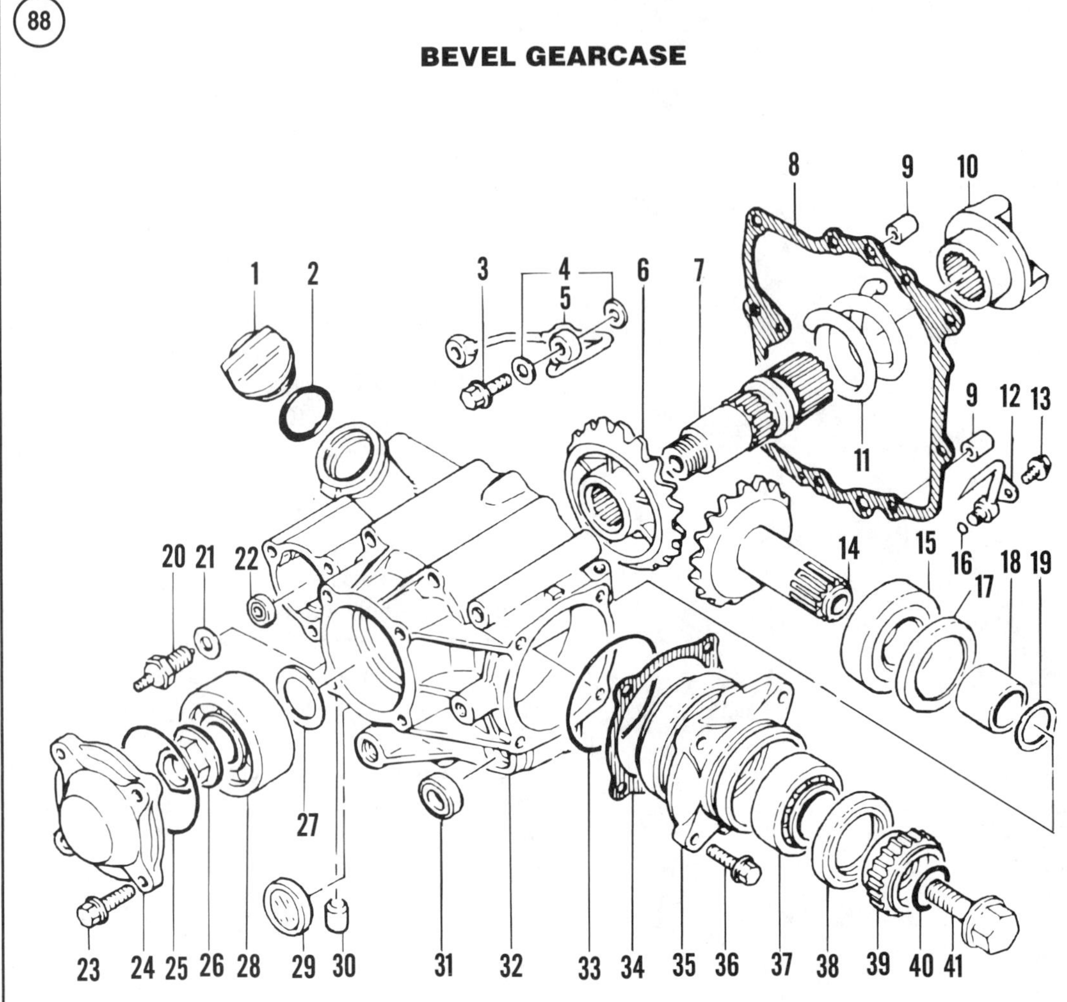

1. Oil filler cap
2. O-ring
3. Banjo bolt
4. Copper washers
5. Oil pipe
6. Bevel drive gear
7. Bevel drive shaft
8. Gasket
9. Dowel
10. Damper cam
11. Spring
12. Oil pipe
13. Oil pipe bolt
14. Bevel driven gear/shaft
15. Bearing
16. O-ring
17. Cup
18. Collar
19. Bevel driven gear spacer
20. Neutral switch
21. Gasket
22. Oil seal
23. Bolt
24. Bevel gear cover
25. O-ring
26. Bevel drive gear nut
27. Bevel drive gear shim
28. Bearing
29. Oil inspection window
30 Plug
31. Oil seal
32. Bevel gearcase
33. O-ring
34. Bearing housing shim
35. Bearing housing
36. Bearing housing bolt
37. Bearing
38. Oil seal
39. Driven coupling
40. O-ring
41. Bevel driven gear bolt

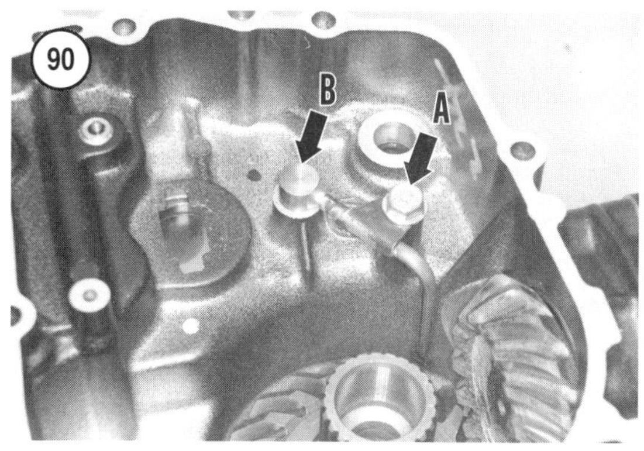

3. Remove the bevel drive gear nut by performing the following:

a. If still installed, remove the bevel gear cover bolts (B, **Figure 80**) and remove the cover (C). Watch for the O-ring (A, **Figure 82**) behind the cover.

b. Unstake the bevel drive gear nut (B, **Figure 82**).

c. Hold the driven coupling with the Kawasaki driven gear holder (**Figure 91**) and remove the bevel drive gear nut.

4. Evenly loosen the bearing housing bolts (A, **Figure 92**) and remove bevel driven gear assembly (B) from the bevel gearcase.

CAUTION
Do not remove the bevel drive shaft, shim or bevel drive gear unless one of these parts or the bearing must be replaced. Pressing the bevel drive shaft from the gearcase can damage the bearing. Have a new bearing on hand before starting this procedure.

5. If necessary, remove the bevel drive shaft, shim and the bevel drive gear by performing the following:

a. Support the bevel gearcase in a hydraulic press.

b. Press the bevel drive shaft (**Figure 93**) from the bearing inner race. Remove the bevel drive shaft, the shim and the bevel drive gear.

6. Use the appropriate size bearing driver or socket to press the bearing from the bevel gearcase.

7. If necessary, refer to *Bevel Driven Gear Disassembly* in this section.

8. Inspect the components as described in this section.

7

Bevel Gearcase Assembly

NOTE
The bevel drive and driven gears are matched. They must be replaced as a set.

1. Press a new bevel drive gear bearing into the bevel gearcase. Use the appropriate size socket or bearing driver and press the bearing outer races until the bearing bottoms in the gearcase.
2. Set the bevel gearcase in the press. Make sure the bearing inner race is supported (**Figure 94**).
3. Install the bevel drive gear onto the shaft and set the shim (use a standard shim if any bearing, gear or shaft is being replaced) into place on the outboard side end of the of the bevel drive shaft.
4. Position the assembly in the bearing inner race and press the shaft (**Figure 95**) through the race until it bottoms.

CAUTION
Changing any part in the gearcase (bearing, shim or gear) affects the gear backlash. When assembling the case, install the bevel drive gear and torque that nut. Set the driven assembly into place and measure the gear backlash while tightening the bearing housing bolts. If gear backlash ever reaches zero, stop tightening the bolts. Disassemble the gearcase and reassemble it with different shims.

5. If a bearing, shim or bevel gear has been replaced, install the standard size bearing housing shim (C, **Figure 92**) onto the bevel driven gear assembly.
6. Set the bevel driven gear assembly into the gearcase so the oil hole in the bearing housing (**Figure 96**) aligns with the oil hole in the gearcase (A, **Figure 97**).

CAUTION
Do not overtighten the bearing housing bolts at this point in the procedure. They must be tight enough so that the bevel driven gear can hold the bevel drive gear while the drive nut is torqued.

7. Make sure the bevel driven gear (B, **Figure 92**) engages the bevel drive gear (B, **Figure 97**) and finger-tighten the bearing housing bolts (A, **Figure**

94

95

96

92). Do not over-tighten the bolts because gear backlash has not been set.

8. Apply molybdenum disulfide grease to the threads and seating surface of the bevel drive gear nut (B, **Figure 82**). Turn the nut onto the bevel drive gear shaft.

9. Hold the driven coupling with the driven gear holder (**Figure 91**) and torque the bevel drive gear nut to 195 N•m (144 ft.-lb.).

10. Stake the bevel drive gear nut (**Figure 98**) to lock it in place.

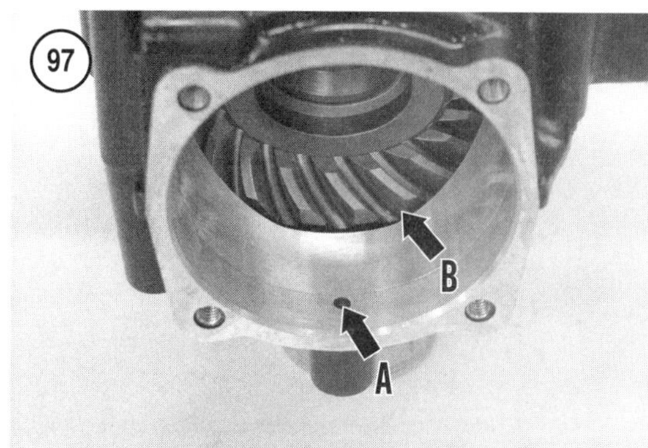

CAUTION
Replacing the bevel gearcase, bearing housing, one or both roller bearings, the bevel gears or a shim affects the gear backlash. Check the backlash after replacing any of these parts.

CAUTION
When assembling the gearcase, measure the gear backlash as you tighten the bearing housing bolts. If gear backlash ever reaches zero, stop tightening the bolts. Disassemble the gearcase and reassemble it with different shims.

11. Measure the gear backlash by performing the following:
   a. Clean any oil or dirt from the teeth of the bevel drive gear and the bevel driven gear.
   b. Install the Kawasaki dial gauge holder onto the gearcase. Set a dial indicator in place so its plunger rests against a tooth of the bevel driven gear as shown in **Figure 99**.
   c. Hold the bevel drive gear nut (**Figure 98**) with a wrench and rotate the driven coupling (**Figure 99**) back and forth. Backlash equals the difference between the lowest and highest reading on the dial indicator.
12. Slowly and evenly tighten the bearing housing bolts to 9.8 N•m (87 in.-lb.). Stop frequently to check the gear backlash. If backlash ever reaches zero. Disassemble the gearcase and replace the bearing housing shim and/or the bevel drive gear shim. Refer to **Table 3**.
13. Once the bearing housing bolts are torqued to specification, measure gear backlash again. If this final measurement is outside the range specified in **Table 1**, adjust the backlash by installing a different bearing housing shim and/or bevel drive gear shim. Refer to **Table 3**. Recheck the backlash with the new shim(s).
14. Check the tooth contact pattern as described below.
15. Install the oil pipe into the bevel gearcase.
   a. Make sure the O-ring is installed on the oil pipe nozzle (B, **Figure 90**).
   b. Lubricate the O-ring with engine oil and seat the nozzle in the gearcase port.
   c. Apply Loctite 242 (blue) to the threads of the mounting bolt (A, **Figure 90**) and torque the oil pipe mounting bolt to 9.8 N•m (87 in.-lb.).

Bevel Gear Tooth Contact

1. Clean any dirt or oil from the teeth of the bevel gears.
2. Apply a thin even coat of marking compound to four or five teeth of the bevel driven gear.
3. Hold the bevel drive gear nut (**Figure 98**) to create a slight drag on the bevel drive gear. Turn the driven coupling (**Figure 99**) and rotate the bevel driven gear through three or four complete revolution in one direction. Reverse direction and rotate

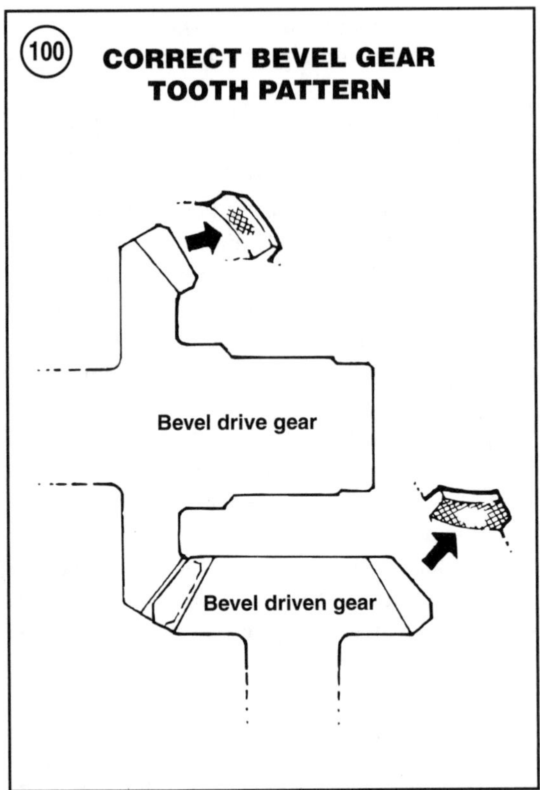

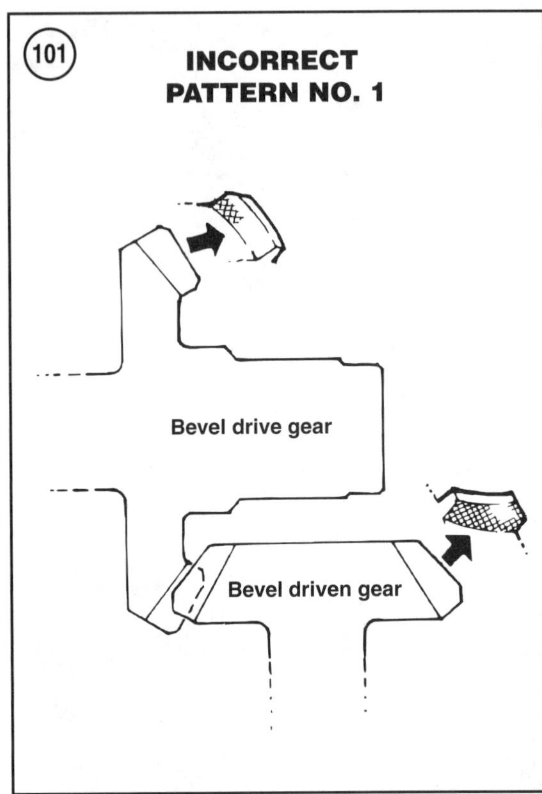

the driven gear through three or four revolutions in the opposite direction.

4. Check the contact pattern on both sides of both the drive and driven gears. The contact pattern should be centered on the face of the tooth as shown in **Figure 100**. If it is, clean all marking compound from both gears.

5. Adjust the tooth contact by moving the bevel gears further into or out of the bevel gearcase.

   a. If the contact pattern appears like the pattern shown in **Figure 101**, decrease the thickness of the bevel drive gear shim(s) by 0.05 mm and increase the thickness of the bearing housing shim(s) by 0.1 mm.

   b. If the contact pattern looks like the pattern shown in **Figure 102**, increase the thickness of the bevel drive gear shims by 0.05 mm and decrease the thickness of the bearing housing shim(s) by 0.1 mm.

   c. Recheck the tooth contact pattern with the new shim(s).

   d. Once the contact pattern is centered (**Figure 100**), wipe the marking compound from both gears and recheck the backlash.

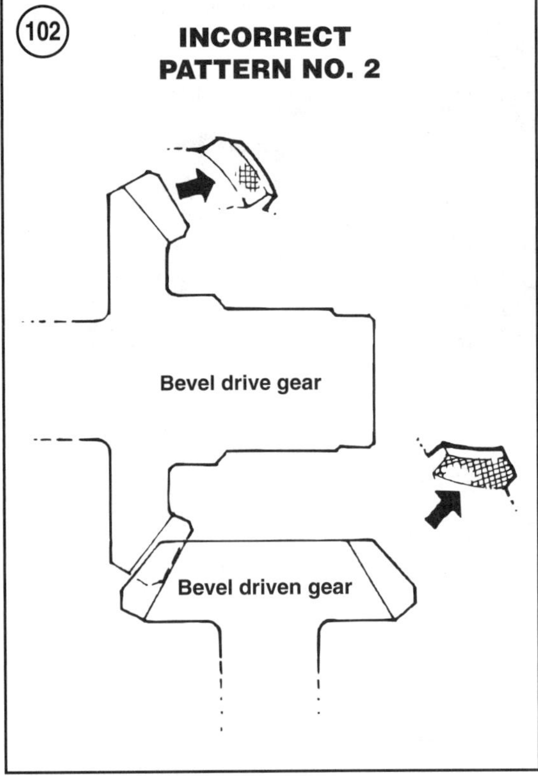

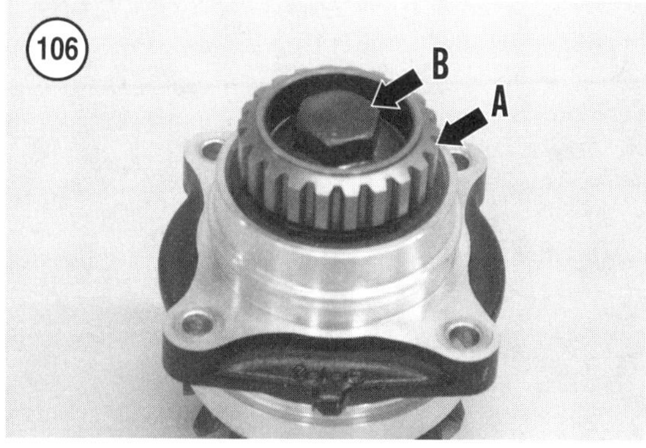

Bevel Gearcase Inspection

During inspection, replace any part that is worn or damaged. The bevel drive gear and the bevel driven gear are mated and must be replaced as a set.

1. Clean all parts and the gearcase in solvent. Dry them thoroughly with compressed air. Make sure no residual solvent remains in the gearcase. It will contaminate the engine oil.
2. Blow all oil galleries clear with compressed air.
3. Check the bevel gearcase for cracks or other damage. Inspect the mating surfaces on the gearcase and on the crankcase. These surfaces must be free of gouges, burrs or other damage that could cause an oil leak.
4. Inspect the teeth of the bevel drive gear.
5. Inspect the splines of the bevel drive shaft.
6. Inspect the shift shaft oil seal (A, **Figure 103**) and the clutch pushrod oil seal (B) for tears, discoloration, hardening or signs of a leak. If a seal requires replacement, perform the following:
   a. Pry the oil seal (**Figure 104**) from the bevel gearcase.
   b. Pack the lips of the new oil seal with grease.
   c. Drive in the new oil seal (**Figure 105**) with an appropriate size socket or seal driver until the seals closed side sits flush with the top of the gearcase.

Bevel Driven Gear Disassembly

1. Secure the bearing housing in a vise with soft jaws.
2. Hold the driven coupling (A, **Figure 106**) with the driven gear holder and remove the driven gear bolt (B). See **Figure 107**.
3. Remove the O-ring (A, **Figure 108**) from the driven coupling (B) and remove the driven coupling from the bearing housing.

NOTE

*The leaf spring provides the spring pressure that acts on the lockpin (**Figure 78**) and locks the engine driveshaft to the driven coupling.*

4. Remove the leaf spring (**Figure 109**) from the driven coupling.
5. Lift the bearing housing from the bevel driven gear/shaft (**Figure 110**).
6. Remove the bevel driven gear spacer (A, **Figure 111**) and remove the collar (B).

7

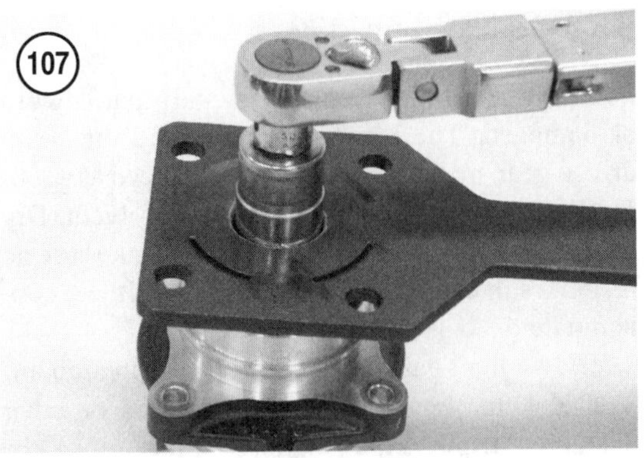

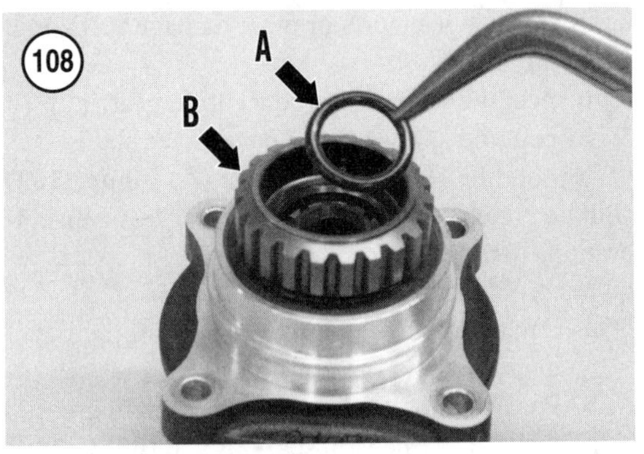

7. Inspect the bevel driven gear assembly as described in this section.

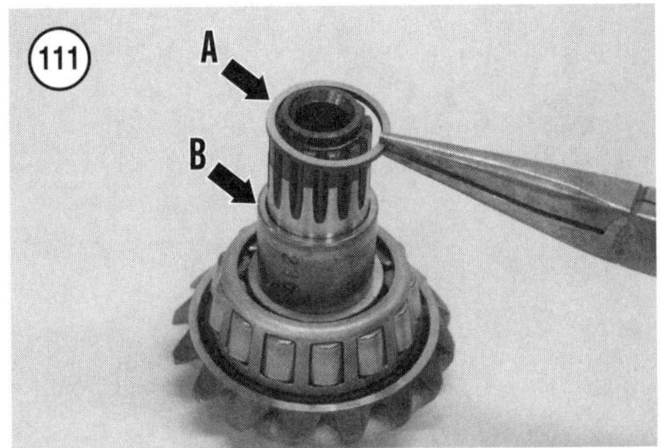

Bevel Driven Gear Assembly

1. Set the bevel driven gear/shaft assembly upright on the bench and install the collar (B, **Figure 111**) and then the spacer (A).
2. Lower the bearing housing over the shaft (**Figure 110**) and seat the housing on the bearing.
3. Install the leaf spring (**Figure 109**) so it is completely seated inside the driven coupling.
4. Install the coupling (B, **Figure 108**) over the bevel driven gear shaft and into bearing housing. Make sure the inner splines of the driven coupling engage the splines of the shaft.
5. Apply oil to the O-ring (A, **Figure 108**) and seat it inside the driven coupling.
6. Oil the shoulder of the driven gear bolt (B, **Figure 106**) so the bolt will not tear the O-ring. Turn the bolt into the driven shaft.
7. Hold the driven coupling with the Kawasaki tool (**Figure 107**). Torque the driven gear bolt to 120

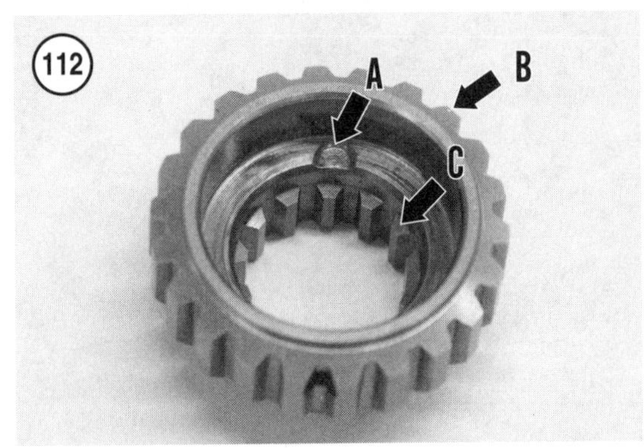

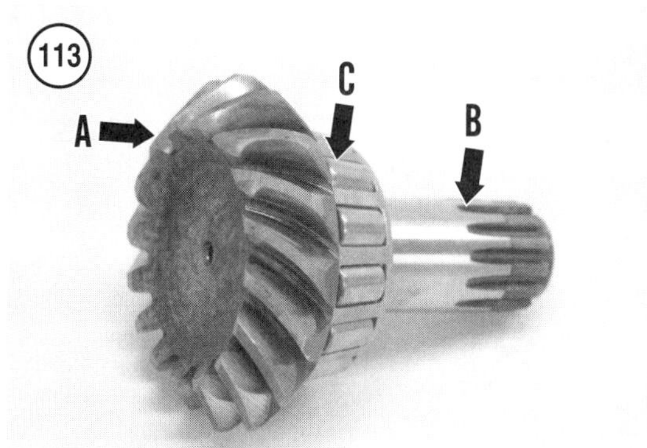

N•m (89 ft.-lb.) and then the stake bolt to the female recess (A, **Figure 112**) in the driven coupling.

7

Bevel Driven Gear Inspection

During inspection, replace any part that is worn or damaged. The bevel drive gear and bevel driven gear are mated. If either bevel gear is worn, replace them both.

1. Inspect the teeth (A, **Figure 113**) of the bevel driven gear for cracks or excessive wear and inspect the splines (B) on the shaft.
2. Spin the bearing (C, **Figure 113**) by hand. It should turn freely without noise or binding. If the bearing must be replaced, perform the following:
   a. Remove the bearing with the Kawasaki bearing puller (part No. 57001-135) or an equivalent bearing puller. See **Figure 114**.
   b. Apply grease to the new bearing.
   c. Drive the bearing onto the shaft with a bearing driver or pipe that matches the diameter of the bearing inner race (**Figure 115**).
3. Inspect the teeth (B, **Figure 112**) and inner splines (C) on the driven coupling.
4. Inspect the leaf spring (**Figure 109**) for cracks or other signs of fatigue.
5. Inspect the oil seal (**Figure 116**) in the bearing housing for tears, discoloration, hardening or signs of leak. If necessary, replace the oil seal by performing the following:
   a. Pry the oil seal from the housing.
   b. Lubricate the lips of the oil seal with grease.
   c. Use the appropriate size seal driver or socket (**Figure 117**) and drive the seal into the bear-

ing housing until its closed side sits flush with the edge of the bearing housing.

NOTE
Kawasaki recommends driving the bearing from the housing. However, the cup inside diameter is smaller than the diameter of the bearing outer race. You cannot get the proper size driver into the housing unless you remove the cup, which will destroy it. Furthermore, you risk damaging the bearing and housing during bearing removal. If the bearing requires replacement, take the housing to a Kawasaki dealership. If you choose to perform this procedure yourself, have new parts on hand before attempting to remove the bearing.

6. Spin the bearing in the bearing housing by hand. It should turn smoothly without noise or binding.
7. Assemble the bevel driven gear assembly without the oil seal and check the bearing preload.

Bevel Driven Gear Bearing Preload

Bearing preload is the amount of force or torque required to turn the bevel driven gear shaft. Bearing preload can be measured with a spring scale or with a beam-type torque wrench. Both methods are described here.

Measure and adjust the bearing preload whenever the bevel driven gear bolt has been loosened and after any bearing has been replaced.

1. Lubricate the bearings with engine oil and assemble the bevel driven gear assembly without the oil seal.
2. Hold the driven shaft with the Kawasaki driven gear holder and torque the driven gear bolt to 120 N•m (89 ft.-lb.). See **Figure 107**.
3. Secure the bearing housing in a vise with soft jaws.
4. Rotate the driven coupling five complete turns to seat the bearings.
5A. To measure bearing preload with a spring scale, perform the following:

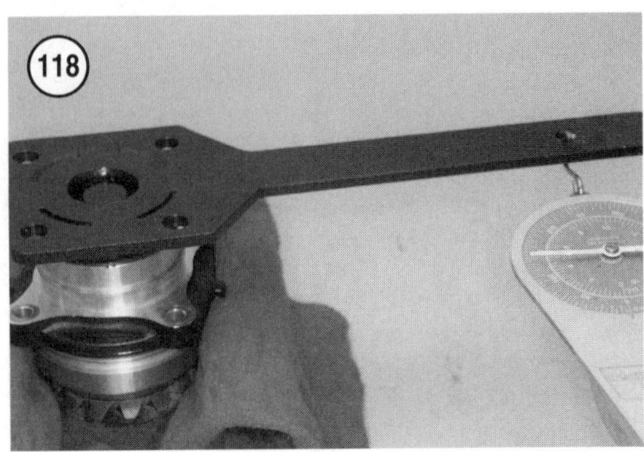

   a. Install the Kawasaki driven gear holder onto the driven coupling (**Figure 118**).

NOTE
The Kawasaki driven gear holder has a hole drilled 200 mm from the center of the bolt for bearing preload measurement.

   b. Hook a spring scale to the handle of wrench so the scale is 200 mm from the center of the shaft.
   c. Gently pull the spring scale until the shaft begins to turn. Record the reading on the scale.

5B. To measure bearing preload with a torque wrench, perform the following:

   a. Set a beam-type torque wrench onto the bevel driven gear bolt.
   b. Hold the torque wrench approximately 200 mm from the center of the shaft.
   c. Apply torque to the wrench until the shaft begins to turn. Record the reading on the torque wrench.

6. If the bearing preload is outside the range specified in **Table 1**. Adjust the preload by installing a new collar, spacer or both in the bevel driven gear assembly. Bearing preload is adjusted by changing the combined length of the bevel driven gear collar and the bevel driven gear spacer. Refer to **Table 2**.

   a. To increase bearing preload, decrease the combined length of the collar and spacer.
   b. To decrease bearing preload, increase the combined length of the collar and spacer.

Table 1 TRANSMISSION, BEVEL GEAR AND SHIFT MECHANISM SPECIFICATIONS

Item	New mm (in.)	Service limit mm (in.)
Transmission ratios		
First gear	3.071 (43/14)	–
Second gear	2.055 (37/18)	–
Third gear	1.590 (35/22)	–
Fourth gear	1.333 (32/24)	–
Fifth gear	1.153 (30/26)	–
Sixth gear	0.965 (28/29)	–
Primary reduction ratio	1.732 (97/56)	
Shift fork finger thickness	4.9-5.0 (0.193-0.197)	4.8 (0.189)
Shift fork guide pin diameter	7.9-8.0 (0.311-0.315)	7.8 (0.307)
Shift drum groove width	8.05-8.20 (0.317-0.323)	8.3 (0.327)
Sliding gear groove width	5.05-5.15 (0.199-0.203)	5.3 (0.209)
Transmission gear lash	0.06-0.23 (0.002-0.009)	0.3 (0.012)
Bevel gear backlash	0.13-0.18 (0.0051-0.007)	–
Bevel driven gear bearing preload		
With spring scale	2.9-4.9 N (0.7-1.1 lb.)	–
With torque wrench	0.6-1.0 N•m (5.3-8.8 in.-lb.	–

Table 2 BEVEL DRIVEN GEAR BEARING PRELOAD

Bevel driven gear collar length mm	Part No.	Bevel driven gear spacer thickness mm	Part No.
22.8	9027-1152	1.70	92025-1072
22.9	9027-1153	1.72	92025-1073
23.0	9027-1154	1.74	92025-1074
23.1	9027-1155	1.76	92025-1075
23.2	9027-1156	1.78	92025-1076
23.3	9027-1157	1.80	92025-1077
23.4	9027-1158	–	–
23.5	9027-1159	–	–
23.6	9027-1160	–	–
23.7	9027-1161	–	–
23.8	9027-1162	–	–
23.9	9027-1163	–	–
24.0	9027-1164	–	–
24.1	9027-1165	–	–

*Standard length/thickness.

Table 3 BEVEL GEAR BACKLASH AND TOOTH CONTACT ADJUSTMENT

Bevel drive gear shim thickness mm	Part No.	Bearing housing shim thickness mm	Part No.
0.10	92025-1016	0.10	92025-1606
0.15	92025-1017	0.15	92025-1607
0.20	92025-1018	0.50	92025-1608
0.30	92025-1019	0.60	92025-1609
0.60	92025-1013	0.70	92025-1610
0.90	92025-1014	0.80	92025-1611
1.20	92025-1015	0.90	92025-1612
–	–	1.00	92025-1613
–	–	1.20	92025-1614

*Standard thickness.

Table 4 BEVEL GEARCASE AND SHIFT MECHANISM TORQUE SPECIFICATIONS

Item	N•m	in.-lb.	ft.-lb.
Bearing housing bolts	9.8	87	–
Bevel gear cover bolts	9.8	87	–
Bevel gearcase oil pipe banjo bolt	12	106	–
Bevel gearcase oil pipe mounting bolt	9.8	87	–
Bevel gearcase-to-driveshaft mounting nut	29	–	22
Bevel drive gear nut	195	–	144
Bevel driven gear bolt	120	–	89
Damper cam nut[2]	225	–	166
Oil pipe mounting bolt[1]	9.8	87	–
Shift pedal bracket bolt (14 mm)	78	–	58
Shift pedal pivot shaft[1]	25	–	18

1. Apply Loctite 242 (blue) or an equivalent medium-strength threadlock.
2. Lubricate the flange and threads with oil containing molybdenum disulfide.

CHAPTER EIGHT

AIR/FUEL, EMISSION AND EXHAUST SYSTEMS

This chapter describes service procedures for the air/fuel system, the emissions control system and the exhaust system.

When servicing these systems, refer to the specifications in **Table 1** and **Table 2** at the end of this chapter. Replace any part that is worn, damaged or out of specification.

WARNING
Some fuel may spill when you work on fuel system components. Work in a well-ventilated area at least 50 feet from any sparks or flames, including gas appliance pilot lights. Do not allow anyone to smoke in the area. Keep a B:C rated fire extinguisher on hand.

FUEL TANK

Removal/Installation

Refer to **Figure 1**.

1. Place the motorcycle on its centerstand.

NOTE
The fuel tank can be removed with the side covers in place. However, the drain and breather hoses can be seen and routed more easily if the side covers are removed.

2. Remove the seat, tool box and both side covers.
3. Disconnect the negative battery cable (**Figure 2**).

CAUTION
The hoses at the rear of the tank are color coded. If these markings are missing or not clear, use colored tape to mark each hose and its fitting on the tank. These hoses must be connected to the correct fitting during assembly.

4. Disconnect the drain hose (A, **Figure 3**, marked white) from the tank fitting.
5. On California models, disconnect the EVAP fuel return hose (B, **Figure 3**, marked red) and the EVAP breather hose, (C, **Figure 3**, marked blue) from the tank fittings.
6. Pull the fuel sender drain hose (D, **Figure 3**) from the frame. Note how this hose is routed so it

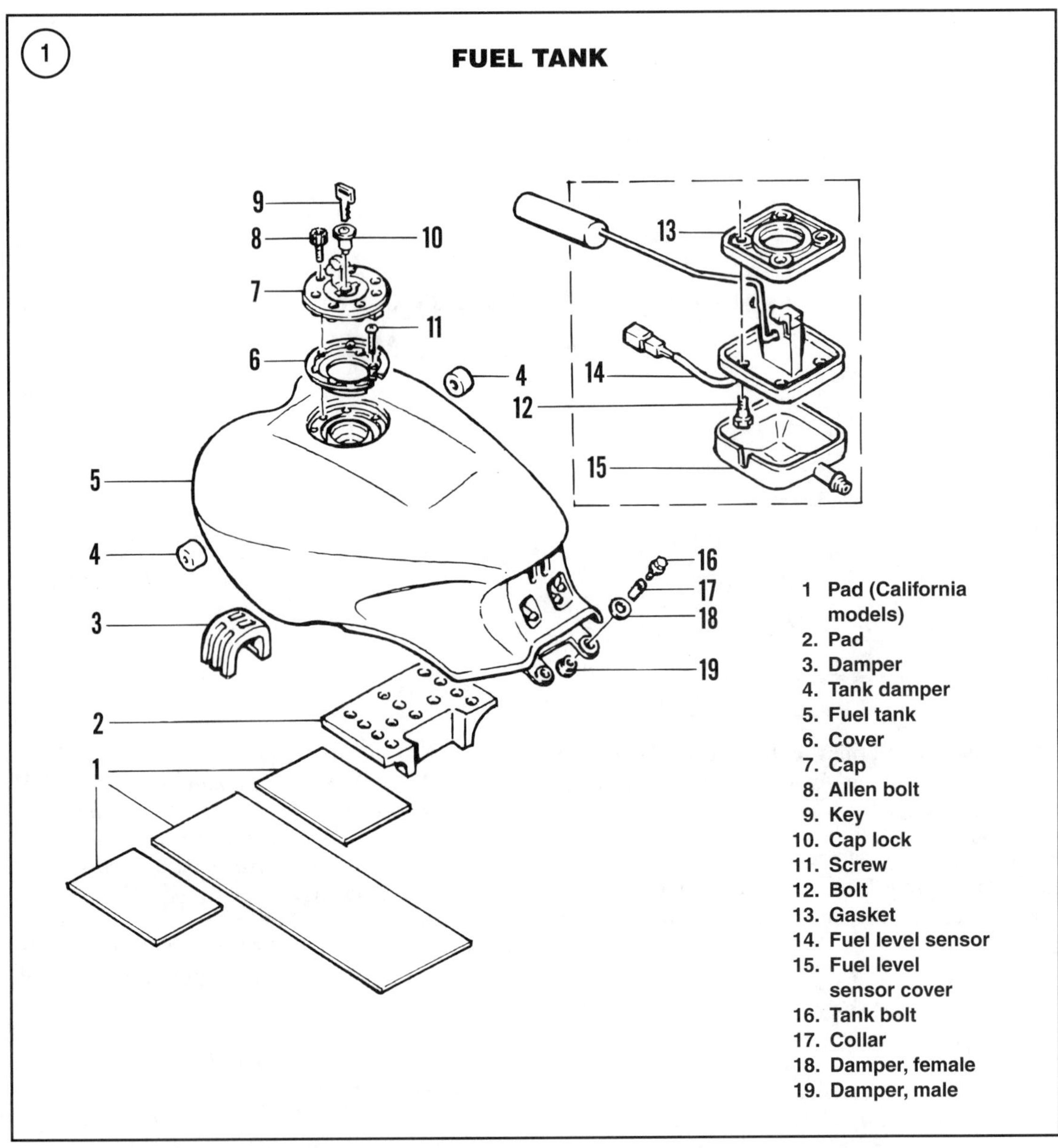

can be rerouted along the same path during installation.

7. Remove the tank bolts (E, **Figure 3**). Watch for the collar and damper installed with each bolt.

8. Pivot the rear of the tank upward and disconnect the fuel sender connector (A, **Figure 4**) from its harness mate.

9. Make sure the fuel valve is on. Disconnect the fuel hose (A, **Figure 5**) and vacuum hose (B) from their fittings on the fuel valve.

10. Lift the tank and pull it rearward.

11. Drain the fuel by performing the following:

   a. Connect a hose to the fuel fitting (the larger fitting) on the fuel valve.

   b. Insert the other end of the hose into a suitable gas can.

   c. Turn the fuel valve to prime and drain the fuel into the gas can.

12. Inspect the fuel tank as described in this chapter.

13. Installation is the reverse of removal; pay attention to the following:

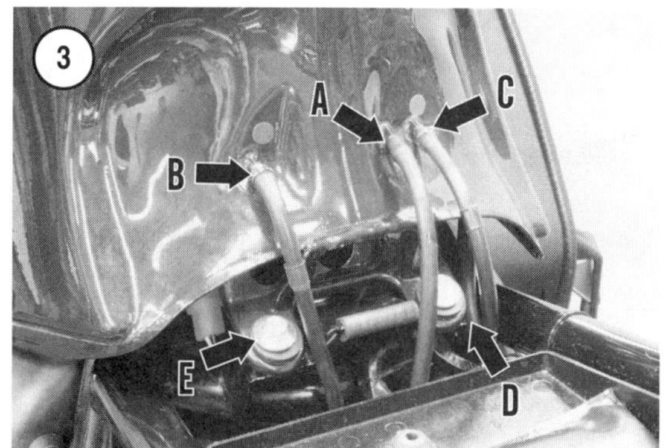

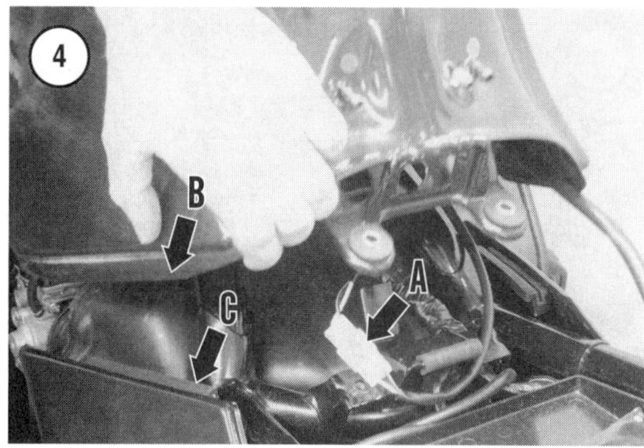

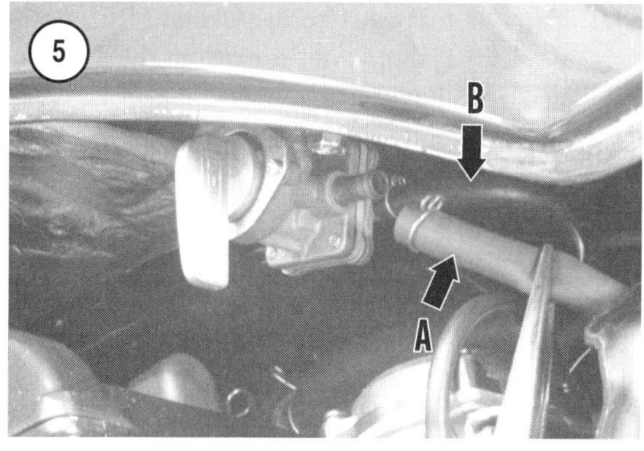

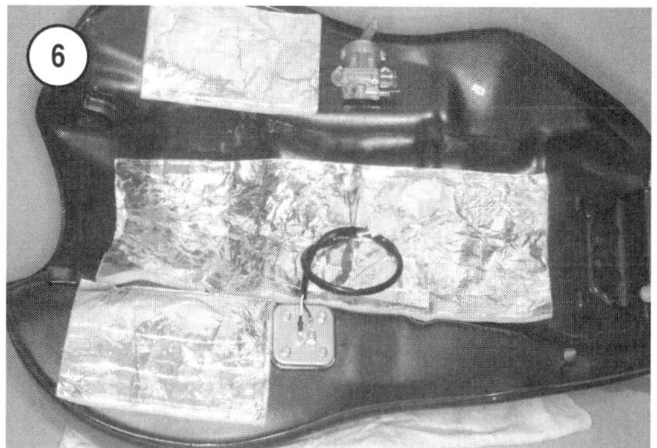

a. Position the tank over the frame. Lower the front of the tank until mounting bosses engage the round dampers on the frame, then lower the rear of the tank into place.

b. Route the fuel sender drain hose (D, **Figure 3**) down the right side of the frame. Follow the same path as the other hoses.

c. Connect each hose to its original fitting on the fuel tank and fuel valve.

d. Secure the hoses in place with their clamps.

e. Lower the fuel tank into place. If the side covers are installed, make sure the edge of the tank (B, **Figure 4**) seats in the grommet (C) on each side cover.

f. Install a collar and damper with each tank bolt. Tighten the bolts securely.

Inspection

1. Inspect all hoses for cracks, deterioration or other damage. The hoses must be flexible and strong enough to withstand engine heat and vibration.

2. Inspect dampers for wear or damage. Replace the dampers if necessary.

3. Inspect the insulation underneath the fuel tank (**Figure 6**). It must be in good condition.

4. Service the fuel valve and fuel level sensor as described in this chapter.

5. Open the tank filler cap and inspect the gaskets. Replace the filler cap if they are damaged or starting to deteriorate.

6. Clean the tank by swirling high-flashpoint solvent around the inside the tank. Pour out the solvent. Let the tank dry thoroughly.

FUEL LEVEL SENSOR

Removal/Installation

The fuel level sensor is part of the fuel gauge circuit. Refer to this circuit in Chapter Nine for fuel level sensor testing.

See **Figure 1** when servicing the fuel level sensor.

1. Remove the tank and drain the fuel as described in this chapter.
2. Remove the cover (A, **Figure 7**) from the fuel level sensor and release the drain hose from the clamp (B).
3. Remove the mounting bolts (**Figure 8**) and pull the fuel level sensor (**Figure 9**) from the tank.
4. Installation is the reverse of removal. Replace the gasket if necessary.

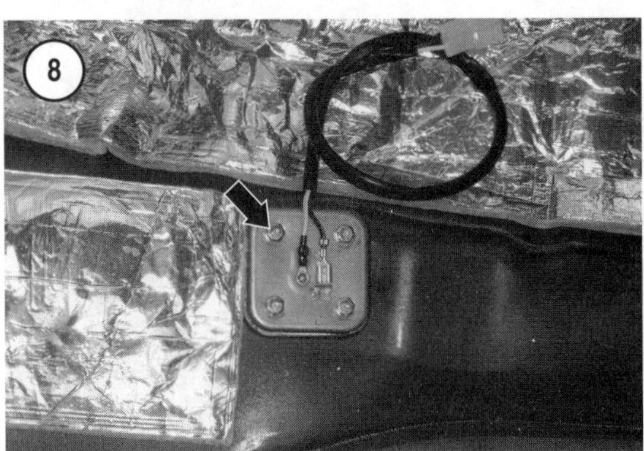

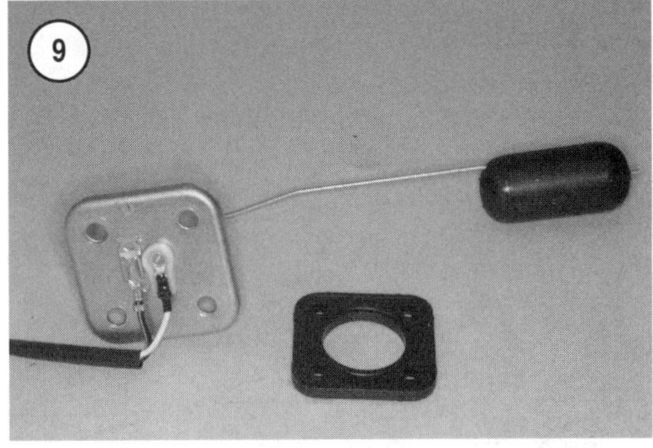

FUEL VALVE

The vacuum-operated fuel valve does not have an off position. When turned to the ON or RESERVE position, fuel should not flow through the valve until the engine is running. In PRI (prime), the fuel flows whether the engine is running or not.

Removal/Installation

Refer to **Figure 10**.

1. Remove the tank and drain the fuel as described in this chapter.
2. Remove the fuel valve mounting bolts (**Figure 11**) with their nylon washers.
3. Remove the fuel valve and its O-ring from the fuel tank.
4. Inspect the fuel valve O-ring.
5. Clean the screen with high-flashpoint solvent.
6. Pour solvent through the valve and clean the valve in each operating position.
7. Dry the fuel valve with compressed air.
8. Installation is the reverse of removal. Note the following:
   a. Make sure the nylon washers are in good condition so fuel will not leak past them. When in doubt, replace the washers.
   b. Do not use steel washers with the mounting bolts. Steel washers will not seal properly.
   c. Add a small amount of fuel to the tank and check for leaks.
   d. Turn the fuel valve to the ON and RES positions. Fuel should not flow from the valve in these positions.

Inspection

1. Refer to **Figure 10** and disassemble the fuel valve.
2. Check the diaphragm. Look for pin holes or other damage. Make sure the diaphragm is clean.

(10)

FUEL VALVE

1. Screw
2. Cover plate
3. Washer
4. Lever
5. O-ring
6. Valve gasket
7. Valve body
8. Bolt
9. Nylon washer
10. O-ring
11. O-ring
12. Diaphragm
13. Spring
14. Diaphragm cover
15. Screw

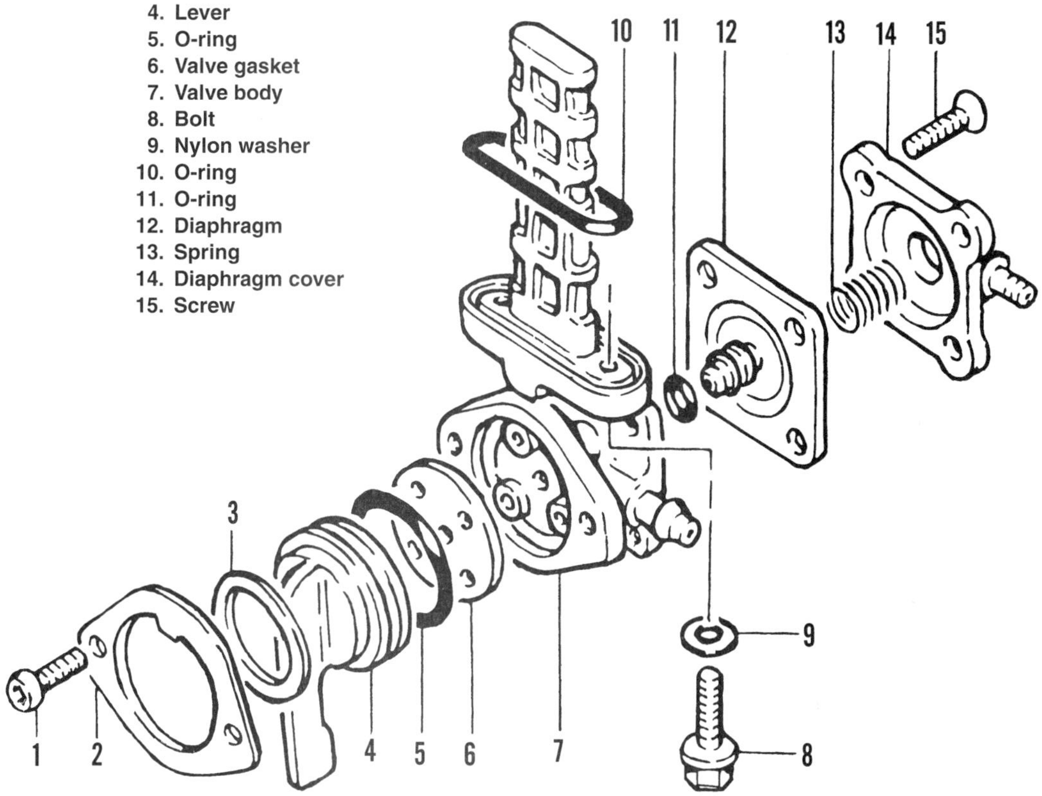

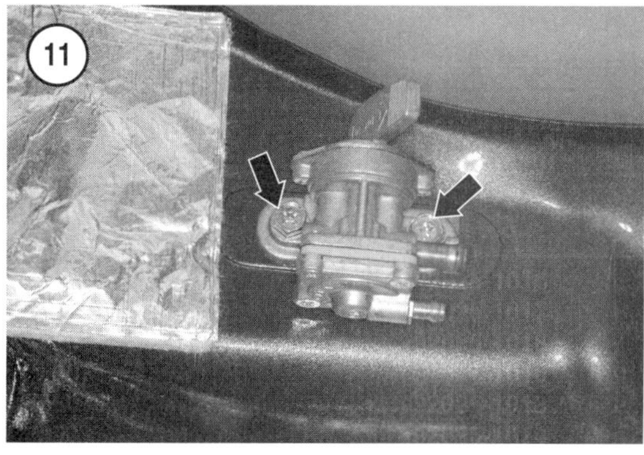

3. Check the O-ring for damage. Clean it carefully. Any debris on the O-ring will prevent the valve from completely closing.

4. If the fuel valve leaks or if fuel flows when the valve is in the on or reserve positions (and the engine is not running), check the O-rings (5, 10 and 11, **Figure 10**) and gasket (6, **Figure 10**). Replace them as necessary.

5. Make sure the diaphragm spring is in place and install the diaphragm cover.

12

AIR FILTER HOUSING ASSEMBLY

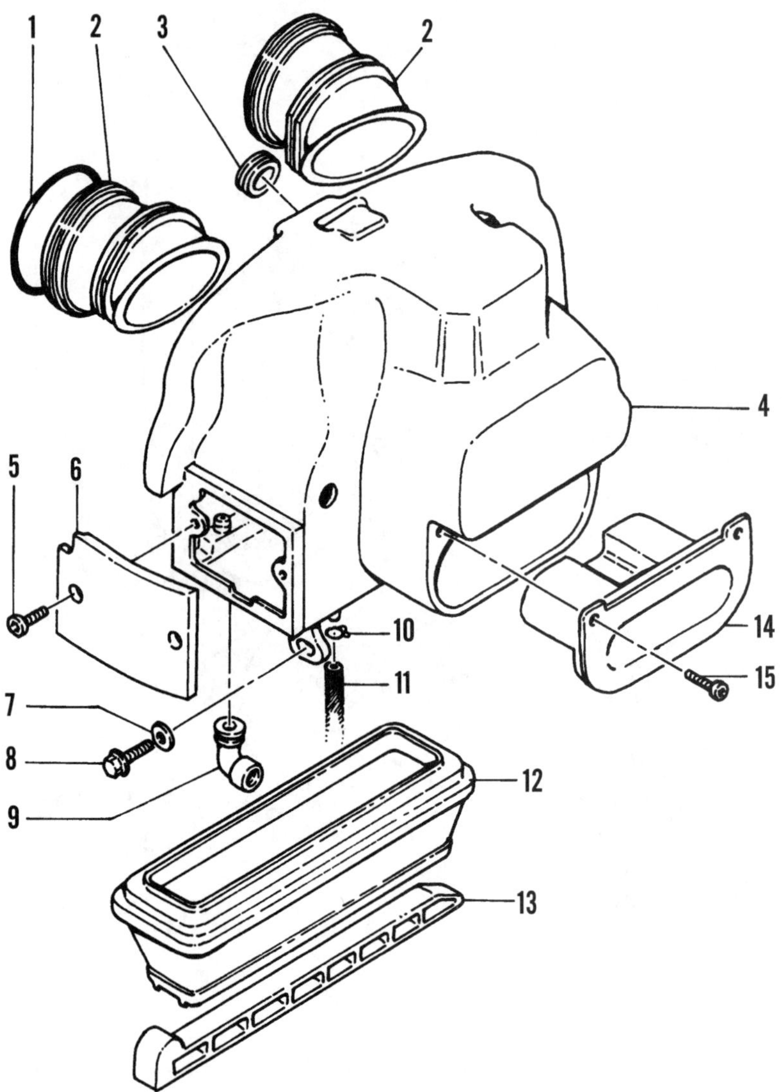

1. Ring clamp
2. Hose
3. Grommet (USA, California, and Switzerland models)
4. Housing
5. Screw
6. Cover
7. Washer
8. Bolt
9. Breather tube
10. Hose clamp
11. Hose
12. Filter element
13. Element holder
14. Intake duct
15. Screw

AIR FILTER HOUSING

Refer to the procedure in Chapter Three for air filter replacement.

Removal

Refer to **Figure 12**.

1. Remove the fuel tank as described in this chapter.
2. Remove the carburetor assembly as described in this chapter.
3. On models with a secondary air system, disconnect the vacuum switch hose (A, **Figure 13**) from the front of the air filter housing if still installed.
4. On California models, disconnect the charcoal canister's green purge hose (A, **Figure 14**) from the upper port on the left side of the air box.
5. Remove the mounting bolt (B, **Figure 14**) and its washer from each side.
6. Note how the air filter breather hose (C, **Figure 14**) is routed between the engine and the swing arm. The hose must be rerouted along the same path during assembly.
7. Slide the housing forward and disconnect the elbow (A, **Figure 15**) from the port (B) on the crankcase breather cover.
8. Remove the air filter housing from the engine.
9. Inspect the air filter housing as described in this section.

Installation

1. Insert the air filter housing into the frame so the elbow on the housing (A, **Figure 15**) aligns with the port (B) on the crankcase breather cover.
2. Slide the housing rearward and connect the elbow to the breather cover.
3. Route the breather hose (C, **Figure 14**) between the engine and swing arm. Follow the same path noted during removal.
4. On California models, connect the charcoal canister's green purge hose (A, **Figure 14**) to the housing.
5. Loosely install the housing mounting bolts (B, **Figure 14**) through the mounting slots. Push the housing rearward as far and possible and tighten the bolts. This provides maximum clearance for carburetor installation. Once the carburetors are installed, the bolts can be loosened and the housing moved forward as necessary.
6. On models with a secondary air system, install the vacuum switch hose (A, **Figure 13**) to the air filter housing once the carburetors are installed.

Inspection

1. If still installed, remove the air filter as described in Chapter Three.

2. Wipe out the inside of the air filter housing and cover with a clean rag.
3. Inspect the housing and cover. Look closely for cracks or other damage that would allow unfiltered air into the engine.
4. Replace any part that is damaged or starting to deteriorate.

SECONDARY AIR SYSTEM

The secondary air system is used on all California, 1998-on U.S. and Switzerland, and 1997-on German models. The system consists of a vacuum switch, two air suction valves (reed valves) and hoses. The system uses vacuum pulses from the carburetor to introduce filtered air into the exhaust ports. The additional air promotes the combustion of any unburned fuel in the exhaust gas, which reduces hydrocarbon and carbon monoxide emissions. During deceleration, however, the vacuum switch closes to prevent backfiring.

The air suction valves on top of the cylinder head cover are one-way valves. They allow fresh air to enter the exhaust ports, but they prevent any air or exhaust gasses from reversing back into the system.

This system requires no regular maintenance, however, periodic inspection is recommended. Make sure all air and vacuum hoses are correctly routed and securely attached to their respective fittings. Inspect the hoses and replace any if necessary.

Vacuum Switch Removal/Installation

The vacuum switch is located on top of the cylinder head cover. To remove it, disconnect the hoses and slide the vacuum switch, with its hoses still attached, from between the frame and cylinder head cover.

NOTE

As a hose is disconnected, label the hose and its fitting. These hoses must be reconnected to the proper fittings during assembly.

1. Remove the fuel tank as described in this chapter.
2. Disconnect the large, vacuum-switch hose (A, **Figure 13**) from the air filter housing.

3. Disconnect each small vacuum-switch hose from the fittings on the front of the No. 1 (B, **Figure 13**) and the No. 4 carburetors.
4. Disconnect the vacuum-switch hose from its fitting (A, **Figure 16**) on each air suction valve cover.
5. Slide the vacuum switch assembly (B, **Figure 16**) and its hoses from the top of the cylinder head. Note that the side of the vacuum switch with the hole faces down. It must be reinstalled in this position during assembly.
6. Installation is the reverse of removal. Make sure each hose is securely connected to the proper fitting noted during removal.

Vacuum Switch Test

Test the vacuum switch when you notice backfiring or other abnormal engine noises during deceleration. A vacuum gauge (Kawasaki part No. 57001-1198) and a syringe are needed for this test.

1. Remove the vacuum switch from the motorcycle.
2. Plug the large hoses as shown in **Figure 17**.
3. Connect the vacuum gauge to one of the vacuum hoses; connect the syringe to the other vacuum hose (**Figure 17**).
4. Connect the battery to the vacuum gauge following the manufacturer's instructions.
5. Operate the vacuum gauge and gradually raise the vacuum. At the same time, use the syringe to pump air into the vacuum hose.
6. When the vacuum is low, the vacuum switch should allow air to flow. When the vacuum rises to 54-68 kPa (410-510 mm HG), the vacuum switch should close and stop the flow of air from the syringe.

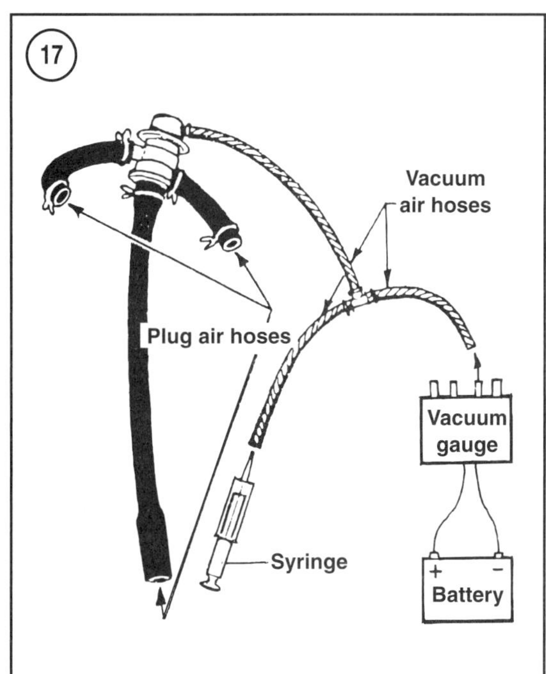

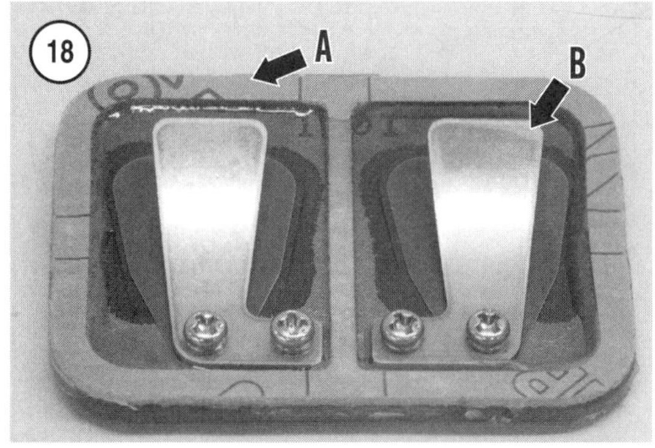

7. Replace the vacuum switch if it fails this test.

Air Suction Valve Removal/Installation

A defective air suction valve(s) can cause rough idle, decreased engine performance and abnormal noise.

1. Remove the fuel tank and vacuum switch as described in this chapter.
2. Remove the cover bolts and lift the air suction valve cover (C, **Figure 16**) from the cylinder head cover.
3. Pry the valve (**Figure 18**) from the cylinder head cover.
4. Check the sealing lip (A, **Figure 18**) around the perimeter of the air suction valve. If must be free of grooves, scratches or signs of damage.

CAUTION
Do not scrape carbon from the reeds or their contact area. The assembly will be damaged.

5. Use solvent to wash any carbon deposits from between each reed (B, **Figure 18**) and the reed contact area.
6. Replace the air suction valve if it is worn or damaged. An air suction valve cannot be repaired.
7. Carefully remove any carbon deposits from the ports in the cylinder head cover.
8. Installation is the reverse of removal.

EVAPORATIVE EMISSION CONTROL SYSTEM (CALIFORNIA MODELS)

The evaporative emission control (EVAP) system (**Figure 19**) captures fuel vapors and stores them in the charcoal canister so they will not be released into the atmosphere. When the engine is started, the stored vapors are drawn from the canister and burned in the engine.

The charcoal canister mounts to the right of the battery box (**Figure 20**). The liquid/vapor separator (**Figure 21**) also sits on the right side just rearward of the clutch cover.

Inspection

WARNING
The EVAP system stores fuel vapors. Make sure the work area is free of all sparks or flames, including gas appliance pilot lights, before working on the system.

1. Disconnect the negative battery cable (**Figure 2**).
2. Remove the side cover from each side of the motorcycle.
3. Make sure all hoses are in good condition and securely attached as indicated in **Figure 22**.
4. Replace any cracked, damaged or brittle hose.
5. Remove and inspect the canister (**Figure 20**) by performing the following:

19

EVAPORATIVE EMISSION CONTROL SYSTEM (CALIFORNIA MODELS)

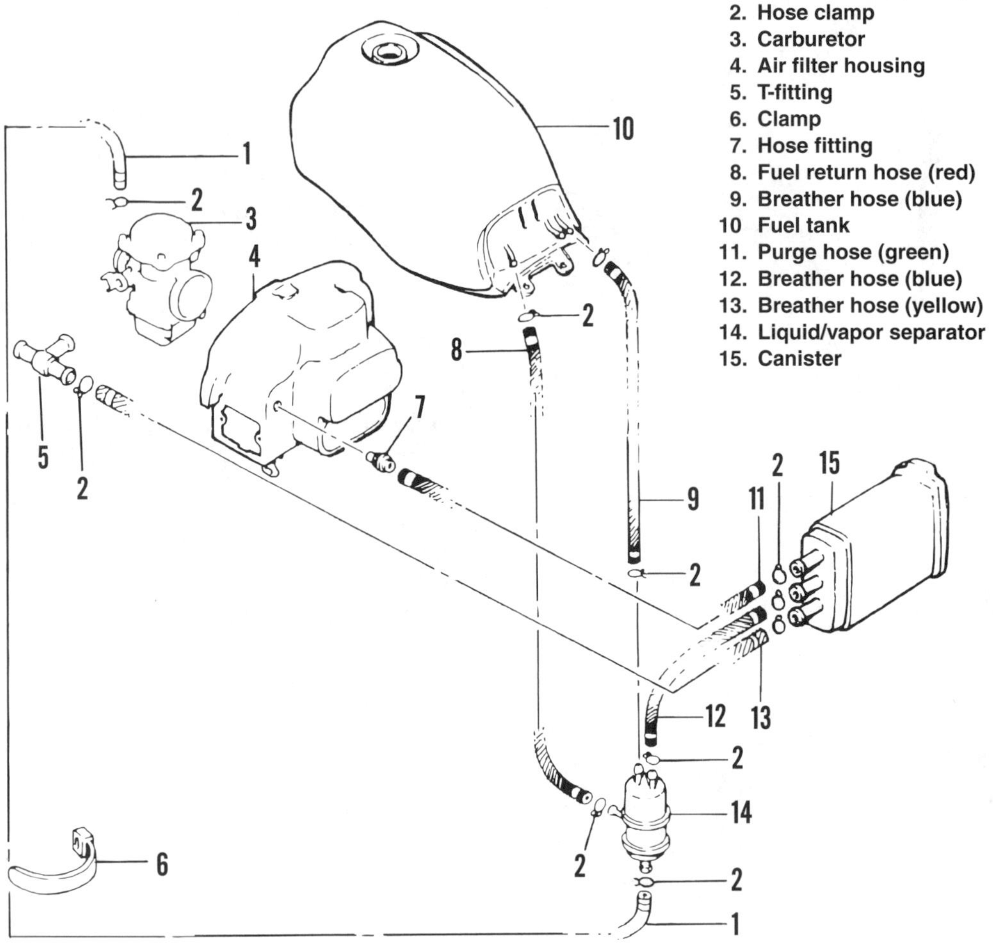

1. Vacuum hose (white)
2. Hose clamp
3. Carburetor
4. Air filter housing
5. T-fitting
6. Clamp
7. Hose fitting
8. Fuel return hose (red)
9. Breather hose (blue)
10. Fuel tank
11. Purge hose (green)
12. Breather hose (blue)
13. Breather hose (yellow)
14. Liquid/vapor separator
15. Canister

20

21

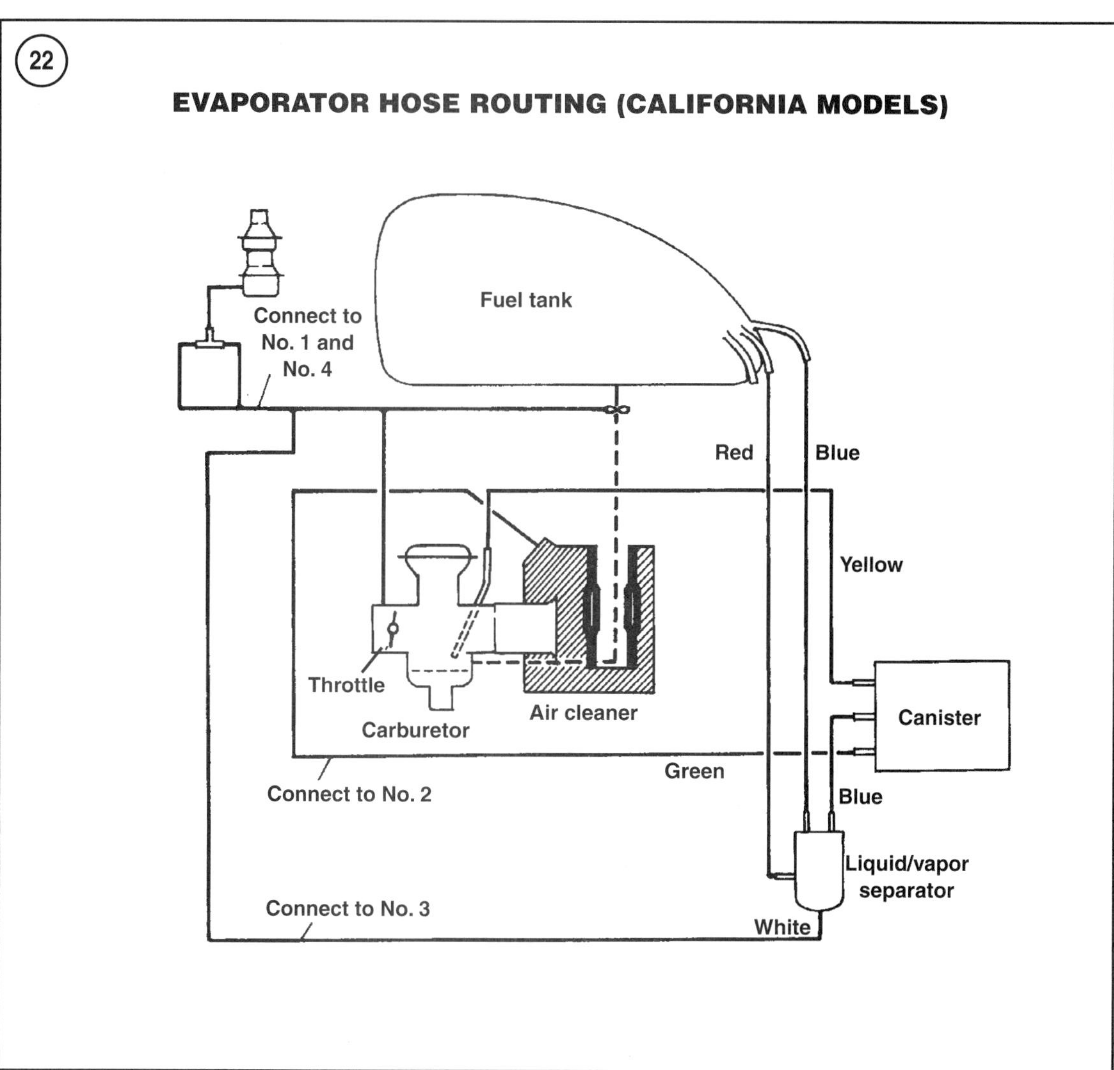

a. Disconnect the hoses from the canister. Label each hose and it fitting so they can be properly connected during installation.
b. Disconnect the rubber mounting band and remove the canister from its mount.
c. Visually inspect the canister for cracks or other sign of damage. Replace the canister if any damage is found.
d. Installation is the reverse of removal.

WARNING
Do not turn the separator upside down or sideways. Doing so will allow gasoline to flow into the canister.

6. Remove and inspect the liquid/vapor separator (**Figure 21**) by performing the following:

a. Disconnect the hoses from the separator. Label each hose and its fitting so they can be properly connected during installation.
b. Lift the rubber mounts from the motorcycle. Visually inspect the liquid/vapor separator for cracks of other sings of damage. Replace it as necessary.
c. Installation is the reverse of removal.

CARBURETOR

Carburetor Removal

NOTE
The carburetors can be accessed with the front fairing installed. However,

8

removing the front fairing provides additional room to work, which is helpful.

1. Remove the lower and middle fairings as described in Chapter Fifteen. If necessary, remove the front fairing.
2. Securely support the motorcycle on a level surface.
3. Remove the seat (Chapter Fifteen) and disconnect the negative battery cable (**Figure 2**).

NOTE
Mark each hose and its fitting during carburetor removal. Each hose must be reconnected to the proper fitting during assembly.

4. Remove the fuel tank (this chapter).
5. Loosen the two clamp screws (A, **Figure 23**) on each intake manifold and pull back the spring (B) on each air box boot.
6. On models with a secondary air system, perform the following:
   a. Disconnect the large, vacuum-switch hose (A, **Figure 13**) from the air filter housing.
   b. Disconnect the small vacuum-switch hoses from the fittings on the No. 1 carburetor (B, **Figure 13**) and on the No. 4 carburetor (A, **Figure 24**).
7. On California models, perform the following:
   a. Disconnect the EVAP canister's vent hose from the fitting between the No. 1 and No 2 carburetors (C, **Figure 13**) and from the fitting between the No.3 and No.4 carburetors (B, **Figure 24**).
   b. Disconnect the liquid/vapor separator's hose from the fitting at the front of the No. 3 carburetor (C, **Figure 24**).
8. Loosen the air box housing bolt (B, **Figure 14**) on each side. Push the housing rearward as far and possible and tighten the bolts. This provides maximum clearance for carburetor removal.
9. Pull each air box boot from its carburetor's horn.
10. Loosen the clamp screw (A, **Figure 25**) and disconnect the choke cable (B) from the choke plate.
11. Grasp the carburetor assembly on both ends. Work the assembly up and down and separate each carburetor from its intake manifold.

12. Pull the assembly from the left side of the motorcycle. Disconnect the carburetor pull cable (A, **Figure 26**) and return cable (B) from their fittings on the carburetor wheel.
13. Stuff clean rags into the intake manifolds and the air box boots to keep debris out of the engine.

Carburetor Installation

1. Set the carburetor assembly onto the left side of the motorcycle.

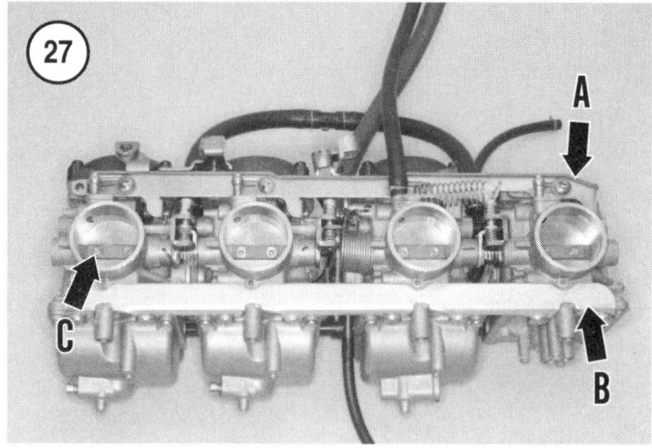

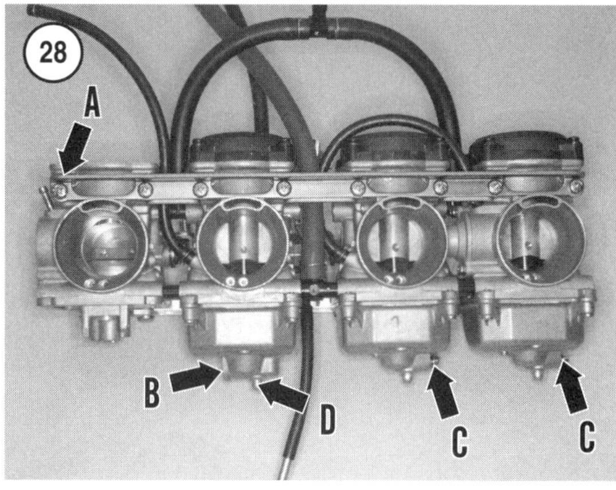

2. Connect the pull (A, **Figure 26**) and return (B) cables to the throttle wheel.

3. Install the carburetors between the intake manifold and the air box boots.

4. Press the carburetor assembly forward and seat each carburetor in its intake manifold.

5. Connect the end of the choke cable (B, **Figure 25**) to the choke plate, secure the cable in the holder and tighten the clamp screw (A).

6. On California models, perform the following:
   a. Connect the EVAP canister's vent hose to the fitting between the No. 1 and No 2 carburetors (C, **Figure 13**) and to the fitting between on the No. 3 and No. 4 carburetors (B, **Figure 24**).
   b. Connect the liquid/vapor separator's hose to the fitting on the front of the No. 3 carburetors (C, **Figure 24**).

7. On models with a secondary air system, perform the following:
   a. Connect the large, vacuum switch hose (A, **Figure 13**) to the air filter housing.
   b. Connect the small vacuum switch hoses to the fittings on the No. 1 carburetor (B, **Figure 13**) and on the No. 4 carburetor (A, **Figure 24**).

8. Fit the air box boot over the carburetors horns. If necessary, loosen the air box housing bolt (B, **Figure 14**) on each side. Push the housing forward as far and possible and tighten the bolts.

9. Secure each boot with its spring (B, **Figure 23**) and tighten the carburetor clamp screws (A, **Figure 23**).

10. Refer to Chapter Three and adjust the following as necessary:
   a. Throttle cable free play.
   b. Choke cable free play.
   c. Idle speed.
   d. Carburetor synchronization.

Carburetor Separation

The carburetors are joined by the choke plate (A, **Figure 27**) and lower plate (B) on the front and by the upper plate (A, **Figure 28**) on the rear. The carburetors can be disassembled without separating the carburetor bodies. Carburetor separation is not necessary unless a carb body must be replaced, it must be cleaned internally, or if a pipe fitting must be replaced.

Refer to **Figure 29**.

1. Remove the carburetor assembly as described in this section.

2. Remove the mounting screws and separate the throttle stop bracket (**Figure 30**) from the No. 1 carburetor body.

CAUTION

Use an impact driver to loosen the holding plate screws. Loosening these

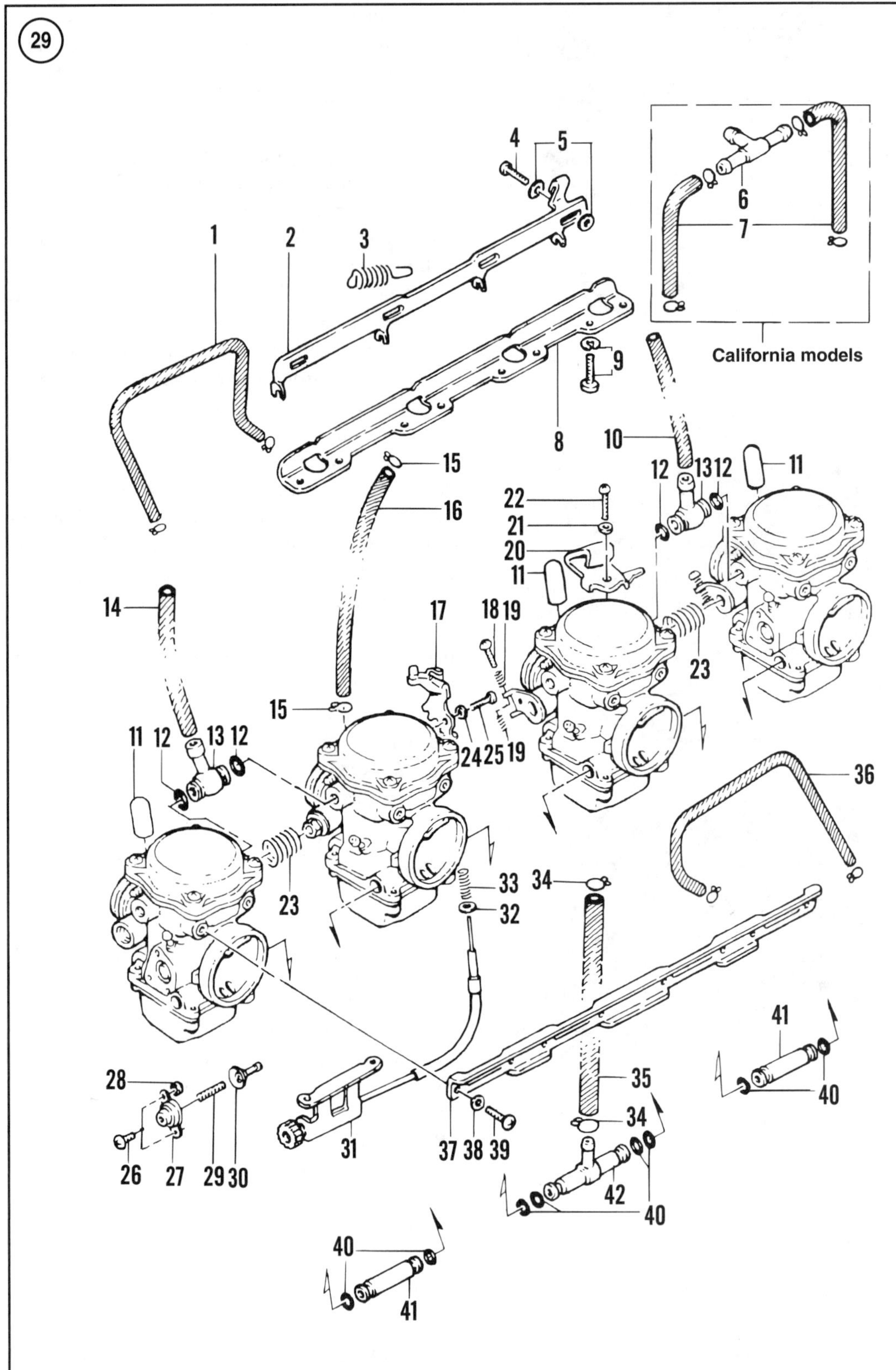
29
1
2
3
4
5
6
7
California models
8
9
10
11
12
13
14
15
16
17
18
19
20
21
22
23
24
25
26
27
28
29
30
31
32
33
34
35
36
37
38
39
40
41
42

CARBURETOR SEPARATION

1. Hose
2. Choke plate
3. Spring
4. Screw
5. Washer
6. T-fitting
7. Hose
8. Lower plate
9. Screw
10. Hose
11. Vacuum plug
12. O-ring
13. T-fitting
14. Hose
15. Clamp
16. Hose
17. Throttle cable bracket
18. Screw
19. Spring
20. Choke cable bracket
21. Washer
22. Screw
23. Spring
24 Washer
25. Screw
26. Screw
27. Air cut valve cover
28. O-ring
29. Spring
30. Diaphragm
31. Throttle stop screw
32. Washer
33. Spring
34. Clamp
35. Hose
36. Hose
37. Upper plate
38. Washer
39. Screw
40. O-ring
41. Hose fitting
42. T-fitting

screws with a Phillips screwdriver may damage the head.

3. Disconnect the spring (A, **Figure 31**) from the choke plate.
4. Remove the mounting screws (B, **Figure 31**), lift the fingers of the choke plate from each starter plunger and lift the choke plate (A, **Figure 27**) from the carburetor bodies. Watch for the washers behind each screw. The washers function as the sliding bearings for the choke plate.
5. Remove the lower plate (B, **Figure 27**) and the upper plate (A, **Figure 28**). Watch for the washer installed on each mounting screw.
6. Carefully separate the carburetors. Note the position of any springs, fittings and pipes.
7. Assembly is the reverse of separation.
   a. Replace all fuel pipe O-rings.
   b. The carburetor bores (**Figure 32**) must be parallel. If necessary, place the assembly on a flat surface and align the centerline of the bores horizontally and vertically.
   c. Make sure the drain screws on the float bowls face the outboard side of the assembly. The screws on the No. 1 and No. 2 carburetors (B,

8

Figure 28) face the left side of the motorcycle. The drain screws on the No. 3 and No. 4 carburetors (C, **Figure 28**) must face the right.

d. Check the operation of the choke plate. It must slide smoothly.
e. Operate the throttle pulley and visually inspect the movement of the butterfly valve (C, **Figure 27**) in each carburetor. Make sure they open and close smoothly. Also visually check the clearance between each valve and its bore. If necessary, use the synchronizing screws (**Figure 33**) to adjust the butterfly valves. See *Carburetor Synchronization* in Chapter Three.

Carburetor Disassembly

Do not mix parts from one carburetor with those of another. To avoid confusing parts; disassemble, clean and reassemble one carburetor and then move on to next.

Refer to **Figure 34**.

1. Remove the carburetor assembly as described in this section.
2. Check the fuel level as described in this section.
3. Drain the float bowl by performing the following:
   a. Connect a hose to the drain fitting (D, **Figure 28**) on the float bowl.
   b. Insert the other end of the hose into a suitable gas container.
   c. Open the drain screw (B, **Figure 28**) and let the fuel drain from the float bowl.
   d. Repeat for the remaining float bowls.
4. Remove the diaphragm cover (**Figure 35**) from the carburetor.
5. Remove the spring (A, **Figure 36**) and the vacuum slide (B).
6. Remove the spring seat (**Figure 37**) from the slide body and remove the jet needle.
7. Remove the air cut valve mounting screw (**Figure 38**) and remove the cover and spring (**Figure 39**).
8. Remove the O-ring (**Figure 40**) and the diaphragm (A, **Figure 41**).
9. Remove the float bowl. On the No. 1 carburetor, the throttle stop bracket (**Figure 30**) will come out once the two rear float blow screws are removed.

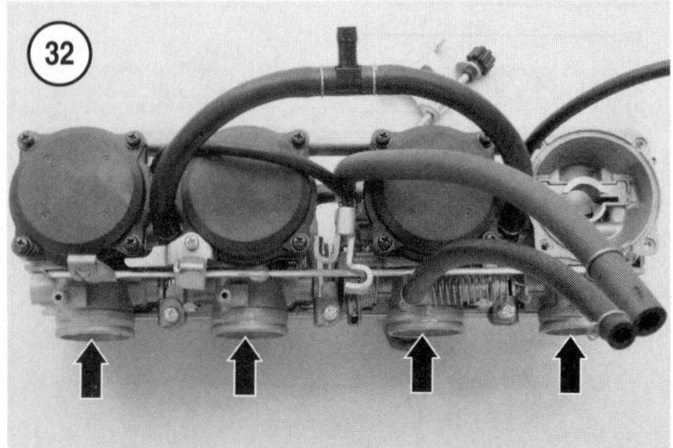

10. Remove the float pin (A, **Figure 42**) and lift the float assembly (B), along with the float valve, from the carburetor.

11A. On all models except U.S., California and Switzerland models, remove the pilot screw (**Figure 43**) by performing the following:
   a. Count the number of turns as you carefully turn the pilot screw in until it *lightly* seats. Record this number. The pilot screw must be reset to this same position during assembly.
   b. Unscrew and remove the pilot screw.

11B. On U.S., California and Switzerland models, the pilot screw is sealed. If necessary, remove it as described in *Pilot Screw* in this section.

12. Unscrew and remove the main jet (A, **Figure 44**) from the needle jet holder (B).
13. Remove the pilot jet (**Figure 45**).
14. Remove the needle jet holder (**Figure 46**).
15. Insert a finger into the carburetor bore. Press the needle jet toward the float bowl and remove the needle jet (**Figure 47**).

34

CARBURETOR

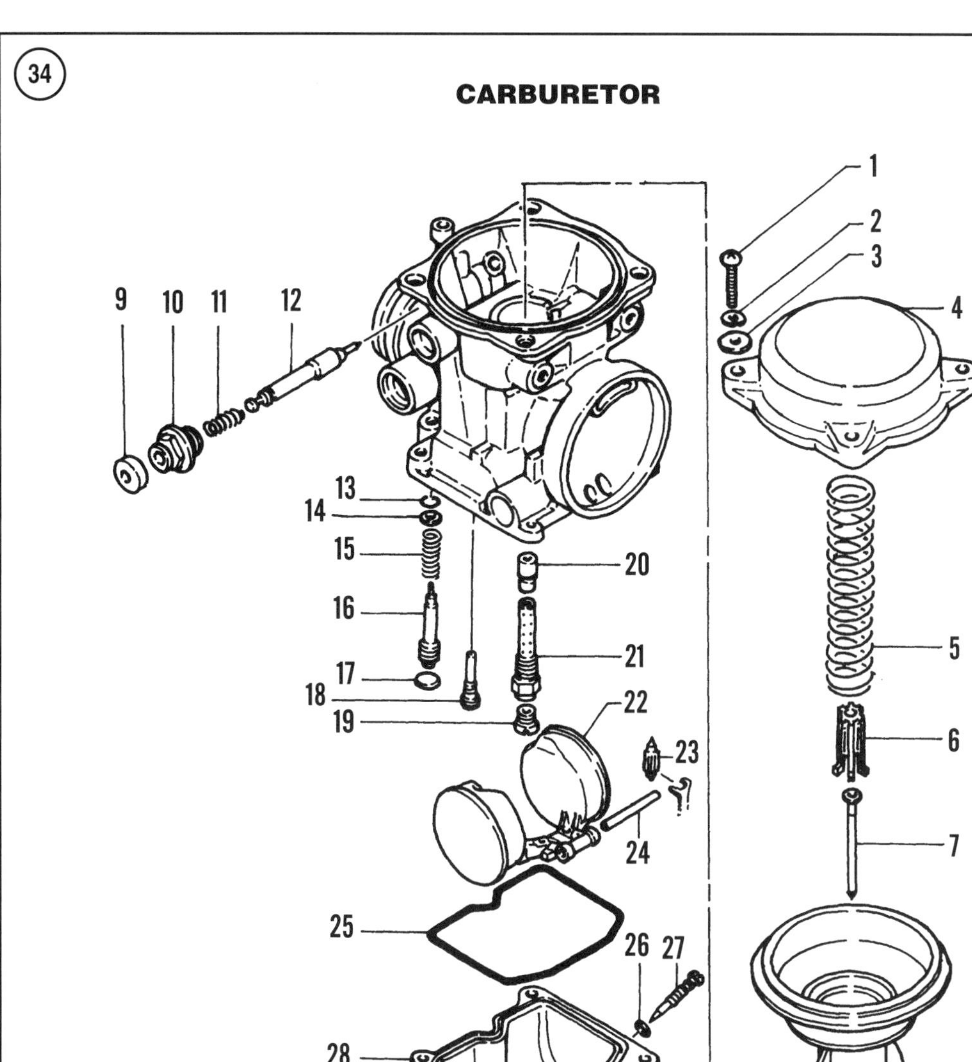

1. Screw
2. Lockwasher
3. Flat washer
4. Diaphragm cover
5. Spring
6. Spring seat
7. Jet needle
8. Vacuum slide
9. Seal
10. Nut
11. Spring
12. Choke shaft
13. O-ring
14. Washer
15. Spring
16. Pilot (idle mixture) screw
17. Plug (U.S. models only)
18. Pilot jet
19. Main jet
20. Needle jet
21. Needle jet holder
22. Float
23. Float valve
24. Float pivot pin
25. O-ring
26. O-ring
27. Drain screw
28. Float bowl
29. Lockwasher
30. Bolt

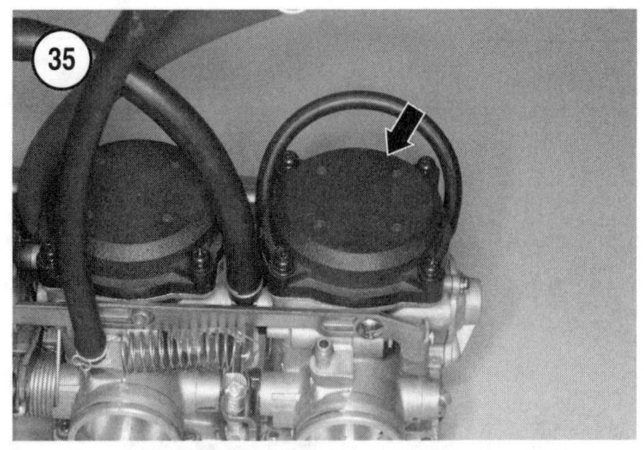

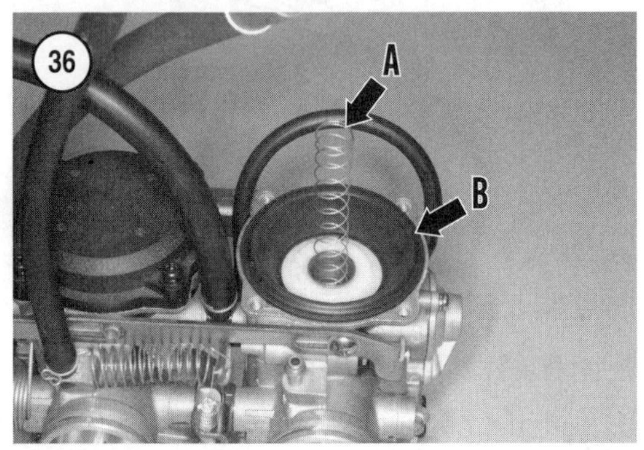

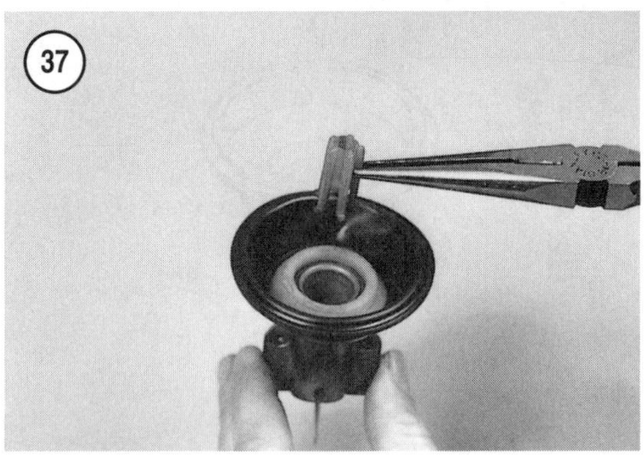

16. Unscrew the starter plunger (**Figure 48**) and remove it from the carburetor.

17. Clean and inspect the carburetor as described in this section.

18. Assemble the carburetor by reversing the disassembly procedure. Note the following:

   a. Install the needle jet (**Figure 47**) so the end with the smaller diameter goes in first.

   b. As the needle jet holder (**Figure 46**) is screwed into the carburetor, it will push the needle jet into the carburetor bore.

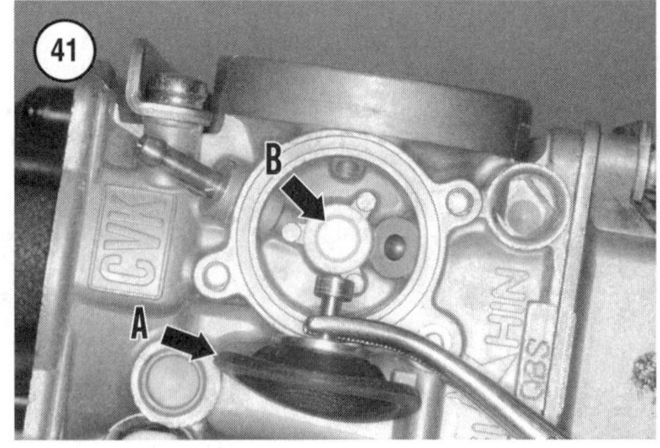

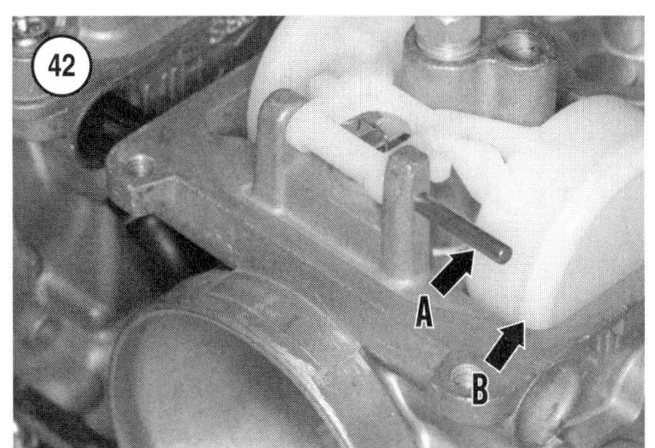

8

c. Turn the pilot screw in (**Figure 43**) until it *lightly* seats in the bore and then back it out the number of turns noted during removal.

d. Install the jet needle (**Figure 49**) through the center hole (A, **Figure 50**) in the vacuum piston.

e. Install the spring seat (**Figure 37**). Rotate the spring seat so it does not block the off-center hole (B, **Figure 50**) in the bottom of the vacuum piston.

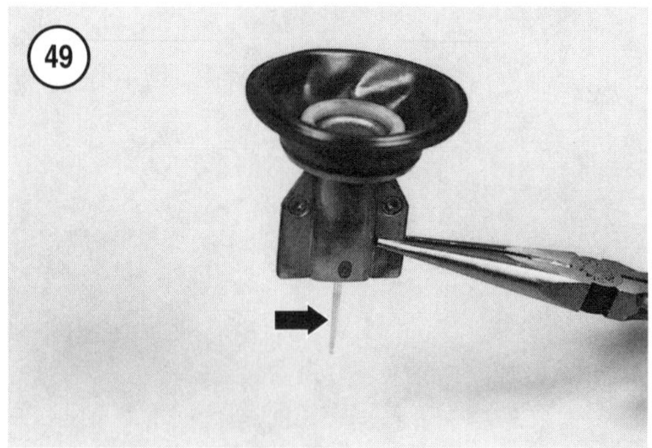

f. Install the vacuum piston cover so the spring engages the boss (**Figure 51**) in the cover.
g. Lower the float into the carburetor so the float valve sits in the valve seat. See **Figure 52**.
h. Install the air cut valve diaphragm so its piston seats in the housing boss (B, **Figure 41**).
i. Check the fuel level as described in this section.

Carburetor Inspection

1. Thoroughly clean and dry all parts. Kawasaki does not recommend the use of a caustic carburetor cleaning solvent. Instead, clean carburetor parts in a petroleum-based solvent and thoroughly rinse them in clean water.

2. Allow the carburetor to dry completely before assembly. Blow out the jets (**Figure 53**) and passages with compressed air.

CAUTION
If compressed air is not available, allow the parts to air dry or dry them with a clean, lint-free cloth. Do not use a paper towel to dry carburetor parts. Small paper particles could plug openings in the carburetor body or jets. Do not use a piece of wire to clean the jets. Minor gouges in a jet can alter the air/fuel mixture.

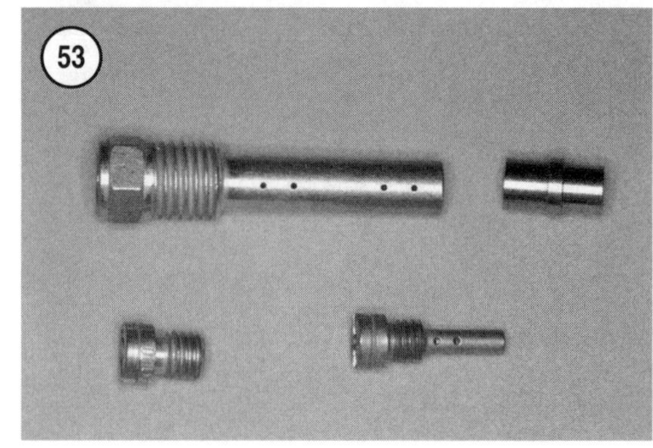

3. Remove the drain bolt from the float bowl.

4. Inspect the needle valve assembly by performing the following:

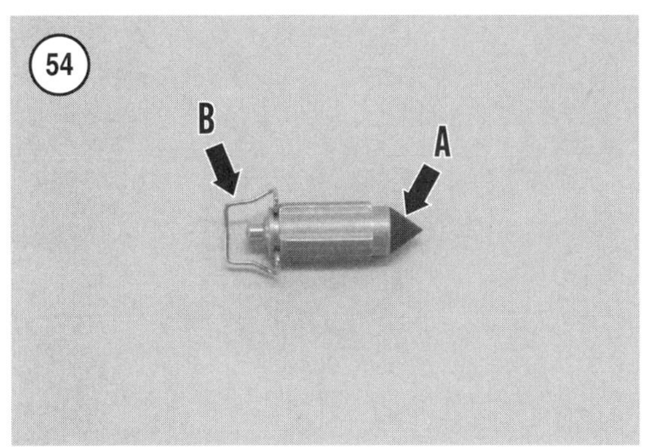

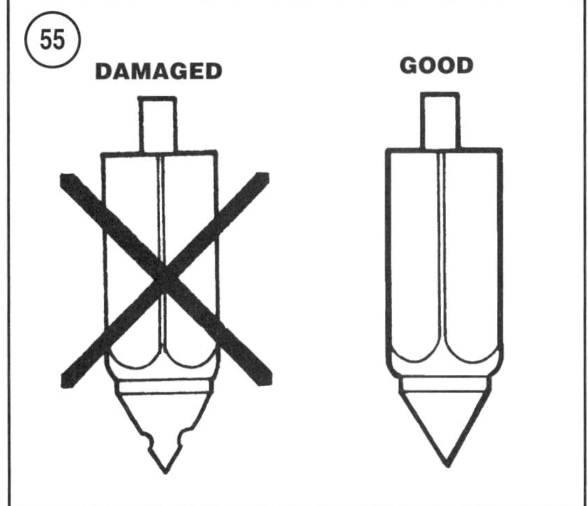

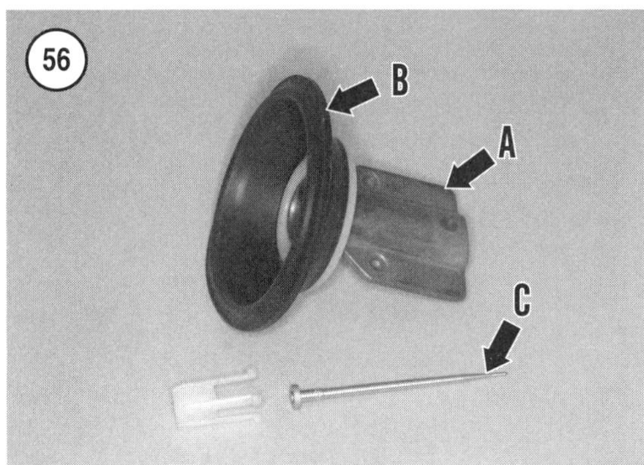

a. Inspect the end of the needle valve (A, **Figure 54**) for wear or damage (**Figure 55**).

b. Check the needle valve wire (B, **Figure 54**). Replace the needle valve as necessary.

c. Check the inside of the needle valve seat in the carburetor. A damaged valve seat or a particle of dirt in the seat results in flooded carburetors.

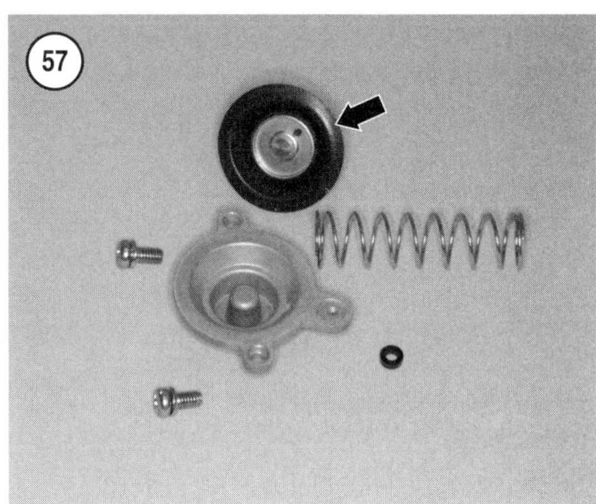

d. If any part is worn or damaged, replace the entire needle valve assembly (needle valve and valve seat) as a set.

5. Make sure all the holes in the jets and holder (**Figure 53**) are clear. Clean them out if they are plugged in any way. Replace any part if you cannot unplug its holes.

6. Make sure all openings in the carburetor body are clear. Clean them out if they are plugged in any way.

7. Inspect the slide bore in the carburetor body. Make sure it is clean and free of any burrs or obstructions that may cause the vacuum piston to hang up during normal operation.

8. Inspect the vacuum piston (A, **Figure 56**) for scoring and wear. Replace the piston if necessary.

9. Inspect the diaphragm (B, **Figure 56**) on the vacuum piston for tears, cracks or other damage. Replace the vacuum piston assembly if the diaphragm is damaged.

10. Inspect the jet needle (C, **Figure 56**) for excessive wear at the tip or for other damage.

11. Inspect the float for deterioration or damage. If you suspect that the float leaks, place it in a container of water and push it down. If the float sinks or if bubbles appear (indicating a leak), the float must be replaced.

12. Inspect the air cut valve diaphragm (**Figure 57**) for tears, cracks or other damage. Replace the diaphragm if any damage is found.

13. If removed, inspect the pilot screw assembly. Pay particular attention to the O-ring.

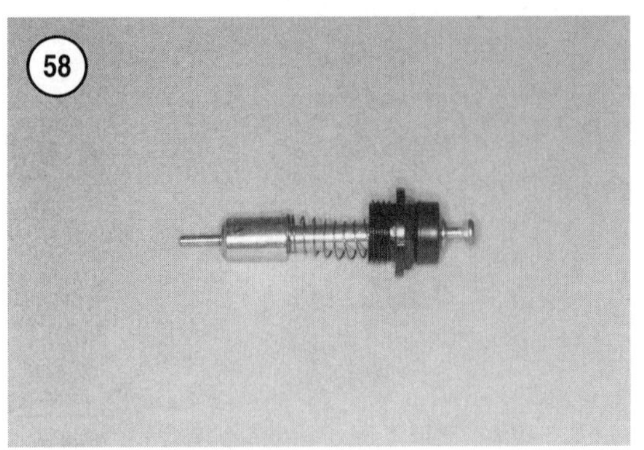

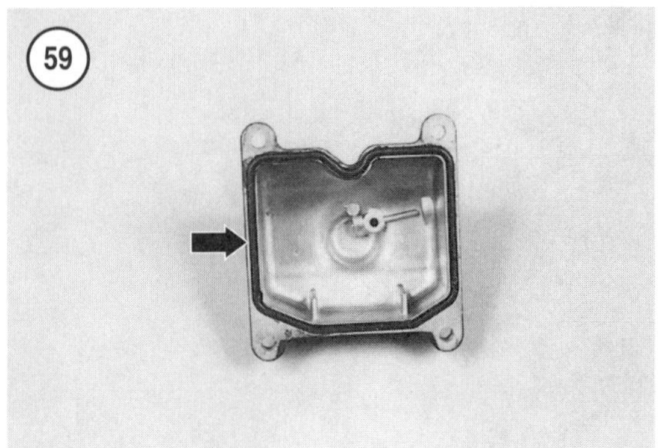

14. Inspect the starter plunger (**Figure 58**).
15. Inspect the float bowl O-ring (**Figure 59**).
16. Inspect the fuel lines for cracks, scoring or other signs of damage. Replace the fuel lines as needed.
17. Replace any carburetor part that is worn, damaged, or plugged.

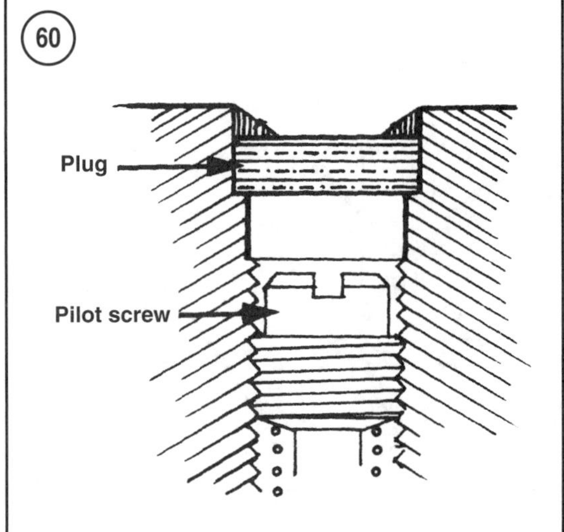

Pilot Screw Adjustment (U.S., California and Switzerland models)

The pilot screws are sealed with a plug inserted into the top of the pilot screw bore (**Figure 60**). The plug must be removed to access the pilot screw.

1. Carefully scrape out the bonding agent from the recess in the pilot screw bore.
2. Use a 5/32 in. drill (**Figure 61**) to drill a hole through the plug. Be prepared to stop drilling as soon as you break through the plug so you will not damage the pilot screw.
3. Turn in a small screw into the hole and use the screw to pull out the plug (**Figure 62**).
4. Count the number of turns as you carefully turn the pilot screw in until it *lightly* seats in the bore. Record this number. The pilot screw must be reset to this same position during assembly.
5. Unscrew and remove the pilot screw (**Figure 43**).
6. To install the pilot screw, turn the pilot screw into the bore until it *lightly* seats.
7. Back out the pilot screw the same number of turns noted during removal.
8. Install a new plug. Secure the plug with a small amount of non-hardening bonding agent.

Fuel Level Inspection

The flow of fuel up from the bowl is affected by the size of the jets, the amount of vacuum at the throttle bore and the by the fuel level on the bowl. A fuel level measurement is more useful than a float height measurement because it measures actual fuel

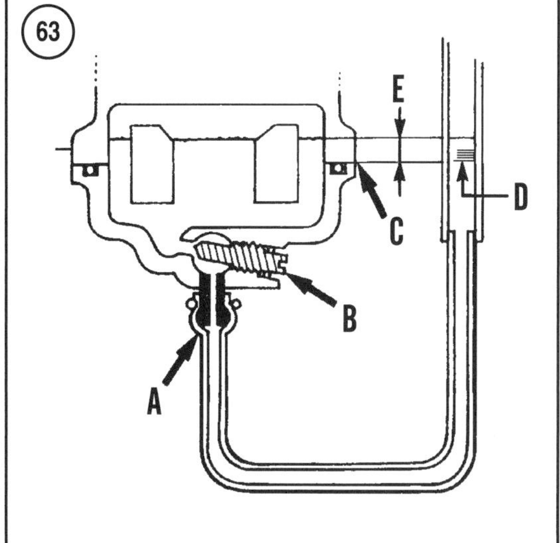

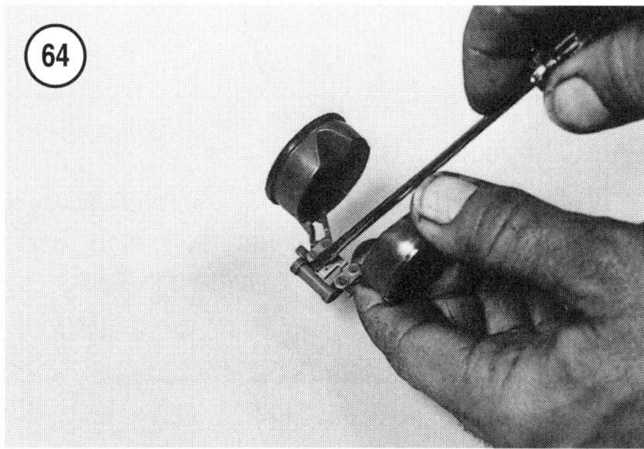

level. Fuel level inspection requires the Kawasaki fuel level gauge (part No. 57001-1017).

The fuel level must be checked with the carburetor assembly removed from the engine. This inspection *cannot* be performed with the carburetors on the motorcycle.

1. Remove the carburetors as described in this section. Secure the carburetors in an upright position.
2. Mount the carburetor assembly vertically in a fabricated wooden stand. Make sure carburetors are perfectly vertical.
3. Securely position the fuel tank on wooden blocks higher than the carburetors. Use a 300 mm length of 6-mm fuel hose to connect the fuel valve outlet to the carburetors.
4. Attach a piece of suitable size clear vinyl tubing to the drain outlet fitting (A, **Figure 63**) on the carburetor float bowl.
5. Connect the Kawasaki fuel level gauge to the end of the vinyl tubing.
6. Hold the fuel level gauge in a vertical position next to the carburetor body. Position the gauge so the *Zero* line is several millimeters higher than the bottom of the carburetor body (C, **Figure 63**).
7. Turn the fuel valve to prime.
8. Unscrew the carburetor drain screw (B, **Figure 63**) several turns to allow fuel to enter the fuel level gauge. Wait until the fuel in the gauge settles.

NOTE

*Do not lower the **Zero** line on the fuel level gauge below the upper edge of the float bowl. If the fuel level gauge is lowered and then raised again, the fuel within the fuel level gauge will be slightly higher than the actual fuel level, resulting in a false reading.*

9. Keep the gauge vertical, slowly lower the fuel level gauge until the *Zero* line (D, **Figure 63**) is even with the bottom of the carburetor body (C). Read the fuel level in the gauge (E, **Figure 63**) and write down the reading.
10. Turn the fuel valve to the on or to the reserve position.
11. Tighten the carburetor drain screw. Drain the fuel in the gauge and hose into a suitable container. Dispose of the fuel properly.
12. If the fuel level is out of specification (**Table 1** or **Table 2**), adjust fuel level as follows:
    a. Remove the float bowl from the carburetor and remove the float.
    b. Bend the float tang (**Figure 64**) as required to get the correct float height.

8

c. Increasing float height lowers the fuel level.

NOTE

If the float tang cannot be adjusted sufficiently to achieve the correct fuel level in the carburetor, either the float and/or the float valve may be faulty. Replace either of these parts as necessary.

d. Install the float and float bowl and recheck the fuel level.

13. Repeat Steps 4-12 for the remaining carburetors.
14. Reinstall the carburetors.

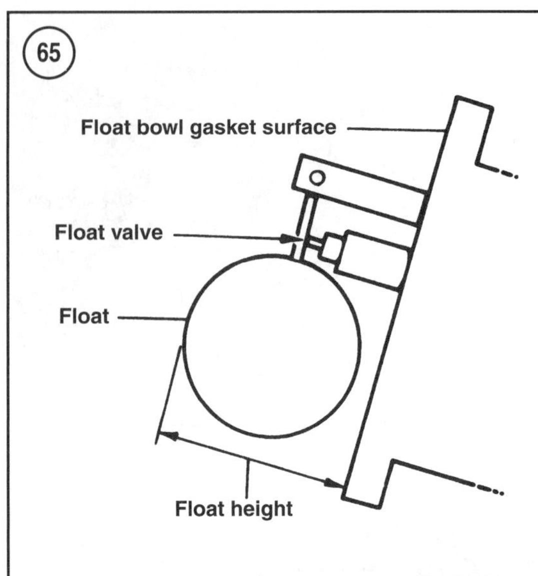

Float Height Inspection/Adjustment

1. Remove the carburetor assembly as described in this section.
2. Drain the fuel from the float bowl into a suitable container.
3. Remove the float bowl from the carburetor body.
4. Hold the float chamber almost vertically so the spring-loaded rod in the float valve needle makes contact with the tang on the float but does not push it down (**Figure 65**).
5. Measure the distance between the top of the float and the gasket surface (**Figure 65**).
6. If the float height is outside of the specification in **Table 1** or **Table 2**, remove the float from the bowl.
7. Bend the float tang (**Figure 64**) *very slightly* until the float height is within specification. Increasing the float height lowers the fuel level; decreasing the float height raises the fuel level.
8. Assemble the carburetor as described in this section.
9. Install the carburetor assembly as described in this section.
10. Check the fuel level as described in this section to verify that the float tang was adjusted correctly.

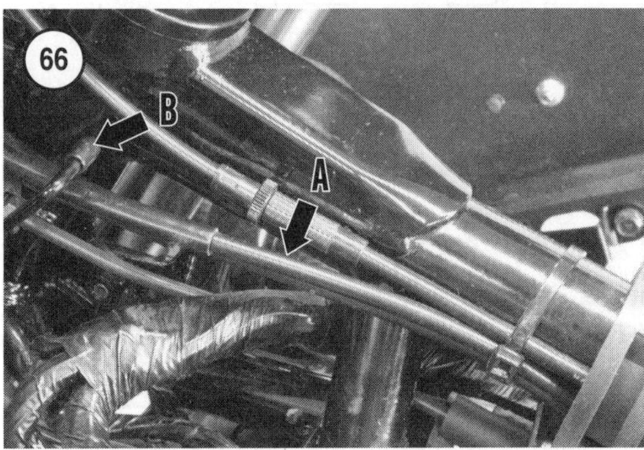

Carburetor Rejetting

1. Do not attempt to solve a poor engine running condition by rejetting the carburetors. Make sure all other systems are operating correctly before considering the carburetors as the source of the problem. If the following list of conditions hold true, rejetting is most likely not the problem.

a. The engine has held a good tune in the past with the standard jetting.

b. The engine has not been modified.

c. The motorcycle is being operated in the same geographical region under the same general climatic conditions as in the past.

d. The motorcycle was and is being ridden at average highway speeds.

2. The following are conditions under which carburetor rejetting may be required:

a. A non-standard type of filter element is being used.

b. A non-standard exhaust system is installed.

c. Any top end component in the engine (pistons, camshafts, valves, compression) has been modified.

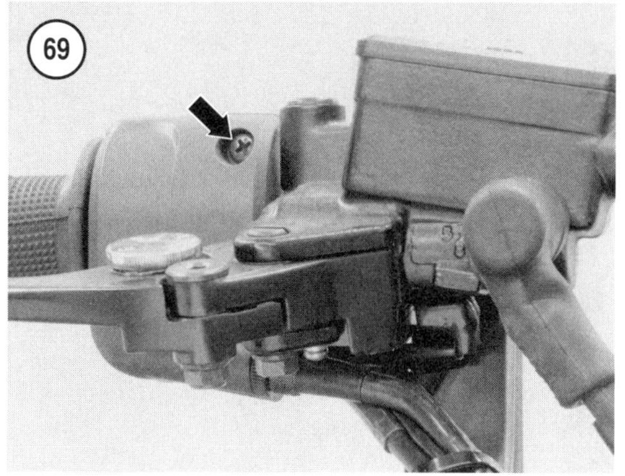

d. The motorcycle is in use at considerably higher or lower elevation or in a considerably hotter or colder climate than in the past.

e. The motorcycle is being operated at considerably higher speeds than before and changing to a colder spark plug heat range does not solve the problem.

f. Someone has previously changed the carburetor jetting. Original equipment jet sizes are listed in **Table 1** or **Table 2**.

g. The motorcycle has never held a satisfactory engine tune.

3. If it is necessary to rejet the carburetor, check with a Kawasaki dealership or motorcycle performance specialist for recommendations on the size of jets to install in specific conditions.
4. If the jets are going to be replaced, do so only one size at a time. After jetting, test ride the motorcycle and inspect the spark plugs as described in Chapter Three.

Idle Speed Adjustment

Refer to Chapter Three when adjusting the idle speed.

THROTTLE CABLE

Free Play

Refer to Chapter Three when checking or adjusting the throttle cable free play.

Replacement

1. Securely support the motorcycle on a level surface.
2. Remove the seat and disconnect the negative battery cable (**Figure 2**).
3. Remove the fuel tank as described in this chapter.
4. Remove the lower and middle fairings (Chapter Fifteen).
5. Note how the throttle cables (A, **Figure 66**) are routed along the left side of the frame, through the cable holder (B) and under the central arm of the fairing bracket (**Figure 67**). The replacement throttle cables must follow the same path as the original cables.
6. Remove the carburetor assembly as described in this chapter. Disconnect the carburetor pull cable (A, **Figure 68**) and return cable (B) from their fittings on the carburetor throttle wheel.
7. Remove the handlebar switch assembly screws (**Figure 69**) and separate the halves of the switch assembly from the right handlebar.
8. Disengage the ends of both the pull and return cables from the throttle drum.
9. Tie a length of heavy string or cord to the ends of the throttle cable at the carburetor. Wrap this end with tape. Do not use an excessive amount of tape. Too much tape could interfere with the cable's pas-

70

EXHAUST SYSTEM

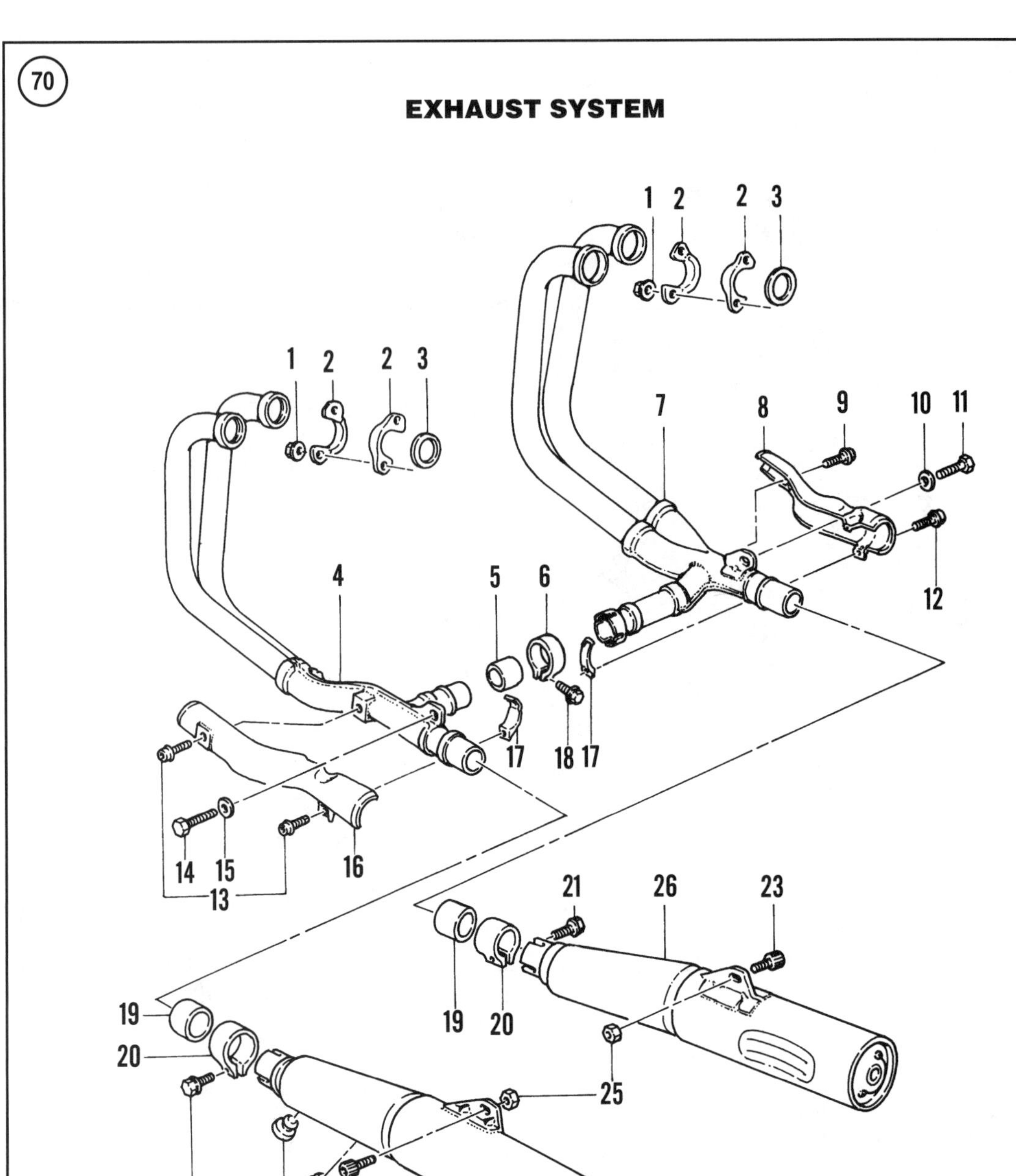

1. Nut
2. Pipe holder
3. Gasket
4. Left exhaust pipe
5. Gasket
6. Clamp
7. Right exhaust pipe
8. Right cover
9. Bolt
10. Washer
11. Bolt
12. Bolt
13. Bolts
14. Bolt
15. Washer
16. Left cover
17. Clamp
18. Bolt
19. Gasket
20. Clamp
21. Bolt
22. Protectors
23. Allen bolt
24. Left muffler
25. Nut
26. Right muffler

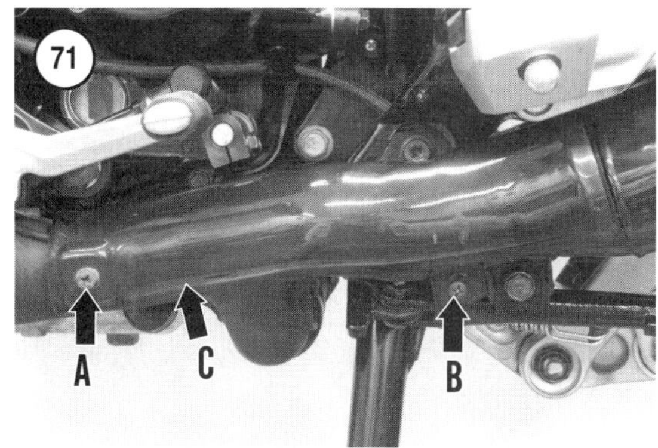

sage through the frame during removal. Tie the other end of the string to the frame.

10. Starting at the handlebar, carefully pull the throttle cables out from under the fairing bracket and along the frame. Make sure the attached string passes through any loops that secure the cables to the frame.

11. Untie the string from the old cable and tie it to the carburetor ends of the new cables.

12. Carefully pull the string back through the frame, routing the new cable through the same path as the old.

13. Remove the string and lubricate the ends of the new cable with grease.

14. Connect the lower cables to the carburetor throttle wheel and fit the cables into position on the cable bracket.

15. At the handlebar, lubricate the ends of the new cable with grease. Connect the cable ends to the throttle drum.

16. Set the right handlebar switch into place over the throttle drum. Secure the switch in place with the mounting screws (**Figure 69**).

17. Operate the throttle grip. Check that the throttle linkage operates correctly without binding. If necessary, check that the cables are correctly attached and that there are no tight bends in the cables.

18. Adjust the throttle cables as described in Chapter Three.

19. Reinstall the carburetor assembly and fuel tank.

20. Start the engine. Turn the handlebar from side to side without operating the throttle. If the engine speed increases as the handlebar is turned, the throttle cable is routed incorrectly. Recheck the cable routing.

8

EXHAUST SYSTEM

Removal/Installation

Refer to **Figure 70**.

1. Securely support the motorcycle on a level surface.
2. Remove the fuel tank as described in this chapter.
3. Remove the lower, middle and front fairings as described in Chapter Fifteen.
4. If installed, remove the saddlebags.
5. Drain the engine oil and the coolant (Chapter Three).
6. Remove the radiator bracket (Chapter Ten).
7. Remove the cover mounting screw (A, **Figure 71**) and the cover clamp screw (B). Lower the exhaust pipe cover (C, **Figure 71**) from the motorcycle.
8. Remove the mufflers as follows:
   a. Loosen the muffler clamps bolt (**Figure 72**).
   b. Remove the muffler hanger bolt (**Figure 73**) and pull the muffler from the exhaust pipe. Remove and discard the muffler gasket (A, **Figure 74**). It may come out with the muffler, or it may remain on the exhaust pipe.
   c. Repeat Steps 6-8 for the other muffler.
9. Remove the header nuts (**Figure 75**) from one exhaust pipe.

10. Remove the lower clamp (**Figure 76**) and then the upper clamp (**Figure 77**).
11. Repeats Steps 9-10 for the remaining header pipes.
12. Remove the exhaust pipe hanger bolt (B, **Figure 74**) from each side.
13. Pull the exhaust pipes forward and disengage each pipe (**Figure 78**) from its exhaust port. Lower the exhaust pipe assembly and rest it on the floor beneath the motorcycle.
14. Loosen the clamp bolt (**Figure 79**) and separate the crossover pipe.
15. Remove one side of the exhaust pipe assembly then the other.
16. Remove and discard the exhaust gasket from each exhaust port.

Installation

1. Set both header pipes loosely together under the engine and connect the crossover tube. Install a new crossover tube gasket and finger-tighten the clamp bolt (**Figure 79**).
2. Install a new exhaust gasket into each exhaust port.
3. Raise the exhaust pipes and fit each header into its exhaust port (**Figure 78**).
4. Raise the rear of the exhaust pipe and loosely install the exhaust pipe hanger bolt (B, **Figure 74**) on each side.
5. Install the upper clamp (**Figure 77**) so its flat side faces the cylinder head.
6. Install the lower clamp (**Figure 76**) so it mates with the upper clamp.
7. Loosely install the header nuts (**Figure 75**).
8. Repeat Steps 5-7 for each header pipe.
9. Install a new muffler gasket (A, **Figure 74**) onto each exhaust pipe.
10. Slide the muffler onto the exhaust pipe and loosely install the muffler hanger bolt (**Figure 73**).
11. Snug down the hardware in the following order:
    a. Evenly snug down the exhaust header nuts (**Figure 75**).
    b. Remove the exhaust pipe hanger bolt (B, **Figure 74**) from one side. Apply Loctite 242 (blue) to threads of the hanger bolt and snug down the bolt. Repeat on the other exhaust pipe hanger bolt.
    c. The muffler hanger bolt (**Figure 73**) on each side.
    d. The crossover pipe clamp bolt (**Figure 79**).

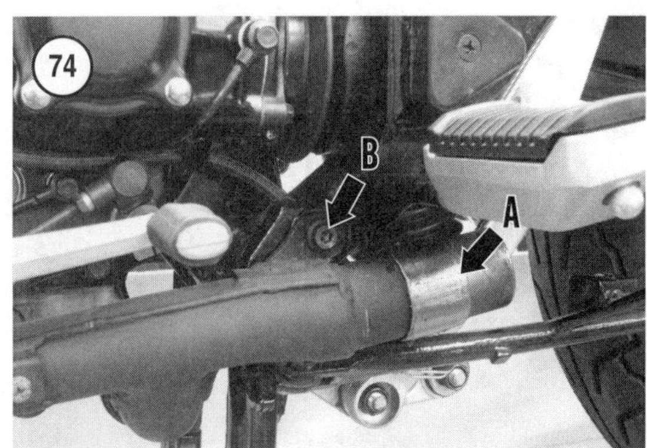

e. The muffler clamp bolt (**Figure 72**) on each side.

12. Securely tighten the hardware in the same order followed in Step 11.

13. Install the exhaust pipe cover (C, **Figure 71**) onto each side.

Inspection

1. Check the exhaust pipes and crossover pipe for cracks or areas that are starting to rust through. A damaged or leaking pipe should be replaced.

2. Check the mufflers for dents or other damage.

3. Check the clamps for damage, corrosion or weakness. Clean or repair clamps as required.

4. Replace any bent, damaged or corroded fasteners.

5. Check the exhaust pipe covers for damage.

6. Store the removed part(s) in a safe place until they are reinstalled.

8

Table 1 FUEL SYSTEM SPECIFICATIONS (USA AND CALIFORNIA MODELS)

Carburetor	Keihin CVK32
Main jet	
California models	130
USA models	125
Main jet (high altitude)	
California models	128
USA models	122
Main air jet	130
Air jet	#85
Jet needle	N52M
Needle jet (2000-on models)	#6
Pilot jet	
Sea level	35
High altitude	32
Pilot air jet	85
Pilot screw*	–
Starter jet	
California models	45
USA models	55
Fuel level	
Sea level	0.5 mm (0.019 in.)
High altitude	1.5 mm (0.059 in.) above carb body to 0.5 mm (0.019 in.) below carb body
Float height	17 mm (0.669 in.)
Idle speed	
California models	1150-1250 rpm
USA models	950-1050 rpm

*The pilot screw is sealed and should not be adjusted unless the carburetor is overhauled.

Table 2 FUEL SYSTEM SPECIFICATIONS (ALL MODELS EXCEPT USA AND CALIFORNIA)

Carburetor	Keihin CVK32
Main jet	
1996-1999 Austria and Switzerland models	125
1996-1999 Europe models except Austria and Switzerland	115
1986-1999 models except those listed above	125
2000-on models except Australia and Canada	115
2000-on Australia and Canada models	125
Main air jet	130
Air jet	#85
Jet Needle	
1990-1993 U.K. models	N52H
1996-1999 Austria and Switzerland models	N52M
1996-1999 Europe models except Austria and Switzerland	N1QM
1986-1999 models except those listed above	N52M
2000-on models except Australia models	N1QM
2000-on Australia models	N52M
Needle jet (2000-on models)	#6
Pilot jet	35
Pilot air jet (1989-on models)	85
Pilot screw	
1986-1987 Switzerland models	1 3/4 turns out
1988-1999 Switzerland models	1 1/4 turns out
1989-1999 Austria models	1 1/2 turns out
All 1996-1999 European models except Austria and Switzerland	1 1/2 turns out
All 1986-1999 models except those listed above	2 turns out
2000-on models except Australia	1 1/2 turns out
2000-on Australia models	2 turns out
Starter jet	55
Fuel level	
1986-1999 models	0.5 mm (0.019 in.)
All 1996-1999 European models except Austria and Switzerland	
Sea level	0.5 mm (0.019 in.)
High altitude	1.5 mm (0.059 in.) above carb body to 0.5 mm (0.019 in.) below carb body
2000-on except Australia and Canada	
Sea level	0.5 mm (0.019 in.) above carb body
High altitude	2.5 mm (0.098 in.) to 0.5 mm (0.019 in.) above carb body
2000-on Australia and Canada models	
Sea level	0.5 mm (0.019 in.)
High altitude	1.5 mm (0.059 in.) above carb body to 0.5 mm (0.019 in.) below carb body
Float height	17 mm (0.669 in.)
Idle speed	
1988-on Switzerland models	1150-1250 rpm
2000-on Eurpoean and French models	1250-1350 rpm
All models except those listed above	950-1050 rpm

CHAPTER NINE

ELECTRICAL SYSTEM

This chapter covers service procedures for the electrical system. When inspecting an electrical component, compare any measurements to the specifications in the tables at the end of this chapter. Replace a component that is worn, damaged or out of specification. During assembly, tighten fasteners to the specified torque.

Refer to *Electrical System Fundamentals* in Chapter One and *Electrical Testing* in Chapter Two for basic information and troubleshooting.

ELECTRICAL COMPONENT REPLACEMENT

Most motorcycle dealerships and parts suppliers will not accept the return of any electrical part. If you cannot determine the *exact* cause of any electrical system malfunction, have a Kawasaki dealership retest that specific system to verify your test results. If you purchase a new electrical component(s), install it and then find that the system still does not work properly, you will probably be unable to return the unit for a refund.

Consider any test results carefully before replacing a component that tests only *slightly* out of specification, especially resistance. A number of variables can affect test results dramatically. These include: the testing meter's internal circuitry, ambient temperature and conditions under which the machine has been operated. All instructions and specifications have been checked for accuracy; however, successful test results depend to a great degree upon individual accuracy.

ELECTRICAL CONNECTORS

Identification

The photographs in this chapter show components on a 2003 model. Component and connector locations may vary for other model years. Refer to **Figures 1-3** for a connector location. Confirm connector identification by comparing the connector wire colors with the appropriate wiring diagram located at the end of the manual.

This is particularly important if someone else has worked on the motorcycle. This person may have positioned the connector someplace other than the original location. To check, follow the wiring harness from the specific component to the connector.

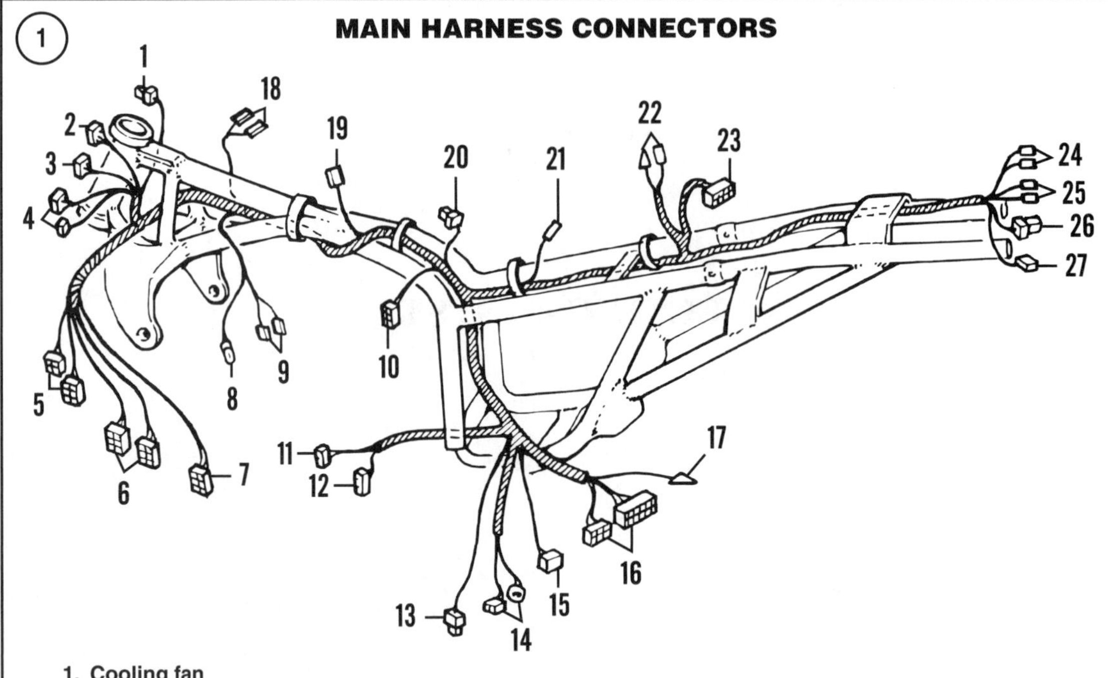

1. Cooling fan
2. Right handlebar switch
3. Main switch
4. Left handlebar switch
5. Meter assembly
6. Fairing harness
7. Reserve lighting device (1986-1993 USA, California and Canada models)
8. Ground wire
9. Ignition coil
10. Pickup coil
11. Neutral switch, oil pressure switch
12. Sidestand switch
13. Alternator
14. Starter relay
15. Fuse box
16. Junction box
17. Battery positive lead
18. Ignition coil
19. Coolant temperature sensor
20. Fan switch
21. Battery negative lead
22. Rear brake light switch
23. IC igniter
24. Left rear turn signal
25. Right rear turn signal
26. Taillight/brake light
27. License plate light

2

FAIRING HARNESS CONNECTORS (1986-1993 MODELS)

1. Horns
2. Right front turn signal
3. Turn signal relay
4. Headlight
5. Reserve lighting device (USA, California and Canada models)
6. Meter assembly
7. Fairing harness

FRONT

LEFT SIDE

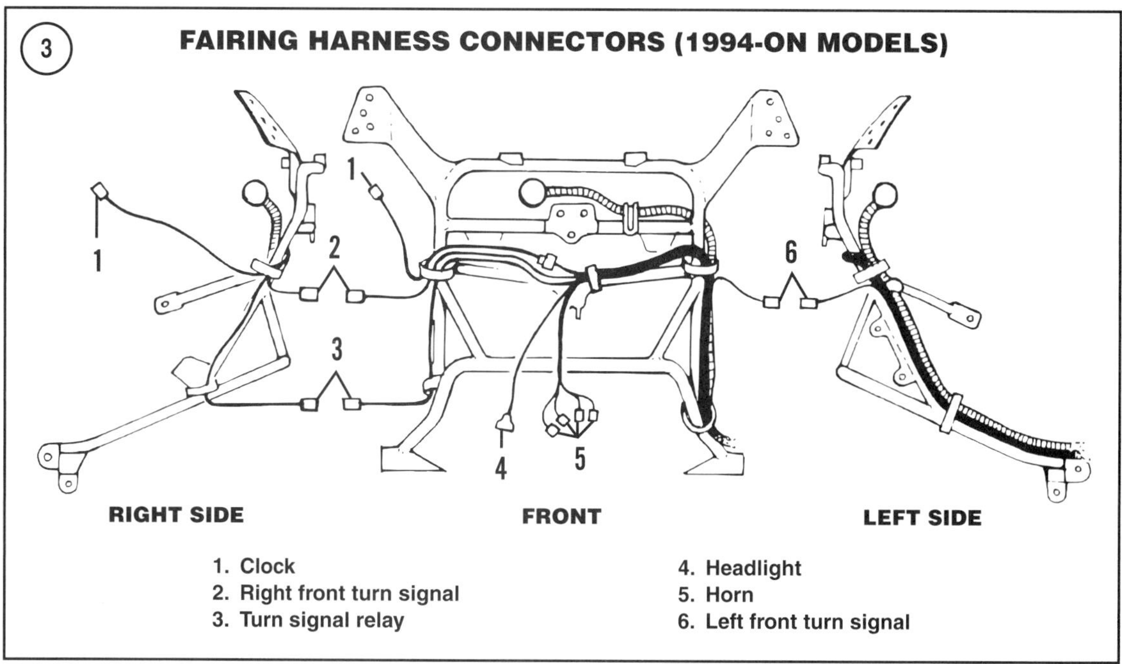

1. Clock
2. Right front turn signal
3. Turn signal relay
4. Headlight
5. Horn
6. Left front turn signal

Maintenance

The electrical system uses a variety of electrical connectors. Moisture can enter these connectors and cause a poor electrical connection. Troubleshooting an electrical circuit with corroded electrical terminals can be time-consuming and frustrating.

To prevent corrosion, pack electrical connectors with dielectric grease when reconnecting them. Dielectric grease is formulated for sealing and waterproofing electrical connectors and it will not interfere with current flow.

Only use dielectric grease or an equivalent compound designed for this specific purpose. Other materials may interfere with the current flow. Do not use silicone sealant.

Thoroughly clean and dry both the male and female connector halves. Pack one of the halves with dielectric grease before joining the two connector halves. Use a fair amount so it will ooze out when the two halves are pushed together. For best results, the compound should fill the entire inner area of the connector.

Also pack the backside of the connector halves to prevent moisture from entering the back of the connector. After the connector is fully packed, wipe excess dielectric grease from the outside of the connector.

In addition to packing electrical connectors, regularly check the ground connections at the various locations on the motorcycle. Make sure the ground connections are tight and free of corrosion.

NEGATIVE BATTERY TERMINAL

Some of the procedures in this manual require disconnecting the negative battery cable from the negative battery terminal for safety.

1. Turn the ignition switch off.
2. Remove the seat and tool box as described in Chapter Fifteen.
3. Disconnect the cable from the negative (–) battery terminal (**Figure 4**).

4. Move the negative cable out of the way so it will not accidentally make contact with the negative terminal.
5. Once the procedure is completed, apply dielectric grease to the battery terminal. Connect the battery negative cable to the terminal and tighten the bolt securely.
6. Install the tool box and seat (Chapter Fifteen).

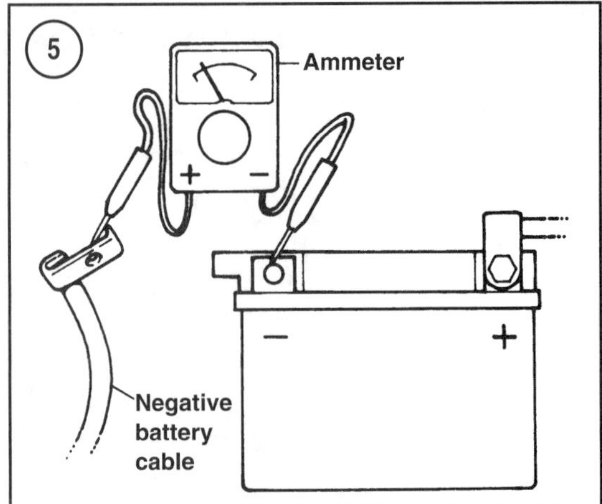

CHARGING SYSTEM

The charging system consists of the battery, main fuse, main relay and alternator. The voltage regulator and the rectifier are integral parts of the alternator.

Alternating current generated by the alternator is rectified to direct current. The voltage regulator maintains the voltage to the battery and additional electrical loads (lights, ignition, etc.) at a constant voltage regardless of variations in engine speed and load.

The alternator mounts to the left side of the engine behind the cylinder block. The voltage regulator, rectifier and brushes can be serviced while the alternator is still installed on the engine. The alternator is shown removed for photographic clarity.

A malfunction in the charging system typically leads to an undercharged battery. Refer to Chapter Three for battery maintenance.

Troubleshooting

Refer to Chapter Two.

Current Draw Test

1. Turn the ignition switch off and disconnect the negative battery cable.
2. Connect an ammeter between the battery negative cable and the negative terminal of the battery (**Figure 5**).
3. The ammeter should read less than 0.1 mA. If the amperage is greater, there is a current draw in the system that will discharge the battery.
4. An excessive current draw suggests a short circuit and a continuous battery discharge. Dirt and/or electrolyte on top of the battery or a crack in the battery case can cause this type of problem by providing a path for battery current to follow. Remove and clean the battery as described in Chapter Three. Reinstall the battery and retest.
5. If the current draw is still excessive, refer to the wiring diagrams at the end of the manual. Then continue to measure the current draw while disconnecting different connectors in the electrical system one by one. When the current draw returns to an acceptable level, the circuit causing the problem is indicated. Test the circuit further to isolate the problem.

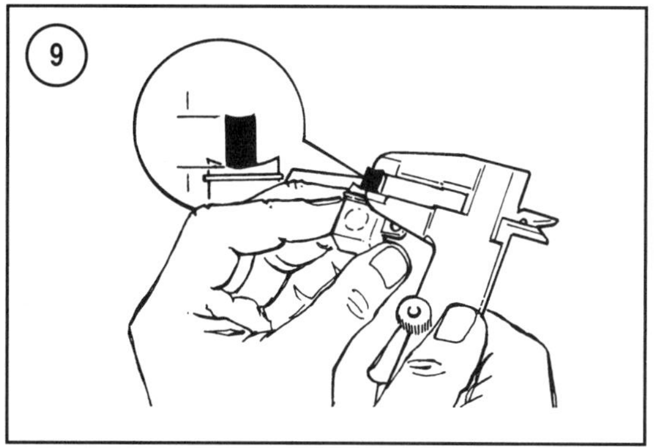

Charging Voltage Test

1. Connect a DC voltmeter across the battery terminals.
2. Start the engine and turn on the headlight.
3. Increase engine speed to approximately 4000 rpm. The measured voltage should equal the charging voltage specified in **Table 1**.
4. If the charging voltage is out of specification, check the stator coil resistance as described in this chapter.

ALTERNATOR

Brush Removal/Inspection/Installation

1. Remove the alternator cover nuts and end cover (A, **Figure 6**) from the alternator.
2. Remove the screws securing brush holder (**Figure 7**) and the brushes and springs. See **Figure 8**.
3. Use a vernier caliper to measure the portion of the brushes that extend beyond the holder (**Figure 9**). Replace both brushes if either is worn to the service limit specified in **Table 1**.
4. Installation is the reverse of removal.

9

Regulator Removal/Installation

1. Remove the alternator cover nuts and remove the end cover (A, **Figure 6**).
2. Remove the brush holder (**Figure 7**) screws and remove the brushes and springs.
3. Remove the screw securing the wire to the regulator (A, **Figure 10**).
4. Remove the regulator mounting screws (A, **Figure 11**) and lift the regulator (B) from the alternator.
5. Installation is the reverse of removal.

Rectifier Removal/Installation

A soldering iron and rosin core solder are needed to complete this task.

1. Remove the alternator cover nuts and remove the end cover (A, **Figure 6**).
2. Remove the brush holder (**Figure 7**) and the brushes and springs.
3. Remove the screw securing the wire to the regulator (A, **Figure 10**) and the screw (B) securing the alternator wire to the rectifier.

4. Unsolder the alternator wire from the rectifier (A, **Figure 12**) and remove the rectifier (B).

5. Installation is the reverse of removal. Note the following:

   a. Only use rosin core solder when soldering the alternator wire to the rectifier (A, **Figure 12**).

   b. Make sure the end cover is secure.

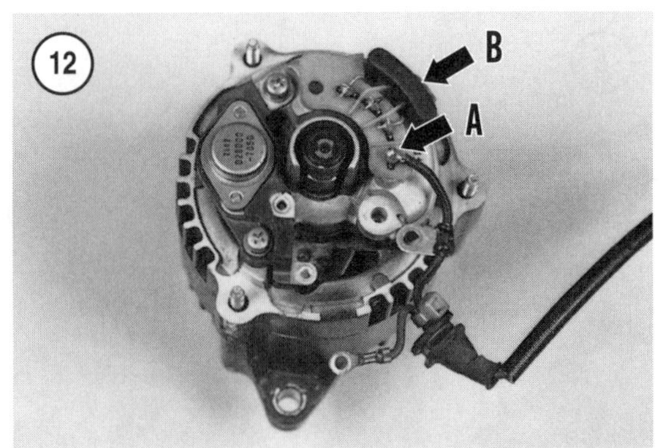

Alternator

Removal/installation

1. Disconnect the negative battery cable.

2. Remove the lower and middle fairings as described in Chapter Fifteen.

3. Follow the alternator electrical lead and disconnect the 2-pin alternator connector from its harness mate. Note how the wire is routed along the frame.

CAUTION

Be careful when pulling the alternator so its does not slam into the cam chain tensioner. Remove the tensioner if necessary (Chapter Four).

4. Remove the alternator mounting bolts (B, **Figure 6**), pull the alternator until it is free of the coupling dampers (A, **Figure 13**) and lower the alternator from the engine.

5. If necessary, remove the dampers (A, **Figure 13**) from the left inner coupling.

6. Check the alternator O-ring (**Figure 14**) for flat spots or wear. Replace the O-ring as necessary.

7. The alternator is grounded through the mounting lugs on the crankcase (B, **Figure 13**) and alternator (A, **Figure 15**). Clean these areas with contact cleaner before installing the alternator.

8. Check the blades (B, **Figure 15**) on the coupling for looseness, cracks or other damage. Replace the coupling as necessary.

10. Installation is the reverse of removal. Pay attention to the following:

   a. Apply a light coat of engine oil to the alternator O-ring (**Figure 14**) and to coupling dampers (A, **Figure 13**).

   b. Position the dampers so there is a gap between each set of dampers as shown in **Figure 13**.

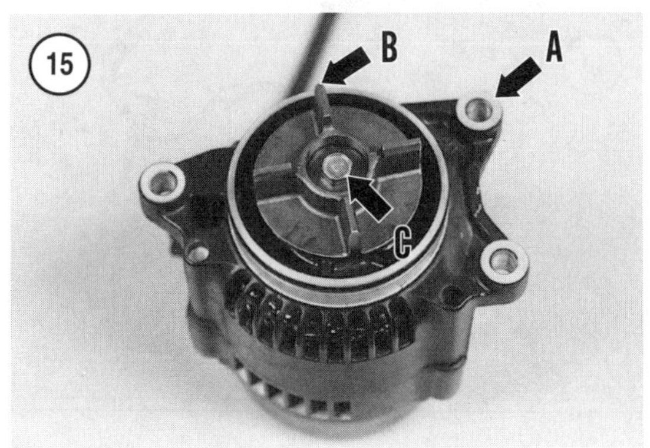

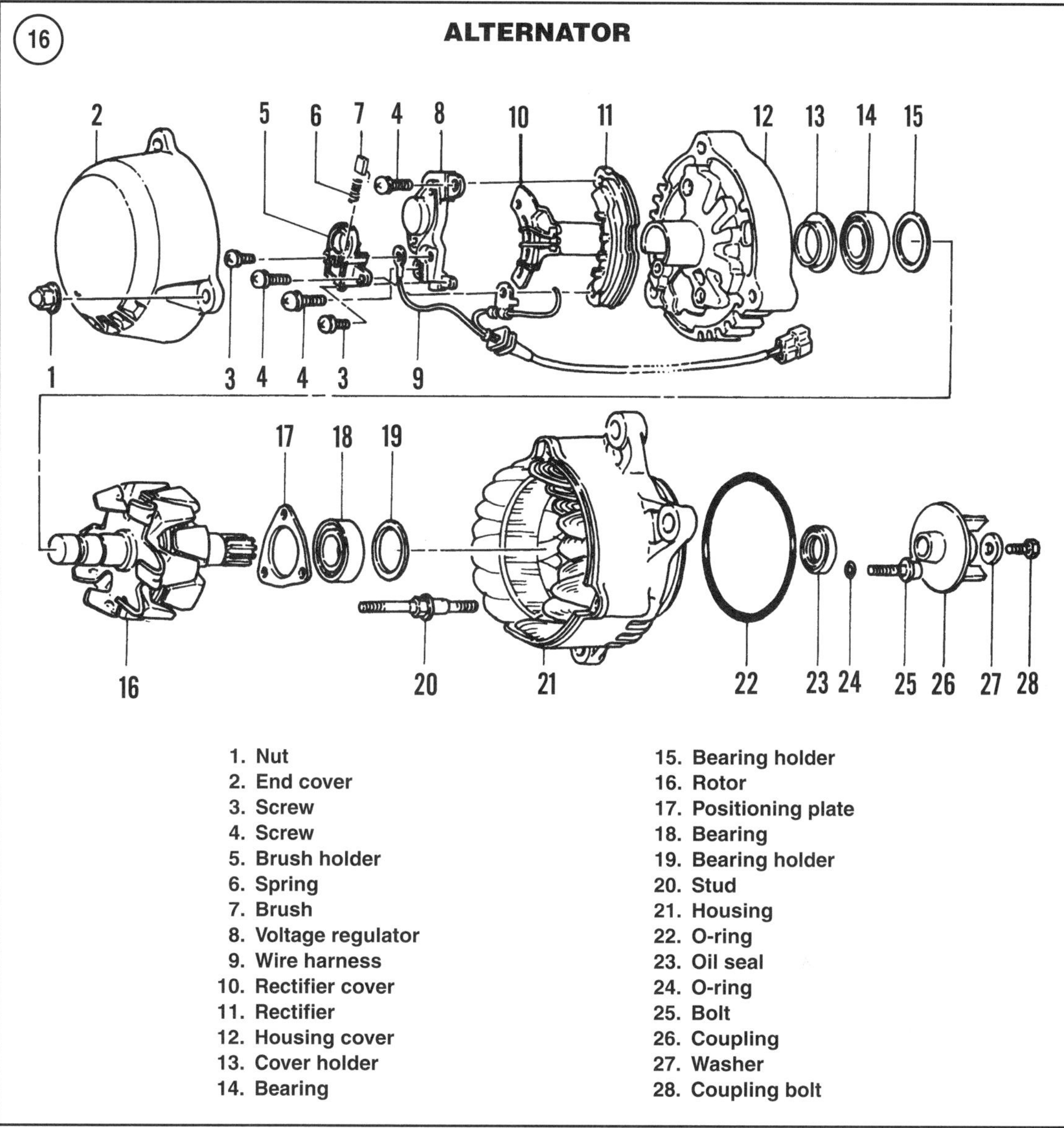

c. Align the alternator coupling blades (B, **Figure 15**) with the slots between the dampers and install the alternator.

d. Apply Loctite 242 (blue) to the threads of the alternator mounting bolts (B, **Figure 6**). Evenly tighten the bolts in a crisscross pattern. Once the alternator is snug against the crankcase, torque the alternator bolts to 25 N•m (18 ft.-lb.).

Disassembly

Refer to **Figure 16**.

1. Remove the alternator as described in this section.

2. Remove the alternator cover nuts and remove the end cover.

3. Remove the brush holder, regulator and rectifier as described in this section.

4. Hold the coupling (B, **Figure 15**) and remove the coupling bolt (C). Pull the coupling from the alternator.

5. Wrap the splines on the alternator shaft with Teflon tape so the splines will not damage the oil seal during disassembly.

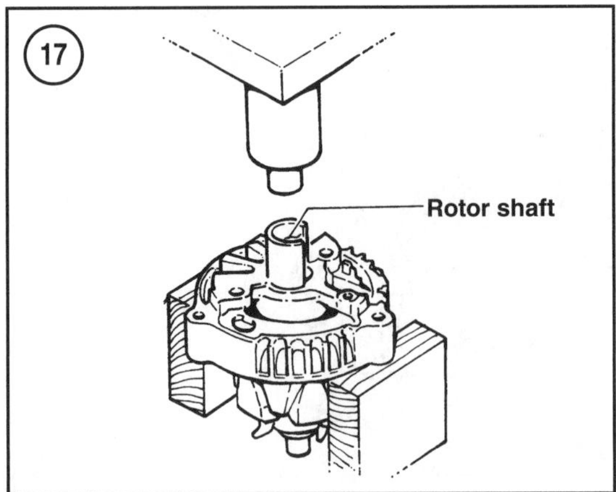

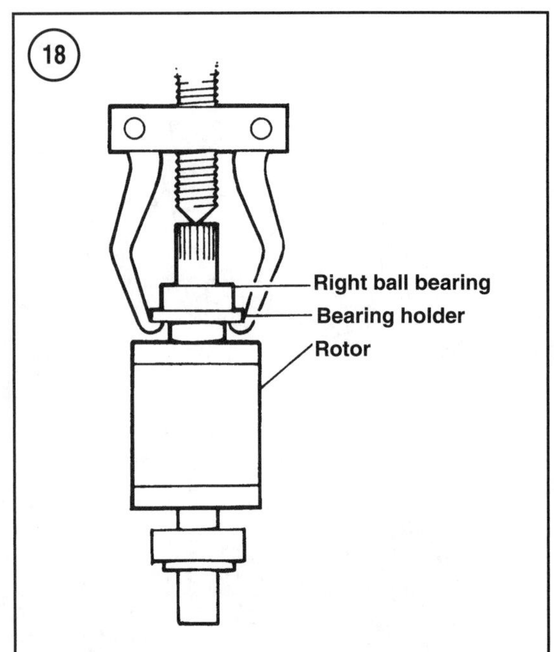

6. Remove the screws securing the housing to the housing cover and pull the housing off the rotor/housing cover assembly.

7. Support the housing cover as shown in **Figure 17** and press the rotor from the cover. Be prepared to catch the rotor so it will not fall to the floor.

NOTE
Label the left and right bearings. If a bearing can be reused, it must be reinstalled in its original location on the rotor shaft.

8. Use a universal bearing puller to remove the right bearing from the rotor shaft (**Figure 18**), then remove the left bearing.

9. Inspect the alternator as described in this section.

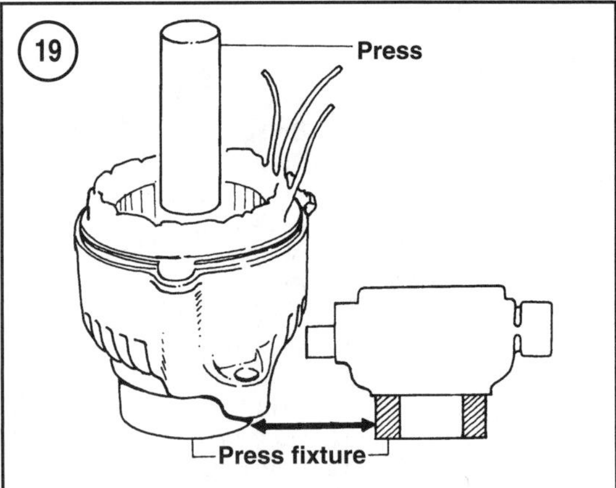

Assembly

1. Support the housing in a press as shown in **Figure 19**.
2. Press the right bearing into the housing.
3. Install the bearing retainer and secure it with its mounting bolts.
4. Support the inner race of the right bearing as shown in **Figure 20**.
5. Press the rotor into the inner race on the right bearing.
6. With the right bearing supported as described in Step 4, press the bearing holder, left bearing and cover holder onto the rotor shaft (**Figure 21**). Make sure the side of the bearing with the ring faces out away from the rotor windings.

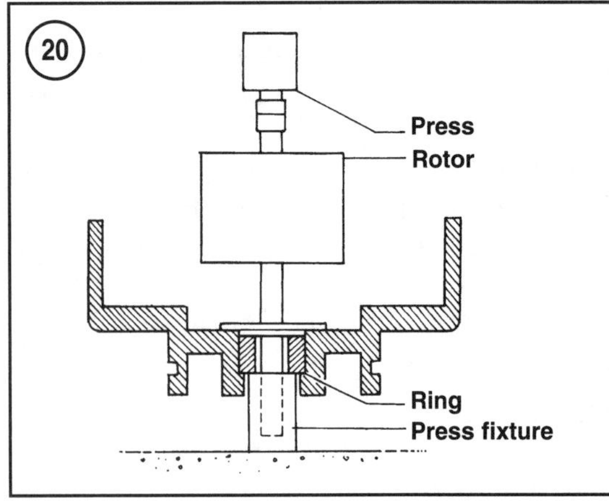

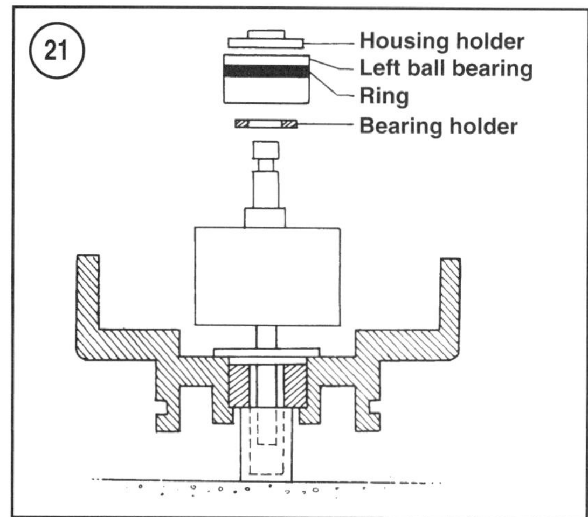

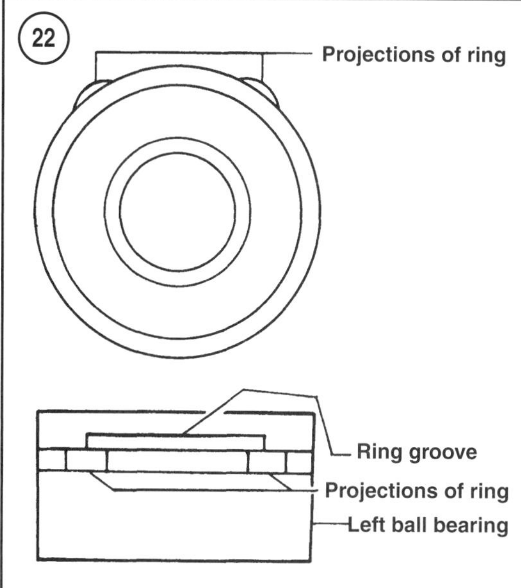

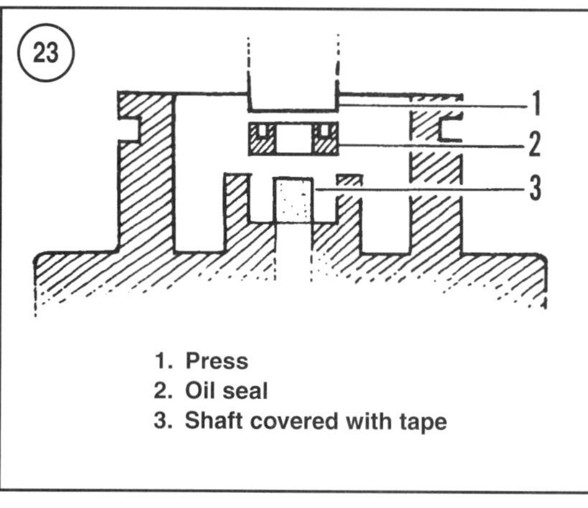

1. Press
2. Oil seal
3. Shaft covered with tape

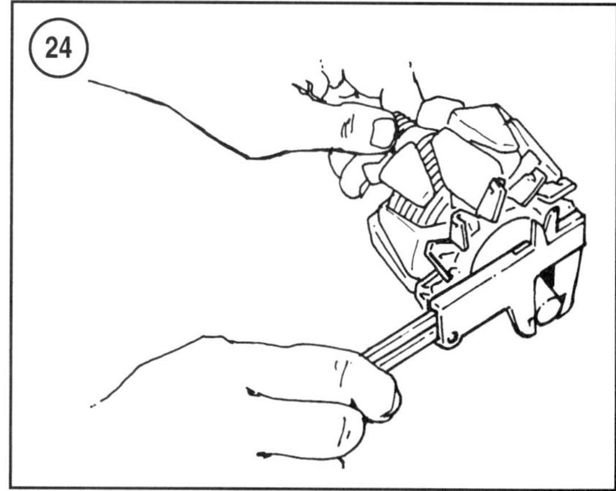

7. Align the bearing ring so its tabs align with the positioning grooves (**Figure 22**) and install the housing cover.

8. If the oil seal was removed from the right cover, replace it by performing the following:

   a. Wrap the splines of the rotor shaft with Teflon tape.
   b. Lubricate the lips of the oil seal.
   c. Position the oil seal so its open side (the side with the spring) faces out.
   d. Press the new oil seal into place (**Figure 23**).

Inspection

1. Check the bearing seal for tears or other damage. Replace the bearings as necessary.
2. Turn the bearing inner races by hand. Replace the bearings if any roughness or excessive noise is noticed.
3. Perform the stator coil resistance check and the stator coil continuity check described in this section. Replace the stator as necessary.
4. Visually inspect the rotor slip rings for pitting corrosion or other signs or abnormal wear. If necessary, dress the slip ring with No. 300 to No. 500 emery cloth.
5. Measure the diameter of the slip rings with a vernier caliper (**Figure 24**). Replace the rotor if the diameter exceeds the service limit specified in **Table 1**.
6. Perform the rotor resistance test and the rotor continuity test described in this section.
7. Perform the rectifier resistance test described in this section.
8. Perform the regulator operational test described in this section.

9

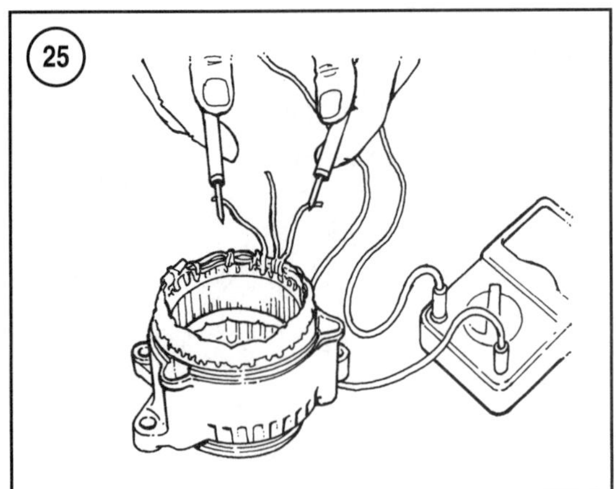

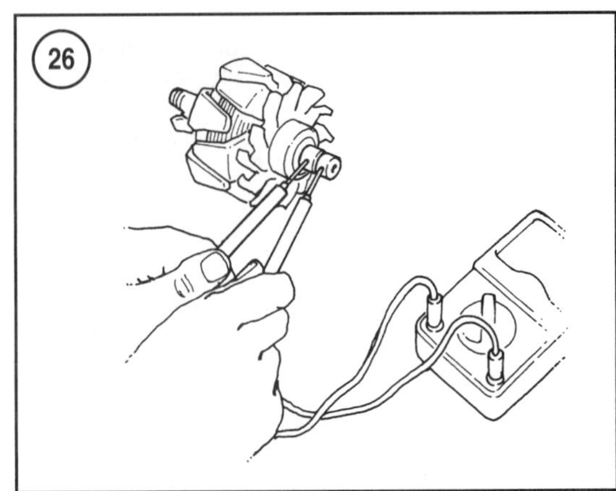

Stator

Resistance test

1. If using an analog ohmmeter, set the meter to the R × 1 scale.
2. Check the resistance between each of the three stator coil wires (**Figure 25**).
3. If any reading is less than the specification in **Table 1**, replace the stator.

Continuity test

1. If using an analog ohmmeter, set the meter to the R × 100 scale.
2. Check the continuity between each winding and the stator core.
3. If any reading shows continuity, the stator coil is shorted; Replace the stator.

Rotor

Resistance test

1. Set an analog ohmmeter to the R × 1 scale.
2. Check the resistance between the slip rings (**Figure 26**).
3. Replace the rotor is the resistance varies considerably from the rotor resistance specified in **Table 1**.

Continuity test

1. If using an analog ohmmeter, set the meter to the R × 100 scale.

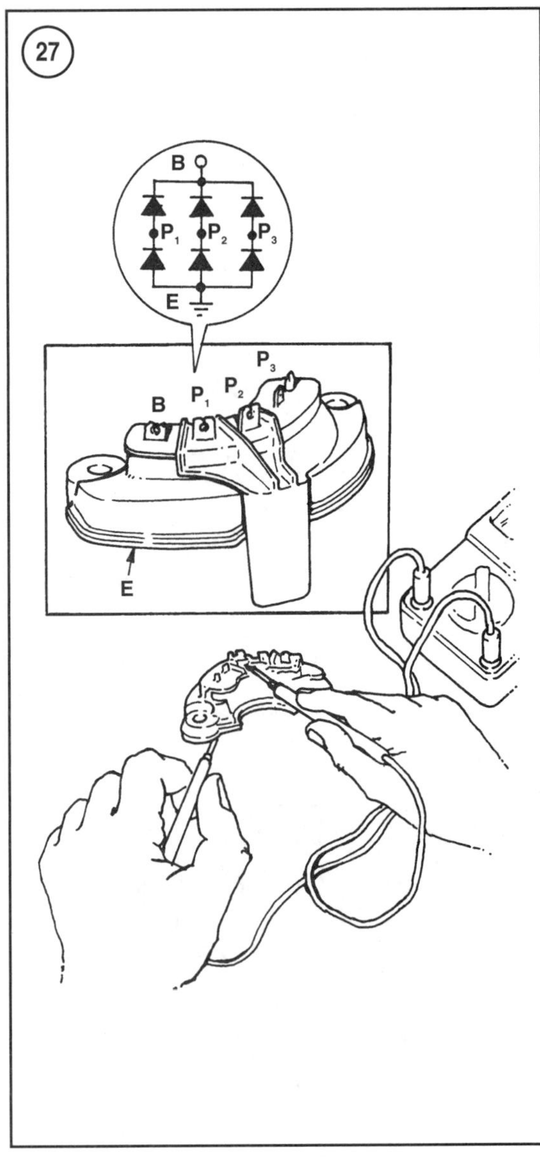

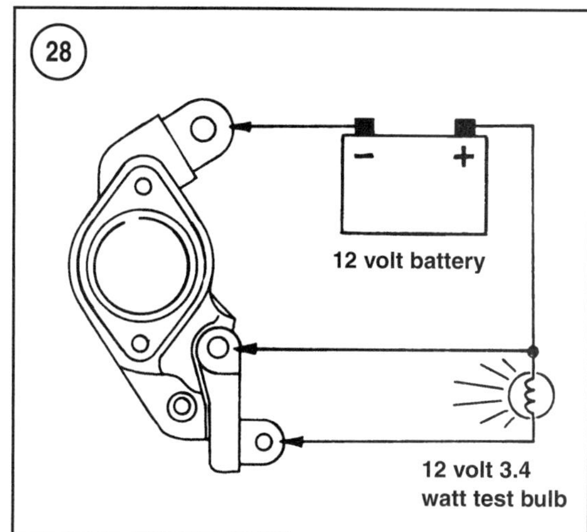

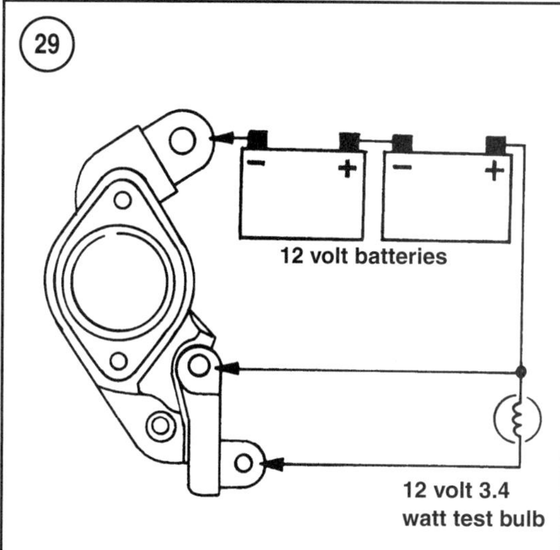

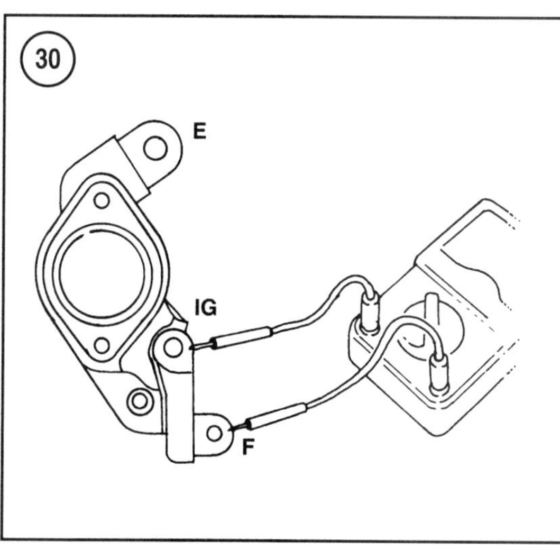

2. Check the continuity between the rotor shaft and each slip ring. There should be no continuity (infinite resistance).
3. If continuity is found between either slip ring and the shaft, the rotor coil is shorted. Replace the rotor.

Rectifier Resistance Test

1. Set an ohmmeter to the R × 1000 scale.
2. Refer to **Figure 27** and check the resistance at the B terminal by performing the following:
   a. Connect one ohmmeter test lead to the rectifier body and connect the other test lead to the B terminal. Record the reading.
   b. Reverse the test leads and record the reading.
   c. The resistance should be low in one direction and more than 10 times higher when the test leads are reversed.
3. Repeat Step 2 for the P1, P2 and P3 terminals.
4. If the readings at any terminal are low or high in both directions, a diode is defective. Replace the rectifier.

9

Regulator Operational Test

A test light (12-volt, 3.4 watt bulb), two 12-volt batteries and three test wires with alligator clips are needed to perform this test.

CAUTION
Do not use an ammeter in place of the test light. The voltage regulator could be damaged. Also, do not let an electrical lead from a battery touch the regulator metal housing.

1. Connect the test light and one 12-volt battery to the regulator as shown in **Figure 28**. The test light should turn on.
2. Connect the test light and two 12-volt batteries to the regulator as shown in **Figure 29**. The test light should *not* turn on.
3. Replace the regulator if it failed either test.
4. Check the internal resistance by performing the following:
   a. See **Figure 30** for the regulator test points.
   b. Connect an ohmmeter to the test points indicated in **Table 2**.
   c. The measured value should be near the indicated specification. If any reading equals zero

or infinity, the regulator is damaged and should be replaced.

IGNITION SYSTEM

All models are equipped with an electronic ignition system. Ignition timing and advance are maintained without adjustment.

When the crankshaft-driven rotor passes the pickup coil, an electrical pulse is generated within the coil. This pulse flows to the switching and distribution circuits in the IC igniter. The IC igniter interrupts current flow through the ignition coil and the magnetic field within the coil collapses. When this happens, a high voltage is induced in the secondary windings of the ignition coil. This voltage is sufficient to jump the gap at the spark plugs.

Troubleshooting

Refer to Chapter Two.

Pickup Coil Cover Removal/Installation

1. Remove the lower and middle fairings as described in Chapter Fifteen.
2. Remove the cover bolts and pull the cover (A, **Figure 31**) from the crankcase.
3. Remove the cover gasket.
4. Installation is the reverse of removal. Pay attention to the following:
   a. Apply sealant where the case halves come together (A, **Figure 32**) and to the grommet (B) for the pickup coil wire.
   b. Install a new gasket if necessary.
   c. Apply Loctite 242 (blue) to the threads of the two indicated cover bolts (B, **Figure 31**). Tighten the bolts securely.

Timing Rotor Removal/Installation

1. Remove the pickup coil cover from the left side of the crankcase as described in this section.
2. Remove the Allen bolt (C, **Figure 32**) and then remove the nut (D).
3. Remove the timing rotor (**Figure 33**).
4. Installation is the reverse of removal. Note the following:

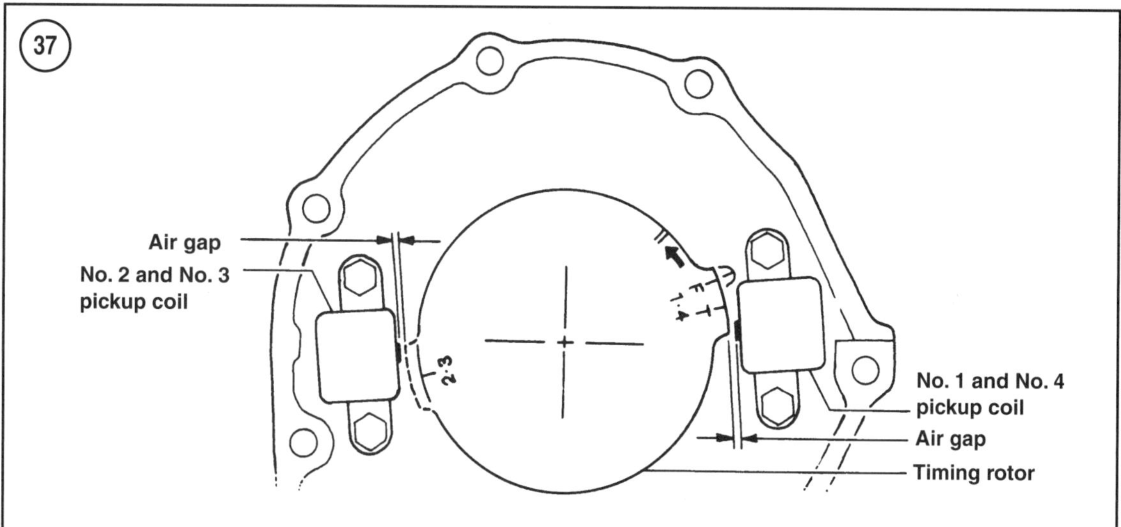

a. Align the dowel on the end of the crankshaft with the slot in the rotor and install the rotor.

b. Install the large nut (D, **Figure 32**) and the Allen bolt (C). Torque the timing rotor Allen bolt to 25 N•m (18 ft.-lb.).

c. Install the pickup coil cover as described in this chapter.

Pickup Coil Removal/Installation

1. Remove the pickup coil cover as described in this section.

2. Follow the pickup coil wire rearward to the pickup coil 4-pin connector (**Figure 34**). Pull the connector out from the behind the frame downtube and disconnect it from its harness mate.

3. Release the pickup coil wire from any clamps that secure it to the engine. Note how the wire is routed so it can be rerouted along the same path.

4. Pull the pickup coil grommet (A, **Figure 35**) from the crankcase.

5. Remove the two mounting screws for each pickup coil (B, **Figure 35**) and remove the pickup coil assembly.

6. Installation is the reverse of removal.

a. Secure the pickup coil grommet (A, **Figure 35**) in the notch in the crankcase.

b. Set the pickup coil air gap as described in this section.

Pickup Coil Air Gap Inspection/Adjustment

1. Remove the pickup coil cover as described in this section.

2. Use the timing rotor nut to rotate the crankshaft (**Figure 36**) counterclockwise until the timing rotor projection aligns with one of the pickup coils. See **Figure 37**.

3. Use a feeler gauge to measure the gap between the timing rotor and pickup coil (**Figure 38**).
4. If the pickup coil air gap is outside the range specified in **Table 1**, loosen that coil's mounting bolts and reposition the coil. Tighten the bolts and recheck the air gap.
5. Repeat for the opposite pickup coil.
6. Install the pickup coil cover as described in this section.

Pickup Coil Resistance Test

1. Follow the pickup coil wire rearward to the pickup coil 4-pin connector (**Figure 34**). Pull the connector out from the behind the frame downtube and disconnect it from its harness mate.
2. Check the resistance between the black and yellow terminals in the harness side of the connector (coil for No. 1 and No. 4 cylinders) and check the resistance between the blue and black/white terminals (coil for No. 2 and No. 3 cylinders).
3. If either reading is outside the range specified in **Table 1**, replace the pickup coil assembly.
4. Check the continuity between each terminal in the pickup coil side of the connector and a good ground. If any test shows continuity, the coil is shorted to ground. Replace the pickup coil assembly.

Ignition Coil Removal/Installation

Two ignition coils are mounted to the side of the main frame tube. The coil on the left side (**Figure 39**) fires the No. 1 and No. 4 cylinders; the right coil fires the No. 2 and No. 3 cylinders.

1. Remove the fuel tank as described in Chapter Eight.
2. Grasp each spark plug lead (**Figure 40**) and pull it from its spark plug.
3. Disconnect the primary leads (A and B, **Figure 39**) from the terminals on the ignition coil.
4. Remove the mounting nuts (C, **Figure 39**) and remove the coils. When removing the left ignition coil, watch for the black/yellow frame ground wire under the front mounting nut.
5. Installation is the reverse of removal. Pay attention to the following:
   a. When installing the left ignition coil, secure the black/yellow ground wire under the front mounting nut. See **Figure 39**.
   b. Connect the red primary wire (A, **Figure 39**) to the positive terminal of the ignition coil.

   c. When installing the left ignition coil, connect the black primary wire (B, **Figure 39**) to the negative terminal on the coil. When installing the right ignition coil, connect the green primary wire to the coil's negative terminal.

Ignition Coil Test

The following describes an ignition coil static test. If the coils pass this test and ignition-related

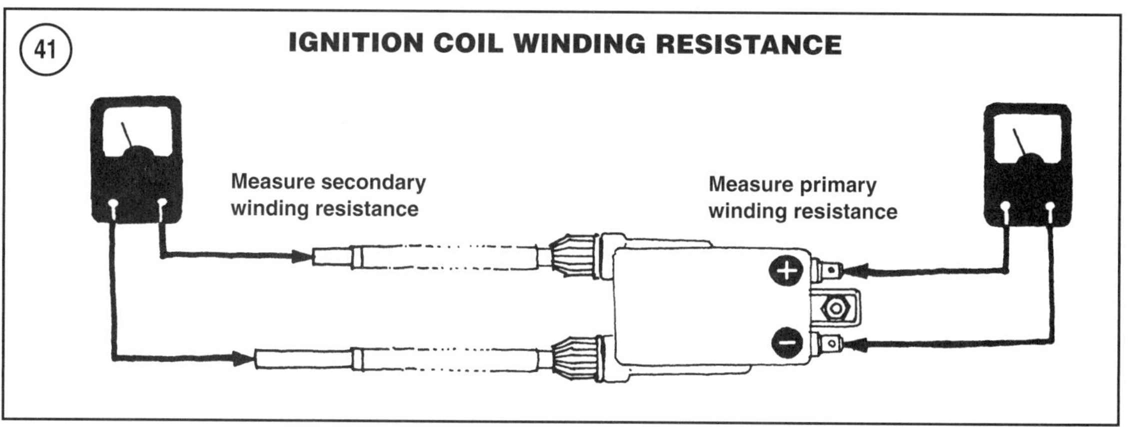

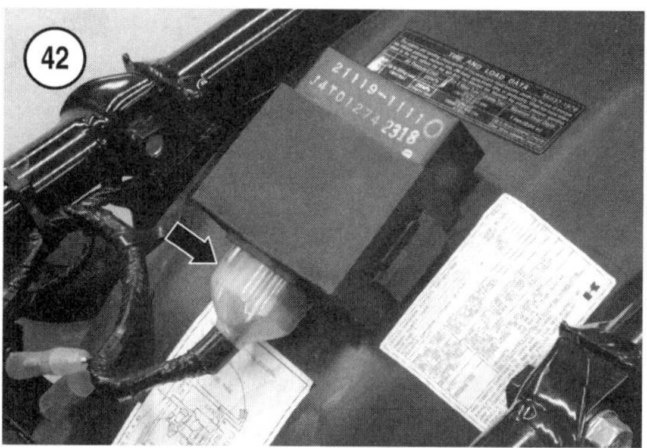

problems are still present, take the ignition coils to a Kawasaki dealership for an ignition coil arc test.

1. Remove the ignition coils as described in this section.
2. Connect an ohmmeter as shown in **Figure 41** and measure the ignition coil's primary winding resistance. Record the reading.
3. Measure the coils secondary winding resistance as shown in **Figure 41**. Record the reading.
4. Replace an ignition coil if the reading is outside the range specified in **Table 1**.

Spark Plugs

Refer to Chapter Three.

IC Igniter Removal/Installation

1. Remove the seat as described in Chapter Fifteen.
2. Unplug the connector (**Figure 42**) and pull the igniter from the mounting damper.
3. Installation is the reverse of removal. Make sure the rubber damper is in good condition. Replace the damper as necessary.

IC Igniter Resistance Test

The Kawasaki Hand Tester (part No. 57001-983) is required to perform this test. Other testers will yield inaccurate results. A tester with a large-capacity battery can damage the igniter. Remove the IC igniter and take it to a Kawasaki dealership or other qualified service shop for testing.

STARTING SYSTEM

The starting system consists of the starter, starter circuit relay, starter relay, starter lockout switch, as well as the neutral and starter switches.

When the starter button is pressed under the correct conditions, control current flows through the starter circuit relay and on to starter relay coil, which energizes the starter relay. The starter relay contacts close and load current flows directly from the battery to the starter.

The starter will only operate when the transmission is in neutral or when the clutch lever is pulled in.

Troubleshooting

Refer to Chapter Two.

Starter Removal/Installation

1. Securely support the motorcycle on a level surface.
2. Disconnect the negative battery cable (**Figure 4**).
3. Remove the lower and middle fairings as described in Chapter Fifteen.
4. Remove the alternator as described in this chapter.
5. Pull back the boot, remove the terminal nut (**Figure 43**) and disconnect the cable from the starter terminal.
6. Remove the starter mounting bolts (**Figure 44**) and pull the starter from the crankcase.
7. Installation is the reverse of removal. Pay attention to the following:
   a. To assure a good ground, use electrical contact cleaner to remove all oil from the mounting lugs on the starter and the crankcase.
   b. Apply engine oil to the starter O-ring (**Figure 45**).
   c. Install the starter so its shaft engages the teeth of the starter idler wheel (**Figure 46**).

Starter Disassembly/Assembly

Refer to **Figure 47**.

1. Loosen and remove the two through bolts and their lockwashers.
2. Remove each end cover and its O-ring from the housing.
3. Slide the lockwasher (A, **Figure 48**) and washers (B) from the armature shaft.
4. Slide the armature from the housing.
5. Partially lift the brush plate from the housing (**Figure 49**). Pull back the spring from each positive brush, remove the positive brushes from their holders and then remove the brush plate.
6. If necessary, remove the terminal bolt/positive brush assembly (A, **Figure 50**) by performing the following:
   a. Remove the terminal nut and washers (B, **Figure 50**) from the terminal bolt.

NOTE
*The quantity, type and placement of washers on the starter may not be the same as shown in **Figure 47**.*

(47)

STARTER

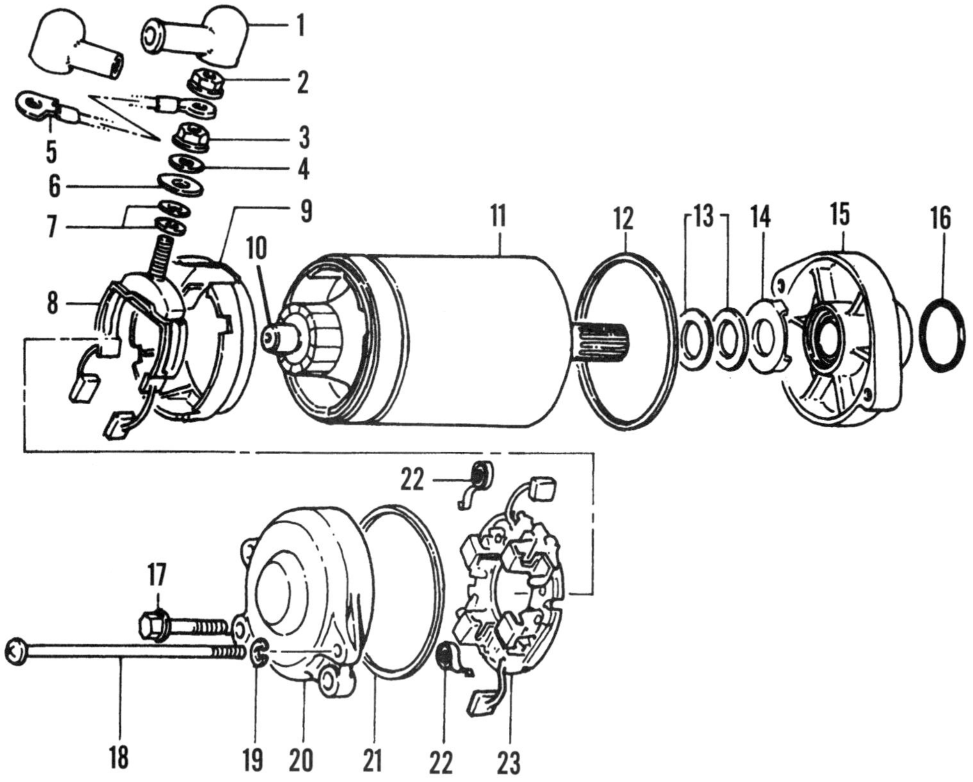

1. Boot
2. Nut
3. Nut
4. Washer
5. Starter cable
6. Large plastic washer
7. Small plastic washers
8. Terminal bolt/positive brush assembly
9. Plastic holder
10. Armature
11. Housing
12. O-ring
13. Washers
14. Lockwasher
15. Right end cover
16. O-ring
17. Mounting bolt
18. Through bolt
19. Lockwasher
20. Left end cover
21. O-ring
22. Spring
23. Brush plate (with negative brushes)

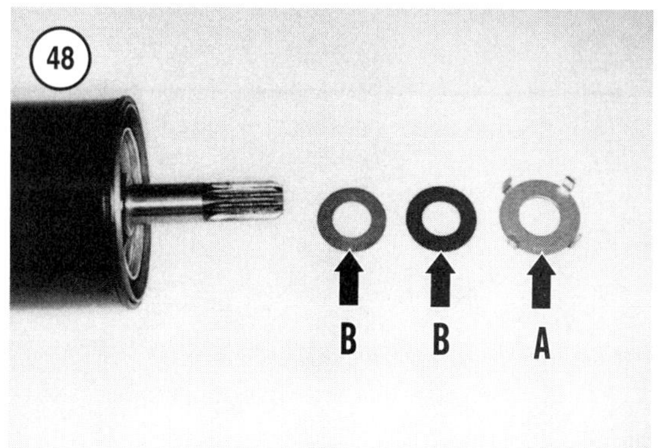

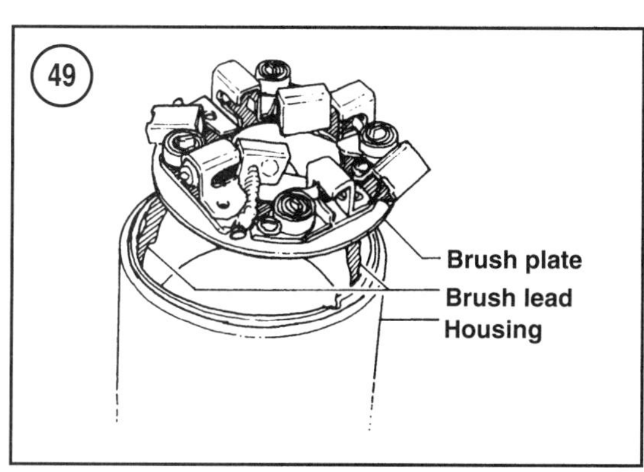

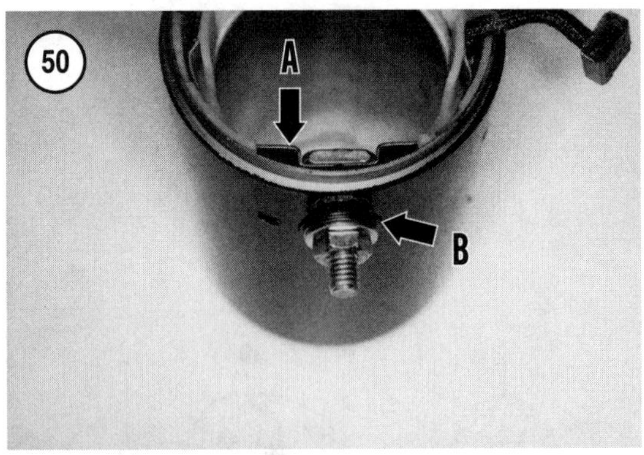

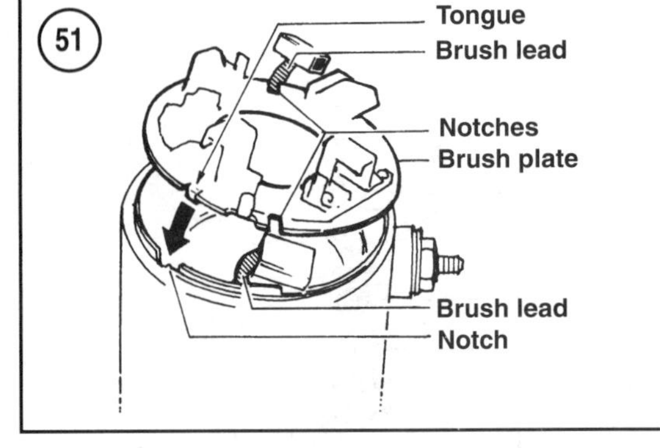

b. Note the number of washers and their order. The washers must be reinstalled in this order during assembly.
c. Pull the terminal bolt from the housing and remove assembly.

7. Clean all grease, dirt and carbon from the armature, housing and end covers.

CAUTION
Do not immerse the brushes or wire windings in solvent. The insulation could be damaged. Clean the windings with electrical contact cleaner or wipe the winding with a cloth lightly moistened with solvent. Dry the windings thoroughly.

8. Inspect the components as described in this section.

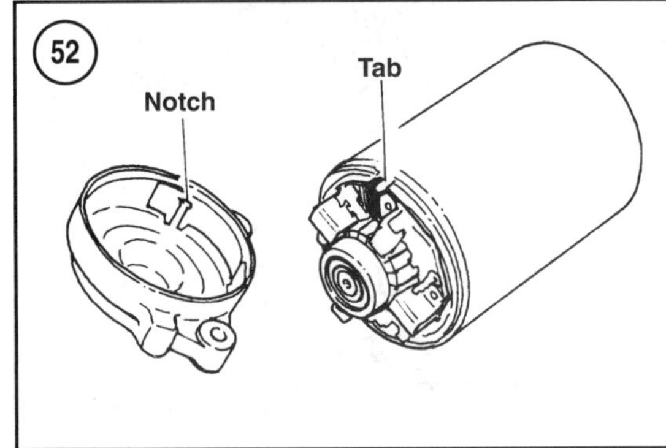

Starter Assembly

1. Install the housing O-rings into the groove at each end of the housing.
2. Set the terminal bolt/positive brush assembly (A, **Figure 50**) into the housing. Secure it to the housing with the terminal nut and washers (B, **Figure 50**). Install the washers in the order noted during removal.
3. Install the brush plate by performing the following:
   a. Seat the positive brush leads into the notches (**Figure 51**) in the brush plate.
   b. Lower the plate onto the housing so the tongue in the plate engages the notch in the housing.
   c. Insert the positive brushes into their respective holders in the brush plate.

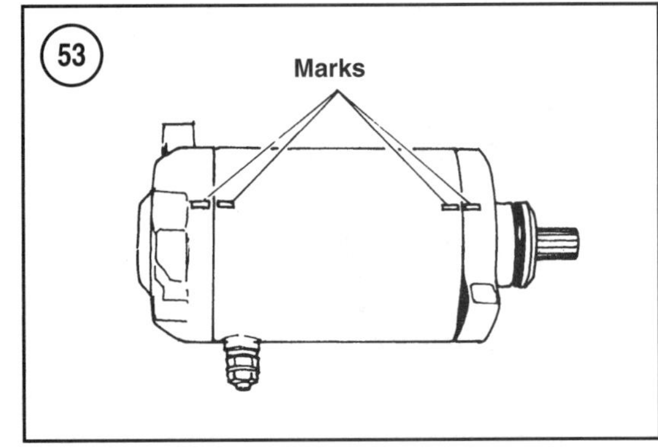

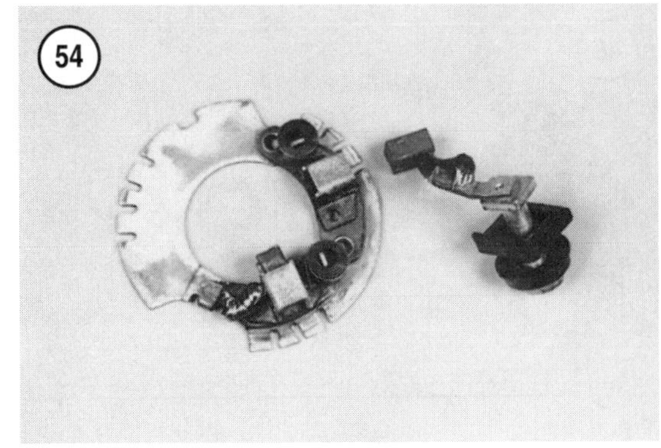

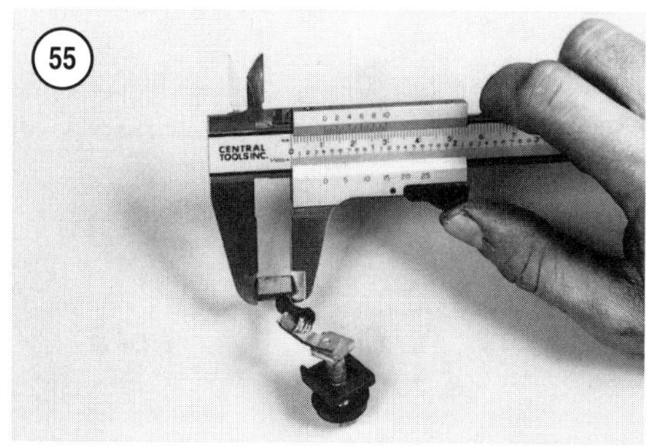

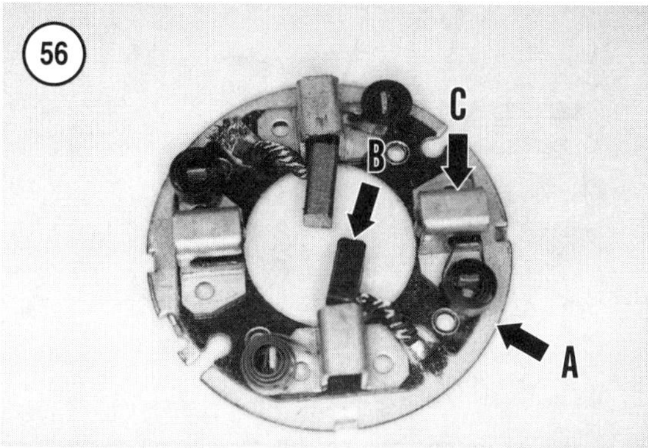

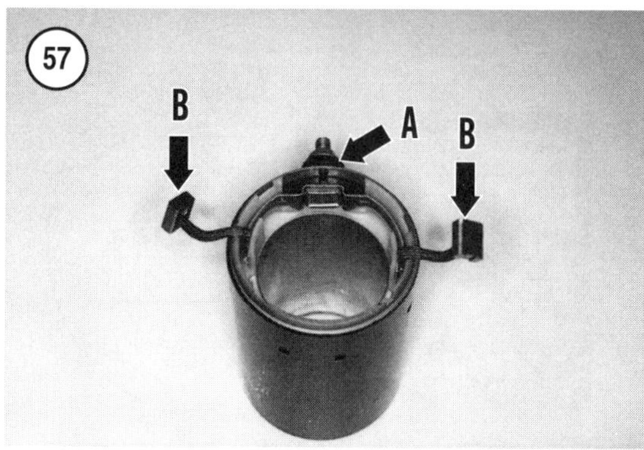

d. Lower the D-shaped portion of the spring half-way onto the spring post. Turn the other half of the spring 1/2-turn clockwise and insert it into the brush groove.

e. Push the spring onto the post until it stops at the stepped portion of the post.

4. Carefully slide the armature into the housing so the brushes engage the commutator properly. Do not damage the brushes during this step.

5. Install the left end cover so the raised tab on the brush plate seats in the cap's notch (**Figure 52**).

6. Install the lockwasher (A, **Figure 48**) so its arms engage the ribs in the right end cover.

7. Both end covers are properly installed when the marks on each cover aligns with the marks on the housing (**Figure 53**).

8. Install the through bolts securely.

Starter Inspection

1. Pull the spring away from any remaining brushes (**Figure 54**) and pull the brushes out of their holders.

2. Measure the length of each brush with a vernier caliper (**Figure 55**). If any brush is worn to the service limit (**Table 1**), replace all the brushes by replacing the brush plate and the positive brush holder. Brushes cannot be replaced individually.

3. Check the continuity between the metal portion of the brush plate (A, **Figure 56**) and each negative brush (B). There should be continuity. Replace the brush plate if no continuity is found.

4. Check the continuity between the metal portion of the brush plate (A, **Figure 56**) and each brush holder (C). There should be no continuity. Replace the brush plate if continuity is found.

5. Check the continuity between the terminal bolt (A, **Figure 57**) and each positive brush (B). There should be continuity. Replace the terminal bolt/positive brush assembly if no continuity is found.

6. Inspect the commutator (**Figure 58**). The mica should be below the surface of the copper bars (**Figure 59**). If the copper bars are worn to the surface of the mica, the commutator must be serviced by a dealership or electrical repair shop.

7. Check the continuity between the commutator bars (**Figure 60**). There should be continuity between the bars. Also check the continuity between each commutator bar and the shaft (**Figure 61**);

there should be no continuity. Replace the armature if it fails either test.

8. Measure the commutator diameter with a vernier caliper. Replace the armature if the commutator diameter is worn to the service limit in **Table 1**.

Starter Operational Test

1. Use jack stands or a scissors jack to securely support the motorcycle on level ground.
2. Remove the starter as described in this section.

WARNING
The jumper wires mentioned in the next step must be as large as the battery cables. Be sure the wires are large enough to handle the current flow from the battery. If a wire is too small, it could melt.

WARNING
The test in the next step will probably produce sparks. Be sure no flammable gas or fluid is in the vicinity of the motorcycle.

3. Apply battery voltage directly to the starter by connecting a jumper from the battery positive terminal to the starter terminal. Use a second jumper to connect the battery negative terminal to the mounting lug on the starter.
4. If the starter does not operate, repair or replace the starter.

Starter Relay Removal/Installation

The starter relay is located on the right side of the motorcycle, just forward of the junction box.

1. Remove the seat and disconnect the negative battery cable.
2. Remove the left side cover as described in Chapter Fifteen.
3. Remove the 2-pin connector (A, **Figure 62**) from the relay.
4. Remove the terminal nuts (B, **Figure 62**). Disconnect the battery cable from the relay positive terminal and pull the starter cable from the relay negative terminal. Label each cable and terminal so the cables can be reconnected properly.
5. Pull the starter relay from its holder and remove it.

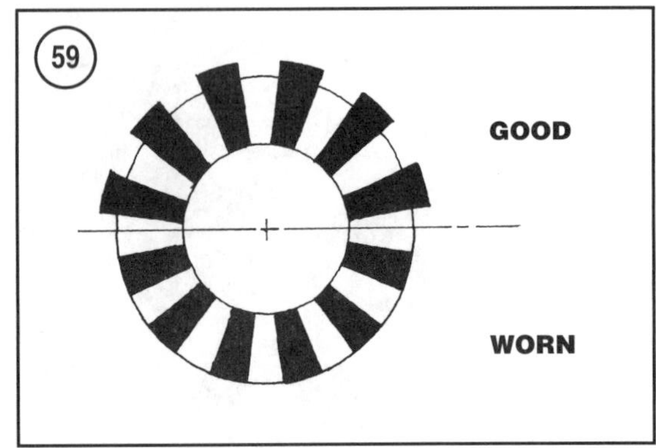

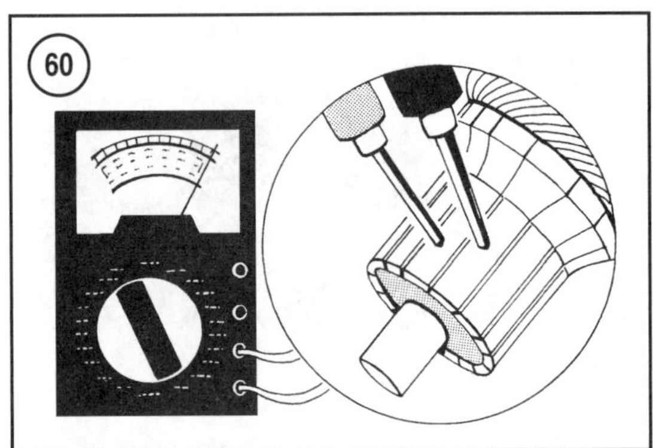

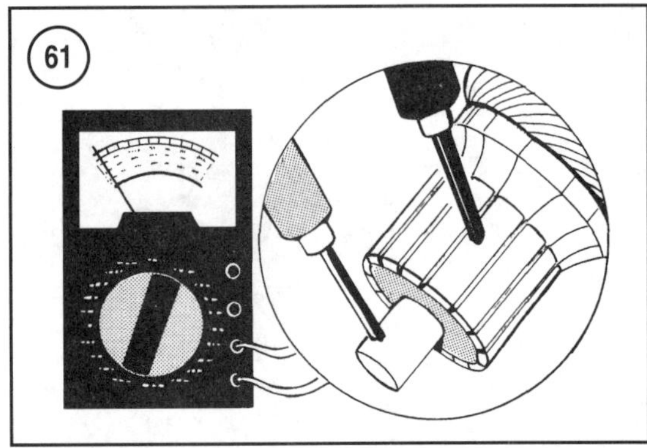

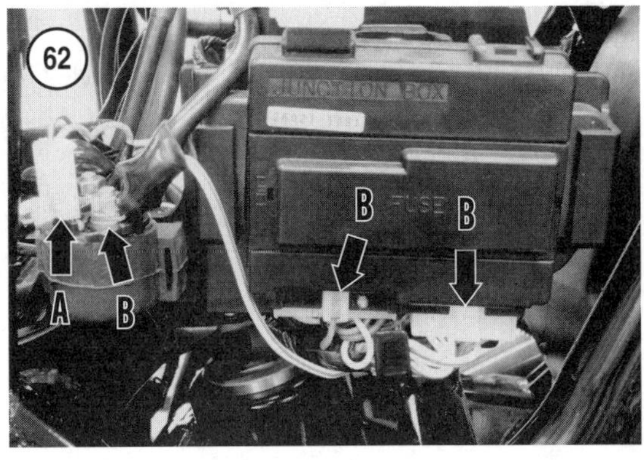

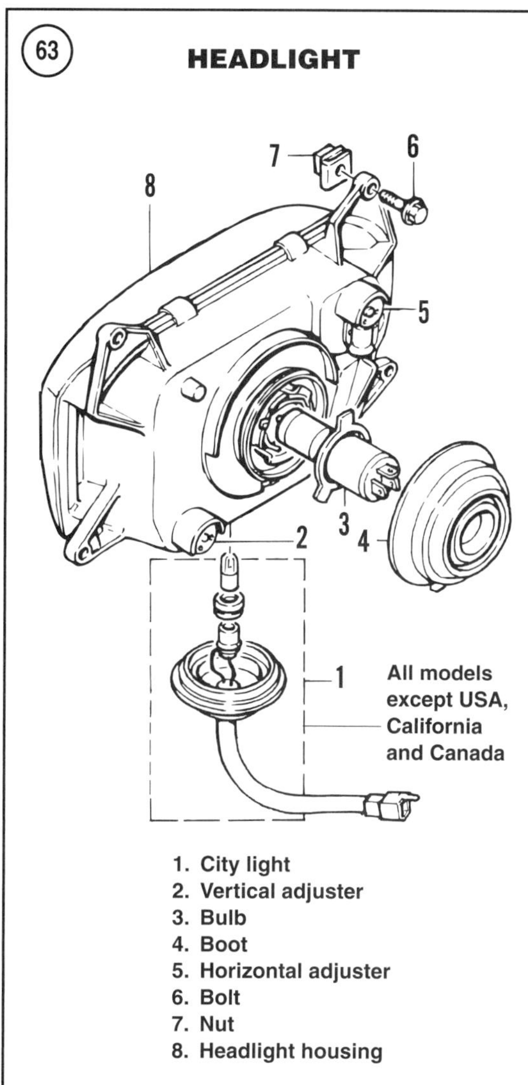

6. Installation is the reverse of removal. Make sure the battery cable is connected to the positive relay terminal.

Starter Relay Test

1. Shift the transmission into neutral and make sure the engine stop switch is in the run position.
2. Remove the left side cover as described in Chapter Fifteen.

CAUTION
Because the battery cable connects directly to the battery, this cable is hot even when the ignition switch is off. Do not allow the end of the cable to touch any part of the motorcycle during this test.

3. Remove the terminal nuts (B, **Figure 62**). Disconnect the battery cable from the relay positive terminal and pull the starter cable from the relay negative terminal. Label each cable and terminal so the cables can be reconnected properly. Do not remove the 2-pin connector (A, **Figure 62**).
4. Connect an ohmmeter across the starter relay terminals.
5. Turn the main switch on and press the starter button. The relay should click and the ohmmeter should read zero resistance. If the relay does not click or if the resistance is anything other than zero, replace the relay.

LIGHTING SYSTEM

The lighting system consists of the headlight, taillight/brake light, turn signals, warning and indicator lights. Whenever troubleshooting a lighting problem, check the affected bulb first. If the bulb is good, check the wiring and connections with a test light.

Headlight Bulb Replacement

WARNING
If the headlight just burned out, it will be HOT. Do not touch the bulb until it cools.

CAUTION
Do not touch the quartz-halogen bulb. Even trace amounts of skin oil on the glass will create hot spots that drastically shorten the life of the bulb. Clean any traces of oil from the bulb with alcohol or lacquer thinner.

The following procedure is shown with the fairing removed for photographic clarity. The bulb can be change with the fairing installed.

Refer to **Figure 63**.

1. Disconnect the connector from the bulb.
2. Remove the rubber boot (**Figure 64**) from the headlight.
3. Release the clip (**Figure 65**) and pivot it away from the bulb.
4. Pull the bulb (**Figure 66**) from the socket.

9

5. Installation is the reverse of removal. Note the following:
   a. Install the bulb so its tabs engage the notches in the bulb socket.
   b. Lock the clip on the socket.
   c. Install the dust cover so the TOP mark faces up.

Headlight Housing Removal/Installation

1. Remove the lower, middle and front fairings as described in Chapter Fifteen.
2. Remove the fairing bracket from the front fairing (Chapter Fifteen).
3. Remove the mounting bolts (A, **Figure 67**) and pull the headlight housing from the fairing.
4. Installation is the reverse of removal. Adjust the headlight beam as described in this section.

Headlight Adjustment

NOTE
The tire pressure must be correct and the fuel tank approximately 1/2 full when the headlight is adjusted. Check with your state or local regulations for headlight beam requirements. They may differ from those given below.

1. Park the motorcycle on a level surface so the front of the headlight is 25 ft. (7.6 m) away from a vertical wall (**Figure 68**).
2. Sit on the motorcycle wearing normal riding gear.
3. Have an assistant measure the distance from the center of the headlight to the ground. Place a horizontal mark on the vertical wall that is the same height above the ground as the center of the headlight.
4. Turn the headlight on and switch to the high beam.
   a. The beam should be pointing straight ahead. If it is not, adjust the headlight horizontally.
   b. The brightest spot on the high beam should be 2 in. (50 mm) below the horizontal mark. If it is not, adjust the headlight vertically.
5. To adjust the headlight, perform the following:
   a. Remove the access panel from the front fairing.
   b. Insert a Phillips screwdriver through the guide on the horizontal adjuster (B, **Figure 67**). Turn the adjuster clockwise or counterclockwise until the beam points straight ahead.

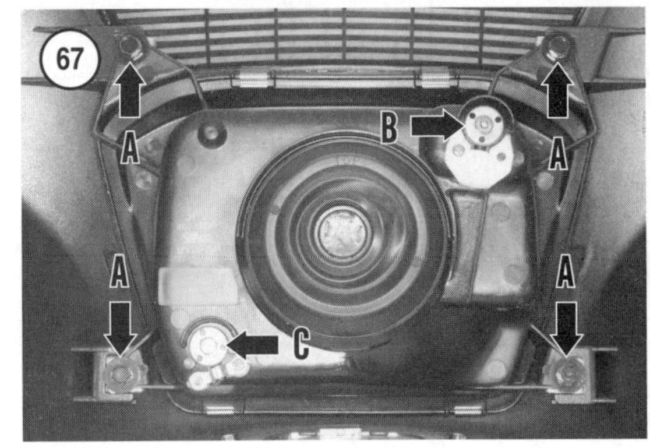

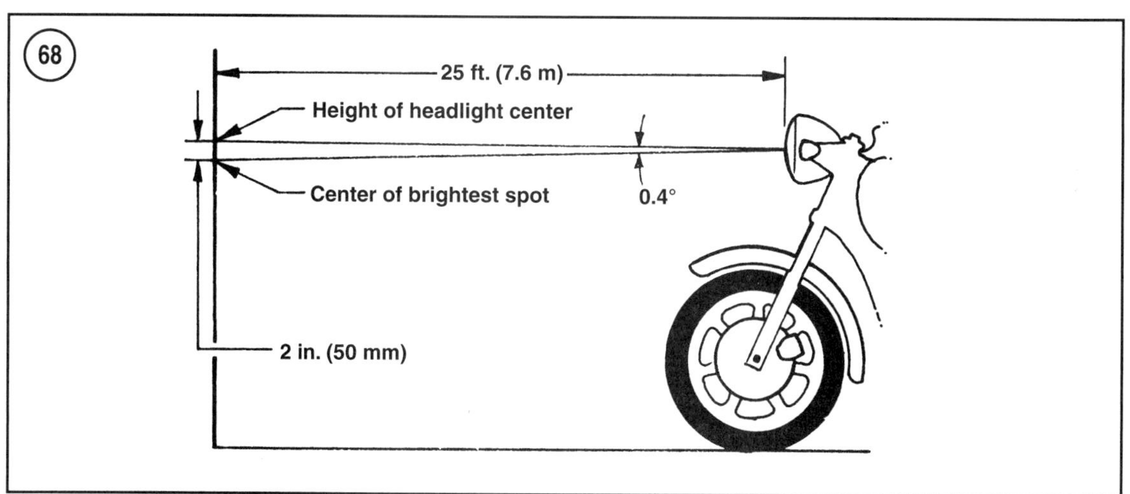

c. Insert a Phillips screwdriver through the guide on the vertical adjuster (C, **Figure 67**). Turn the adjuster clockwise or counterclockwise until the brightest spot of the beam is 2 in. (50 mm) below the horizontal mark.

Headlight Reserve Lighting System

1986-1993 U.S., California and Canada models are equipped with a reserve headlight device that alerts the rider when a filament burns out.

If the high beam filament burns out, the headlight-failure indicator lamp illuminates and the device turns on the low beam filament when the dimmer switch is turned to HI. Conversely, when the low beam filament burns out, the headlight-failure indicator lamp illuminates and the device turns on the high beam filament when the dimmer switch is turned to LOW. Replace the headlight bulb as soon as possible whenever the headlight failure indicator light turns on.

U.S., California and Canada models also include a headlight relay. The headlight turns on when the engine is started and remains on until the engine is turned off.

Consider the reserve headlight device when troubleshooting a headlight circuit problem on these models. If the wiring and other components in the headlight circuit are working, the reserve headlight device is defective. The reserve lighting device is mounted on the fairing bracket. See **Figure 2**. The headlight relay is part of the junction box.

Taillight/Brake Light

Refer to **Figure 69**.

1. To replace the taillight/brake light assembly, perform the following:
   a. Remove the tail cover as described in Chapter Fifteen.
   b. Disconnect the 3-pin taillight/brake light connector (A, **Figure 70**) from its harness mate.
   c. Remove the nut (B, **Figure 70**) from each stud and pull the assembly from the frame. Watch for the collar and damper installed on each mount.
   d. Installation is the reverse of removal.
2. To replace a bulb, perform the following:
   a. Remove the screws (A, **Figure 71**) and pull the lens (B).
   b. Replace the bulb as necessary and reinstall the lens. Make sure the gasket is properly seated.

License Plate Light

Refer to **Figure 69**.

1. If replacing the socket, remove the seat and disconnect the 2-pin license plate connector (A, **Figure 72**) from its harness mate.
2. Remove the mounting screws and remove the outer cover (**Figure 73**) from the rear fender.
3. Remove the mounting screws and lower the lens (**Figure 74**) from the light.
4. Replace the bulb or socket as necessary.
5. Installation is the reverse of removal. Make sure the TOP on the lens faces up.

69

TAILLIGHT AND LICENSE PLATE LIGHT ASSEMBLIES

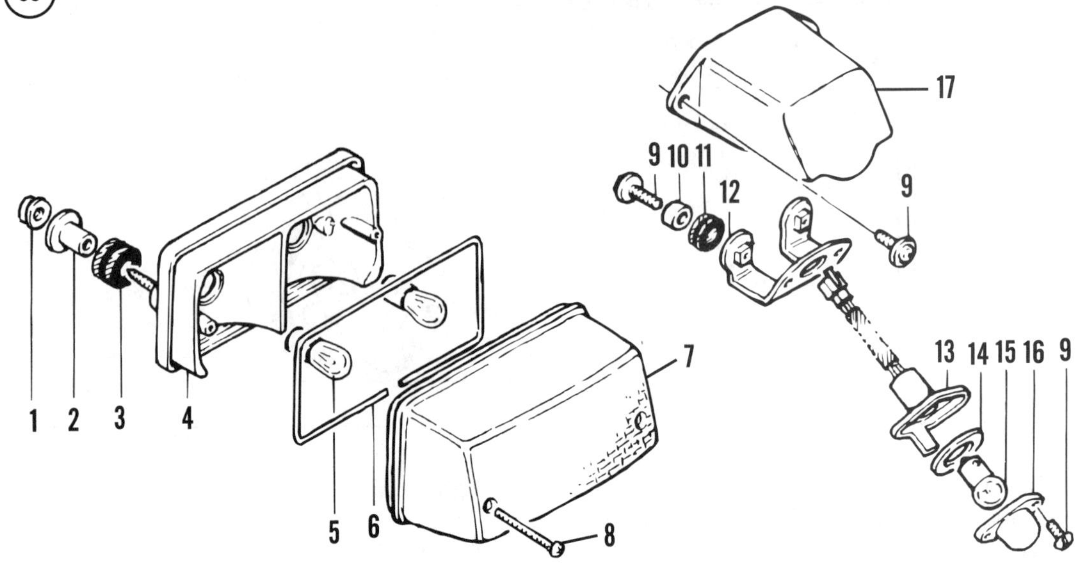

1. Nut
2. Collar
3. Damper
4. Socket assembly
5. Bulb
6. Gasket
7. Lens
8. Screw
9. Screw
10. Collar
11. Damper
12. Bracket
13. Socket
14. Gasket
15. Bulb
16. Lens
17. Outer cover

70

72

71

73

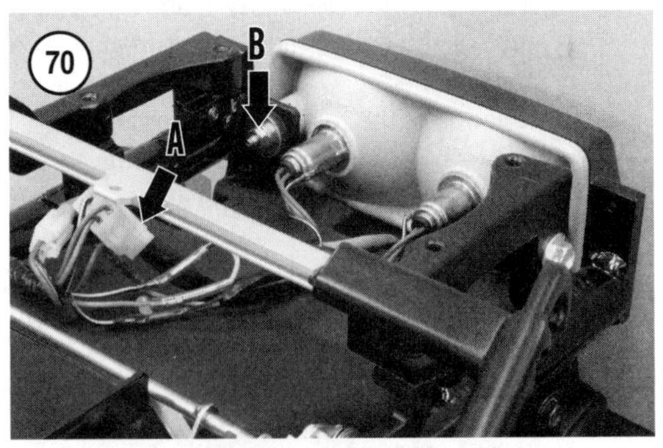

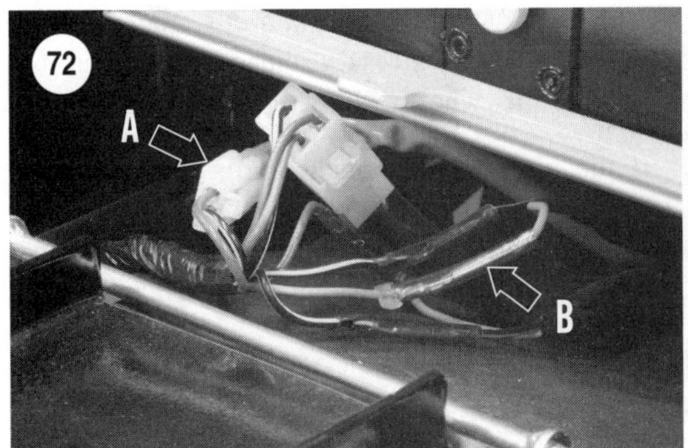

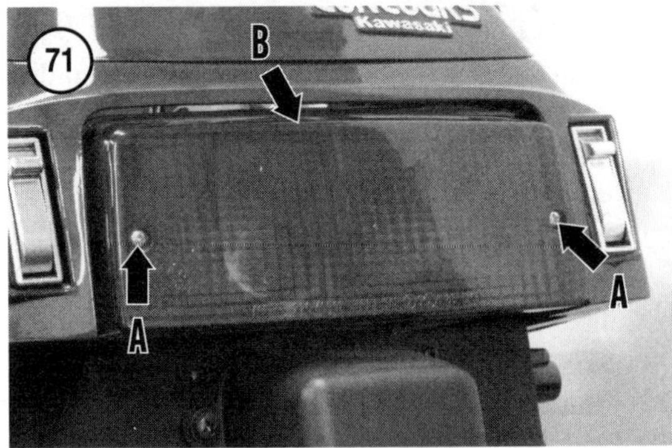

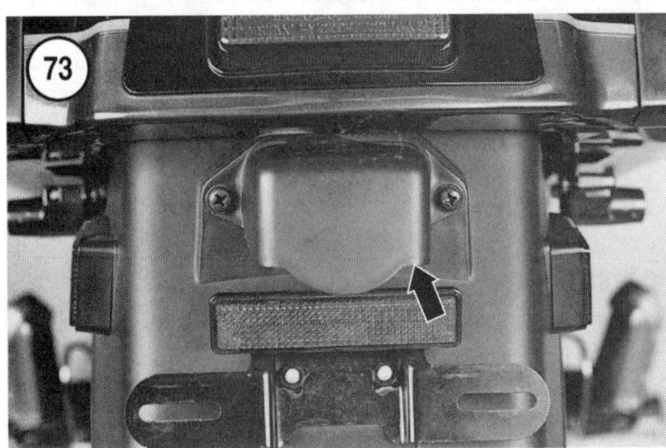

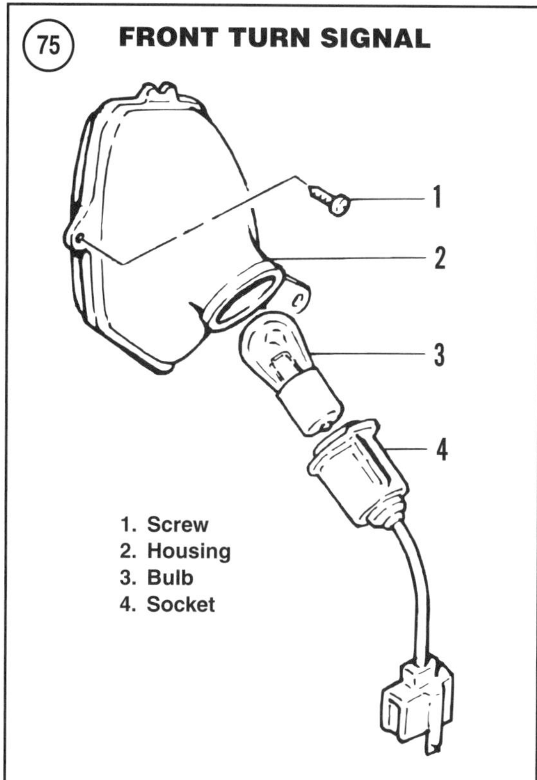

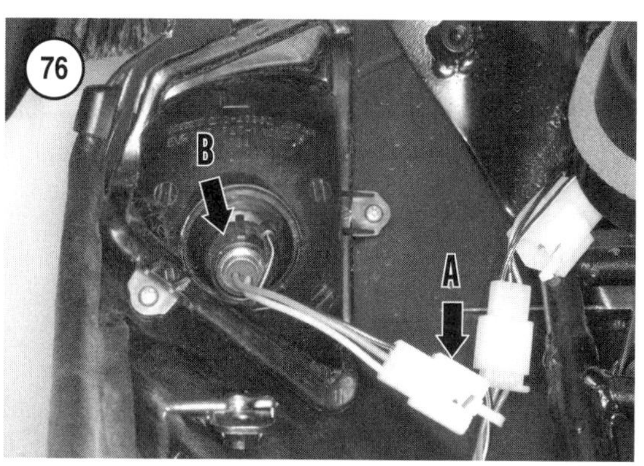

Front Turn Signal

Refer to **Figure 75**.

1. Disconnect the turn signal connector (A, **Figure 76**) from its harness mate.
2. Turn the socket (B, **Figure 76**) counterclockwise and remove it from the turn signal assembly.
3. Replace the bulb or socket as necessary.

Rear Turn Signal

Refer to **Figure 77**.

1. If replacing the socket assembly, remove the seat and disconnect the turn signal's two bullet connectors (B, **Figure 72**).
2. Remove the screw from the front of the housing.
3. Pull the socket assembly from the housing.
4. Turn out the lens screws and remove the lens and gasket.
5. Replace the bulb or socket as necessary.
6. Installation is the reverse of removal. Make sure the gasket is in place.

9

METER ASSEMBLY

The meter assembly contains the speedometer, tachometer, fuel gauge, temperature gauge as well as meter and indicator lights.

Two types of meter assemblies (**Figure 78** and **Figure 79**) are used. The following photographs show a later (1994-on) style meter.

Removal/Installation

1. Refer to *Front Fairing Removal* in Chapter Fifteen and remove the windshield and fairing shroud.
2. Disconnect the meter 4-pin and 9-pin connectors (A, **Figure 80**) from their mates on the wiring harness.
3. Disconnect the speedometer cable, if not already done.
4. Remove the meter bracket bolts (B, **Figure 80**) and lower the meter assembly and its bracket from the fairing bracket.
5. If necessary, pull a light socket (A, **Figure 81**) from the meter assembly and replace the bulb.
6. Installation is the reverse of removal.

77

DIRECTIONAL SIGNAL

1. Lens
2. Gasket
3. Bulb
4. Socket assembly
5. Screw
6. Housing
7. Screw

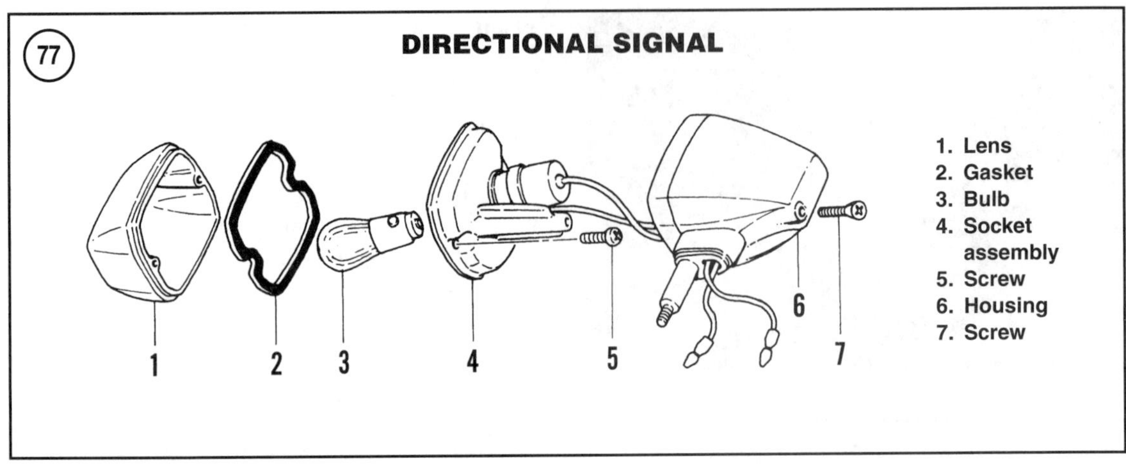

78

METER ASSEMBLY (1986-1993 MODELS)

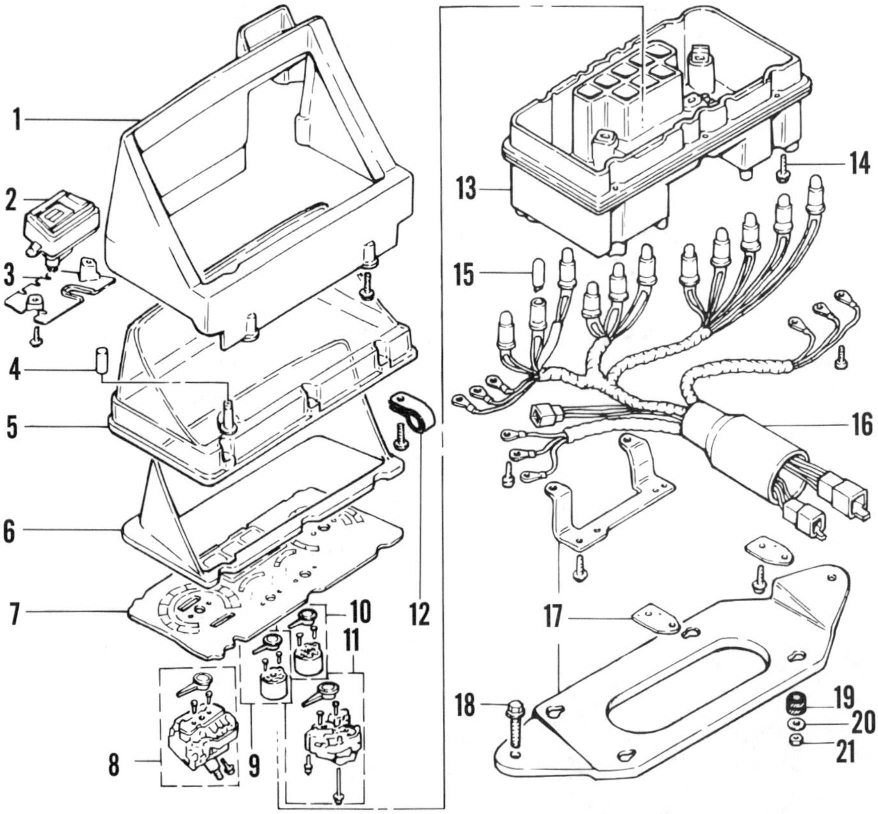

1. Shroud
2. Clock
3. Cover
4. Reset knob
5. Upper housing
6. Meter cover
7. Meter face
8. Speedometer
9. Fuel gauge
10. Temperature gauge
11. Tachometer
12. Clamp
13. Lower housing
14. Screw
15. Bulb
16. Harness
17. Bracket
18. Bolt
19. Damper
20. Washer
21. Nut

79

METER ASSEMBLY (1994-ON MODELS)

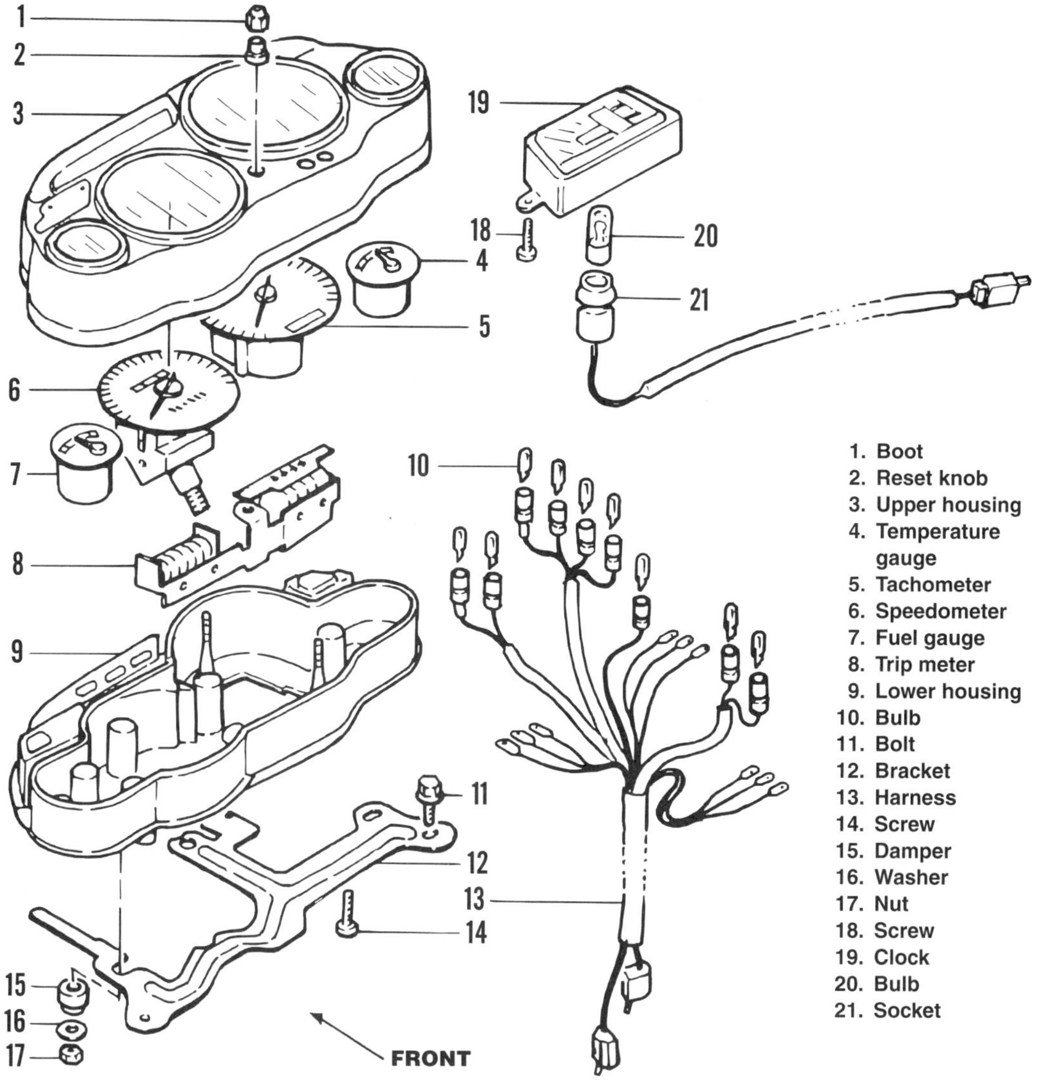

FRONT

1. Boot
2. Reset knob
3. Upper housing
4. Temperature gauge
5. Tachometer
6. Speedometer
7. Fuel gauge
8. Trip meter
9. Lower housing
10. Bulb
11. Bolt
12. Bracket
13. Harness
14. Screw
15. Damper
16. Washer
17. Nut
18. Screw
19. Clock
20. Bulb
21. Socket

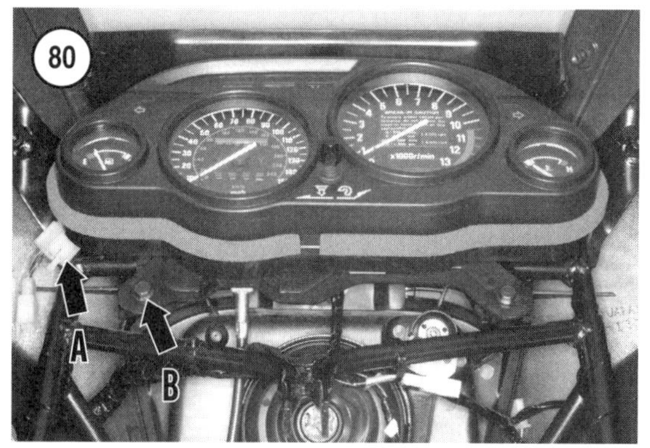

Disassembly

The meter assembly contains the speedometer, tachometer, fuel gauge and temperature gauge.

1. Remove each nut (B, **Figure 81**) and pull the meter bracket (C). Watch for the damper and washer installed with each nut.

2. Release the harness from any clamps that secure it to the meter assembly.

3. Remove the screws (D, **Figure 81**) and separate the upper and lower housings.

4. Remove any gauge that needs replacement. Refer to *Gauge Replacement* for 1986-1993 models.

5. Installation is the reverse of removal. Check the damper installed beneath each bracket-mounting nut (B, **Figure 81**). Replace any damper that is cracked or deteriorated.

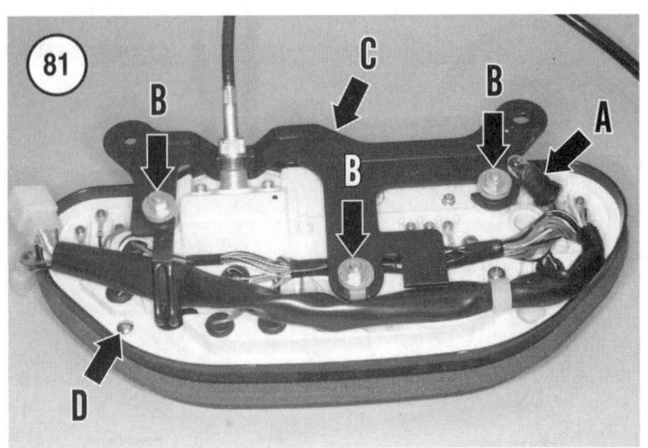

Gauge Replacement (1986-1993 Models)

Refer to **Figure 82**.

1. Remove and disassemble the meter assembly as described in this section.

2. Grasp the pointer on the gauge and loosen the cap.

3. Pull the retainer and the pointer from the meter spindle.

4. Remove the gauge from the dial face and mount its replacement.

5. Install the pointer so it engages the notch on the spindle.

6. Press the retainer over the pointer. Hold the pointer and tighten the cap.

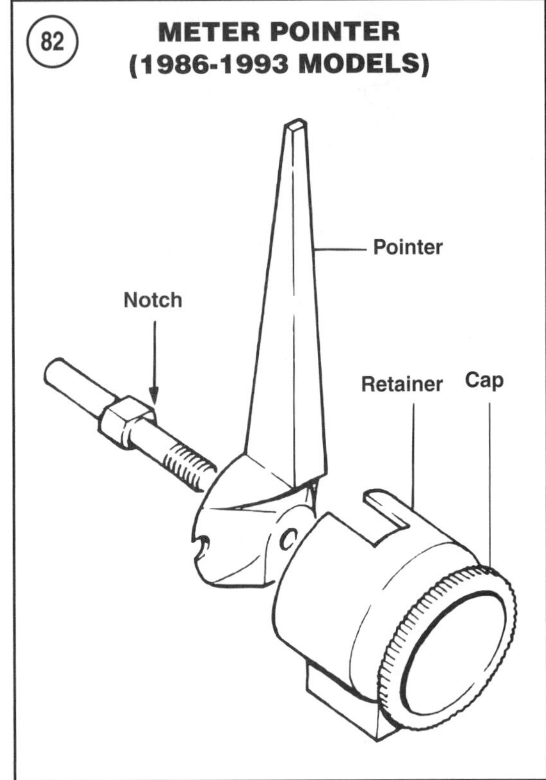

Clock Removal/Installation

1. Refer to *Front Fairing Removal* in Chapter Fifteen and remove the windshield and fairing shroud.

2. Disconnect the 3-pin clock connector and the 2-pin clock-light connector from their harness mates.

3. Remove the mounting screws (**Figure 83**) from the fairing shroud and pull the clock. On 1986-1993 models, remove the cover and the clock.

4. Installation is the reverse of removal.

Horn Removal/Installation

1. Remove the front fairing and remove the fairing bracket as described in Chapter Fifteen.

2. Unplug the connectors (**Figure 84**) from the horn terminals.

3. Remove the mounting bolts (**Figure 85**) and lower the horns from the shroud.

4. Installation is the reverse of removal.

84

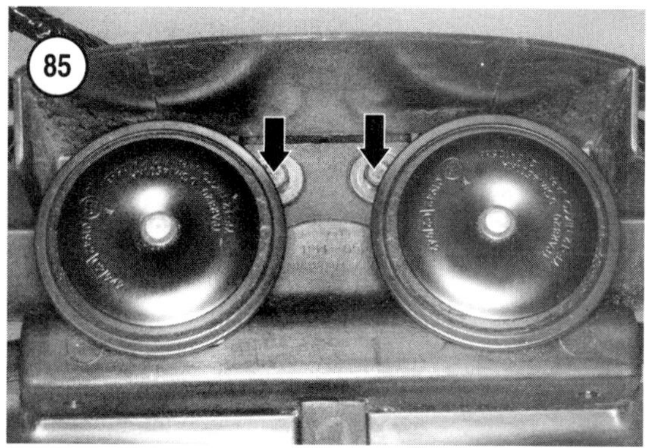
85

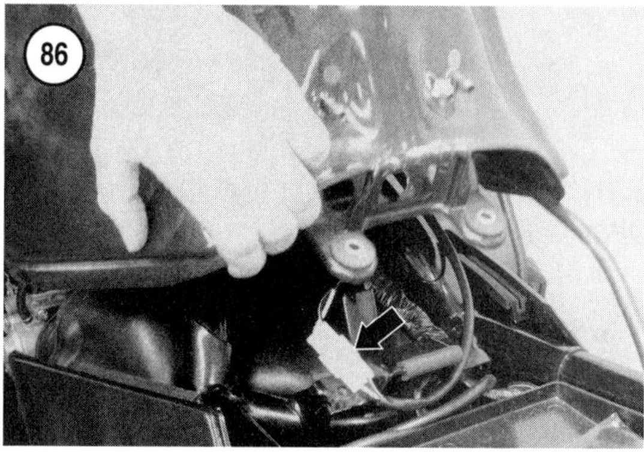
86

GAUGES

This section describes testing procedures for the tachometer, fuel level gauge and coolant temperature gauge. Refer to *Meter Assembly* in this chapter when removing or installing a particular gauge.

Tachometer Test

1. Check the mounting dampers at the meter assembly bracket. They must be in good condition. Replace the dampers if they are cracked, brittle or deteriorated in any way.
2. Refer to the wiring diagrams at the end of the manual and perform the following:
   a. Check the continuity of the circuit as described in *Wiring and Connectors* in this chapter.
   b. If the wiring and connectors are in good operating condition, replace the tachometer.

Fuel Gauge Test

1. Refer to the wiring diagrams at the end of the manual and perform the operational tests.
   a. See Chapter Eight and remove the tank bolts. Watch for the collar and damper installed with each bolt.
   b. Pivot the rear of the tank upward and disconnect the fuel sensor 2-pin connector (**Figure 86**) from its harness mate.
   c. Turn the ignition switch on. The fuel gauge should read empty.
   d. Connect a jumper across the two terminals in the harness side of the 2-pin connector. The fuel gauge should read full when the ignition switch is on.
   e. The fuel level sensor is faulty if both indicated reading were obtained. If the system failed one or both tests, the wiring and/or fuel gauge is faulty. Proceed to Step 2.
2. Check the continuity of the circuit as described in *Wiring and Connectors* later in this chapter. If the wiring and connectors are in good operating condition, replace the fuel gauge.

Fuel Level Sensor Test

1. Remove the fuel level sensor as described in Chapter Eight.
2. Pivot the float arm up and down (**Figure 87**). The arm should move smoothly without any binding. Raise the float arm all the way up and release it. The arm should smoothly drop under its own weight. Replace the sensor as necessary.
3. Connect an ohmmeter to the sensor side of the 2-pin fuel sensor connector (**Figure 86**).
4. Raise the float to its full position. Record the resistance.
5. Lower the float to the empty position. Record the resistance.

6. Replace the fuel level sensor if either resistance is outside the range specified in **Table 1**.

Coolant Temperature Gauge Test

1. Refer to the wiring diagrams at the end of the manual and perform the following:
   a. Disconnect the yellow/white connector (**Figure 88**) from the coolant temperature sensor.
   b. Turn the ignition switch on. The coolant temperature gauge should read cold.

CAUTION
Do not ground the sensor wire longer than necessary. The gauge could be damage. Stop the test as soon as the needle moves to hot.

   c. Use a jumper wire to connect the yellow/white connector to a good engine ground and turn the ignition switch on. The temperature gauge should read hot.
   d. The coolant temperature sensor is faulty if both indicated readings were obtained. If the system failed one or both tests, the wiring and/or coolant temperature gauge is faulty. Proceed to Step 2.

2. Check the continuity of the circuit as described in *Wiring and Connectors* in this chapter. If the wiring and connectors are in good operating condition, replace the coolant temperature gauge.

Cooling Fan Operational Test

1. Remove the lower, middle and upper fairings as described in Chapter Fifteen.
2. Follow the cooling fan electrical lead to the 2-pin fan connector.
3. Disconnect the fan connector from its harness mate.
4. Connect a 12-volt battery to the device side of the fan connector.
   a. Use a jumper to connect the positive battery terminal to the blue terminal in the fan side of the connector.
   b. Use a second jumper to connect the negative battery terminal to the black terminal in the fan side of the connector.
5. The fan motor should run freely with no grinding or excessive noise.

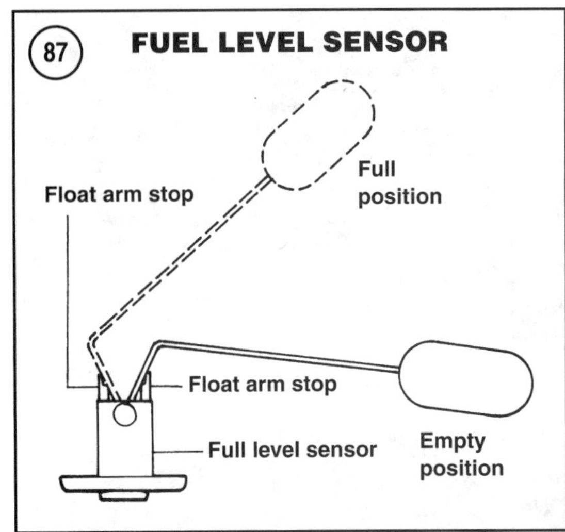

6. If the fan motor does not operate correctly, replace it.

Fan Switch Test

The thermostatic fan switch controls the radiator fan based on engine coolant temperature.

1. Remove the fan switch as described in Chapter Ten.
2. Fill a beaker or pan with water and place it on a stove or hot plate.
3. Mount the fan switch so that the temperature sensing tip and the threaded portion of the body are submerged as shown in A, **Figure 89**.

NOTE
The thermometer and the switch must not touch the container sides or bottom. If either does, it will result in a false reading.

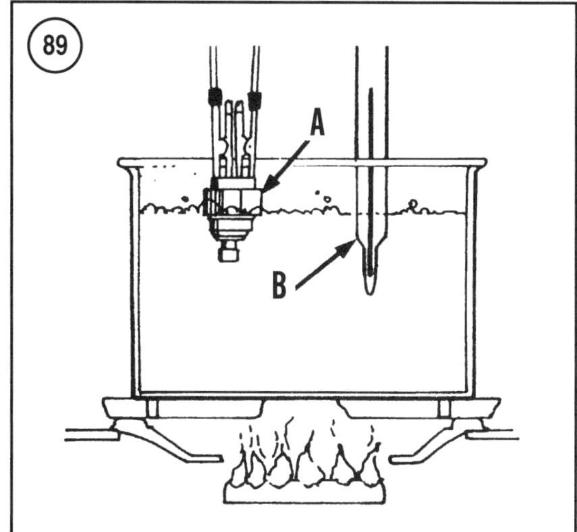

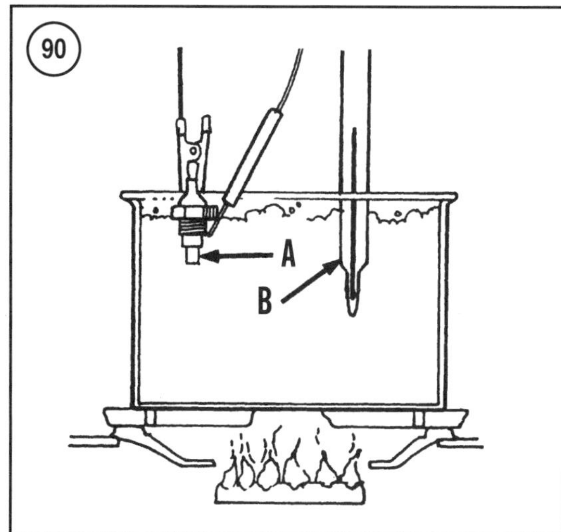

4. Place a thermometer (B, **Figure 89**) in the pan of water (use a cooking or candy thermometer that is rated higher than the test temperature).

5. Attach the leads of an ohmmeter to the fan switch terminals as shown in A, **Figure 89**.

6. Check the resistance as follows:

   a. Turn on the heat and gradually heat the water.

   b. When the temperature rises to 93-103° C (199-217° F), the resistance should be 0.5 ohms or less.

   c. Turn the heat off and let the water cool.

   d. When the temperature falls to 91-95° C (196-203° F), the resistance should be greater than 1000 ohms.

Replace the fan switch (Chapter Ten) if it fails either portion of the test.

Coolant Temperature Sensor Test

1. Remove the coolant temperature sensor as described in Chapter Ten.
2. Fill a beaker or pan with water and place it on a stove or hot plate.
3. Mount the sensor so that the temperature sensing tip and the threaded portion of the body are submerged as shown in A, **Figure 90**.

NOTE
The thermometer and the switch must not touch the container sides or bottom. If either does, it will result in a false reading.

4. Place a thermometer (B, **Figure 90**) in the pan of water (use a cooking or candy thermometer that is rated higher than the test temperature).
5. Attach the one lead of an ohmmeter to the sensor terminal. Connect the other test lead to the sensor body as shown in A, **Figure 90**.
6. Check the resistance as follows:
   a. Turn on the heat and gradually heat the water.
   b. When the temperature reaches 80° C (176° F), the resistance should read approximately 52 ohms.
   c. Continue heating the water.
   d. When the temperature reaches 100° C (212° F), the resistance should be approximately 27 ohms.
7. Replace the coolant temperature sensor (Chapter Ten) if it fails either portion of the test.

9

WIRING AND CONNECTORS

Many electrical problems can be traced to damaged wiring or to contaminated or loose connectors.
1. Visually inspect the wiring for fraying, burning and other signs of problems.
2. Service the connectors in a circuit by disconnecting them and cleaning the terminals with electrical contact cleaner. Make sure the terminals are not damaged. Pack multipin connectors with dielectric grease and reconnect them.
3. Check the continuity of the individual wires in the circuit by performing the following:

   a. Disconnect the negative battery cable (**Figure 4**).
   b. Starting at one end of the circuit, check the continuity of each individual wire from one connector to the next. If no continuity is found (high resistance), an open exists between the two test points.

4. If necessary, make sure the connector is not the location of an open circuit. With the connector connected, insert the test probes through the back of each connector half. Make sure the test probes contact the correct terminals on each side of the connector.

SWITCHES

Testing

1. When testing switches, note the following:
   a. First check the fuses in the relevant circuit as described in this chapter.
   b. Check the battery as described in Chapter Three. Charge the battery to the correct state of charge, if required.
   c. When checking continuity, disconnect the negative cable from the battery if the switch connectors are not disconnected from the circuit.

CAUTION
Do not attempt to start the engine with the battery negative cable disconnected. This will damage the wiring harness.

   d. When separating two connectors, pull the connector housings and not the wires.
   e. Check the connectors to make sure they are clean and properly connected. Check all wires going into a connector housing to make sure each wire is properly positioned and that the wire end is not loose.
   f. When replacing a handlebar switch assembly, make sure the cables are routed correctly so that they are not crimped when the handlebar is turned from side to side.

2. Test the switches for continuity with an ohmmeter (see Chapter Two) as follows:
   a. Disconnect the switch connector and check for continuity at the terminals on the switch side of the connector. If the connector connects directly to the switch, check for continuity directly at the switch.
   b. Operate the switch in each operating position and compare the results to the switch continuity diagrams within the wiring diagrams at the end of the manual.
   c. For example, **Figure 91** shows a continuity diagram for the horn button. The line indicates there should be continuity between the black/white and black yellow terminals when the horn button is pressed. There should be no continuity between these two terminals when the horn button is free.

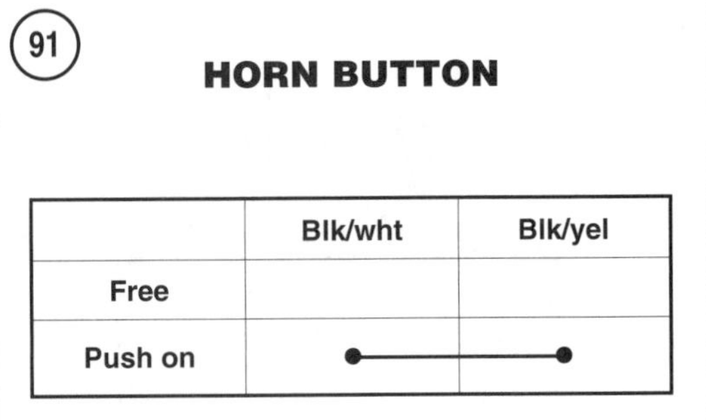
91

HORN BUTTON

	Blk/wht	Blk/yel
Free		
Push on	●	●

Left Handlebar Switch Replacement

1. The left handlebar switch housing includes the following switches:
   a. Headlight dimmer switch.
   b. Turn signal switch.
   c. Horn switch.
   d. Hazard switch.
   e. Starter lockout switch, which mounts to the clutch lever.
   f. Passing switch (all models except U.S., California and Canada models).
2. Remove the lower, middle and front fairings as described in Chapter Fifteen.
3. Follow the switch cable and disconnect the 10-pin left handlebar switch connector from its harness mate.
4. Disconnect the 2-pin connector (A, **Figure 92**) from the starter lockout switch.
5. Remove any cable tie that secures the switch cable to the motorcycle. Note the position of each cable tie so a new tie can be installed in the same location.

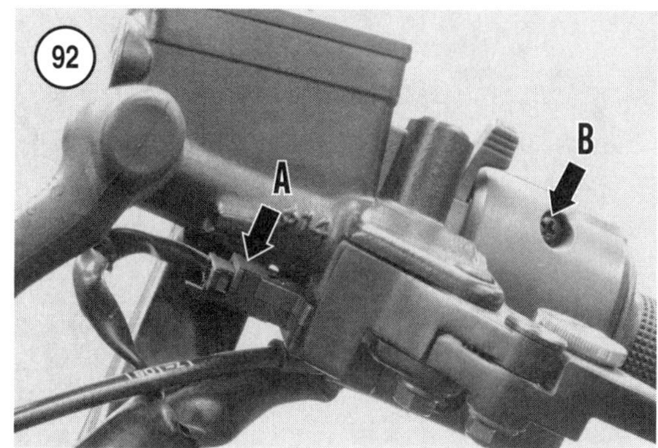

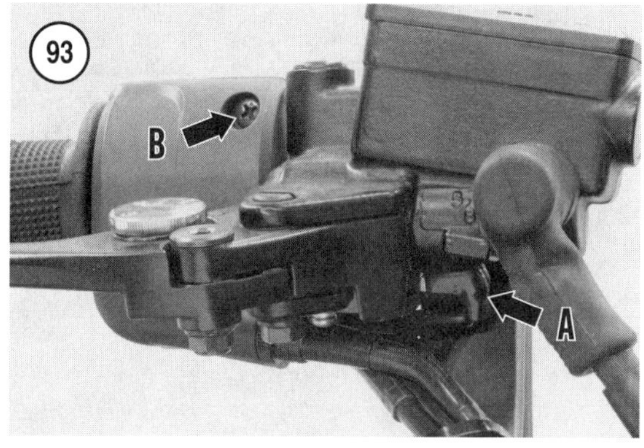

6. Remove the screws (B, **Figure 92**) and separate the housing halves from the handlebar.

7. Pull the choke cable from the housing and remove the switch housing and its wiring cable.

8. Installation is the reverse of these steps. Note the following:

   a. Position the switch assembly onto the handlebar so its tab engages the hole in the handlebar.

   b. Pack the electrical connectors with dielectric grease and securely connect them to their mates.

   c. Adjust the choke cable free play (Chapter Three).

Starter Lockout Switch Replacement

The starter lockout switch mounts beneath clutch master cylinder. Disconnect the electrical connector (A, **Figure 92**) from the starter lockout switch, remove the switch screw and lower the switch from the master cylinder. Install by reversing this procedure.

Right Handlebar Switch Replacement

1. The right handlebar switch housing includes the following switches:
   a. Engine stop switch.
   b. Starter switch.
   c. Front brake switch, which mounts to the brake lever assembly.
   d. Headlight switch (all models except U.S., California and Canada models).
2. Remove the lower, middle and front fairings as described in Chapter Fifteen.
3. Follow the switch cable and disconnect right handlebar switch connector.
   a. On U.S., California and Canada models, disconnect the 6-pin connector from its harness mate.
   b. On all models except U.S., California and Canada, disconnect the 6-pin and 4-pin connectors from their harness mates.
4. Disconnect the connectors (A, **Figure 93**) from the front brake light switch.
5. Remove the switch assembly screws (B, **Figure 93**) and separate the halves of the right handlebar switch.
6. Disengage the end the pull cable and the return cable from the throttle drum. Remove each cable from the switch housing and remove the housing.
7. Installation is the reverse of removal. Note the following:
   a. Lubricate the throttle cable ends with grease.
   b. Feed the cables through the ports on the switch housing and connect them to the throttle drum.
   c. Route the electrical cable along the same path noted during removal.
   d. Position the switch assembly onto the handlebar so its tab engages the hole in the handlebar.
   e. Pack the right handlebar switch connectors with dielectric grease and securely connect it to its harness mate.
   f. Adjust the throttle cable free play (Chapter Three).

Front Brake Switch Replacement

The front brake light switch mounts beneath the front brake master cylinder.

9

1. Disconnect the spade connectors (A, **Figure 93**) from the front brake switch.
2. Remove the switch mounting screw and lower the switch from the master cylinder.
3. Install by reversing this procedure. Check switch operation. The brake light should come on when the front brake lever is applied.

Rear Brake Switch Replacement

The rear brake switch mounts to the inside of the brake pedal/footpeg assembly.

1. Follow the rear brake switch electrical lead along the right side of the frame and disconnect the switch's two bullet connectors (**Figure 94**). Note how the wire is routed, then release the wire from any clamps or ties that secure it to the frame.
2. Remove the brake pedal/footpeg assembly as described in Chapter Fourteen.
3. Disconnect the spring (A, **Figure 95**) from the boss on the brake pedal and remove the switch (B) from the bracket.
4. Installation is the reverse of removal. Note the following:
   a. Pack the bullet connectors with dielectric grease.
   b. Connect the spring to the brake pedal boss.
   c. Adjust the rear brake switch as described in Chapter Three.

Ignition Switch Replacement

1. Remove the lower, middle and front fairings as described in Chapter Fifteen.
2. Disconnect the ignition switch 6-pin connector (A, **Figure 96**) from its harness mate. On U.S., California and Canada models also disconnect the ignition switch bullet connector (B, **Figure 96**).
3. Turn out the mounting screws (**Figure 97**) and lift the cover from the steering head.
4. Remove each ignition switch bolt (A, **Figure 98**) and remove the switch (B) from the mounting bracket.
5. Installation is the reverse of these steps. Note the following:
   a. Make sure the electrical connectors are free of corrosion.
   b. Pack the connector(s) with dielectric grease and connect it securely to its mate.

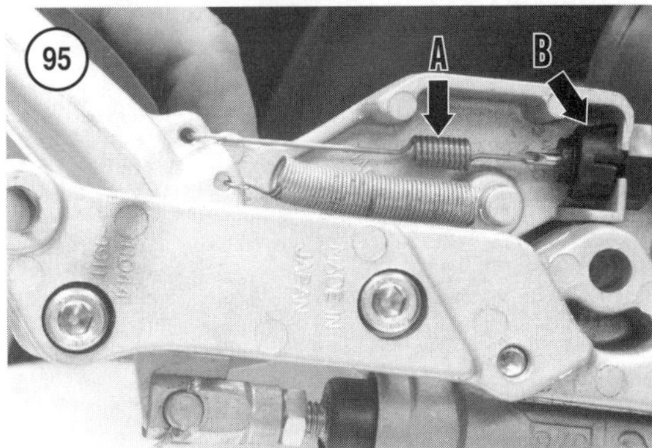

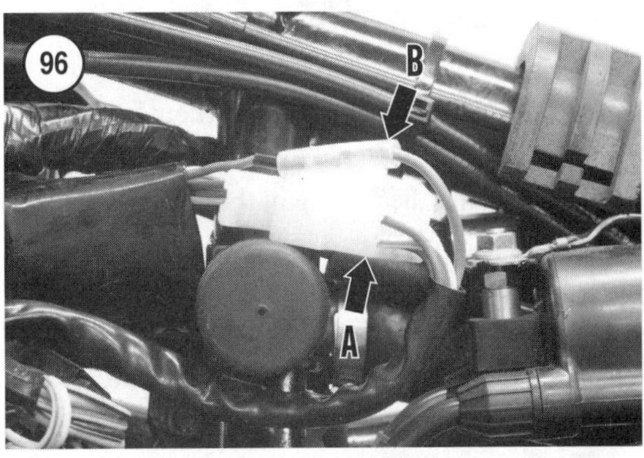

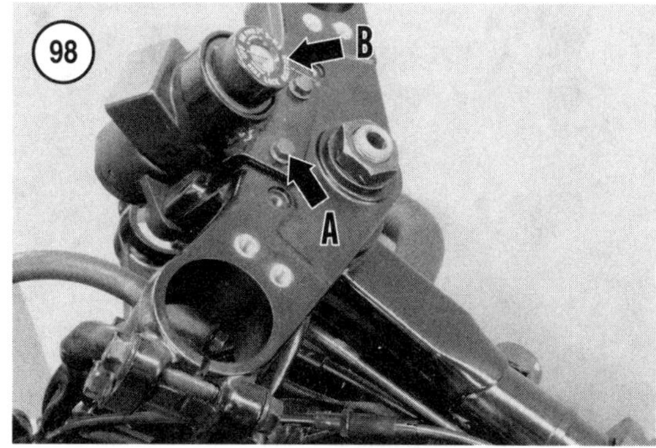

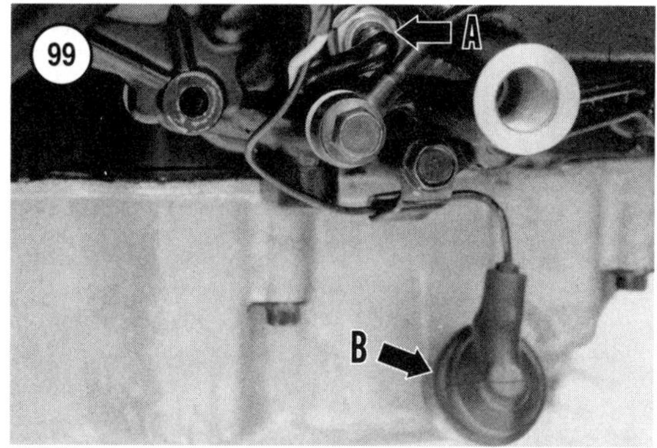

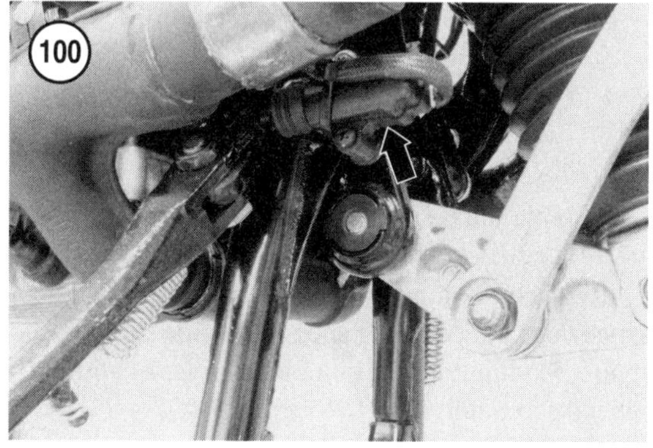

Neutral Switch Replacement

1. Securely support the motorcycle on level ground.
2. Drain the engine oil as described in Chapter Three.
3. Disconnect the electrical connector from the neutral switch (A, **Figure 99**).
4. Remove the neutral switch and its O-ring from the bevel gearcase.
5. Install by reversing these removal steps while noting the following:
   a. Install a new O-ring and torque the neutral switch to 15 N•m (11 ft.-lb.).
   b. Make sure the electrical connector is free of corrosion and is tight.

Oil Pressure Switch Replacement

1. Securely support the motorcycle on level ground.
2. Drain the engine oil as described in Chapter Three.
3. Disconnect the electrical connector from the oil pressure switch (B, **Figure 99**).
4. Remove the oil pressure switch from the oil pan.
5. Install by reversing these removal steps while noting the following:
   a. Apply Loctite 242 (blue) to the threads of the oil pressure switch and torque the switch to 15 N•m (11 ft.-lb.).
   b. Make sure the electrical connector is free of corrosion and is tight.

Sidestand Switch Replacement

1. Securely support the motorcycle on its centerstand.
2. Lower the sidestand so the switch (**Figure 100**) is accessible.
3. Follow the switch wire to the sidestand switch connector on the frame and disconnect the connector from the wiring harness. Release the wire from cable tie(s) that secure it to the frame. Note how the wire is routed along the frame.
4. Remove the two screws securing the sidestand switch to the sidestand bracket and remove the switch.
5. Installation is the reverse of these steps. Note the following:
   a. Apply dielectric grease to the electrical connectors prior to reconnecting them. This helps seal out moisture.
   b. Route switch electrical wire along the same path noted during removal.
   c. Secure the switch wire to the same points on the frame noted during removal.

JUNCTION BOX

The junction box (J-box) contains fuses, diodes and the starter circuit relay, main relay and headlight relay (USA, California and Canada models, 2000-on International models). The diodes and relays cannot be replaced individually. If any of these components fail, replace the junction box.

Refer to the junction box diagrams at the end of this manual

NOTE

Over the years, the internal circuitry in the junction box has changed on some models. Consequently, all portions of the tests described in this section may not apply to all models. If a tested junction box does not yield the specified results, take the unit to a Kawasaki dealership for further testing. Confirm that the junction box is faulty before purchasing a replacement.

Removal/Installation

1. Disconnect the negative battery cable.
2. Remove the left side cover as described in Chapter Fifteen.
3. Slide the junction box (A, **Figure 101**) from its mounts on the motorcycle.
4. Disconnect the 8-pin and 14-pin connectors (B, **Figure 101**) from the junction box.
5. Installation is the reverse of removal. Make sure the damper is in place on each junction box ear.

Relay Circuit Test

1. Remove the junction box as described in this section.
2. Refer to **Table 3** and perform relay circuit test 1 as follows:
   a. Connect the test probes of an ohmmeter to the two junction-box terminals listed in the *Test terminals* column.
   b. Note the resistance. It should equal the value specified in the *Resistance (ohms)* column.
   c. Repeat this test for each pair of terminals.
   d. When measuring the resistance across terminals 10 and 13 U.S., California and Canadian models, measure the resistance in both directions. Resistance should be low in one direction and more than 10 times as much in the opposite direction.
3. Refer to **Table 4** and perform relay circuit test 2 as follows:

   a. Connect a battery to the junction-box terminals as indicated in the *Battery* columns.
   b. Connect the test probes of an ohmmeter to the two junction-box terminals indicated in the *Test terminals* column.
   c. Note the resistance. It should equal the value specified in the *Resistance* column (**Table 4**).
4. Replace the junction box if any measured resistance does not equal the specified value. Neither the main, headlight or starting circuit relays can be replaced separately.

Diode Circuit Test

1. Remove the junction box as described in this section.
2. Measure the resistance across the following sets of junction box terminals: 14 and 12, 14 and 15, and 14 and 16. On U.S., California and Canada models, also check terminals 9 and 13, and 10 and 13.
   a. At each pair of terminals, measure the resistance in one direction.
   b. Reverse the ohmmeter probes and measure the resistance in the opposite direction.

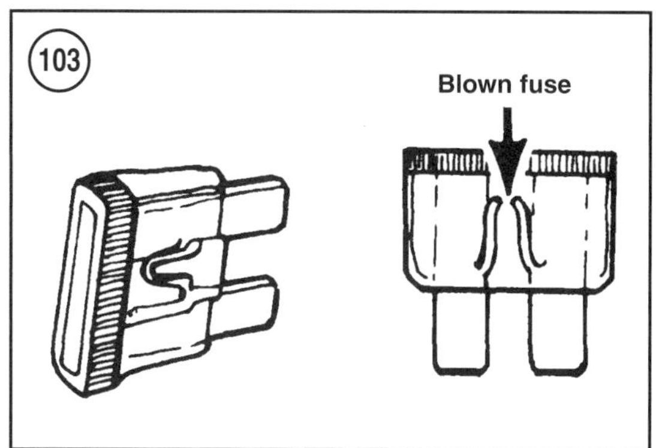

c. The resistance should be low in one direction but more than 10 times as great in the opposite direction. Replace the junction box if any diode is defective.

Fuse Circuit Inspection

1. Remove the junction box as described in this section.
2. Refer to **Table 5** and check the continuity of the fuse circuits by performing the following:
   a. Connect the test probes of an ohmmeter to the junction box terminals indicated in the *Test Terminals* column. Each set of terminals should have continuity (zero volts).
   b. Connect a 12-volt battery to the No. 6 and No. 7 terminals and check the continuity across the last three sets of terminals listed in **Table 5**. Each set of terminals should have continuity.
3. Replace the junction box is any set of terminals fails this test.

FUSES

Whenever a fuse blows, determine the reason for the failure before replacing the fuse. Usually, the trouble is a short in the wiring. This may be caused by worn-through insulation or by a disconnected wire shorting to ground.

CAUTION
Never substitute metal foil or wire for a fuse. Never use a higher amperage fuse than specified. An overload could result in fire and complete loss of the motorcycle.

1. The following fuses are found in or on the junction box:
   a. Accessory fuse—10 amp.
   b. Main fuse—30 amp.
   c. Headlight fuse—10 amp.
   d. Taillight fuse—10 amp.
   e. Ignition/horn fuse—10 amp.
   f. Turn signal relay fuse—10 amp.
   g. Spare.
2. The 10-amp cooling fan fuse is located on top of the junction box.

9

Inspection

1. Grasp the front side of the junction box and pull out the fuse box cover (**Figure 102**).
2. Remove the suspect fuse by pulling it out of the holder with a needlenose pliers.
3. Visually inspect the fuse (**Figure 103**). Replace the fuse if it is blown or cracked.
4. If necessary, check the continuity across the two spade connectors. Replace a fuse that does not have continuity (low resistance).
5. A replacement fuse must have the same amperage rating as the original.

If a fuse continuously blows and a short cannot be located, perform the junction box *Fuse Circuit Inspection* described in this chapter.

Tables 1-6 are on the following pages.

Table 1 ELECTRICAL SPECIFICATIONS

Battery	Yuasa YB18L-A
Capacity	12 V 18 AH
Alternator	Three-phase AC, regulator and rectifier in housing
Rated output	14 V, 28.6 A @ 6000 rpm
Charging voltage	13.5 V @ 4000 rpm (with headlight on)
Stator resistance	Less than 1.0 ohm
Rotor resistance	Approx. 4 ohms
Slip ring diameter	
New	14.4 mm (0.567 in.)
Service limit	14.0 mm (0.551 in.)
Brush length	
New	10.5 mm (0.413 in.)
Service limit	4.5 mm (0.177 in.)
Pickup coil resistance	390-590 ohms
Pickup coil air gap	0.5-0.9 mm (0.020-0.035 in.)
Ignition coil	
Arcing distance	7 mm (0.28 in.) or more
Primary winding resistance	1.8-2.8 ohms
Secondary winding resistance	10-16 K ohms
Spark plug gap	0.6-0.7 mm (0.024-0.028 in.)
Starter	
Brush length	
New	12-12.5 mm (0.472-0.492 in.)
Service limit	6 mm (0.236 in.)
Commutator diameter	
New	28 mm (1.102 in.)
Service limit	27 mm (1.063 in.)
Fuel level sensor resistance	
Full position	4-10 ohms
Empty position	90-100 ohms
Ignition timing	Refer to Chapter Three
Thermostatic fan switch resistance	
Temperature rises to 93-103° C (199-217° F)	Less than 0.5 ohms
Temperature falls 91-95° C (196-203° F)	More than 1000 ohms
Coolant temperature sensor resistance	
80° C (176° F)	Approx. 52 ohms
100° C (212° F)	Approx. 27 ohms

Table 2 REGULATOR RESISTANCE SPECIFICATIONS

Test connections (positive lead to negative lead)	Specification (ohms)
F to E	200-650
E to F	4.5-14.5
IG to E	750-2300
E to IG	2-6.5
F to IG	2.5-8
IG to F	200-600

Table 3 RELAY CIRCUIT TEST 1

Test terminals	Resistance (ohms)
3 and 8	Infinity
8 and 9*	Infinity
11 and 13	Infinity
6 and 7	Approximately 320
10 and 13*	Low in one direction; more than 10 times the value in the other direction
11 and 12	Approximately 320
3 and 7	Infinity
8 and 13*	Infinity
12 and 13	Infinity

*U.S., California and Canada models only.

Table 4 RELAY CIRCUIT TEST 2

Battery (pos.)	Battery (neg.)	Test terminals	Resistance (ohms)
6	7	3 and 8	0
10	13	8 and 9*	0
11	12	11 and 13	0

*U.S., California and Canada models only.

9

Table 5 FUSE CIRCUIT TEST

Test terminals	Resistance (ohms)	Battery connection
1 and 3	0	none
1 and 2B	0	none
19 and 20	0	none
3 and 8	0	6 and 7
3 and 17	0	6 and 7
3 and 18	0	6 and 7

Table 6 ELECTRICAL SYSTEM TORQUE SPECIFICATIONS

Item	N•m	in.-lb.	ft.-lb.
Alternator coupling brades bolt	9.8	87	–
Alternator cover cap nut	4.9	43	–
Alternator mounting bolts[1]	25	–	18
Coolant temperature sensor[2]	7.8	69	–
Fan switch	27	–	20
Neutral switch	15	–	11
Oil pressure switch[1]	15	–	11
Spark plug	14	–	10
Starter cable terminal	4.9	43	–
Timing rotor Allen bolt	25	–	18

1. Apply Loctite 242 or an equivalent medium-strength threadlock.
2. Apply silicone sealant (Kawasaki Bond part No. 56019-120 or equivalent) to the threads.

NOTES

CHAPTER TEN

COOLING SYSTEM

10

This chapter describes repair and replacement of cooling system components. Refer to Chapter Three for routine cooling system maintenance procedures. When inspecting cooling system components, compare any measurements to the cooling system specifications in **Table 1** at the end of this chapter. During assembly, tighten fasteners to the specified torque.

The pressurized cooling systems includes the radiator, water pump, thermostat, cooling fan and coolant reservoir.

Check the coolant level at the upper reservoir mark (A, **Figure 1**) when the engine is cold. If necessary, remove the fairing cover (B, **Figure 1**) and add coolant to the reservoir. If the cooling system requires repeated refilling, there is probably a leak somewhere in the system. Inspect the cooling system as described in Chapter Three.

The cooling system must be cool before any component is removed from the system.

WARNING

*Do not remove the radiator cap (**Figure 2**) when the engine is hot. The coolant is under pressure and ex-*

tremely hot. Severe scalding could result if the coolant contacts your skin.

WARNING
The cooling fan and fan switch connect directly to the battery. Whenever the engine is warn or hot, the fan may operate, even with the ignition switch off. Never work around the fan or touch the fan until the engine is completely cool.

HOSE CLAMPS

There are different types of hose clamps used on various locations throughout the cooling system. The clamping screw type is released by turning the screw with a screwdriver. The clamping-band type must be pinched with a pair of pliers to be released. These clamps are used at specific locations due to space limitations. Be sure to install the correct type of clamp at each location.

The small diameter coolant hoses are very stiff and can be difficult to install. Before installing one of these hoses, lubricate the inside of the hose with a small amount of antifreeze. It will slide onto the fitting much more easily.

Some parts of the cooling system must be sealed with silicone sealant. Apply Kawasaki Bond (part No. 56019-120) or an equivalent silicone sealant to these components before installing them.

COOLING SYSTEM CHECKS

Perform the following checks before troubleshooting any cooling system malfunction.

1. Run the engine until it reaches operating temperature. While the engine is running, a pressure surge should be felt when the upper radiator hose is squeezed.
2. Watch for white steam immediately after the engine is started. If substantial coolant loss is noted, the cylinder head gaskets may be leaking. If so, coolant could leak into a cylinder and cause hydraulic lock. If coolant is entering a combustion chamber, white steam will be observed at the mufflers when the engine is first started.
3. Check the engine oil for coolant. In severe cases, coolant may enter the crankcase and contaminate the oil. If the oil has a white, foamy appearance, coolant is probably in the oil. Extensive engine damage will soon result if coolant is in the engine oil. Therefore, any internal coolant leak must be corrected immediately.

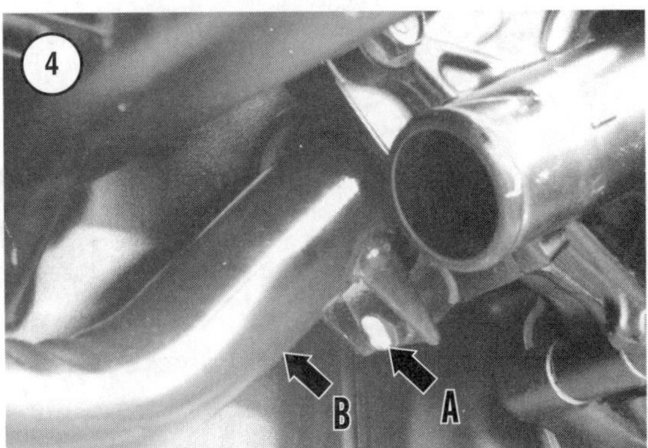

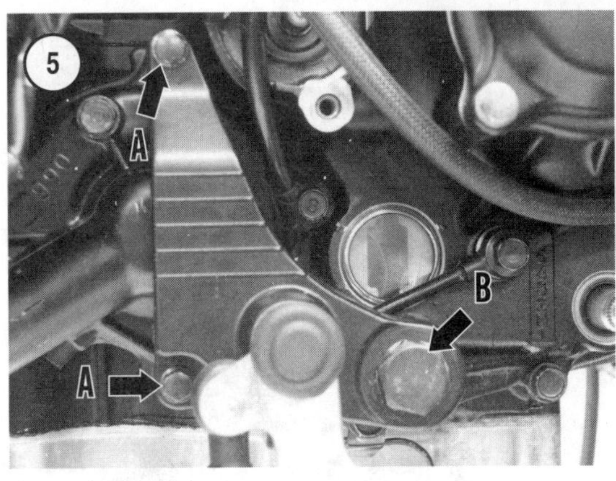

CAUTION
After the cooling system problem is corrected, drain and thoroughly flush the engine oil system to eliminate all coolant residue. Refill the engine with fresh engine oil. Refer to Chapter Three.

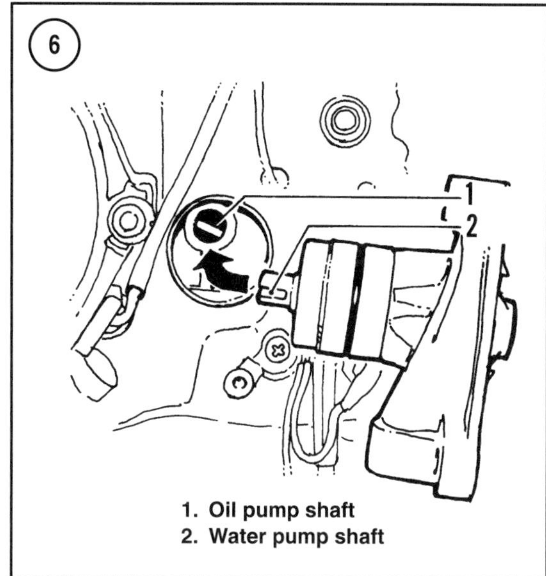

1. Oil pump shaft
2. Water pump shaft

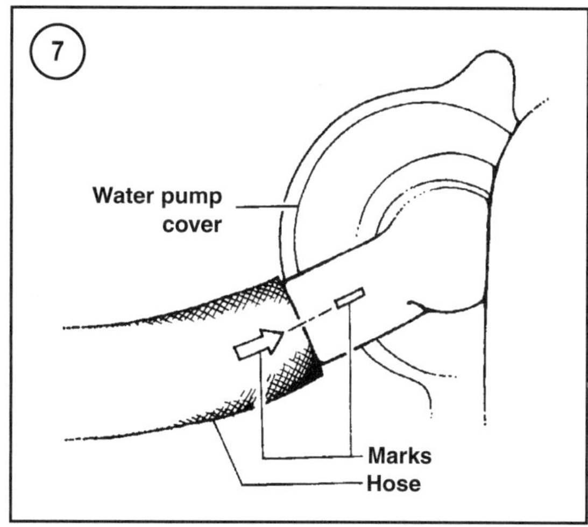

FLUSHING THE SYSTEM

1. Drain the coolant as described in Chapter Three.
2. Fill the cooling system (Chapter Three) with a flushing compound mixed with distilled water.
3. Start the engine and let it warm up for about 10 minutes.
4. Stop the engine and drain the flushing compound from the engine.
5. Fill the system with distilled water.
6. Warm up the engine and drain the water.
7. Repeat Steps 3 and 4.
8. Fill the system with coolant as described in Chapter Three.

WATER PUMP

Removal/Installation

1. Remove the lower and middle fairings as described in Chapter Fifteen.
2. Drain the engine oil and the cooling system (Chapter Three).
3. Remove the clutch slave cylinder (Chapter Six).
4. Loosen the hose clamp and pull the radiator hose from the input fitting on the water pump. Note that the index mark on the hose (A, **Figure 3**) aligns with the index mark on the water pump fitting (B).
5. Remove the mounting bolt (A, **Figure 4**) and pull the coolant manifold pipe (B) from the water pump output port. Watch for the O-ring installed on the pipe.

NOTE

*The water pump is secured to the crankcase by two of the shift pedal bracket bolts (A and B, **Figure 5**).*

6. Remove the shift pedal bracket (Chapter Seven).
7. Pull the water pump housing from the crankcase.
8. Inspect the water pump as described in this section.
9. Installation is the reverse of removal.
   a. Install the water pump into the crankcase so the slot in the water pump shaft engages the tab on the oil pump shaft. See **Figure 6**.
   b. Install a new O-ring on the coolant manifold pipe (B, **Figure 4**).
   c. Install the shift pedal bracket bolts (A and B, **Figure 5**). Torque the 14-mm bolt (B, **Figure 5**) to 78 N•m (58 ft-lb.). Tighten the other bolts (A, **Figure 5**) securely.
   d. Align the index mark on the radiator hose (A, **Figure 3**), with the index mark on the water pump input fitting (B). See **Figure 7**.
   e. Add engine oil as described in Chapter Three.
   f. Add coolant and bleed the system (Chapter Three).

Inspection

NOTE

The water pump is sold as a complete assembly. If any part is worn or damaged, replace the water pump. The O-rings, however, can be purchased separately.

10

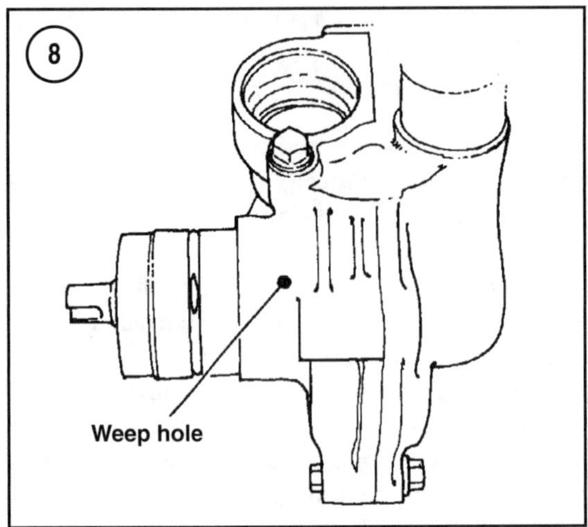

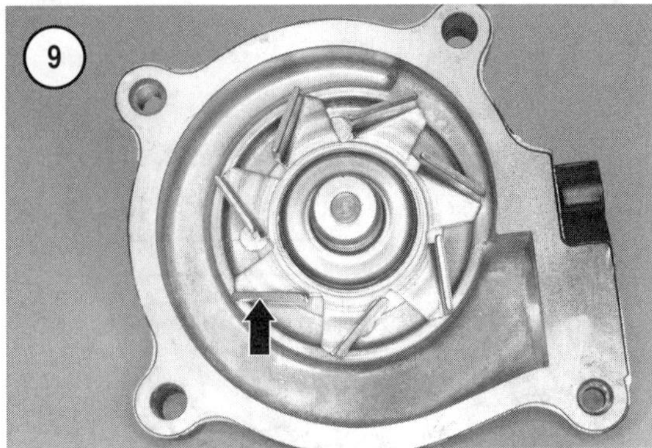

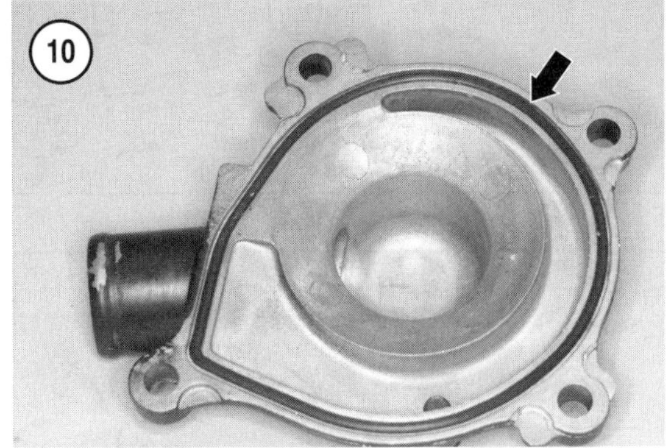

1. If the coolant level has been dropping, inspect the water pump weep hole (**Figure 8**) for signs of leaks. If leakage is noted, an internal seal is worn; replace the water pump. If no leaks are found, reinstall the water pump and pressure test the system as described in *Cooling System Inspection* in Chapter Three.
2. Inspect the bearing by manually turning the impeller shaft. It should turn smoothly without any noise. Replace the water pump if the bearing worn.
3. Inspect the water pump input and output ports for corrosion or sludge. Clean minor corrosion from a port. Replace the water pump if any port is severely corroded or pitted.
4. Remove the two cover bolts and separate the water pump cover from the housing.
5. Check the impeller blades (**Figure 9**) for signs of corrosion or damage. Minor corrosion can be cleaned from the blades. If the blades are severely corroded, cracked or broken, replace the water pump.
6. Check the O-rings (**Figure 10** and **Figure 11**) for flat spots, tears or other signs of damage. Replace the O-rings as necessary.
7. Fit the cover onto the housing and install the two pump cover bolts.

THERMOSTAT ASSEMBLY

Removal/Installation

Refer to **Figure 12**.

1. Remove the lower, middle and front fairings as described in Chapter Fifteen.
2. Drain the coolant (Chapter Three).
3. Remove the fuel tank and carburetor assembly (Chapter Eight).
4. Disconnect the electrical connector from the coolant temperature sensor (A, **Figure 13**).
5. Loosen the hose clamp (B, **Figure 13**) and disconnect the hose from the thermostat cover.
6. Remove the mounting bolts (C, **Figure 13**) and pull the thermostat assembly from the cylinder head. Watch for the O-rings on the thermostat pipe fittings.

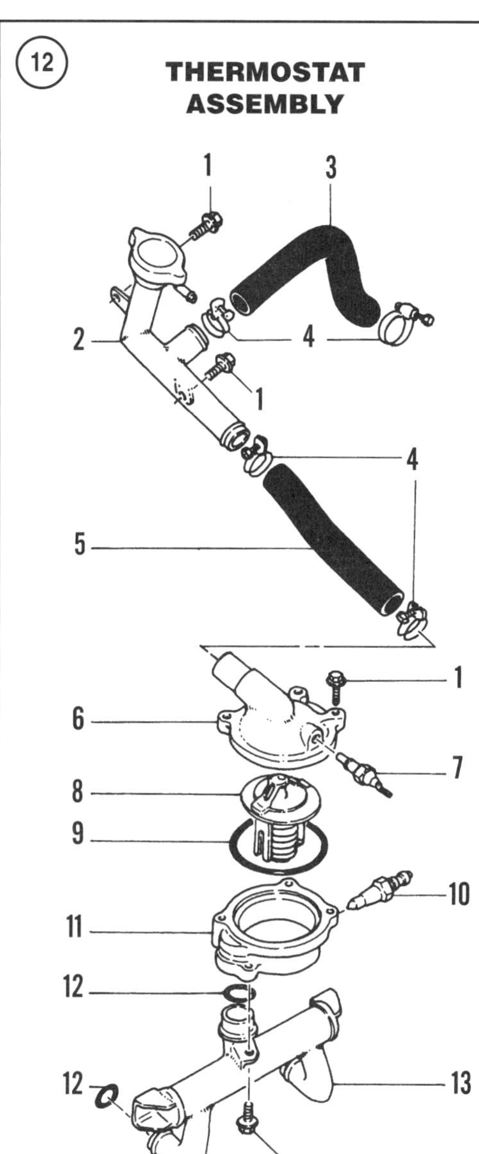

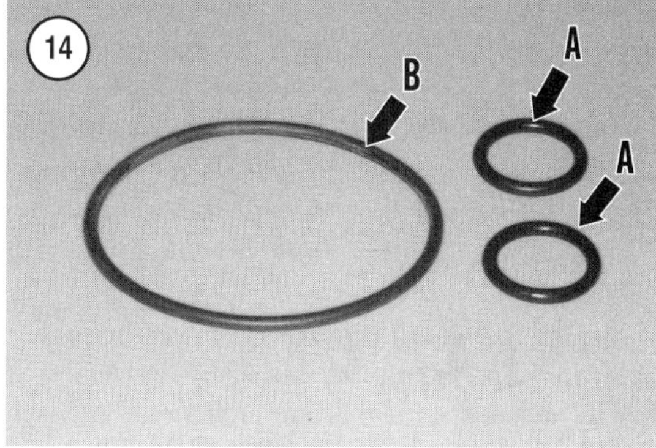

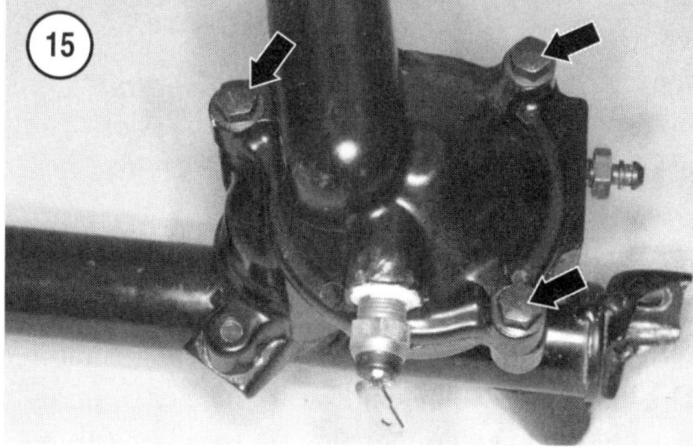

7. Installation is the reverse of removal.
   a. Replace the O-ring (A, **Figure 14**) on each thermostat pipe fitting.
   b. Add coolant and bleed the system as described in Chapter Three.

Disassembly/Assembly

1. Remove the thermostat assembly as described in this section.
2. Remove the cover bolts (**Figure 15**) and remove the thermostat cover and O-ring.

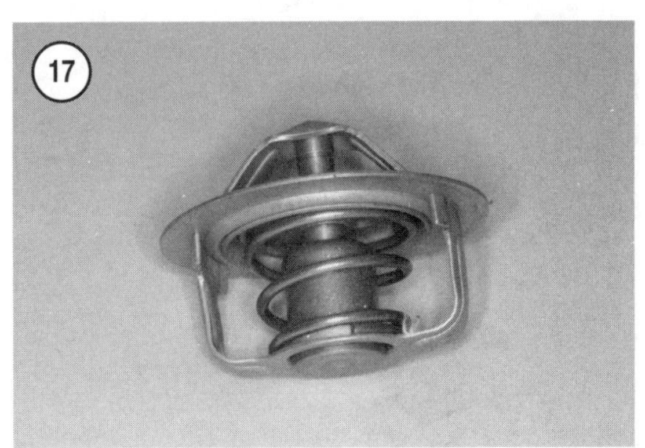

3. Remove the thermostat (**Figure 16**) from the housing.
4. Test the thermostat as described in this section.
5. Assembly is the reverse of removal. Install a new thermostat cover O-ring (B, **Figure 14**).

Thermostat Testing

Test the thermostat (**Figure 17**) to ensure proper operation. The thermostat should be replaced if it remains open at normal room temperature or stays closed after the specified temperature has been reached during the test procedure.

NOTE
The thermometer and the thermostat must not touch the container sides or bottom during this test. If either does, it will result in a false reading.

Suspend the thermostat and thermometer in a pan of water (**Figure 18**). Use a cooking or candy thermometer rated higher than the test temperature. Gradually heat and gently stir the water until it reaches the opening temperature listed in **Table 1**. At this temperature, the thermostat valve should start to open. Once the water temperature reaches the specified fully open temperature, the thermostat valve should be fully opened. The valve lift should equal the minimum specified value.

NOTE
Valve operation is sometimes sluggish. It may take 3-5 minutes for the valve to operate.

If the valve fails to operate at the specified temperatures or if the valve lift is below the minimum specification, the thermostat should be replaced (it cannot be serviced). Make sure to replace the thermostat with one that has the same temperature rating.

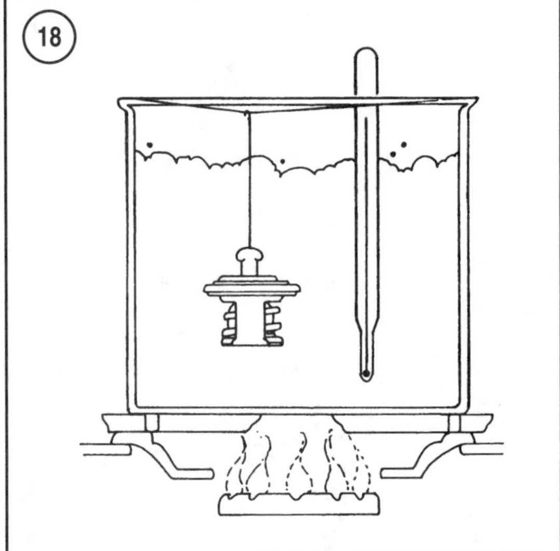

COOLANT TEMPERATURE SENSOR

Removal/Installation

1. Remove the fuel tank as described in Chapter Eight.
2. Remove the lower and middle fairings (Chapter Fifteen).
3. Drain the engine coolant (Chapter Three).
4. Disconnect the electrical connector from the coolant temperature sensor (A, **Figure 13**).
5. Unscrew and remove the coolant temperature sensor from the thermostat cover.
6. Install the coolant temperature sensor by reversing the removal procedures.

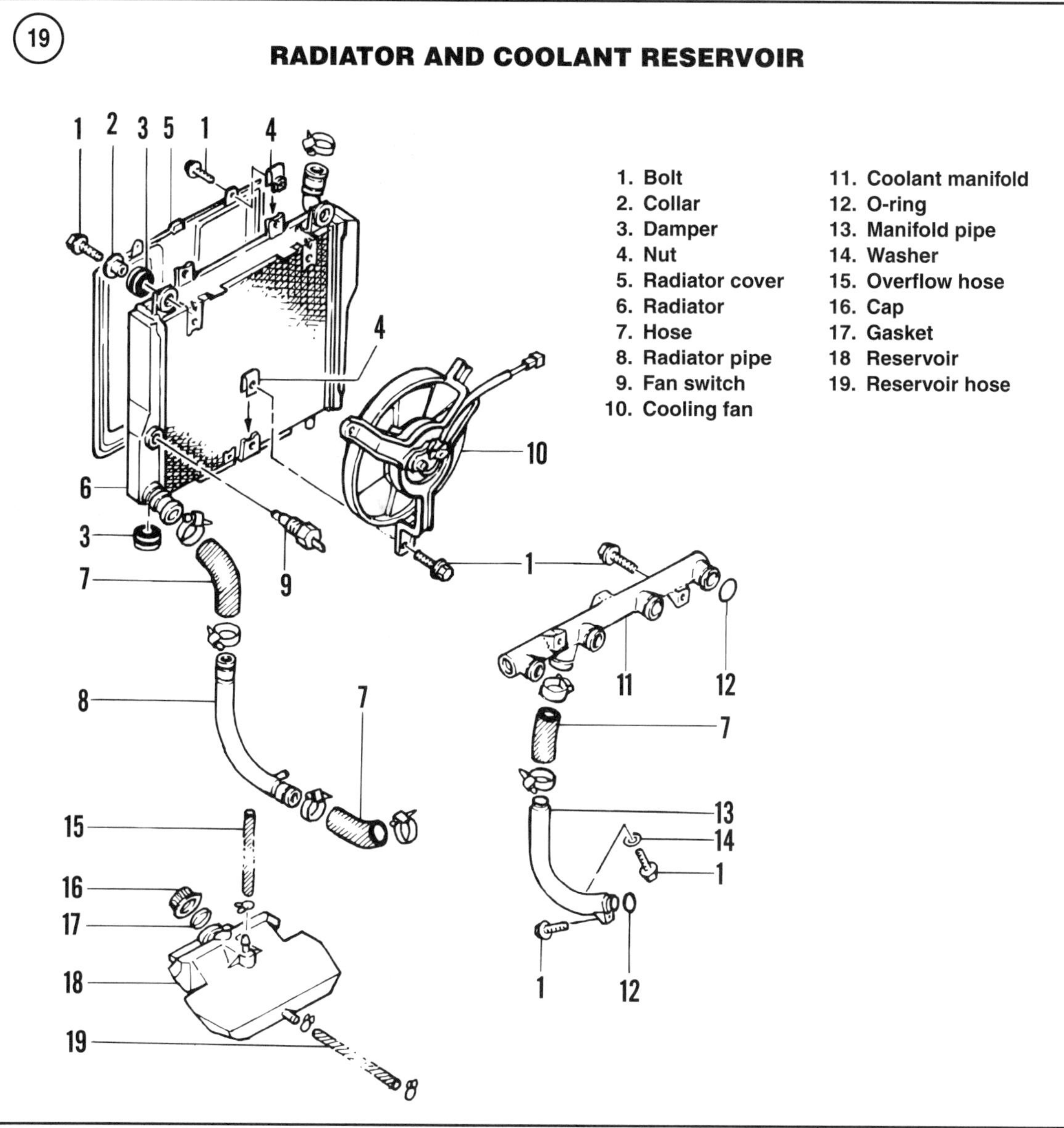

a. Apply silicone sealant to the threads of the temperature sensor.

b. Thread the sensor into the thermostat cover and torque the coolant temperature sensor to 7.8 N•m (69 in.-lb.).

c. Add coolant and bleed the system as described in Chapter Three.

Testing

Follow the test procedure described in Chapter Nine.

COOLANT RESERVOIR

Removal/Installation

Refer to **Figure 19**.

1. Remove the middle and lower fairings as described in Chapter Fifteen.
2. Drain the coolant as described in Chapter Three.

NOTE
Be prepared to catch residual coolant as each hose is removed from the coolant reservoir.

3. Disconnect the reservoir hose from the rear fitting on the reservoir (A, **Figure 20**). Note the zip tie (B, **Figure 20**) that secures this hose to the oil cooler pipe. This tie keeps the hose away from the exhaust pipe. If this zip tie is removed, install a new one during assembly.
4. Note how the overflow hose (A, **Figure 21**) is routed up behind the oil cooler, over the clutch cover (**Figure 22**) and then secured to the swing arm. This hose must be rerouted along the same path during assembly.
5. Remove the reservoir bracket bolts (B, **Figure 21**), and then lower the reservoir and its bracket from the radiator bracket.
6. Disconnect the overflow hose from the fitting on the top of the coolant reservoir. Remove the reservoir. Pour out any coolant from the reservoir.
7. Installation is the reverse of removal. Note the following:
   a. Make sure the overflow hose follows the same path noted during removal.
   b. If removed, secure the reservoir hose to the oil pipe with a new zip tie (B, **Figure 20**).

COOLANT MANIFOLD

Removal/Installation

Refer to **Figure 19**.

1. Remove the lower, middle and front fairings as described in Chapter Fifteen.
2. Drain the engine oil and coolant (Chapter Three).
3. Remove the radiator and radiator bracket (this chapter).
4. Remove the exhaust pipes (Chapter Eight).
5. Remove the bolt (A, **Figure 4**) that secures the coolant manifold pipe (B) to the output fitting on the water pump.
6. Remove the main oil pipe (**Figure 23**) by performing the following:
   a. Remove the banjo bolts (**Figure 24**) that secure the main oil pipe to the cylinder head. Watch for the two sealing washers installed with each banjo bolt.
   b. Remove the banjo bolt (**Figure 25**) that secures the main oil pipe to the oil pan.
   c. Remove the mounting bolt (A, **Figure 26**) that secures the main oil pipe to the coolant manifold and pull the oil pipe from the engine.

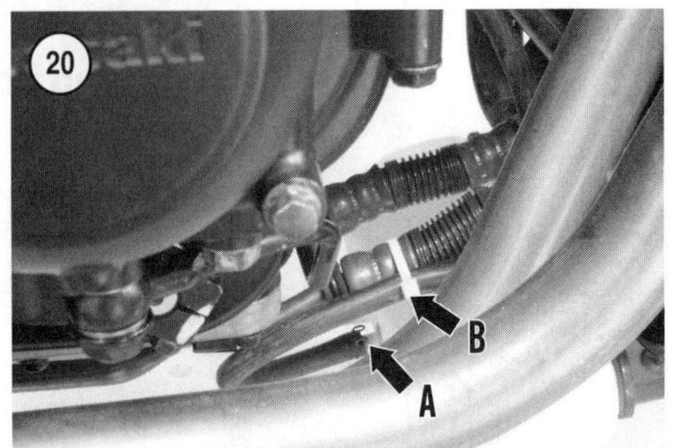

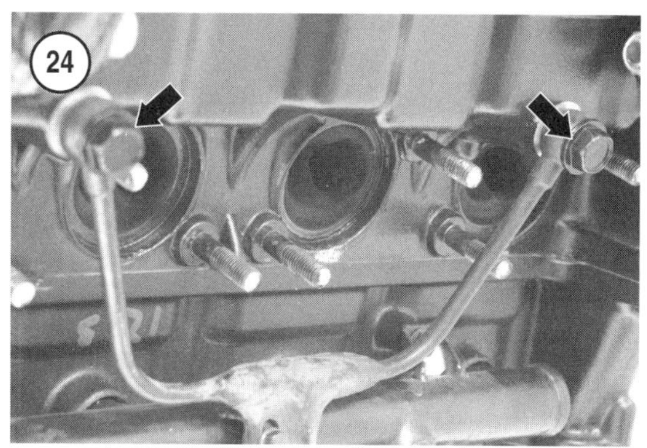

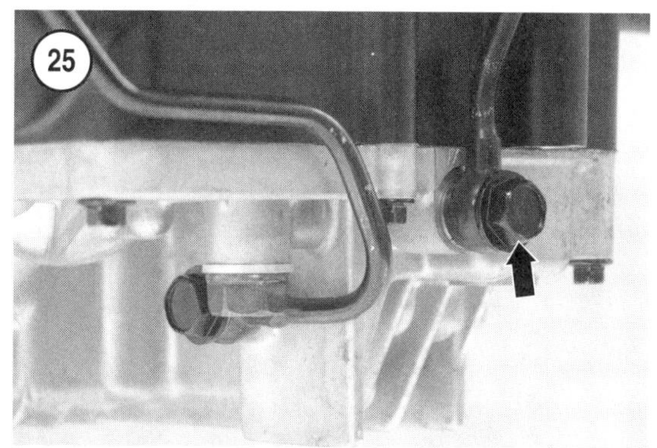

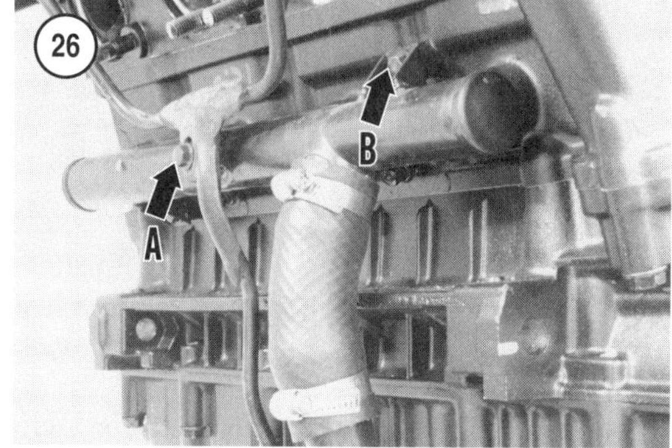

7. Remove the coolant manifold bolt (B, **Figure 26**) from each side.

8. Pull the manifold forward and disconnect it from each port in the cylinder head. Watch for the O-ring installed on each manifold fitting.

9. Installation is the reverse of removal. Install a new O-ring on each manifold fitting.

10. Install the main oil pipe (**Figure 23**). Use a new sealing washer on each side of the oil pipe fittings, and torque the banjo bolts to 25 N•m (18 ft.-lb.). Tighten the oil pipe mounting bolt securely.

RADIATOR

Removal/Installation

Refer to **Figure 19**.

1. Remove the lower, middle and front fairings as described in Chapter Fifteen.

2. Remove the drain bolt and drain the coolant from the radiator and engine (Chapter Three).

3. Remove the reservoir hose (A, **Figure 20**) from the fitting at the rear of the coolant reservoir.

4. Clip the zip tie (B, **Figure 20**) that secures the reservoir hose to the oil cooler pipe.

5. Disconnect the reservoir hose (A, **Figure 27**) from fitting on the filler neck. Pull the hose through the holder behind the fuel tank damper and from the holders on the right side of the radiator. Note how the reservoir hose is routed. It must be rerouted along the same path during assembly.

6. Loosen the clamp (B, **Figure 27**) and remove the hose from the upper fitting on the radiator.

7. Pull the electrical connectors (A, **Figure 28**) from the fan switch and disconnect the hose (B) from the lower fitting on the radiator.

8. Remove the radiator mounting bolt (C, **Figure 27**) from each side. Watch for the collar and damper installed with each bolt.
9. Lean the radiator forward and rest it against the fork legs.
10. Disconnect the fan connector (A, **Figure 29**) from its harness mate.
11. Disengage the heat shield from the tabs (B, **Figure 29**) on the radiator and remove the heat shield.
12. Lift the radiator feet from their seats (**Figure 30**) in the radiator bracket and remove the radiator.
13. Installation is the reverse of removal. Note the following:
   a. Set the radiator feet into the dampers (**Figure 30**) on the radiator bracket. Rest the radiator against the fork legs.
   b. Secure the heat shield to the tabs (B, **Figure 29**) on the radiator and connect the fan connector (A) to its harness mate.
   c. Tilt the radiator rearward, seat each radiator foot in its damper and install each radiator mounting bolt (C, **Figure 27**). Include a collar and damper with each bolt.
   d. Connect the reservoir hose (A, **Figure 27**) to the fitting on the filler neck. Following the path notes during removal, route the reservoir hose through the holders on the right side of the radiator, through the holder behind the fuel tank damper and connect the hose to the rear fitting (A, **Figure 20**) on the coolant reservoir.
   e. Secure the reservoir hose to the oil cooler pipe with a new zip tie (B, **Figure 27**).
   f. Add coolant and bleed the cooling system as described in Chapter Three.

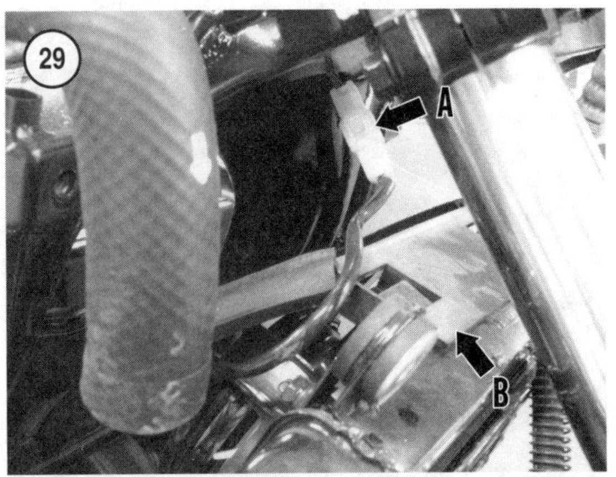

Inspection

1. If necessary, remove the mounting bolts (A, **Figure 31**) and lift the fan motor from the radiator.
2. Flush the exterior of the radiator with a garden hose on low pressure. Spray both the front and the back to remove all debris. Carefully use a whisk broom or stiff paint brush to remove any stubborn dirt.

CAUTION
Do not press too hard or the cooling fins and tubes may be damaged.

3. Carefully straighten out any bent cooling fins with a broad-tipped screwdriver or putty knife.

NOTE
If the radiator has been damaged across approximately 20% or more of the frontal area, the radiator should be recored or replaced.

4. Check for cracks or signs of leakage (usually a moss-green colored residue) at the filler neck, the inlet and outlet hose fittings, and along the tank seams.
5. If the condition of a radiator is doubtful, pressure check it as described in *Cooling System Inspection* in Chapter Three. Radiators can be pressure checked while removed or when mounted on the motorcycle.
6. If paint is worn off any area of the radiator, repaint the area with a quality black spray paint. This helps prolong the radiator life by cutting down on oxidation from the outside. Do not apply too much paint to the cooling fin area. Excessive paint will reduce the radiator's cooling efficiency.
7. Make sure the rubber dampers (B, **Figure 31**) in the upper radiator mounts are in good condition. Replace them as necessary.

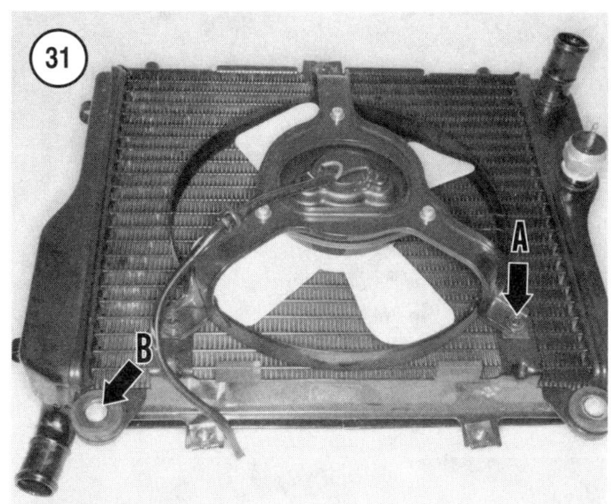

8. Inspect the rubber seals on the radiator cap. Replace the cap if the seals are hard or starting to deteriorate. Pressure test the radiator cap as described in Chapter Three.

COOLING FAN MOTOR

Testing

Test the cooling fan by performing the cooling fan operational test described in Chapter Nine.

Removal/Installation

1. Remove the radiator as described in this chapter.
2. Remove the mounting fan bolts (A, **Figure 31**) and lift the fan from the radiator.
3. Installation is the reverse of removal. Apply Loctite 242 (blue) to the threads of the fan mounting bolts and tighten the bolts securely.

FAN SWITCH

Removal/Installation

1. Remove the lower and middle fairings as described in Chapter Fifteen.
2. Drain the coolant (Chapter Three).
3. Disconnect each connector (A, **Figure 28**) from the fan switch.
4. Unscrew the fan switch and remove it from the radiator.
5. Installation is the reverse of removal. Note the following:
   a. Apply a silicon sealant to the threads of the fan switch.
   b. Torque the fan switch to 27 N•m (20 ft.-lb.).
   c. Refill and bleed the system as described in Chapter Three.

Testing

Follow the test procedure described in Chapter Nine.

10

RADIATOR BRACKET

The radiator, coolant reservoir and oil cooler mount to the radiator bracket. The following procedure describes bracket removal with the coolant reservoir and oil cooler mounted to the bracket.

Removal/Installation

1. Remove the lower, middle and front fairings as described in Chapter Fifteen.
2. Drain the engine oil and coolant (Chapter Three).
3. Remove the radiator (this chapter).
4. Disconnect the reservoir overflow hose from the fitting on top of the coolant reservoir.
5. Remove the banjo bolt (**Figure 32**) that secures each oil pipe to the oil pan. Watch for the two copper washers installed with each bolt.

CAUTION

Watch the oil pipes as the radiator bracket is lowered from the engine and slid from the motorcycle. The oil pipes must not be strained or bent.

6. Remove the radiator bracket bolts from the upper and lower mounts (**Figure 33**) on each side. Carefully lower the radiator bracket from the motorcycle so the oil cooler pipes are not damaged.
7. Installation is the reverse of removal. Note the following:
   a. Slide the radiator bracket between the engine and front wheel so the oil cooler pipes sit beneath the oil pan.
   b. Lift the radiator bracket so the oil cooler pipes are in position beneath their ports on the oil pan (**Figure 34**).
   c. Loosely install the bracket mounting bolts (**Figure 33**) to hold the radiator bracket in place.
   d. Secure the oil pipes to the oil pan with the banjo bolts (**Figure 32**). Install a new copper washer on each side of an oil pipe fitting and torque the oil cooler banjo bolts to 34 N•m (25 ft.-lb.).
   e. Tighten the radiator bracket bolts securely.

Table 1 COOLING SYSTEM SPECIFICATIONS

Coolant quantity (to the upper mark)	3.1 L (3.27 U.S. qt. [2.73 Imp. qt.])
Radiator cap relief pressure	93-123 kPa (13.2-17.9 psi)
Fan switch	
Off-to-on	93-103° C (199-217° F)
On-to-off	91-95° C (196-203° F)
Coolant temperature resistance	
80° C (176° F)	Approx. 52 ohms
100° C (212° F)	Approx. 27 ohms
Thermostat	
Opening temperature	80-84° C (176-183° F)
Full opening lift	8 mm (0.315 in.) @ 95° C (203° F)

Table 2 COOLING SYSTEM TORQUE SPECIFICATIONS

Item	N•m	in.-lb.	ft.-lb.
Cooling system drain bolt	7.8	69	–
Coolant temperature sensor*	7.8	69	–
Fan switch	27	–	20
Oil cooler pipe banjo bolts	34	–	25
Main oil pipe banjo bolt	25	–	18
Shift pedal bracket 14-mm bolt	78	–	58

*Apply silicone sealant (Kawasaki Bond part No. 56019-120 or equivalent) to the threads.

CHAPTER ELEVEN

WHEELS AND TIRES

This chapter describes repair and maintenance procedures for the wheels and tires. When inspecting any of the components in this chapter, compare all measurements to the tire and wheel service specifications in the tables at the end of this chapter. Replace any component that is damaged, worn to the service limit or out of specification. During assembly, tighten fasteners to the specified torque.

BIKE STAND

Many procedures in this chapter require that the motorcycle be supported with a wheel off the ground. A quality motorcycle front end stand (**Figure 1**) or a swing arm stand does this safely and effectively. Before purchasing or using a stand, check the manufacturer's instructions to make sure the stand will work on your motorcycle. If the motorcycle or stand require any modifications or adjustment, perform the required service before lifting the motorcycle. When using a motorcycle stand, have an assistant standing by.

An adjustable centerstand can also be used to support the motorcycle with a wheel off the ground. Again, check the manufacturer's instructions and perform any necessary modifications before supporting the motorcycle with the adjustable centerstand.

Some means to tie down one end of the bike is also needed when lifting a motorcycle. Regardless of the method used, be sure the motorcycle is properly supported before walking away from it.

BRAKE ROTOR PROTECTION

Be careful when removing, handling and installing a wheel with a disc brake rotor. Brake rotors are thin in order to dissipate heat and to minimize unsprung weight. A rotor is designed to withstand tremendous rotational loads, but it can be damaged when subjected to side impacts.

Protect the rotor when servicing a wheel. Never set a wheel down on the brake rotor. It may be bent or scratched. When a wheel must be placed on its side, support the wheel on wooden blocks (**Figure 2**). Position the blocks along the outer circumference of the wheel so the rotor lies between the blocks and does not rest on them.

Also protect the rotor when transporting a wheel to a dealership or tire specialist for tire service. Do *not* place a wheel in a car trunk or truck bed without protecting the rotor from side impact.

If the rotor is knocked out of true by a side impact, you will feel a pulsation in the brake lever or pedal when braking. Since brake rotors are too thin to be trued, damaged rotors must be replaced.

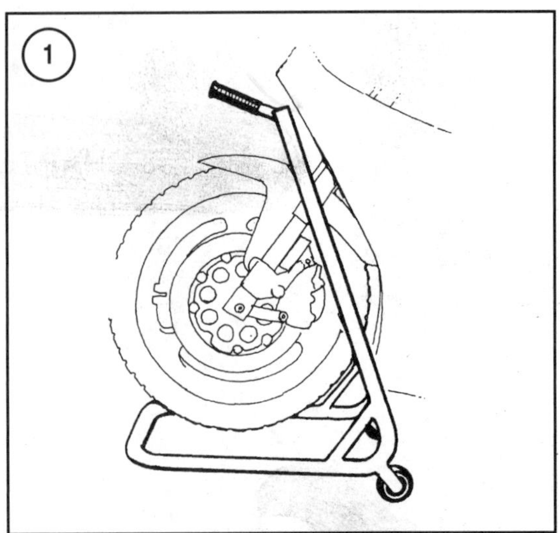

FRONT WHEEL

Removal/Installation

1. Place wooden block(s) under the crankcase to securely support the motorcycle with the front wheel off the ground. Make sure the wheel is high enough so it will clear the front fender once the axle is removed.
2. Check the wheel bearings by performing these preliminary tests:
   a. Hold the wheel along its side (180° apart) and try to rock it back and forth. If any play is noticed at the axle, the wheel bearings are worn or damaged.
   b. Have an assistant apply the brake while you rock the wheel again. On wheels with severely worn bearings, play will be detected even though the wheel is locked in position.
   c. Spin the wheel and listen for excessive wheel bearing noise. Grinding or catching noises indicate worn bearings.
   d. If either bearing is worn or damage, replace both wheel bearings as a set. Refer to the hub procedures in this chapter.
3. Remove the speedometer cable (A, **Figure 3**) from the speedometer gear housing.

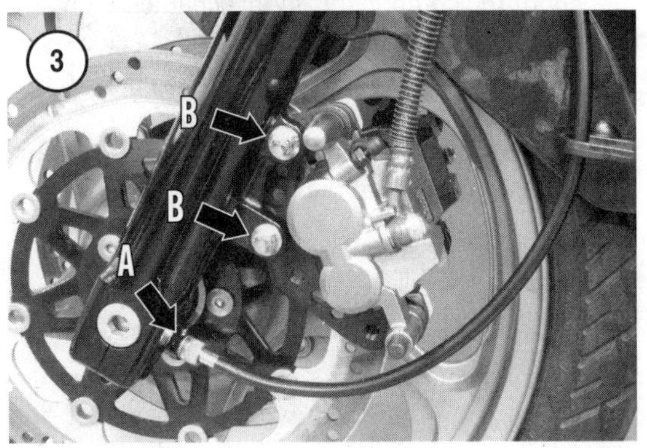

NOTE

If the brake lever is applied while the calipers are off the front wheel, both calipers must be disassembled to reseat the caliper pistons and the brakes must be bled. A wooden block between the brake lever and the handlebar prevents the accidental application of the brakes.

4. Insert a wooden block between the brake lever and the handlebar grip. Use a rubber band to hold the block in place.
5. Remove the brake caliper from the wheel by performing the following:
   a. Remove the caliper mounting bolts (B, **Figure 3**) from the caliper.

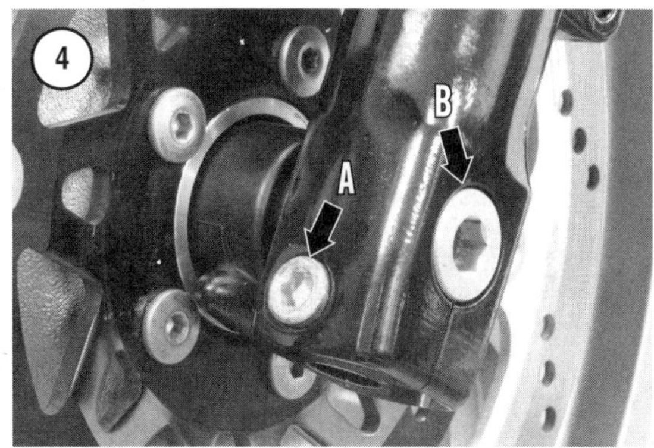

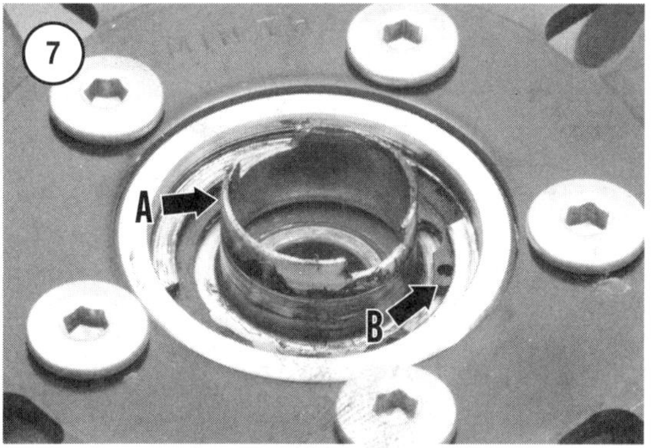

b. Rotate the caliper off the brake disc. Use a stiff wire or bungee cord to suspend the caliper from the motorcycle.
c. Place a shop rag around the caliper so the front fender will not be scratched. Secure the rag with a zip tie or rubber band.

6. Repeat Step 5 for the other front brake caliper.
7. Loosen the clamp bolt (A, **Figure 4**) on each fork leg.
8. Hold the axle (A, **Figure 5**) and remove the axle nut (B, **Figure 4**) from the left fork leg.
9. Pull the axle from the right fork leg and lower the wheel. Watch for the collar (**Figure 6**) in the right side of the hub.
10. Roll the wheel from between the fork legs. Remove the speedometer gear housing from the left side of the hub; remove the collar (**Figure 6**) from the right side.

CAUTION
Do not lay a wheel on the brake disc. The disc could be scratched or bent.

11. If the wheel must be set down on its side, place wooden blocks (**Figure 2**) beneath the tire.
12. Inspect the wheel as described in this section.
13. Installation is the reverse of removal. Pay attention to the following:
    a. Apply a coat of antiseize compound to the axle.
    b. Install the speedometer gear housing into the left side of the hub. Align the tabs in the speedometer gear housing with the slots (A, **Figure 7**) in the receiver.
    c. Make sure the collar is in place on the right side of the hub (**Figure 6**).
    d. Position the wheel between the fork legs. Make sure the lug on the speedometer gear housing engages the locating boss on the left fork slider.
    e. Install the axle (A, **Figure 8**) from the right side.
    f. Tighten the axle nut (B, **Figure 4**) to 88 N•m (65 ft.-lb.).
    g. Carefully fit each front brake caliper onto the brake disc. Torque the caliper mounting bolts (B, **Figure 3**) to 32 N•m (24 ft.-lb.).
    h. Rotate the wheel several times to make sure it turns freely. Apply the front brake as many

11

times as necessary to make sure the brake pads properly engage the brake disc.

i. Apply the front brake and pump the forks several times to ensure the fork legs slide smoothly. On 1986-1993 models, torque each axle clamp bolt (A, **Figure 4**) to 20 N•m (15 ft.-lb.); on 1994-on models, torque the clamp bolts to 35 N•m (26 ft.-lb.).

Wheel Inspection

During inspection, compare all measurements to the specification in **Table 1**. Replace any part that is damaged, out of specification or worn to the service limit.

1. Inspect the speedometer gear housing (**Figure 9**) for wear or damage. Replace it if necessary. Clean old grease from the gear housing and apply a high-temperature grease.
2. Inspect the seals for excessive wear, hardness, cracks or other damage. If necessary, replace the seals as described in the appropriate hub disassembly section in this chapter.
3. Remove any corrosion from the axle (A, **Figure 8**), collar (B) or axle nut (C) with a piece of fine emery cloth.

WARNING

Do not attempt to straighten a bent axle.

4. Place the axle on V-blocks set 100 mm (4 in.) apart and measure the runout with a dial indicator. If runout exceeds the service limit but is less than the repair limit (**Table 1**), have it straightened at the dealership or machine shop. If runout exceeds the repair limit, replace the axle.
5. Install the wheel on a truing stand. Check wheel runout by performing the following:
   a. Measure the radial (up and down) runout of the wheel rim with a dial indicator as shown in **Figure 10**.
   b. Measure the axial (side to side) runout of the wheel rim with a dial indicator as shown in **Figure 10**.
6. If the radial or axial runout exceeds specification (**Table 1**), inspect the wheel bearings as described in the appropriate hub disassembly section in this chapter.
   a. If the wheel bearings are good, the wheel must be replaced.
   b. If either wheel bearing is worn, disassemble the hub and replace both bearings as a set.
7. Check the tightness of the brake disc bolts. If a bolt is loose, remove and reinstall the bolts with Loctite 242 (blue). Clean the old threadlocking compound from the threads and torque the bolt to 23 N•m (17 ft.-lb.).

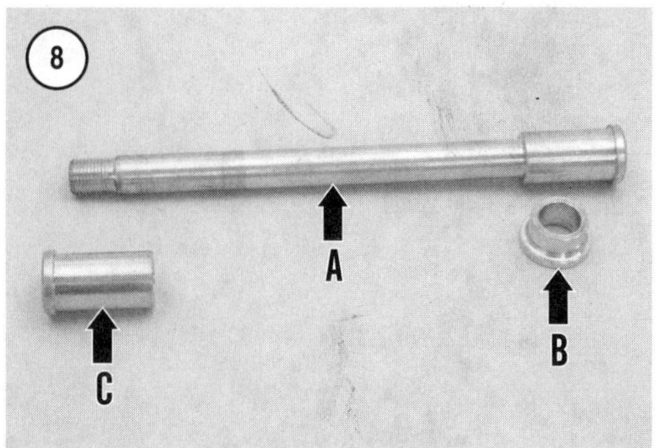

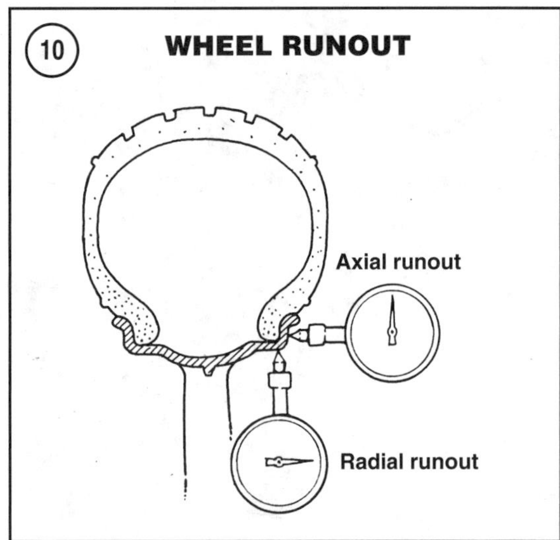

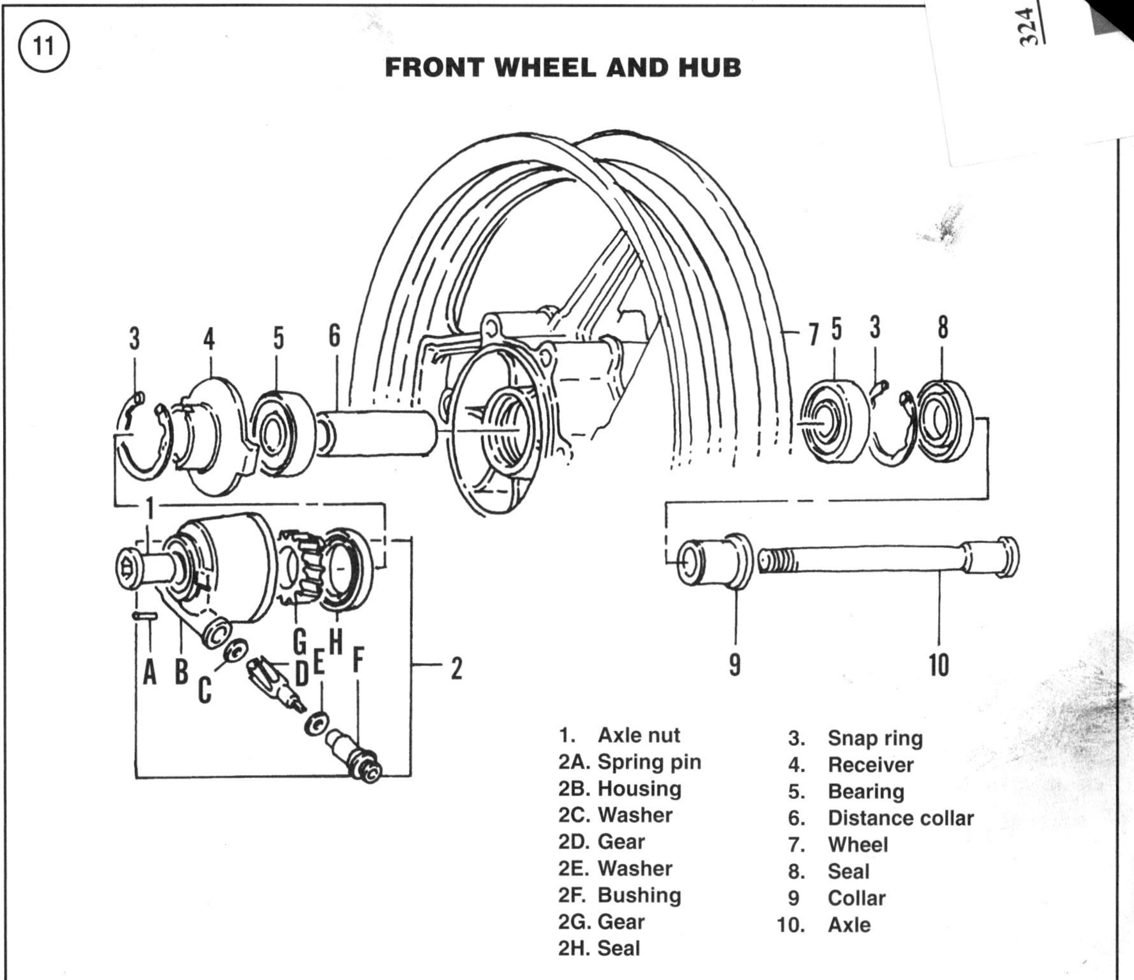

8. Visually inspect the brake discs and measure the brake disc deflection as described in Chapter Fourteen. If deflection is excessive, measure wheel runout. If runout is within specification, replace the brake disc. Refer to the procedure in Chapter Fourteen.

9. Visually inspect the wheel rim for dents, bending or cracks. Check the rim and rim sealing surface for scratches that are deeper than 0.5 mm (0.01 in.). If any of these conditions are present, replace the wheel.

FRONT HUB

Disassembly/Inspection/Assembly

Refer to **Figure 11**.

1. Remove the front wheel as described in this chapter.
2. If still installed, remove the collar (**Figure 6**) from the right side of the hub and remove the speedometer gear housing from the left.

CAUTION

Do not lay a wheel on the brake disc. The disc could be scratched or bent.

3. Use wooden blocks to support the wheel. Place the tire on the blocks so the brake disc will not be damaged (**Figure 2**).
4. Remove the snap ring (B, **Figure 7**) and remove the receiver (A) from the hub.
5. Pry the oil seal (**Figure 12**) from the right side of the hub and remove the snap ring.
6. Inspect the bearings by performing the following:

12

a. Turn each bearing inner race by hand. The bearing must turn smoothly with no roughness, binding or excessive noise. Some axial play (**Figure 13**) is normal, but radial play must be negligible.

b. Check the bearing's outer seal for buckling or other damage that would admit dirt.

c. If either bearing is damaged, replace both bearings as a set.

7. If necessary, remove the bearings as described in *Bearing Removal* in this chapter.

8. Clean the distance collar and hub in solvent. Thoroughly dry them with compressed air.

9. Install the bearings by performing the following:

a. Place the new bearings in a freezer overnight.

b. Remove the bearings from the freezer and pack the unsealed side of the front bearings with grease.

c. Carefully drive the right bearing into place. Use a bearing driver or socket that matches the diameter of the outer bearing race.

d. Install the snap ring so it is seated in the hub groove.

e. Install the distance collar and install the left bearing.

10. Install a new right-side seal. Drive the seal in squarely with seal driver or a large diameter socket (**Figure 14**) seated on the outer portion of the seal.

11. Align the tabs on the speedometer receiver with the slots in the hub and install the receiver (A, **Figure 7**). Secure it in place with the snap ring (B, **Figure 7**). Make sure the snap ring is completely seated in the hub groove.

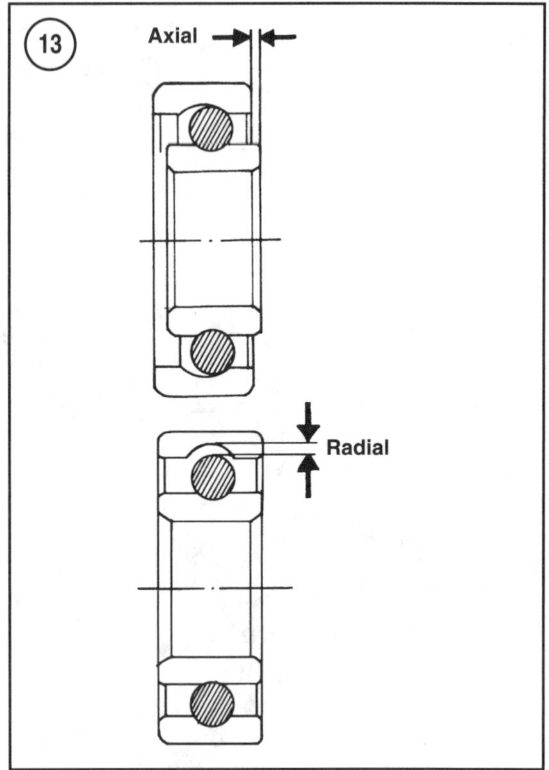
13

14

Bearing Removal

1. Disassemble the hub as described in this section.

WARNING
Be sure to wear safety glasses while using the wheel bearing remover set.

NOTE
*The Kowa Seiki Wheel Bearing Remover (**Figure 15**) can be used to remove the wheel bearings. This tool set can be ordered through a Kawasaki*

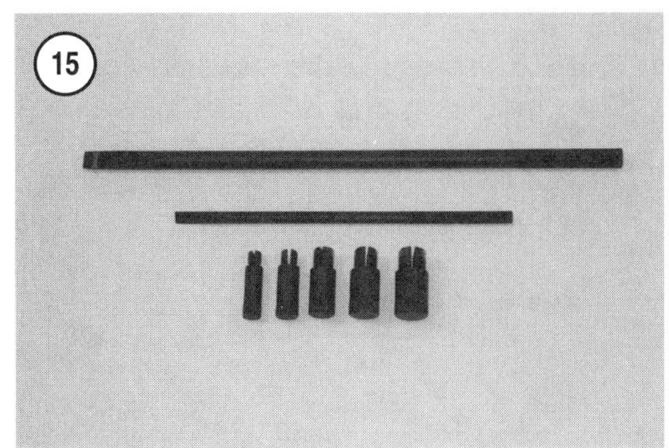
15

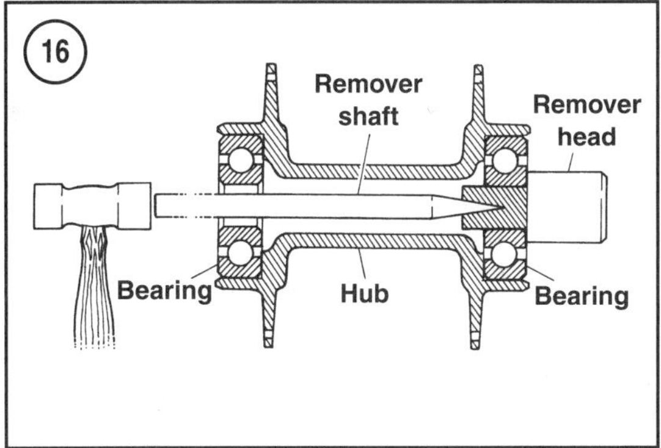

16

17

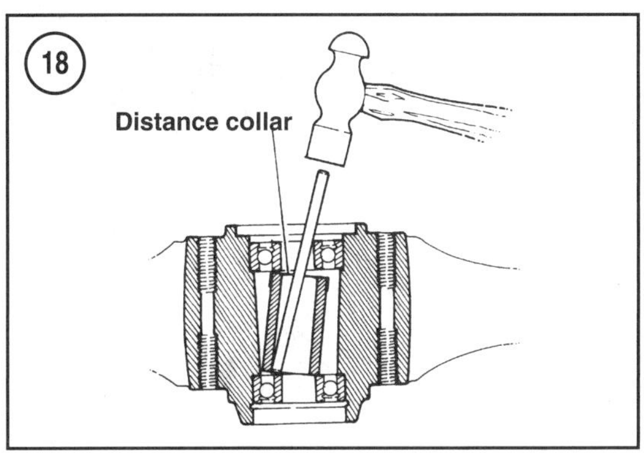

18

dealership or from K & L Supply Co. in Santa Clara, CA.

2A. Remove the bearings with the Kowa Seiki Wheel Bearing Remover by performing the following:

a. Select the correct size remover head and insert it into the outside bearing (**Figure 16**).
b. From the opposite side of the wheel, insert the remover shaft into the slot in the backside of the remover head. Position the wheel so that the remover head rests against a solid surface. Tap the remover shaft and force it into the slot in the remover head. This tightens the remover head against the bearings inner race.

CAUTION
Do not set the wheel down on the brake disc. If necessary, support the rim with wooden blocks.

c. Reposition the wheel. Using a hammer, tap the remover shaft to drive the bearing out of the wheel (**Figure 17**). Slide the bearing and tool assembly out of the hub. Tap the remover head to release it from the bearing.
d. Remove the distance collar from the wheel.
e. Repeat the above procedure and remove the opposite bearing.

2B. If the Kowa Seiki or similar tool is not available, remove the bearings by performing the following:

a. Using a long drift and hammer, tilt the distance collar away from one side of the right bearing (**Figure 18**) and then drive the right bearing out of the hub.
b. Remove the distance collar and turn the hub over.
c. Use the drift to drive out the left bearing.

REAR WHEEL

Removal

1. Remove the cotter pin and loosen the rear axle nut (A, **Figure 19**).
2. Remove the torque arm nut (B, **Figure 19**), pull the bolt and lift the torque arm off the caliper bracket.
3. Release the brake hose from the holders (C, **Figure 19**) on the swing arm.

4. Securely support the motorcycle with the rear wheel off the ground.
5. Remove the axle nut from the axle.
6. Pull the axle (A, **Figure 20**) and its seal (B) from the left side.

NOTE
Insert vinyl tubing or a piece of wood between the brake pads in the caliper. That way, if the brake pedal is inadvertently applied, the pistons will not be forced out of the cylinders. If this does happen, the caliper will have to be disassembled to reseat the pistons and the system will have to be bled.

7. Lift the brake caliper and its bracket from the brake disc. Use a wire or bungee cord to suspend the caliper from the motorcycle.
8. Remove the collar (**Figure 21**) from the right side of the hub.
9. Move the wheel to the right to disengage it from the final gearcase, roll the wheel rearward and remove it.
10. Inspect the wheel as described in *Wheel Inspection* in this chapter.
11. If necessary, disassemble the hub as described in this chapter.

Installation

1. Apply a coat of anti-seize compound to the axle.
2. Apply grease to the splines of the coupling and final gearcase.
3. Roll the rear wheel into position in the swing arm (**Figure 22**).
4. Slide the wheel to the left until the splines on the rear wheel coupling completely engage those in the final gearcase (**Figure 23**).
5. Install the collar (**Figure 21**) into the right side of the hub.
6. Carefully lower the brake caliper onto the brake disc. Make sure the caliper bracket sits between the swing arm and the collar in the right side of the hub as shown in A, **Figure 24**.
7. Install the axle (A, **Figure 20**) and seal (B) from the left side. Make sure the axle passes through the final gearcase, the hub, collar, caliper bracket and emerges from the swing arm (B, **Figure 24**).
8. Loosely install the axle nut onto the right side of the axle.

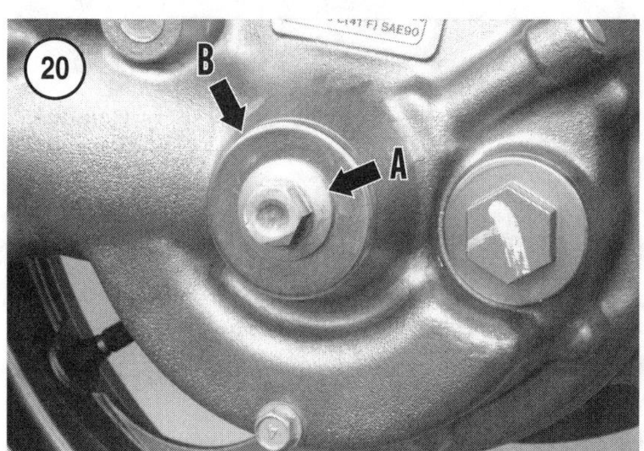

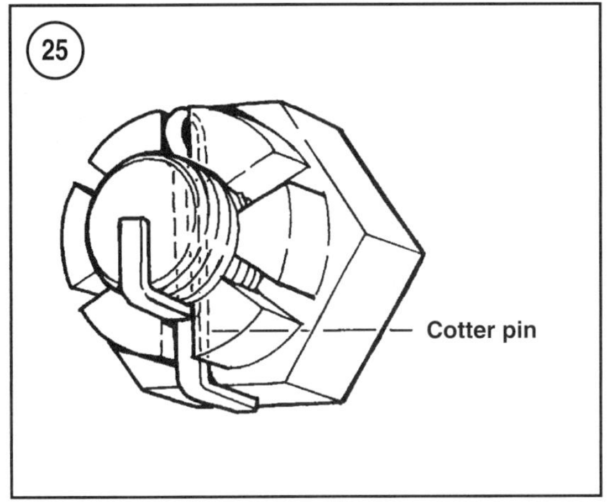

9. Lower the torque arm so it engages the caliper bracket. Install the torque arm bolt and nut (B, **Figure 19**). Tighten the torque arm nut to 29 N•m (22 ft.-lb.).

10. Secure the brake hose to the swing arm with the holders (C, **Figure 19**).

11. Torque the axle nut (A, **Figure 19**) to 110 N•m (81 ft.-lb.) and install a new cotter pin. Bend the cotter pin arms as shown in **Figure 25**.

REAR HUB

Preliminary Inspection

CAUTION
Do not remove the wheel bearings for inspection purposes. The bearings are damaged during removal and cannot be reused. Remove the wheel bearings only if they must be replaced.

1. Remove the rear wheel as described in this chapter.
2. The condition of the rear wheel bearings is critical to the tracking and acceleration performance of the motorcycle. Check the wheel bearings whenever the wheel is removed or as one of the first steps when diagnosing handling or noise problems.
3. Inspect the each bearing by performing the following:
   a. If still in place, remove the collar (**Figure 21**) from the right side of the rear hub.
   a. Turn the bearing inner race by hand. The bearing must turn smoothly with no roughness, binding or excessive noise. Some axial play (**Figure 13**) is normal, but radial play must be negligible.
   b. Check the bearing fit in the hub by trying to move the bearing laterally by hand. The bearing should be tight in the bore. Loose bearings allow the wheel to wobble. If the bearing is loose, the bearing bore in the hub is probably worn or damaged.
4. Check for a worn or damaged seal.
5. If either bearing is damaged, disassemble the hub and replace both bearings.

Disassembly

Refer to **Figure 26**.

1. Remove the retaining ring (A, **Figure 27**) and pull the rear wheel coupling (B) from the hub. If the coupling will not come out, spray soap solution through the holes to lubricate the rubber dampers and the coupling ribs.
2. Remove the dampers (**Figure 28**) and O-ring from the hub.
3. Pry the seal from the right side of the hub and remove the snap ring.

26

REAR HUB

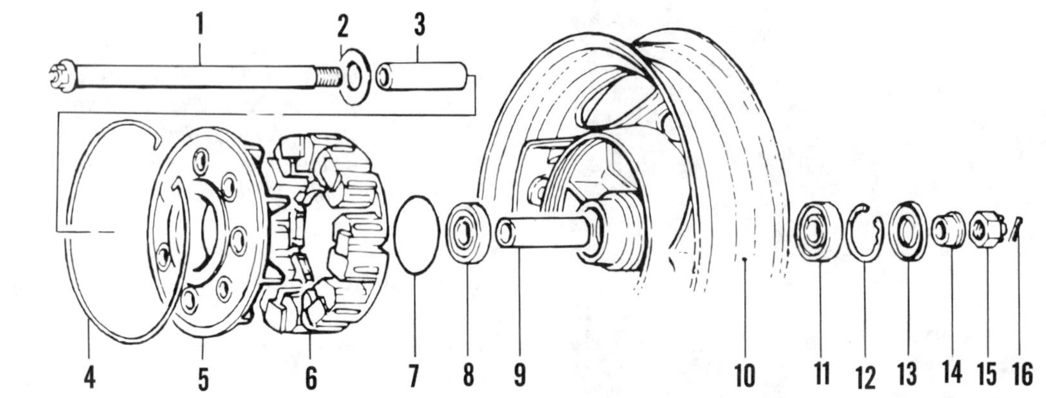

1. Rear axle
2. Seal
3. Distance collar
4. Retaining ring
5. Coupling
6. Damper
7. O-ring
8. Bearing
9. Distance collar
10. Wheel
11. Bearing
12. Snap ring
13. Seal
14. Collar
15. Nut
16. Cotter pin

4. Drive out the bearings as described in *Bearing Removal* in this chapter.

5. Inspect the rear hub as described in this section.

Assembly

1. Install the bearings by performing the following:
   a. Place the new bearings in a freezer overnight.
   b. Set a bearing into place on the right side of the hub. Use a socket or driver that matches the outside diameter of the bearing (**Figure 29**) and drive the bearing until it is seated in the hub.
   c. Install the snap ring so it is completely seated in the hub groove.
   d. Turn the hub over and install the distance collar.
   e. Drive the left bearing into place as described in substep b.

2. Lubricate the new seal with grease. Use the socket or driver used to install the bearings and seat the seal in the hub.

3. Install a new O-ring into the hub.

27

28

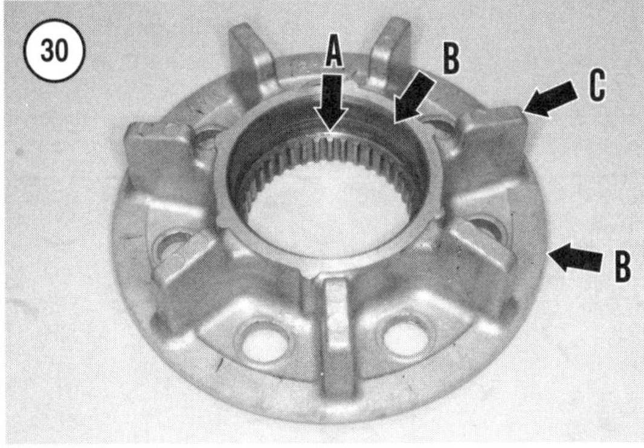

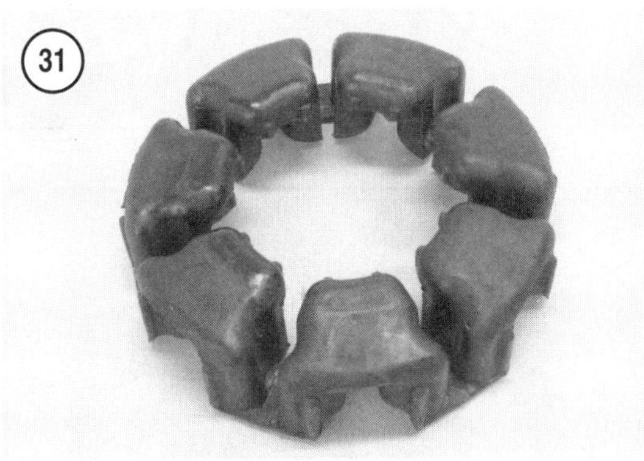

4. Install the damper assembly (**Figure 28**) into the hub so the smooth side faces down into the hub. Make sure each damper straddles a rib in the hub. Press them into the hub so they are completely seated.
5. Apply grease to the coupling splines (A, **Figure 30**) and to the inner and outer circumferences (B) of the coupling.
6. Lubricate the coupling ribs (C, **Figure 30**) with soap solution.
7. Set the coupling onto the hub so its ribs sit in the gap between the dampers.
8. Use a plastic mallet to evenly tap the coupling into the hub until it bottoms, then install the retaining ring (A, **Figure 27**).

Inspection

During inspection, replace any part that is damaged, worn or out of specification.
1. Visually inspect the rear hub dampers (**Figure 31**). If any damper is worn, cracked or becoming brittle, replace the damper assembly.
2. Inspect the ribs (C, **Figure 30**) on the coupling for nicks, roughness or other damage.
3. Inspect the splines (A, **Figure 30**) on the coupling. If damage is noted, inspect the mating splines in the final gearcase.
4. Inspect the ribs (**Figure 32**) in the hub for nicks, roughness or other damage.

11

WHEEL BALANCE

An unbalanced wheel is unsafe. Depending upon the degree of unbalance and the speed of the motorcycle, the rider may experience anything from a mild vibration to a violent shimmy that may result in loss of control.

Kawasaki offers balance weights of 10, 20 and 30 grams each. Before you attempt to balance the wheel, check to be sure that the wheel bearings are in good condition and properly lubricated. The wheel must rotate freely.

NOTE
When balancing the wheels, do so with the brake disc attached. The disc rotates with the wheel and affects the balance.

1. Remove the wheel as described in this chapter.

2. Mount the wheel on an inspection stand as shown in (**Figure 33**) so it can rotate freely.
3. Give the wheel a spin and let it coast to a stop. Mark the tire at the lowest point (6 o'clock).
4. Spin the wheel several more times. If the wheel keeps coming to rest at the same point, it is out of balance.

NOTE
Adhesive test weights are available from motorcycle dealerships. These adhesive-backed weights can be cut to the desired length and attached directly to the rim.

5. Loosely attach a balance weight (or tape a test weight) at the upper or light side (12 o'clock) of the wheel.
6. Rotate the wheel 1/4 turn (3 o'clock). Release the wheel and observe the following:
   a. If the wheel does not rotate (if it stays at the 3 o'clock position), the correct balance weight was installed. The wheel is balanced.
   b. If the wheel rotates and the weighted portion goes up, replace the weight with the next heavier size.
   c. If the wheel rotates and the weighted portion goes down, replace the weight with the next lighter size.
   d. Repeat this step until the wheel remains at rest after being rotated 1/4 turn. Rotate the wheel another 1/4 turn and another 1/4 turn and another turn to see if the wheel is correctly balanced.
7. Firmly crimp the balance weight in place with a pair of pliers. If you used adhesive weights, remove the adhesive weight and crimp the proper sized balance weight to the rim.

TIRE REPAIRS

WARNING
Do not install an inner tube inside a tubeless tire. The tube will cause an abnormal heat buildup in the tire.

Only use tire plugs as an emergency repair. Follow the manufacturer's instructions and note the motorcycle weight and speed restrictions. A combination plug/patch (**Figure 34**) applied from the inside is preferred to a plug applied from the outside. After performing an emergency tire repair with a

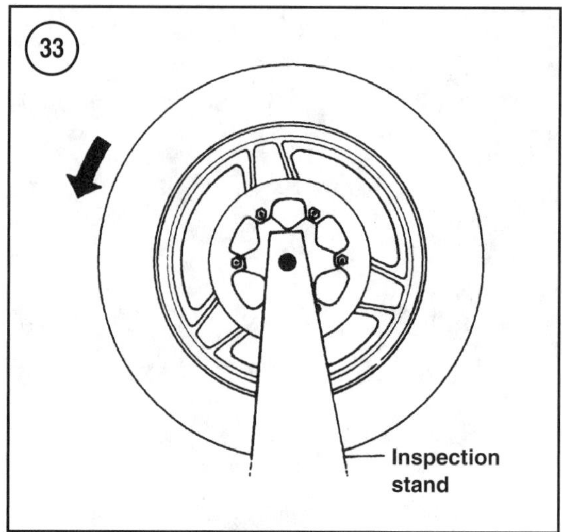

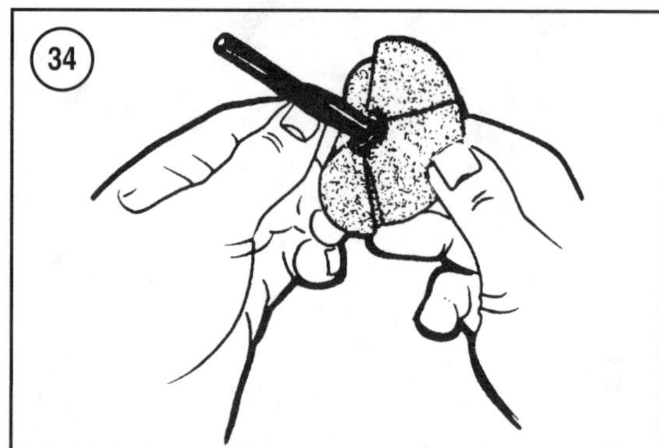

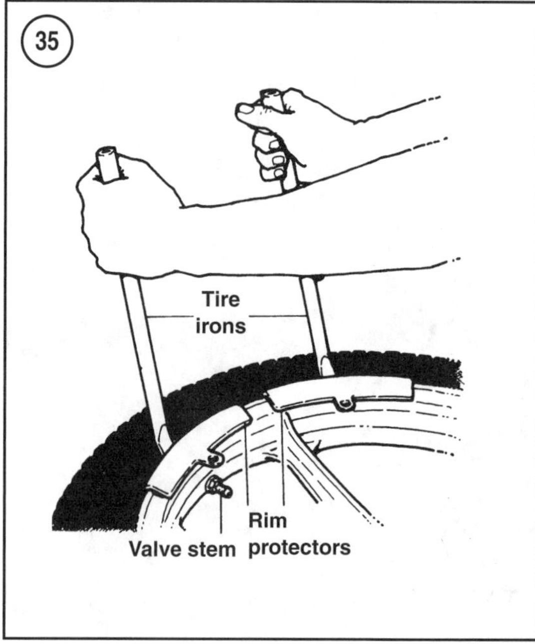

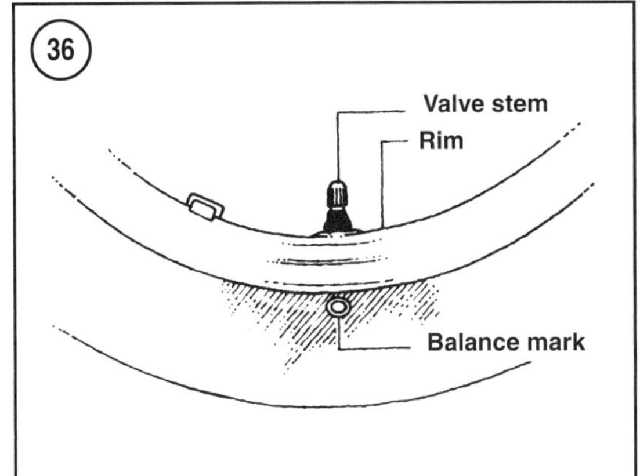

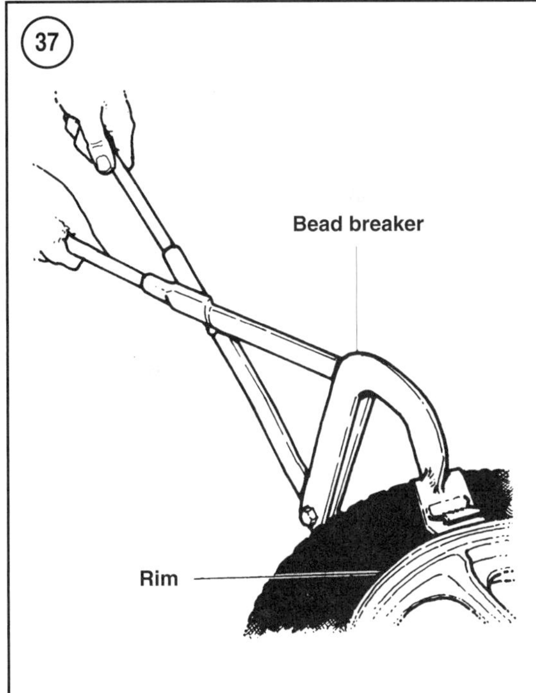

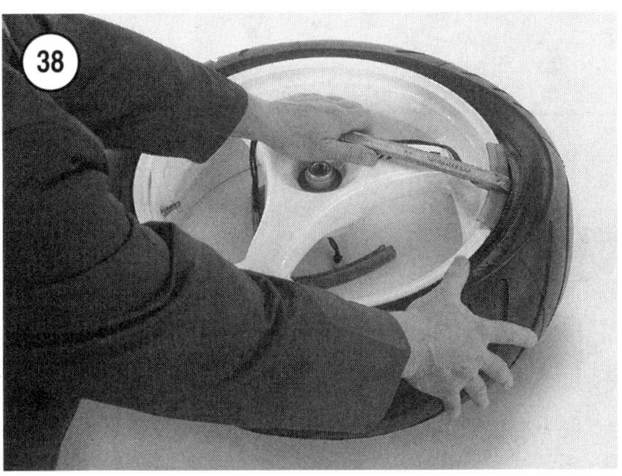

plug, consider the repair temporary and replace the tire at the earliest opportunity.

TIRE CHANGING

The wheels can easily be damaged during tire removal. Special care must be taken with tire irons to avoid scratching and gouging the outer rim surface. Protect the rim by inserting scraps of leather between the tire iron and the rim (**Figure 35**). The cast wheels are designed for use with tubeless tires.

When removing a tubeless tire, take care not to damage the tire beads, inner liner of the tire or the wheel rim flange. Use tire levers or flat-handled tire irons with rounded ends.

Removal

NOTE
*While removing a tire, support the wheel on two blocks of wood (**Figure 2**), so the brake disc does not contact the floor.*

1. Mark the valve stem (**Figure 36**) location on the tire sidewall, so the tire can be reinstalled in the same position for easier balancing. 11
2. Remove the valve core to deflate the tire.

CAUTION
*Removal of tubeless tires from their rims can be very difficult because of the exceptionally tight bead/rim seal. Breaking the bead seal may require the use of a special tool (**Figure 37**). If you have trouble breaking the seal, take the tire to a motorcycle dealer to avoid damaging the wheel. The inner rim and tire bead are sealing surfaces on a tubeless tire. Do not scratch the inside of the rim or damage the tire bead.*

3. Press the entire bead on both sides of the tire into the center of the rim.
4. Lubricate the beads with soapy water.
5. Insert the tire iron under the bead next to the valve stem. Force the bead on the opposite side of the tire into the center of the rim and pry the bead over the rim with the tire iron (**Figure 38**).

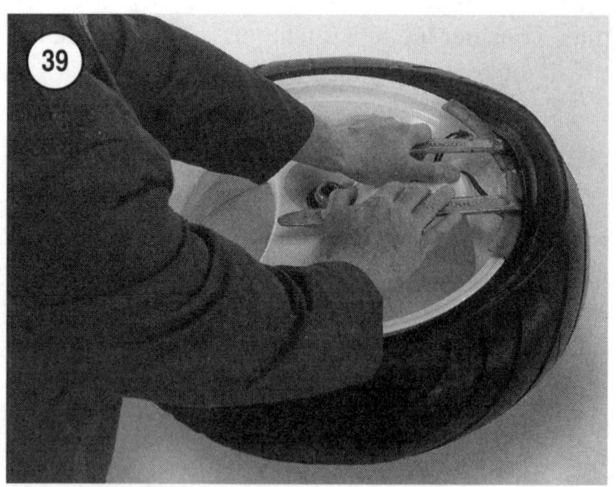

6. Insert a second tire iron next to the first to hold the bead over the rim (**Figure 39**). Then work around the tire with the first tool prying the bead over the rim.

7. Set the wheel on its edge. Insert a tire tool between the second bead and the same side of the rim that the first bead was pried over (**Figure 40**). Force the bead on the opposite side from the tool into the center of the rim. Pry the second bead off the rim, working around the wheel with two tire irons as with the first.

8. Inspect the valve stem seal. Because rubber deteriorates with age, it is advisable to replace the valve stem when replacing a tire.

Installation

1. Carefully inspect the tire for any damage, especially inside.

2. A new tire may have balancing rubbers inside. These are not patches and should not be disturbed.

3. A colored spot near the bead indicates a lighter point on the tire. Install the tires so this balance mark sits opposite the valve stem (**Figure 36**).

4. Most tires have directional arrows on the sidewall that indicate the direction of rotation. Install the tire so it will rotate in the indicated direction.

5. Lubricate both beads of the tire with soapy water.

6. Place the backside of the tire into the center of the rim. The lower bead should go into the center of the rim and the upper bead outside.

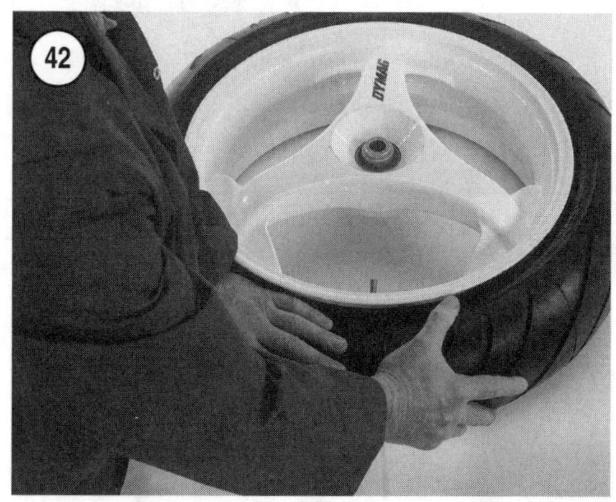

Work around the tire in both directions (**Figure 41**).

7. Starting at the side opposite the valve stem, press the upper bead into the rim (**Figure 42**).

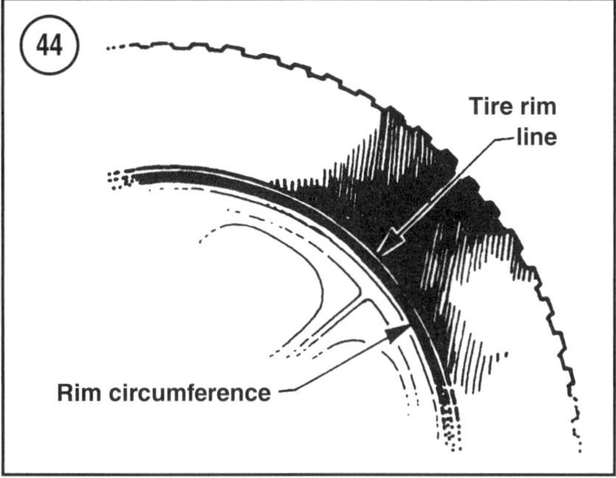

8. Pry the bead into the rim on both sides of the initial point with a tire tool, working around the rim to the valve (**Figure 43**).

9. Check the bead on both sides of the tire for an even fit around the rim.

10. Place an inflatable band around the circumference of the tire. Slowly inflate the band until the tire beads are pressed against the rim. Inflate the tire enough to seat it against the rim. Deflate and remove the band.

WARNING

Never exceed 386 kPa (56 psi) inflation pressure as the tire could burst causing severe injury. Never stand directly over the tire while inflating it.

11. After inflating the tire, check to see that the beads are fully seated and that the tire rim lines are the same distance from the rim all the way around the tire (**Figure 44**). If the beads will not seat, deflate the tire, re-lubricate the rim and beads with soapy water and re-inflate the tire.

12. Inflate the tire to the required pressure. Refer to tire inflation pressure specifications listed in **Table 1**. Screw on the valve stem cap.

13. Balance the wheel assembly as described in this chapter.

11

Table 1 TIRE AND WHEEL SPECIFICATIONS

Front tire	Tubeless
Size, manufacturer	
1986-1993 models	110/80 VR18, Dunlop K105F or 110/80 V18, Metzeler ME33 Laser
1994-1999 Germany models	110/80 V18, Pirelli MT09 or 120/70 ZR18, Bridgestone Battrax BT54F
All 1994-1999 models except Germany models	120/70 R18 59V, Dunlop K 701F
2000-on models	120/70 R18 59V, Dunlop K 701F
Rear tire	Tubeless
Size, manufacturer	
1986-1993 models	150/80 VR16, Dunlop K700G or 150/80 VB16, Metzeler ME99 A2
1994-1999 Germany models	150/80 VB16, Pirelli MT08 or 150/80 VR16 V250, Bridgestone Battrax BT53V R
All 1994-1999 models except Germany models	150/80 R16 71V, Dunlop K 700J
2000-on models	150/80 R16 71V, Dunlop K 700J
Minimum tread depth	
Front	1.0 mm (0.04 in.)
Rear	
Under 130 km/h	2.0 mm (0.08 in.)
Over 130 km/h	3.0 mm (0.12 in.)

(continued)

Table 1 TIRE AND WHEEL SPECIFICATIONS (continued)

Wheel runout	
Axial	0.5 mm (0.020 in.)
Radial	0.8 mm (0.031 in.)
Axle runout	
New	Less than 0.05 mm (0.002 in.)
Service limit	0.2 mm (0.009 in.)
Repair limit	0.7 mm (0.028 in.)

Table 2 TIRE INFLATION PRESSURE[1]

	Load[2]	Pressure (cold)
1986-1999 models		
Front tire	–	250 kPa (36 psi [2.5 kg/cm^2])
Rear tire		
USA, California, Canada, Australia and South Africa models	0-200 kg (0-441 lb.)	290 kPa (41 psi [2.9 kg/cm^2])
All models except USA, California, Canada, Australia and South Africa models	0-97.5 kg (215 lb.)	250 kPa (36 psi [2.5 kg/cm^2])
	97.5-183 kg (215-404 lb.)	290 kPa (41 psi [2.9 kg/cm^2])
2000-on models		
Front tire	–	250 kPa (36 psi [2.5 kg/cm^2])
Rear tire		
USA, California, Canada and Australia models	0-200 kg (0-441 lb.)	290 kPa (41 psi [2.9 kg/cm^2])
All models except USA, California, Canada, and Australia	0-97.5 kg (215 lb.)	250 kPa (36 psi [2.5 kg/cm^2])
	97.5-183 kg (215-404 lb.)	290 kPa (41 psi [2.9 kg/cm^2])

1. Tire inflation pressures apply to original equipment tires only. Aftermarket tires may require different pressures. Refer to the tire manufacturer's specifications.
2. Load equals the total weight of the rider, passenger, accessories and all cargo.

Table 3 WHEEL TORQUE SPECIFICATIONS

	N•m	in.-lb.	ft.-lb.
Brake disc mounting bolts	23	–	17
Front axle nut	88	–	65
Front axle clamp bolts			
1986-1993 models	20	–	15
1994-on models	35	–	26
Front caliper bolts	32	–	24
Rear axle nut	110	–	81
Rear caliper bolts	34	–	25
Torque arm nut	29	–	22

CHAPTER TWELVE

FRONT SUSPENSION AND STEERING

This chapter described the procedures for servicing the front fork, handlebar and steering head. When inspecting these components, compare any measurements to the specifications in the tables at the end of this chapter. Replace any part that is worn, damaged or out of specification. During assembly, tighten fasteners to the specified torque.

FRONT FORK

Before concluding there are major problems with the fork, drain the fork oil from each fork leg, and refill them with the proper type and quantity of fork oil. Refer to *Removal/Disassembly (Fork Leg Requires Service)* in this chapter.

To simplify fork service and prevent the mixing of parts, service one fork leg at a time.

Removal/Installation (Fork Will Not Be Serviced)

1. Remove the lower, middle and front fairings as described in Chapter Fifteen.
2. Place wooden block(s) under the crankcase to securely support the motorcycle with the front wheel off the ground. Make sure the wheel is high enough so it will clear the front fender once the axle is removed.
3. Remove the front wheel (Chapter Eleven) and the front fender (Chapter Fifteen).
4. Note that the top of the fork tube aligns with the top of the handlebar bracket (**Figure 1**). The fork tube must be reinstalled to this position.
5. On 1986-1993 models, loosen the air balancer clamp on each fork leg.
6. If both fork legs will be removed, label them left and right so they can be easily identified during installation.
7. Remove any zip ties (A, **Figure 2**) that secure a brake, clutch or electrical line to a fork leg. Note the location of these zip ties. They must be reinstalled during installation.

8. Loosen the upper fork bridge clamp bolts (B, **Figure 2**).
9. Loosen the lower fork bridge clamp bolts (**Figure 3**).
10. Rotate the fork leg slightly while pulling it from the upper and lower fork bridges.
11. Repeat Steps 7-10 and remove the other fork leg.
12. Installation is the reverse of removal. Note the following:
   a. On 1986-1993 models, make sure the air balancer and clamp are in place between the lower and upper fork bridges.
   b. Slide the fork leg up through the lower fork bridge, through the air balancer and clamp (1986-1993 models only) and align the top of the fork tube with the top of the handlebar bracket (**Figure 1**).
   c. Torque the upper-fork-bridge clamp bolts (B, **Figure 2**) to 16 N•m (12 ft.-lb.).
   d. Torque the lower-fork-bridge clamp bolts (**Figure 3**) to 21 N•m (15 ft.-lb.).
   e. On 1986-1993 models, lower the air balancer to the lower fork bridge and tighten the clamp securely.

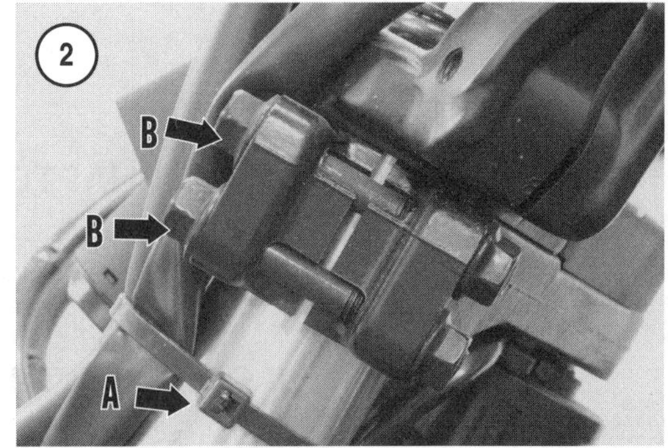

Removal/Disassembly (Fork Leg Requires Service)

Special tools

The following Kawasaki special tools, or their equivalent, are required to service the fork legs.

1. Damper rod T-handle: 57001-183.
2. Damper rod holder: 57001-1011.
3. Fork seal driver: 57001-1219.
4. Driver weight: 57001-1218.

NOTE
The fork leg Allen bolt can be removed without using the damper rod holder. However, the Allen bolt cannot be torqued without this tool.

Procedure

Refer to **Figure 4**.

1. Remove the lower, middle and front fairings as described in Chapter Fifteen.
2. Place wooden block(s) under the crankcase to securely support the motorcycle with the front wheel off the ground. Make sure the wheel is high enough so it will clear the front fender once the axle is removed.
3. Remove the front wheel (Chapter Eleven) and the front fender (Chapter Fifteen).

4A. On 1986-1993 models, perform the following:
   a. Pry the fork cap from the fork leg. Depress the valve and release the air pressure from both fork legs.
   b. Loosen the air balancer clamp on each fork leg.

4B. On 1994-on models, turn out the spring preload adjuster to its completely released position.

5. Note that the top of the fork tube aligns with the top of the handlebar bracket (**Figure 1**). The fork leg must be reinstalled to this same position.
6. Remove any zip ties (A, **Figure 2**) that secure a brake, clutch or electrical line to a fork leg. Note the location of these zip ties. They must be reinstalled during installation.
7. On 1986-1993 models, place a drain pan beneath the fork leg, remove the oil drain bolt and drain the fork oil into the pan.
8. Remove the Allen bolt by performing the following:
   a. Place a drain pan beneath the fork leg.

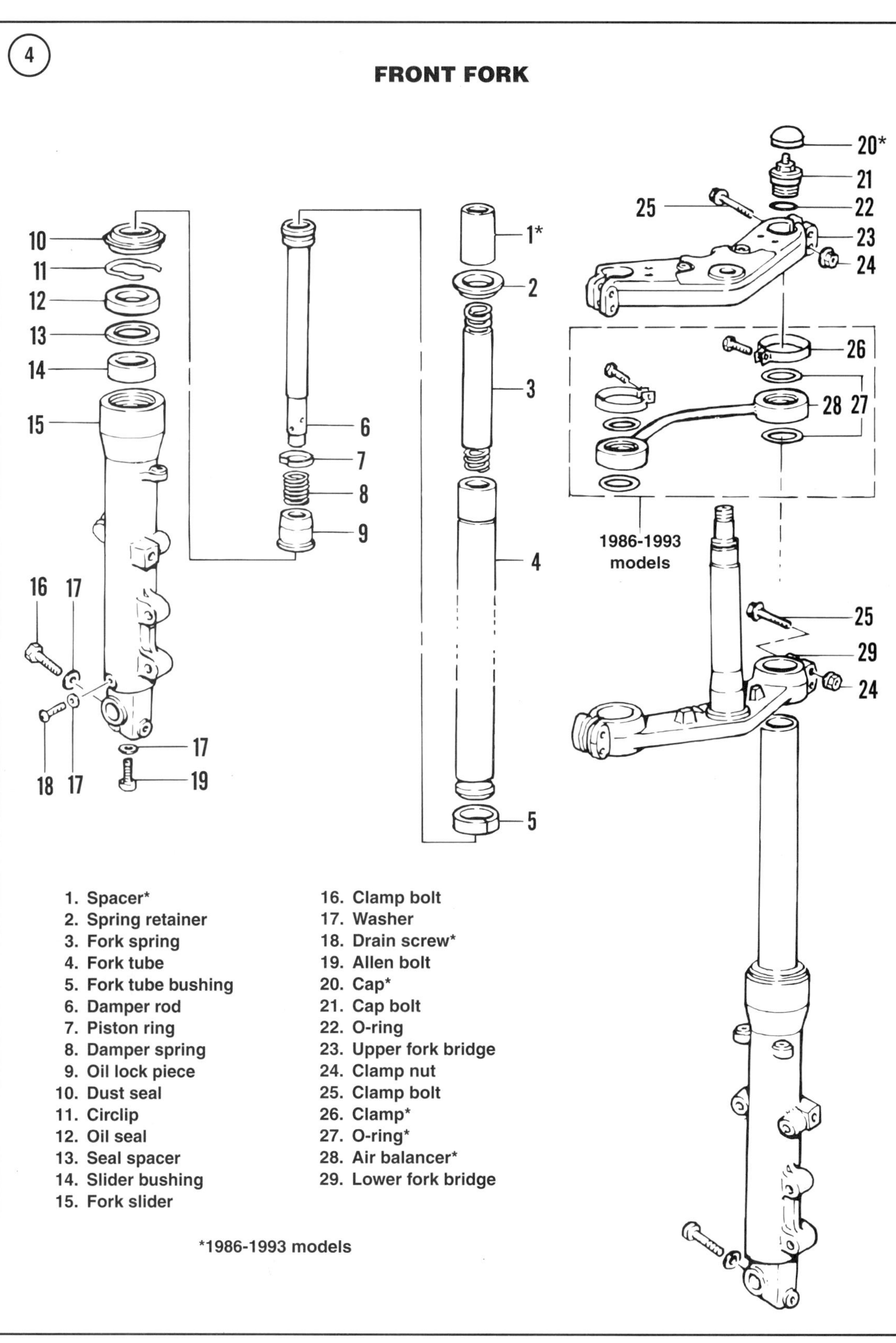
4
FRONT FORK
1*
2
3
4
5
6
7
8
9
10
11
12
13
14
15
16
17
18
19
20*
21
22
23
24
25
26
27
28
29
1986-1993
models
1. Spacer*
2. Spring retainer
3. Fork spring
4. Fork tube
5. Fork tube bushing
6. Damper rod
7. Piston ring
8. Damper spring
9. Oil lock piece
10. Dust seal
11. Circlip
12. Oil seal
13. Seal spacer
14. Slider bushing
15. Fork slider
16. Clamp bolt
17. Washer
18. Drain screw*
19. Allen bolt
20. Cap*
21. Cap bolt
22. O-ring
23. Upper fork bridge
24. Clamp nut
25. Clamp bolt
26. Clamp*
27. O-ring*
28. Air balancer*
29. Lower fork bridge
*1986-1993 models

b. Insert the axle through both fork legs. The axle holds the sliders in position while the Allen bolt is loosened.

c. Use an impact wrench to loosen and remove the Allen bolt from the bottom of the fork leg. If the Allen bolt cannot be loosened, use the damper rod holder mentioned in Step 10.

9. Pull out the fork slider and fully extend the fork leg.

WARNING

*The cap bolt (A, **Figure 5**) is under spring pressure. Exercise caution while removing the cap bolt.*

10. Slowly loosen the cap bolt (A, **Figure 5**). Remove the cap bolt and the spring retainer (B, **Figure 5**). On 1986-1993 models, also remove the spacer.

11. If the Allen bolt could not be loosened during Step 8, remove it now by performing the following:

a. Place a drain pan beneath the fork leg.

b. Install the damper rod holder onto the T-handle.

c. Insert the holder into the fork tube until the holder engages the damper rod (A, **Figure 6**), and remove the Allen bolt (B) and its washer from the bottom of the slider.

d. Let the oil drain from the fork. If necessary, pump the fork to expel any residual oil.

12. Remove the dust seal and the circlip from the fork slider. Slide the dust seal and circlip up the fork tube. Zip tie the circlip to the leg to keep it out of the way. (See **Figure 7**).

NOTE

It may be necessary to slightly heat the area on the slider around the oil seal prior to removal. Heat the area with a rag soaked in hot water. Do not apply a flame directly to the fork slider.

13. There is an interference fit between the bushing in the fork slider and the bushing on the fork tube. In order to remove the fork slider from the fork tube, firmly grasp the slider (**Figure 8**). Pull hard on the slider using quick in-and-out strokes (**Figure 9**) and pull the slider off the fork tube (**Figure 10**).

14. Invert the slider and remove the oil lock piece.

15. Loosen the upper (B, **Figure 2**) and lower clamp bolts (**Figure 3**), and pull the fork tube from

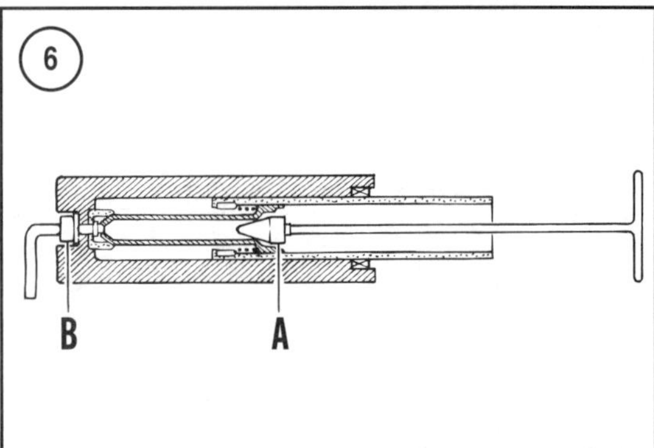

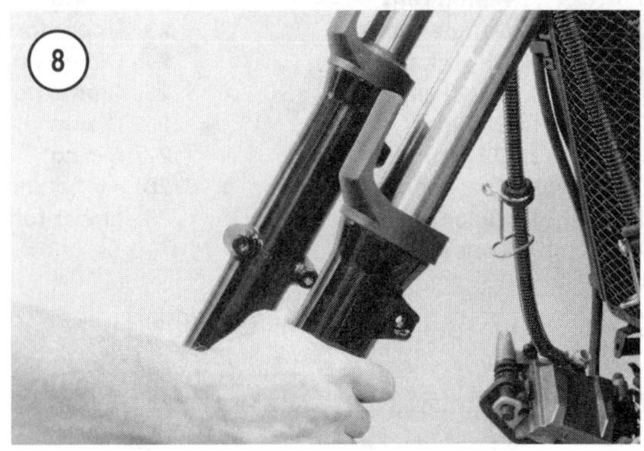

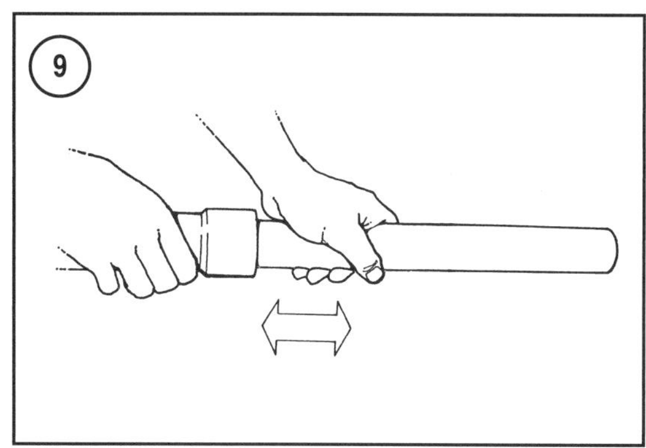

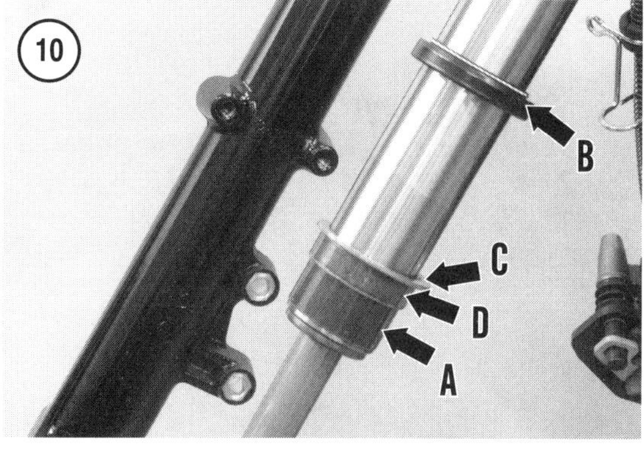

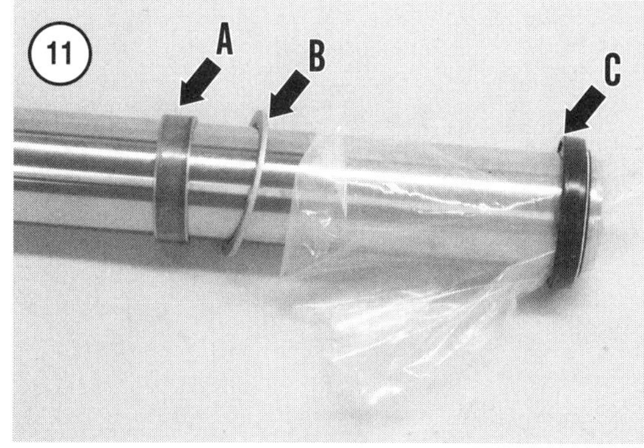

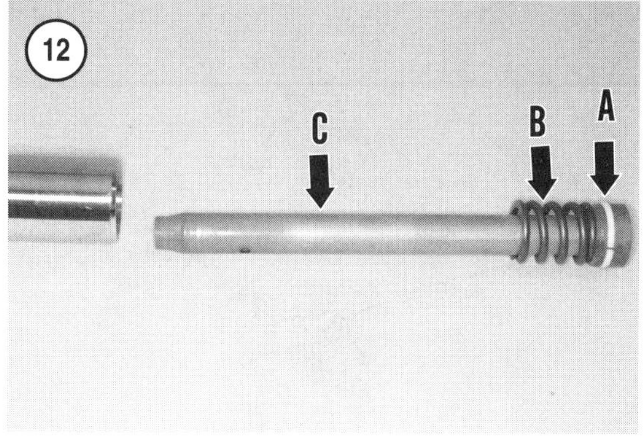

the upper and lower fork bridges. Remove the fork tube and take it to the bench for further disassembly.

16. Remove the fork spring from the fork tube. Note that the closer wound coils face the top of the tube.

17. Remove the damper rod and the rebound spring.

NOTE

*Do not remove the fork tube bushing (A, **Figure 10**) unless it is going to be replaced. Inspect it as described in this chapter.*

18. Slide the oil seal (B, **Figure 10**), seal spacer (C) and the slider bushing (D) from the fork tube.

19. Inspect all parts as described below in this section.

Installation/Assembly

1. Coat all parts with fresh fork oil before installing them.
2. On 1986-1993 models, perform the following:
   a. Clean all liquid gasket residue from the threads of the drain screw and from the internal threads in the fork leg drain hole.
   b. Apply liquid gasket to the threads of the drain screw.
   c. Install the screw and washer. Torque the drain screw to 1.5 N•m (13 in.-lb.).
3. Slide the slider bushing (A, **Figure 11**) and seal spacer (B) down the fork tube.
4. Install a new oil seal (C, **Figure 11**) by performing the following:
   a. Wrap the end of the fork tube with plastic wrap. Liberally coat the plastic wrap with fork oil.
   b. Pack the lips of the oil seal with grease.
   c. Slide the oil seal (C, **Figure 11**) down the fork tube. Make sure the manufacturer's marks face up.
5. If removed, install the piston ring (A, **Figure 12**) and the rebound spring (B) onto the damper rod (C).
6. Slide the damper rod through the fork tube until the rod emerges from the end of the tube. Press the oil lock piece (**Figure 13**) onto the end of the damper rod.
7. Lubricate the fork tube with fork oil and install the fork tube into the slider (**Figure 14**).

8. Install the Allen bolt and washer by performing the following:
   a. Insert the damper rod holder until it engages the damper rod inside the fork slider. See **Figure 6**.
   b. Apply Loctite 242 to the threads of the Allen bolt, insert the Allen bolt and washer into the bottom of the slider (**Figure 15**), and thread the bolt into the oil lock piece.
   c. Hold the damper rod with the holder (A, **Figure 6**) and torque the Allen bolt (B) to 39 N•m (29 ft.-lb.).
9. Seat the slider bushing and seal spacer by performing the following:
   a. Slide the slider bushing and the spacer into the slider.
   b. Use a fork seal driver (**Figure 16**) to drive the bushing into the place until it is completely seated in the bushing bore in the slider.
   c. Lift the seal spacer from the slider bushing and inspect the bushing. The top of the bushing should be even with the top of the bushing bore.
   d. Set the seal spacer back onto the bushing.
10. Slide the oil seal down the fork seal and drive it into the slider with the fork seal driver (**Figure 16**). Drive the seal until the circlip groove in the slider is visible above the top of the oil seal.
11. Slide the circlip (A, **Figure 17**) down the fork tube and install it into the slider. Make sure the circlip is completely seated in the slider's circlip groove.
12. Slide the dust seal (B, **Figure 17**) down the fork tube and seat it in the slider. If necessary, use the fork seal driver to seat the dust seal.
13. Slide the fork leg up through the lower fork bridge, through the air balancer and clamp (1986-1993 models only), and align the top of the fork tube with the top of the handlebar bracket (**Figure 1**).
14. Torque the upper-fork-bridge clamp bolts (B, **Figure 2**) to 16 N•m (12 ft.-lb.), and torque the lower-fork-bridge clamp bolts (**Figure 3**) to 21 N•m (15 ft.-lb.).
15. On 1986-1993 models, lower the air balancer to the lower fork bridge and tighten the clamp securely.
16. Add oil and set the oil level as described in *Fork Oil Adjustment* in this section.

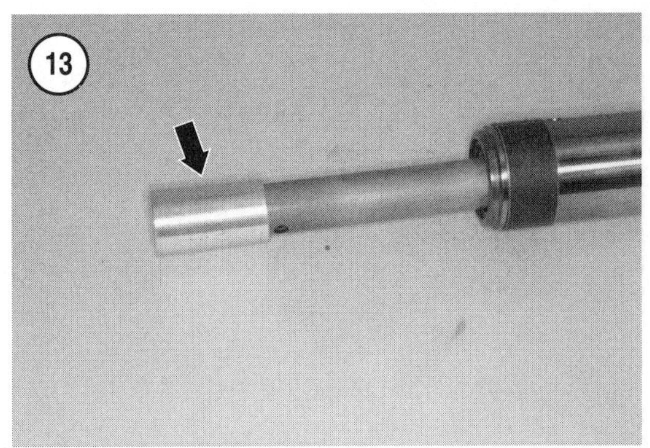

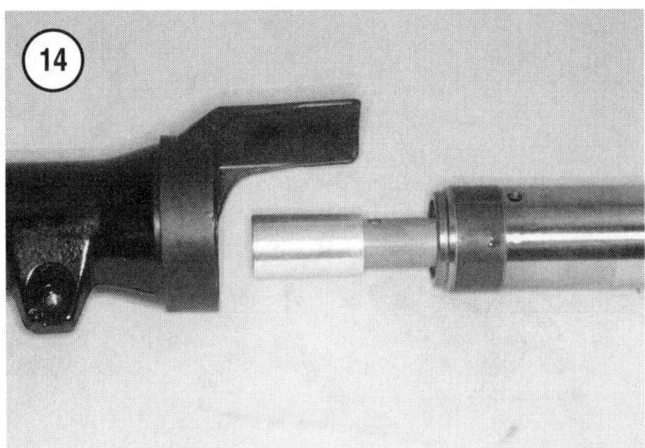

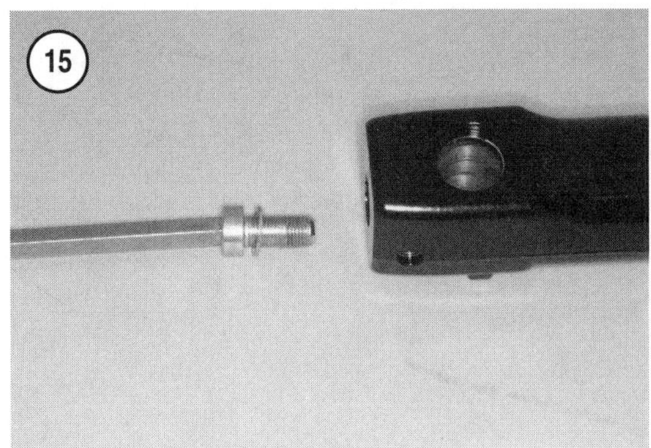

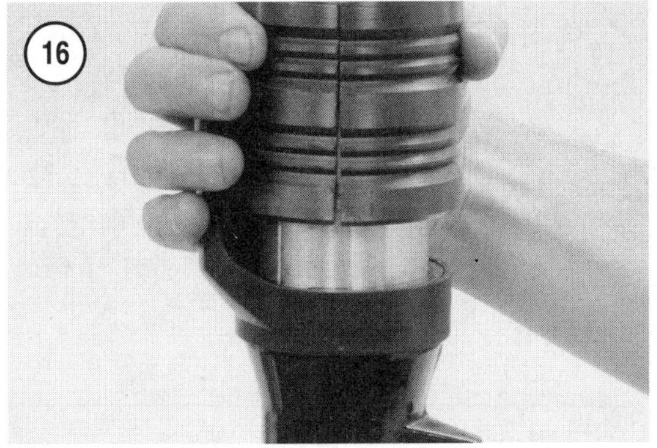

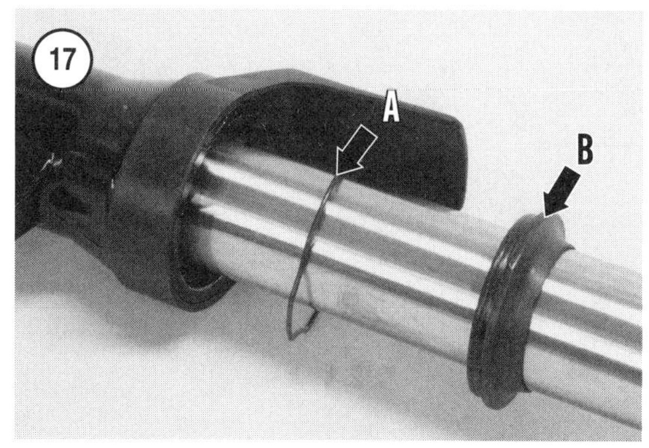

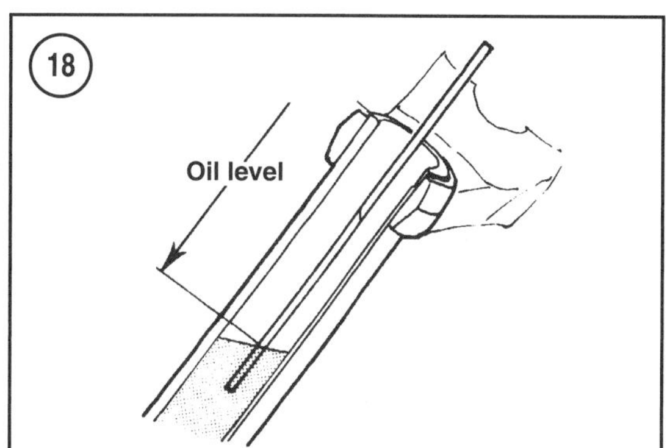

Fork Oil Adjustment

1. Refer to **Table 1** and slowly add the recommended amount of fork oil to the fork leg.
2. Slowly pump the slider up and down several times to distribute the fork oil.

3A. On 1986-1993 models, pull the slider from the fork tube and fully extend the fork leg.

3B. On 1994-on models, press the slider up the fork tube and fully compress the fork leg.

4. Once the oil settles, insert a tape measure or rod down the center of the fork tube and measure the oil level. See **Figure 18**. Remove or add oil as necessary. Let the oil completely settle and recheck the oil level measurement.
5. Fully extend the fork leg. Install the fork spring (**Figure 19**) so the end with the closer wound coils sits up at the top of the fork tube.
6. Install spring retainer (**Figure 20**).
7. On 1986-1993 models, install the spacer.
8. Lubricate a new O-ring (A, **Figure 21**) with clean fork oil and install it onto the cap bolt.
9. Install the cap bolt (A, **Figure 5)** while pushing down on the spring retainer (B). Start the bolt slowly. Do not cross-thread it. Torque the fork cap to 23 N•m (17 ft-lb.).

10A. On 1986-1993 models, add air to the air valve.

10B. On 1994-on models, set the preload as described in Chapter Three.

Inspection

During inspection compare any measurements to the specifications in **Table 1**. Replace any part that is damaged, worn to the service limit or out of specification. Simply cleaning and reinstalling unserviceable fork components will not improve the performance of the front suspension.

1. Thoroughly clean all parts in solvent and dry them with compressed air.
2. Check the damper rod by performing the following:
   a. Remove the rebound spring (B, **Figure 12**) from the damper rod.
   b. Check damper rod runout by rolling the rod along a surface plate or a piece of glass. If the damper rod is not straight, replace it.
   c. Make sure the oil holes in the damper rod are clear. Clean them out if necessary.
   d. Inspect the damper rod (C, **Figure 12**) and piston ring (A) for wear or damage. Replace as necessary.
4. Inspect the fork tube (A, **Figure 22**).
   a. Check the fork tube for straightness. If the tube is bent or severely scratched, it should be replaced.
   b. Check the fork tube for chrome flaking or creasing. This condition will damage oil seals.
   c. Check the fork tube for scratches of other damage that will admit dirt and cause an oil leak.
   d. Check the threads in the top of the fork tube for wear or damage.
5. Inspect the fork slider (**Figure 23**).
   a. Check the slider for dents or exterior damage that may cause the upper fork tube to hang up during riding.
   b. Inspect the inner surfaces in the slider for damage or burrs. Pay particular attention to the circlip groove and the oil seal areas. Clean the slider if necessary.
   c. Check for cracks or damage to the brake caliper and fender mounting bosses on the slider.
   d. Inspect the front axle boss in the slider for damage.
   e. Replace the slider as necessary.
6. Measure the uncompressed length of the fork spring (not rebound spring) as shown in **Figure 24**. Replace the fork spring if it has sagged to the service limit listed in **Table 1**.
7. Inspect the fork tube bushing (B, **Figure 22**) and the slider bushing (A, **Figure 11**). If a bushing is scratched or scored, it must be replaced. If the Teflon coating is worn off so that the copper base material is showing on approximately 3/4 of the total surface, the bushing must be replaced.

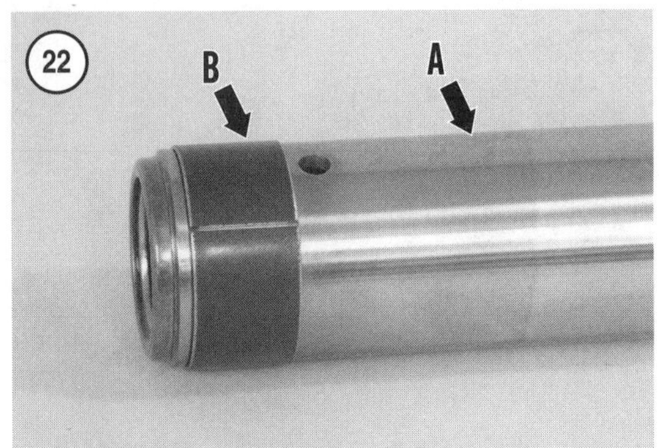

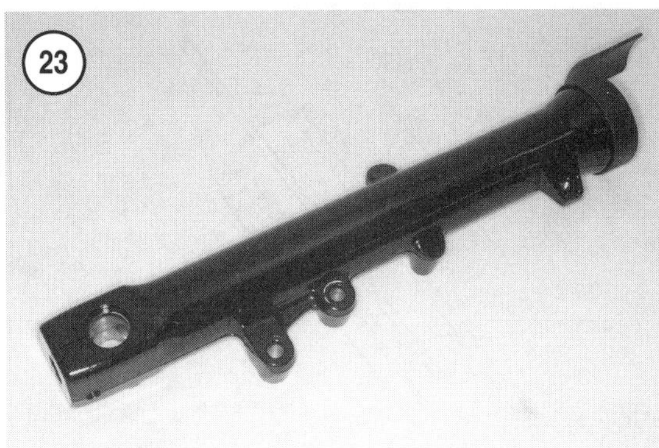

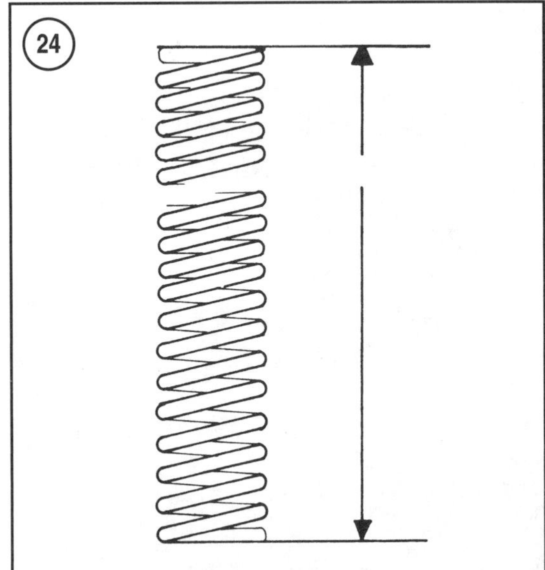

8. To replace the fork tube bushing (B, **Figure 22**), open the bushing slot with a screwdriver and slide the bushing off the fork tube. Lubricate a new bush-

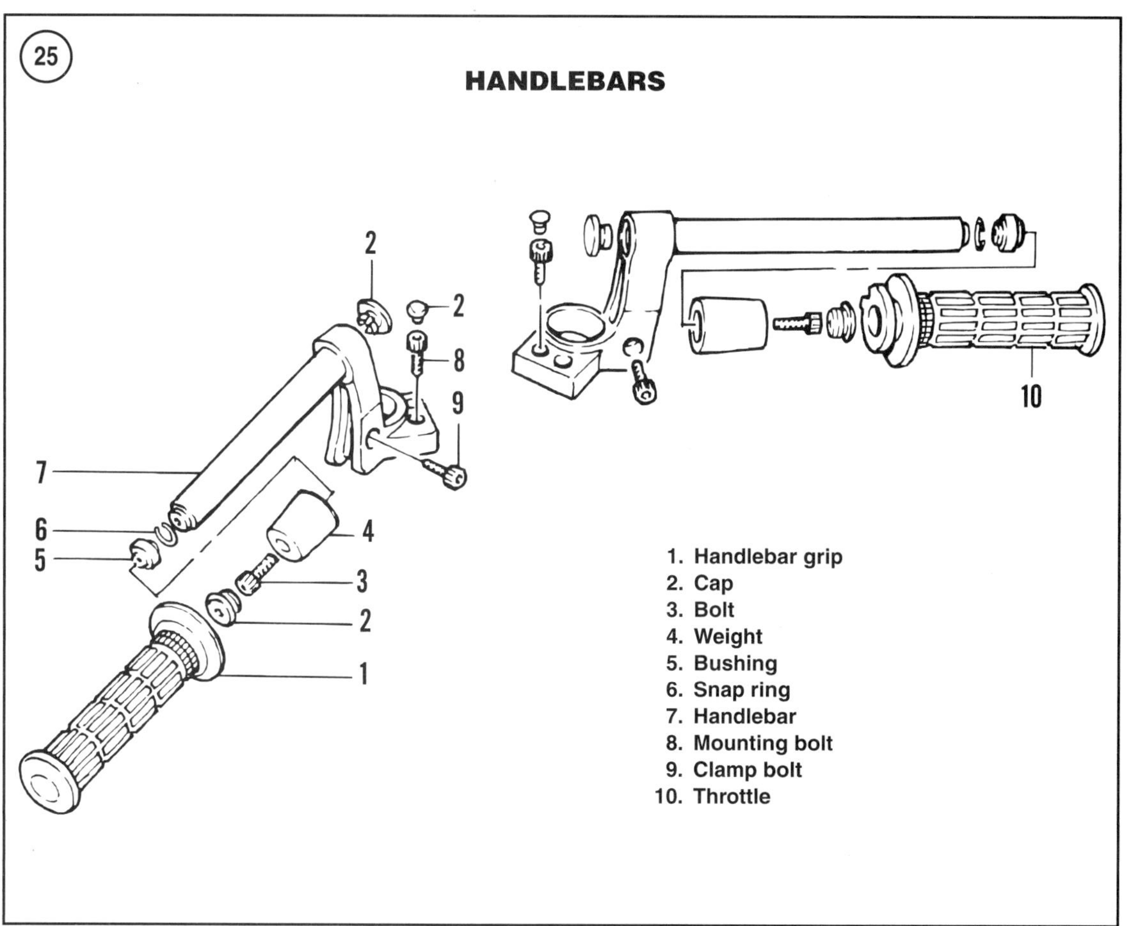

ing with fresh fork oil, open its slot slightly and slide the bushing onto the fork tube slot.

9. Inspect the threads of the cap bolt (**Figure 21**) for wear or damage.

HANDLEBARS

Removal/Installation

Steps 1-3 describe the procedure for removing and replacing the handlebar. If handlebar replacement is not required, proceed to Step 4.

Refer to **Figure 25**.

1. Disconnect the cable from the negative battery terminal.
2. Remove any cable ties securing a cable or hydraulic line to the handlebar.

CAUTION

Cover the front wheel with a heavy cloth or plastic tarp to protect them from brake fluid spills. Brake fluid damages the finish on painted, plated or plastic surfaces. Immediately wash spilled brake fluid with soapy water and rinse the area thoroughly.

3A. When replacing the right handlebar perform the following:

a. Remove the front brake master cylinder as described in Chapter Fourteen.
b. Remove the right handlebar switch (Chapter Nine).
c. Remove the handlebar weight and slide the throttle grip from the handlebar end.

3B. When replacing the left handlebar perform the following:

a. Remove the clutch master cylinder as described in Chapter Six.
b. Remove the left handlebar switch (Chapter Nine).

4. Remove the mounting screws (**Figure 26**) and lift the steering head cover from the motorcycle.
5. Loosen the handlebar clamp bolt (A, **Figure 27**).
6. Remove the caps from the handlebar mounting bolts.
7. Remove the handlebar mounting bolts (B, **Figure 27**) and lift the handlebar from the upper fork bridge.
8. Installation is the reverse of removal. Pay attention to the following:
   a. Seat the handlebar squarely over the fork tube.
   b. Torque the handlebar mounting bolts (B, **Figure 27**) to 19 N•m (14 ft.-lb.).
   c. Torque the handlebar clamp bolt (A, **Figure 27**) to 19 N•m (14 ft.-lb.).

Inspection

Check the handlebar along the entire mounting area for cracks or damage. Replace a bent or damaged handlebar immediately. If the motorcycle has been involved in a crash, examine the handlebars, steering stem and front fork carefully.

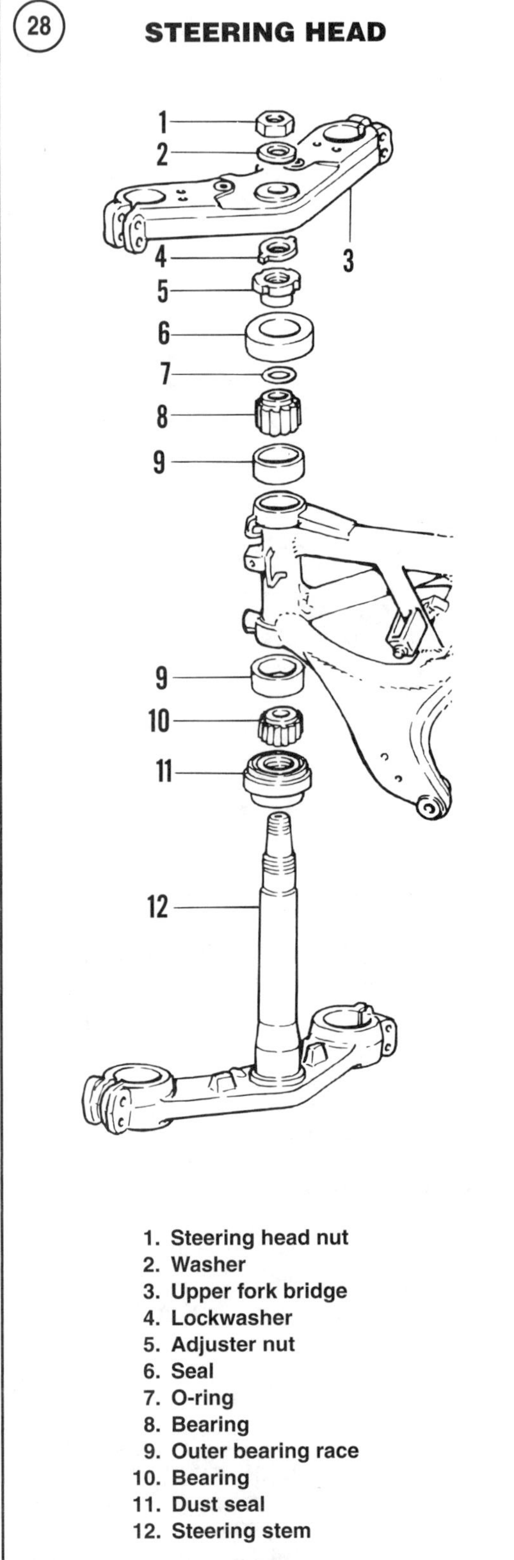

1. Steering head nut
2. Washer
3. Upper fork bridge
4. Lockwasher
5. Adjuster nut
6. Seal
7. O-ring
8. Bearing
9. Outer bearing race
10. Bearing
11. Dust seal
12. Steering stem

29

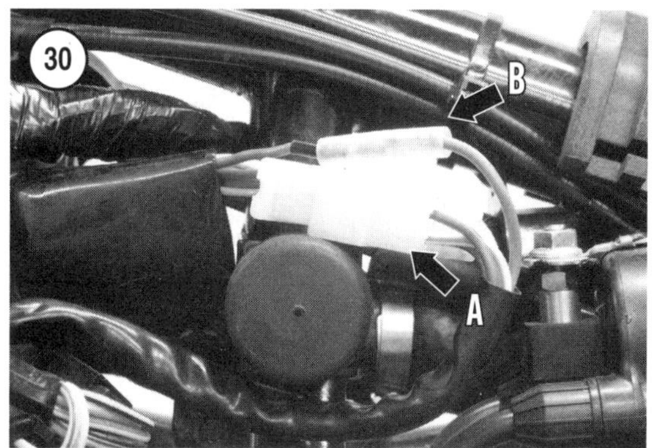

30

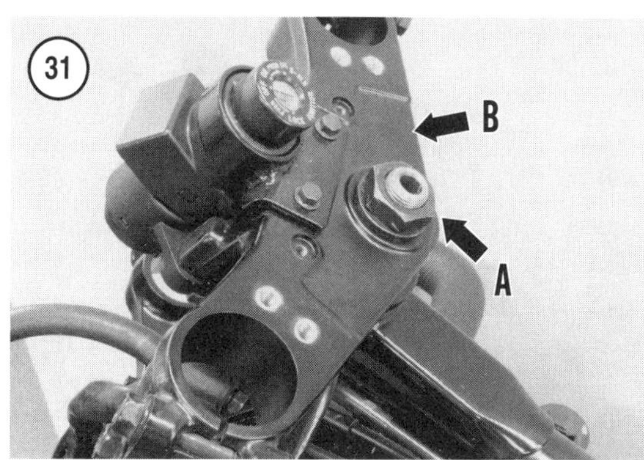

31

HANDLEBAR LEFT GRIP REPLACEMENT

NOTE
The right grip is part of the throttle grip assembly and cannot be replaced separately.

1. Remove the end cap and screw and remove the handlebar weight.
2. Slide a thin screwdriver between the left grip and handlebar. Spray electrical contact cleaner into the opening under the grip.
3. Pull the screwdriver out, quickly twist the grip to break its bond with the handlebar, then slide off the grip.
4. Clean the handlebar of all rubber or sealer residue.
5. Install the new grip following the manufacturer's directions. Apply an adhesive, such as ThreeBond Griplock, between the grip and handlebar. When applying an adhesive, follow the manufacturer's instructions for drying time before operating the motorcycle.
6. Install the handlebar weight.

STEERING HEAD

The Kawasaki steering stem wrench (part No. 57001-1100) or its equivalent are required to adjust the steering stem.

Disassembly

Refer to **Figure 28**.

1. Securely support the motorcycle on level ground.
2. Remove the lower, middle and front fairings as described in Chapter Fifteen.
3. Remove the front wheel (Chapter Ten) and front fender (Chapter Fifteen).
4. Remove the mounting bolts (**Figure 29**) and the brake hose union from the lower fork bridge. Use a bunjee cord or wire to suspend the union from the motorcycle.
5. Remove both fork legs as described in *Fork Leg Removal/Installation (Fork Will Not Be Serviced)* in this chapter.
6. Remove the handlebars as described in this chapter.
7. Disconnect the ignition switch 6-pin connector (A, **Figure 30**) from its harness mate. On U.S., California and Canada models also disconnect the ignition switch bullet connector (B, **Figure 30**).
8. Remove the steering head nut (A, **Figure 31**) and washer. Lift the upper fork bridge (B, **Figure 31**) from the steering stem.
9. Remove the lockwasher (**Figure 32**) from the adjuster nut.

10. Hold onto the lower end of the steering stem assembly and loosen the adjuster nut (A, **Figure 33**). Remove the nut and seal assembly (B, **Figure 33**) from the steering stem.
11. Lower the steering stem assembly (A, **Figure 34**) from the steering head.
12. Remove the upper bearing (B, **Figure 34**) from the steering head. Watch for the O-ring (C, **Figure 34**) in the bearing's groove.
13. Inspect the steering head as described in this section.

Assembly

1. Liberally apply grease to the bearings and races (**Figure 35**).
2. Insert the steering stem (A, **Figure 34**) up through the steering head until the lower bearing seats in the lower race.
3. Install the upper bearing (B, **Figure 34**) into the upper race.
4. Install the O-ring (C, **Figure 34**) and seat it in the groove in the bearing.
5. Press the adjuster nut (A, **Figure 36**) into the seat in the seal (B) and turn the seal/adjuster nut onto the steering stem. See **Figure 33**.

NOTE

Use the Kawasaki steering stem wrench (part no. 57001-1100) or its equivalent when tightening and adjusting the adjuster nut.

6. Tighten the adjuster nut (A, **Figure 33**) to seat the bearings and races. You should feel a light resistance when turning the steering stem from left to right.
7. Adjust the bearings by performing the following:
   a. Completely loosen the adjuster nut and then retighten the nut until there is little or no free play in the bearings and no preload.
   b. To check for bearing free play, grasp one fork clamp area on the lower fork bridge and try to rock the side of the lower fork bridge up and down. There should be little or no bearing free play, that is, little or no rocking in the steering head. If any play is felt, tighten the adjuster nut 1/8 of a turn. Recheck the play.
   c. Check the bearing preload by turning the steering stem from side-to-side. It should turn smoothly from lock-to-lock without drag or

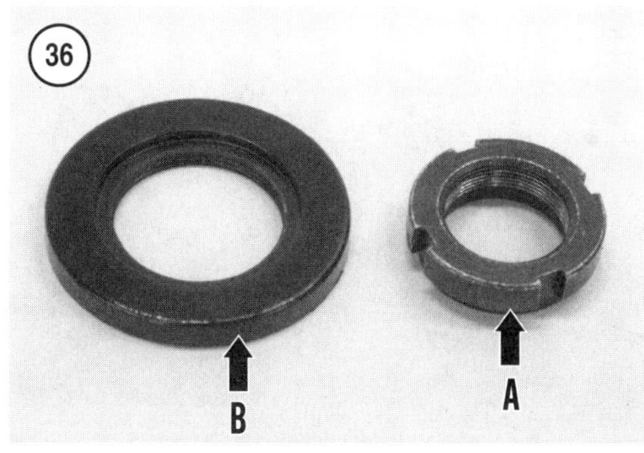

binding. There should be no preload. If necessary, loosen the adjuster nut in 1/8-turn increments and recheck the preload.

d. Repeatedly turn the adjuster nut in 1/8-turn increments and check the bearing free play and preload. The steering head bearings are properly adjusted when you feel little or no free play and absolutely no preload.

8. Install the lockwasher (**Figure 32**) so its fingers sits in the slots of the adjuster nut.

9. Set the upper fork bridge in place on the steering stem and install the washer (**Figure 37**).

10. Install and finger-tighten the steering head nut (A, **Figure 31**).

11. Install the handlebars onto the upper fork bridge. Snug down the mounting bolts (B, **Figure 27**) at this time.

12. Install the brake hose union and tighten the bolts (**Figure 29**) securely. Install the hose holder on the side with the white dot (under the left bolt). Position the holder so it faces down.

13. Install each fork leg so the top of the fork tube aligns with the top of the handlebar bracket (**Figure 38**). On 1986-1993 models, make sure the air balancer sits between the upper and lower fork bridges.

CAUTION

The hardware must be tightened in the order given below. The fork tubes and fork bridge will be unduly stressed if the hardware is not tightened in the proper order.

14. Torque both clamp bolts on each side of the lower fork bridge (**Figure 39**) to 21 N•m (15 ft.-lb.).

15. Torque the steering head nut (B, **Figure 31**) to 39 N•m (29 ft.-lb.).

16. Torque the upper fork bridge clamp bolts (**Figure 40**) to 16 N•m (12 ft.-lb.).

17. Torque the handlebar mounting bolts (B, **Figure 27**) to 19 N•m (14 ft.-lb.). Install the caps onto the bolts.

18. Torque the handlebar clamp bolt (A, **Figure 27**) to 19 N•m (14 ft.-lb.).

19. On 1986-1993 models, lower the air balancer to the lower fork bridge and tighten the clamp securely.

Routine Adjustment

Use the following the procedure when adjusting the steering head bearings as part of routine maintenance.

1. Remove the fuel tank as described in Chapter Eight.
2. Remove the lower, middle and upper fairings (Chapter Fifteen).
3. Remove the mounting screws (**Figure 26**) and lift the steering head cover from the motorcycle.
4. Loosen the clamp bolts (**Figure 40**) on the upper fork bridge. Do not loosen the lower-fork-bridge clamp bolts.
5. Loosen, but do not remove the steering head nut (A, **Figure 41**).
6. Insert a ring nut wrench under the upper fork bridge (B, **Figure 41**). Tighten or loosen the adjuster nut in 1/8-turn increments. Recheck the bearing free play and preload. Repeatedly adjust the nut in 1/8-turn increments and check the bearings. The bearings are properly adjusted when you feel absolutely no bearing preload and little or no bearing free play.
7. Torque the steering head nut (A, **Figure 41**) to 39 N•m (29 ft.-lb.).
8. Torque the upper fork bridge clamp bolts (**Figure 40**) to 16 N•m (12 ft.-lb.).

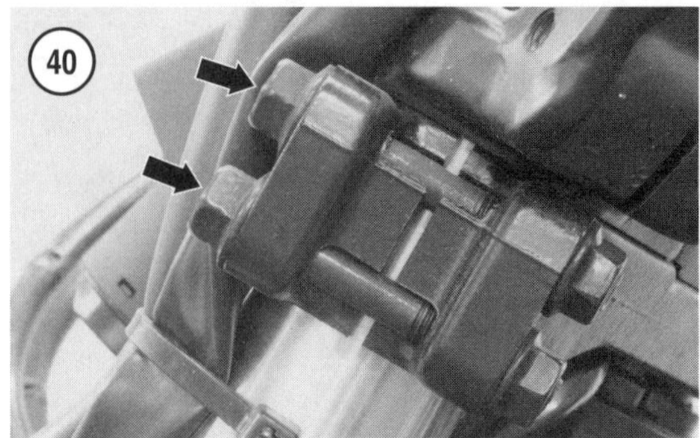

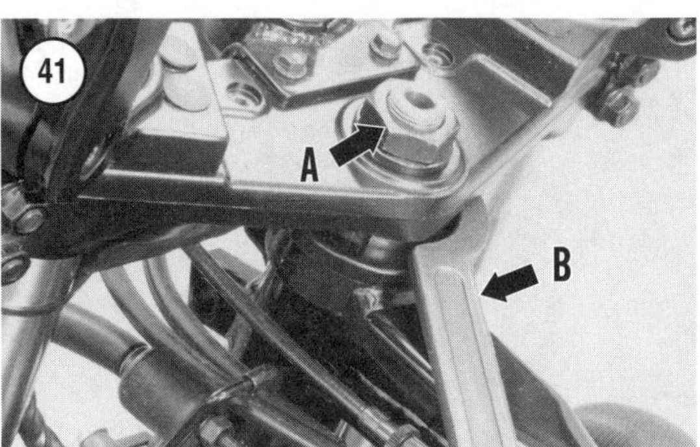

Inspection

1. Clean the upper and lower bearings in a bearing degreaser. Hold onto the bearing so it will not spin and thoroughly dry both bearings with compressed air. Make sure all solvent is removed from the lower bearing installed on the steering stem (**Figure 42**).
2. Wipe the old grease from the outer races located in the steering head (**Figure 35**) and then clean the outer races with a rag soaked in solvent. Thoroughly dry the races with a lint-free cloth. Check the races for pitting, galling and corrosion. If any of these conditions exist, replace the races as described in this chapter.
3. If any race is worn or damaged, replace the race and bearing as an assembly. Follow the procedure described in this chapter.
4. Check the welds around the steering head for cracks and fractures. If any damage is found, have the frame repaired at a competent frame or welding shop.

5. Check the bearings (**Figure 43**) for pitting, scratches or discoloration indicating wear or corrosion. Replace the bearing if any roller is less than perfect.

6. If the bearings are in good condition, pack them thoroughly with grease. To pack the bearings, spread some grease in the palm of your hand and scrape the open side of the bearing across your palm until the bearing is completely full of grease. Spin the bearing a few times to determine if there are any open areas; repack if necessary.

43

44

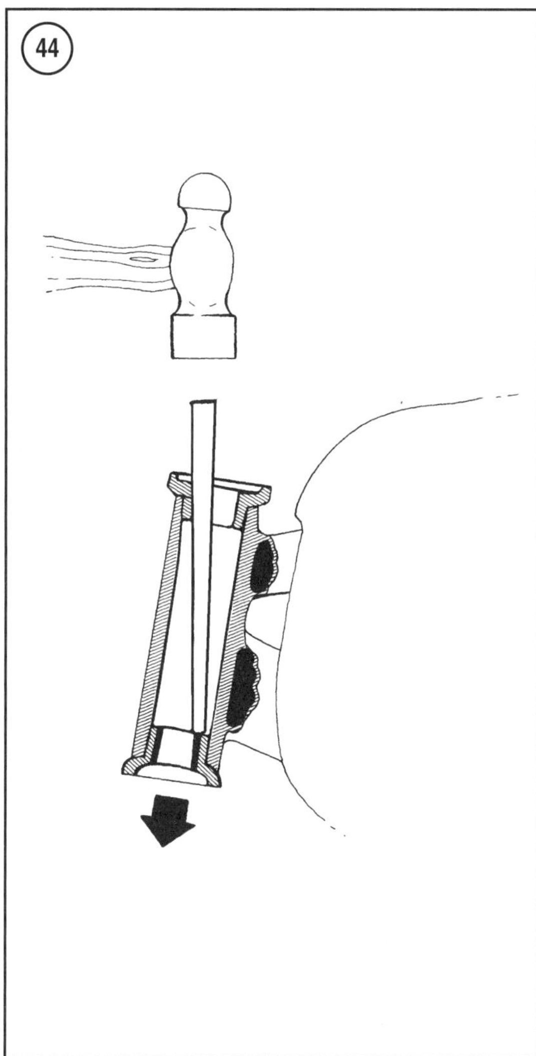

7. Thoroughly clean all mounting parts in solvent. Dry them completely.

8. Inspect the adjuster nut (A, **Figure 36**) and seal (B) for wear or damage. Inspect the nut threads. If necessary, clean them with an appropriate size metric tap or replace the nut(s). If the threads are damaged, inspect the appropriate steering stem thread(s) for damage. If necessary, clean the threads with an appropriate size metric die.

9. Check the underside of the steering head nut for damage. Replace the nut as necessary.

10. Inspect the steering stem and the lower fork bridge for cracks or other damage. Make sure the fork bridge clamping areas are free of burrs and that the bolt holes are in good condition.

11. Inspect the upper fork bridge for cracks or other damage. Check both the upper and lower surface of the fork bridge. Make sure the fork bridge clamping areas are free of burrs and that the bolt holes are in good condition.

Steering Head Bearing Races

Special tools

The following Kawasaki special tools or their equivalent are required to replace the bearing races:

1. Outer race remover: 57001-1107.
2. Outer race press shaft: 57001-1075.
3. Outer race driver: 57001-1106.
4. Outer race driver: 57001-1076.

Procedure

The upper (**Figure 35**) and lower bearing outer races must not be removed unless they are going to be replaced. These races are pressed into place and are damaged during removal. If removed, replace both the outer race and the bearings as a set. Never reuse an outer race that has been removed. It is no longer true and will damage the bearings if reused.

1. Chill the new bearing races overnight in a freezer to shrink the outer diameter of the race as much as possible.
2. Remove the steering stem as described in this section.
3. Use the Kawasaki outer race remover to remove the lower race from the steering head. If this tool is not available, insert an aluminum drift into the steering head and carefully tap the lower race out from the steering head (**Figure 44**). Repeat this procedure for the upper race.
4. Clean the race seats in the steering head. Check for cracks or other damage.

12

5. Apply grease to a new upper race and insert the race into the steering head with the tapered side facing out. Square the race with the race bore.

CAUTION
When installing the bearing outer races with the threaded rod or similar tool, do not let the rod or tool contact the face of the bearing race. It could damage the race.

6. Insert the installer through the race and steering head and assemble the tool according to the manufacturer's instructions. Recheck the aligment of the race and tool before applying pressure (**Figure 45**, typical).
7. Hold the end of the installer shaft and turn the nut to press the upper race into the steering head. Continue until the race bottoms in the bore.
8. Remove the installer and inspect the bearing race. It should be bottomed in the steering head as shown in **Figure 35**.
9. Turn the special tool over and repeat this procedure for the lower bearing outer race.

LOWER BEARING REPLACEMENT

Do not remove the lower bearing and lower dust seal unless they are going to be replaced. The bearing can be difficult to remove. If it cannot be easily removed as described in this procedure, have a dealership service department replace the bearing and seal.

Never reinstall a bearing that has been removed; it is no longer true and will damage the rest of the bearing assembly if reused.

1. Install the adjuster nut and the steering stem nut onto the top of the steering stem to protect the threads.

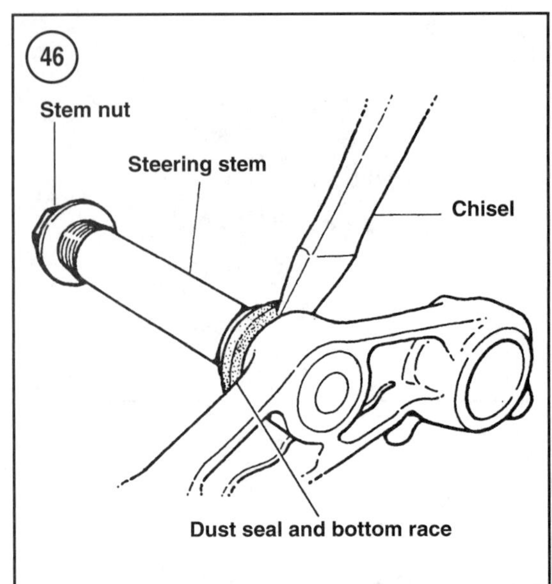

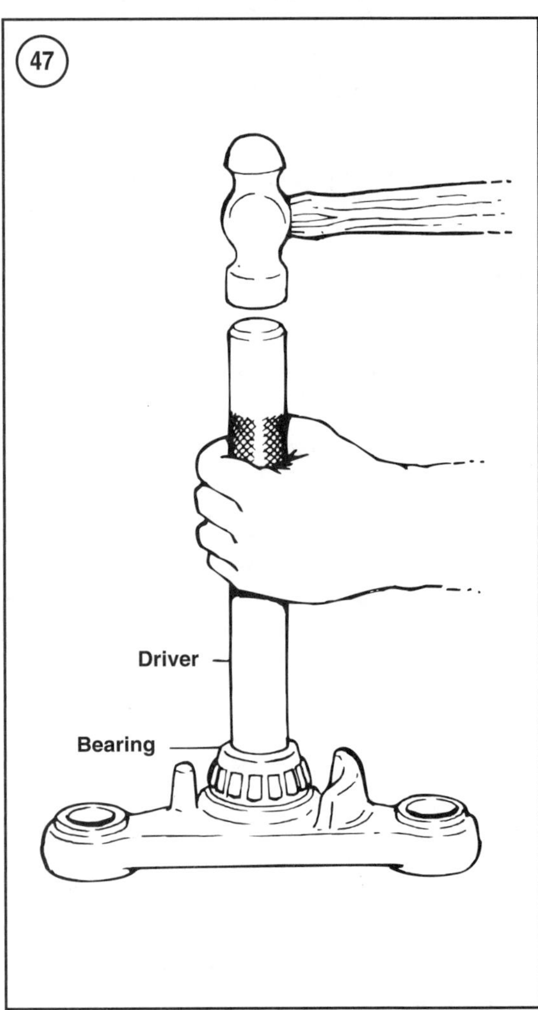

2. Use a chisel to drive the bearing/seal assembly from the steering stem (**Figure 46**). Work around in a circle and slowly drive the assembly from the shoulder on the steering stem. Remove the bearing and seal. Discard them both.
3. Clean the steering stem with solvent and dry it thoroughly.
4. Slide a new dust seal and the lower bearing onto the steering stem.
5. Align the bearing inner race with the machined shoulder on the steering stem.
6. Drive the bearing onto the steering stem shoulder with a driver or piece of pipe that matches the diameter of the inner race (**Figure 47**).

Table 1 FRONT SUSPENSION SPECIFICATIONS

Front fork air pressure	50 kPa (7.1 psi)
Fork oil viscosity	SAE 10W-20 fork oil
Oil capacity per leg	
1986-1993 model	
When empty	Approx. 388 ml (13.1 U.S. oz. [13.7 Imp oz.])
Oil change	Approx. 330 ml (11.2 U.S. oz. [11.6 Imp. oz.])
Oil level each leg (measured from top of the fully extended fork tube without spring)	355 mm (13.97 in.)
1994-on models	
When empty	Approx 379 ml (112.82 U.S. oz. [13.13 Imp. oz.])
Oil change	Approx. 330 ml (11.2 U.S. oz. [11.6 Imp. oz.])
Oil level each leg (measured from the top of the fully compressed fork tube without spring)	171 mm (6.73 in.)
Fork spring free length	
1986-1993 models	
New	514 mm (20.24 in)
Service limit	504 mm (19.84 in.)
1994-on models	
New	545.3 mm (21.47 in.)
Service limit	533 mm (20.98 in.)

12

Table 2 FRONT SUSPENSION AND STEERING TORQUE SPECIFICATIONS

Item	N•m	in.-lb.	ft.-lb.
Fork Allen bolt[1]	39	–	29
Fork cap bolt	23	–	17
Fork bridge clamp bolts			
Lower	21	–	15
Upper	16	–	12

(continued)

Table 2 FRONT SUSPENSION AND STEERING TORQUE SPECIFICATIONS (continued)

Item	N•m	in.-lb.	ft.-lb.
Fork drain screw[2]	1.5	13	–
Front axle nut	88	–	65
Front axle clamp bolts			
1986-1993 models	20	–	15
1994-on models	35		26
Front caliper bolt	32	–	24
Handlebar clamp bolt	19	–	14
Handlebar mounting bolts	19	–	14
Steering head nut	39	–	29

1. Apply Loctite 242 (blue) or an equivalent medium-strength threadlock.
2. Apply liquid gasket.

CHAPTER THIRTEEN

REAR SUSPENSION AND FINAL DRIVE

This chapter covers repair procedures for servicing the rear shock absorber, swing arm and final drive assembly.

When inspecting rear suspension and final drive components, compare any measurements to the specifications in **Table 1** at the end of this chapter. Replace parts that are damaged, worn, or out of specification. During assembly, tighten fasteners to the specified torque.

SHOCK ABSORBER

The shock absorber can be adjusted to suit various riding conditions by adjusting air pressure and/or rebound damping. Refer to the procedures in Chapter Three.

Removal/Installation

Refer to **Figure 1**.

1. Securely support the motorcycle with the rear wheel off the ground so the shock absorber is not compressed.
2. Remove the side cover from the right side as described in Chapter Fifteen.
3. Remove the air hose nut (A, **Figure 2**) and washer (B) and release the air hose from the frame bracket.
4. Unthread the damper adjuster (C, **Figure 2**) from the damper rod.
5. Loosen the locknut and remove the damper rod from the shock absorber.
6. Remove the nut (A, **Figure 3**) from the left side of the rocker arm. Remove the center rocker arm bolt (A, **Figure 4**) and release the tie rods from the rocker arm.
7. Remove the nut (B, **Figure 3**) from the lower shock mount. Remove the rear rocker arm bolt (B, **Figure 4**) and lower the rocker arm from the shock mount.
8. Remove the nut (**Figure 5**) from the left side of the upper shock mount. Pull the upper shock absorber bolt (**Figure 6**).
9. Lower the shock absorber from the frame, through the swing arm and remove it.
10. Install the shock absorber by reversing the removal procedures. Pay attention to the following:
   a. Apply molybdenum disulfide grease to the needle bearings in the rocker arm.
   b. Install all bolts from the right side, nuts from the left.

SHOCK ABSORBER

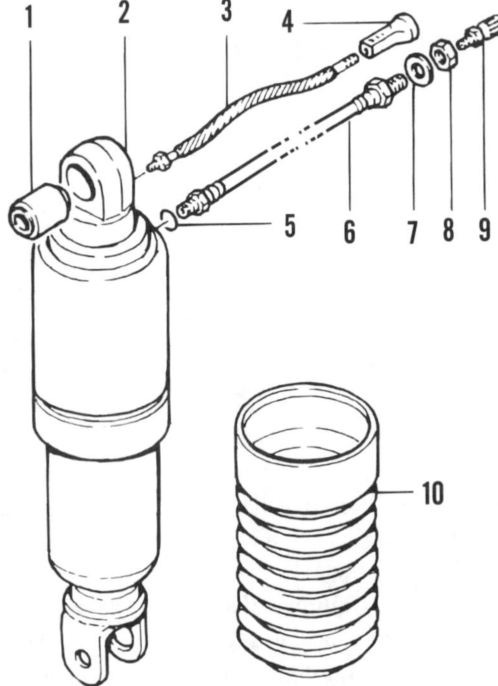

1. Bushing
2. Shock absorber
3. Damper rod
4. Damper adjuster
5. O-ring
6. Hose
7. Washer
8. Nut
9. Air valve
10 Boot

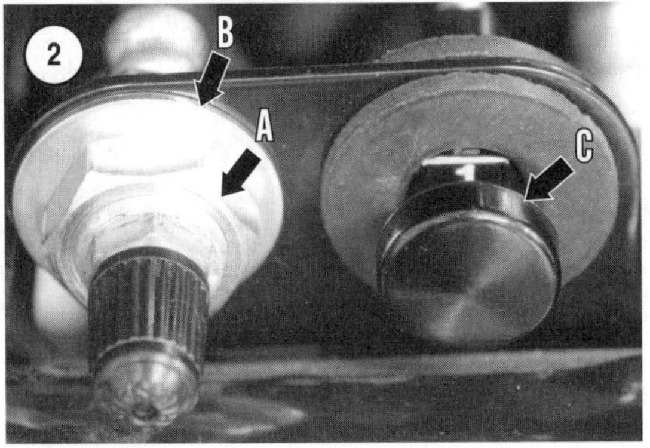

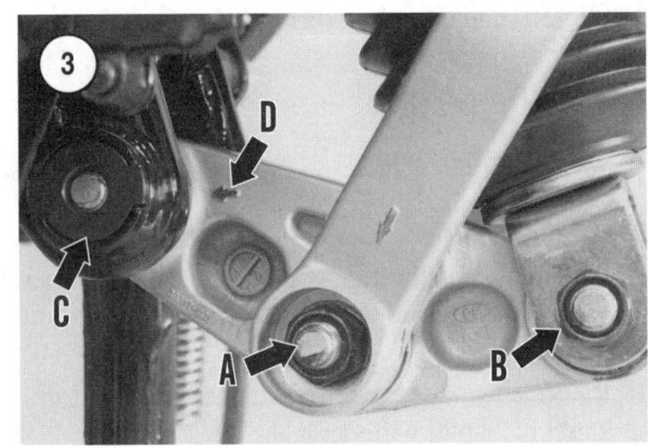

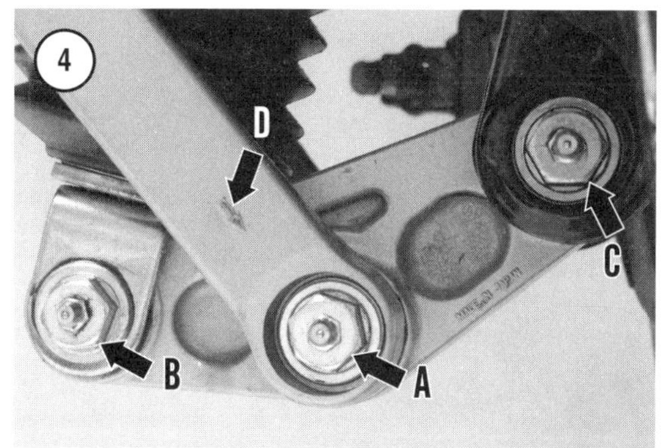

c. Slide the shock up through the swing arm and into the upper mount. Make sure the shock's air hose faces the right side.

d. Secure the lower shock mount to the rear mount on the rocker arm.

e. Secure the tie rods to the middle mount on the rocker arm. Check that the arrow on each tie rod (D, **Figure 5**) points down. If necessary, remove and reinstall the tie rods on the swing arm.

f. Torque the rocker arm nuts (A and B, **Figure 4**) to 59 N•m (44 ft.-lb.).

g. Torque the upper shock absorber nut (**Figure 6**) to 39 N•m (29 ft.-lb.).

h. Turn the damper rod into the shock absorber until the outboard end of the rod sits in the center (**Figure 7**) of the frame mount. Tighten the rod locknut.

i. Apply Loctite 242 to the threads of the damper rod and turn the adjuster (C, **Figure 2**) onto the rod.

j. Insert the air valve through its frame mount and secure it in place with the washer (B, **Figure 2**) and nut (A). Tighten the nut securely and install the valve cap.

k. Adjust the air pressure and rebound damper (Chapter Three).

13

Inspection

1. Clean and dry the hardware, mounting studs and the mounts on the shock absorber.

2. Pull back the boot (**Figure 8**) and inspect the shock absorber for dents, damage or oil leaks. Replace the shock absorber if necessary.

3. Inspect the bushing in the upper shock mount (**Figure 9**) for excessive wear of damage. The bushing must fit tightly within the mount. Replace the bushing as necessary.
4. Inspect the lower shock mount (**Figure 10**) for elongation, cracks or other damage. If damage is found, replace the shock.
5. Inspect the air hose and valve (**Figure 11**) for cracks, damage or signs of leaking. When replacing the hose, install a new O-ring and torque the hose-to-shock nut to 12 N•m (106 in.-lb.).

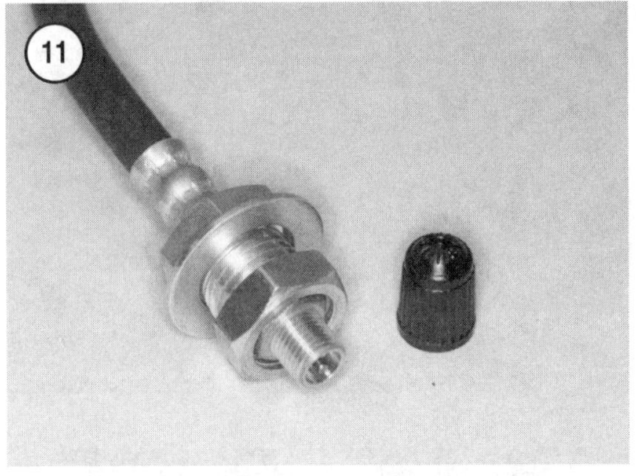

REAR SUSPENSION LINKAGE

Refer to **Figure 12**.

Rocker Arm Removal/Installation

NOTE
*A needle bearing and its related rocker-arm or tie-rod bolt (**Figure 13**) must be replaced as a set. Label each bolt (front, middle or rear rocker-arm bolt; left or right tie-rod bolt) as it is removed so it can be identified if its bearing must be replaced.*

1. Remove the shock absorber as described in this chapter.
2. Turn out the forward rocker arm bolt (C, **Figure 5**) and lower the rocker arm from the frame mount.
3. Remove the special nut (C, **Figure 4**) from the frame mount.
4. Inspect the rocker arm as described in *Linkage Inspection* in this section.
5. Installation is the reverse of removal. Note the following:
   a. Apply molybdenum disulfide grease to the needle bearings in the rocker arm.
   b. Fit the special nut into the frame mount so the nut's ears (**Figure 14**) engage the slots in the mount.
   c. Slip the rocker arm in its frame mount so the arrow (D, **Figure 4**) sits on the left side and points forward.
   d. Torque the forward rocker arm bolt (C, **Figure 5**) to 59 N•m (44 ft.-lb.).

Tie Rod Removal/Installation

NOTE
*A needle bearing and its related rocker-arm or tie-rod bolt (**Figure 13**) must be replaced as a set. Label each bolt (front, middle or rear rocker-arm bolt; left or right tie-rod bolt) as it is removed so it can be identified if its bearing must be replaced.*

(12)

REAR SUSPENSION LINKAGE

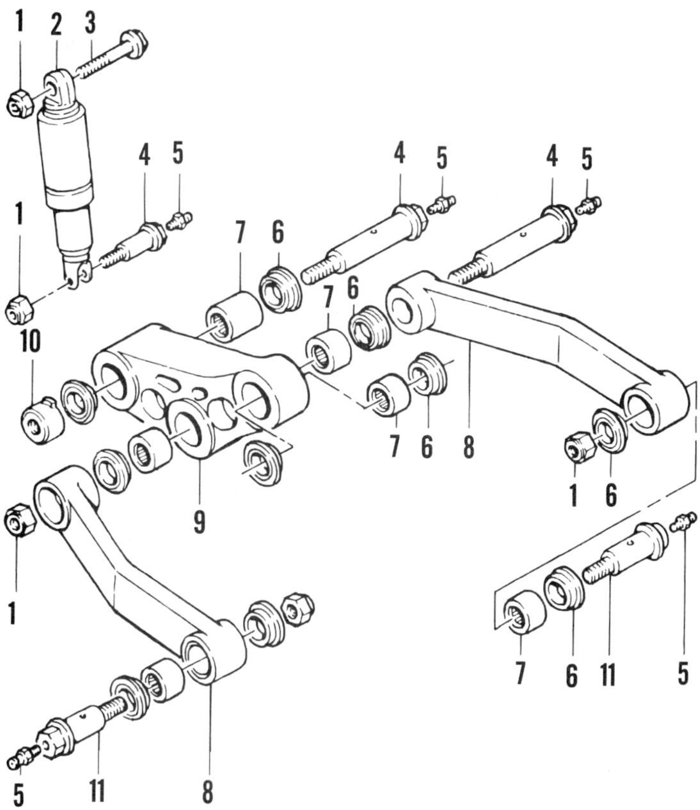

1. Nut
2. Shock absorber
3. Upper shock mount bolt
4. Rocker arm bolt
5. Grease nipple
6. Dust seal
7. Needle bearing
8. Tie rod
9. Rocker arm
10. Special nut
11. Tie rod bolt

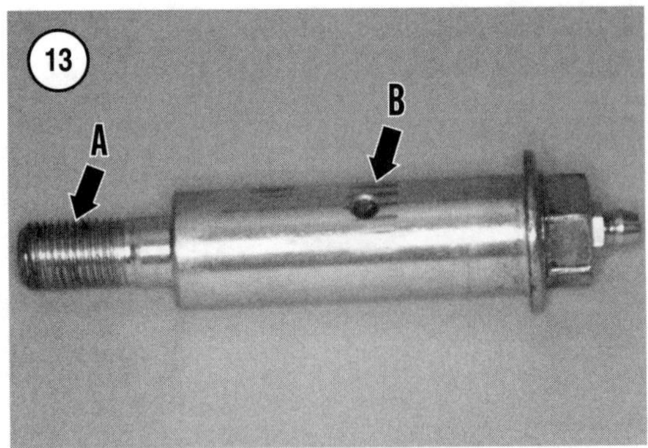

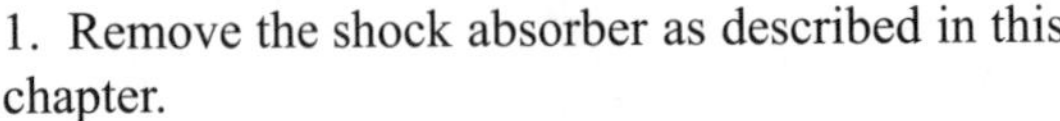

1. Remove the shock absorber as described in this chapter.

NOTE
The swing arm is shown removed for photographic clarity. The tie rods can be removed while the swing arm is installed on the motorcycle.

2. Remove the nut and tie rod bolt (A, **Figure 15**) and lower the tie rod from the swing arm.
3. Repeat Step 2 for the remaining tie rod.
4. Installation is the reverse of removal. Note the following:
   a. Apply molybdenum disulfide grease to the tie rod needle bearings.
   b. Insert the tie rod end (B, **Figure 15**) into the swing arm mount so the OUT on the tie rod faces the outboard side of the swing arm and the arrow on the tie rod points away from the swing arm mount. See **Figure 16**.
   c. Install the tie rod bolt (A, **Figure 15**) and nut. Torque the tie rod nut to 59 N•m (44 ft.-lb.).

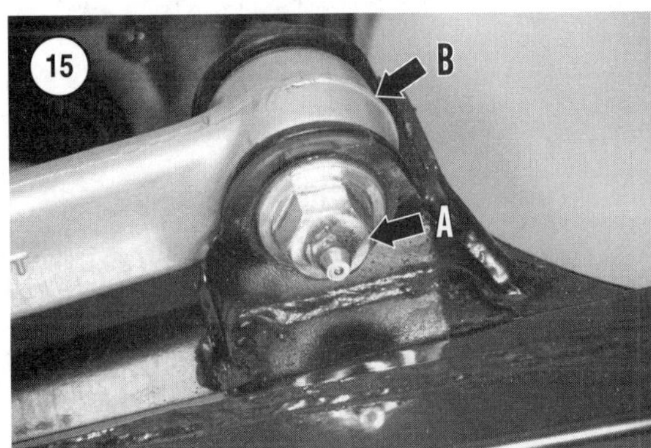

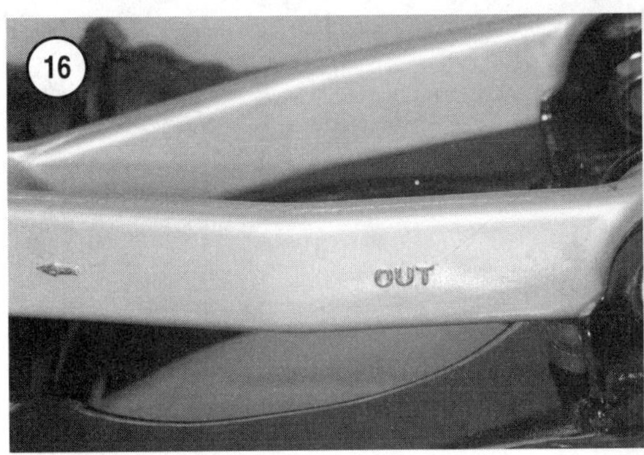

Linkage Inspection

1. Inspect the dust seals (A, **Figure 17**) for tears cracks or other signs of damage. Replace any seal that is damaged or brittle. See *Needle Bearing Replacement* in this section.
2. Inspect the needle bearings (B, **Figure 17**) in the rocker arm and tie rods. Check the needles and the cage for abrasion, color change or other signs of overheating. Turn the bearings by hand. They should rotate smoothly without binding or excessive noise. If damage is noted, replace the bearing and its rocker-arm or tie-rod bolt (**Figure 13**) as a set.

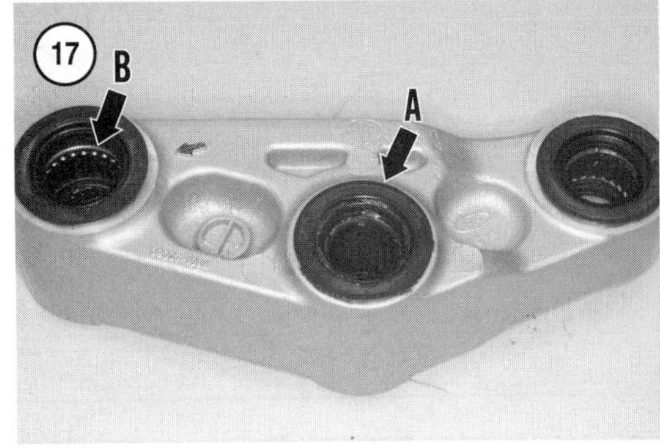

18

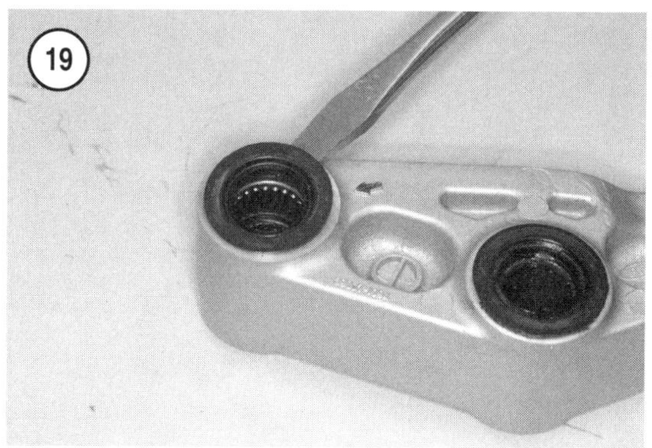
19

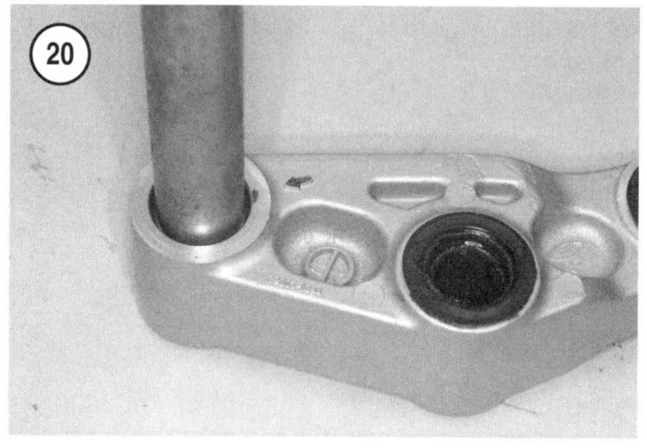
20

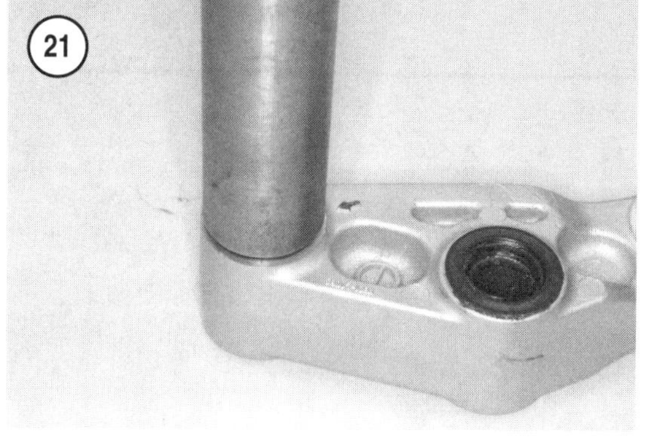
21

3. Inspect the threads of the rocker-arm and tie-rod bolts (A, **Figure 13**). Minor damage can be cleaned with the appropriate size metric die.
4. Inspect the bolt's sleeve (B, **Figure 13**) for scoring, abrasion or other signs of overheating. If damage is noted, replace the bolt and its related needle bearing.
5. Inspect the threads of the special nut (**Figure 18**). Minor damage can be cleaned with the appropriate size metric tap. Make sure the ears or the special nut and its mated slots in the frame mount are not rounded.

Needle Bearing Replacement

1. Pry the dust seal (**Figure 19**) from each side of the needle bearing.
2. Each bearing is set to a specific depth in the its bore. Use a vernier caliper to measure that depth. Record the reading. The new bearings must be set to the same depth during assembly.
3. Support the rocker arm or tie rod in a hydraulic press. Support the opposite end of the assembly so it will not cock sideways when the press ram is applied.
4. Use a suitable size driver (**Figure 20**) and press the bearing from the rocker arm or tie rod.
5. Clean the bearing bore with solvent. Dry it thoroughly with compressed air.
6. Support the rocker arm or tie rod in the press and drive the bearing to the same depth noted during removal. Drive the bearing with the same driver used during removal.
7. Apply molybdenum disulfide grease to the needles.
8. Use the appropriate size driver to install a new seal (**Figure 21**) into each side of the bearing bore.

SWING ARM

Removal

Refer to **Figure 22**.

1. Securely support the motorcycle on level ground.
2. Remove the mufflers as described in Chapter Eight.
3. Remove the rear wheel (Chapter Eleven).
4. Remove the shock absorber (this chapter).

SWING ARM

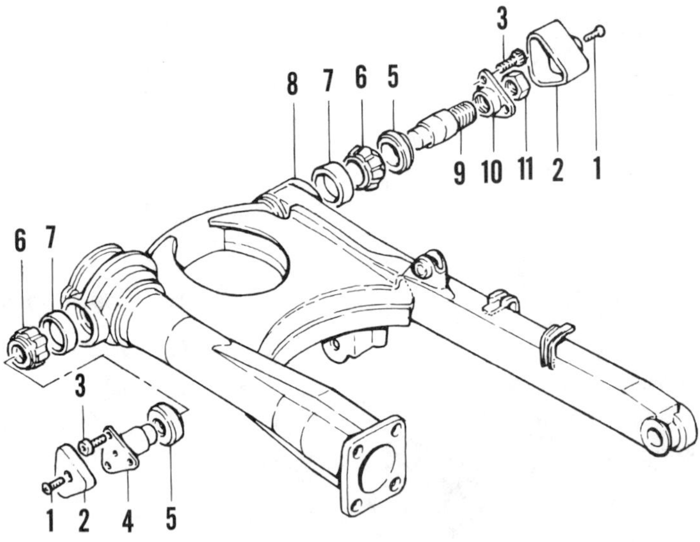

1. Screw
2. Pivot cover
3. Pivot mounting bolt
4. Non-adjustable pivot
5. Seal
6. Bearing
7. Outer bearing race
8 Swing arm
9. Adjuster bolt
10. Adjustable pivot
11. Locknut

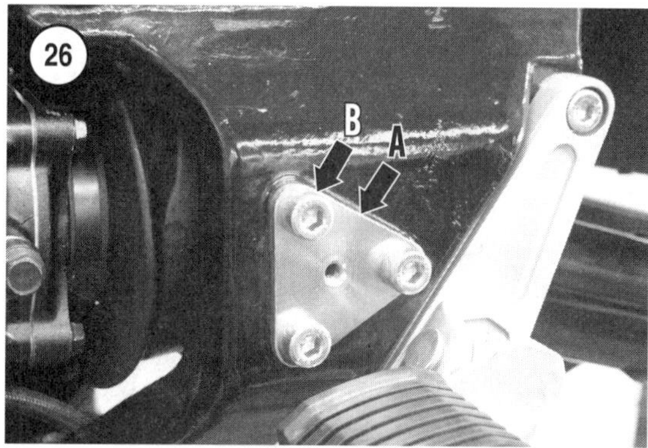

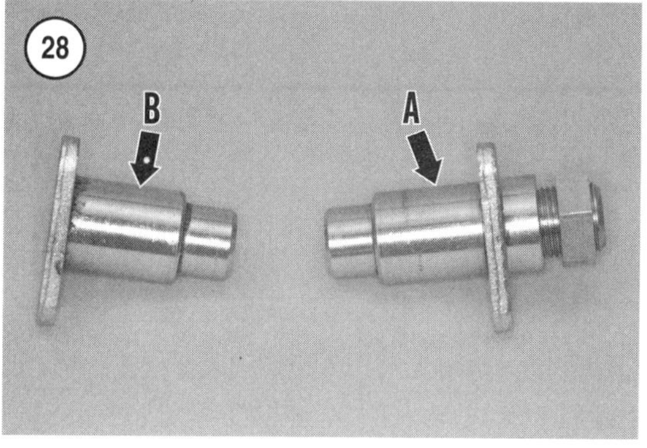

5. Check the swing arm bearings by performing the following:
   a. Grasp both ends of the swing arm and move it up and down. The swing arm should move smoothly. If any binding or abnormal noise is noted, the bearings are worn and must be replaced.
   b. Try to move the swing arm from side to side in a horizontal arc. If more than a slight amount of movement is felt, the bearings are worn and must be replaced.
6. Remove the final gearcase (this chapter). If the gearcase is full of oil, set it aside so the breather hole sits up (**Figure 23**).
7. Note the location of any cable ties that secure wires or hoses to the swing arm and release the cable ties.
8. Roll the rubber U-joint boot forward and off the swing arm.
9. Support the swing arm with a hydraulic jack.
10. Remove the swing arm pivot cover from each side of the frame.
11. Remove the adjustable swing arm pivot from the right side by performing the following:
   a. Remove the mounting bolts (A, **Figure 24**) from the adjustable swing arm pivot (B) on the right side.
   b. Turn a 6-mm bolt into the pivot and pull the pivot from the frame (**Figure 25**).
12. Repeat Step 11 and remove the non-adjustable swing arm pivot (A, **Figure 26**) from the left side.
13. Pull the swing arm rearward (**Figure 27**), slide it off the driveshaft and remove the swing arm.
14. Inspect the swing arm as described in this chapter.

Installation

1. Apply molybdenum disulfide grease to the swing arm pivots (**Figure 28**) and to the mounts in the frame.
2. Position the U-joint boot so its cutouts sit on the left and right side as shown in **Figure 29**.
3. Slide the swing arm over the driveshaft (**Figure 27**) and position swing arm between the frame pivots.
4. Insert the swing arm pivot assemblies into the frame and through the swing arm bearing on each side. The adjustable pivot (B, **Figure 24**) goes on

the right side; the non-adjustable pivot (A, **Figure 26**) on the left.

5. Turn the swing arm pivot mounting bolts (B, **Figure 26** and A, **Figure 24**) into each pivot. Torque the mounting bolts to 23 N•m (17 ft.-lb.).

6. Turn the adjuster bolt (A, **Figure 30**) until it bottoms and torque adjuster bolt to 27 N•m (20 ft.-lb.).

7. While holding the adjuster bolt (A, **Figure 30**), torque the locknut (B) to 52 N•m (38 ft.-lb.).

8. Pull the U-joint boot over the swing arm.

9. Install the shock absorber and final gearcase as described in this chapter.

10. Install the rear wheel (Chapter Eleven) and the mufflers (Chapter Eight).

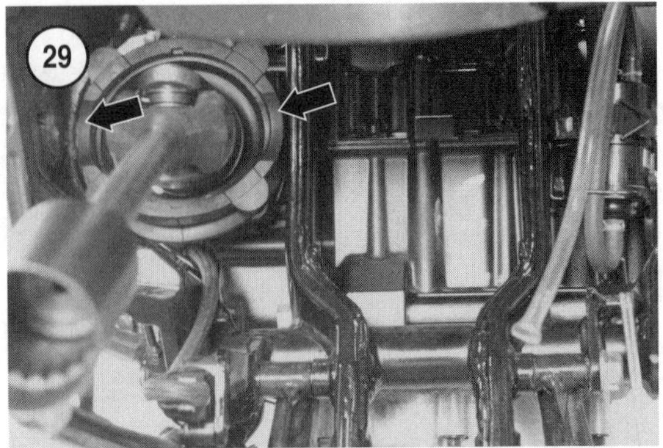

Disassembly/Inspection

1. Check the swing arm (**Figure 31**) for cracks or twisting. Also check the welds for cracks or fractures. Take the swing arm to a competent welding shop for any needed repairs.

2. Check the adjustable (A, **Figure 28**) and non-adjustable pivots (B) for bends. A bent pivot will restrict the movement of the swing arm. Replace as necessary.

3. Inspect the pivot threads on each side of the frame. Clean and dress the threads as necessary.

4. Inspect the seals in the swing arm. Replace a seal if it is worn or damaged.

5. Turn the bearing by hand. The bearing should turn smoothly without excessive play or noise.

6. Pry the seal (**Figure 32**) from the bearing bore. Place a rag beneath the pry tool to protect the swing arm.

7. Remove the bearings (**Figure 33**). Mark the pivot bearing so it can be reinstalled in its original location.

8. Check the bearing rollers for evidence of wear, pitting or rust.

9. Use a lint-free cloth to remove surface grease from the bearing outer race (**Figure 34**).

10. Inspect the outer race in the swing arm for scoring, wear or damage.

11. Repeat Steps 5-10 for the bearing on the opposite side. If either bearing or outer race is damaged, replace both bearings and outer races as a set.

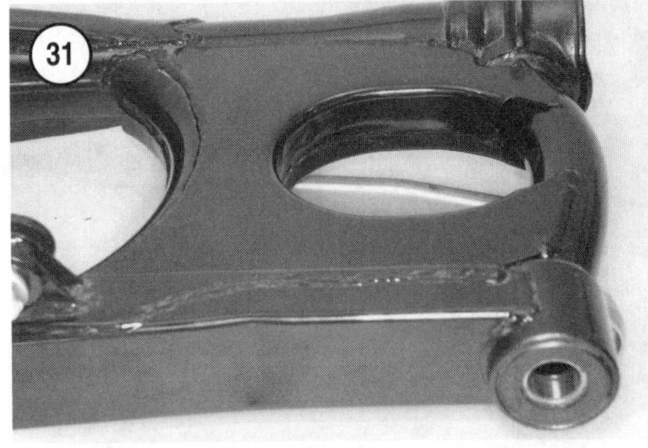

Assembly

A slide hammer and the Kawasaki outer race remover (part No. 57001-1058) are needed to remove the bearing races from the swing arm.

1. If the bearings and races are being reused, clean them with a degreaser and let them dry thoroughly.
2. If the races need replacing, perform the following:
   a. Use a slide hammer and the Kawasaki outer race remover or an equivalent tool to move the bearing outer race from each side of the swing arm (**Figure 35**).
   b. Clean the bore with solvent and dry it completely.
   c. Set a new outer race into the bearing bore with the narrow taper facing into the bore.
   d. Use the appropriate size driver to press or drive the race into the bore until the race bottoms.
3. Install the bearings by performing the following:
   a. Pack the bearings with molybdenum disulfide grease. Thoroughly work the grease between the bearing rollers and inner race.
   b. Liberally apply molybdenum disulfide grease to each outer race in the bearing bore.
   c. Install the bearings into the outer races (**Figure 33**). If reusing the old bearings and races, set each bearing into its original location.
4. Pack the lips of a new seal with molybdenum disulfide grease and drive it into place in the bearing bore (**Figure 36**).

DRIVESHAFT

Removal/Installation

The driveshaft is pinned to the coupling in the bevel gearcase. This lockpin must be released before the driveshaft can be removed.

Refer to **Figure 37**.

1. Remove the final gearcase and swing arm as described in this chapter.
2. Pull the U-joint boot forward to expose the driveshaft.
3. If necessary, rotate the driveshaft until the release hole (**Figure 38**) is visible.
4. Insert an awl or similar tool into the hole. Press the lockpin approximately 3 mm (1/8 in.) into the coupling and release the driveshaft.

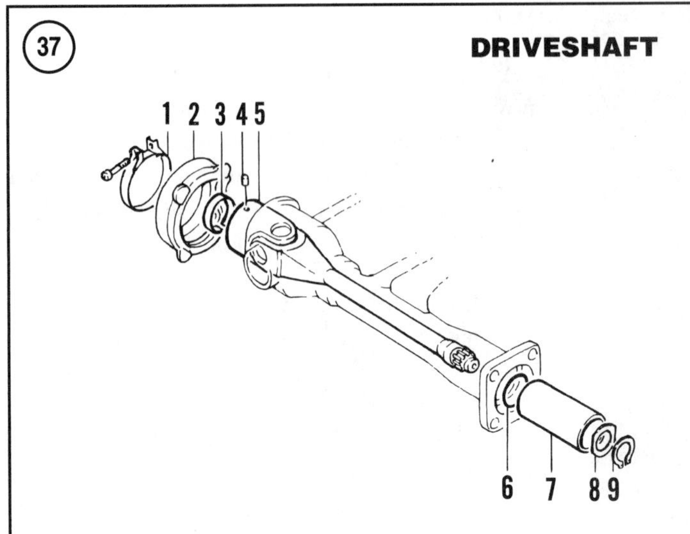

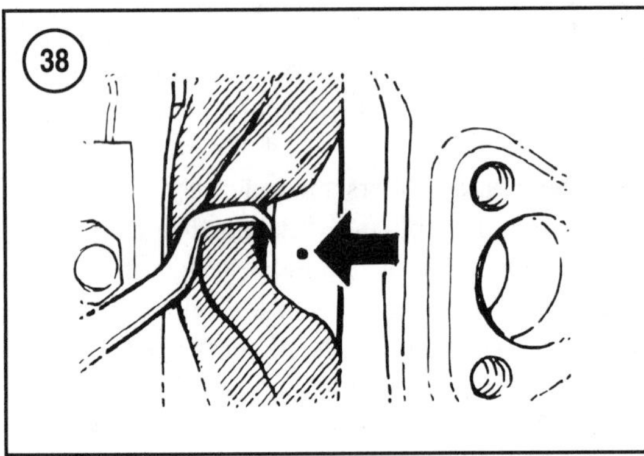

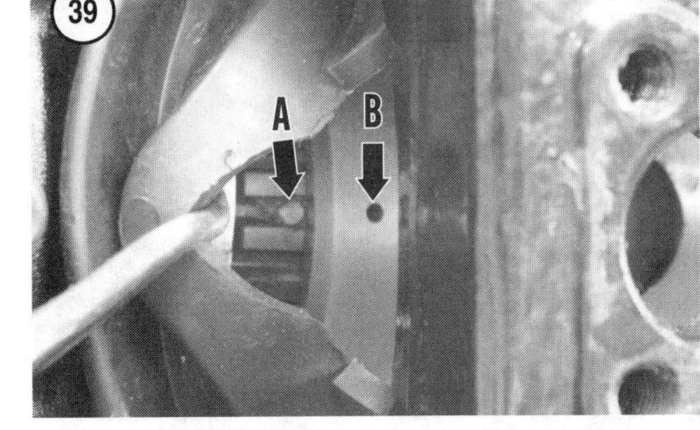

5. While holding the pin in, pull the driveshaft rearward.

6. When the driveshaft clears the lockpin (A, **Figure 39**), remove the awl and pull the driveshaft from the bevel gearcase coupling.

NOTE
Once the driveshaft is removed, the lockpin can easily slip from the coupling.

7. Use a magnet to remove the pin from the bevel gearcase coupling. Store the pin in a labeled, sealable plastic bag.

8. Disassemble and inspect the driveshaft as described in this section.

9. Installation is the reverse of removal. Note the following:

a. Insert the lockpin (A, **Figure 39**) into the bevel gearcase drive coupling.

b. Apply a high-temperature grease to the splines of the driveshaft (A, **Figure 40**).

c. Align the splines of the driveshaft with those of the bevel gearcase coupling.

d. Slide the driveshaft forward. Make sure the release hole on the driveshaft (B, **Figure 39**) aligns with the lockpin (A) in the coupling.

e. Depress the lockpin and slide the driveshaft forward until the pin snaps into the release hole.

f. Pull the driveshaft rearward to assure it is properly locked to the bevel gearcase coupling.

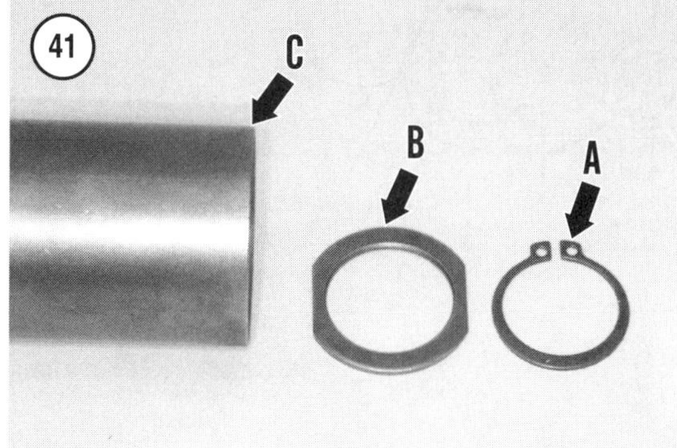

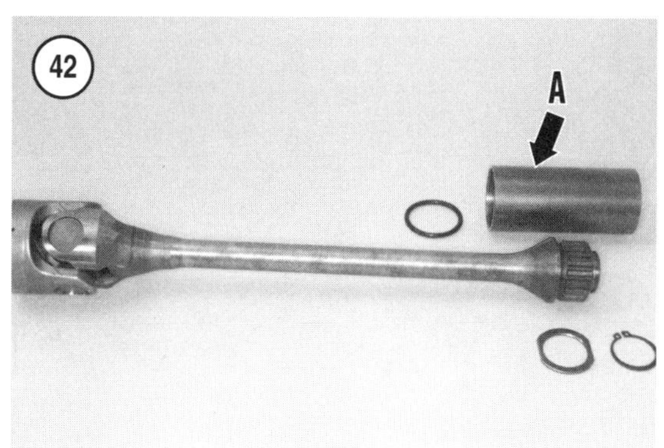

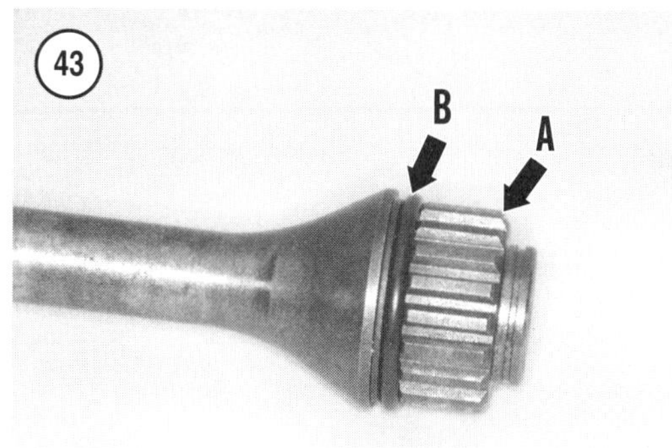

Disassembly/Inspection

1. Remove the snap ring (A, **Figure 41**) and the spacer (B) from the end of the coupling.
2. Pull the coupling (A, **Figure 42**) from the end of the driveshaft.
3. Wipe the old grease from the internal splines of the coupling (A, **Figure 42**) and from the splines on the front (A, **Figure 40**) and rear (A, **Figure 43**) of the driveshaft.
4. Inspect the splines for abrasion, damage or other signs of excessive wear. Replace the driveshaft as necessary.
5. Check the operation of the driveshaft U-joint (B, **Figure 40**). Make sure it moves smoothly. If any noise or binding is noted, the bearings are worn. Replace the driveshaft.
6. Remove and discard the O-ring (B, **Figure 43**).

13

Assembly

1. Install a new O-ring onto the end of the driveshaft (B, **Figure 43**).
2. Pack the internal splines of the coupling (A, **Figure 42**) with 20 cc (16 grams) of high-temperature grease.
3. Apply a thin coat of high-temperature grease to the splines of the driveshaft (A, **Figure 43**).

NOTE
The side of the coupling with the shallow splines goes onto the rear of the driveshaft.

4. Align the splines of the coupling with those of the driveshaft and slide the coupling onto the driveshaft until the coupling bottoms (**Figure 44**).

FINAL GEARCASE

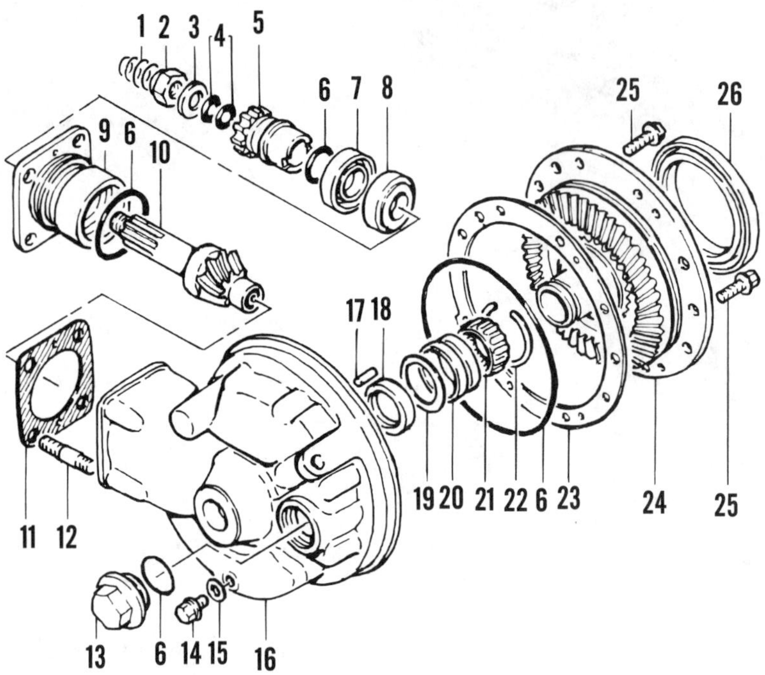

1. Spring
2. Pinion gear nut
3. Washer
4. Bearing preload shim(s)
5. Pinion gear coupling
6. O-ring
7. Oil seal
8. Bearing
9. Bearing housing
10. Pinion gear
11. Pinion gear shim(s)
12. Stud
13. Filler bolt
14. Drain bolt
15. Washer
16. Final gearcase
17. Pin
18. Oil seal
19. Washer
20. Outer bearing race
21. Bearing
22. Circlip
23. Ring gear shim(s)
24. Ring gear
25. Bolt
26. Oil seal

46

47

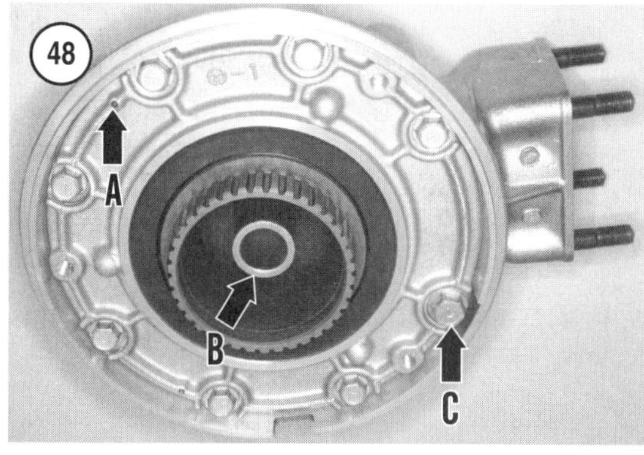

48

5. Install the spacer (B, **Figure 41**) into the end of the coupling (C) and install a new snap ring (A). Make sure the snap ring is completely seated within its groove.

FINAL GEARCASE

Final Gearcase Removal/Installation

Refer to **Figure 45**.

1. Securely support the motorcycle on a level surface.
2. If the final gearcase will be disassembled, drain the gearcase oil as described in Chapter Three.
3. Remove the rear wheel (Chapter Eleven).
4. Support the final gearcase with a hydraulic jack or wooden blocks.
5. Evenly loosen and remove the final gearcase mounting nuts (**Figure 46**).
6. Pull the final gearcase rearward until the splines of pinion gear coupling (A, **Figure 47**) disengage from those of the driveshaft coupling in the swing arm. Watch for the spring (B, **Figure 47**) on the pinion gear nut.
7. If the final gearcase has not been drained, securely support the gearcase so its breather hole sits up. (A, **Figure 48**).
8. Installation is the reverse of removal. Note the following:
   a. Install the spring (B, **Figure 47**) onto the pinion gear shaft so the small end of the spring faces the nut.
   b. Smear molybdenum disulfide grease onto the splines of the pinion gear coupling (A, **Figure 47**) and slide the final gearcase onto the swing arm.
   c. Manually rotate the ring gear as necessary to align the splines of the pinion gear coupling with those of the driveshaft coupling. Press the final gearcase forward until it bottoms against the swing arm.
   d. Evenly tighten final gearcase mounting nuts and torque them to 29 N•m (22 ft.-lb.).
   e. Install the rear wheel (Chapter Eleven).

Final Gearcase Disassembly

Disassembly and reassembly of the final gearcase requires the Kawasaki pinion gear holder (part No. 57001-1165) and blind bearing/seal remover (part No. 57001-1058) or their equivalent.

In addition to the special tools, a considerable amount of expertise is required to set the bearing preload and backlash. General practice is to have this type of repair performed by a specialist. If the final gearcase requires overhaul, determine if the cost of tools and/or labor, and the replacement parts would exceed the cost of replacing the unit with a new one.

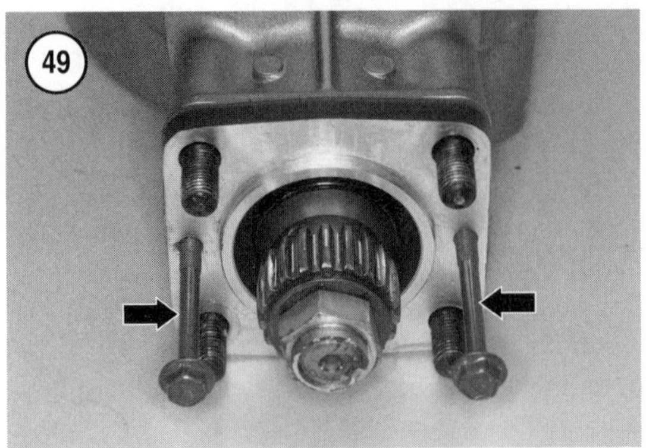

1. If necessary, remove the pinion gear assembly by performing the following:
   a. Turn two 6-mm bolts (**Figure 49**) into the holes of the bearing housing.
   b. Pull these bolts and remove the pinion gear assembly (A, **Figure 50**) and the pinion gear shim pack (B) from the final gearcase.
   c. If necessary, disassemble the pinion gear assembly as described in this section.
2. Remove the collar (B, **Figure 48**) from the ring gear.
3. Remove the ring gear mounting bolts. Lift the ring gear assembly from the final gearcase. One of the mounting bolts (C, **Figure 48**) is larger (10 mm) than the others (8 mm). Note its position.
4. Remove the ring gear shims (**Figure 51**). Note the number and order of shim(s).
5. Remove the needle bearing (**Figure 52**).
6. Remove the circlip (**Figure 53**).
7. Remove the ring gear oil seal by performing the following:

CAUTION
The ring gear must be evenly heated. Do not use a torch on the ring gear as it will warp.

   a. Use a shop oven or hot plate to heat the ring gear to 120-150° C (248-302° F).
   b. Pry the oil seal from the ring gear (**Figure 54**).
8. Remove the oil seal and outer bearing race from the final gearcase by performing the following:

CAUTION
The final gearcase must be evenly heated. Do not use a torch on the final gearcase as it will warp.

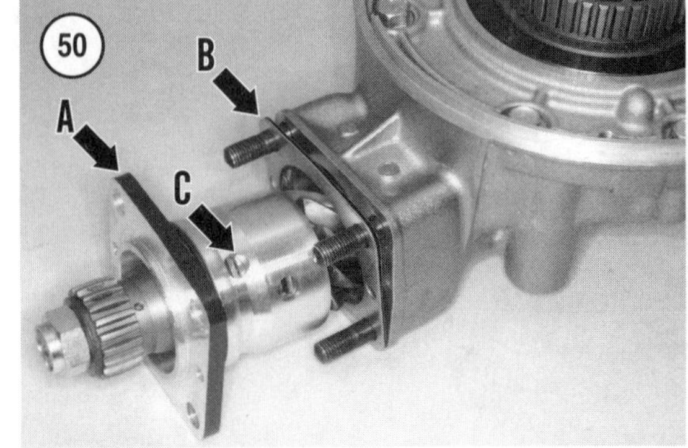

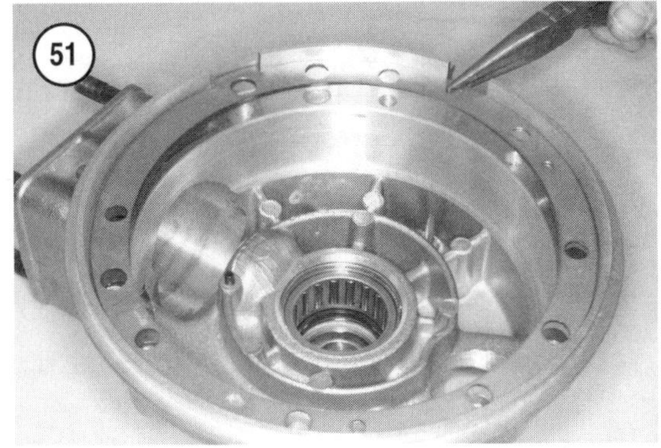

   a. Use a shop oven or hotplate to heat the final gearcase to approximately 100° C (212° F).
   b. Use a blind bearing remover (**Figure 55**) and simultaneously pull out the oil seal, washer and outer race. Discard all three parts. They are damaged during removal and cannot be reused.
9. Inspect the final gearcase as described in this section.

Final Gearcase Assembly

1. Use a shop oven to heat the final gearcase to approximately 100° C (212° F). With the appropriate size drivers, install the new oil seal, new washer and new bearing outer race. When installing the outer race, align the hole in the race with the hole in the final gearcase.
2. Install the circlip (**Figure 53**) and completely seat it in the circlip groove.
3. Install the needle bearing (**Figure 52**) into the final gearcase.

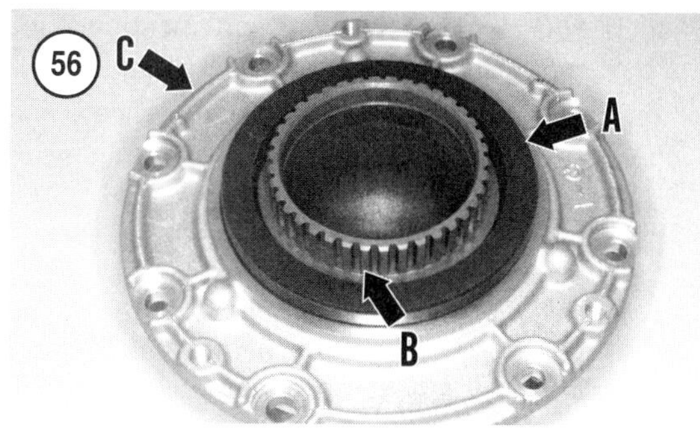

4. Use a shop oven to heat the ring gear to 120-150° C (248-302° F). Set a new oil seal (A, **Figure 56**) onto the ring gear and drive the seal into place.

CAUTION
Final gear backlash and tooth contact must be checked whenever the ring and pinion gears, ring gear cover, pinion gear bearing or the final gearcase are replaced.

5. If the ring gear, pinion gear, ring gear cover, pinion gear bearings or the final gearcase were replaced, select the new ring gear shim(s) by checking the final gear backlash, then select the new pinion gear shim(s) by checking the final gear tooth contact. Refer to the procedures described in this section.

6. Install the appropriate size and number of pinion gear shims (B, **Figure 50**) onto the final gear case studs.

   a. If you are replacing any part mentioned in Step 5, install the new pinion gear shim(s).

   b. If none of the above mentioned parts are being replaced, install the original shim(s).

7. Squirt final gear oil into the holes (C, **Figure 50**) in the pinion gear assembly. Rotate the shaft to fully lubricate the assembly. Slide the pinion gear assembly over the studs and seat it in the final gearcase. See **Figure 47**.

8. Install the small end of the spring (B, **Figure 47**) onto the pinion gear nut.

9. Smear molybdenum disulfide grease onto the splines of the pinion gear coupling (A, **Figure 47**) and slide the final gearcase onto the swing arm. Make sure the splines of the pinion gear coupling engage those of the driveshaft coupling in the swing arm. Torque the final gearcase mounting nuts (**Figure 46**) to 29 N•m (22 ft.-lb.).

10. Align the bolt holes in the ring gear shim(s) and install the shims so their tabs engages the slots (**Figure 51**) in the gearcase.

a. If you are replacing any part mentioned in Step 5, install the new ring gear shim(s).
b. If none of the above mentioned parts are being replaced, install the original ring gear shim(s).

CAUTION
If installing a new ring gear, also replace the pinion gear. The ring and pinion gears are mated and must be replaced as a set.

11. Apply oil to the shaft of the ring gear and insert the shaft into the needle bearing. Align the large bolt hole (**Figure 57**) in the ring gear cover with the forward-most slot in the gearcase and seat the ring gear cover in the gearcase.
12. Install the ring gear mounting bolts by performing the following:
   a. Apply Loctite 242 (blue) to the threads of the ring gear bolts.
   b. Install the 10-mm bolt (C, **Figure 48**) into the large hole opposite the forward slot.
   c. Secure a dial indicator to the final gearcase so its plunger rests against a spline on the ring gear.

CAUTION
*Constantly check the gear backlash as you tighten the ring gear mounting bolts. If the backlash ever reaches zero, stop and remove the ring gear. Refer to **Table 3** and select a thicker shim.*

   d. Evenly tighten the bolts in a crisscross pattern. Regularly check the dial indicator as you do so.
   e. Torque the 10-mm bolt to 34 N•m (25 ft-lb.); torque the 8-mm bolts to 24 N•m (18 ft.-lb.).

13. Insert the collar (B, **Figure 48**) into the ring gear.

Final Gearcase Inspection

1. Inspect the ring gear (**Figure 58**) for scored, chipped or damage teeth. Replace the ring gear and the pinion gear if any damage is noted.

2. Inspect the splines (B, **Figure 56**) on the ring gear.

3. Inspect the ring gear cover (C, **Figure 56**) and the final gearcase for cracks or other signs of damage. Replace the ring gear or gearcase as necessary.

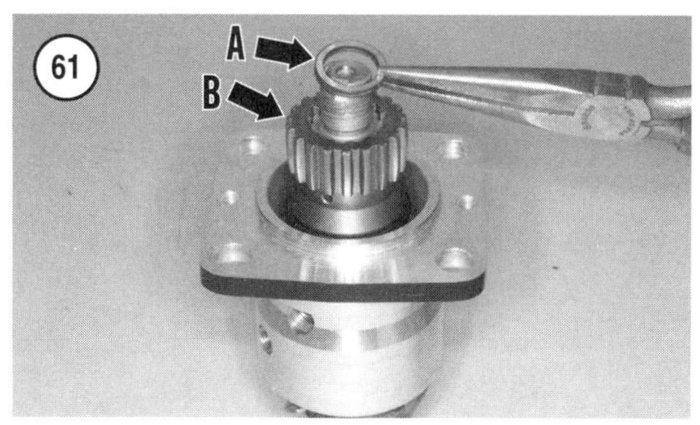

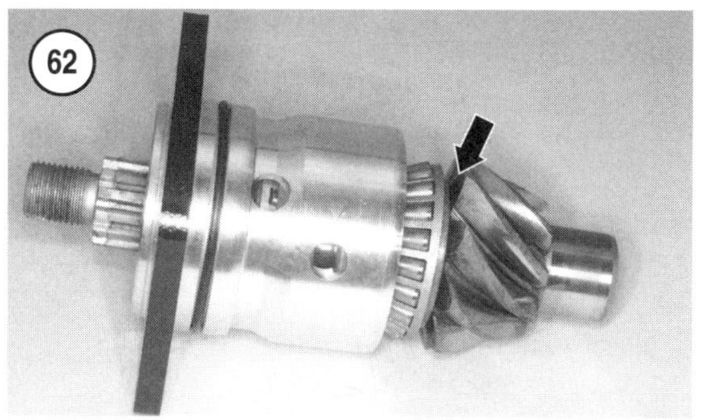

Pinion Gear Disassembly

1. Pry the lip of the pinion gear nut away from the cutout in the gear shaft.
2. Hold the pinion gear with the pinion gear holder and remove the nut (**Figure 59**). Discard the nut.
3. Remove the washer (**Figure 60**) and remove the bearing preload shim(s) (A, **Figure 61**).
4. Slide the pinion gear coupling (B, **Figure 61**) from the pinion shaft.
5. Pull the pinion gear with its bearing (**Figure 62**) from the bearing housing.

NOTE
The pinion gear bearing preload must be adjusted whenever the pinion gear nut has been loosened, even if no parts have been replaced. The oil seal must be removed to measure the preload.

6. Pry the oil seal from the bearing housing (**Figure 63**).
7. Inspect the pinion gear assembly as described in this section.
8. Check the pinion gear bearing preload as described in this section.

13

Pinion Gear Assembly

1. Use the appropriate size driver to install a new oil seal (**Figure 64**) into the bearing housing.
2. Lubricate the bearings with final gear oil and slide the pinion gear into the bearing housing.
3. Install a new O-ring (**Figure 65**) onto the pinion gear coupling.
4. Align the coupling's internal splines with the external splines of the pinion gear shaft and slide the coupling (B, **Figure 61**) onto the shaft.

NOTE
In Step 5, install the shims that were removed or install those calculated during bearing preload adjustment.

5. Use the shims selected during pinion gear bearing preload adjustment and install the bearing preload shim pack (A, **Figure 61**) onto the pinion gear shaft.
6. Apply Loctite 242 (blue) to the threads of a new pinion gear nut and install the nut (**Figure 66**).
7. Hold the pinion gear with the Kawasaki pinion gear holder (**Figure 59**) and torque the pinion gear nut to 120 N•m (89 ft.-lb.).
8. Stake the nut to lock it in place. See **Figure 66**.

Pinion Gear Inspection

1. Clean the pinion gear (**Figure 67**) and bearing housing (**Figure 68**) with a high-flashpoint solvent.
2. Visually inspect the oil seal. Replace the seal if it is discolored, its lips are deformed, or if the seal has become brittle.
3. Visually inspect the bearings for scoring, abrasion or other signs of damage. If either bearing requires replacement, replace both as a set. Perform the following:
   a. Use the appropriate size bearing driver to drive the bearing (**Figure 69**) from the bearing housing.
   b. Use the Kawasaki bearing puller (part No. 57001-135) or its equivalent (**Figure 70**) to pull the bearing from the pinion gear.
   c. Use the appropriate size driver to install a new bearing into the bearing housing.
   d. Use a pipe that matches the inside diameter of the bearing race and install a new bearing (A, **Figure 67**) onto the pinion gear.
4. Inspect the splines (B, **Figure 67**) and threads (C) on the pinion gear shaft.
5. Inspect the internal and external splines on the pinion gear coupling (**Figure 65**).

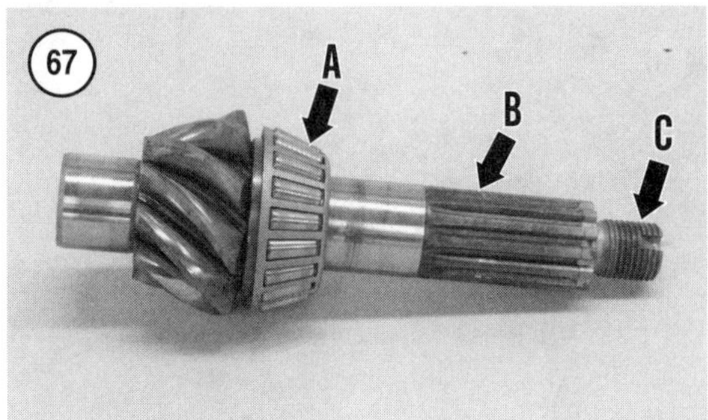

Pinion Gear Bearing Preload

Bearing preload is the amount of force or torque required to turn the pinion gear shaft. Bearing preload can be measured with a spring scale or with a beam-type torque wrench. Both methods are described here.

Measure and adjust the pinion gear preload whenever the pinion gear nut has been loosened, even if no parts have been replaced.

NOTE
Pinion gear bearing preload is measured without the oil seal installed in the bearing housing.

1. Apply final gear oil to the bearing in the bearing housing (**Figure 68**) and the bearing (A, **Figure 67**) on the pinion gear shaft.
2. Insert the pinion gear into the bearing housing (**Figure 62**).

NOTE
*Refer to **Table 2** and select the bearing preload shim(s). Start with shim(s) that leave the bearings just snug in the housing with no free play and no*

69

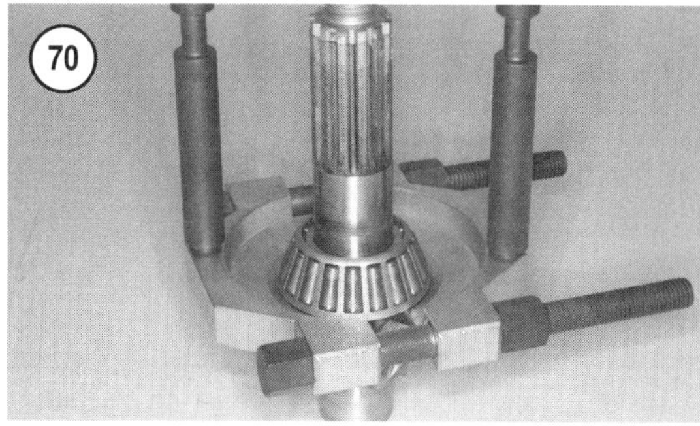
70

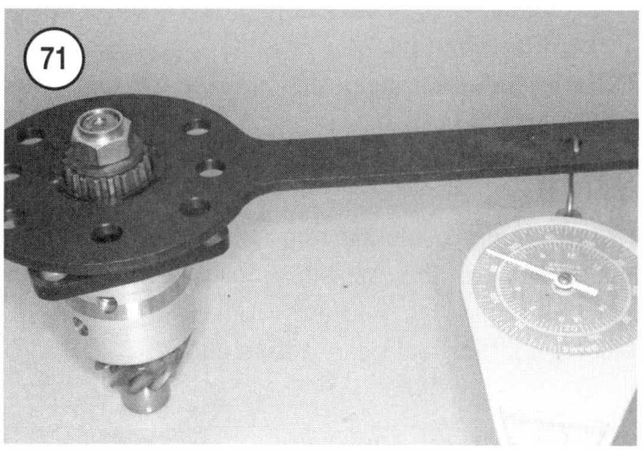
71

preload. Excessive preload could damage the bearings.

3. Install the coupling (B, **Figure 61**) and bearing preload shim (A) onto the pinion gear shaft.
4. Install the washer (**Figure 60**) and pinion gear nut.
5. Hold the pinion gear with the Kawasaki pinion gear holder (**Figure 59**) and torque the nut to 120 N•m (89 ft.-lb.).
6. Secure the bearing housing in a vise with soft jaws.
7. Rotate the pinion gear shaft five complete turns to seat the bearings.
8A. To measure bearing preload with a hook scale, perform the following:

a. Install the Kawasaki pinion gear holder onto the pinion gear coupling.

NOTE

The Kawasaki pinion gear holder has a hole drilled 200 mm from the center of the bolt for bearing preload measurement.

b. Hook a spring scale to the handle of holder so the scale is 200 mm from the center of the shaft.
c. Gently pull the spring scale until the shaft begins to turn. Record the reading on the scale (**Figure 71**).

8B. To measure bearing preload with a torque wrench, perform the following:

a. Set a beam-type torque wrench onto the pinion gear nut.
b. Hold the torque wrench approximately 200 mm from the center of the shaft.
c. Apply torque to the wrench until the shaft begins to turn. Record the reading on the torque wrench.

9. If the bearing preload is outside the range specified in **Table 1**, adjust the thickness of the bearing preload shim pack (A, **Figure 61**).

a. To increase bearing preload, decrease the thickness of the shim pack.
b. To decrease bearing preload, increase the thickness of the shim pack.

10. Once the proper shim(s) have been identified, disassemble the pinion gear assembly, install the oil seal and reassemble the pinion gear as described in *Pinion Gear Assembly* in this section.

Final Gear Backlash

1. Clean any dirt or oil from the teeth of the ring gear and the pinion gear.
2. Perform Steps 1-4 of the *Final Gearcase Assembly* procedure described in this section.
3. Refer to **Table 4** and install the standard size pinion gear shim (B, **Figure 50**) onto the final gear studs.
4. Install the pinion gear assembly into the final gearcase. (**Figure 47**).
5. Temporarily install the final gearcase onto the swing arm and torque the mounting nuts (**Figure 46**) to 29 N•m (22 ft.-lb.).

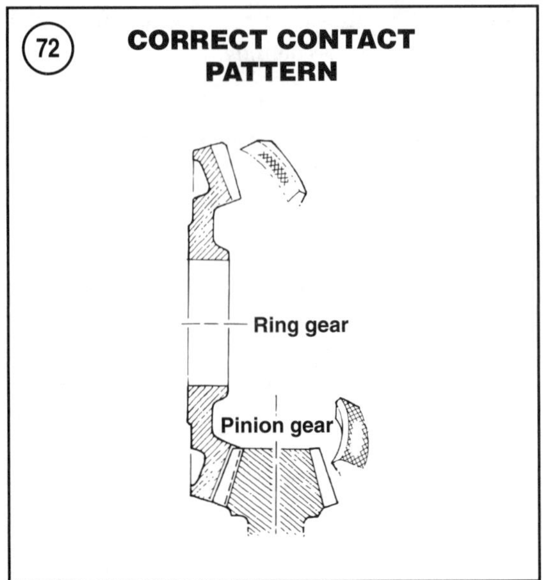

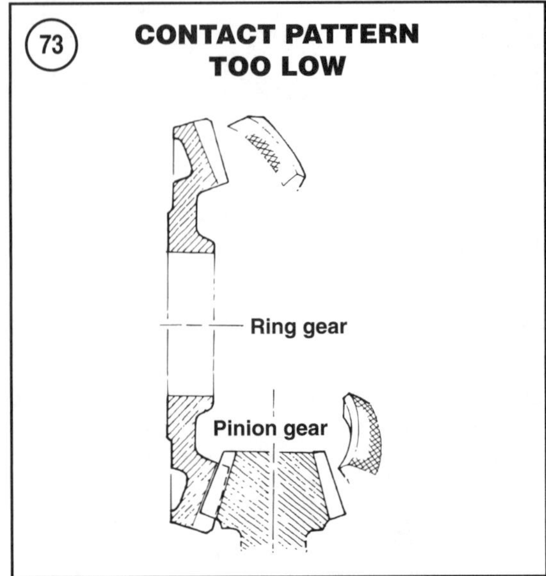

6. Install a standard size ring gear shim (**Table 3**) so it tabs engages the slots (**Figure 51**) in the gearcase.
7. Apply oil to the shaft of the ring gear and insert the shaft into the needle bearing. Align the large bolt hole in the ring gear cover with the forward-most slot in the gearcase and seat the ring gear cover in the gearcase.
8. Install and finger-tighten the ring gear mounting bolts. Install the 10 mm bolt (C, **Figure 48**) into the large hole opposite the forward slot.
9. Secure a dial indicator to the final gearcase so its plunger rests against a spline of the ring gear.
10. Make sure the transmission is in gear.
11. Check the gear backlash by rocking the ring gear back and forth while reading the dial indicator. Write down the reading.

CAUTION
*Constantly check the gear backlash as you tighten the ring gear mounting bolts. If the backlash ever reaches zero, stop and remove the ring gear. Refer to **Table 3** and select a thicker shim.*

12. Evenly tighten the bolts in a crisscross pattern. Torque the 10-mm bolt (C, **Figure 48**) to 34 N•m (25 ft-lb.); torque the 8-mm bolts to 24 N•m (18 ft.-lb.).
13. Once the bolts have been torqued to specification, rock the ring gear back and forth and check the backlash. If backlash is outside the range specified in **Table 1**, adjust the thickness of the ring gear shim pack.
   a. To decrease backlash, decrease the thickness of the shim pack.
   b. To increase backlash, increase the thickness of the backlash.
14. Remove the ring gear and check the backlash with the new shims.
15. Continue to change the shims and check the backlash until the measured backlash is within specification.
16. Check the final gear tooth contact.

Final Gear Tooth Contact

1. Adjust the final gear backlash as described above.
2. Remove the final gearcase from the swing arm.
3. Turn two 6-mm bolts into the pinion gear bearing housing (**Figure 49**) and pull the pinion gear from the final gearcase.
4. Apply a thin, even coat of marking compound to four or five teeth of the pinion gear (**Figure 62**).
5. Install the pinion gear shim(s) selected during backlash check (B, **Figure 50**) and install the pinion gear assembly (A) into the final gearcase. See **Figure 47**.
6. Temporarily install the final gearcase onto the swing arm and torque the mounting nuts (**Figure 46**) to 29 N•m (22 ft.-lb.).
7. Shift the transmission into neutral.

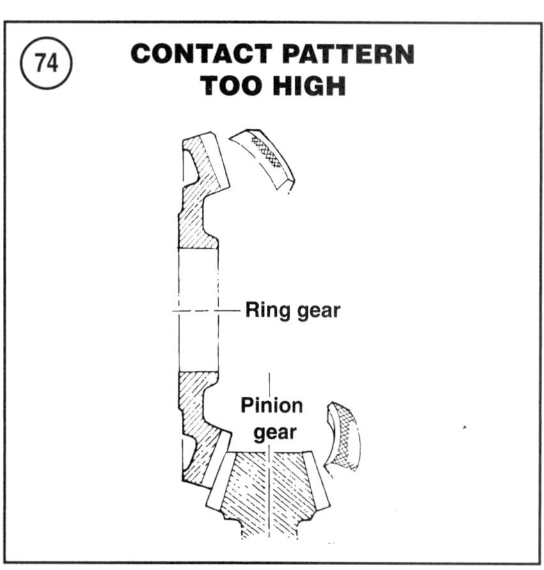

8. Turn the ring gear one complete revolution. Reverse direction and rotate the ring gear one complete revolution in the opposite direction.

9. Remove the final gearcase from the swing arm.

10. Turn two 6-mm bolts into the pinion gear bearing housing (**Figure 49**) and pull the pinion gear from the final gearcase.

11. Check the contact pattern on both sides of the pinion gear. The contact pattern should be centered between the top and bottom of the tooth as shown in **Figure 72**. If it is, clean all marking compound from both gears.

12. Adjust the tooth contact by moving the pinion gear further into or out of the final gearcase.

a. If the contact pattern appears like the pattern shown in **Figure 73**, increase the thickness of the pinion gear shim(s) by 0.05 mm.

b. If the contact pattern looks like the pattern shown in **Figure 74**, decrease the thickness of the pinion gear shim(s) by 0.05 mm.

c. Recheck the tooth contact pattern with the new shim(s).

d. Once the contact pattern is centered (**Figure 72**), wipe the marking compound from both gears and recheck the backlash.

Table 1 REAR SUSPENSION AND FINAL DRIVE SPECIFICATIONS

Final gear backlash	0.13-0.18 mm (.005-.007 in.)
Final gearcase oil	
Viscosity	
Temperature above 5° C (41° F)	SAE 90
Temperature below 5° C (41° F)	SAE 80
Grade	API GL-5 hypoid gear oil
Capacity	220 ml (7.4 U.S. oz. [7.7 Imp. oz.])
Pinion gear bearing preload	
With spring scale	2.9-4.9 N (0.7-1.1 lb.[0.20-0.50 kg])
With torque wrench	0.6-1.0 N•m (5.2-8.7 in.-lb.)
Shock absorber air pressure	
Solo rider no load	50 kPa (7.1 psi)
Rider with load and/or passenger	200-350 kPa (28-50 psi)

Table 2 BEARING PRELOAD SHIM

Shim thickness (mm)	Part No.
0.1	92025-1219
0.2	92025-1220
0.3	92025-1221
0.5	92025-1222
0.6	92025-1223
0.7	92025-1224
0.8	92025-1225

(continued)

Table 2 BEARING PRELOAD SHIM (continued)

Shim Thickness (mm)	Part No.
0.9*	92025-1226
1.0	92025-1227
1.30	92025-1214
1.32	92025-1215
1.34	92025-1216
1.36	92025-1217
1.38	92025-1218

*Standard thickness.

Table 3 RING GEAR SHIM

Shim Thickness (mm)	Part No.
0.1	92025-1625
0.15	92025-1626
0.2	92025-1627
0.3*	92025-1628
0.6	92025-1629
0.9	92025-1630
1.2	92025-1631

*Standard thickness.

Table 4 PINION GEAR SHIM

Shim Thickness (mm)	Part No.
0.15	92025-1052
0.5	92025-1053
0.6	92025-1054
0.7*	92025-1055
0.8	92025-1056
0.9	92025-1057
1.0	92025-1058
1.2	92025-1059

*Standard thickness.

Table 5 REAR SUSPENSION AND FINAL DRIVE TORQUE SPECIFICATIONS

Item	N•m	in.-lb.	ft.-lb.
Air hose (to shock absorber)	12	106	–
Final gearcase mounting nuts	29	–	22
Final gearcase oil drain bolt	17	–	12
Pinion gear nut*	120	–	89
Ring gear 8 mm mounting bolts*	24	–	18
Ring gear 10 mm mounting bolt*	34	–	25
Rocker arm bolt/nut	59	–	44
Shock absorber air valve hose	12	106	–
Shock absorber mounts			
Lower	59	–	44
Upper	39	–	29
Swing arm locknut	52	–	38
Swing arm adjuster bolt	27	–	20
Swing arm pivot mounting bolts	23	–	17
Tie rod nut	59	–	44

*Apply Loctite 242 (blue) or an equivalent medium-strength threadlocking compound.

CHAPTER FOURTEEN

BRAKES

This chapter describes repair and replacement procedures for brake system components.

The brake system on all models consists of dual front disc brakes and a single rear disc brake.

When inspecting brake components, compare any measurements to the brake system specifications in **Table 1** at the end of this chapter. Replace any part that is damaged, worn to the service limit, or out of specification. During assembly, tighten brake fasteners to the specified torque.

BRAKE SERVICE

When working on hydraulic brakes, all tools and the work area must be absolutely clean. Caliper or master cylinder components can be damaged by even tiny particles of grit that enter the brake system. Do not use sharp tools inside the master cylinders, calipers or on the pistons. Sharp tools could damage these surfaces and interfere with brake operation.

If there is any doubt about your ability to service the brake components safely and correctly, take the job to a Kawasaki dealership or brake specialist.

Consider the following when servicing the front and rear brake systems:

1. Disc brake components rarely require disassembly. Do not disassemble them unless necessary.
2. When adding brake fluid, only use brake fluid clearly marked DOT 4 from a sealed container. Other grades of brake fluid may vaporize and cause brake failure.
3. Always use the same brand of brake fluid. One manufacturer's brake fluid may not be compatible with another's. Do not mix different brands of brake fluids.
4. Brake fluid absorbs moisture, which greatly reduces its ability to perform correctly. Purchase brake fluid in small containers and properly discard any small leftover quantities. Do not store a container of brake fluid with less than 1/4 of the fluid remaining. This small amount absorbs moisture very rapidly.

WARNING

Do not use silicone-based (DOT 5) brake fluid on the models covered in this manual. Silicone-based fluid can cause brake component damage leading to brake system failure.

WARNING

Never reuse brake fluid. Contaminated brake fluid can cause brake failure.

5. Always keep the master-cylinder reservoir cover installed to keep dust or moisture out of the system.

6. Use only DOT 4 brake fluid or isopropyl alcohol to wash parts. Never use petroleum-based solvents of any kind on the brake system's internal components. The seals will swell and distort. They will have to be replaced.

7. Whenever any brake banjo bolt or brake line nut is loosened, the system is opened and must be bled to remove air. If the brakes feel spongy, this usually means air has entered the system. For safe operation, refer to *Bleeding the Brakes* in this chapter.

WARNING

*Whenever working on the brake system, do **not** inhale brake dust. It may contain asbestos, which can cause lung injury and cancer. Wear a mask that meets OSHA requirements for trapping asbestos particles. Also, wash your hands and forearms thoroughly after completing the work.*

WARNING

*Do not use compressed air to clean any part of the brake system. This releases harmful brake pad dust. Use an aerosol brake cleaner **(Figure 1)** to clean parts when servicing any component still installed on the motorcycle.*

PREVENTING BRAKE FLUID DAMAGE

Brake fluid will damage most surfaces on a motorcycle. To prevent brake fluid damage, note the following:

1. Protect the motorcycle before beginning any service requiring draining, bleeding or handling of brake fluid. Anticipate which parts are likely to dribble brake fluid and use a large tarp or piece of plastic to cover the areas beneath those parts. Even a few drops of brake fluid can extensively damage painted, plated or plastic surfaces.

2. Keep a bucket of soap and water nearby while working on the brake system. If brake fluid spills on any surface of the motorcycle, immediately wash the area with soap and water and rinse it thoroughly.

3. To help control the flow of brake fluid when refilling the reservoirs, punch a small hole into the seal of a new container. Put this hole next to the edge of the pour spout.

BRAKE BLEEDING TIPS

Bleeding the brakes removes air from the brake system. Air in the brakes increases brake lever or brake pedal travel and it makes the brakes feel soft or spongy. Under extreme circumstances, it can cause complete loss of brake pressure.

The brakes can be bled manually or with the use of a vacuum pump. Both methods are described here. Only use fresh DOT 4 brake fluid when bleeding the brakes. Do not reuse old brake fluid and do not use DOT 5 (silicone-based) brake fluid.

1. Clean the bleed valve and area around the valve before beginning. Make sure the opening in the valve is clear.

2. Use a box-end wrench to open and close the bleed valve. This prevents damage to the valve especially when it is rusted in place.

3. Replace a bleed valve with damaged threads or with a rounded hex head. A damaged valve is difficult to remove and it cannot be properly tightened.

NOTE

*The catch hose **(Figure 2)** is the hose installed between the bleed valve and the catch bottle.*

4. Use a clear catch hose so the fluid can be seen as it leaves the bleed valve. Air bubbles in the catch hose indicate air may be trapped in the brake system.

5. Open the bleed valve just enough to allow fluid to pass through the valve and into the catch bottle. If a bleed valve is too loose, air can be drawn into the system through the valve threads, In this case, apply silicone brake grease around the valve where it emerges from the caliper. The grease should seal the

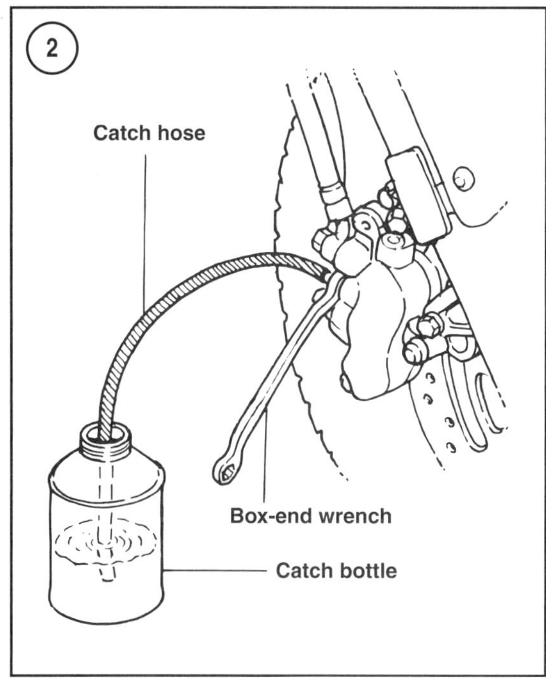

valve and prevent the entry of air. Wipe away the grease once the brakes have been bled.

6. If the system is difficult to bleed, tap the banjo bolt on the master cylinder a few times. This should dislodge air bubbles that may have become trapped at the hose connection. Also tap the banjo bolts at the brake hose union (beneath the lower fork bridge), at the calipers and any other hose connections in the brake line.

BLEEDING THE BRAKES

Manual Bleeding

1. Check all banjo bolts in the system, they must be tight.

2. Remove the dust cap from the bleed valve on the caliper assembly.

3. Connect a length of clear tubing to the bleed valve (**Figure 2**, typical). Place the other end of the tube into a clean container. Fill the container with enough fresh brake fluid to keep the end submerged. The tube should be long enough so that its loop is higher than the bleed valve. This prevents air from being drawn into the caliper during bleeding.

NOTE
When bleeding the front brakes, turn the handlebars to level the front master cylinder.

4. Clean all debris from the top of the master cylinder reservoir. Remove the top cover, diaphragm plate (1992-on models) and the diaphragm from the reservoir.
5. Add brake fluid to the reservoir until the fluid level reaches the reservoir upper limit. Loosely install the diaphragm and the cover. Leave them in place during bleeding to keep dirt out of the system and so brake fluid cannot spurt out of the reservoir.
6. Pump the brake lever or brake pedal a few times and then release it.
7. Apply the brake lever or pedal until it stops and hold it in this position.
8. Open the bleed valve with a wrench (**Figure 2**, typical). Let the brake lever or pedal move to the limit of its travel, then close the bleed valve. Do not release the brake lever or pedal while the bleed valve is open.

NOTE
As brake fluid enters the system, the fluid level in the reservoir drops. Add brake fluid as necessary to keep the fluid level 10 mm (3/8 in.) below the reservoir top so air will not be drawn into the system.

9. Repeat Steps 6-8 until the brake fluid flowing from the hose is clear and free of air. If the system is difficult to bleed, tap the master cylinder or caliper with a soft mallet to release trapped air bubbles.
10. Test the feel of the brake lever or pedal. It should feel firm and offer the same resistance each time it is operated. If the lever or pedal feels soft, air is still trapped in the system. Continue bleeding the system.

NOTE
The setting on the front brake lever adjuster affects bleeding. Initially bleed the front brakes with the adjuster turned to the softest setting. Once the brakes feel solid, check the feel with the adjuster in several different settings. If the lever feels soft at any setting or if the lever hits the handlebar, air is still trapped in the system. Continue bleeding the system.

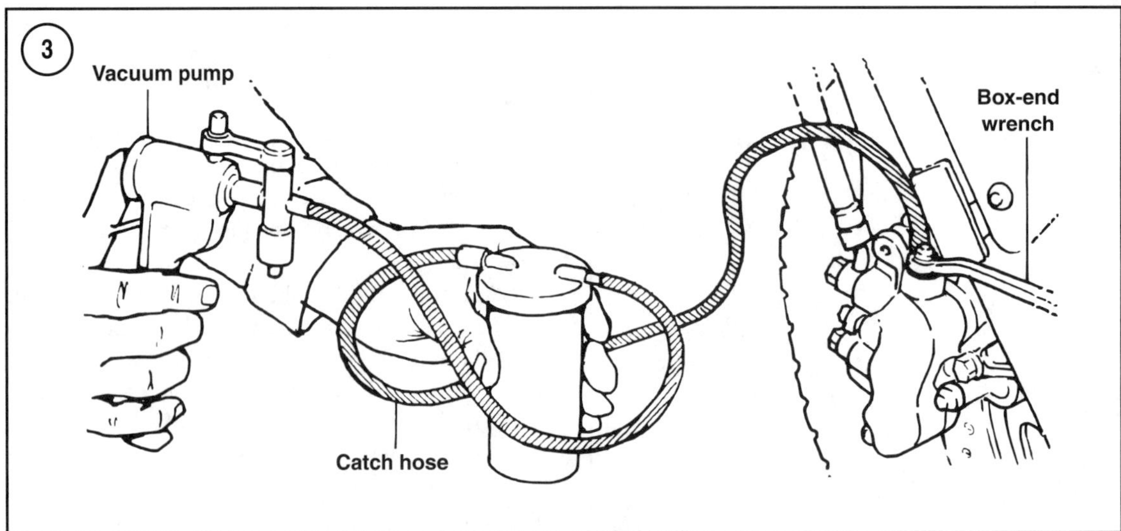

11. When bleeding is complete, disconnect the hose from the bleed valve. Torque the bleed valve to 7.8 N•m (69 in.-lb.).
12. When bleeding the front brakes, repeat Steps 1-11 on the opposite front caliper.
13. Add brake fluid to the master cylinder to correct the fluid level.
14. Install the diaphragm, diaphragm plate (1992-on models) and top cap. Be sure the cap is secured in place.

WARNING
Do not ride the motorcycle until front and rear brakes as well as the brake light are working properly.

15. Test ride the motorcycle slowly at first to make sure the brakes are operating properly.

Vacuum Bleeding

1. Check all banjo bolts in the system. They must be tight.
2. Remove the dust cap from the bleed valve on the caliper.

NOTE
When bleeding the front brakes, turn the handlebars to level the front master cylinder.

3. Clean all debris from the top of the master cylinder reservoir. Remove the top cover, diaphragm plate (1992-on models) and the diaphragm from the reservoir.
4. Add brake fluid to the reservoir until the fluid level reaches the reservoir upper limit. Loosely install the diaphragm and the cover. Leave them in place during this procedure to keep dirt out of the system and so brake fluid cannot spurt out of the reservoir.
5. Assemble the vacuum tool following the manufacturer's instructions.
6. Connect the pump's catch hose to the bleed valve on the brake caliper (**Figure 3**).

NOTE
When using a vacuum pump, keep an eye on the brake fluid level in the reservoir. It will drop quite rapidly. This is particularly true for the rear reservoir, which does not hold as much brake fluid as the front reservoir. Stop often and check the brake fluid level. Maintain the level at 10 mm (3/8 in.) from the top of the reservoir so air will not be drawn into the system.

7. Operate the vacuum pump to create vacuum in the hose.
8. Use a wrench to open the bleed valve. The vacuum pump should pull fluid from the system. Close the bleed valve before the brake fluid stops flowing from the system or before the master cylinder reservoir runs empty. Add fluid to the reservoir as necessary.
9. Operate the brake lever or brake pedal a few times and release it.

10. Repeat Steps 7-9 until the fluid leaving the bleed valve is clear and free of air bubbles. If the system is difficult to bleed, tap the master cylinder and caliper housing with a soft mallet to release trapped air bubbles.

NOTE
The setting on the front brake lever adjuster affects bleeding. Initially bleed the front brakes with the adjuster turned to the position 1 setting. Once the brakes feel solid, check the feel with the adjuster in several settings. If the lever feels soft at any setting or if the lever hits the handlebar, air is still trapped in the system. Continue bleeding the system.

11. Test the feel of the brake lever or brake pedal. It should feel firm and offer the same resistance each time it is operated. If the lever or pedal feels soft, air is still trapped in the system. Continue bleeding the system.
12. When bleeding is complete, disconnect the hose from the bleed valve. Torque the bleed valve to 7.8 N•m (69 in.-lb.).
13. When bleeding the front brakes, repeat Steps 1-12 on the opposite front caliper.
14. Add brake fluid to the master cylinder to correct the fluid level.
15. Install the diaphragm, diaphragm plate (1992-on models) and top cap. Be sure the cap is secured in place.

WARNING
Do not ride the motorcycle until both brakes and the brake light are working properly.

16. Test ride the motorcycle slowly at first to make sure the brakes are operating properly.

BRAKE FLUID DRAINING

Before disconnecting a front or rear brake hose, drain the brake fluid. Draining the fluid reduces the amount of fluid that can spill out when system components are removed.

This section describes two methods for draining the brake system: manual and vacuum.

Manual Draining

An empty bottle, a length of clear hose and a wrench is required when performing this procedure.

1. Remove the dust cap from the bleed valve. Remove all dirt from the valve and its outlet port.
2. Connect a length of clear hose to the bleed valve on the caliper. Insert the other end into a container (**Figure 2**, typical).
3. Apply the front brake lever or the rear brake pedal until it stops. Hold the lever or pedal in this position.
4. Open the bleed valve with a wrench and let the lever or pedal move to the limit of its travel. Close the bleed valve.
5. Release the lever or pedal and repeat Step 3 and Step 4 until brake fluid stops flowing from the bleed valve.
6. If draining the front brakes, repeat this on the other brake caliper.
7. Discard the brake fluid.

Vacuum Draining

A hand-operated vacuum pump is required when performing this procedure.

1. Connect the pump's catch hose to the bleed valve on the brake caliper (**Figure 3**).
2. Operate the vacuum pump to create vacuum in the hose.
3. Use a wrench to open the bleed valve. The vacuum pump should pull fluid from the system.
4. When fluid has stopped flowing through the hose, close the bleed valve.
5. Repeat Steps 2-4 until brake fluid no longer flows from the bleed valve.
6. If draining the front brake system, repeat this procedure on the opposite caliper.
7. Discard the brake fluid.

BRAKE PAD REPLACEMENT

Pad wear depends greatly upon riding habits and conditions. Periodically check brake pads for wear.

To maintain even brake pressure on the disc, always replace both pads in a caliper at the same time. If any front brake pad is worn to the service limit, replace all four front brake pads as a set.

Please note that the brake hose does not need to be disconnected from the caliper during brake pad replacement. If the hose is removed, the brakes will have to be bled. Disconnect the hose only when servicing the brake caliper.

WARNING
Use brake fluid clearly marked DOT 4 from a sealed container. Other types may vaporize and cause brake failure. Always use the same brand of brake fluid. Do not mix brake fluids from different manufacturers. They may not be compatible.

CAUTION
*Check the pads more frequently when the wear grooves (**Figure 4**) approach the disc. On some pads, the wear grooves are very close to the metal backing plate. If pad wear happens to be uneven, the backing plate may contact the disc and cause damage.*

Front Pad Replacement

The following photographs show brake pad replacement on a dual piston caliper used on 1994-on models. The procedure is identical for 1986-1993 models with a single piston caliper.

1. Remove the caliper bolts (A, **Figure 5**) and rotate the caliper off the brake disc.
2. Push the caliper holder (A, **Figure 6**) toward the piston until the holder posts clear the ears in the inboard pad (B). Lift the inboard pad from the caliper.
3. Lift the outboard pad (**Figure 7**) from the caliper. Note that the ears of the pad sit beneath the stopper springs on the caliper holder.
4. Remove the pad spring (A, **Figure 8**) from the caliper.

NOTE
If any front brake pad needs replacing, replace both brake pads in both front calipers. All four front brake pads must be replaced as a set.

5. Inspect the brake pads as described in this section.
6. During new pad installation, the master cylinder brake fluid level rises as the caliper pistons are repositioned. Perform the following:
   a. Clean all debris from the top of the master cylinder.

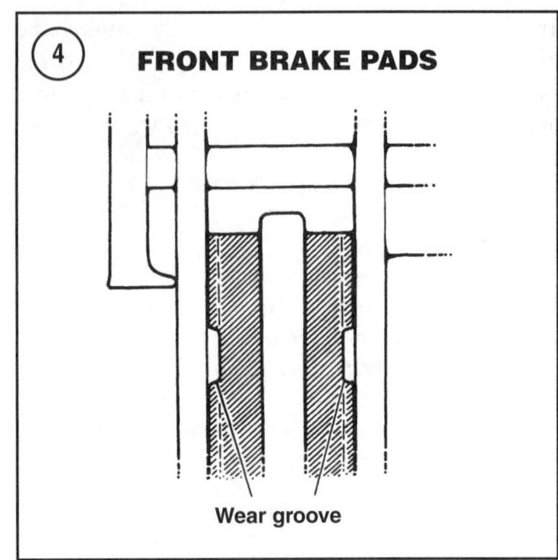

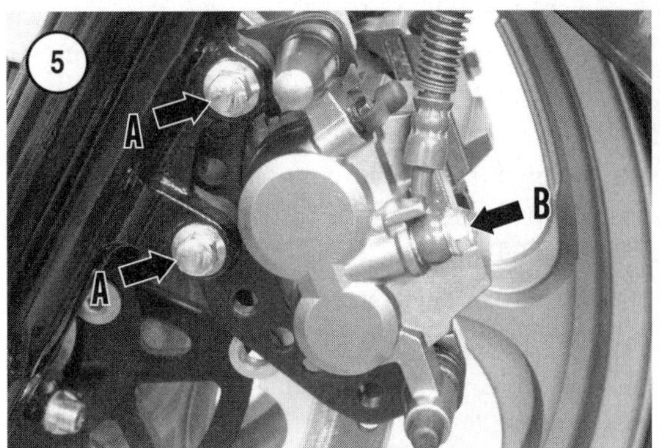

   b. Remove the master cylinder top cover, diaphragm plate (1992-on models) and the diaphragm from the master cylinder.
   c. Set the old outboard pad (**Figure 7**) into the caliper. Slowly push the pad against the pistons until they bottom in their cylinders. If the

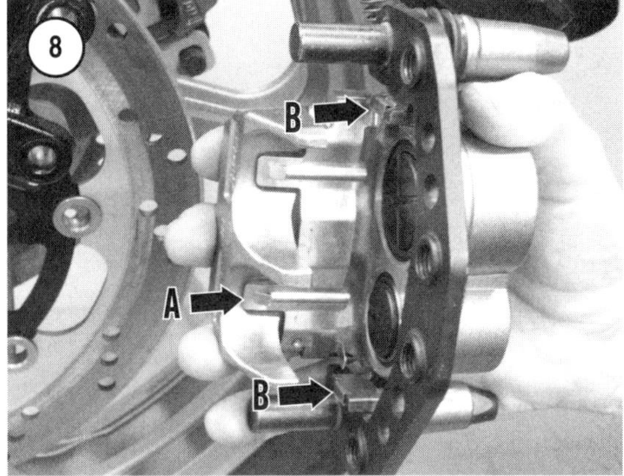

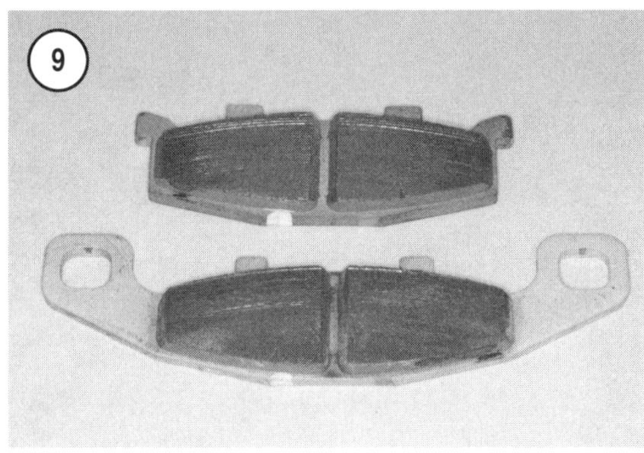

pistons do not move smoothly without sticking, disassemble and service the caliper as described in this chapter.

d. Constantly monitor the fluid level in the reservoir so brake fluid does not overflow. Remove brake fluid if necessary.

e. Remove and discard the old inboard pad.

7. Make sure the stopper springs (B, **Figure 8**) are securely installed on the caliper holder.

8. Install the pad spring (A, **Figure 8**) into the caliper.

9. Fit the outboard brake pad (**Figure 7**) into the caliper so the pad's ears sit beneath the stopper springs. The pad's backing plate must face the pistons.

10. Press the caliper holder (A, **Figure 6**) toward the pistons until the holder bottoms against the housing.

11. Fit one ear of the inboard pad over a post on the caliper holder and pivot the pad into place (A, **Figure 6**). Pull the pad holder out slightly so its posts engage both holes of the inboard pad.

12. Lower the caliper onto the brake disc. Be careful not to damage the leading edges of the brake pads during installation.

13. Install the caliper bolts (A, **Figure 5**) and torque them to 32 N•m (24 ft.-lb.).

14. Support the motorcycle with the front wheel off the ground. Spin the wheel and pump the brake lever until the pads are seated against the disc.

WARNING
Use brake fluid clearly marked DOT 4 from a sealed container. Other types may vaporize and cause brake failure. Always use the same brand of brake fluid. Do not intermix brake fluids. Many brands are not compatible with one another.

15. Check the fluid level in the master cylinder reservoir. Add brake fluid as necessary to correct the fluid level. Install the diaphragm and top cover.

WARNING
Do not ride the motorcycle until you are sure the brakes are operating correctly with full hydraulic advantage. If necessary, bleed the brakes as described in this chapter.

Brake Pad Inspection

1. Inspect the brake pads (**Figure 9**) by performing the following:

a. Inspect the friction material for light surface dirt, grease and oil contamination. Remove light contamination with sandpaper. If contamination has penetrated the surface, replace the brake pads.

   b. Inspect the brake pads for excessive wear or damage. Replace the brake pads if they are worn to the service limit (**Figure 10**).
   c. Inspect the friction material for uneven wear, damage or contamination. Both pads should show approximately the same amount of wear. If the pads are wearing unevenly, the caliper may not be operating correctly.
   d. Inspect the metal plate on the back of each pad for corrosion and damage.

NOTE
Cleaning the brake disc is especially important if new pads are being installed. Many brake pad compounds are not compatible.

2. Use brake parts cleaner and a fine grade emery cloth to remove all road debris and brake pad residue from the brake disc surface.
3. Inspect the brake disc as described in this chapter.
4. Check the friction surface of the new pads for any foreign matter or manufacturing residue. If necessary, clean the pads with an aerosol brake cleaner.
5. Check the pad spring (**Figure 11**) for wear or fatigue. Replace the pad spring if it shows any sign of damage or excessive wear.

Rear Pad Replacement

1. Remove the saddlebag from the right side.
2. Remove the muffler from the right side (Chapter Four).
3. Remove the caliper bolts (A, **Figure 12**) and rotate the caliper off the brake disc.
4. Remove the outboard pad from the caliper (**Figure 13**).
5. Press the caliper holder toward the piston until the inboard pad clears the posts on the holder (**Figure 14**) and remove the inboard pad.
6. Remove the pad spring from the caliper.
7. Inspect the brake pads as described in this chapter.
8. When new pads are installed in the caliper, the master cylinder brake fluid level rises as the caliper pistons are repositioned. Perform the following:
   a. Clean all dirt and debris from the top of the master cylinder.
   b. Remove the master cylinder top cover and the diaphragm from the master cylinder.

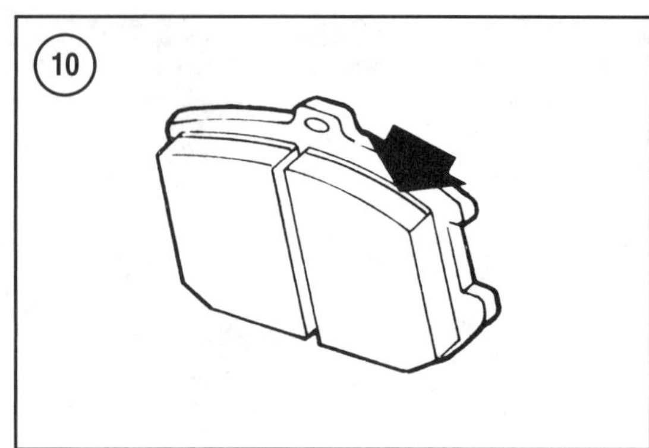

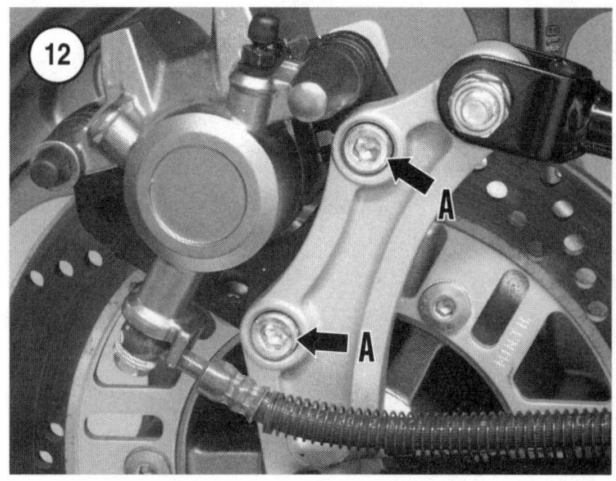

   c. Set the old inboard pad into the caliper. Slowly push the pad toward the caliper until the piston bottoms. If the piston does not move smoothly without sticking, disassemble and service the caliper as described in this chapter.
   d. Constantly monitor the fluid level in the reservoir so brake fluid does not overflow. Remove brake fluid if necessary.
   e. Remove and discard the old inboard pad.

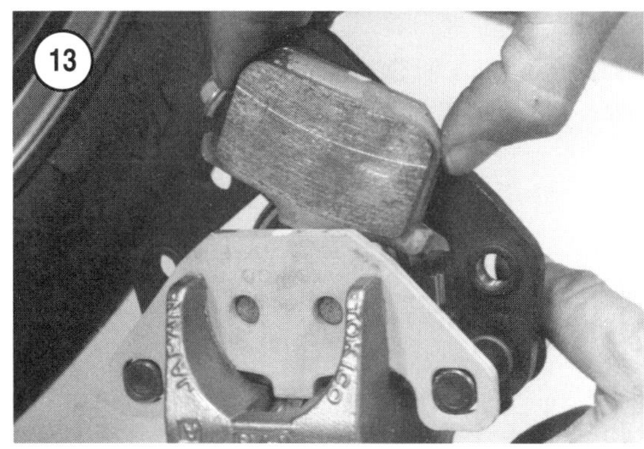

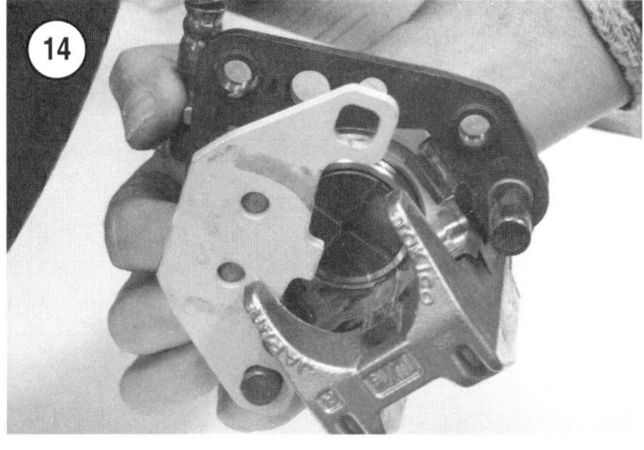

9. If necessary, install a new pad spring into the caliper.
10. Push the caliper holder toward the piston until the holder bottoms against the housing.
11. Set one ear of the inboard piston onto a holder post (**Figure 14**) and install the pad.
12. Set the outboard brake pad (**Figure 13**) into the caliper. The pad's backing plate must face the piston.
13. Pull the caliper holder out slightly until its posts engage the holes in the ears of the inboard pad.
14. Lower the caliper onto the brake disc. Be careful not to damage the leading edges of the brake pads during installation.
15. Align the mounting holes on the caliper holder with those on the bracket and install the caliper bolts (A, **Figure 12**). Torque the bolt to 34 N•m (25 (ft.-lb.).
16. Support the motorcycle with the front wheel off the ground. Spin the wheel and pump the brake lever until the pads are seated against the disc.

WARNING
Use brake fluid clearly marked DOT 4 from a sealed container. Other types may vaporize and cause brake failure. Always use the same brand of brake fluid. Do not intermix brake fluids. Many brands are not compatible with one another.

17. Check the fluid level in the master cylinder reservoir. Add brake fluid as necessary to correct the fluid level. Install the diaphragm and top cover.

WARNING
Do not ride the motorcycle until you are sure the brakes are operating correctly with full hydraulic advantage. If necessary, bleed the brakes as described in this chapter.

FRONT BRAKE CALIPERS

Removal/Installation

Two types of front calipers have been used on the Concours. A single piston caliper is found on 1986-1993 models, dual piston calipers on 1994-on models. The following photographs show the removal of a dual piston caliper. The procedure is identical for single piston calipers.

1. Securely support the motorcycle on a level surface.

NOTE
If the brake lever is applied while a caliper is off the front wheel, both calipers must be disassembled to reseat the caliper pistons and the brakes must be bled. A wooden block between the brake lever and the handlebar prevents an accidental application of the brakes.

2. Insert a wooden block between the brake lever and the handlebar grip. Use a rubber band to hold the block in place.
3. Drain the brake fluid as described in this chapter.
4. Remove the banjo bolt (B, **Figure 5**) from the caliper. Remove and discard the two copper washers, one on each side of the brake hose fitting. New washers must be used during installation.
5. Insert the end of the brake hose into a reclosable plastic bag so brake fluid will not dribble onto the motorcycle.

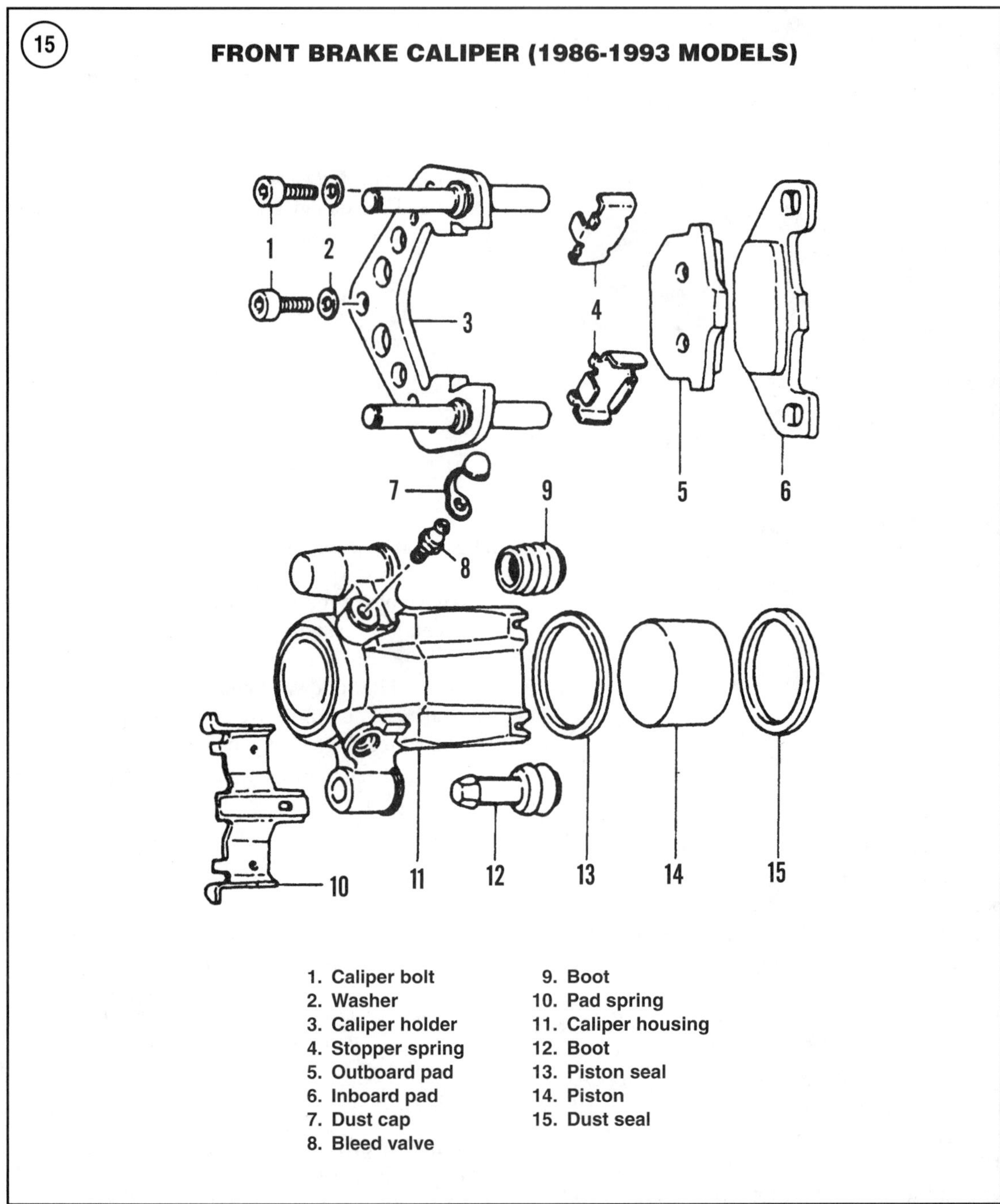

6. Remove the caliper bolts (A, **Figure 5**) and rotate the caliper off the brake disc.

7. Disassemble the caliper as described in this chapter.

8. Installation is the reverse of removal. Note the following:

a. Torque the caliper bolts (A, **Figure 5**) to 32 N•m (24 ft.-lb.).

b. Position the brake hose fitting so its neck sits on the inboard side of the caliper indexing post. See **Figure 5**.

c. Install a new copper washer on each side of the brake hose fitting.

16

17

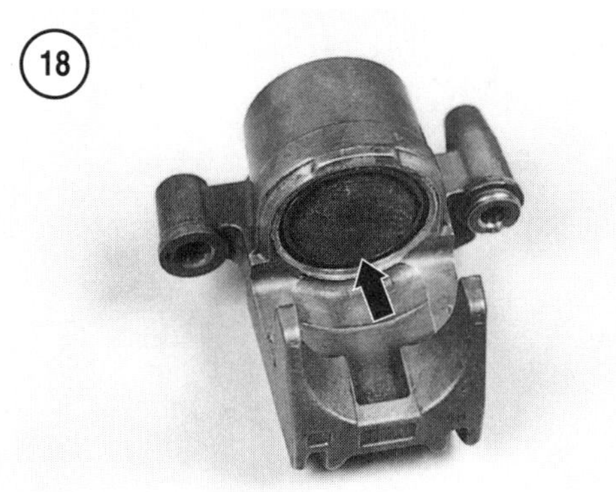

18

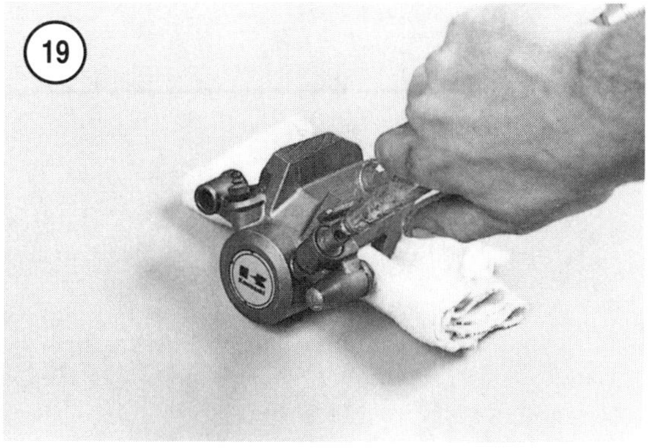

19

20

d. Torque the banjo bolt to 25 N•m (18 ft.-lb.).

Disassembly (1986-1993 Models)

NOTE
Compressed air is required to completely disassemble the caliper.

Refer to **Figure 15**.

1. Remove the brake caliper and brake pads as described in this chapter.
2. Remove the pad spring from the caliper.
3. Slide the caliper holder (**Figure 16**) from the boots in the caliper housing.
4. Remove the stopper springs from the caliper holder.
5. Pull the rubber boots (**Figure 17**) from the caliper.

WARNING
*Keep your fingers and hands away from the caliper bore when removing the piston (**Figure 18**). It could blow out of the bore with considerable force and crush your fingers.*

6. Pad the piston with shop rags or a wooden block as shown in **Figure 19**. Apply compressed air through the brake hose port and blow the piston (**Figure 20**) out of the bore.
7. Remove the dust seal (**Figure 21**) and the piston seal (**Figure 22**) from the caliper bore. Discard the seals. New ones must be installed during assembly.
8. Inspect the caliper parts as described in *Inspection* in this section.

Assembly (1986-1993 Models)

1. Soak the new piston and dust seals in clean DOT 4 brake fluid.
2. Coat the caliper cylinder with clean DOT 4 brake fluid.
3. Install the piston seal (A, **Figure 23**) into the inside groove in the cylinder (**Figure 22**).
4. Seat the dust seal (B, **Figure 23**) into the outer groove in the cylinder (**Figure 21**).
5. Apply clean DOT 4 brake fluid to the outside of the piston.
6. Align the piston with the cylinder as shown in **Figure 20** and press the piston into the cylinder until the piston bottoms.
7. Install the rubber boots (**Figure 17**) into the caliper housing.
8. Apply a light coat of brake grease to the sliding shafts in the caliper holder. Align the sliding shafts with the rubber boots and slide the shafts into the boots. Remove any excess grease so it will not contaminate the brake pads.
9. Install a stopper spring onto each end of the caliper holder.
10. Install the pad spring into the caliper housing.
11. Install the brake pads as described earlier in this chapter.

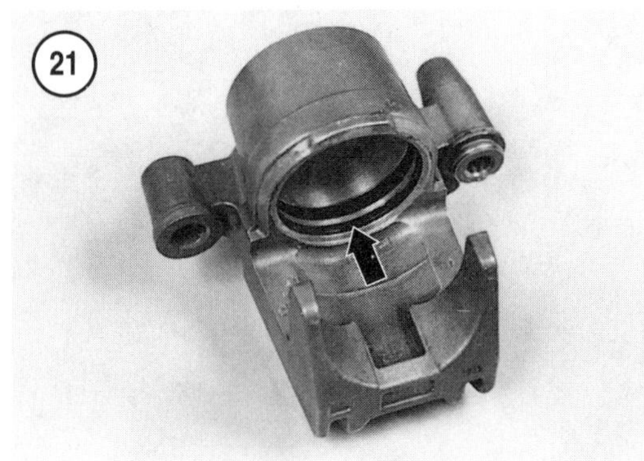

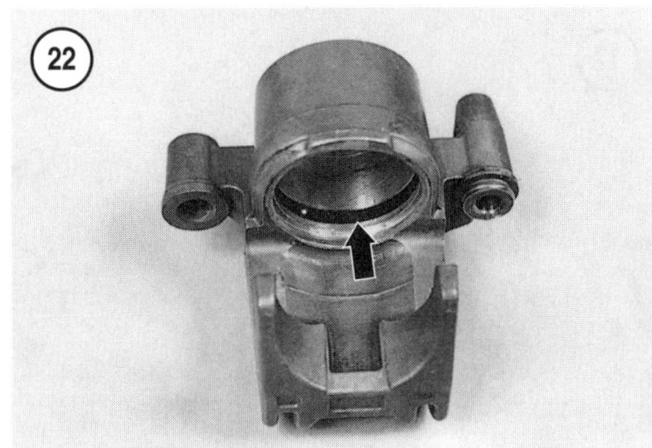

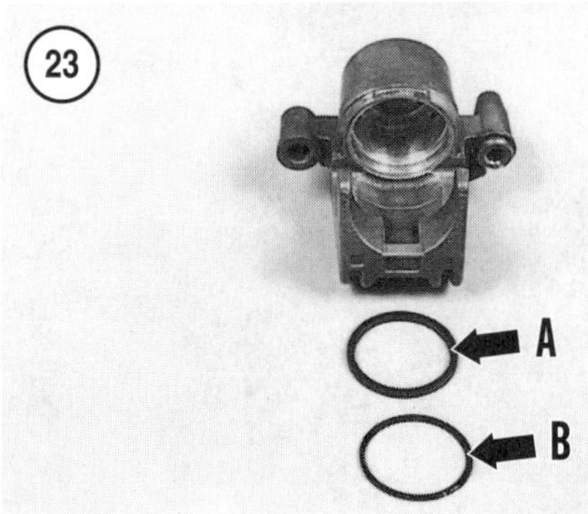

Inspection (1986-1993 Models)

When inspecting a brake caliper, replace any part that is worn, damaged or exceeds the service limit specified in **Table 1**.

1. Clean all parts (except brake pads) with clean DOT 4 brake fluid. Place the cleaned parts on a lint-free cloth.
2. Inspect the caliper housing by performing the following:
   a. Inspect the caliper cylinder (**Figure 24**) for scratches, scoring, corrosion or other signs of wear.
   b. Inspect the seal grooves in the cylinder for damage or corrosion.
   c. Inspect the caliper housing for scratches, corrosion or other signs of damage. Replace the caliper assembly if necessary.
3. Inspect the piston (**Figure 25**) for scratches, scoring or other damage. If rusty or corroded, replace the pistons.

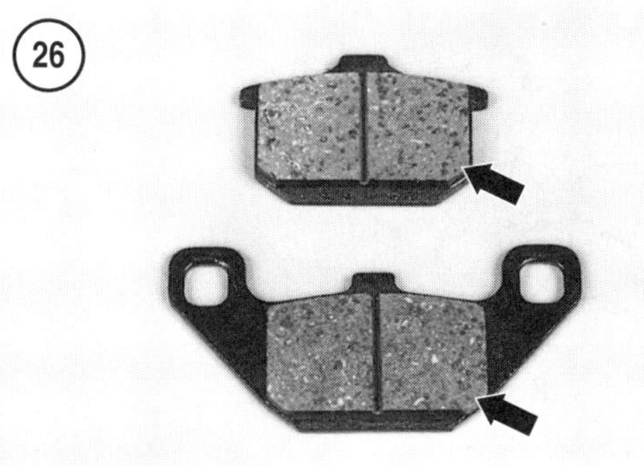

27

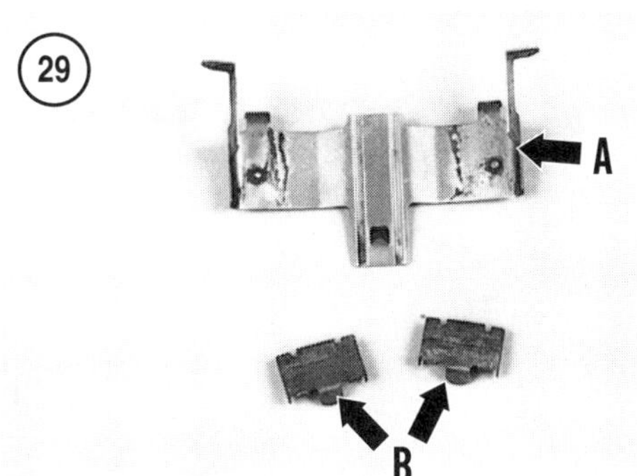

4. Measure the brake pad friction material (**Figure 26**) with a caliper. Replace both brake pads if either is worn to the service limit (**Table 1**). When servicing a front caliper, replace both brake pads in both front calipers.

5. Inspect the caliper holder (**Figure 27**) for cracks or other damage. Pay particular attention to the mounting holes. Make sure they are not cracked or elongated.

6. Check the rubber boots (**Figure 28**) for tears or damage. If either boot is damaged, replace both boots and the caliper holder.

7. Inspect the pad spring (A, **Figure 29**) and stopper springs (B) for cracks, wear or other signs of fatigue. Replace both stopper springs as a set.

8. Inspect the threads in the brake hose fitting. The threads must be clean and in good condition. Replace the caliper as necessary

9. Remove the bleed valve from caliper body. Apply compressed air to the opening and make sure it is clear. If necessary, clean out the bleed screw with fresh brake fluid.

10. Inspect the fluid opening in the base of each cylinder bore. Apply compressed air to the opening and make sure it is clear. Clean out the opening with fresh brake fluid if necessary.

11. Inspect the threads of the banjo bolt and the caliper bolts for wear or damage. Clean up any minor thread damage. Replace the bolts and the caliper assembly if necessary.

Disassembly (1994-on Models)

Refer to **Figure 30**.

1. Remove the brake caliper and the brake pads as described in this chapter.

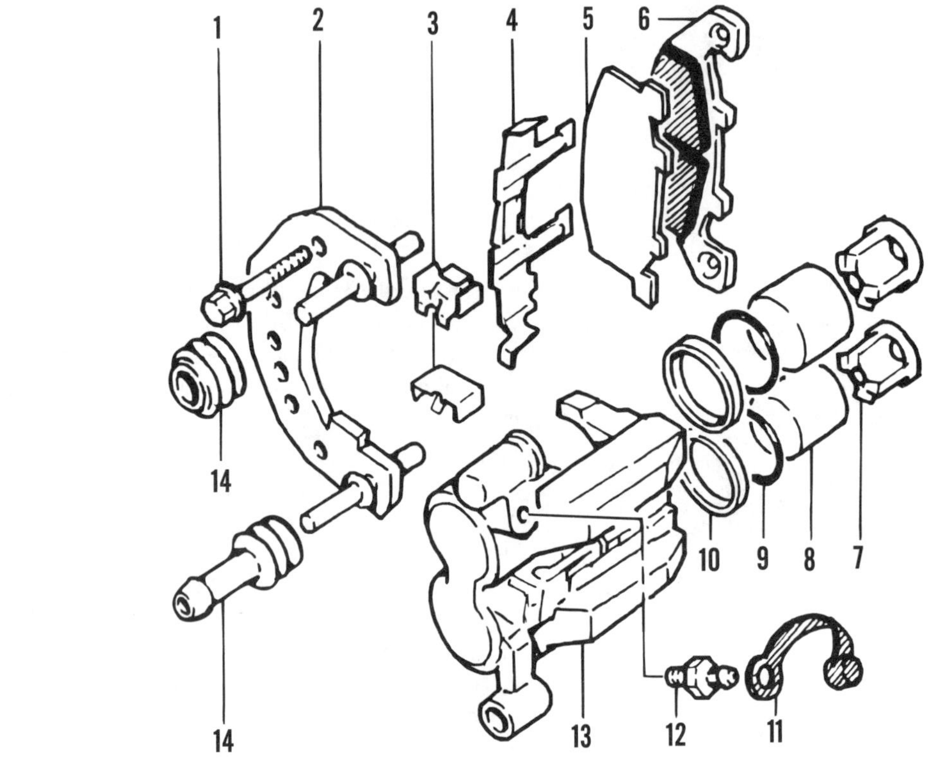

30
FRONT BRAKE CALIPER (1994-ON MODELS)
1
2
3
4
5
6
14
10
9
8
7
14
13
12
11

1. Caliper bolt
2. Caliper holder
3. Stopper spring
4. Pad spring
5. Outboard pad
6. Inboard pad
7. Insulator
8. Piston
9. Dust seal
10. Piston seal
11. Dust cap
12. Bleed valve
13. Caliper housing
14. Boot

2. Slide the caliper holder (A, **Figure 31**) from the boots in the caliper housing.
3. Remove the stopper springs from the caliper holder.
4. Pull the rubber boots (A, **Figure 32**) from the caliper.
5. Remove the insulator (B, **Figure 32**) from each piston.

WARNING
Keep your fingers and hands away from the caliper bore when removing

31
B
A

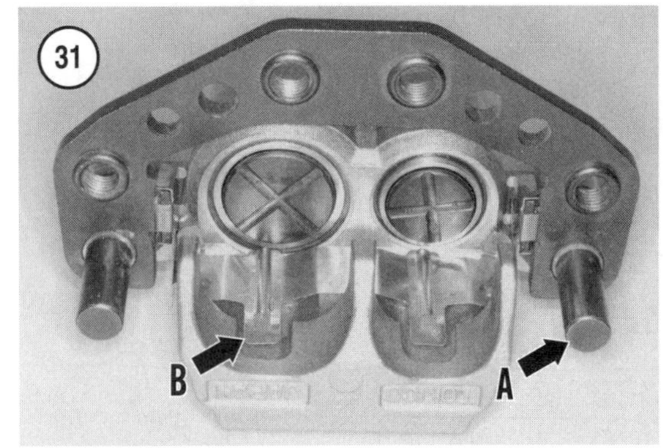

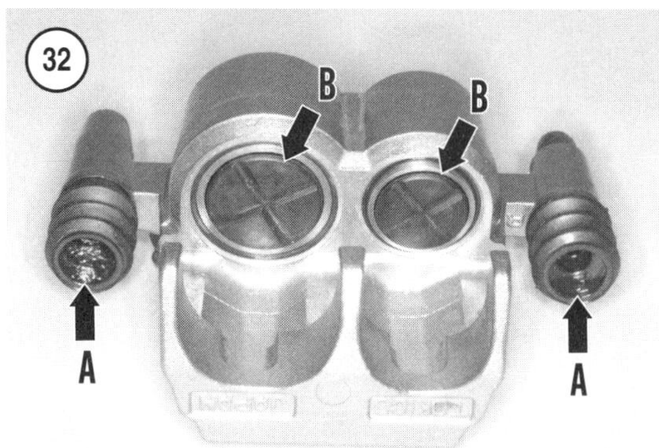

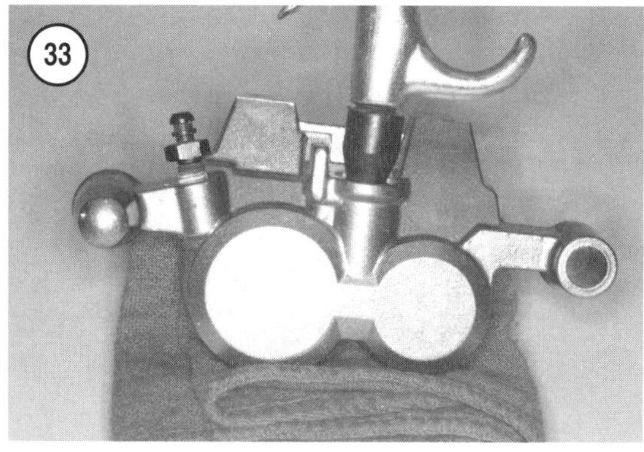

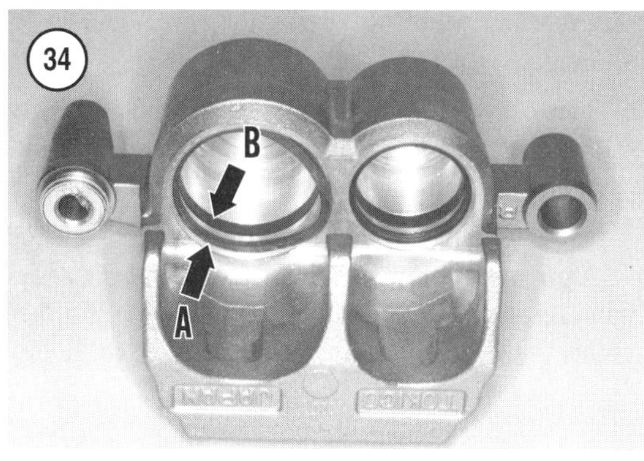

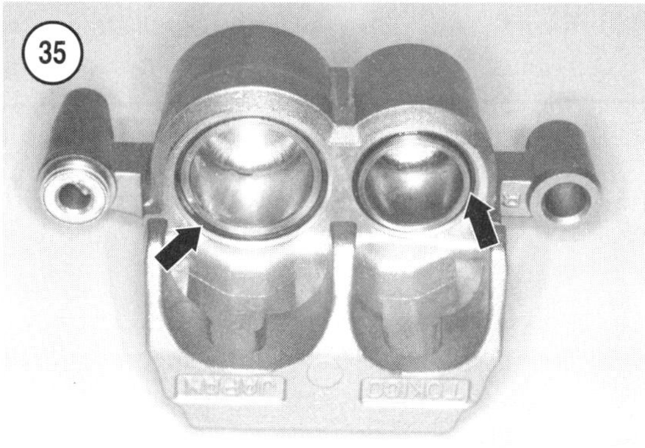

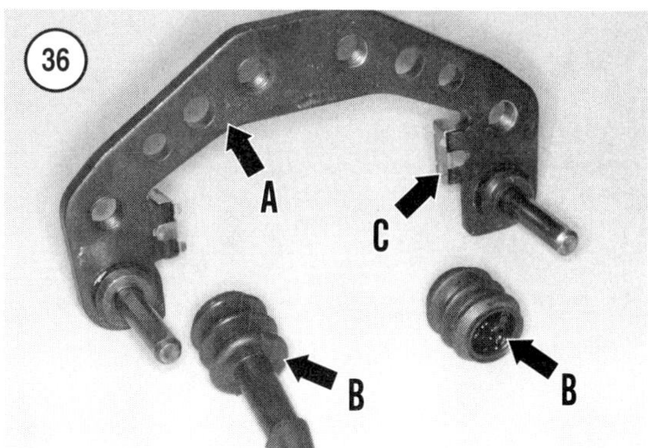

*the piston (**Figure 33**). It could blow out of the bore with considerable force and crush your fingers.*

6. Pad the piston with shop rags or a wooden block. Apply compressed air through the brake hose port (**Figure 33**) and blow the pistons out of the cylinder bores.
7. Remove the dust seal (A, **Figure 34**) and the piston seal (B) from their grooves in each cylinder. Discard the seals. New ones must be installed during assembly.
8. Inspect the caliper parts as described in *Inspection* in this section.

Assembly (1994-on Models)

1. Soak the new piston and dust seals in clean DOT 4 brake fluid.
2. Coat the caliper cylinder with clean DOT 4 brake fluid.
3. Install the piston seal (B, **Figure 34**) into the inner groove in the cylinder and the dust seal into the outer groove (A).
4. Apply clean DOT 4 brake fluid to the outside of the piston.
5. Slide the pistons into the cylinders (**Figure 35**) so their open sides face out. Make sure each piston bottoms in its cylinder.
6. Install the insulators (B, **Figure 32**) into the pistons until the insulators bottom in their pistons.
7. Install the boots (A, **Figure 32**) into the receivers in the caliper. The long boot goes into the open receiver.
8. Install the stopper springs (C, **Figure 36**) on the caliper holder.

9. Apply a light coat of brake grease to the sliding shafts in the caliper holder. Align the sliding shafts with the rubber boots and slide the shafts into the boots. Remove any excess grease so it will not contaminate the brake pads.
10. Install the pad spring (B, **Figure 31**) into the caliper housing.
11. Install the brake pads as described in this chapter.

Inspection (1994-on Models)

When inspecting a brake caliper, replace any part that is worn, damaged or exceeds the service limit specified in **Table 1**.

1. Clean all parts (except brake pads) with clean DOT 4 brake fluid. Place the cleaned parts on a lint-free cloth.
2. Inspect the caliper housing by performing the following:
   a. Inspect the caliper cylinders (**Figure 37**) for scratches, scoring, corrosion or other signs of wear.
   b. Inspect the seal grooves in the cylinders for damage or corrosion.
   c. Inspect the caliper housing for scratches, corrosion or other signs of damage. Replace the caliper if necessary.
3. Inspect the pistons (**Figure 38**) for scratches, scoring or other damage. If rusty or corroded, replace the pistons.
4. Measure the brake pad friction material with a vernier caliper. Replace both brake pads in both front calipers if either is worn to the service limit (**Table 1**).
5. Inspect the caliper holder (A, **Figure 36**) for cracks or other damage. Pay particular attention to

39

the mounting holds. Make sure they are not cracked or elongated.

6. Check the rubber boots (B, **Figure 36**) for tears or damage. If either boot is damaged, replace both boots and the caliper holder.

7. Inspect the pad spring and both stopper springs (C, **Figure 36**) for cracks, wear or other signs of fatigue. Replace the stopper springs as a set if either requires replacement.

8. Inspect the insulators (**Figure 39**) for excessive wear or signs of heat damage. Replace as necessary.

9. Inspect the threads in the brake hose fitting. The threads must be clean and in good condition. Replace the caliper as necessary.

10. Remove the bleed valve from caliper body. Apply compressed air to the opening and make sure it is clear. If necessary, clean out the bleed valve with fresh brake fluid.

11. Inspect the fluid opening in the base of each cylinder bore. Apply compressed air to the opening and make sure it is clear. Clean out the opening with fresh brake fluid if necessary.

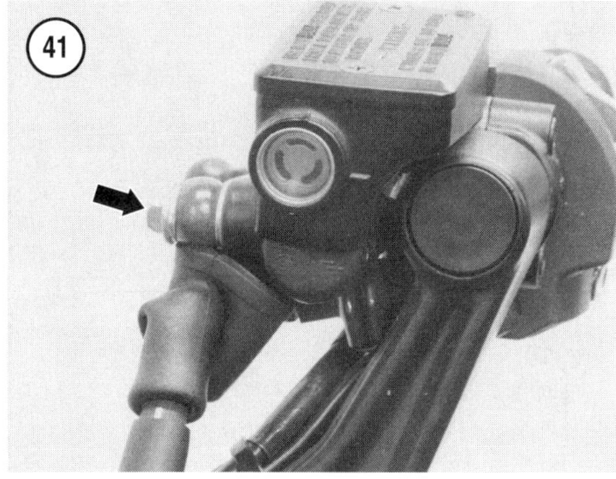

12. Inspect the threads of the banjo bolt and the caliper bolts for wear or damage. Clean up any minor thread damage. Replace the bolts and the caliper assembly if necessary.

FRONT BRAKE MASTER CYLINDER

Removal/Installation

CAUTION
Brake fluid will damage the finish of any painted, plated or plastic surface. Wash spilled from these surfaces immediately. Use soapy water and rinse the area completely.

1. Remove the lower, middle and front fairings (Chapter Fifteen) to protect them from brake fluid spills.
2. Securely support the motorcycle on a level surface.
3. Protect the front fender with a heavy cloth or plastic tarp.

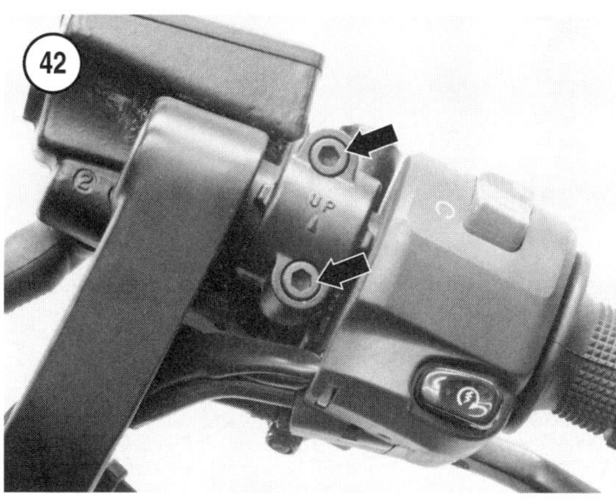

4. Drain the brake fluid from the front brakes as described in this chapter.
5. Disconnect the electrical leads (A, **Figure 40**) from the front brake light switch.
6. Pull back the boot (B, **Figure 40**) from the brake hose fitting.
7. Place a rag beneath the banjo bolt (**Figure 41**) and remove the bolt from the master cylinder reservoir. Separate the brake hose from the master cylinder. Remove and discard the two copper washers from either side of the hose fitting. New washers must be installed during assembly.
8. Place the loose end of the brake hose into a reclosable plastic bag so brake fluid will not dribble onto the motorcycle. Tie the loose end of the hose up to the handlebar.
9. Remove the front master cylinder clamp bolts (**Figure 42**) and pull the clamp. Lower the master cylinder from the handlebar.
10. Drain any residual brake fluid from the master cylinder reservoir. Dispose of fluid properly.
11. If the master cylinder will not to be serviced, place it in a reclosable plastic bag to protect it from foreign matter.
12. Installation is the reverse of removal. Pay attention to the following:
   a. Set the front master cylinder onto the right handlebar.
   b. Position the clamp so its arrow points up and install the front master cylinder clamp bolts (**Figure 42**). Tighten the clamp bolts to 8.8 N•m (78 in.-lb.). Torque the upper clamp bolt first and then torque the lower bolt.
   c. Install the brake hose onto the master cylinder. Install a new copper washer onto each

(43)

FRONT BRAKE MASTER CYLINDER

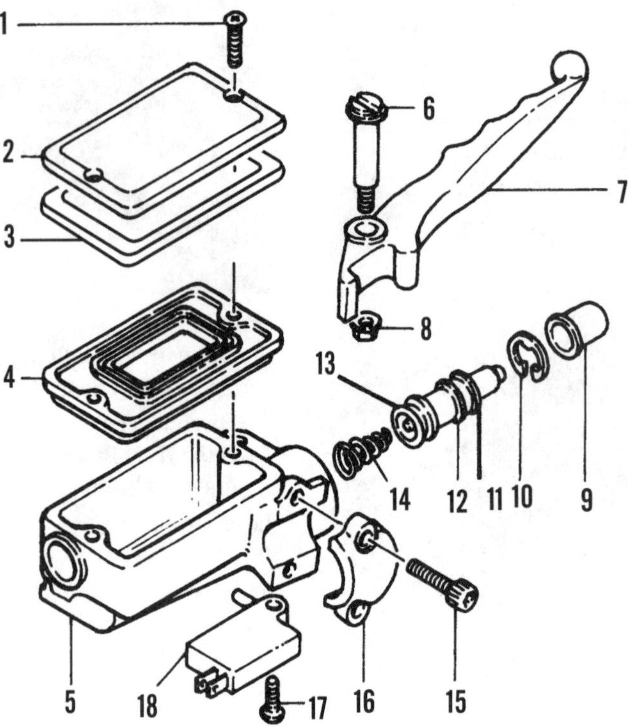

1. Screw
2. Cover
3. Diaphragm plate (1992-on models)
4. Diaphragm
5. Master cylinder body
6. Pivot bolt
7. Brake lever
8. Nut
9. Boot
10. Snap ring
11. Piston
12. Secondary cup
13. Primary cup
14. Spring
15. Clamp bolt
16. Clamp
17. Screw
18. Brake light switch

(44)

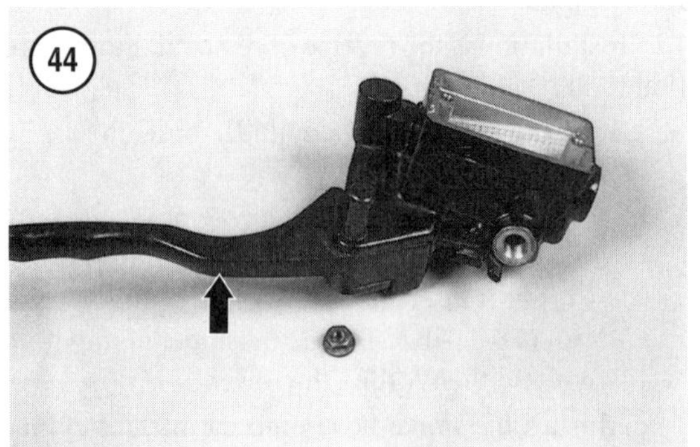

(45)

46

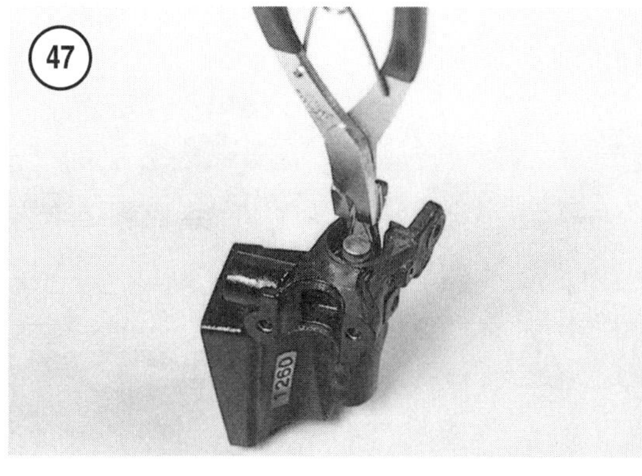

47

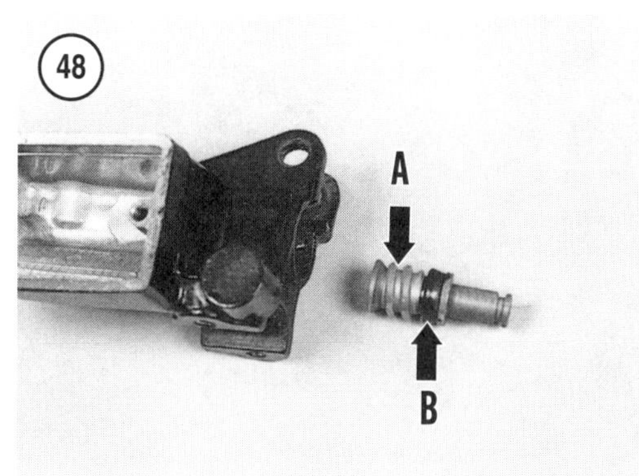

48

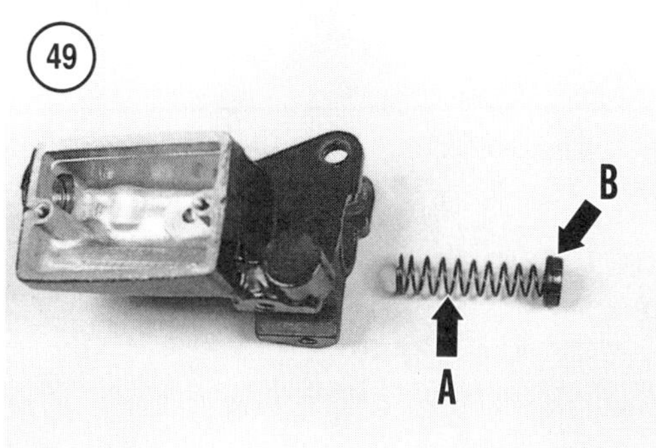

49

side of the hose fitting and torque the banjo bolt (**Figure 41**) to 25 N•m (18 ft.-lb.).

d. Reconnect the electrical connectors (A, **Figure 40**) to the front brake light switch.

WARNING
Do not ride the motorcycle until the front and rear brakes operate with full hydraulic advantage.

e. Refill the master cylinder reservoir with fresh DOT 4 brake fluid and bleed the brake system as described in this chapter.

Disassembly

Refer to **Figure 43**.

1. Remove the master cylinder as described in this section.
2. If still in place, remove the cover, diaphragm plate (1992-on models) and the diaphragm. Pour out and discard any the remaining brake fluid.
3. Remove the nut from the lever pivot bolt. Turn out the pivot bolt and pull the brake lever (**Figure 44**) from its boss on the master cylinder body.
4. If necessary, remove the mounting screw (A, **Figure 45**) and lift the front brake switch (B) from the master cylinder body.
5. Roll the boot (**Figure 46**) from the master cylinder bore.
6. Remove the snap ring (**Figure 47**) from its groove in the cylinder bore.
7. Remove the piston (A, **Figure 48**) with the secondary cup (B). Do not remove the secondary cup from the piston. The cup will be destroyed.
8. Remove the spring (A, **Figure 49**) with the primary cup (B).

Assembly

1. Soak the new cups and the new master piston in fresh DOT 4 brake fluid for at least 15 minutes to make them pliable. Coat the inside of the cylinder bore with fresh brake fluid.
2. Fit the new primary cup (B, **Figure 49**) onto the spring (A). Insert the spring and primary cup assembly spring first into the master cylinder.

CAUTION
When installing the piston and secondary cup assembly, do not allow the sec-

ondary cup to turn inside out. This will damage the cup and allow brake fluid to leak within the cylinder bore.

3. Install the piston and secondary cup assembly (**Figure 48**) into the cylinder.
4. Press the piston into the bore and secure it in place with a new snap ring (**Figure 47**). Seat the snap ring in the groove inside the cylinder bore.
5. Lubricate the boot with fresh DOT 4 brake fluid and carefully roll the boot over the piston so the boot seals the master cylinder bore. See **Figure 46**.
6. If removed, fit the brake light switch (B, **Figure 45**) to the bottom of the master cylinder reservoir. Secure the switch in place with the screw (A).
7. Apply a light coat of grease to the brake lever bushing (A, **Figure 50**) and to the piston-mating surface (B) on the lever.
8. Slide the brake lever into place on the master cylinder body.
9. Lightly lubricate the pivot bolt with grease and secure the brake lever to the body with the pivot bolt (**Figure 44**). Install the nut and torque the brake lever pivot nut to 5.9 N•m (52 in.-lb.).
10. Install the diaphragm, diaphragm plate (1992-on models) and cover after the master cylinder has been installed on the handlebar.

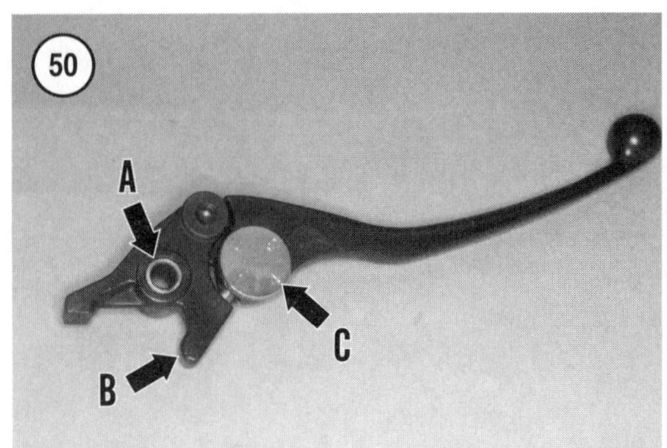

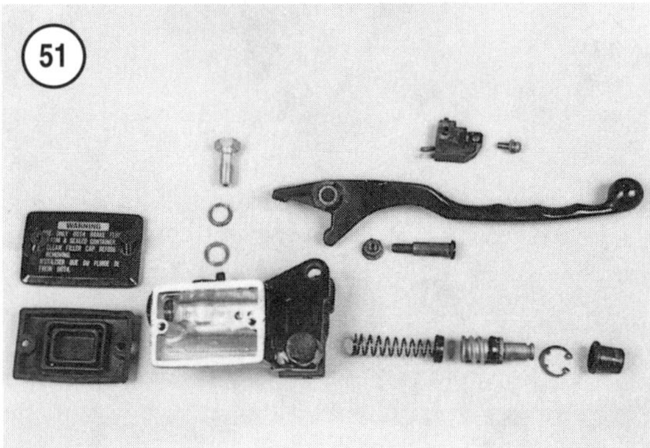

Inspection

1. Clean all parts (**Figure 51**) in fresh DOT 4 brake fluid. Place the master cylinder components on a clean, lint-free cloth.
2. Inspect the cylinder bore and piston contact surfaces for scratches, wear or other signs of damage. Replace the master cylinder body if necessary.
3. Inspect the inside of the reservoir for scratches, wear or other signs of damage. Replace the master cylinder body if necessary.
4. Make sure the passages in the bottom of the brake fluid reservoir (**Figure 52**) are clear.

NOTE
The spring, primary cup, piston and secondary cup are sold as the master piston kit. If any part is worn or damaged, they all must be replaced.

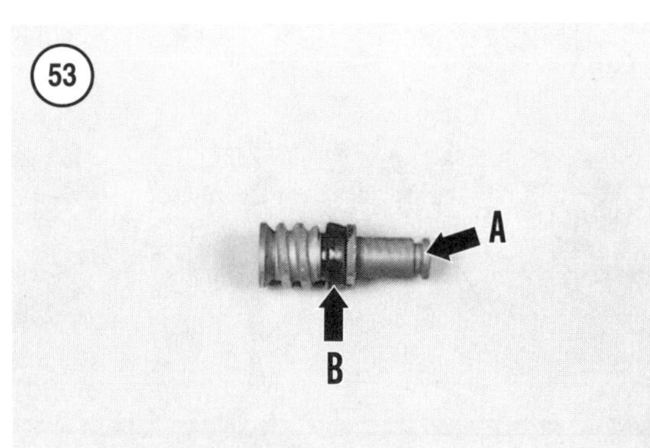

5. Check the end of the piston (A, **Figure 53**) for wear. Check the secondary cup (B, **Figure 53**) for

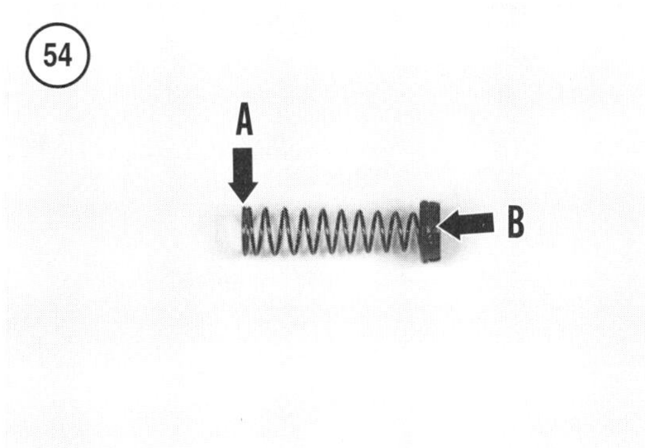

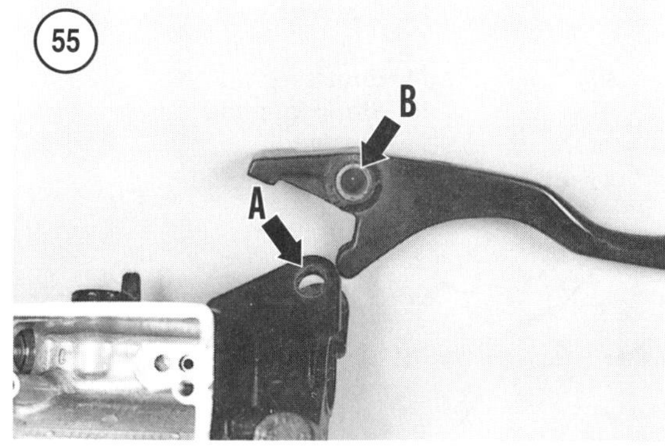

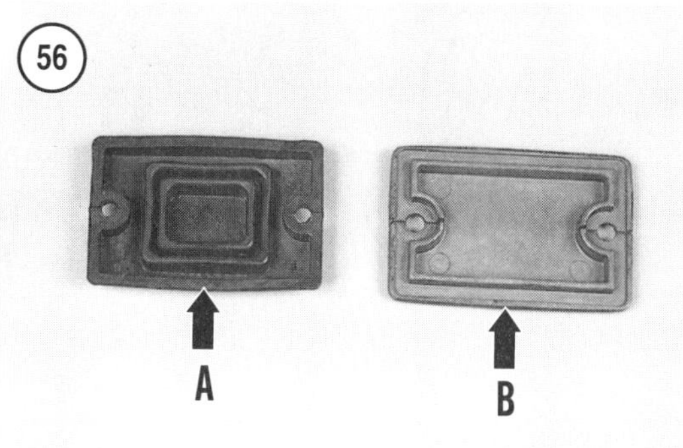

damage, softness or swelling. Install the master piston kit if necessary.

6. Check the spring (A, **Figure 54**) for fatigue. Check the primary cup (B, **Figure 54**) for damage, softness or swelling. Install the master piston kit if necessary.

7. On 1995-on models, check the brake lever adjuster (C, **Figure 50**) for signs of wear.

8. Inspect the brake lever spring, where used. Replace the spring if it is worn or shows signs of fatigue.

9. Inspect the brake lever pivot hole in the master cylinder boss (A, **Figure 55**) and in the brake lever (B). Replace either part if the pivot is worn or elongated.

10. Check the reservoir diaphragm (A, **Figure 56**), cover (B) and diaphragm plate (1992-on models) for damage and deterioration. Replace if necessary.

11. Inspect the threads in the master cylinder port (**Figure 57**). If the threads are damaged or partially stripped, replace the master cylinder body.

12. Inspect the threads of the banjo bolt. Replace the bolt if the threads are worn or damaged.

REAR BRAKE CALIPER

Removal/Installation

Refer to **Figure 58**.

1. Drain the brake fluid as described in this chapter.
2. Remove the banjo bolt (A, **Figure 59**) from the caliper. Remove and discard the two copper washers, one on each side of the brake hose fitting. New washers must be used during installation.
3. Insert the end of the brake hose into a reclosable plastic bag so brake fluid will not dribble onto the motorcycle.
4. Remove the caliper bolts (B, **Figure 59**) and remove the brake caliper from the disc.
5. Disassemble the caliper as described in this chapter.
6. Installation is the reverse of removal. Note the following:
   a. Torque the caliper bolts (B, **Figure 59**) to 34 N•m (25 ft.-lb.).
   b. Position the brake hose fitting so its neck sits on the inboard side of the caliper indexing post. See **Figure 59**.
   c. Install a new copper washer on each side of the brake hose fitting.
   d. Torque the banjo bolt (A, **Figure 59**) to 25 N•m (18 ft.-lb.).

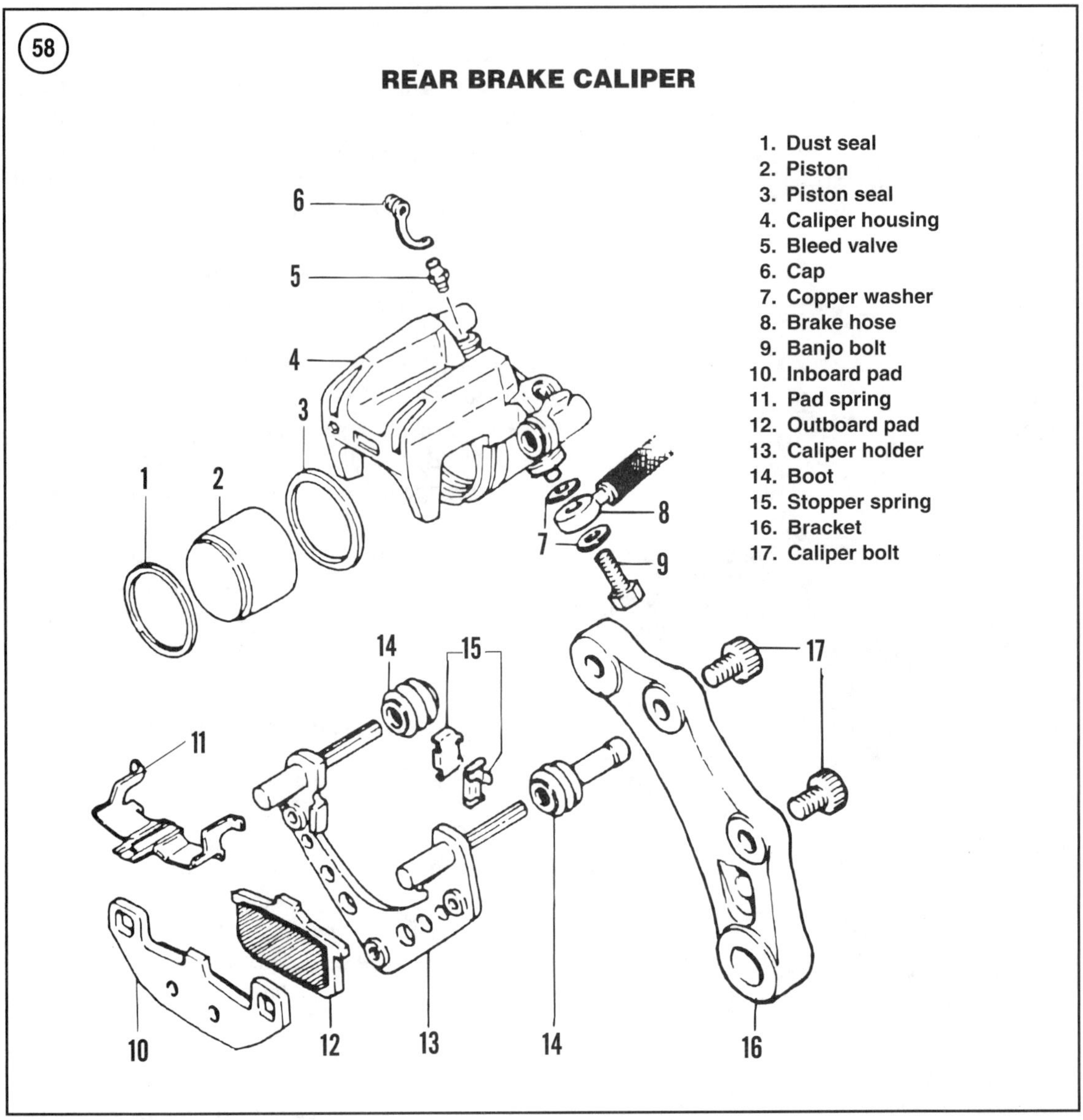

58

REAR BRAKE CALIPER

1. Dust seal
2. Piston
3. Piston seal
4. Caliper housing
5. Bleed valve
6. Cap
7. Copper washer
8. Brake hose
9. Banjo bolt
10. Inboard pad
11. Pad spring
12. Outboard pad
13. Caliper holder
14. Boot
15. Stopper spring
16. Bracket
17. Caliper bolt

Disassembly/Inspection/Assembly

Except for the location of the brake hose port, the rear brake caliper is identical to the front brake caliper used on 1986-1993 models. Refer to the disassembly, inspection and assembly procedures for that caliper in this chapter.

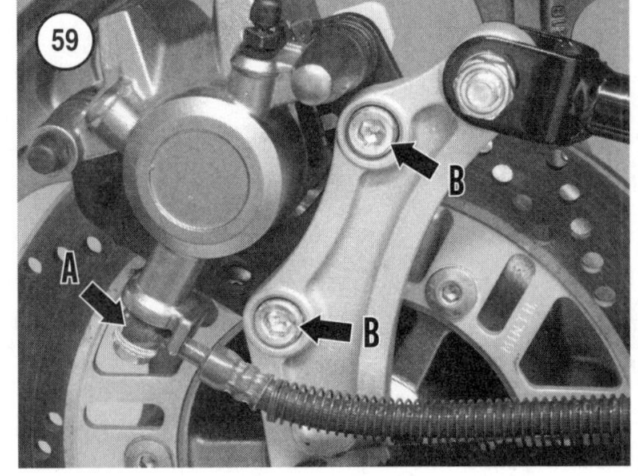

REAR BRAKE MASTER CYLINDER

Removal/Installation

Refer to **Figure 60**.

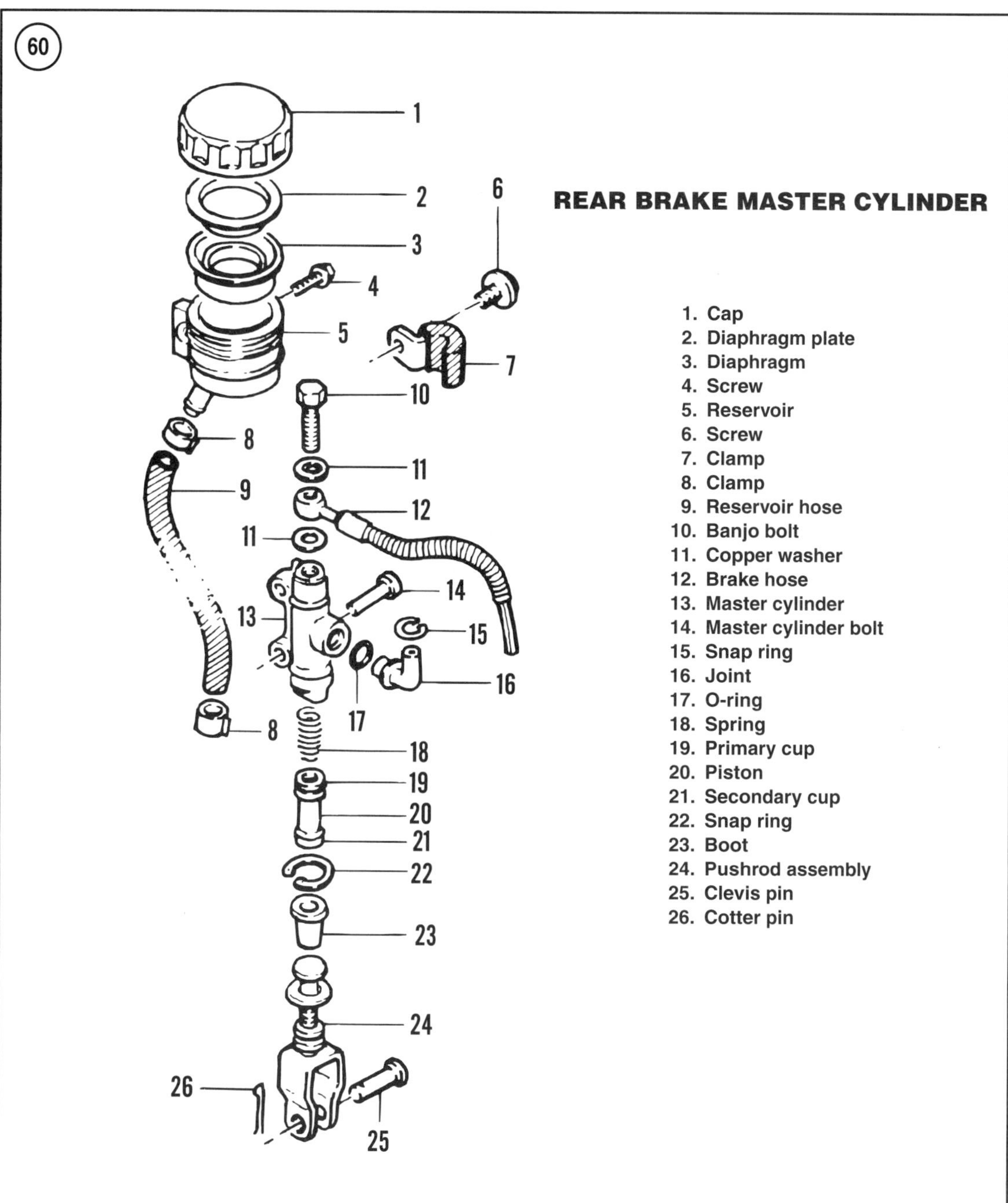

1. Remove the right side cover (Chapter Fifteen).

2. Drain the brake fluid from the rear brakes as described in this chapter.

3. Loosen the hose clamp and separate the reservoir hose from the hose joint on the master cylinder. Secure a sealable plastic bag over the reservoir hose so brake fluid will not dribble on the motorcycle.

4. Remove the banjo bolt and pull the brake hose from the port on the master cylinder. Discard the copper washer that sits on each side of the hose fitting. Insert the brake hose into a sealable plastic bag.

5. Loosen the master cylinder bolts (A, **Figure 61**) now while the footpeg bracket is still on the motorcycle.

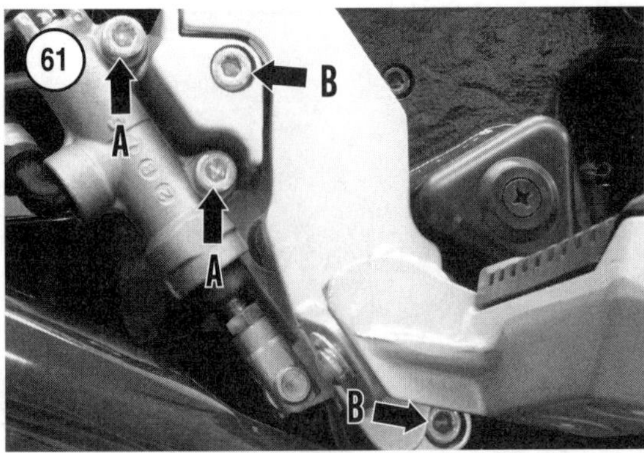

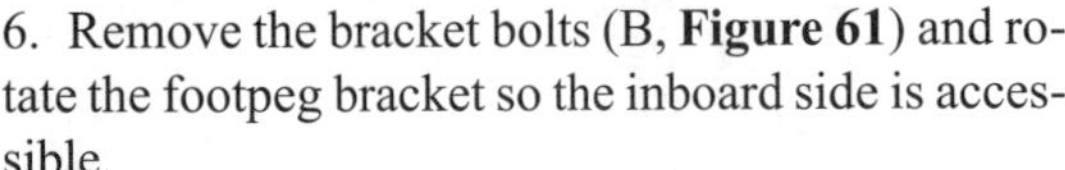

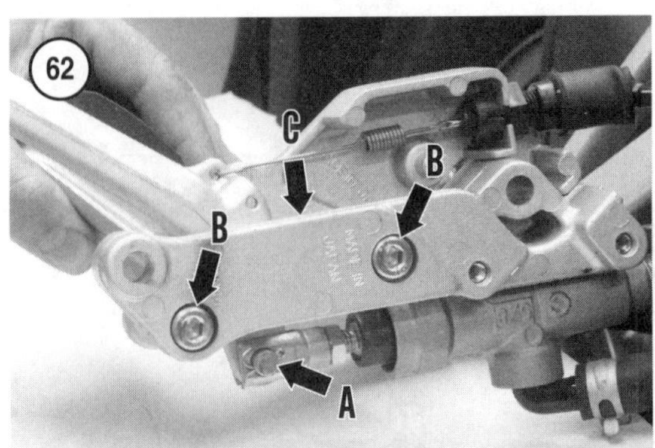

6. Remove the bracket bolts (B, **Figure 61**) and rotate the footpeg bracket so the inboard side is accessible.
7. Remove the cotter pin (A, **Figure 62**), pull the clevis pin and separate the pushrod clevis from the brake pedal.
8. Remove the master cylinder bolts loosened earlier (A, **Figure 61**) and remove the master cylinder from the motorcycle.
9. If necessary, remove the reservoir by performing the following:
   a. Remove the clamp (A, **Figure 63**) that secures the reservoir hose to the frame.
   b. Remove the mounting screw (B, **Figure 63**) and lift the reservoir and hose from the right side of the motorcycle.
10. Installation is the reverse of removal.

WARNING
Do not ride the motorcycle until the front and rear brakes operate with full hydraulic advantage.

   a. Torque the rear master cylinder bolts (A, **Figure 61**) to 23 N•m (17 ft.-lb.).
   b. Position the brake hose so its neck sits on the inboard side of the indexing post on the top of the master cylinder.
   c. Place a new copper washer on each side of the brake hose fitting.
   d. Torque the banjo bolt to 25 N•m (18 ft.-lb.).
   e. Refill the system with fresh DOT 4 brake fluid and bleed the rear brake as described in this chapter.
   f. Measure the pushrod length as described in this section. Adjust the length as necessary.
   g. Adjust the rear brake light switch as described in Chapter Three.

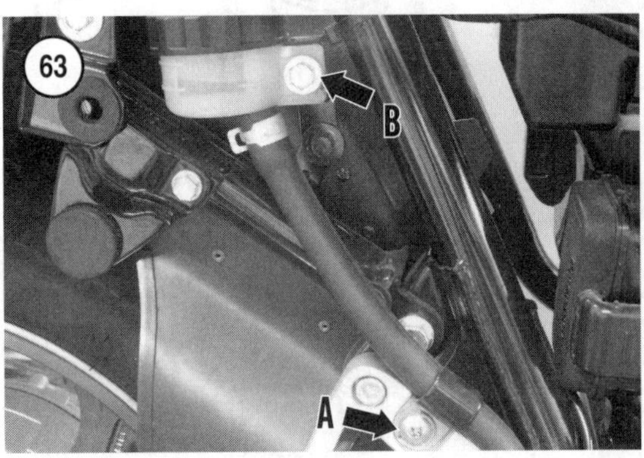

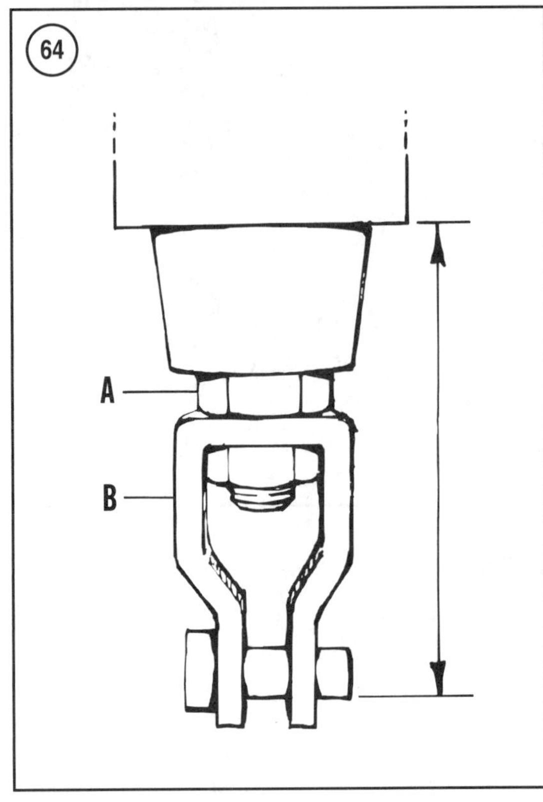

65

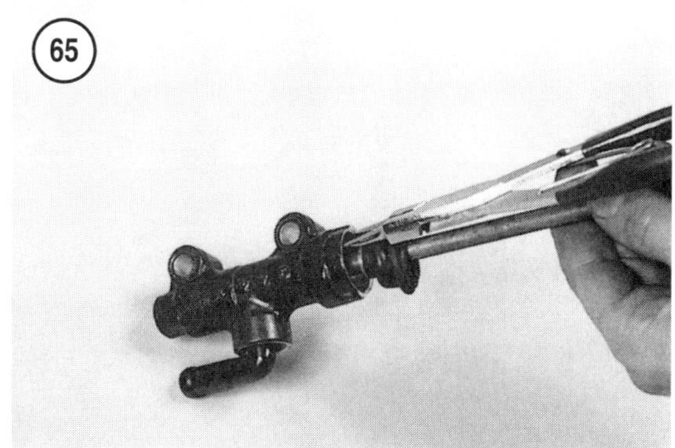

66

67

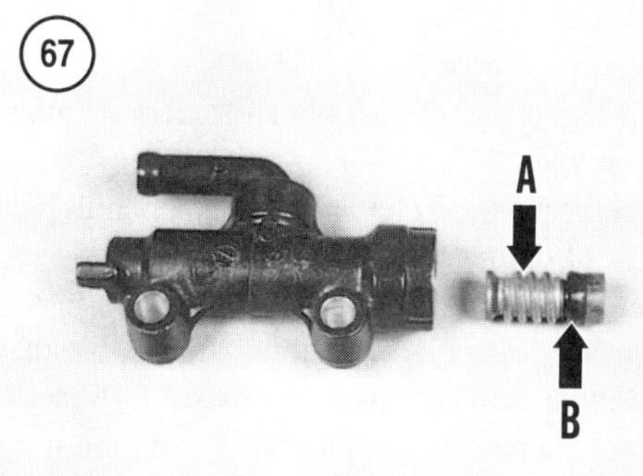

68

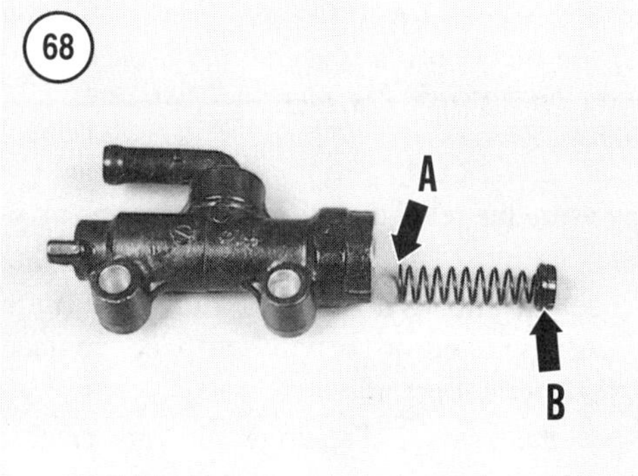

Pushrod Adjustment

1. While the brake pedal is in the released position, measure the distance from the bottom of the clevis pin to the bottom of the master cylinder body. See **Figure 64**. If the measurement is outside the range specified in **Table 1**, continue with Step 2.
2. Remove the bracket bolts (B, **Figure 61**) and rotate the footpeg bracket so the inboard side is accessible.
3. Remove the cotter pin (A, **Figure 62**), pull the clevis pin and separate the pushrod clevis from the brake pedal.
4. Loosen the master cylinder locknut (A, **Figure 64**).
5. Raise or lower the adjust nut by rotating the clevis (B, **Figure 64**) until the rear master cylinder pushrod length is within specification.
6. Tighten the locknut.
7. Secure the pushrod clevis to the brake pedal with the clevis pin and install a new cotter pin (A, **Figure 62**).
8. Fit the brake pedal bracket into place on the right side and tighten the bracket bolts securely.

Disassembly

Refer to **Figure 60**.

1. Remove the rear master cylinder as described above in this section.
2. Slide back the dust boot and remove the snap ring from its groove in the cylinder bore (**Figure 65**).
3. Remove the pushrod assembly (**Figure 66**) from the master cylinder.
4. Remove the piston and secondary cup from the cylinder (**Figure 67**).
5. Remove the spring (A, **Figure 68**) and the primary cup (B).
6. If necessary, remove the snap ring and separate the hose joint from the master cylinder. Discard the hose joint O-ring. A new one must be installed during assembly.
7. Inspect the master cylinder and reservoir as described in this section.

Assembly

1. Soak the primary and secondary cups in brake fluid for at least 15 minutes.

2. Coat the inside of the cylinder with fresh brake fluid prior to assembling the parts.
3. Fit the primary cup (B, **Figure 68**) onto the narrow end of the spring (A) and install the spring and primary cup into the master cylinder.

CAUTION
*When installing the piston, do not allow the secondary cup (B, **Figure 67**) to turn inside out. This will damage the cup and allow brake fluid to leak within the cylinder bore.*

4. Install the piston (A, **Figure 67**) into the master cylinder.
5. Place a dab of grease onto the end of the pushrod (**Figure 66**) and slowly push the piston into the master cylinder with the pushrod assembly. Make sure the end of the push rod engages the seat in the piston.
6. Install the snap ring (**Figure 65**). The snap ring must be completely seated in its groove in the master cylinder.
7. Check the operation of the master cylinder and the slide the dust boot into position. Make sure it is firmly seated against the master cylinder.
8. If removed, install the hose joint into its port on the master cylinder. Use a new O-ring and secure the joint in place with the snap ring.
9. Install the master cylinder as described in this section.

Inspection

The piston, the spring, primary cup and secondary cup are sold as a kit. Individual parts are not available. If any of these parts are faulty, the piston kit must be purchased.

1. Clean all parts in fresh DOT 4 brake fluid. Place the master cylinder components on a clean lint-free cloth.
2. Check the end of the piston (A, **Figure 69**) where it contacts the pushrod for wear.
3. Check the spring (A, **Figure 70**) for fatigue, cracks or other damage.
4. Check the secondary cup (B, **Figure 69**) and primary cup (B, **Figure 70**) for damage, softness or swelling.
5. If any of the parts inspected in Steps 2-4 are worn or damaged, replace all of them by installing a piston kit.

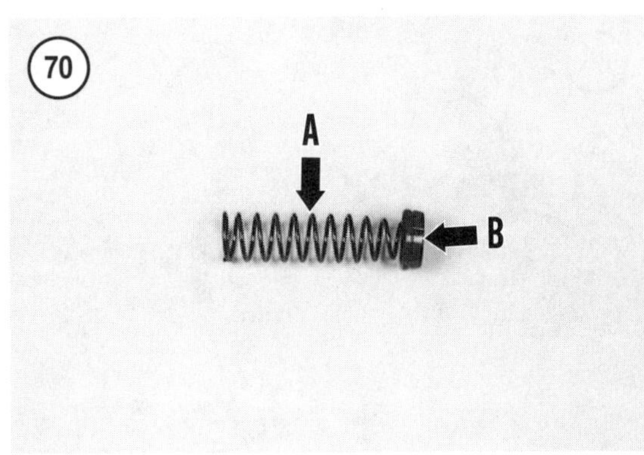

6. Inspect the end of the pushrod where it contacts the piston for damage.
7. Inspect the pushrod dust boot for tears or other signs of damage.
8. Inspect the pushrod clevis for cracks, bending or other signs of damage.
9. Inspect the cylinder bore (**Figure 71**) and piston contact surfaces for signs of wear or damage. If either part is less than perfect, replace the master cylinder.
10. Inspect the master cylinder body and mounting bolt holes for cracks or damage. If damaged in any way, replace the master cylinder assembly.

NOTE
If the relief port is plugged, the brake can be applied, but they will not release.

11. Make sure the relief and supply ports in the master cylinder are clear. Clean them with compressed air.
12. Inspect the threads in the brake fluid port. If the threads are damaged or partially stripped, replace the master cylinder assembly.
13. Inspect the reservoir diaphragm for tears, cracks, or other signs of damage. Replace as necessary.

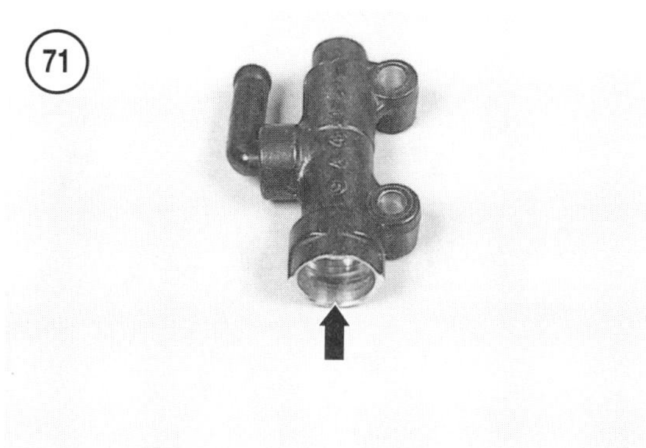

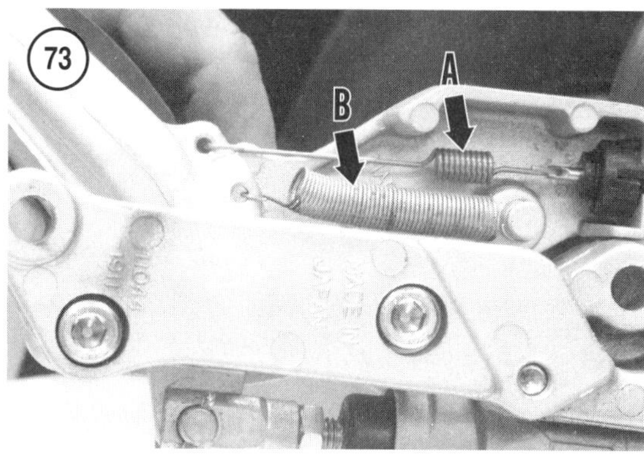

14. Inspect the reservoir, reservoir cap, diaphragm plate and hose for cracks, wear or other signs of damage. Replace as necessary.

BRAKE PEDAL/FOOTPEG ASSEMBLY

Removal/Installation

1. Follow the rear brake switch electrical lead along the right side of the frame and disconnect the switch's two bullet connectors (**Figure 72**). Note how the wire is routed and release the wire from any clamps or ties that secure it to the frame.
2. If the brake pedal or footpeg require service, loosen the master cylinder bolts (A, **Figure 61**) now while the footpeg bracket is still on the motorcycle.
3. Remove the bracket bolts (B, **Figure 61**) and rotate the footpeg bracket so the inboard side is accessible.
4. Remove the cotter pin (A, **Figure 62**), pull the clevis pin and separate the pushrod clevis from the brake pedal.
5. If necessary, disassemble the brake pedal/footpeg assembly by performing the following:
   a. Remove the master cylinder bolts loosened earlier (A, **Figure 61**) and remove the master cylinder. Use a bunjee cord or wire to suspend it from the motorcycle.
   b. Disconnect the brake light spring (A, **Figure 73**) and the return spring (B) from the brake pedal.
   c. Remove the brake pedal bolts (B, **Figure 62**) and separate the footpeg bracket (C) from the footpeg holder.
   d. Lift the brake pedal from its pivot post.
6. Installation is the reverse of removal.

BRAKE DISC

Inspection

A brake disc can be inspected while it is installed on the wheel. Small nicks and marks on the disc are not important, but radial scratches deep enough to snag a fingernail reduce braking effectiveness and increase brake pad wear. If these grooves are evident and the brake pads are wearing rapidly, the disc should be replaced. The specifications for the standard thickness and service limits are listed in **Table 1**.

NOTE
Disc thickness can be measured with the wheel installed or removed from the motorcycle.

1. Clean any rust or corrosion from the disc and wipe it clean with brake parts cleaner. Never use oil-based solvents on a brake disc. They may leave an oil residue on the disc.
2. Measure the thickness of the disc at several locations around the disc with a vernier caliper or a mi-

crometer (**Figure 74**). The disc must be *replaced* if the thickness in any area is equal to or less than the service limit specified in **Table 1**.

3. Check the disc runout by performing the following:
   a. Make sure the disc mounting bolts are tight prior to running this check.
   b. Mount a dial indicator as shown in **Figure 75**.
   c. Slowly rotate the wheel and watch the dial indicator. Replace the disc if runout is out of specification.
4. If the disc runout is greater than the service limit it is likely the disc has been overheated. Check for the following:
   a. The caliper is binding on the caliper holders due to excessive wear. This prevents the caliper from floating on the disc.
   b. The caliper piston seals are worn or damaged.
   c. The master cylinder relief port is plugged.
   d. The master cylinder primary cup is worn or damaged.

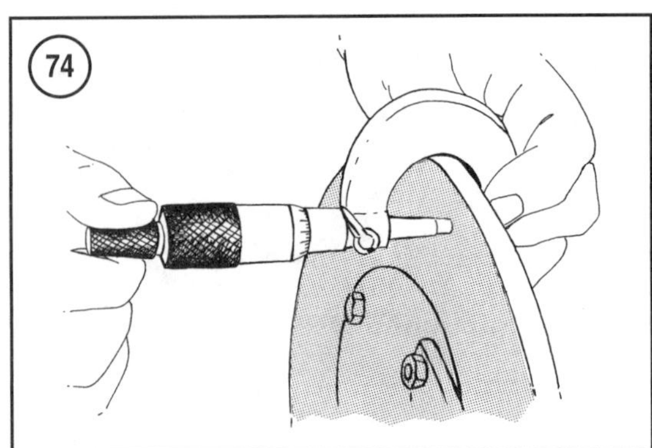
74

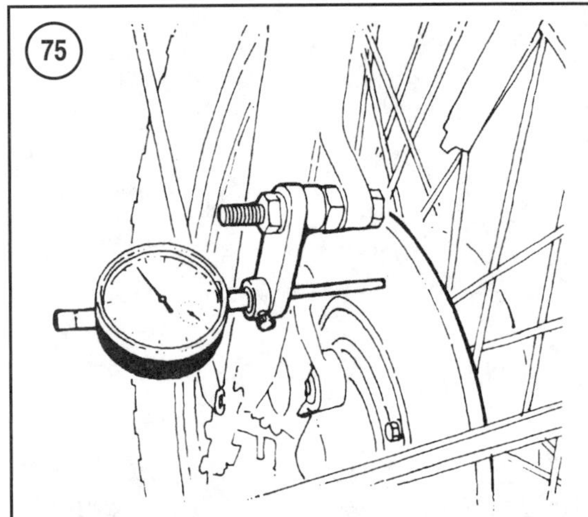
75

Removal/Installation

1. Remove the front or rear wheel as described in Chapter Eleven.

CAUTION
Set the tire on two wooden blocks. Do not set the wheel down on the disc surface. It could be scratched or damaged.

NOTE
Insert a piece of wood or vinyl tube between the pads in the caliper(s). This way, if the brake lever or pedal is inadvertently applied, the pistons will not be forced out of the cylinders. If this does happen, the caliper might have to be disassembled to reseat the pistons and the system will have to be bled. By using the wood or vinyl tube in place of the disc, you will not have to bleed system when installing the wheel.

2. Remove the brake disc bolts (**Figure 76**) and lift the brake disc from the hub.
3. Clean the threaded holes in the hub.

76

4. Clean the brake disc mounting surface on the hub.
5. Reverse the removal procedures to install the brake disc. Note the following:
   a. The brake disc bolts are specifically designed for this application. If the bolts require replacement, make sure they are replaced with original equipment bolts.

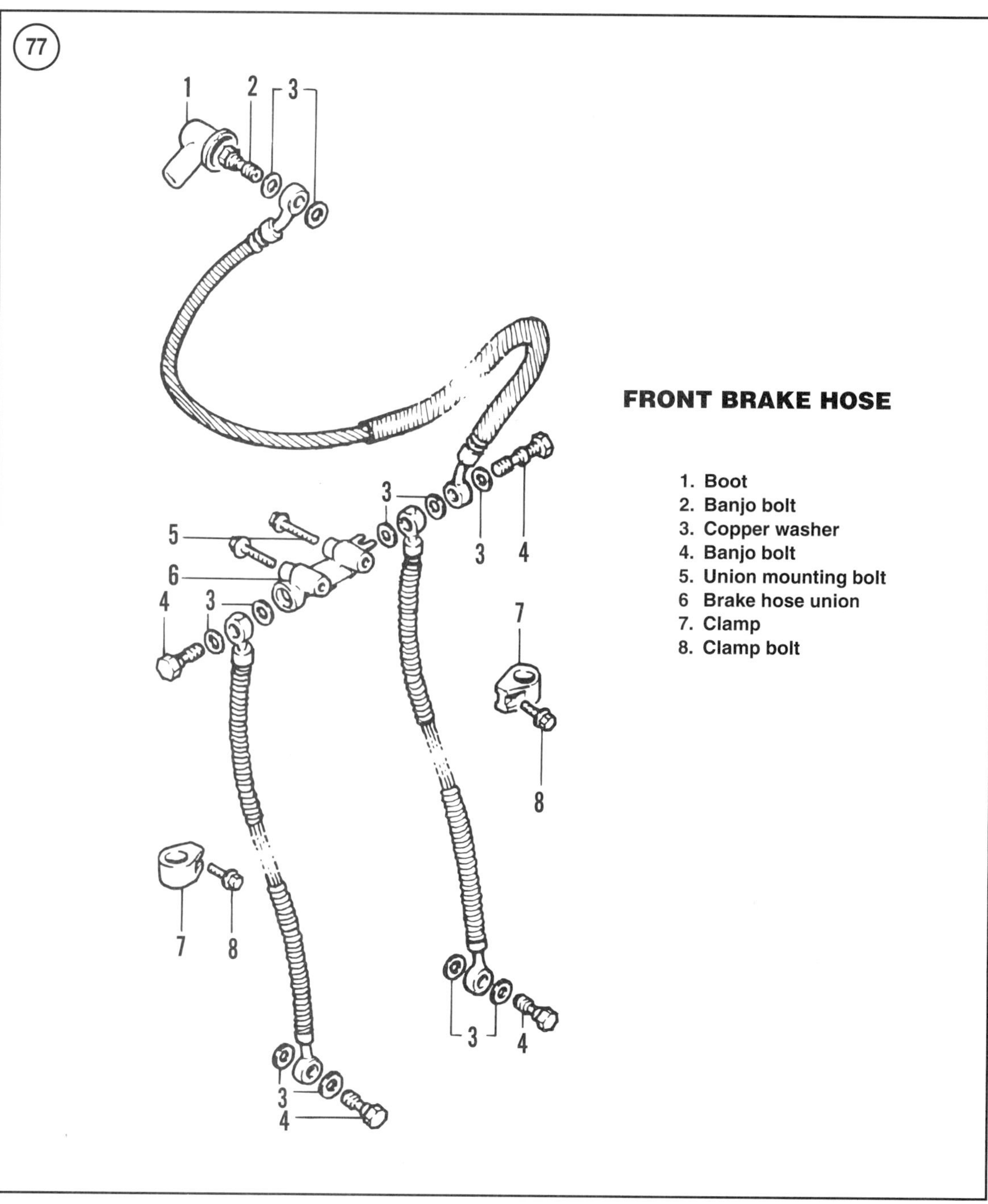

b. Install a disc so its arrow points in the direction of forward rotation.

c. Place a small amount of Loctite 242 on the brake disc bolts prior to installation.

d. Evenly tighten the brake disc bolts in a crisscross pattern. Torque the bolts to the 23 N•m (17 ft.-lb.).

BRAKE HOSE REPLACEMENT

Check the brake hoses at the brake system inspection intervals listed in Chapter Three. Replace any brake hose that is cracked, bulging or shows signs of chafing, wear or other damage.

Refer to **Figure 77** when replacing the front brake hoses.

1. Use a tarp or plastic drop cloth to cover areas of the motorcycle where brake fluid could spill.
2. Follow the procedures described in this chapter and drain the brake fluid from the front or rear brake system.
3. Note how the brake line is routed through the motorcycle. Make a drawing so the new line can be routed along the same path as the original hose or pipe.
4. Remove any clamps or ties securing the line to the motorcycle.
5. Note how a hose fitting is installed on a master cylinder or caliper. The new hose fitting must sit on the same side of the index post.
6. Remove the banjo bolt securing the hose fitting on each end of the hose. Discard the copper washer on each side of a hose fitting (**Figure 78**).
7. Reverse these steps to install a new brake hose. Note the following:
   a. Compare the new and old hoses. Make sure they are the same.
   b. Clean the banjo bolts and hose ends to remove any contamination.
   c. Refer to the notes made during removal and route the new hose along the same path as the original hose. Secure the hose to the motorcycle at the same locations noted during removal.
   d. Replace any banjo bolt with a damaged head or threads.
   e. Install a new copper washer on each side of a brake hose fitting (**Figure 78**).
   f. When connecting the front master cylinder hose to the brake hose union (**Figure 79**), make sure the hose neck sits between the indexing posts on the union.
   g. Tighten the banjo bolts to 25 N•m (18 ft.-lb.).

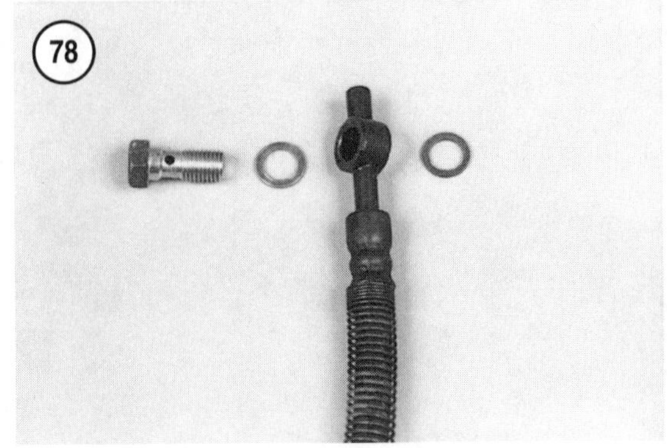

   h. After replacing a front brake line, turn handlebars from side to side to make sure the hose does not rub against any part or pull away from its brake component.
   i. Refill the master cylinders and bleed the brakes as described in this chapter.

WARNING

Before riding the motorcycle, confirm that the brake lights work and that the front and rear brakes operate properly with full hydraulic advantage.

Table 1 BRAKE SYSTEM SPECIFICATIONS

Item	New mm (in.)	Service limit mm (in.)
Brake pad thickness (front and rear)		
Front		
1986-1993 models	4.85 (0.191)	1.0 (0.039)
1994-on models	4.5 (0.177)	1.0 (0.039)
Rear		
1986-1993	4.85 (0.191)	1.0 (0.039)
1994-on	5.0 (0.197)	1.0 (0.039)
Brake fluid	DOT 4	–
Disc thickness		
Front		
1986-1993 models	4.8-5.1 (0.189-0.201)	4.5 (0.177)
1994-on	4.3-4.6 (0.169-0.181)	4.0 (0.157)
Rear	6.8-7.1 (0.268-0.280)	6.0 (0.236)
Disc runout (front and rear)	Less than 0.15 (0.006)	0.3 (0.12)
Rear master cylinder pushrod length	43.5-45.5 (1.71-1.79)	–

Table 2 BRAKE SYSTEM TORQUE SPECIFICATIONS

Item	N•m	in.-lb.	ft.-lb.
Bleed valve	7.8	69	–
Brake hose banjo bolt			
1986-2004	25	–	18
2005-on	34	–	25
Brake lever pivot nut	5.9	–	52
Disc mounting bolts*	23	–	17
Front caliper bolts	32	–	24
Front master cylinder clamp bolts	8.8	78	–
Rear caliper bolts	34	–	25
Rear master cylinder bolts	23	–	17
Torque arm nut	29	–	22

*Apply Loctite 242 or an equivalent medium-strength thread locking compound.

NOTES

CHAPTER FIFTEEN

BODY AND FRAME

This chapter described the procedures for removing and installing the body panels, fenders and footpegs. The photographs in this chapter show the panels on a 2003 model. The location and assembly on other models may differ.

Study an assembly closely before starting work. Take photographs and/or notes. Pay particular attention to the washers, collars and dampers used to install the part. These items must be reinstalled in the proper location during assembly.

SIDE COVER

Removal/Installation

Refer to **Figure 1**.

1. Remove the side cover screw and washer.
2. Pull out the rear of the cover and release its studs from their grommets.
3. Installation is the reverse of removal. If the fuel tank is installed on the motorcycle, make sure the damper (1, **Figure 1**) engages the edge of the fuel tank.

FOOTPEGS

Removal/Installation

Refer to **Figure 2** and **Figure 3**.

1. Remove the E-clip from the clevis pin.
2. Pull the pin and separate the footpeg from its holder.
   a. When removing a riders footpeg, watch for the spring.
   b. When removing a passenger footpeg, watch for the spring, collar and stepped washer.
3. Installation is the reverse of removal.

LOWER FAIRING

Removal/Installation

Refer to **Figure 4**.

1. Securely support the motorcycle on level ground.
2. Remove the mounting screws and lift the reservoir cover (**Figure 5**) from the fairing.
3. Remove the mounting screws and lower the air scoop (A, **Figure 6**) from the fairing.
4. Pull the trim (B, **Figure 6**) from the lower fairing.
5. Repeat Steps 3 and 4 on the other side.
6. Remove the mounting screws (C, **Figure 6**) from each side. Note the location of any washers, dampers or collars. Each screw must be reinstalled with the same hardware.
7. Remove the two screws that secure the lower fairing to the bottom of the radiator bracket.
8. Slide the lower fairing rearward to disengage its front tangs (**Figure 7**) from the scoop formed by the middle fairing and remove the lower fairing.

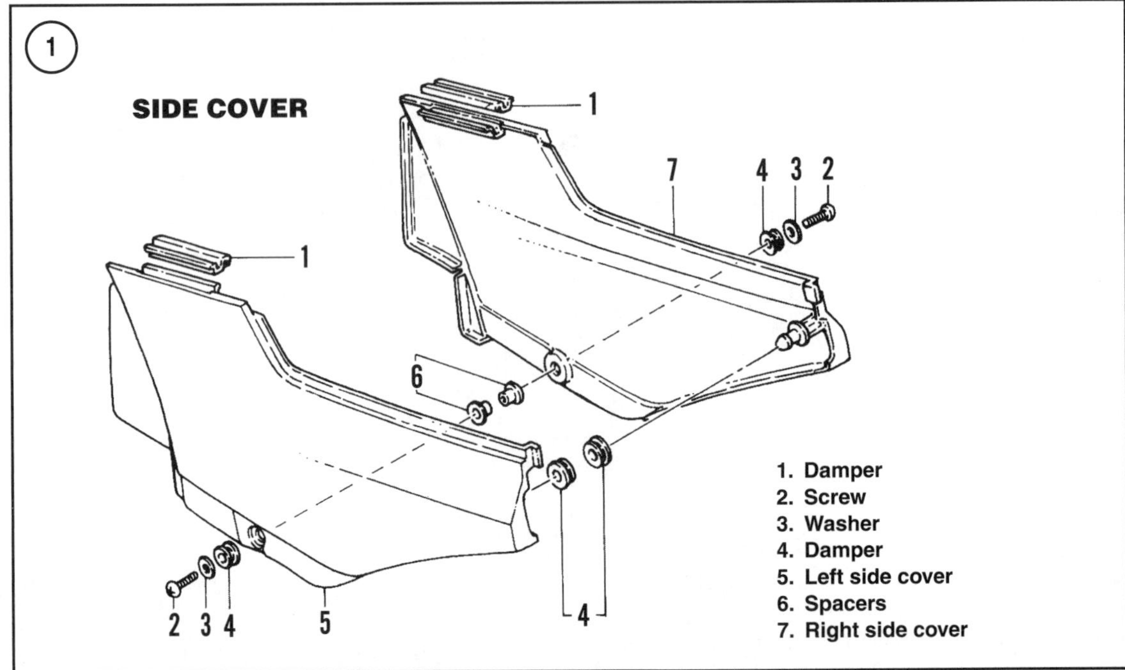

9. Installation is the reverse of removal. Pay attention to the following:
   a. Seat the lower fairing tangs (**Figure 7**) on the air scoop formed by the middle fairing.
   b. Loosely install all the hardware, including any related washer, collar or dampers and then evenly tighten the mounting screws.
   c. Firmly press the trim and trim clips into place.

MIDDLE FAIRING

Removal/Installation

Refer to **Figure 8**.

1. Remove the lower fairing as described in this chapter.
2. Remove the mounting screw (A, **Figure 9**) and release the rear of the air duct from the heat guard (B). Repeat this on the other side.
3. Remove the two heat guard bolts and lower the heat guard from the oil pan. Note that the arrow cutout (**Figure 10**) in the guard points forward.
4. The rear fairing pocket screw (A, **Figure 11**) secures the fairing pocket and the middle fairing to the fairing rod (A, **Figure 12**). Remove the rear fairing pocket screw (A, **Figure 11**) on each side and pull the fairing rod from the engine.
5. Remove the middle fairing-pocket screw (B, **Figure 11**).
6. Remove the trim (A, **Figure 13**) from the middle fairing.
7. Release the front of the middle fairing from the radiator bracket by removing the 6 × 18-mm screw (**Figure 14**) and its grommet.
8. Remove the 6 × 22-mm screws (B, **Figure 13**) and lower the middle fairing panel (C) from the motorcycle. Watch for the washer behind each screw.
9. Repeat Steps 5-8 and remove the middle fairing panel from the other side.
10. Remove the front air duct screws (A, **Figure 15**) and air duct (B) from the motorcycle.
11. Installation is the reverse of removal. Pay attention to the following:
   a. Install the air duct (B, **Figure 15**) by installing the front air duct screws (A). Temporarily set the rear of the air duct (C, **Figure 15**) on the exhaust pipe.
   b. Insert the fairing rod (A, **Figure 12**) through the engine. Position the fairing rod mount behind the tab on the middle fairing (B). Set the fairing pocket over the tab and install the rear fairing-pocket screw (A, **Figure 11**).
   c. Loosely install all the hardware, including any related washers, collars or dampers and then evenly tighten the mounting screws.

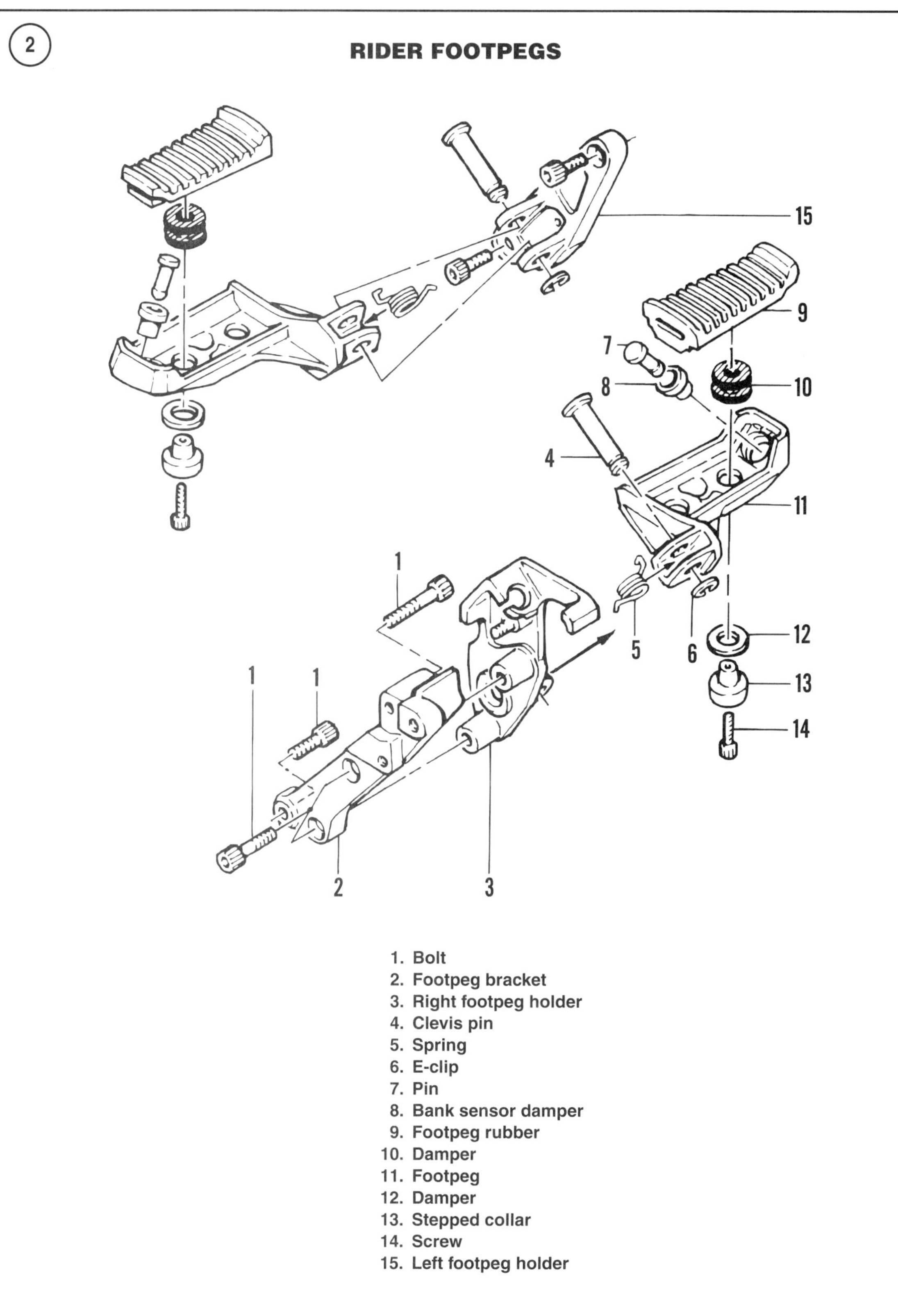

1. Bolt
2. Footpeg bracket
3. Right footpeg holder
4. Clevis pin
5. Spring
6. E-clip
7. Pin
8. Bank sensor damper
9. Footpeg rubber
10. Damper
11. Footpeg
12. Damper
13. Stepped collar
14. Screw
15. Left footpeg holder

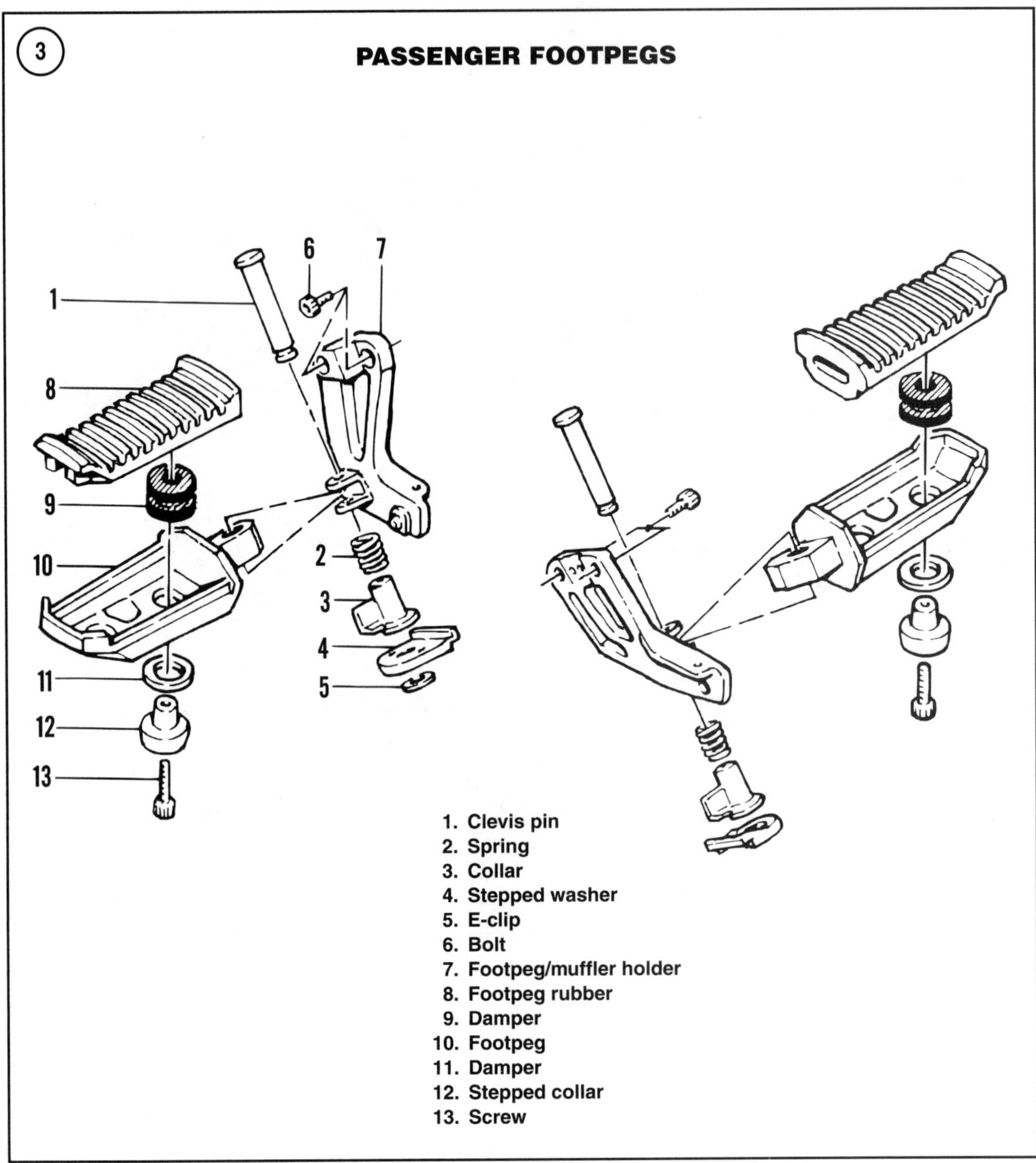

d. Firmly press the trim (A, **Figure 13**) into place along the edge of the middle fairing.

FRONT FAIRING

Removal/Installation

Refer to **Figure 16** and **Figure 17**.

NOTE
Pay attention to any dampers, collars and washers installed with the mounting hardware. Each screw or bolt must be reinstalled with the same damper, collar or washer found during removal.

1. Remove the lower and middle fairings as described in this chapter.
2. Cover the front fender so it will not be damaged.

4

LOWER FAIRING

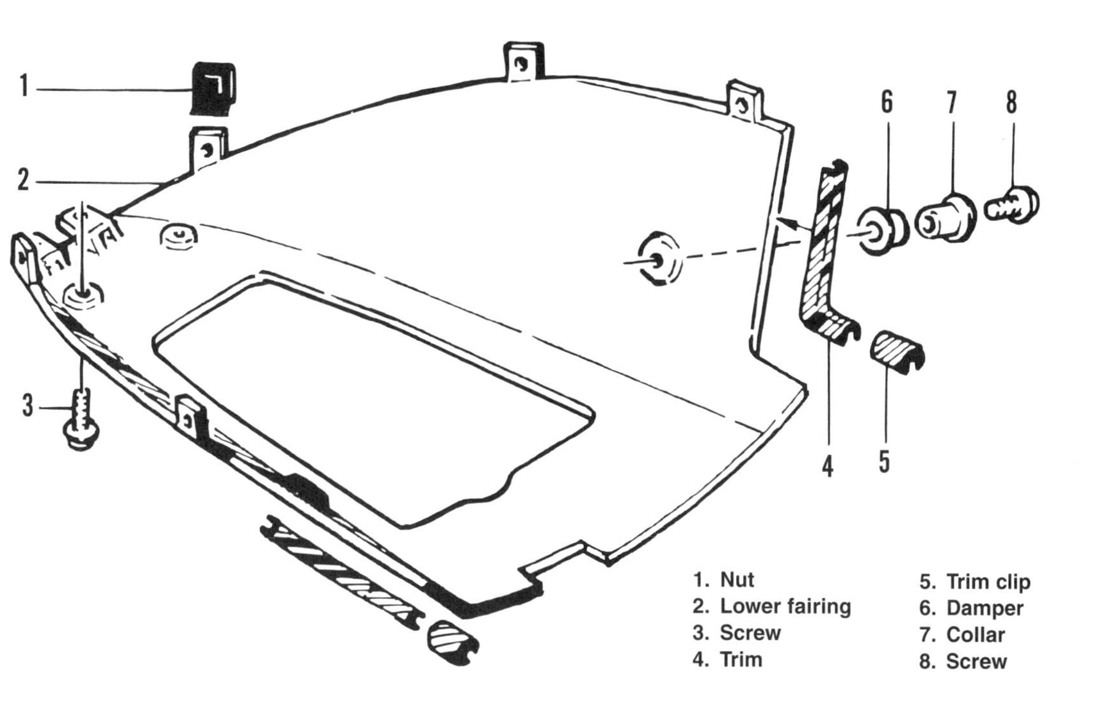

1. Nut
2. Lower fairing
3. Screw
4. Trim
5. Trim clip
6. Damper
7. Collar
8. Screw

5

7

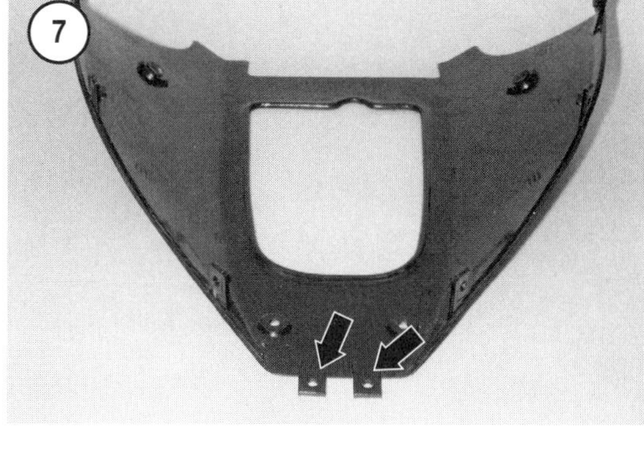

6

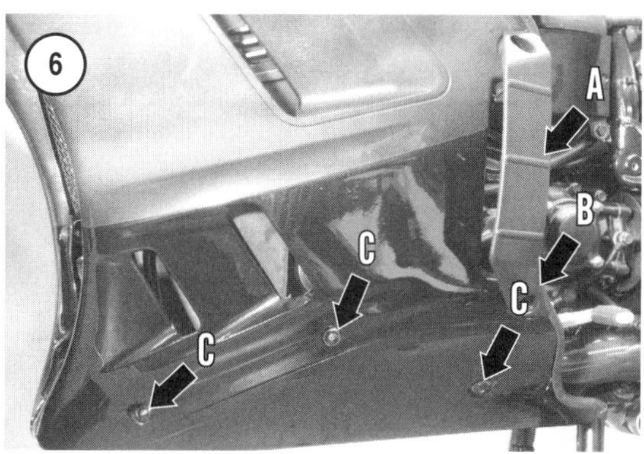

NOTE
*On 1994-on models, the pocket cover can be removed from the hinge. To do so, squeeze the hinge tabs (**Figure 18**) together and slide the cover from the hinge.*

3. Open the pocket cover and remove the fairing pocket screws (**Figure 19**). Lift the pocket from the fairing. Repeat this for the pocket on the other side.

4. Remove the trim clips and the trim from the windshield.

15

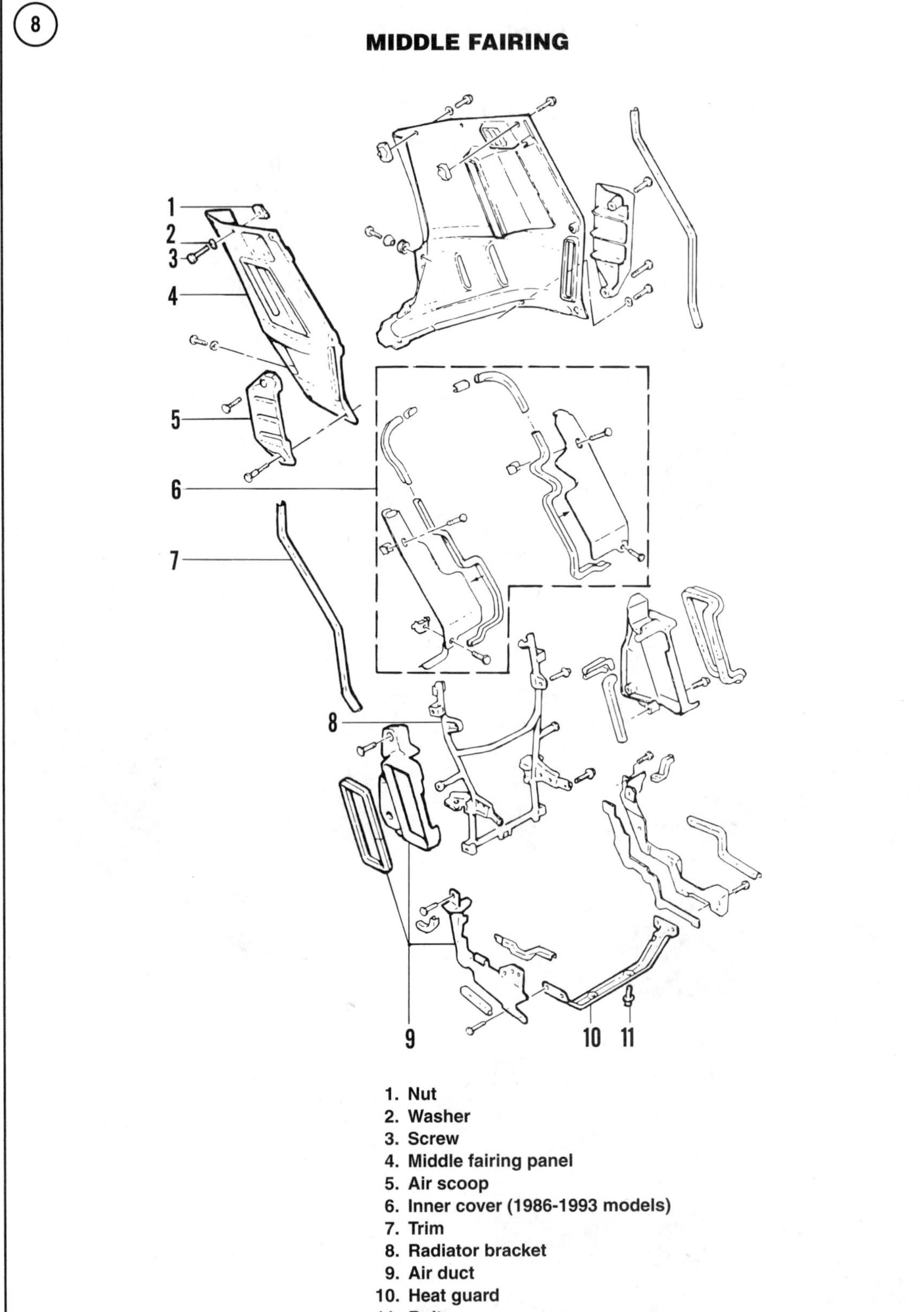
8
MIDDLE FAIRING
1
2
3
4
5
6
7
8
9
10
11
1. Nut
2. Washer
3. Screw
4. Middle fairing panel
5. Air scoop
6. Inner cover (1986-1993 models)
7. Trim
8. Radiator bracket
9. Air duct
10. Heat guard
11. Bolt

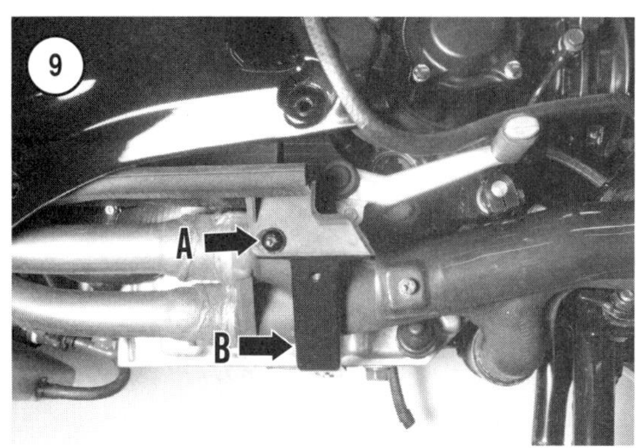

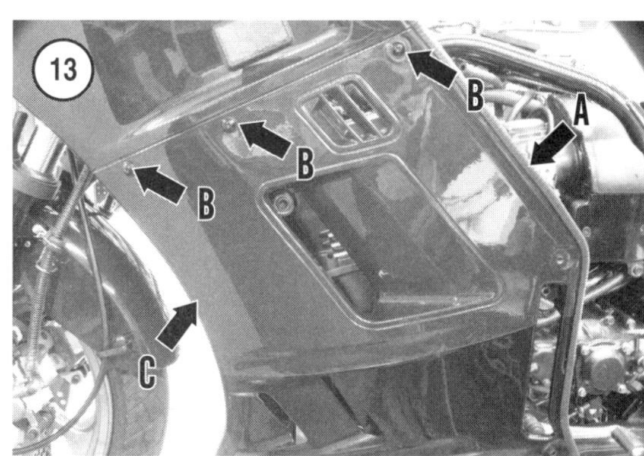

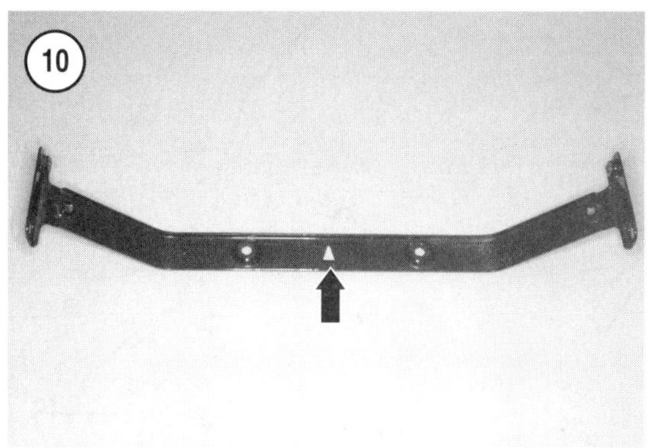

5. Evenly loosen and remove the windshield screws and their washers (A, **Figure 20**). Note that the two outside screws (B, **Figure 20**) on each side are shorter than the other windshield screws.

6. Remove the windshield from the fairing.

7. Disconnect the three-pin clock connector and the two-pin clock-light connector from their harness mates.

8. Remove the single shroud screw (**Figure 21**) and lift the shroud (**Figure 22**) from the fairing. Note how the clock and clock light wires are routed

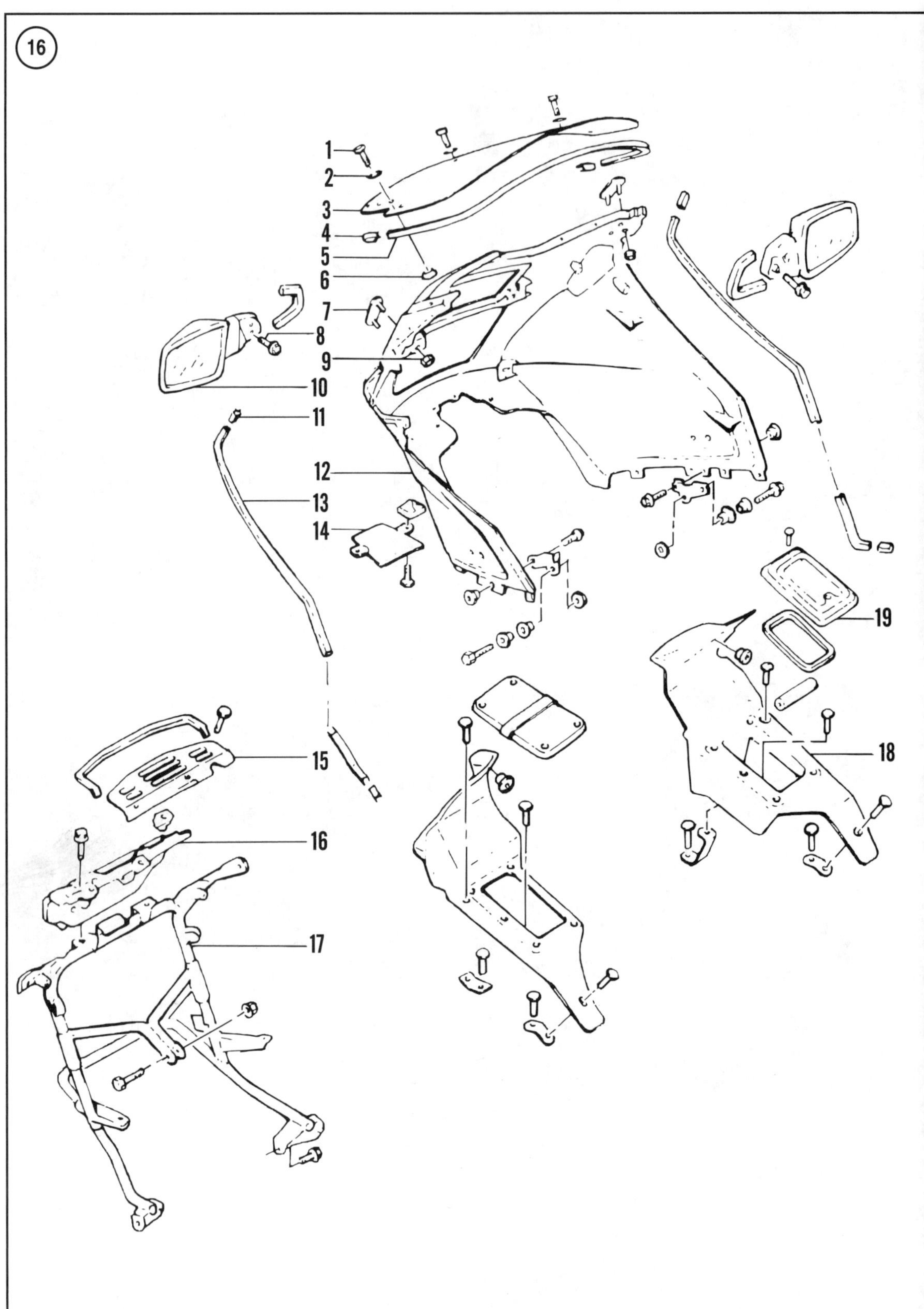
16
1
2
3
4
5
6
7
8
9
10
11
12
13
14
15
16
17
18
19

FRONT FAIRING (1986-1993 MODELS)

1. Screw
2. Washer
3. Windshield
4. Trim clip
5. Trim
6. Nut
7. Bolt plate
8. Bolt
9. Nut
10. Mirror
11. Trim clip
12. Front fairing
13. Trim
14. Access panel
15. Inner cover
16. Horn cover
17. Fairing bracket
18. Fairing pocket
19. Pocket cover

along the frame. They must be rerouted along the same path during assembly.

9. Disconnect the following electrical connectors from their harness mates.
   a. The three-pin left turn signal connector (A, **Figure 23**).
   b. The six-pin and ten-pin fairing-to-main-harness connectors (B, **Figure 23**).
   c. The three-pin and eight-pin instrument cluster connectors (C, **Figure 23**).
   d. The three-pin right turn signal connector.

10. Disconnect the speedometer cable from the speedometer drive on the front wheel. Pull the cable through the holder on the fender and out through the cable holder on the brake union (D, **Figure 23**).

11. Visually inspect the fairing to ensure all electrical lines and cables are free.

12. Remove the rear fairing bolt (A, **Figure 24**) from the right side and remove the bracket bolt (B) from each side.

NOTE
The front fairing and fairing bracket are removed as an assembly. To do this, you need an assistant to hold the right side of the fairing away from the bracket (A, ***Figure 25****) so the bracket can pass under the coolant hose (B). If an assistant is not available, drain the coolant (Chapter Three) and remove the hose.*

13. Remove the nut from the central arm bolt (A, **Figure 26**). Pull the bolt and separate the bracket arm (B, **Figure 26**) from the frame mount.

14. Have an assistant hold the right side of the fairing away from the bracket. Move the fairing assembly forward until the fairing bracket (A, **Figure 25**) and the fairing mount (C) clear the coolant hose (B). Remove the fairing.

15. Installation is the reverse of removal. Pay attention to the following:
   a. Set the fairing assembly into place. Have an assistant pull the right side of the fairing away from the bracket (A, **Figure 25**) so the bracket can pass under and inside the coolant hose (B) while the fairing (C) passes outside the hose.
   b. Route the throttle cables (C, **Figure 26**) under the central arm (B) of the fairing bracket.
   c. Install the bolt (A, **Figure 26**) and secure the central arm to the frame mount.

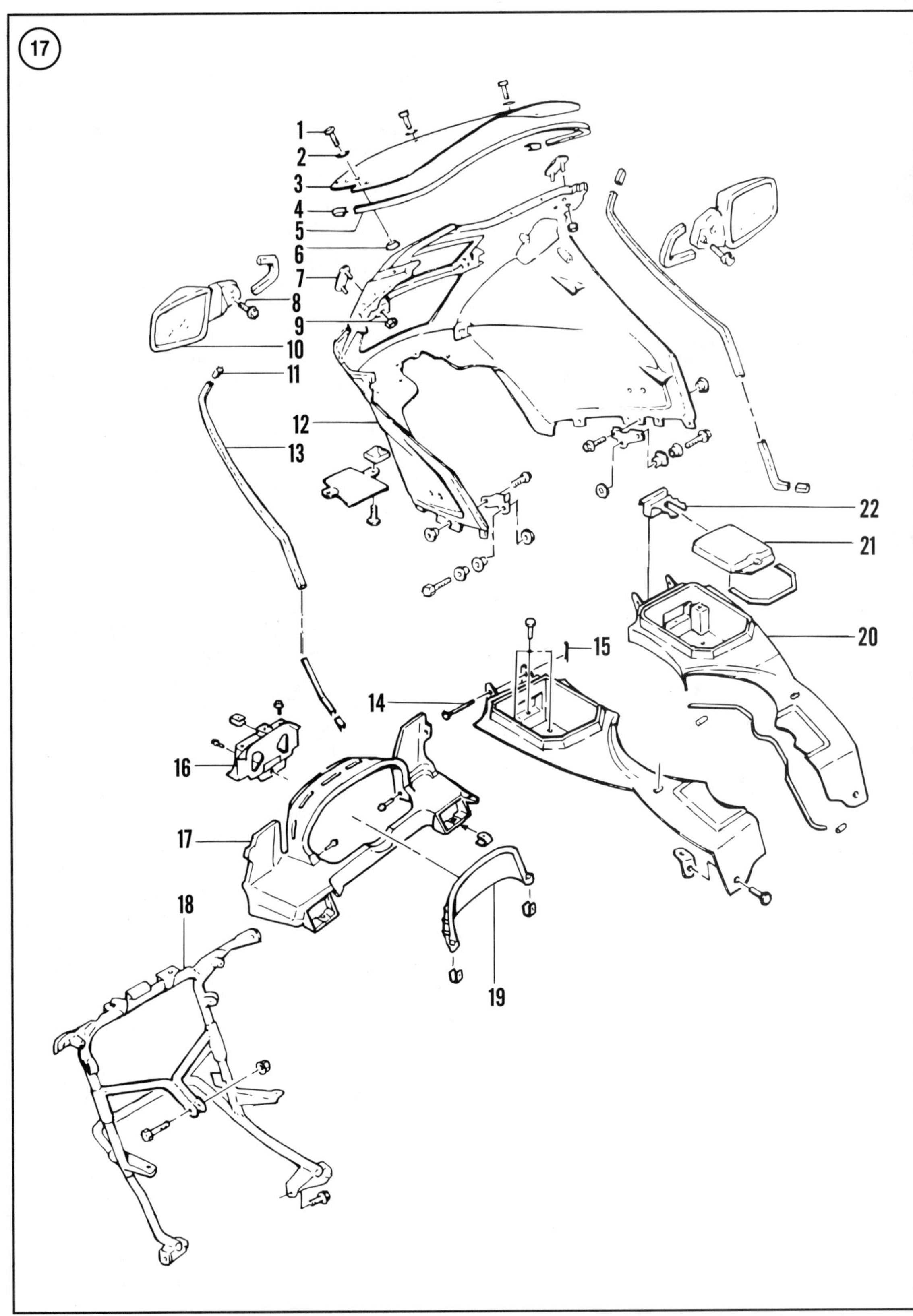
17
1
2
3
4
5
6
7
8
9
10
11
12
13
14
15
16
17
18
19
20
21
22

FRONT FAIRING (1994-ON MODELS)

1. Screw
2. Washer
3. Windshield
4. Trim clip
5. Trim
6. Nut
7. Bolt plate
8. Bolt
9. Nut
10. Mirror
11. Trim clip
12. Front fairing
13. Trim
14. Hinge pin
15. Cotter pin
16. Meter assembly
17. Shroud
18. Fairing bracket
19. Visor
20. Fairing pocket
21. Pocket cover
22. Hinge

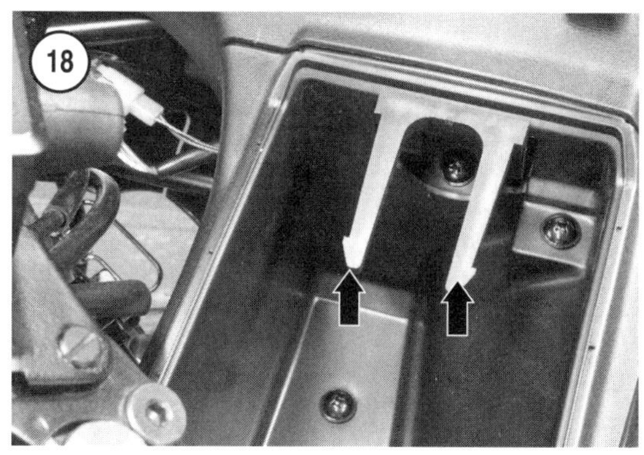

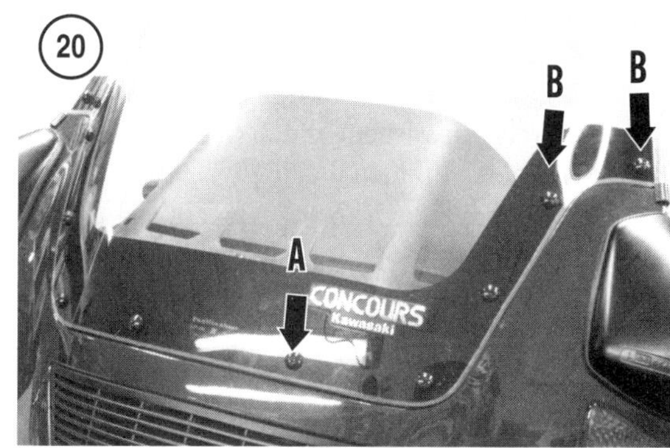

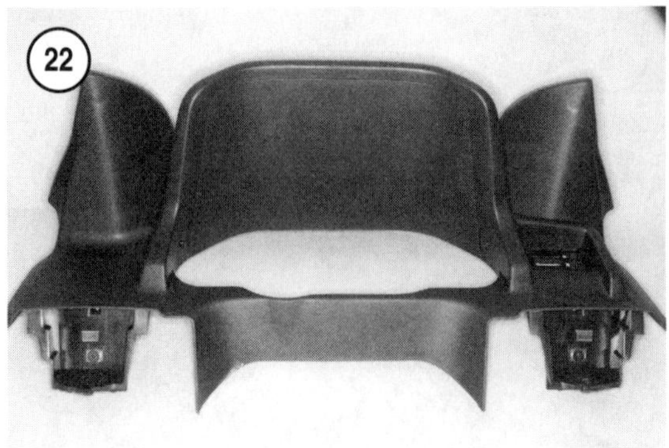

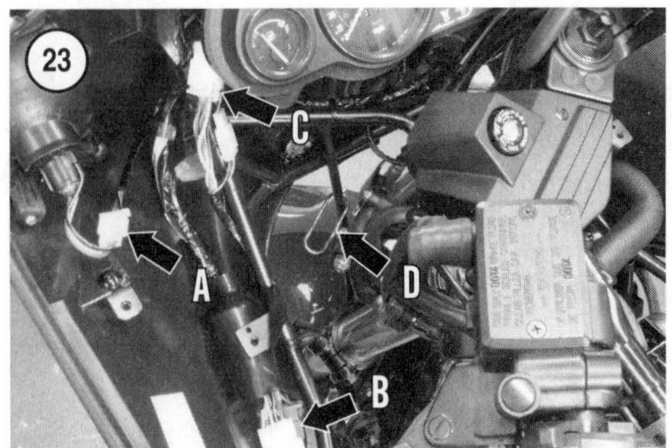

d. Route the speedometer cable through the cable holder (D, **Figure 23**) on the brake union, though the holder on the fender and connect it to the speedometer drive on the front wheel.
e. Connect the electrical connectors to their harness mates.
f. Place a washer under each windshield screw. Install the four shorter screws in the two outside holes (B, **Figure 20**) on each side. Tighten the windshield screws evenly and securely. Do not overtighten them. The plastic windshield can easily crack.
g. Set each fairing pocket into place and secure it to the mounts (**Figure 27**) with the screws (**Figure 19**).
h. Loosely install all the hardware, including any related washers, collars or dampers and then evenly tighten the hardware.
i. Firmly press the trim and trim clips along the windshield.

FAIRING BRACKET

Removal/Installation

1. Remove the front fairing as described in this chapter.
2. Unplug the electrical connector (**Figure 28**) from the headlight bulb.
3. Remove the mirror bolts (A, **Figure 29**) with their washers and remove the mirror (B) from the fairing.
4. Remove the two nuts (A, **Figure 30**), pull the bolt plate (**Figure 31**) from the side of the fairing and separate the fairing from the bracket (B, **Figure 30**).
5. Repeat Steps 3-4 on the other side of the fairing.
6. Remove the rear mount (**Figure 32**) from each side. Lift the fairing bracket, with the meter assem-

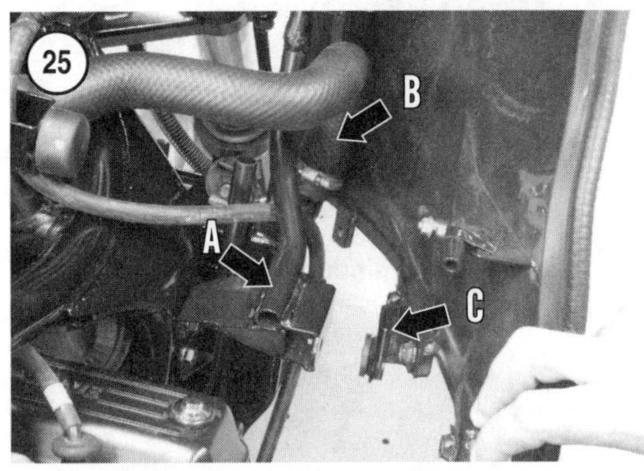

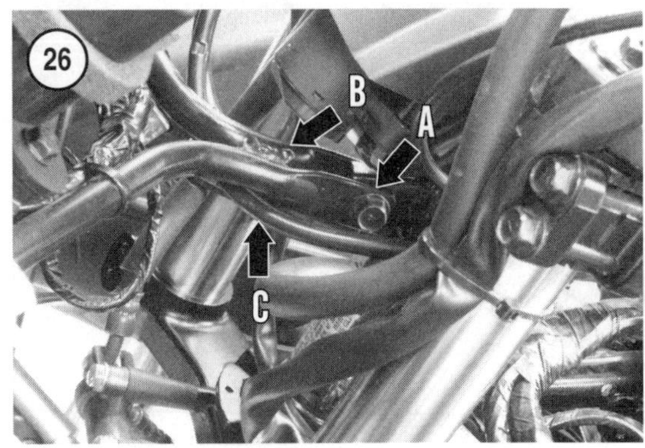

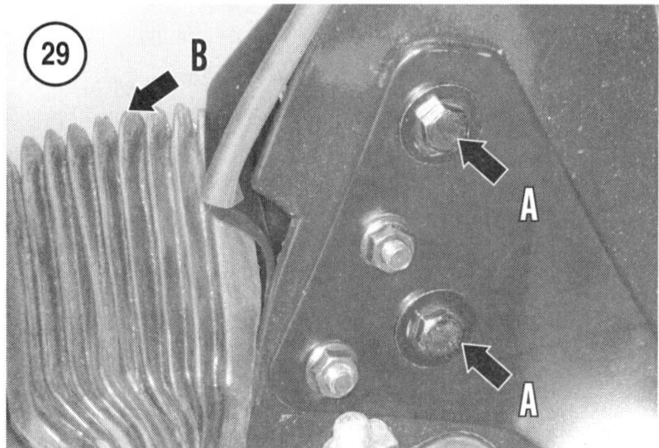

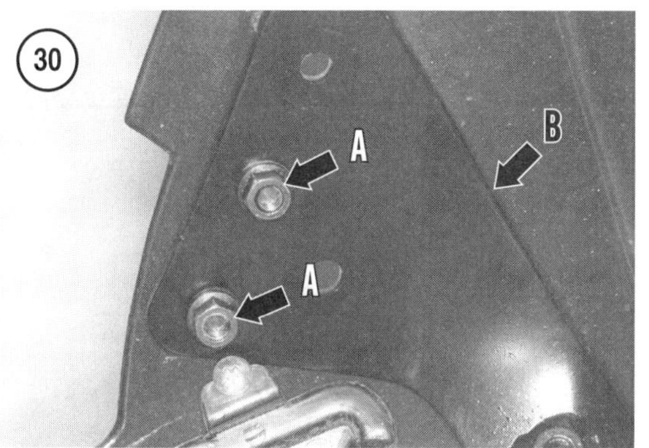

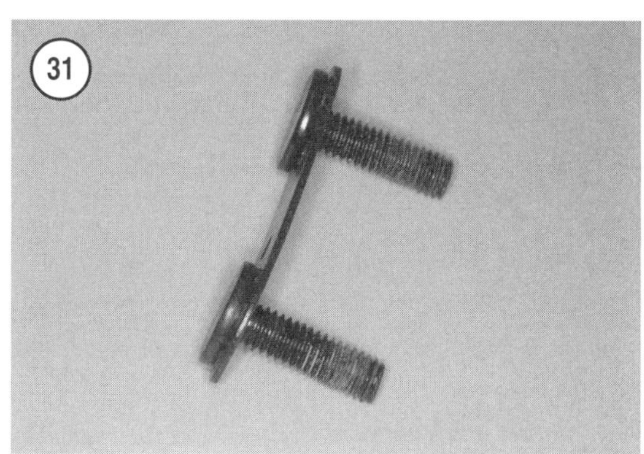

bly, from the front fairing. Note how the meter wiring is routed through the bracket. It must be rerouted along the same path during installation.

CAUTION

Store the fairing bracket so the meters remain upright. A meter can be damaged if it is left sideways or upside down for a period of time.

7. Installation is the reverse of removal. Route the meter wiring along the same path noted during removal.

TAIL COVER

Removal/Installation

Refer to **Figure 33**.

1. Remove the side cover (this chapter) and saddlebag from each side.
2. Turn out the thumb screw and remove the rack cover from the motorcycle.
3. Pry the buttons (A, **Figure 34**) from the rack bolt, unscrew the bolts and lift the rack (B) from the tail cover.

33

TAIL COVER

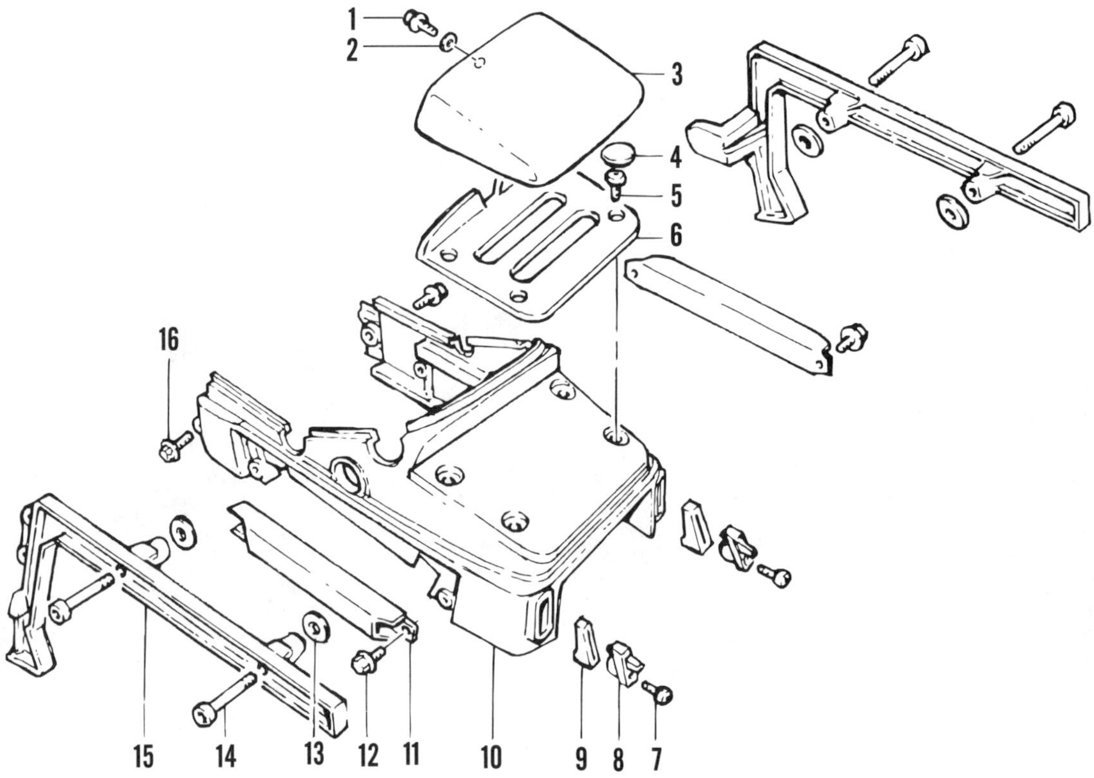

1. Thumb screw
2. Washer
3. Rack cover
4. Button
5. Rack bolt
6. Rack
7. Allen bolt
8. Tie down hook
9. Damper
10. Tail piece
11. Rail bracket
12. Rail bracket bolt
13. Washer
14. Saddlebag holder bolt
15. Saddlebag holder
16. Tail piece bolt

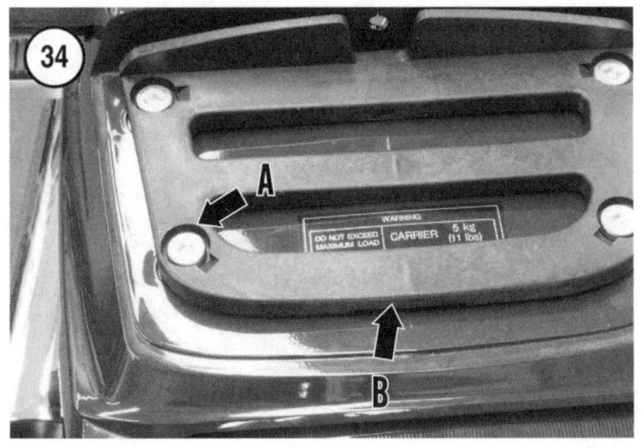

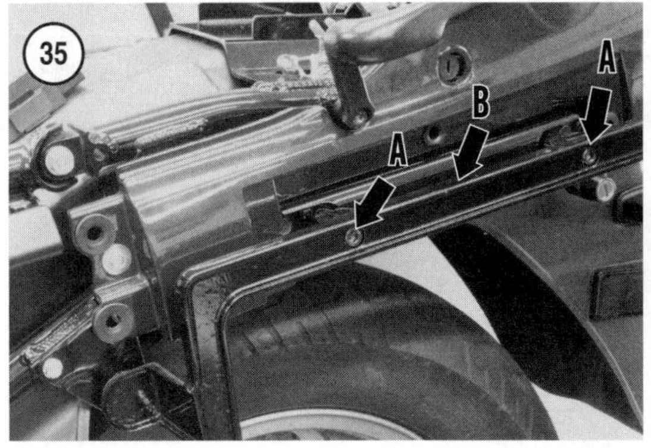

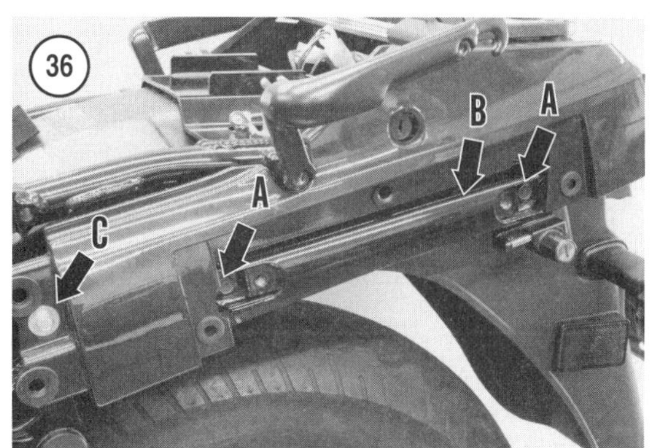

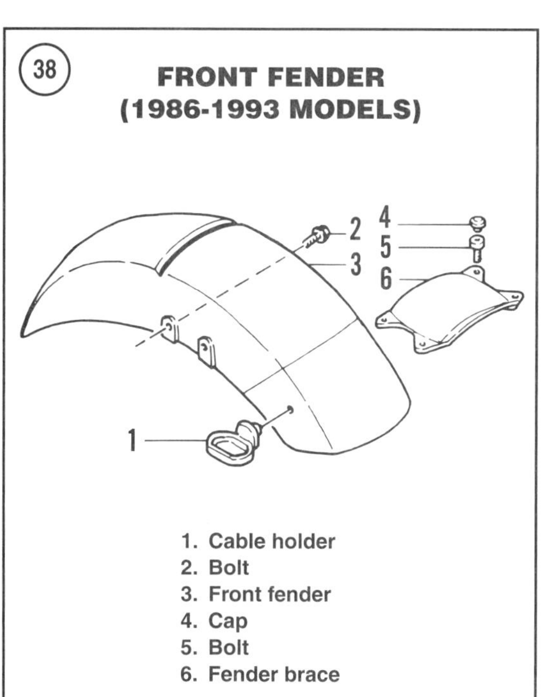

FRONT FENDER (1986-1993 MODELS)

1. Cable holder
2. Bolt
3. Front fender
4. Cap
5. Bolt
6. Fender brace

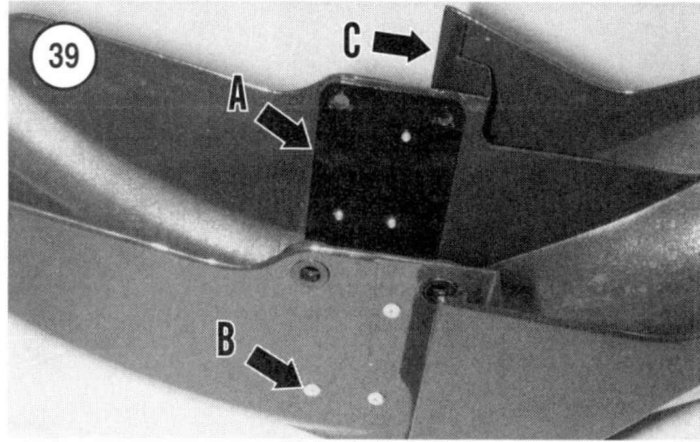

4. Remove the mounting bolts (A, **Figure 35**) and lower the saddlebag holder (B) from one side of the motorcycle. Watch for the washers behind the holder.
5. Remove the rail bracket bolts (A, **Figure 36**) and pull the rail bracket (B) from the tail cover.
6. Turn out the front tail cover bolt (C, **Figure 36**).
7. Repeat Steps 4-6 on the other side.
8. Pull out the tie down hook, unthread the Allen bolt (**Figure 37**) and remove each hook from the tail cover.
9. Spread the front of the tail piece, carefully pull it rearward and remove the tail piece.
10. Installation is the reverse of removal.

FRONT FENDER

Removal/Installation (1986-1993 Models)

Refer to **Figure 38**.

1. Disconnect the speedometer cable from the gear housing on the front wheel.
2. Pull the speedometer cable from the holder on the front fender.
3. Remove the fender brace bolts and lift the fender brace from between the fork legs. Note the side with the raised lip faces rearward. The brace must be reinstalled with this orientation during assembly.
4. Remove the front fender bolts and lift the front fender from between the fork legs.
5. Installation is the reverse of removal. Install the front fender brace so the side with the raised lip faces rearward.

15

Removal/Installation (1994-on Models)

The fender brace (A, **Figure 39**) on these models mounts inside the front fender.

1. Remove the front wheel as described in Chapter Eleven.

REAR FENDER

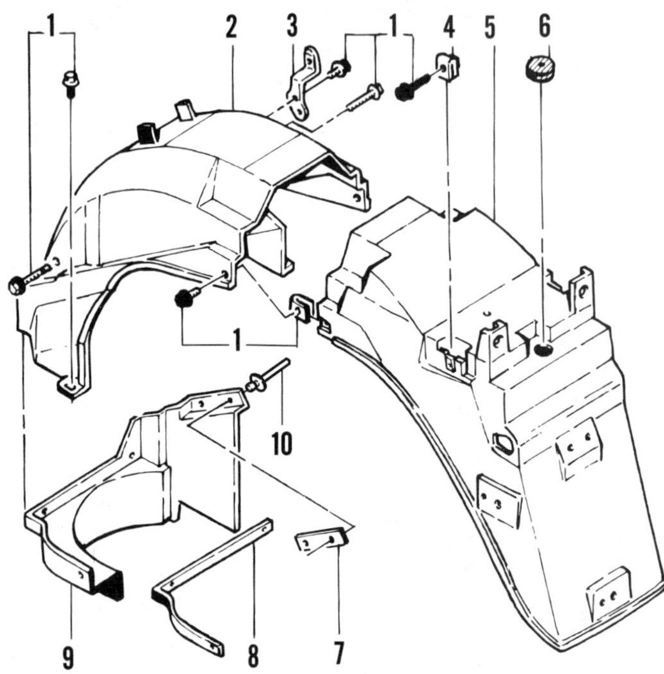

1. Bolt
2. Fender front half
3. Rear brake reservoir bracket
4. Nut
5. Fender rear half
6 Damper
7. Plate
8. Bracket
9. Mud guard
10. Rivet

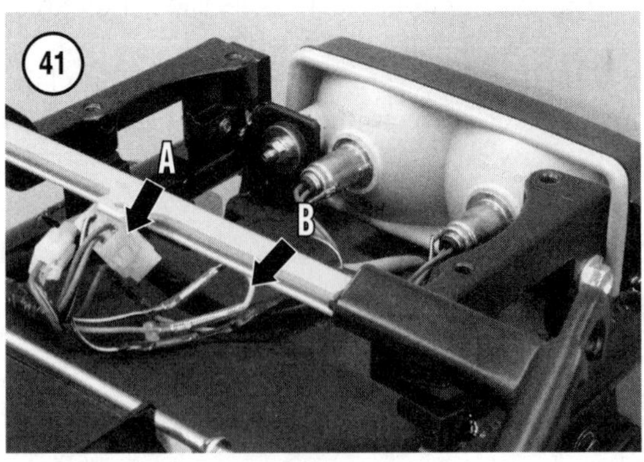

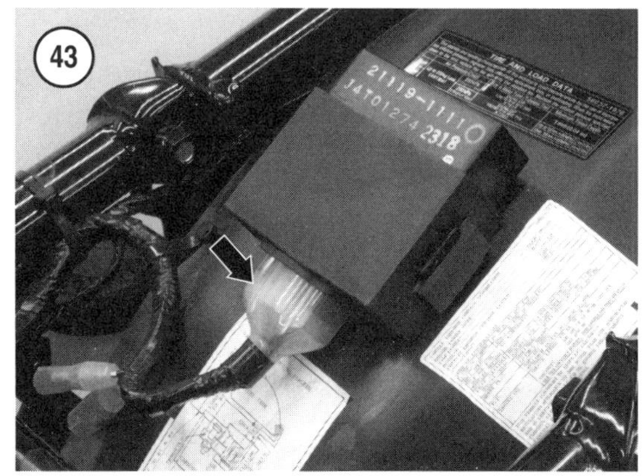

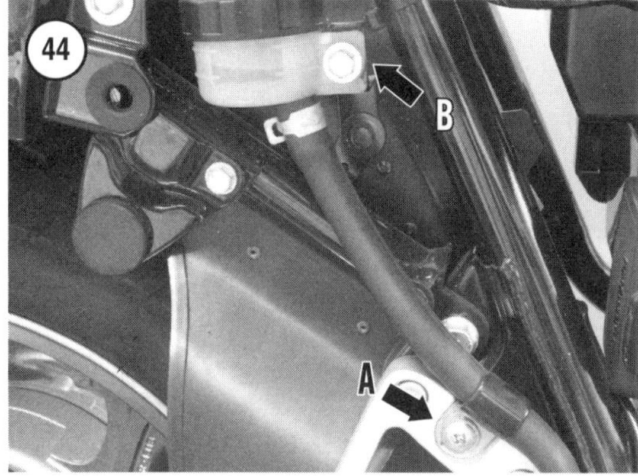

NOTE
The fender bolts sit on the inside of the front fender and turn into threaded holes in the fork legs.

2. Remove the fender bolts from the inside of the fender. Remove the fender from between the fork legs.
3. If necessary, drill out the rivets (B, **Figure 39**) and remove the fender brace (A) from the fender.
4. Installation is the reverse of removal. Install the fender so the flared end (C, **Figure 39**) sits against the front of the fork legs.

REAR FENDER

Rear Half Removal/Installation

Refer to **Figure 40**.

1. Remove the tail cover as described in this chapter.
2. Disconnect the tail/brake light connector (A, **Figure 41**) and turn signal bullet connectors (B) from their harness mate.
3. Remove the mounting bolts (A, **Figure 42**) from each side. Pull the rear half (B, **Figure 42**) of the fender rearward and remove it from the motorcycle. Note how the turn signal connectors are routed. They must be rerouted along the same path during assembly.
4. Installation is the reverse of removal.

Front Half Removal/Installation

1. Remove the rear half of the fender as described in this chapter.
2. Disconnect the connector (**Figure 43**) from the IC igniter.
3. Remove the clamp (A, **Figure 44**) that secures the reservoir hose to the frame.
4. Remove the mounting screw (B, **Figure 44**) and lower the reservoir and hose from the right side of the motorcycle. Suspend the reservoir from the frame with a wire or bunjee cord.
5. Remove the mounting bolts (C, **Figure 42**) from each side of the motorcycle and pull the front half of the fender from the motorcycle.
6. Installation is the reverse of removal. Make sure the cutout on the reservoir bracket engages the tab on the front half of the fender.

SEAT

Removal/Installation

1. Insert the key into the seat lock (**Figure 45**). Turn the key clockwise (rearward) to unlock the seat.

2. Lift the rear of the seat and pull the seat rearward.

TOOL BOX

Removal/Installation

1. Remove the seat.
2. Remove the tool box screws (**Figure 46**) and lift the tool box from the frame.
3. Installation is the reverse of removal.

REAR FRAME

Removal/Installation

Refer to **Figure 47**.

1. Remove the seat and side covers as described in this chapter.

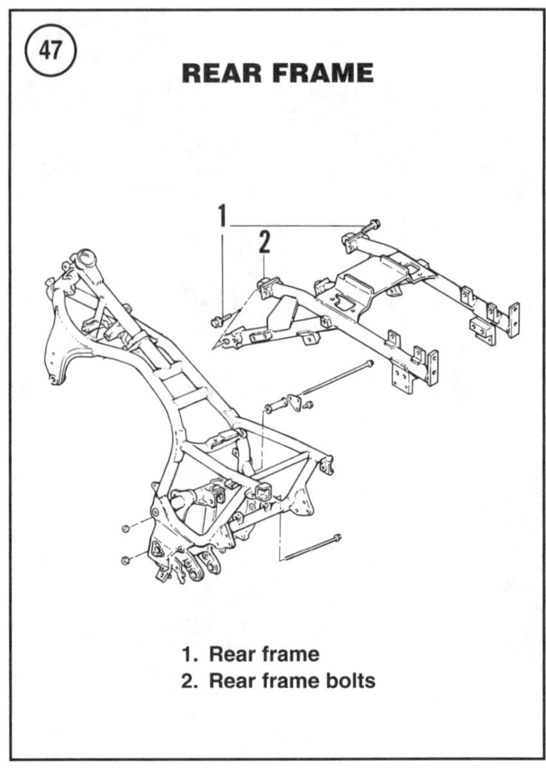

2. Remove the tail cover and the front and rear halves of the rear fender (this chapter).

3. Remove the mounting bolts from each side and pull the rear frame from the frame.

4. Installation is the reverse of removal. Torque the rear frame bolts to 34 N•m (25 ft.-lb.).

INDEX

16

G

H

I

J

L

M

O

P

R

V

W

1986-1993 U.S., CALIFORNIA AND CANADA MODELS

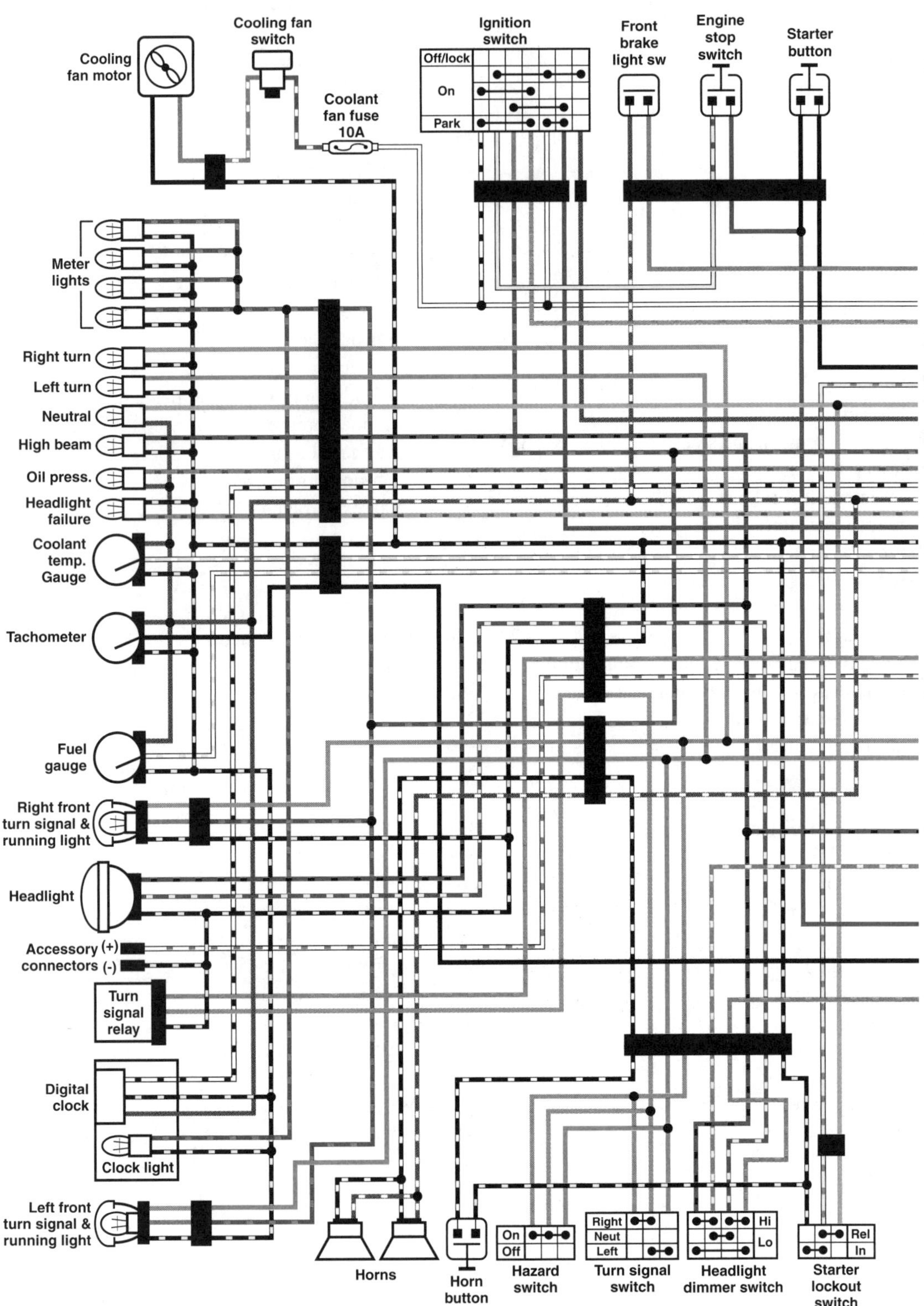

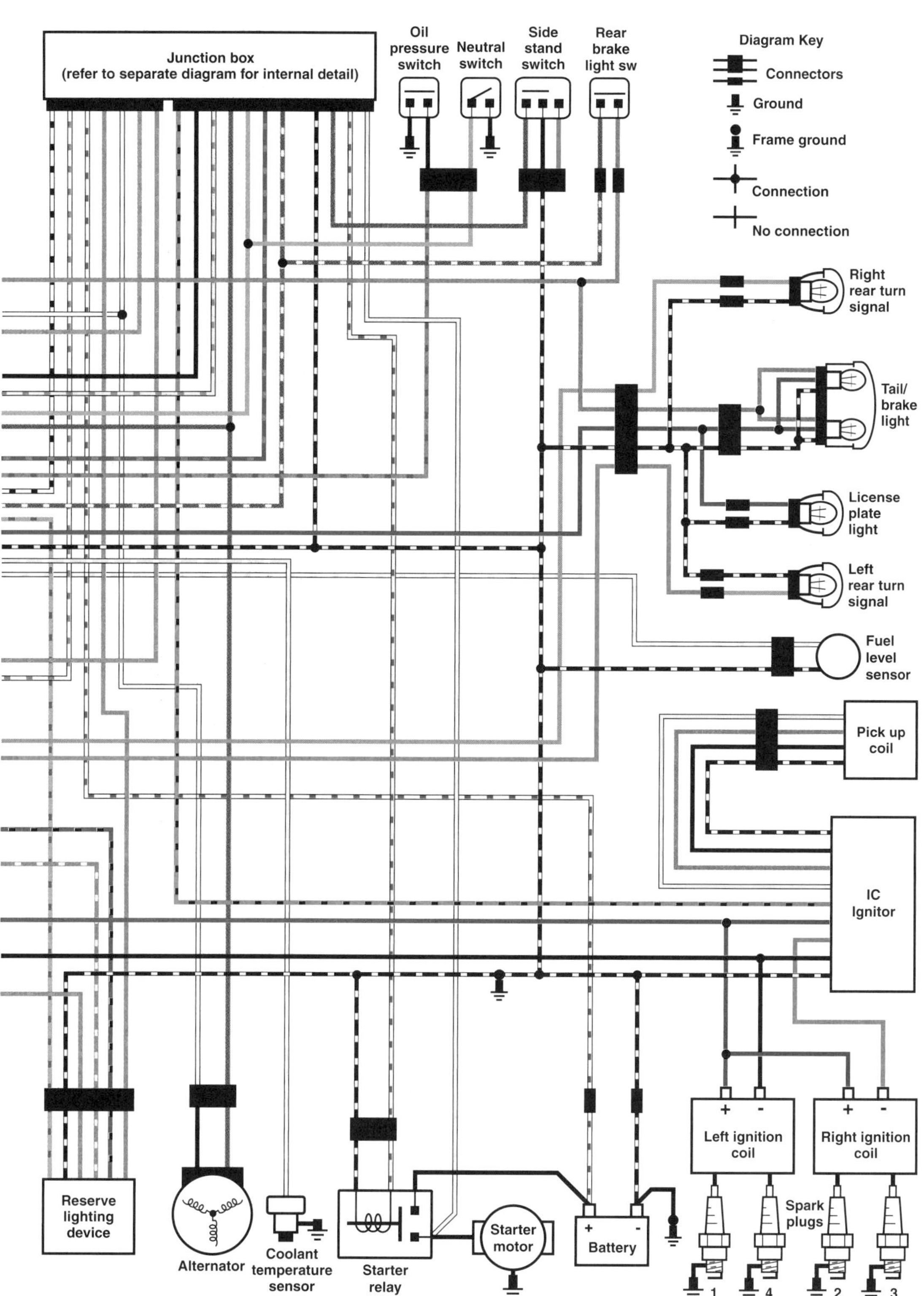
Junction box
(refer to separate diagram for internal detail)
Oil pressure switch
Neutral switch
Side stand switch
Rear brake light sw
Diagram Key
Connectors
Ground
Frame ground
Connection
No connection
Right rear turn signal
Tail/ brake light
License plate light
Left rear turn signal
Fuel level sensor
Pick up coil
IC Ignitor
+
-
Left ignition coil
+
-
Right ignition coil
Spark plugs
1
4
2
3
Reserve lighting device
Alternator
Coolant temperature sensor
Starter relay
Starter motor
+
-
Battery

1994-2000 U.S., CALIFORNIA AND CANADA MODELS

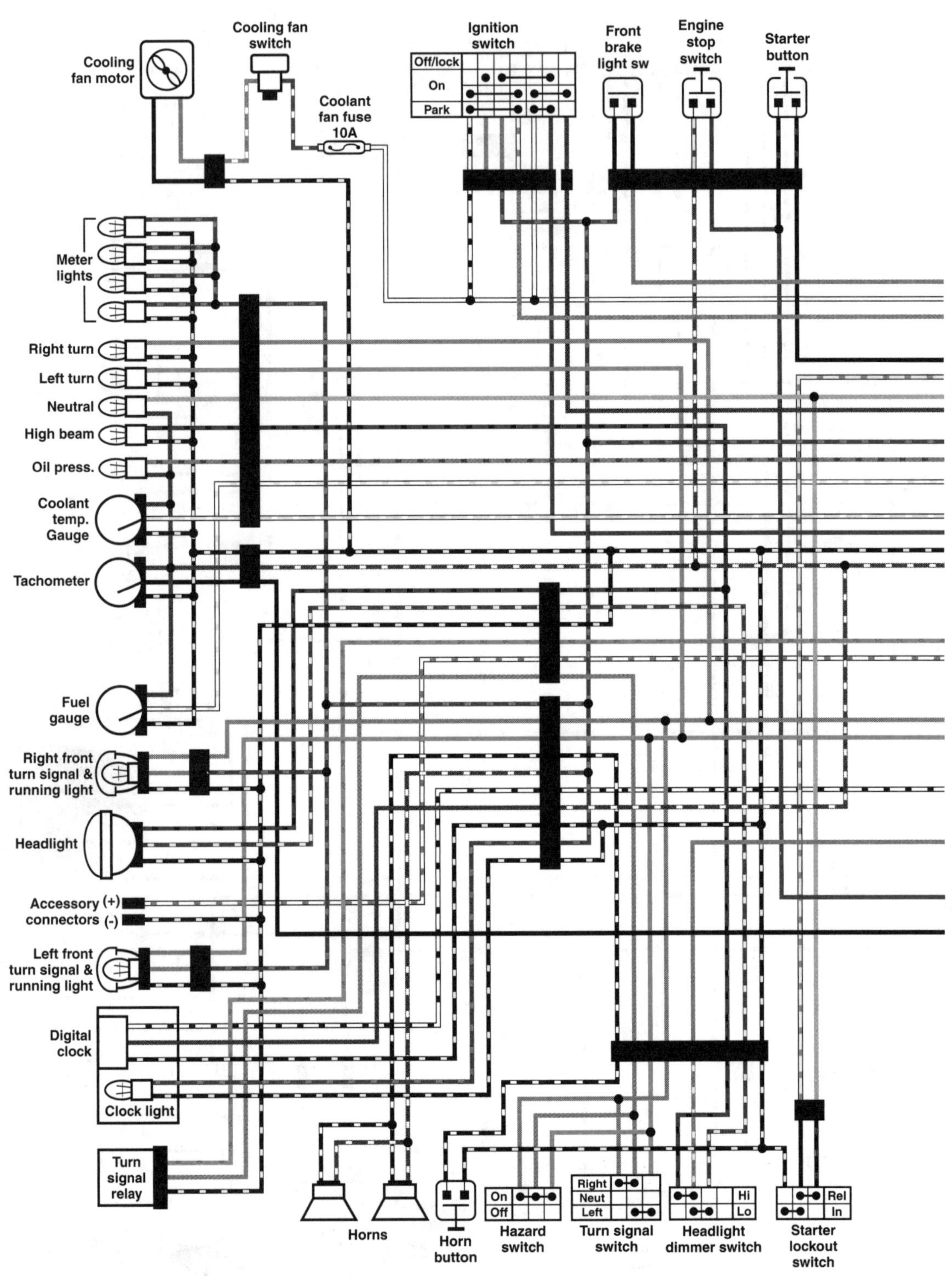

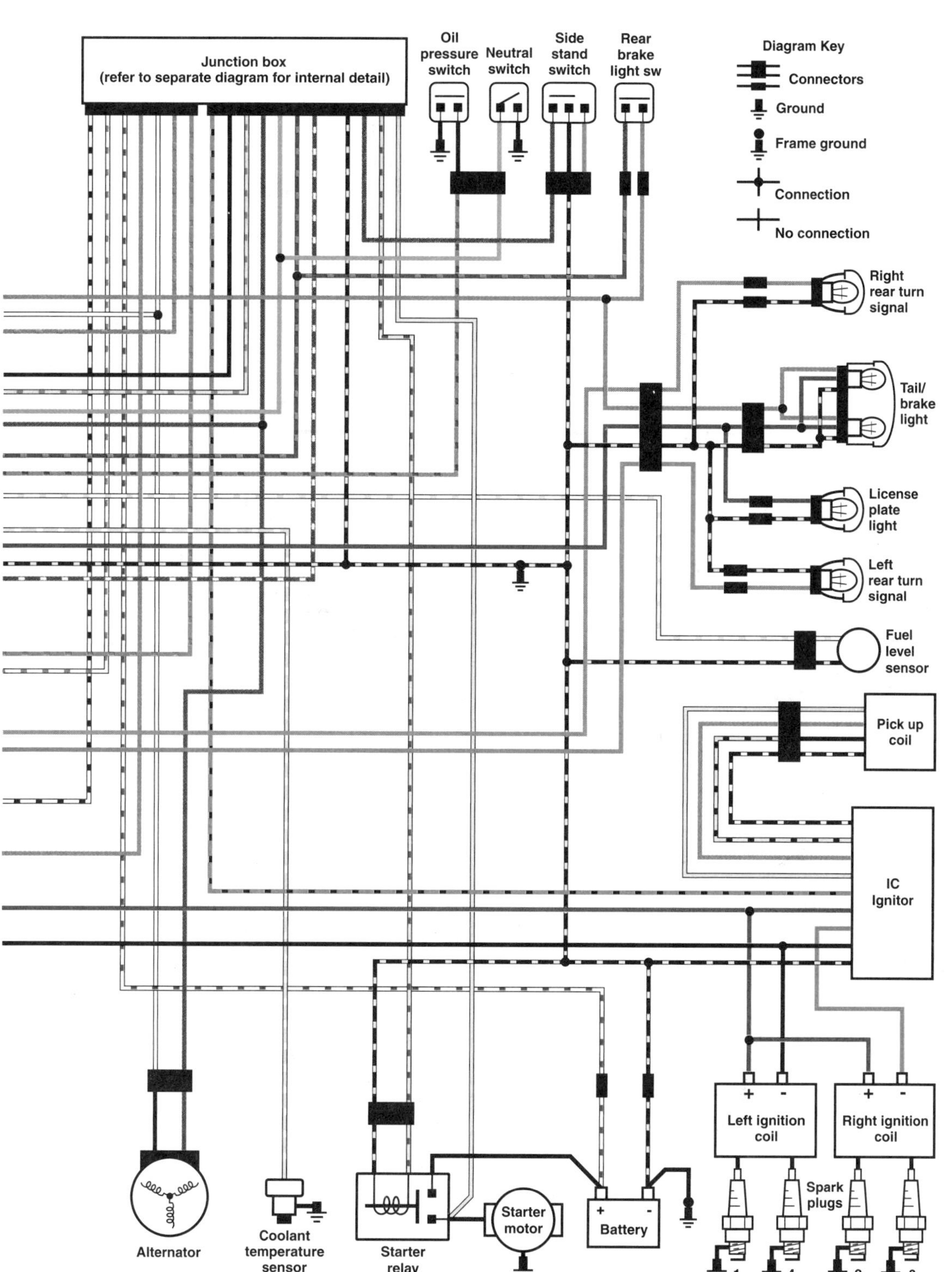
Junction box
(refer to separate diagram for internal detail)
Oil pressure switch
Neutral switch
Side stand switch
Rear brake light sw
Diagram Key
Connectors
Ground
Frame ground
Connection
No connection
Right rear turn signal
Tail/ brake light
License plate light
Left rear turn signal
Fuel level sensor
Pick up coil
IC Ignitor
Left ignition coil
Right ignition coil
Spark plugs
1
4
2
3
Alternator
Coolant temperature sensor
Starter relay
Starter motor
Battery

2001-2006 U.S., CALIFORNIA AND CANADA MODELS

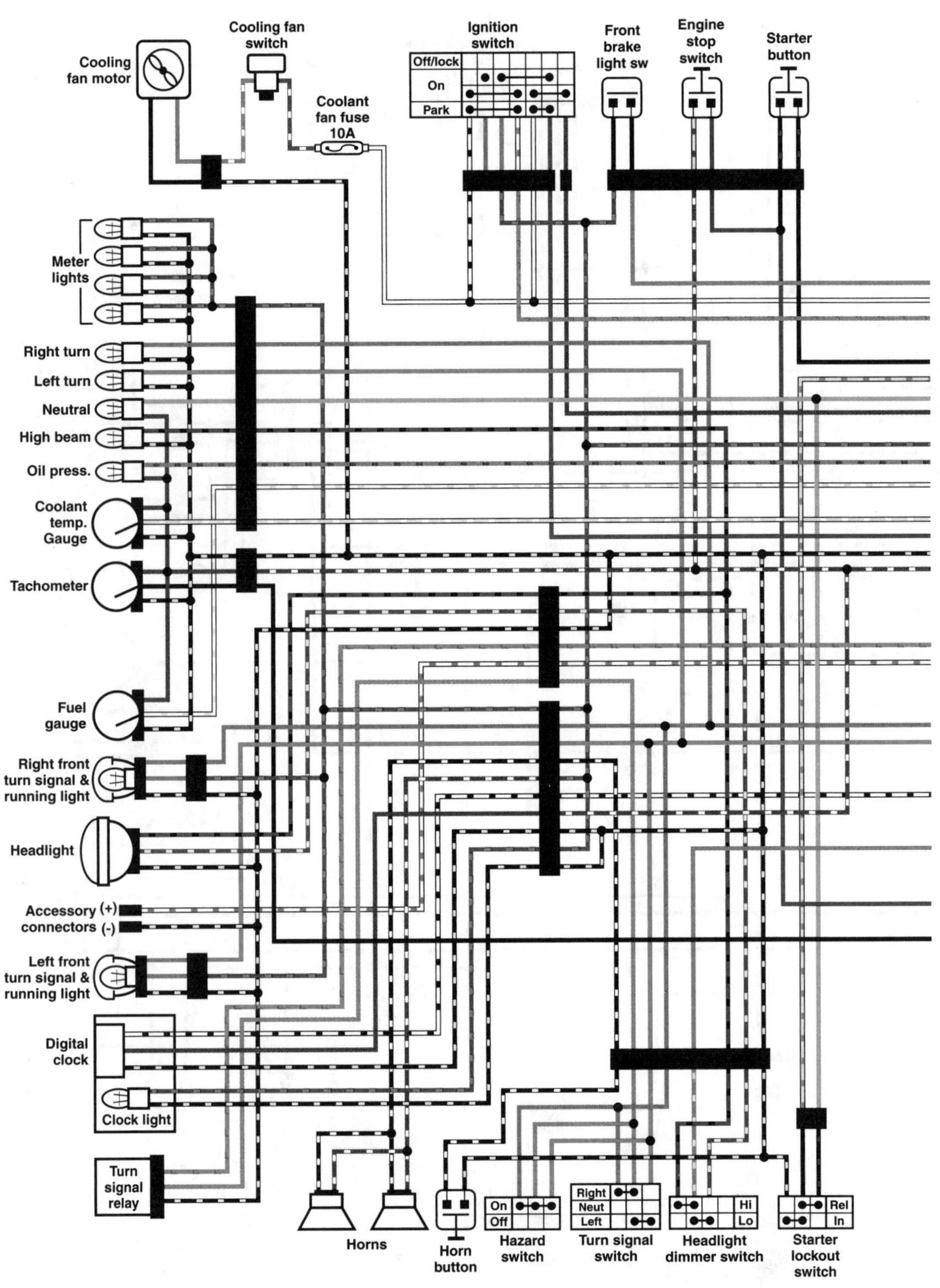

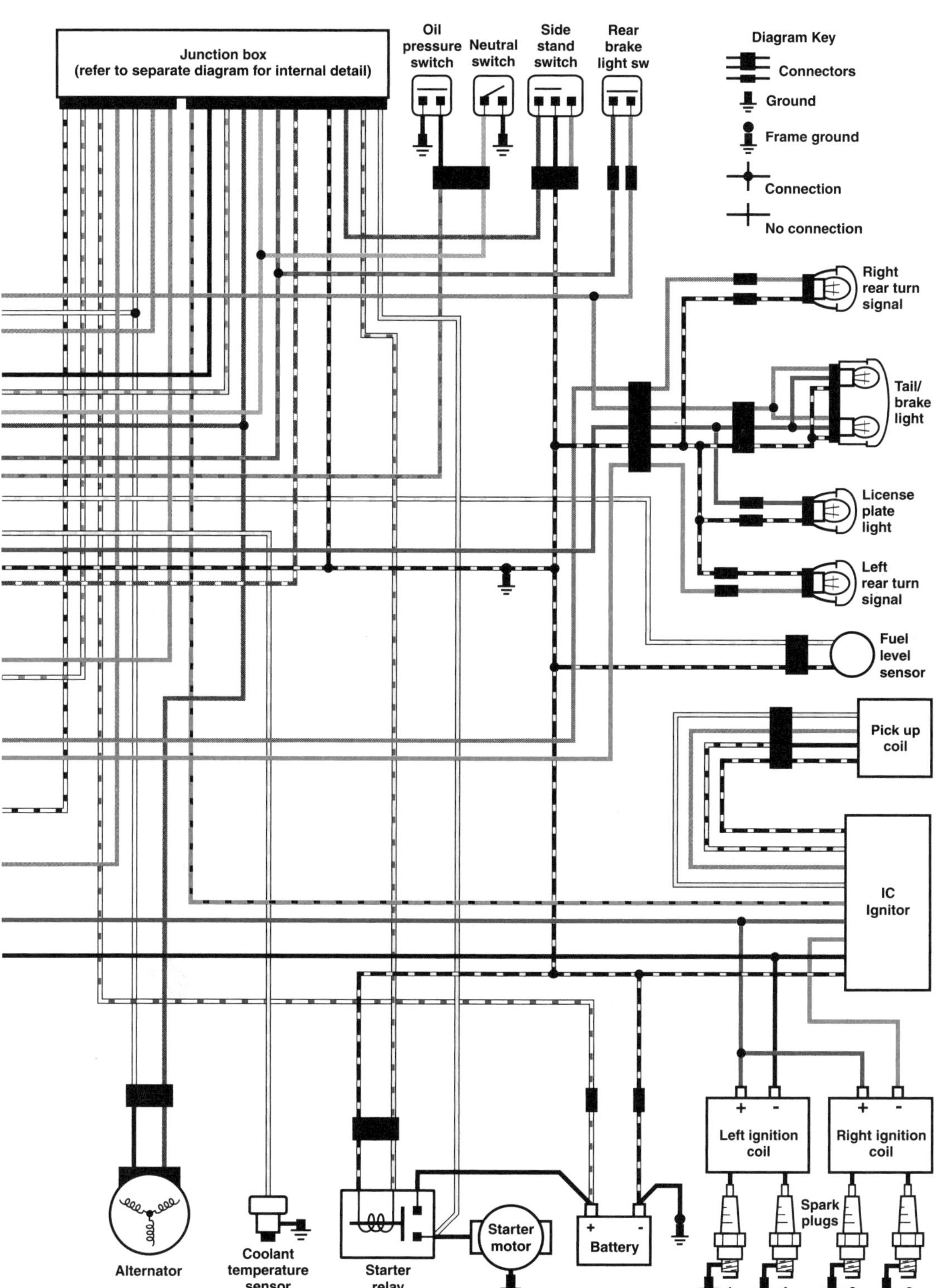
Junction box
(refer to separate diagram for internal detail)
Oil pressure switch
Neutral switch
Side stand switch
Rear brake light sw
Diagram Key
Connectors
Ground
Frame ground
Connection
No connection
Right rear turn signal
Tail/ brake light
License plate light
Left rear turn signal
Fuel level sensor
Pick up coil
IC Ignitor
Left ignition coil
Right ignition coil
Spark plugs
1
4
2
3
Battery
Starter motor
Starter relay
Coolant temperature sensor
Alternator

1986-1993 INTERNATIONAL MODELS

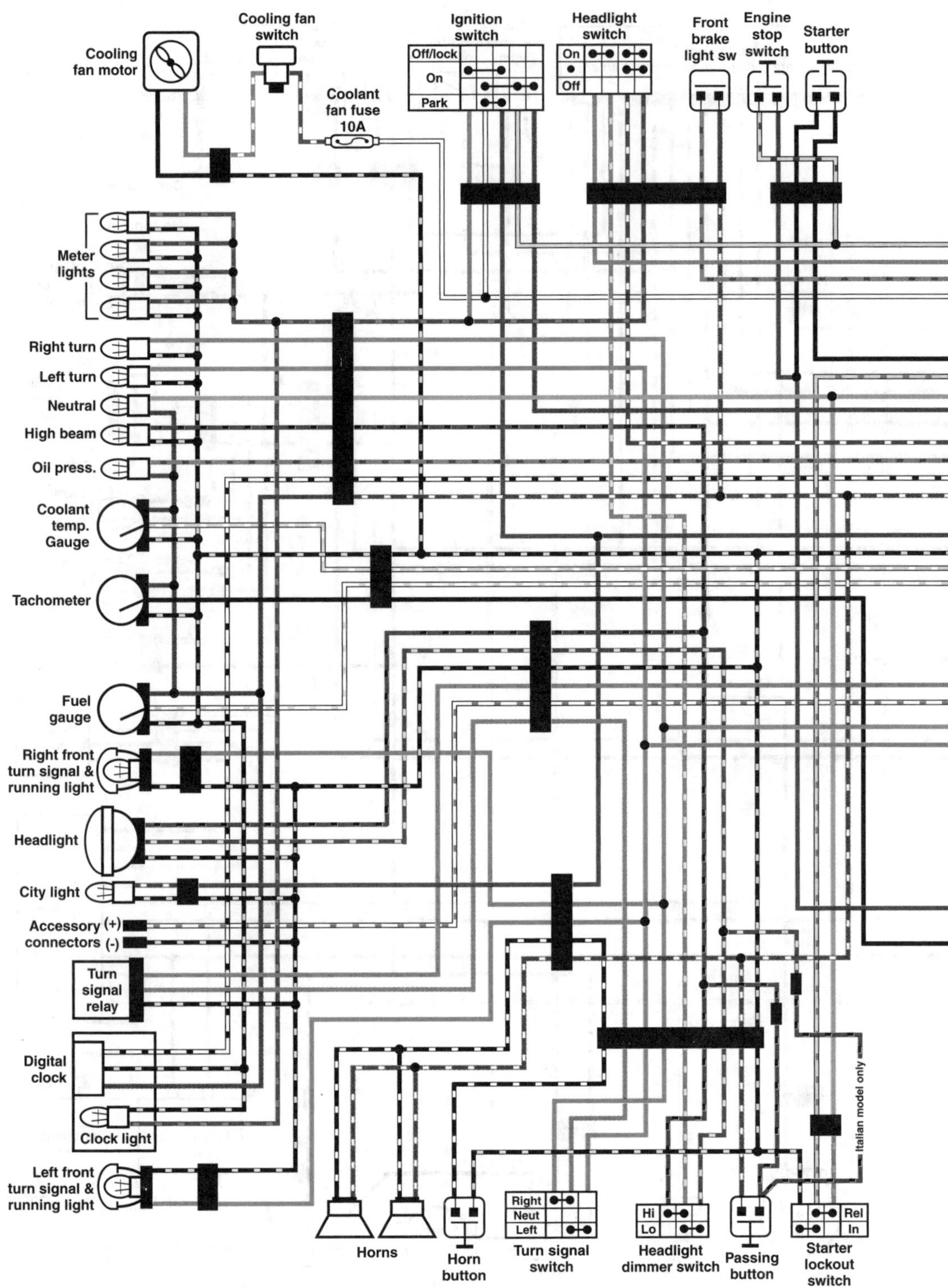

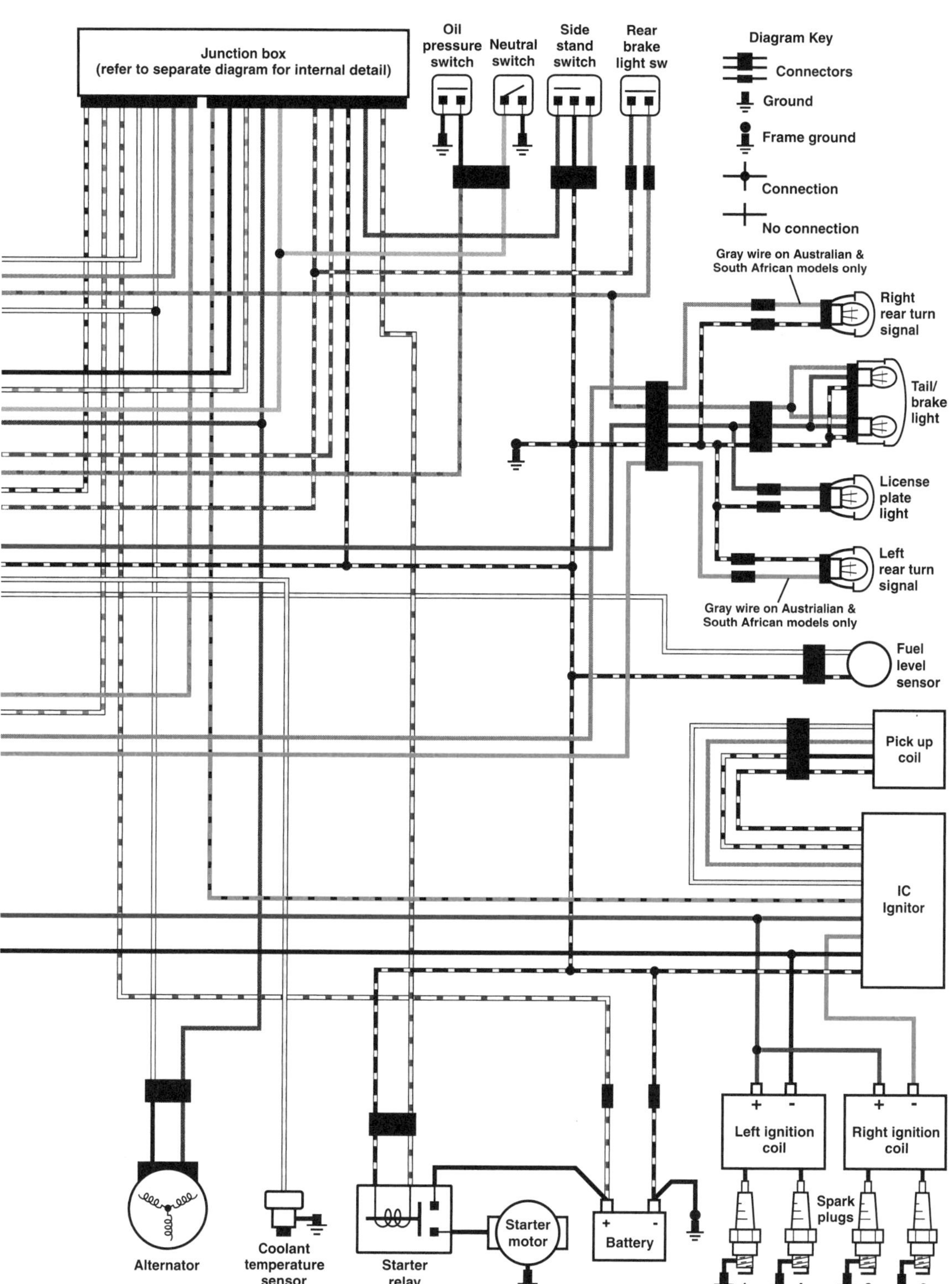
Junction box
(refer to separate diagram for internal detail)
Oil pressure switch
Neutral switch
Side stand switch
Rear brake light sw
Diagram Key
Connectors
Ground
Frame ground
Connection
No connection
Gray wire on Australian & South African models only
Right rear turn signal
Tail/ brake light
License plate light
Left rear turn signal
Gray wire on Austrialian & South African models only
Fuel level sensor
Pick up coil
IC Ignitor
Left ignition coil
Right ignition coil
Spark plugs
1
4
2
3
Alternator
Coolant temperature sensor
Starter relay
Starter motor
Battery

1994-1999 ALL INTERNATIONAL MODELS EXCEPT AUSTRALIA

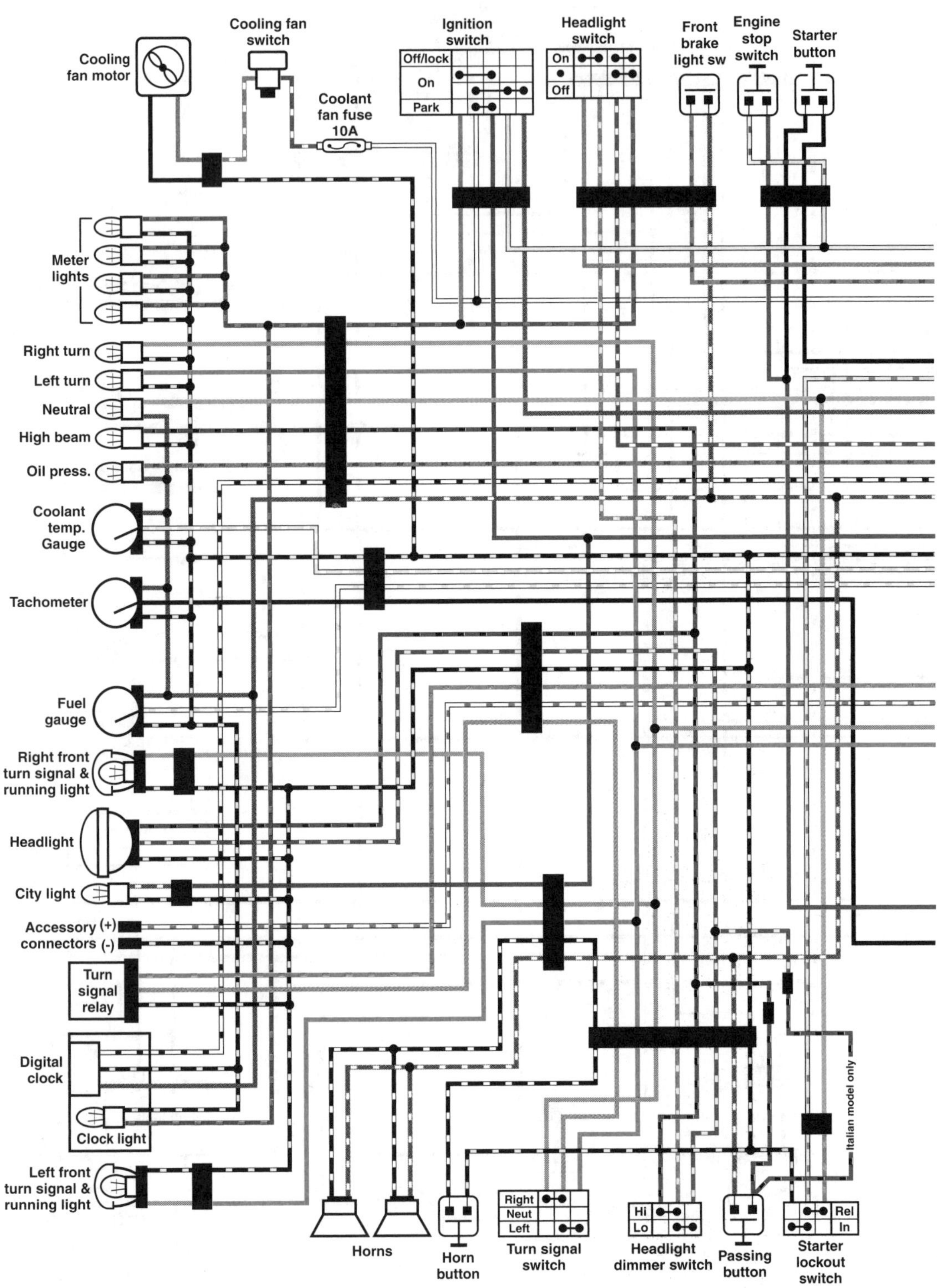

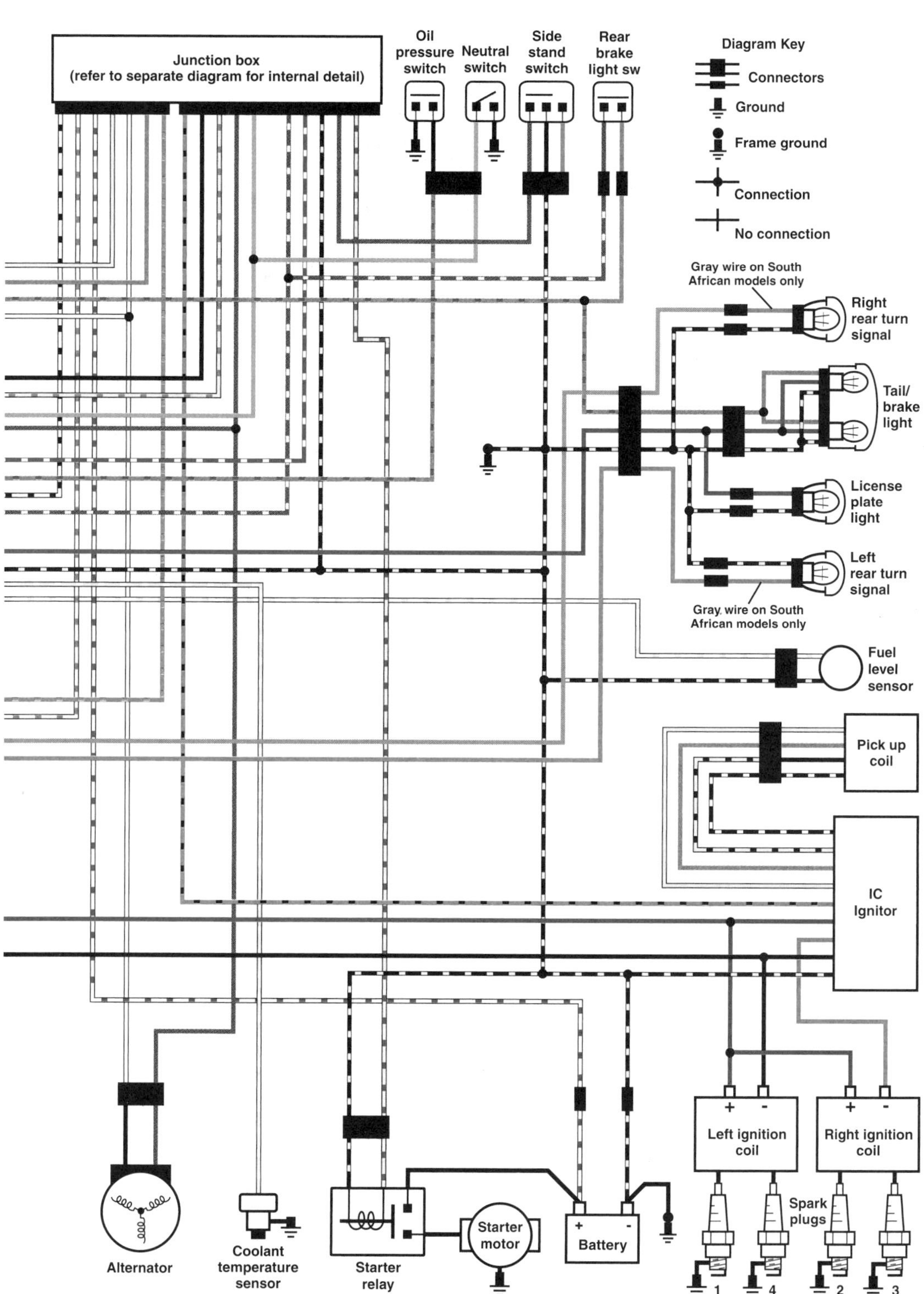
Junction box
(refer to separate diagram for internal detail)
Oil pressure switch
Neutral switch
Side stand switch
Rear brake light sw
Diagram Key
Connectors
Ground
Frame ground
Connection
No connection
Gray wire on South African models only
Right rear turn signal
Tail/ brake light
License plate light
Left rear turn signal
Gray wire on South African models only
Fuel level sensor
Pick up coil
IC Ignitor
Left ignition coil
Right ignition coil
Spark plugs
1
4
2
3
Alternator
Coolant temperature sensor
Starter relay
Starter motor
Battery

2000-2006 ALL INTERNATIONAL MODELS EXCEPT AUSTRALIA

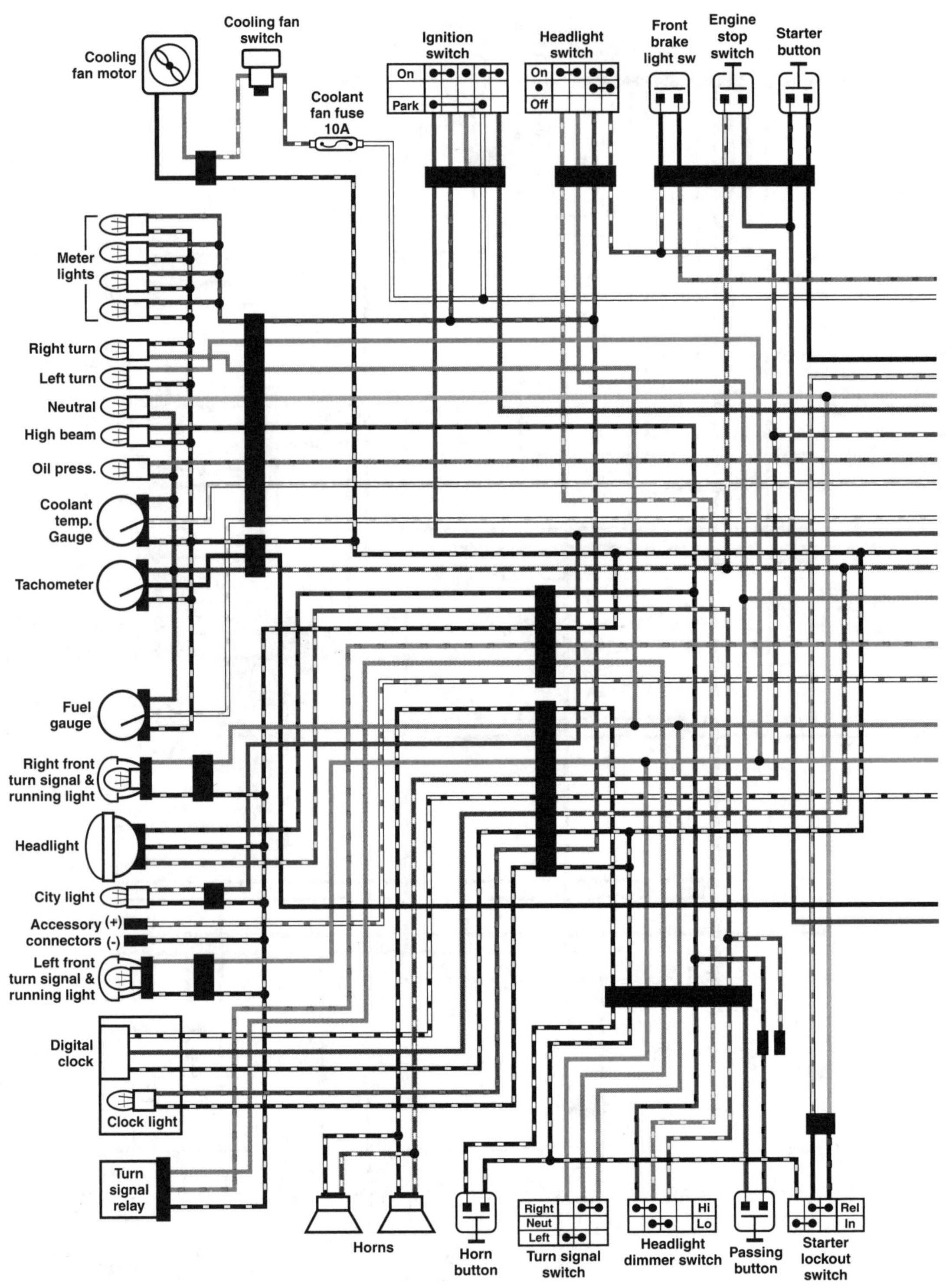

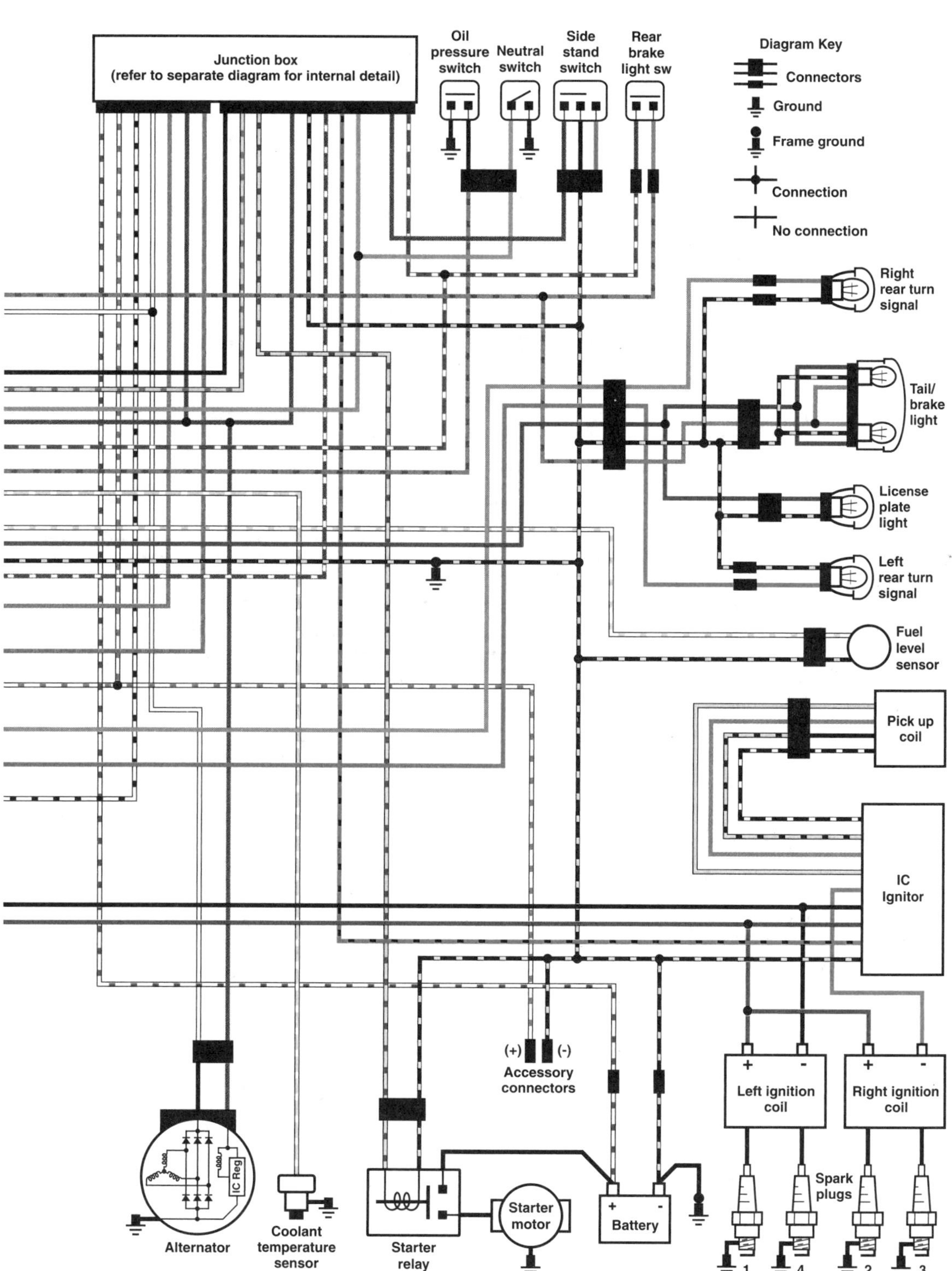

Junction box
(refer to separate diagram for internal detail)
Oil pressure switch
Neutral switch
Side stand switch
Rear brake light sw
Diagram Key
Connectors
Ground
Frame ground
Connection
No connection
Right rear turn signal
Tail/ brake light
License plate light
Left rear turn signal
Fuel level sensor
Pick up coil
IC Ignitor
(+)
(-)
Accessory connectors
+
-
Left ignition coil
Right ignition coil
Spark plugs
IC Reg
Alternator
Coolant temperature sensor
Starter relay
Starter motor
Battery
1
4
2
3

1994-1999 AUSTRALIA MODELS

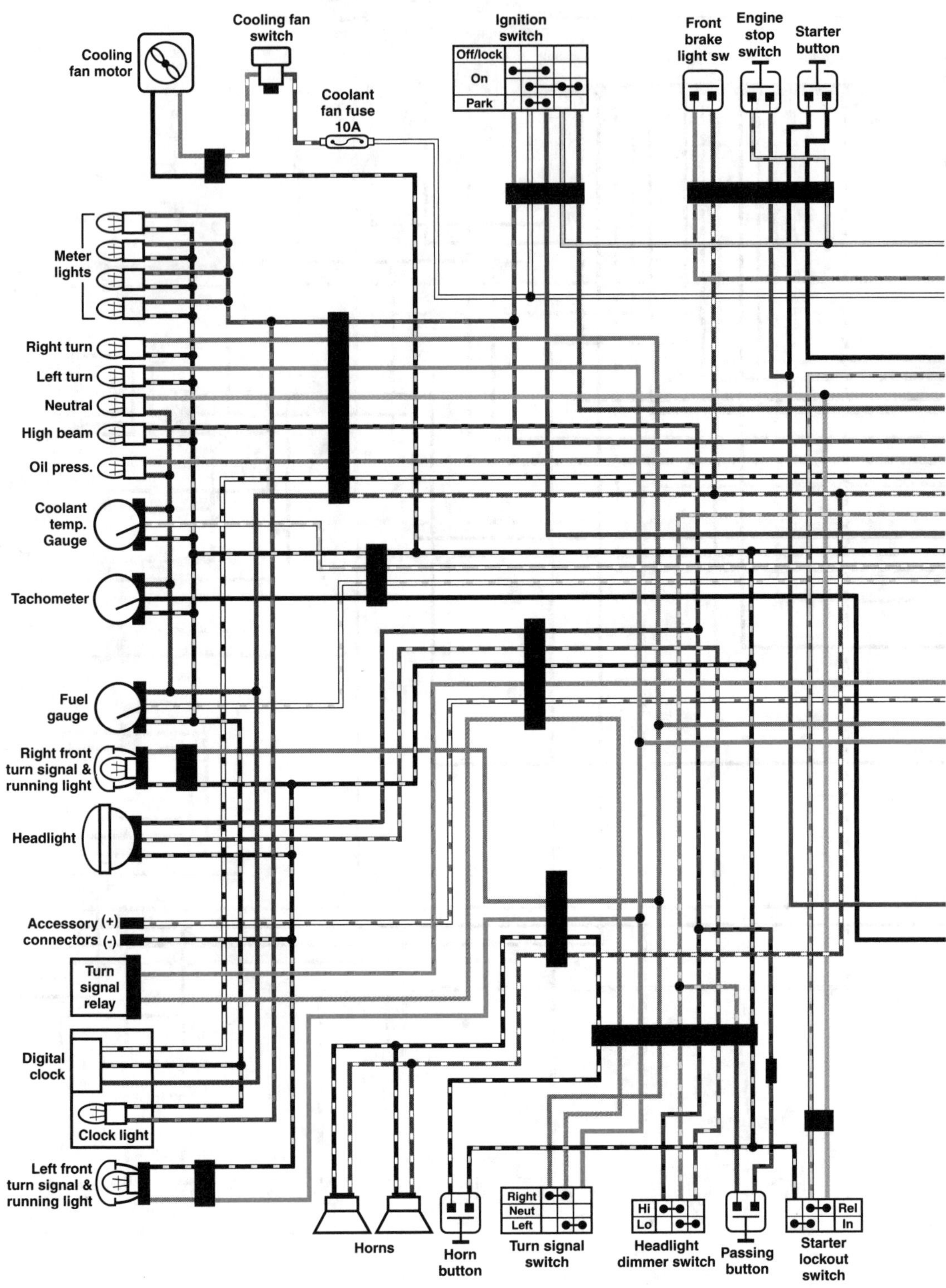

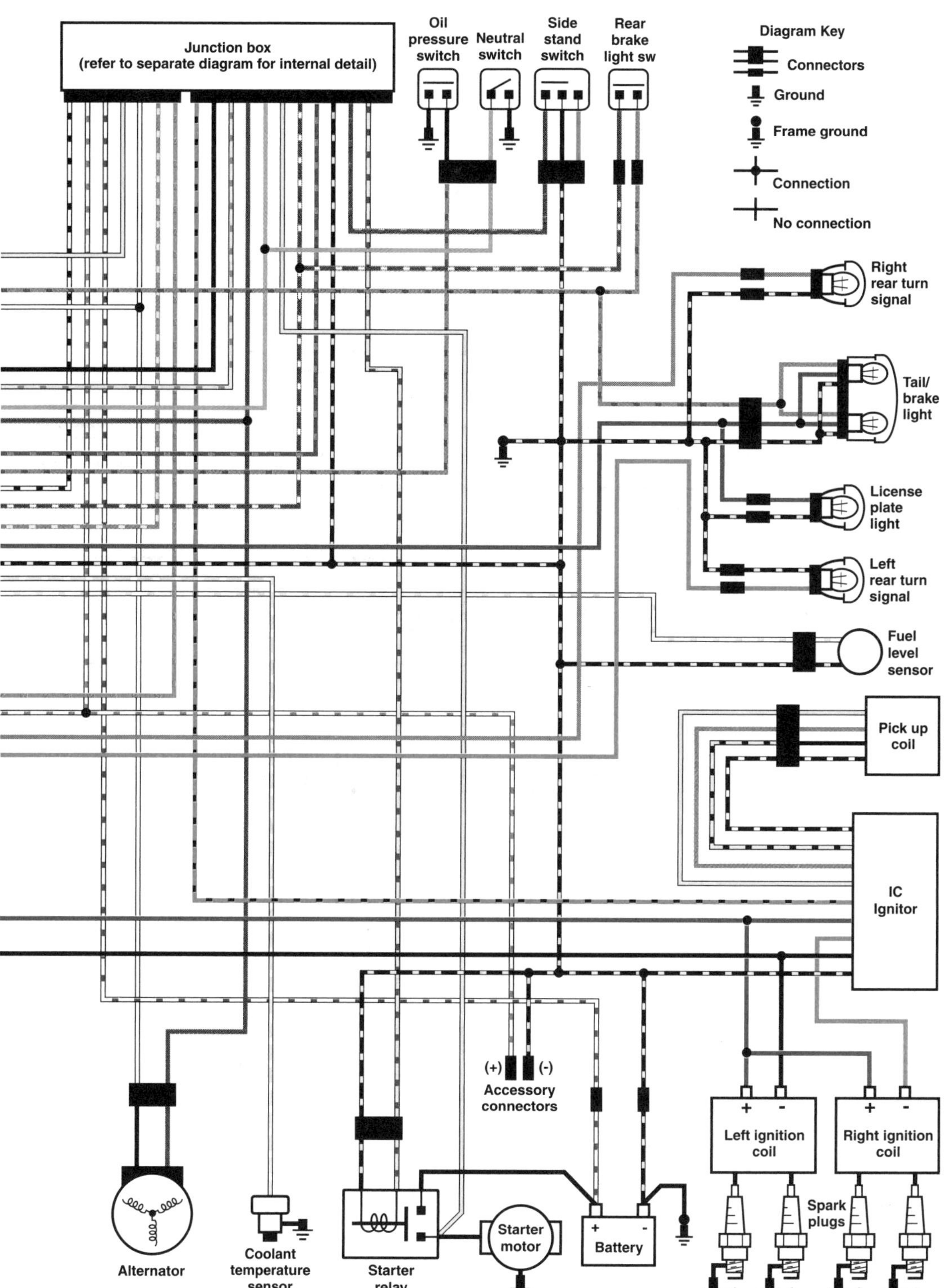
Junction box
(refer to separate diagram for internal detail)
Oil pressure switch
Neutral switch
Side stand switch
Rear brake light sw
Diagram Key
Connectors
Ground
Frame ground
Connection
No connection
Right rear turn signal
Tail/ brake light
License plate light
Left rear turn signal
Fuel level sensor
Pick up coil
IC Ignitor
(+)
(-)
Accessory connectors
+
-
Left ignition coil
+
-
Right ignition coil
Spark plugs
1
4
2
3
Alternator
Coolant temperature sensor
Starter relay
Starter motor
+
-
Battery

2000-2006 AUSTRALIA MODELS

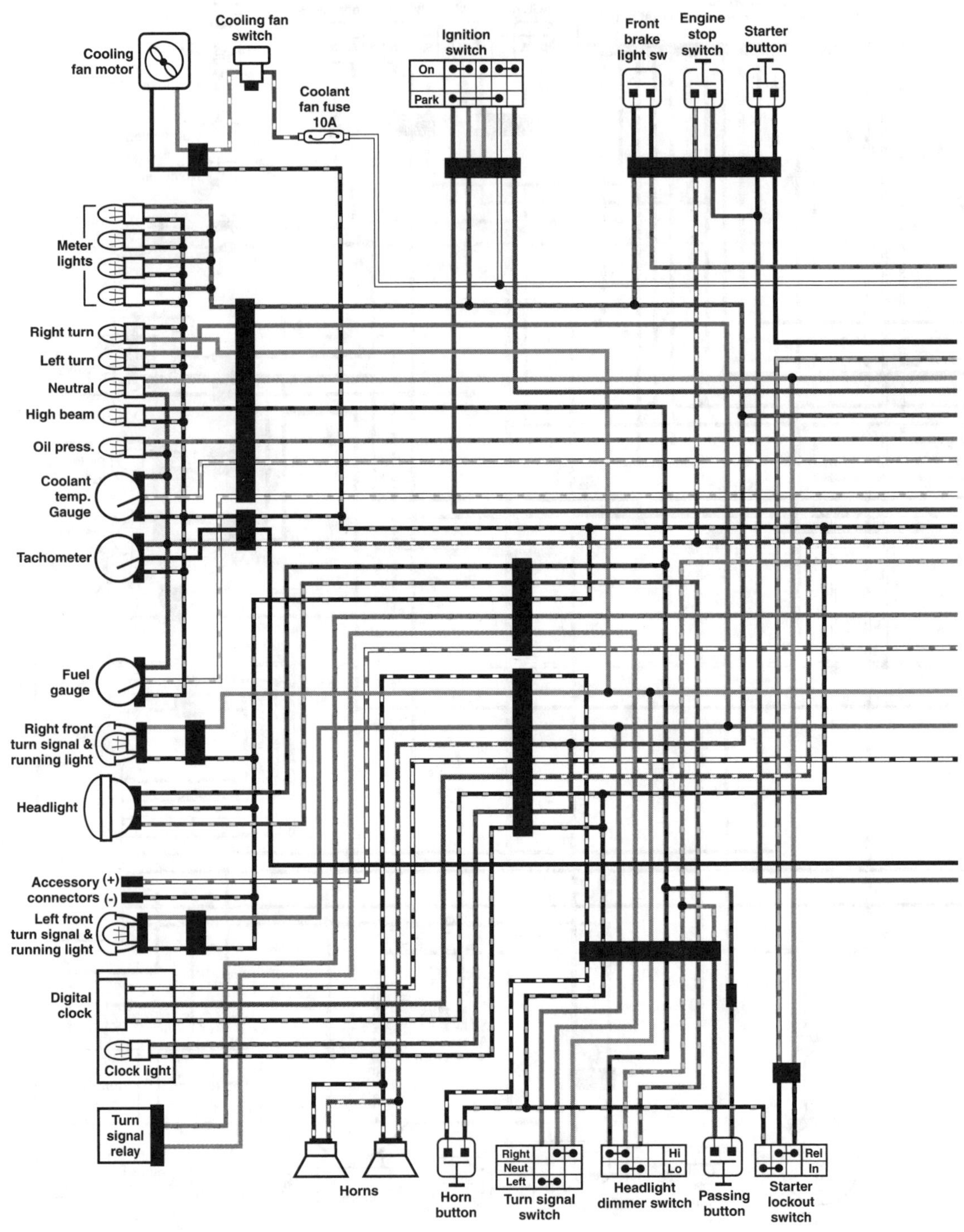

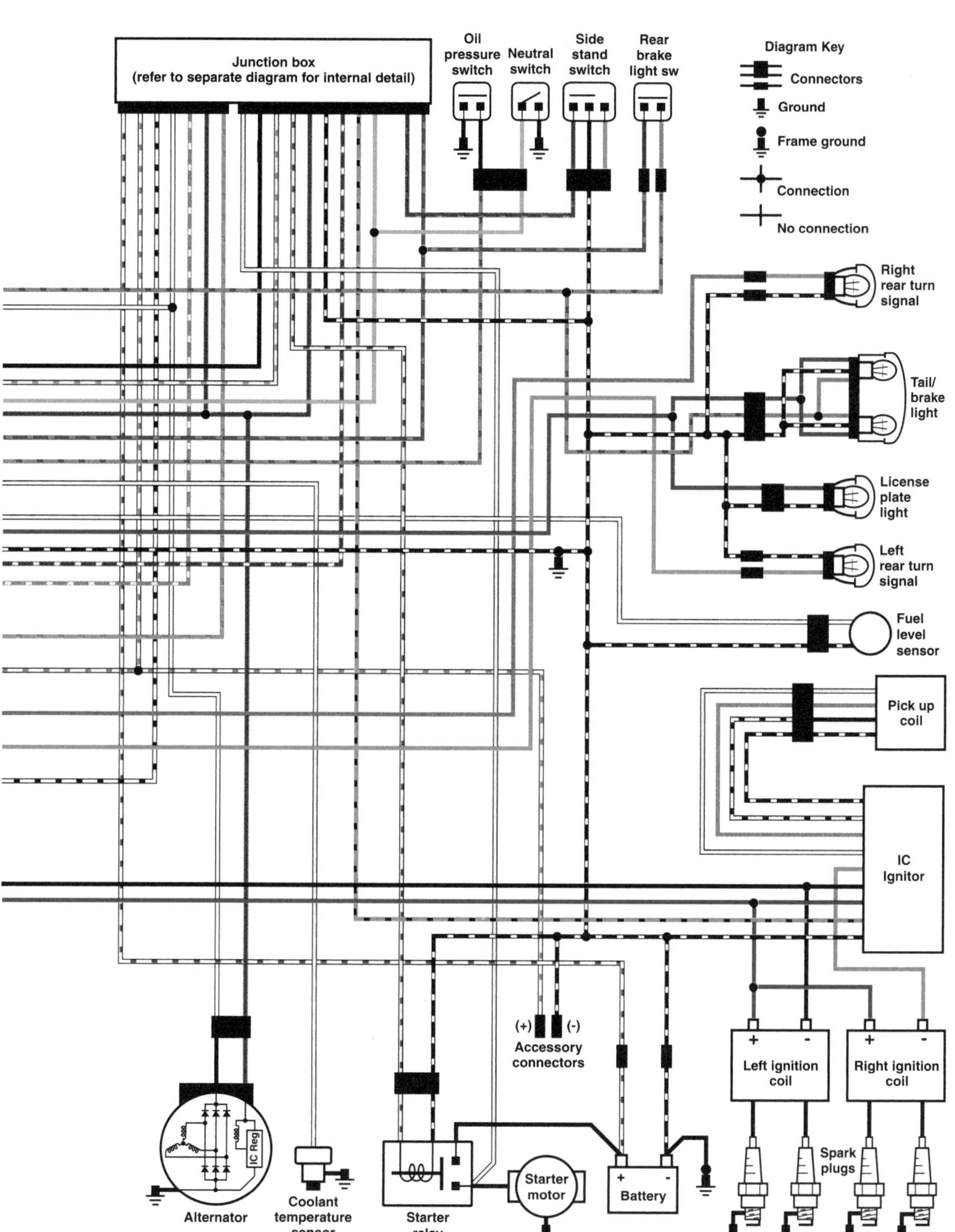
Junction box
(refer to separate diagram for internal detail)
Oil pressure switch
Neutral switch
Side stand switch
Rear brake light sw
Diagram Key
Connectors
Ground
Frame ground
Connection
No connection
Right rear turn signal
Tail/ brake light
License plate light
Left rear turn signal
Fuel level sensor
Pick up coil
IC Ignitor
(+)
(-)
Accessory connectors
+
-
Left ignition coil
Right ignition coil
Spark plugs
1
4
2
3
IC Reg
Alternator
Coolant temperature sensor
Starter relay
Starter motor
Battery

2003-2006 MODELS WITH CITY LIGHT AND NO CATALYTIC CONVERTER

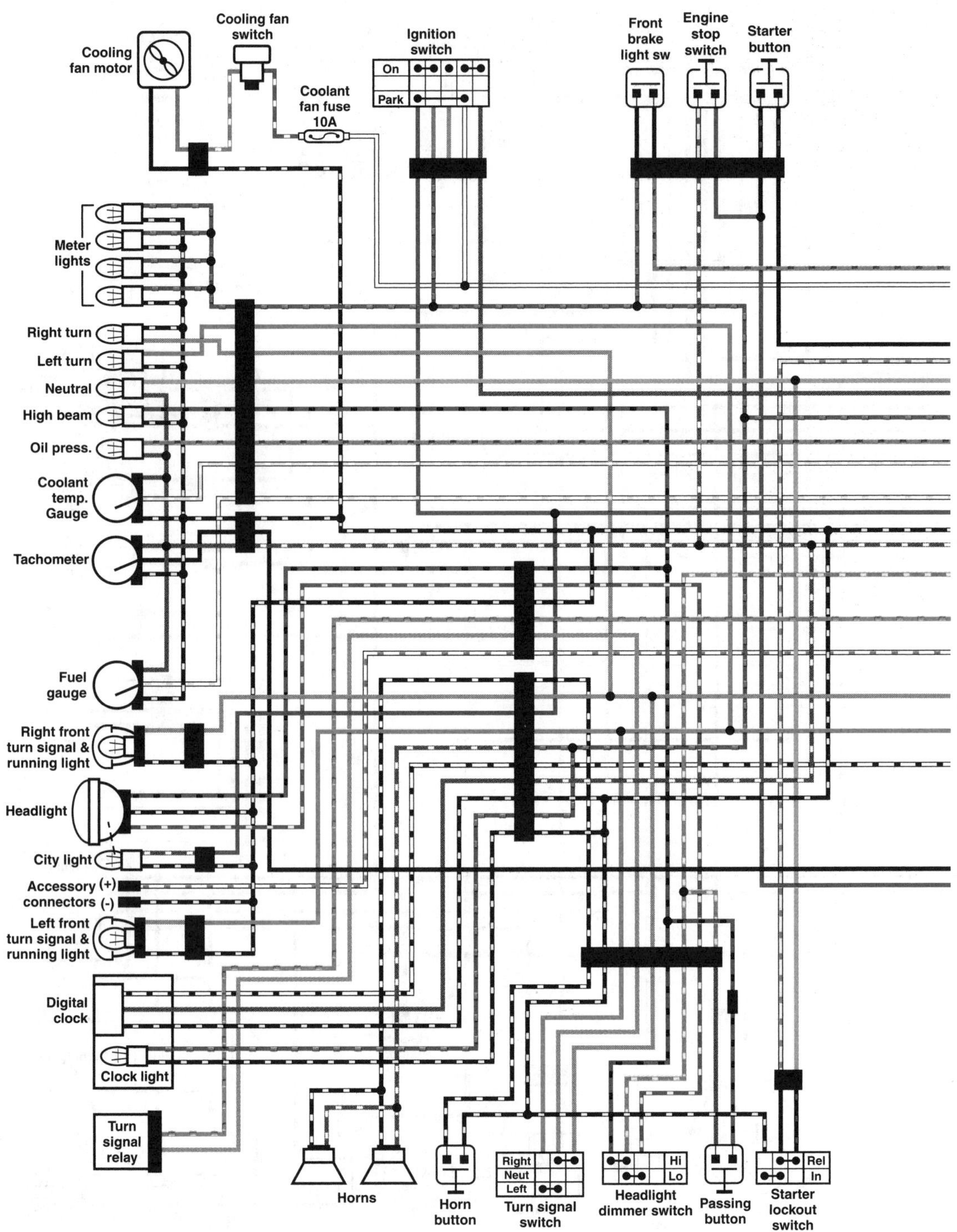

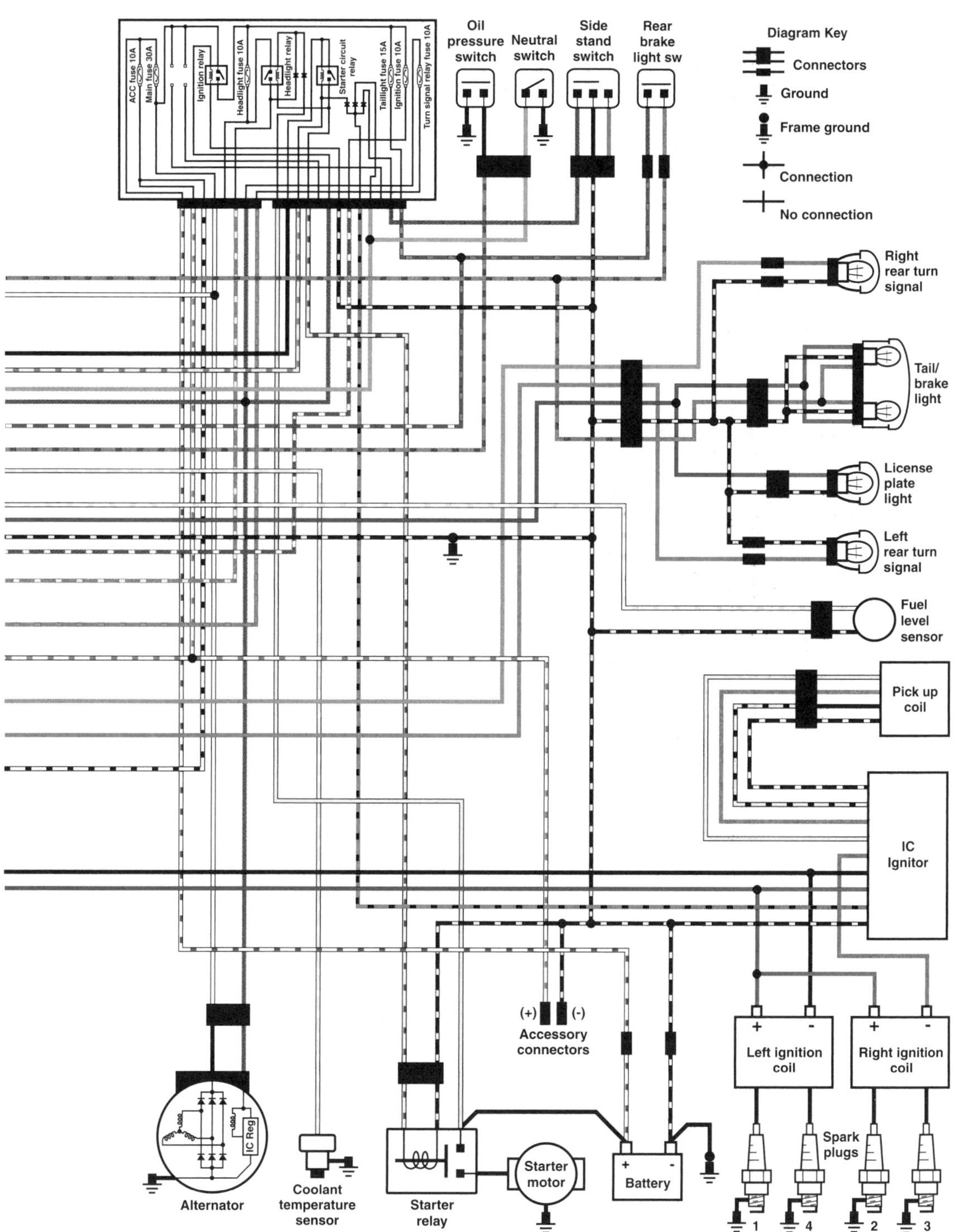

ACC fuse 10A
Main fuse 30A
Ignition relay
Headlight fuse 10A
Headlight relay
Starter circuit relay
Taillight fuse 15A
Ignition fuse 10A
Turn signal relay fuse 10A
Oil pressure switch
Neutral switch
Side stand switch
Rear brake light sw
Diagram Key
Connectors
Ground
Frame ground
Connection
No connection
Right rear turn signal
Tail/ brake light
License plate light
Left rear turn signal
Fuel level sensor
Pick up coil
IC Ignitor
(+)
(-)
Accessory connectors
Left ignition coil
Right ignition coil
Spark plugs
1
4
2
3
IC Reg
Alternator
Coolant temperature sensor
Starter relay
Starter motor
Battery

ALL U.S., CALIFORNIA AND CANADA MODELS, 1986-1999 INTERNATIONAL MODELS

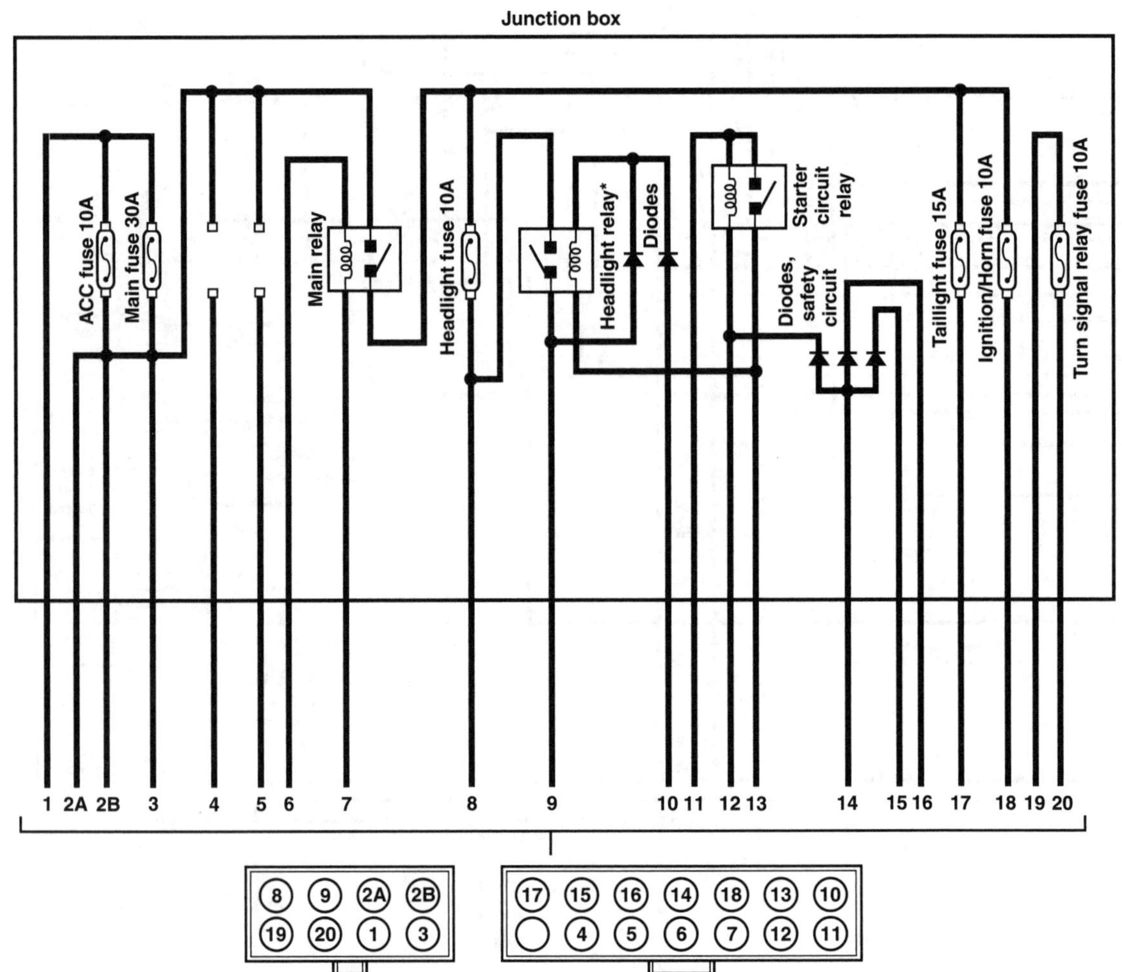

2000-ON INTERNATIONAL MODELS EXCEPT AUSTRALIA

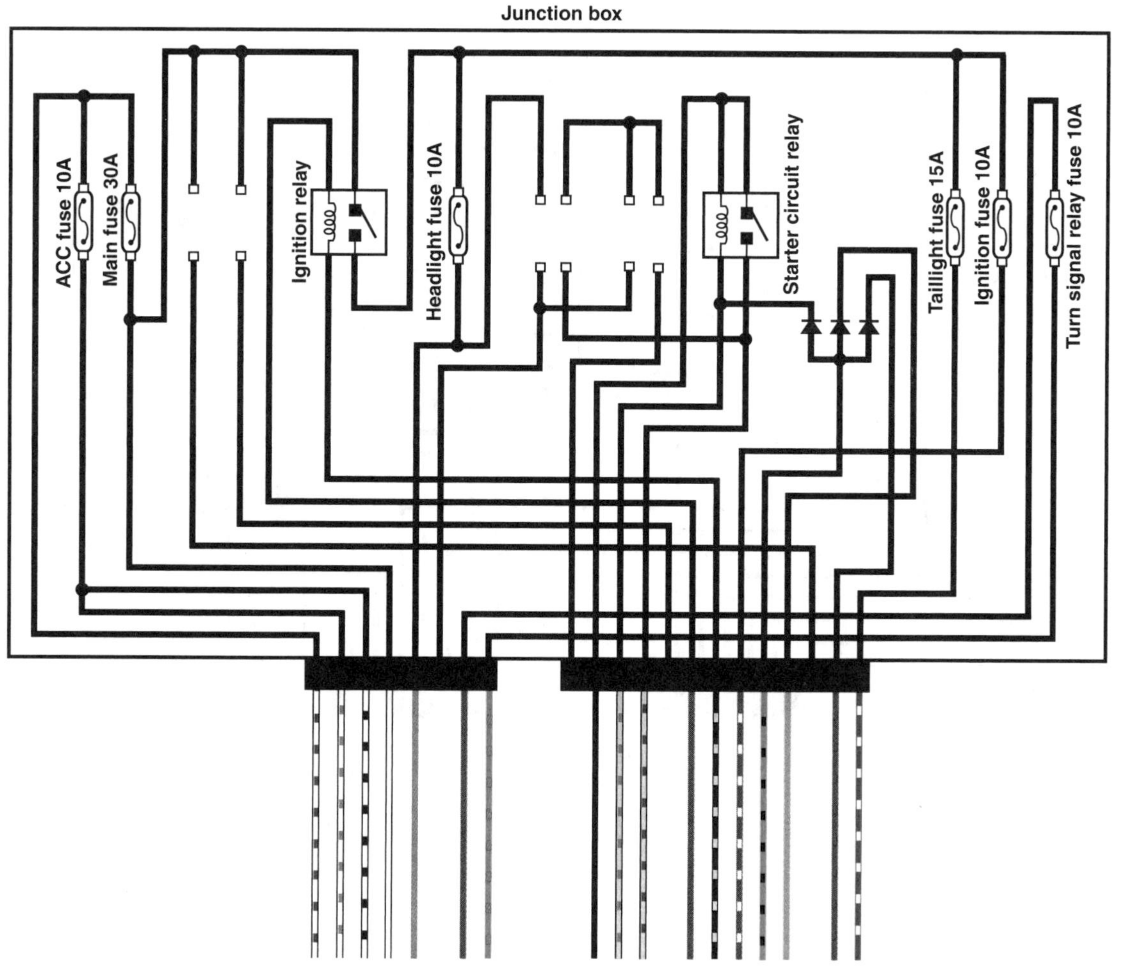

2000-ON AUSTRALIA MODELS

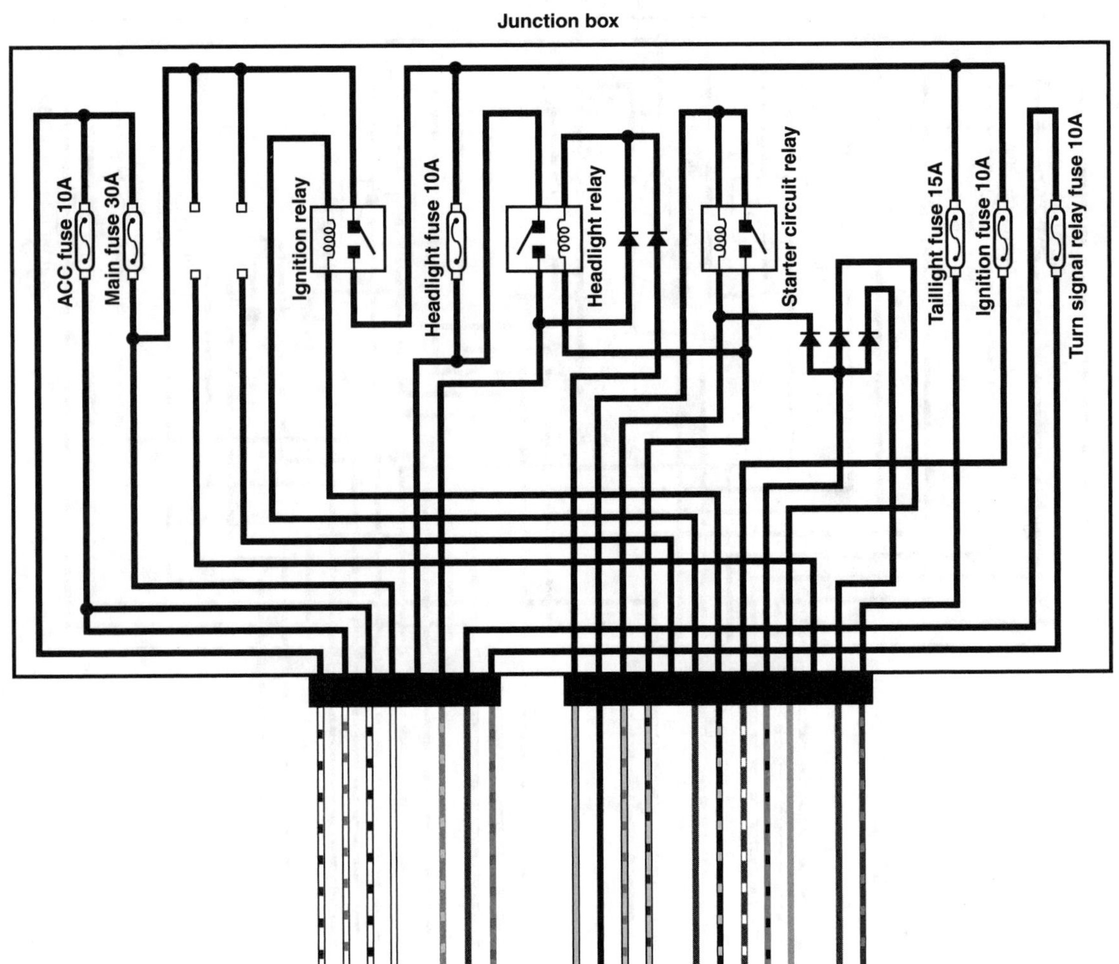

NOTES

NOTES

NOTES

NOTES

NOTES

NOTES

MAINTENANCE LOG

Date	Miles	Type of Service